Mastering
Microsoft® Windows® 7
Administration

Mastering
Microsoft® Windows® 7 Administration

William Panek

Tylor Wentworth

WILEY

Wiley Publishing, Inc.

Acquisitions Editor: Agatha Kim
Development Editor: Jennifer Leland
Technical Editor: Rodney R. Fournier
Production Editor: Christine O'Connor
Copy Editor: Elizabeth Welch
Editorial Manager: Pete Gaughan
Production Manager: Tim Tate
Vice President and Executive Group Publisher: Richard Swadley
Vice President and Publisher: Neil Edde
Book Designer: Maureen Forys, Happenstance Type-O-Rama and Judy Fung
Proofreader: Nancy Bell
Indexer: Ted Laux
Project Coordinator, Cover: Lynsey Stanford
Cover Designer: Ryan Sneed
Cover Image: Pete Gardner/DigitalVision/Getty Images

Library of Congress Cataloging-in-Publication Data

Panek, William, 1970-
  Mastering Microsoft Windows 7 administration / William Panek, Tylor Wentworth.
    p. cm.
  ISBN 978-0-470-55984-0 (paper/website)
  1. Microsoft Windows (Computer file) 2. Operating systems (Computers) I. Wentworth, Tylor, 1962- II. Title.
  QA76.76.O63P3365 2010
  005.4'32–dc22

                                                                            2009043726

Dear Reader,

Thank you for choosing *Mastering Microsoft Windows 7 Administration*. This book is part of a family of premium-quality Sybex books, all of which are written by outstanding authors who combine practical experience with a gift for teaching.

Sybex was founded in 1976. More than 30 years later, we're still committed to producing consistently exceptional books. With each of our titles, we're working hard to set a new standard for the industry. From the paper we print on, to the authors we work with, our goal is to bring you the best books available.

I hope you see all that reflected in these pages. I'd be very interested to hear your comments and get your feedback on how we're doing. Feel free to let me know what you think about this or any other Sybex book by sending me an email at nedde@wiley.com. If you think you've found a technical error in this book, please visit http://sybex.custhelp.com. Customer feedback is critical to our efforts at Sybex.

Best regards,

Neil Edde
Vice President and Publisher
Sybex, an Imprint of Wiley

Acknowledgments

I would like to thank my wife Crystal and my two daughters, Alexandria and Paige, for all of their love and support during the writing of all my books. They make it all worthwhile.

I have to thank my coauthor of this book, Tylor Wentworth. He is a business partner, a confidant, a GREAT family man, but most importantly, my friend. I always end up laughing every time we get together and that's important in this world.

I want to thank my family and especially my brothers Rick, Gary, and Rob. They have always been there for me.

I would like to thank Jeremy Hodgson, my training partner, who spends more time with me on the road than anyone else. His sense of humor keeps me smiling even when I am homesick.

I want to thank one of my close friends, Todd Lammle, for his inspiration and friendship when we get together every month. He is truly one of the great ones in this industry.

I want to thank another close friend, Dennis Gibbs, for always being there when I needed him and for all his pushing to get me to the gym every time I am on the road.

Finally, I want to thank everyone from Sybex who backed me up on this book: especially Jennifer Leland, who constantly pushed to make this the best book possible; Rodney Fournier, who has been my technical editor on multiple books, including this one, because he always has my back; Christine O'Connor, who did a great job keeping all the edits organized; and finally, Agatha Kim, who was the lead for the entire book. She was always there for us and she was great to write for. Thanks to you all and everyone else behind the scenes on this book.

— *William Panek*

I would like to acknowledge and thank my wife and best friend, Julie. Without her support, understanding, and putting up with me walking around in a daze most of the time, I would not have been able to complete this project.

My son Travis and daughter Jessie were also instrumental in maintaining my day-to-day sanity.

I would like to thank my personal motivator and writing/business partner, Will Panek, who kept me focused and going down the correct path; I couldn't possibly have done this without him.

The editing staff at Wiley Publishing has been extremely easy to work with and I thank them as well. I would like to especially thank Jen Leland for her help, her patience with me, and her guidance; she has allowed me to see just how much I didn't know about writing and given me the opportunity to learn it in an enjoyable dialogue during our editing process.

— *Tylor Wentworth*

About the Authors

William Panek (MCP®, MCP+I®, MCSA®, MCSA® w/Security & Messaging, MCSE – NT (3.51 & 4.0)®, MCSE – 2000 & 2003®, MCSE w/Security & Messaging, MCDBA®, MCT®, MCTS®, MCITP®, CCNA®, CHFI®) After many successful years in the computer industry and a degree in computer programming, William Panek decided that he could better use his talents and his personality as an instructor. He started teaching for such schools as Boston University, Clark University, and GlobalNet, just to name a few.

In 1998 William Panek started Stellacon Corporation. Stellacon has become one of New England's most respected training companies. Stellacon is also a two-time winner of the Best Computer School award in Portsmouth, New Hampshire.

William brings years of real-world expertise to the classroom and strives to ensure that each and every student has an understanding of the course material.

William currently lives in New Hampshire with his wife and two girls. In his spare time he likes to golf, ski, and snowmobile. William is also a commercially rated helicopter pilot.

Tylor Wentworth (MCP, MCSA, MCSA /Security & Messaging, MCSE – NT4.0, MCSE – 2000 & 2003, MCSE w/Security & Messaging, MCTS, MCITP, MCT, CEH, CHFI, CSI, CCNA, CCNP, BSEE, FCC RF Licensed) is a member of the IEEE, with membership in the standards committee. Tylor has been involved in computers and networking for over 17 years.

Tylor has provided training for companies such as CA Inc., Liberty Mutual, Time Warner, FairPoint Communications, Enterasys, and many more. He has shared his networking knowledge and experience while developing and delivering custom curriculum for numerous network infrastructure classes as well as security classes.

Tylor delivers Microsoft Official Curriculum both publicly and privately on a regular basis. Tylor and his wife Julie own Intelligence Quest LLC, which offers customized training solutions for several training centers as well as for corporate clients. Intelligence Quest LLC offers a wide range of official training for multiple vendors as well.

Tylor currently lives in Maine with his wife Julie and their two dogs. Tylor's son Travis is enrolled in a chemical engineering graduate program, and his daughter Jessie is pursuing several avenues in business while focusing on Intelligence Quest LLC.

Contents at a Glance

Contents

Introduction

This book was written with over 40 years of IT experience between the two authors, William Panek and Tylor Wentworth. The authors have taken that experience and translated it into a Windows 7 book that will help you develop a clear understanding of how to install and configure Windows 7 while avoiding the possible configuration pitfalls.

Many Microsoft books just explain the Windows operating system but with this *Mastering* book, the authors take it a step further, with many in-depth, step-by-step procedures together with real-world examples that back up the explanations.

Microsoft Windows 7 is the newest version of Microsoft's client operating system software. Microsoft has taken the best of Windows XP and Windows Vista and combined them into their latest creation, Windows 7. Along with the best of Windows XP and Vista, Microsoft has added several new features to Windows 7 — features like Device Stage — to make more functionality available to users from one location.

Windows 7 eliminates many of the problems that plagued Windows Vista, and includes a much faster boot time and shutdown. It is also easier to install and configure, and barely stops to ask the user any questions during installation. We will show you what features are installed during the automated installation and where you can make changes if you need to be more in charge of your operating system and its features.

This book takes you through all the ins and outs of Windows 7, including installation, configuration, Group Policy Objects, auditing, backups, Windows Server 2008, virtualization and Hyper-V, and so much more.

Windows 7 has improved on Microsoft's desktop environment, made home networking easier, enhanced searchability, improved performance, built in wireless support, and even built in touchscreen capabilities — and that's only scratching the surface.

There have been several enhancements that allow Windows 7 to better serve the end user in terms of getting Remote Assistance from others. Windows 7 even adds a simple Easy Connect feature. We will show you the enhancements to Remote Desktop, making the user experience even better than it was before.

When all is said and done, this is a technical book for IT professionals who want to take Windows 7 to the next step. Most IT people just get a copy of Windows 7 and try to learn it. With this book, you will not only learn Windows 7 but you will become a Windows 7 Master.

Who Should Read This Book

This book is intended for mid- to high-level administrators of networks that use Microsoft operating systems. Such people probably fall into a few basic groups:

◆ Administrators who are responsible for client operating systems and are looking to implement the Microsoft Windows 7 operating system

♦ Server administrators or IT managers who are responsible for deciding which operating systems to use and what functionality they need

♦ Help desk administrators who are responsible for supporting the Windows 7 operating system

This book will help anyone who has to administer Windows 7 in a corporate environment, but it will also help anyone who wants to learn the real ins and outs about the Windows 7 operating system.

What's Inside

Here is a glance at what's in each chapter:

Chapter 1: Overview of Windows 7   This chapter begins by explaining many of the new features of Windows 7, together with some features of Windows XP and Vista that have been included with Windows 7.

Chapter 2: Installing Windows 7   We take you through the requirements and multiple ways to install the Windows 7 operating system in this chapter.

Chapter 3: Automating the Windows 7 Installation   This chapter shows you how to install Windows 7 without the need of user intervention and also how to install multiple copies of Windows 7 quickly and easily.

Chapter 4: Configuring Disks   In this chapter you are taken through the process of configuring and managing your physical disks.

Chapter 5: Managing the Windows 7 Desktop   We show you how to manage your desktop environment, including customizing the taskbar and Start Menu, creating shortcuts, setting display properties for themes, and configuring Windows Gadgets in this chapter.

Chapter 6: Managing the Interface   We examine the process of configuring the Windows 7 environment in this chapter, including an overview of the main configuration utilities, including Control Panel and the Registry.

Chapter 7: Using Remote Assistance and Remote Desktop   This chapter explains the new features and benefits to using Remote Assistance and Remote Desktop within Windows 7 and how to support end users, and implement group policy and scripting.

Chapter 8: Configuring Users and Groups   We take you through the different ways to create and manage your users and groups on the Windows 7 operating system in this chapter.

Chapter 9: Managing Security   You will see how to configure different types of security on Windows 7, including Local Group Policy Objects (LGPOs), shared permissions, and NTFS security.

Chapter 10: Configuring Hardware and Printers   This chapter explains how to install and configure new hardware, drivers, and printers by using the different installation applets. A discussion of the new Device Stage feature is included as well.

Chapter 11: Configuring Network Connectivity   We explain in this chapter how to set up hardware to provide network connectivity, connect to network devices, set up peer-to-peer networking, and configure network protocols.

Chapter 12: Networking with Windows Server 2008   This great chapter shows you how to configure Windows Server 2008 to allow Windows 7 to connect properly. This chapter also explains using Windows 7 in a virtualized environment.

Chapter 13: Configuring Internet Explorer 8   You will see how to configure Internet Explorer 8 including Accelerators and Web Slices, pop-up blockers, InPrivate Security features, and security for Internet Explorer 8 in this chapter.

Chapter 14: Installing and Configuring Applications   This chapter shows you how to add and configure many applications that are installed on Windows 7, together with how to install new applications on the Windows 7 operating system. A discussion of Live Mail and Calendar from the online Live Essentials download is also included.

Chapter 15: Maintaining and Optimizing Windows 7   In this exciting chapter you will learn how to monitor, maintain, troubleshoot, and optimize Windows 7 using Performance Monitor, Reliability Monitor, System Information, Task Manager, System Tool, System Configuration, Task Scheduler, and Event Viewer.

The Mastering Series

The *Mastering* series from Sybex provides outstanding instruction for readers with intermediate and advanced skills, in the form of top-notch training and development for those already working in their field and clear, serious education for those aspiring to become pros. Every *Mastering* book includes:

◆ Real-World Scenarios, ranging from case studies to interviews, that show how the tool, technique, or knowledge presented is applied in actual practice

◆ Skill-based instruction, with chapters organized around real tasks rather than abstract concepts or subjects

◆ Self-review test questions, so you can be certain you're equipped to do the job right

How to Contact Sybex

Sybex strives to keep you supplied with the latest tools and information you need for your work. Please check their website at www.sybex.com, where we'll post additional content and updates that supplement this book should the need arise. Enter **Windows 7** in the Search box (or type the book's ISBN — **9780470559840**), and click Go to get to the book's update page.

Chapter 1

Overview of Windows 7

In this chapter we'll explore new features and benefits of using Windows 7. You'll learn the differences between Windows 7 and previous client operating system software. We'll also examine the Windows 7 architecture.

All of the Windows 7 features are explained in greater detail throughout this book. This chapter is just an overview of many of the improvements and features.

This chapter will help us build a good foundation for the rest of this book.

In this chapter, you'll learn how to:

◆ Choose a client operating system

◆ Understand the newest features of Windows 7

◆ Explain the Windows 32-bit and 64-bit architecture

Introducing Windows 7

Unless you've been living on another planet, you know that Windows 7 is not Microsoft's first client operating system. Before we start explaining Windows 7, it's good to know about some of the features of Windows XP and Windows Vista and how they affect Windows 7.

Overview of Windows XP

Microsoft introduced Windows XP in 2001. Microsoft Windows XP was a replacement for the Millennium operating system. Windows XP was a stable environment that catered to both the home and work environment user.

Windows XP was the first operating system to introduce the dual column Start menu, as shown in Figure 1.1. The Windows XP operating system also redesigned how Control Panel was structured.

Windows XP was also the first operating system to use the new core called the kernel. Previous versions of Microsoft used a 9x version of the core systems, but the new kernel was more stable and ran more efficiently.

Windows XP also introduced Remote Assistance (which is still in use in Windows 7). Remote Assistance allows an administrator to accept an invitation from a user and then connect to that user's machine to help the user technically from a remote location.

Windows XP made it easy to keep your machine up-to-date with the ability to schedule Windows updates with the Microsoft website (this feature is also included with Windows 7).

Automatic updates allows users to ensure that their machines are always running with the latest security patches and also with the latest versions of the XP system files.

FIGURE 1.1
Windows XP's Start
menu

Another feature that was introduced with the XP operating system (and that's still used in Windows 7) is Driver Signing. If the manufacturer of a device did not adhere to Microsoft's standards and the devices were not digitally signed, you had the ability to stop the installation of the drivers.

As Microsoft developed Windows Vista, they incorporated some new features. These features are only available for Windows XP if you install Service Pack 3; these features are included with Windows 7.

Windows XP Service Pack 3

With the release of Windows XP Service Pack 3 (SP3), the operating system obtained some new benefits over the basic XP system. First, SP3 includes all previous service pack fixes and patches. It also includes all required security fixes. The following features are some of the enhancements of using SP3:

Network Access Protection (NAP)   Network Access Protection (NAP) is a compliancy-checking platform that is included with Windows 2008 Server, Windows Vista, Windows 7, and Windows XP with SP3. NAP allows you to create compliancy policies that check computers before allowing them access to the network.

Windows Product Activation   Users have the ability to install the complete integrated operating system with SP3 without the need of a product key. The operating system will ask the user to provide a product key at a later time.

Microsoft Cryptographic Module   The rsaenh.dll file has been redesigned with the SHA2 hashing algorithms (SHA256, SHA382, and SHA512) and X.509 certificate validation already included.

Overview of Windows Vista

Windows Vista was the next generation of Microsoft's client operating system to be released. Since the majority of the IT market did not switch to Windows Vista, it's important to understand some basics about Windows Vista. Windows 7 has many of the same features and attributes.

There were many new features and changes from Windows XP to Windows Vista. Let's take a look at some of these new features:

Improved Desktop   Windows Vista introduced a new Desktop called Windows Aero. Windows Aero offers Vista Home Premium, Vista Business, Vista Ultimate, and Vista Enterprise users a more stable Desktop. Computers running Windows Aero require a compatible graphics adapter. Windows 7 also includes the Windows Aero Desktop.

Windows Sidebar   Windows Vista introduced a new vertical bar that's displayed on the side of the Desktop; this bar is called the Windows Sidebar. The Windows Sidebar has mini-applications running within the bar called *gadgets*. Windows 7 has removed the Windows Sidebar, but you can still add gadgets to the Windows 7 Desktop.

Gadgets are mini-applications that allow you to easily perform and see some useful functions such as a clock, a slide show, an Internet feed, a calendar, weather reports, a stocks feed, currency exchange, and so forth. Many downloadable gadgets are available from Microsoft's website. Gadgets will be explained in detail in Chapter 5, "Managing the Windows Desktop."

Parental Controls   Parental Controls allows the computer administrator (or parent) to configure how other family members will be able to use the computer system. You can set which sites specific users can visit and what times a specific user can use the computer system. Parental Controls have been improved and are still included on Windows 7.

Improved Windows Firewall   Firewalls are hardware devices or software applications that either restrict or allow users and data from an internal or external source. Microsoft Vista included an improved version of the software-based firewall, as shown in Figure 1.2.

FIGURE 1.2
Windows Vista Firewall

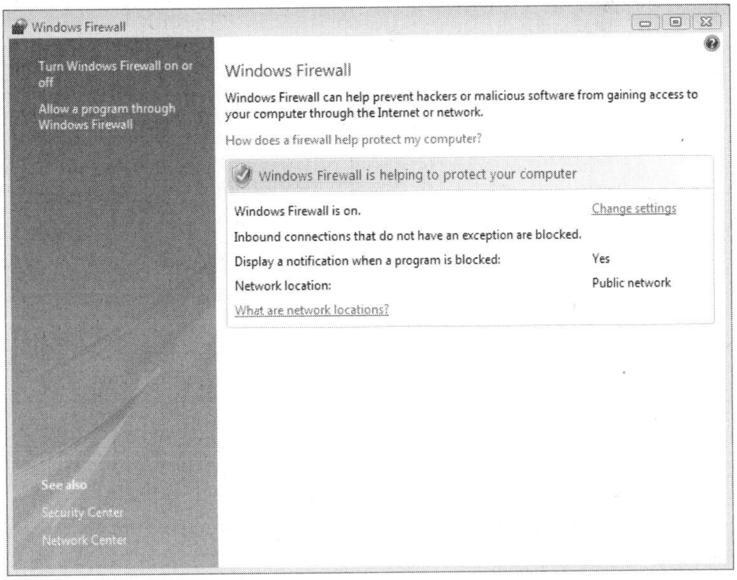

This improved version helps protect your computer system by restricting operating system resources if they operate in an unusual way. For example, let's say that you have an application that uses a particular port number to function properly. If that application tries to use a different port, the system stops the application, thus protecting other computer systems from possible problems. Windows 7 also includes the Windows Firewall.

Windows Vista User Account Control   Introduced with Windows Vista and Windows Server 2008, the User Account Control (UAC) allows a standard user to perform many functions without an Administrator account.

Windows Search   Windows Search, also included with Windows 7, allows you to search files or applications quickly and easily from anywhere in Windows Vista. One of the nice features of Windows Search is that when you begin typing in your search, all files, folders, and applications that have those letters start to appear. For example, if you start typing **No**, all files starting with *no*, including *notepad*, appear.

Live Icons   If you have a compatible video adapter and choose to run Windows Aero (also included with Windows 7), you have the ability to use live icons. Live icons are icons that show you what's in the application or folder when you hover your mouse over the icon.

Windows Vista is easy to install, but you must verify that the machine that you are loading Vista onto can handle the installation. Table 1.1 lists the requirements for a Windows Vista–capable PC as well as the requirements for Windows Vista Premium.

TABLE 1.1:   Hardware Requirements (Non-network Installation)

COMPONENT	WINDOWS VISTA–CAPABLE PC	WINDOWS VISTA PREMIUM PC
Processor	800 MHz 32-bit (*x86*) or 64-bit (*x64*) processor; Intel Core/Pentium/Celeron, AMD, Via, or compatible	1 GHz 32-bit (*x86*) or 64-bit (*x64*) processor; Intel Core/Pentium/Celeron, AMD, Via, or compatible
Memory	512 MB	1 GB
Disk space	20 GB hard drive with 15 GB of free disk space	40 GB hard drive with 15 GB free disk space
Graphics	DirectX 9 video card capable of SVGA at 800×600 resolution (Windows Display Driver Model support recommended)	DirectX 9 video card that supports a WDDM driver, Pixel Shader 2.0 in hardware, and 32 bits per pixel; graphics card memory dependent on desired resolution

PROCESSORS WITH WINDOWS VISTA

Windows Vista supports computers with one or two physical processors. Windows Vista Starter, Windows Vista Home Basic, and Windows Vista Home Premium support one physical processor. Windows Vista Business, Windows Vista Enterprise, and Windows Vista Ultimate support two physical processors. There's no limit to the number of processor cores these editions support, so you can use quad-core processor architectures with Windows Vista.

Now that we've looked at Windows XP and Windows Vista, it's time to look at some of the features of Windows 7.

Microsoft Vista did not take off the way that Microsoft had anticipated. Vista got a bad reputation from the get-go due to its high-end machine requirements. To allow Vista to run properly, you needed a dual-core processor and a beefed-up machine.

Many smaller IT departments did not even have dual-core processors in their servers, and they were not able to purchase all new client machines. In addition, Vista took much more hard disk space compared to its earlier cousin, XP. Therefore, many organizations held off installing Vista.

Microsoft heard the masses and started building a new operating system. What they came up with is now called Windows 7. Microsoft Windows 7 is the newest version of Microsoft's client operating system software. Microsoft has taken the best of XP and Vista and combined them into its latest creation.

Microsoft currently offers six versions of the Windows 7 operating system:

◆ Windows 7 Starter

◆ Windows 7 Home Basic

◆ Windows 7 Home Premium

◆ Windows 7 Professional

◆ Windows 7 Enterprise

◆ Windows 7 Ultimate

WINDOWS 7 REQUIREMENTS

I discuss in detail the Windows 7 hardware requirements in Chapter 2, "Installing Windows 7."

New Features in Windows 7

Windows 7 has improved on many of the problems that were plaguing Windows Vista. Windows 7 has a much faster boot time and shutdown compared to Windows Vista. It is also easier to install and configure.

The Windows 7 operating system functions are also faster than its previous counterparts. Opening, moving, extracting, compressing, and installing files and folders are more efficient than previous versions of Microsoft's client operating systems.

Let's take a look at some of the improvements and features of Windows 7. This is just an overview of some of its benefits.

Windows 7 Taskbar   In the previous versions of Windows, you had a Quick Launch bar on the left side and on the right side you could see which programs were loaded and running. The Quick Launch bar has been replaced by the Windows 7 Taskbar and Jump List, as shown in Figure 1.3.

Windows Taskbar allows users to quickly access the programs they use the most. One advantage to having the applications on the Windows 7 Taskbar is you have fewer icons on the Desktop, thus allowing for a more manageable desktop environment.

FIGURE 1.3
Windows 7 Taskbar

Jump Lists Jump Lists are a new feature to the Windows lineup. They allow you to quickly access files that you have been working on. For example, if you have the Microsoft Word icon in the taskbar, you can right-click it and it will show you all the recent files that you have been working with.

Another advantage to using Jump Lists is that you can preset certain applications, like Windows Media Player. For Internet Explorer, you could view all the recent websites that you have visited.

New Preview Pane Windows XP and Windows Vista have a Preview pane, but Windows 7 has improved on the Preview pane by allowing you to view text files, music files, pictures files, HTML files, and videos. Another new advantage is if you have installed Microsoft Office and Adobe Acrobat Reader, you also have the ability to view Office and PDF files.

Windows Touch This is one of the coolest features included with Windows 7. Windows Touch allows you to control the operating system and its applications by using a touchscreen.

For example, you can open a picture and then move it around, make it larger or smaller, or place it anywhere on the Desktop all with the touch of your fingers on the screen.

Touchscreens are included on laptops, tabletops, GPS devices, phones, and now on the Windows 7 operating system.

Windows XP Mode Microsoft realizes that many organizations are running Windows XP. Also, many of these same organizations run older applications on these Windows XP systems. This is where Windows XP Mode comes into play. Windows XP Mode gives an organization that chooses to upgrade to Windows 7 the ability to run older Windows XP applications on their new system.

To run Windows XP Mode, Windows 7 uses virtualized technology to run a virtual XP operating system to allow for the use of the older applications.

Simpler Home Networking Windows 7 networking has been made easier with the improvement of HomeGroups. HomeGroups are an easy way to set up a network using Windows 7. Windows 7 searches for your home network, and if one is found, it connects after you enter the HomeGroup password.

If a home network is not found, a networking wizard automatically creates a password for the HomeGroup. This password lets you connect all of your other computers to the same network. The password can be changed any time after the installation of Windows 7.

Device Stage Device Stage is new to the Windows operating systems family. Device Stage enables you to connect a compatible device to your PC and a picture of the device appears. Device Stage allows you to easily share files between devices and computers.

Before Windows 7 Device Stage, when you connected a device to the PC, you might see multiple devices shown. For example, when you add a multifunction printer (printer, scanner, and copier) the device might be added as three separate devices. Device Stage helps resolve this issue.

Another feature of the Device Stage is that the device vendors can customize the icons for the Device Stage, so that the same multifunction printer can have the ability to order ink from the Device Stage.

View Available Networks (VAN)   If you have used a laptop, you have used this feature. When you use a wireless network adapter and you right-click the icon in the system tray, you can choose the wireless network that you want to connect to. You connect to a wireless network through the wireless network adapter. Now that same functionality is built into the Windows 7 operating system.

Windows Internet Explorer 8   Windows 7 includes the newest version of Internet Explorer (IE8). IE8, as shown in Figure 1.4, allows a user to work faster and more efficiently on the Internet due to new search features, address bars, and favorites.

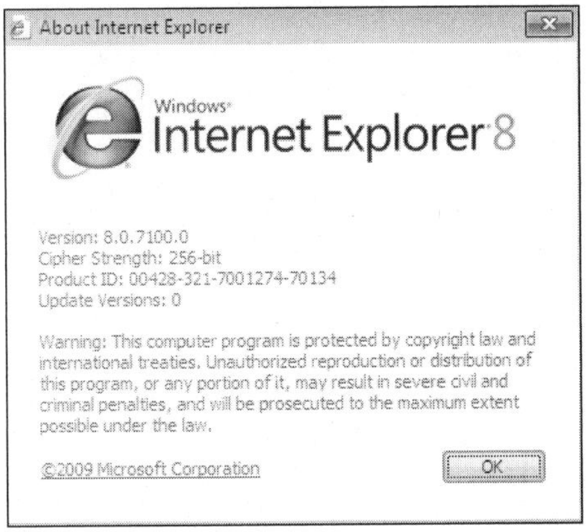

FIGURE 1.4
Internet Explorer 8 lets you work faster and more efficiently.

Some of the new features of IE8 include:

Instant Search   This feature lets you quickly access search requests without typing the entire search criteria. As you start typing in the search request, you'll see suggestions for your search.

The advantage to the Instant Search is that it will also use your browsing history to narrow down the suggestions. After you see what you're looking for, you can make your selection without having to finish the query.

Accelerators   This new feature allows you to accelerate actions on Internet services and applications. For example, if you are looking for a street address and you click the blue Accelerator icon, a map will appear right there on the screen.

Microsoft Accelerators can be used for email, searching, and so forth. Also other websites like eBay and Facebook offer Accelerators for their services.

Web Slices   Web Slices are instances on a website that you want to access without accessing the site. For example, say you want to get stock quotes, sports scores, or auction items without visiting the sites; this is the advantage of using Web Slices. As the information that you are watching changes, the updates will show immediately.

⊕ **Real World Scenario**

CHOOSING AN APPROPRIATE OPERATING SYSTEM

Your client wants to stay on the leading edge of technology, but they may not have the money to replace all of their equipment. In this case, you have to convince the client that it is better to slowly migrate their equipment.

Try presenting a timeline to your customers that shows the migration to Windows 7. Your clients will be happy and that gives you the time needed to perform the migration.

I understand that this is a Windows 7 book and you are reading this book so that you can install Windows 7 into your organization. But it is important to realize that not all of your machines will be able to run Windows 7, so it is important to know the minimum requirements for Windows XP and Vista as well.

Windows 7 Architecture

Windows 7 is built on the Windows Vista core, but Windows 7 has limited the files that load at startup to help with the core performance of the operating system. They have also removed many of the fluff items that Windows Vista used, thus allowing for better performance.

When Microsoft first released Windows 7 as a beta, there was a 64-bit version but no 32-bit version. This did not go over well with the Internet bloggers. I even saw a petition online to have a 32-bit version released.

The funny thing is that I also saw a petition asking Microsoft not to release a 32-bit version. The logic behind this was it would force users and manufacturers to upgrade everything to 64-bit. Well, Microsoft has released Windows 7 as both a 32-bit and a 64-bit version.

Microsoft could not just release a 64-bit version of Windows 7. This would alienate many users with 32-bit computer systems, and it would cost Microsoft a large share of the client-side software market. Users already have to deal with the PC vs. Mac commercials! So Windows 7 users have a choice of either 32-bit or 64-bit.

32-Bit vs. 64-Bit

When you hear the terms 32-bit and 64-bit, this is referring to the CPU or processor. The number represents how the data is processed. It is processed either as 2^32 or as 2^64. The larger the number, the larger the amount of data that can be processed at any one time.

Think of a large highway that has 32 lanes. Vehicles can travel on those 32 lanes only. When traffic gets backed up, they can only use these lanes, and this can cause traffic delays. But now think of a 64-lane highway and how many more vehicles can travel on that highway. This is an easy way of thinking of how 32-bit and 64-bit processors operate.

The problem here is that if you have a 32-lane highway, you can't just set up 64 vehicles on this highway and let them go. You need to have the infrastructure to allow for 64 vehicles by having 64 lanes. This is the same with computers. Your computer has to be configured to allow you to run a 64-bit processor.

So what does all of this mean to the common user or administrator? Well, it's all about RAM. A 32-bit operating system can handle up to 4 GB of RAM and a 64-bit processor can handle up to 16 exabytes of RAM. The problem here is that Windows and most motherboards can't handle this much RAM.

None of this is new — 64-bit is just starting to become accepted with Windows, but other operating systems, like Apple, have been using 64-bit processors for many years.

So, should you switch all of your users to 64 bit? The answer is no. Most users do not need to have large amounts of RAM, and the real problem here is that many manufacturers do not have 64 bit–compliant components.

For example, I am writing this book on a 64-bit computer, but if I open Internet Explorer and go to any website that uses Adobe Flash Player, it will not work. Currently, Adobe does not have a 64-bit Flash Player.

MEASUREMENT UNITS USED IN PROCESSORS

Computer processors are typically rated by speed. The speed of the processor, or CPU, is rated by the number of clock cycles that can be performed in one second. This measurement is typically expressed in gigahertz (GHz). One GHz is one trillion cycles per second. Keep in mind that processor architecture must also be taken into account when considering processor speed. A processor with a more efficient pipeline will be faster than a processor with a less efficient pipeline at the same CPU speed.

The Bottom Line

Choose a client operating system.   Choosing the right client operating system is a task that all IT professionals will have to face. The proper operating system is dependent on the client's hardware and job function.

> **Master It**   You are a consultant who needs to set up a new Windows Server 2008 network for one of your clients. The end-user machines must be able to work on the new network, but new equipment is not possible due to financial constraints. How should you determine which operating systems will go on each machine?

Understand the newest features of Windows 7.   There are many new features in Windows 7, among them a new Windows Taskbar and Jump Lists, Preview pane, Windows Touch, XP Mode, simpler home networking, and Device Stage.

> **Master It**   You are a consultant who needs to quickly set up a home network for one of your clients. Which operating system would you use?

Explain the Windows 32-bit and 64-bit architecture.   The terms 32-bit and 64-bit refer to the CPU, or processor. The number represents how the data is processed. It is processed as 2^{32} or 2^{64}. The larger the number, the larger the amount of data can be processed at any one time.

> **Master It**   How do you decide which operating system, 32-bit or 64-bit, you want to assign to your users?

Chapter 2

Installing Windows 7

In this chapter you'll learn how to install Windows 7 because, as you already know, before you can master any Microsoft product, you must first know how to properly install it.

Preparing for the installation of Windows 7 involves making sure that your hardware meets the minimum requirements and that it's supported by the operating system. Another consideration is whether you're going to upgrade from a previous version of Windows or install a clean copy on your computer. An upgrade attempts to preserve existing settings; a clean install puts a fresh copy of the operating system on your computer. Installation preparation also involves making choices about your system's configuration, such as selecting a disk-partitioning scheme.

To complete the Windows 7 installation, you need to activate the product through Windows Activation. This process is used to reduce software piracy. After Windows 7 is installed, you can keep the operating system up-to-date with postinstallation updates.

Also consider whether the computer will be used for dual-boot or multiboot purposes. Dual-booting or multibooting allows you to have your computer boot with operating systems other than Windows 7.

After you complete all the planning, you are ready to install Windows 7. This is a straightforward process that's highly automated and user friendly.

In this chapter, you'll learn how to:

◆ Determine the hardware requirements for Windows 7

◆ Determine which version of Windows 7 to install

◆ Install the Windows 7 operating system

◆ Migrate users from Windows XP to Windows 7

Preparing to Install Windows 7

Installing Windows 7 is simple thanks to the installation wizard. The wizard walks you through the entire installation of the operating system.

The hardest part of installing Windows 7 is preparing and planning for the installation. An hour of planning will save you days of work. Planning a Windows 7 rollout is one of the most important tasks that you will perform when you install Windows 7.

You must make many decisions before you insert the Windows 7 media into your machine. The first decision is which edition of Windows 7 you want to install.

Users' job functions or requirements may determine which edition of Windows 7 you should use. Do they need their computer for home use or just work? These are some of the factors that you'll take into account when deciding which edition to install. Let's take a look at the various editions of Windows 7.

Windows 7 Editions

Microsoft offers six editions of the Windows 7 operating system. This allows an administrator to custom-fit a user's hardware and job function to the appropriate edition:

◆ Windows 7 Starter

◆ Windows 7 Home Basic

◆ Windows 7 Home Premium

◆ Windows 7 Professional

◆ Windows 7 Enterprise

◆ Windows 7 Ultimate

Many times Microsoft releases multiple editions of the operating system contained within the same Windows 7 media disk. You can choose to unlock the one that you want based on the product key that you have. Let's take a closer look at the various editions of Windows 7.

WINDOWS 7 STARTER

The Windows 7 Starter Edition was designed for small notebook PCs and is now available worldwide. This is a change from the previous versions of the Windows Starter Editions. Previously, the Starter Editions were only available to certain locations. Windows 7 Starter Edition has some features that will work well on small notebook PCs, such as:

◆ A safe, reliable, and supported operating system

◆ HomeGroup, which allows a user to easily share media, documents, and printers across multiple PCs in homes or offices without a domain

◆ Improved Windows Taskbar and Jump Lists over Windows Vista.

◆ Broad application and device compatibility with unlimited concurrent applications

---

THREE CONCURRENT APPLICATIONS RESTRICTION

Currently, the three concurrent applications restriction was removed. If you plan on using the Windows 7 Starter Edition, check Microsoft's website at www.microsoft.com/windows7 for any possible changes to this restriction.

The Windows 7 Starter Edition has many limitations and *excludes* the following features:

◆ Aero Glass; you are only allowed to use the Windows Basic or other opaque themes. Also, you can't use the Taskbar Previews or Aero Peek.

- Personalization features that allow you to change desktop backgrounds, window colors, or sound schemes.

- The ability to easily switch between users. You must log off to change users.

- Multimonitor support.

- DVD playback or Windows Media Center for watching recorded TV or other media

- Remote Media Streaming for streaming your videos, music, and recorded TV from your home computer.

- Domain support for business customers.

- XP Mode for those who want the ability to run older Windows XP programs on Windows 7.

WINDOWS 7 HOME BASIC

The Windows 7 Home Basic Edition will be issued to limited areas throughout the world only. Currently, the Home Basic Edition is not available to US customers. Only emerging markets will be able to purchase the Home Basic Edition so that they can have an inexpensive edition of Windows 7. The Home Basic Edition has some of the following features:

- Broad application and device compatibility with unlimited concurrent applications

- A safe, reliable, and supported operating system

- The ability to share media, documents, and printers using HomeGroup without a domain

- Improved Taskbar and Jump Lists from Windows Vista.

- Live thumbnail previews and an enhanced visual experience

- Advanced networking support (ad hoc wireless networks and Internet connection sharing)

- Windows Mobility Center (shows the most frequently used mobile settings in a single location).

WINDOWS 7 HOME PREMIUM

Windows 7 Home Premium is the main operating system for the home user. Windows 7 Home Premium offers many features, including:

- Broad application and device compatibility with unlimited concurrent applications

- A safe, reliable, and supported operating system

- HomeGroup, which offers the ability to share media, documents, and printers without a domain

- Improved Taskbar and Jump Lists over Windows Vista

- Live thumbnail previews and an enhanced visual experience

- Advanced networking support (ad hoc wireless networks and Internet connection sharing)

- Windows Mobility Center

- Windows Aero transparent glass design and advance Windows navigation
- Easy networking and sharing across all your PCs and devices
- Improved media format support and enhancements to Windows Media Center and media streaming, including Play To
- Multi-touch (built-in touch screen capabilities)
- Improved handwriting recognition

WINDOWS 7 PROFESSIONAL

Windows 7 Professional was designed with the small business owner in mind. Microsoft has designed Windows 7 Professional so that you can get more done and safeguard your data. Windows 7 Professional offers some of the following features:

- Broad application and device compatibility with unlimited concurrent applications
- A safe, reliable, and supported operating system
- HomeGroup, which offers the ability to share media, documents, and printers without a domain
- Improved Taskbar and Jump Lists over Windows Vista
- Live thumbnail previews and an enhanced visual experience
- Advanced networking support (ad hoc wireless networks and Internet connection sharing)
- Windows Mobility Center
- The ability to resolve many IT issues yourself with Action Center
- Aero transparent glass design and advanced Windows navigation
- Easy networking and sharing across all your PCs and devices
- Improved media format support as well as enhancements to Windows Media Center and media streaming, including Play To
- Multi-touch
- Improved handwriting recognition
- Domain Join for simple and secure server networking
- An encrypting file system that protects data with advanced network backup
- Location Aware Printing, for finding the right printer when moving between the office and home
- Windows XP Mode, for running many Windows XP productivity applications

Windows 7 Enterprise and Ultimate

These are the two editions of Windows 7 designed for mid-sized and large organizations. These two operating systems have the most features and security options of all Windows 7 editions. Some of these features include:

◆ Broad application and device compatibility with unlimited concurrent applications

◆ A safe, reliable, and supported operating system

◆ HomeGroup, which offers the ability to share media, documents, and printers without a domain

◆ Improved Taskbar and Jump Lists over Windows Vista

◆ Live thumbnail previews and an enhanced visual experience

◆ Advanced networking support (ad hoc wireless networks and Internet connection sharing)

◆ Windows Mobility Center

◆ Aero transparent glass design and advanced Windows navigation

◆ Easy networking and sharing across all your PCs and devices

◆ Improved media format support and enhancements to Windows Media Center and media streaming, including Play To.

◆ Multi-touch

◆ Improved handwriting recognition

◆ Domain Join, which enables simple and secure server networking

◆ An encrypting file system that protects data with advanced network backup

◆ Location Aware Printing, which helps find the right printer when moving between the office and home

◆ Windows XP Mode, for running many Windows XP productivity applications

◆ BitLocker, which protects data on removable devices

◆ DirectAccess, which links users to corporate resources from the road without a virtual private network (VPN)

◆ BranchCache, which makes it faster to open files and web pages from a branch office

◆ AppLocker, for restricting unauthorized software and also enabling greater security

---

Windows 7 Multilanguage Pack

Windows 7 Ultimate also includes the multilanguage pack, but Windows 7 Enterprise does not.

Table 2.1 compares all the Windows 7 editions and lists what they include. We compiled this information from Microsoft's website and TechNet. This table is only a partial representation of all the features and applications that are included.

TABLE 2.1:   Windows 7 Edition Comparison

	STARTER EDITION	HOME BASIC EDITION	HOME PREMIUM EDITION	PROFESSIONAL EDITION	ENTERPRISE AND ULTIMATE EDITION
Processor (32-bit or 64-bit)	Both	Both	Both	Both	Both
Multiprocessor support	No	No	Yes	Yes	Yes
32-bit maximum RAM	4 GB	4 GB	4 GB	4 GB	4 GB
64-bit Maximum RAM	8 GB	8 GB	16 GB	192 GB	192 GB
Windows HomeGroup	Yes	Yes	Yes	Yes	Yes
Jump Lists	Yes	Yes	Yes	Yes	Yes
Internet Explorer 8	Yes	Yes	Yes	Yes	Yes
Media Player 12	Yes	Yes	Yes	Yes	Yes
System Image	Yes	Yes	Yes	Yes	Yes
Device Stage	Yes	Yes	Yes	Yes	Yes
Sync Center	Yes	Yes	Yes	Yes	Yes
Windows Backup	Yes	Yes	Yes	Yes	Yes
Remote Desktop	Yes	Yes	Yes	Yes	Yes
ReadyDrive	Yes	Yes	Yes	Yes	Yes
ReadyBoost	Yes	Yes	Yes	Yes	Yes
Windows Firewall	Yes	Yes	Yes	Yes	Yes
Windows Defender	Yes	Yes	Yes	Yes	Yes
Taskbar previews	No	Yes	Yes	Yes	Yes

TABLE 2.1:   Windows 7 Edition Comparison *(CONTINUED)*

	STARTER EDITION	**HOME BASIC EDITION**	**HOME PREMIUM EDITION**	**PROFESSIONAL EDITION**	**ENTERPRISE AND ULTIMATE EDITION**
Mobility Center	No	Yes	Yes	Yes	Yes
Easy user switching	No	Yes	Yes	Yes	Yes
Windows Aero Glass	No	No	Yes	Yes	Yes
Multi-touch	No	No	Yes	Yes	Yes
DVD playback	No	No	Yes	Yes	Yes
Windows Media Center	No	No	Yes	Yes	Yes
XP Mode	No	No	No	Yes	Yes
Encrypting file system (EFS)	No	No	No	Yes	Yes
BitLocker	No	No	No	No	Yes
AppLocker	No	No	No	No	Yes
BranchCache	No	No	No	No	Yes
DirectAccess	No	No	No	No	Yes

Now that we have seen what each edition of Windows 7 can accomplish, let's take a look at the hardware requirements needed to install Windows 7.

Hardware Requirements

Before you can insert the Windows 7 DVD and install the operating system, you first must make sure that the machine's hardware can handle the Windows 7 operating system.

To install Windows 7 successfully, your system must meet or exceed certain hardware requirements. Table 2.2 lists the requirements for a Windows 7–compatible PC.

HARDWARE REQUIREMENTS

The hardware requirements listed in Table 2.2 were those specified at the time of this writing. Always check Microsoft's website at www.microsoft.com/windows7 for the most current information.

TABLE 2.2:   Hardware Requirements

COMPONENT	REQUIREMENTS
CPU (processor)	1 GHz 32-bit or 64-bit processor
Memory (RAM)	1 GB of system memory
Hard disk	16 GB of available disk space
Video adapter	Support for DirectX 9 graphics with 128 MB of memory (to enable the Aero theme)
Optional drive	DVD-R/W drive
Network device	Compatible network interface card

The Windows 7–compatible PC must meet or exceed the basic requirements to deliver the core functionality of the Windows 7 operating system. These requirements assume that you're installing only the operating system without any premium functionality. For example, you may be able to get by with the minimum requirements if you're installing the operating system just to learn the basics of the software. Remember, the better the hardware, the better the performance.

Besides the basic hardware requirements that are needed to install Windows 7, the requirements for the graphic card depend on the resolution at which you want to run. The required amount of memory is as follows:

◆ 64 MB is required for a single monitor at a resolution of 1,310,720 pixels or less, which is equivalent to a 1280 × 1024 resolution.

◆ 128 MB is required for a single monitor at a resolution of 2,304,000 pixels or less, which is equivalent to a 1920 × 1200 resolution.

◆ 256 MB is required for a single monitor at a resolution larger than 2,304,000 pixels.

In addition, the graphics memory bandwidth must be at least 1,600 MB per second, as assessed by the Windows 7 Upgrade Advisor.

 **Real World Scenario**

DECIDING ON MINIMUM HARDWARE REQUIREMENTS

The company you work for has decided that everyone will have their own laptop running Windows 7. You need to determine the new computers' specifications for processor, memory, and disk space.

The first step is to learn which applications will be used. Typically, most users will work with an email program, a word processor, a spreadsheet, presentation software, and maybe a drawing or graphics program. Additionally, an antivirus application will probably be used. Under these demands, a 1 GHz Celeron processor and 1 GB of RAM will make for a very slow-running machine. So for this usage, you can assume that the minimum baseline configuration would be higher than a 1 GHz processor with at least 2 GB of RAM.

Based on your choice of baseline configuration, you should then fit a test computer with the applications that will be used on it and test the configuration in a lab environment simulating normal use. This will give you an idea whether the RAM and processor calculations you have made for your environment are going to provide suitable response.

Today's disk drives have become capable of much larger capacity while dropping drastically in price. So for disk space, the rule of thumb is to buy whatever is the current standard. Currently, 500 GB drives are commonplace, which is sufficient for most users. If users plan to store substantial graphics or video files, you may need to consider buying larger-than-standard drives.

Also consider what the business requirements will be over the next 12 to 18 months. If you'll be implementing applications that are memory or processor intensive, you might want to spec out the computers with hardware sufficient to support upcoming needs, to avoid costly upgrades in the near future.

Setting the hardware requirements for Windows 7 on your machine can sometime be a difficult task. You may ask yourself, "Does the hardware you currently have support Windows 7?" Microsoft understands this concern and has a tool called the Hardware Compatibility List to help you figure out if your machines will work with Windows 7.

The Hardware Compatibility List

Along with meeting the minimum requirements, your hardware should appear on the Hardware Compatibility List (HCL). The HCL is an extensive list of computers and peripheral hardware that have been tested with the Windows 7 operating system.

Windows 7 requires control of the hardware for stability, efficiency, and security. The hardware and supported drivers on the HCL have been put through rigorous tests to ensure their compatibility with Windows 7. Microsoft guarantees that the items on the list meet the requirements for Windows 7 and do not have any incompatibilities that could affect the stability of the operating system.

If you call Microsoft for support, the first thing a Microsoft support engineer will ask about is your configuration. If you have any hardware that is not on the HCL, you may not be able to get support from Microsoft.

To determine if your computer and peripherals are on the HCL, check the most up-to-date list at https://winqual.microsoft.com/HCL/Default.aspx.

The HCL will let you know if your hardware is compatible with Windows 7. Besides the basic RAM, video, hard drive, and CPU requirements, there are some other areas of the computer that you should examine for compatibility.

BIOS COMPATIBILITY

Before you install Windows 7, verify that your computer has the most current BIOS (Basic Input/Output System). This is especially important if your current BIOS doesn't include support for Advanced Configuration and Power Interface (ACPI) functionality. ACPI functionality is required for Windows 7 to function properly. Check the computer's vendor for the latest BIOS version information.

DRIVER REQUIREMENTS

To successfully install Windows 7, you must have the critical device drivers for your computer, such as the hard drive device driver. The Windows 7 media comes with an extensive list of drivers. If your computer's device drivers are not on the Windows 7 installation media, check the device manufacturer's website. If you can't find the device driver on the manufacturer's website and no other compatible driver exists, you are out of luck. Windows 7 won't recognize devices that don't have Windows 7 drivers.

If your hardware does not have drivers for Windows 7, be sure to check the hardware manufacturers' websites often because new drivers for Windows 7 are released frequently.

After you have made sure that the hardware for your machine is compatible for Windows 7, the next decision to make is how you're going to install the operating system.

New Install or Upgrade?

When installing Windows 7, you have two choices: you can install a fresh copy of Windows 7 or you can upgrade from Windows Vista.

An upgrade allows you to retain your existing operating system's applications, settings, and files. If you currently have a computer with Windows Vista, you are eligible to use an upgrade copy of Windows 7.

However, the bad news is you must always perform a clean install with Windows XP or earlier editions of Windows. You can, however, use the Windows Easy Transfer utility to migrate files and settings from Windows XP to Windows 7 on the same computer. The steps to do this are shown later in the section, "Upgrading from Windows XP to Windows 7."

Another possibility is to upgrade your Windows XP machine to Windows Vista and then upgrade the new Vista operating system to Windows 7.

You can perform an upgrade to Windows 7 if the following conditions are true:

◆ You are running Windows Vista.

◆ You want to keep your existing applications and preferences.

◆ You want to preserve any local users and groups you've created.

You must perform a clean install of Windows 7 if any of the following conditions are true:

◆ There is no operating system currently installed.

◆ You have an operating system installed that does not support an in-place upgrade to Windows 7 (such as DOS, Windows 9x, Windows NT, Windows Me, Windows 2000 Professional, or Windows XP).

◆ You want to start from scratch, without keeping any existing preferences.

◆ You want to be able to dual-boot between Windows 7 and your previous operating system.

Table 2.3 shows the Vista operating systems that can be upgraded and to which edition of Windows 7 it should be updated to.

TABLE 2.3: Windows Vista Upgrade Options

WINDOWS VISTA EDITION	WINDOWS 7 EDITION
Home Basic Edition	Home Basic Edition
Home Premium Edition	Home Premium Edition
Business Edition	Professional Edition
Ultimate Edition	Ultimate Edition

Before you decide if you should upgrade or install a clean Windows 7 operating system, let's take a look at some of the things you need to consider about upgrades.

UPGRADE CONSIDERATIONS

Almost all Windows Vista applications should run with the Windows 7 operating system. However, there are a few possible exceptions to this statement:

◆ Applications that use file system filters, such as antivirus software, may not be compatible.

◆ Custom power-management tools may not be supported.

Before you upgrade to Windows 7, be sure to stop any antivirus scanners, network services, or other client software. These software packages may see the Windows 7 install as a virus and cause installation issues.

If you're performing a clean install to the same partition as an existing edition of Windows, the contents of the existing Users (or Documents and Settings), Program Files, and Windows directories will be placed in a directory named `Windows.old`, and the old operating system will no longer be available.

HARDWARE COMPATIBILITY ISSUES

Ensure that you have Windows 7 device drivers for your hardware. If you have a video driver without a Windows 7–compatible driver, the Windows 7 upgrade will install the Standard VGA driver, which will display the video with an 800 × 600 resolution. After you get the Windows 7 driver for your video, you can install it and adjust video properties accordingly.

APPLICATION COMPATIBILITY ISSUES

Not all applications that were written for earlier editions of Windows will work with Windows 7. After the upgrade, if you have application problems, you can address the problems as follows:

◆ If the application is compatible with Windows 7, reinstall the application after the upgrade is complete.

- If the application uses dynamic link libraries (DLLs) and there are migration DLLs for the application, apply the migration DLLs.

- Use the Microsoft Application Compatibility Toolkit (ACT) to determine the compatibility of your current applications with Windows 7. ACT will determine which applications are installed, identify any applications that may be affected by Windows updates, and identify any potential compatibility problems with User Account Control and Internet Explorer. Reports can be exported for detailed analysis.

- If applications were written for earlier editions of Windows but are incompatible with Windows 7, use the Windows 7 Program Compatibility Wizard. From Control Panel click the Programs icon and then click the Run Programs From Previous Versions link to start the Program Compatibility Wizard.

- If the application is not compatible with Windows 7, upgrade your application to a Windows 7–compliant version.

WINDOWS 7 UPGRADE ADVISOR

To assist you in the upgrade process, the Windows 7 Setup program can check the compatibility of your system, devices, and installed applications and then provide the results to you. You can then analyze these results to determine whether your hardware or software applications will port properly from the Windows Vista edition to Windows 7.

You can download the Windows 7 Upgrade Advisor from Microsoft's website at `www.microsoft.com/downloads`. The Windows 7 Upgrade Advisor is compatible with Windows 7, Windows Vista, and Windows XP with Service Pack 2 or higher.

When you're running the Upgrade Advisor on a machine running Windows XP, if you do not have .NET Framework 2.0, you are asked to download and install it. After the .NET Framework is installed, you can restart the Upgrade Advisor installation.

After your computer is scanned, the Upgrade Advisor determines whether any incompatibilities exist between your computer and Windows 7. It also tells you which edition of Windows 7 seems to be best for your computer. However, you are by no means limited to upgrading to the recommended edition. The Upgrade Advisor Compatibility reports are broken up into the following three categories:

System Requirements The System Requirements report alerts you to any shortcomings your system might have when running certain editions of Windows Vista. For example, our lab computer should have no problems accessing all the features of Windows Vista Business, but it won't be able to access all of the features of Windows Vista Home Premium or Windows Vista Ultimate because it doesn't have a TV tuner card.

Devices The Drivers report alerts you to any potential Windows Vista driver issues. Each device in your system will be listed in this section either as a device to be reviewed or as a device that should automatically work after Windows 7 is installed. We will need a driver for the network card after Windows 7 is installed.

Programs The Programs report alerts you to any potential application compatibility issues.

You can also save or print a task list that tells you the most compatible Windows 7 edition, your current system configuration, and the steps you need to take before and after you install Windows 7.

Perform the following steps to download and run the Windows 7 Upgrade Advisor:

1. Go to www.microsoft.com/downloads and download the Windows 7 Upgrade Advisor.

2. After the download is complete, run the .msi installation.

3. The Windows 7 Upgrade Advisor Setup Wizard starts, as shown in Figure 2.1. Click the Next button.

FIGURE 2.1
Upgrade Advisor
Setup Wizard

FIGURE 2.1 Upgrade Advisor Setup Wizard

Windows 7 Upgrade Advisor

Welcome to the Windows 7 Upgrade Advisor Setup Wizard

Windows 7 Upgrade Advisor checks your system to see if it's ready to run Windows 7.

This program will install Windows 7 Upgrade Advisor on your computer.

WARNING: This computer program is protected by copyright law and international treaties. Unauthorized duplication or distribution of this program, or any portion of it, may result in severe civil or criminal penalties, and will be prosecuted to the maximum extent possible under the law.

Cancel   < Back   Next >

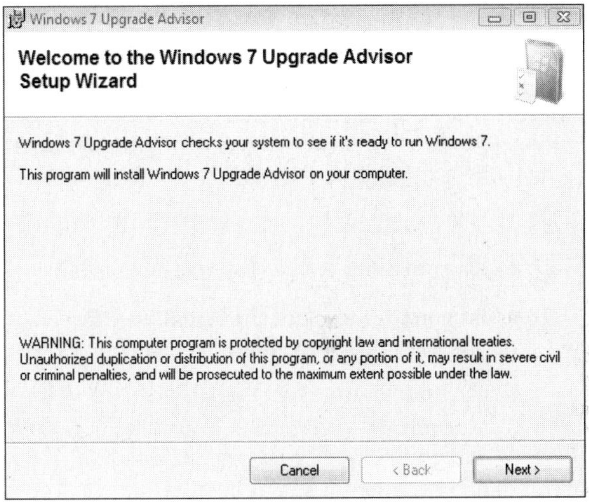

4. At the License screen, click the I Accept The License Terms check box and click Next.

5. At the Select Installation Folder screen, accept the defaults or choose a directory location where you want this program installed, as shown in Figure 2.2. Click Install.

FIGURE 2.2
The Select Installation Folder screen

Windows 7 Upgrade Advisor

Select installation folder

Where do you want to install Windows 7 Upgrade Advisor?

Folder:

C:\Program Files (x86)\Microsoft Windows 7 Upgrade Advisor\   Browse...

Disk Cost...

☑ Create a shortcut on my desktop

Cancel   < Back   Install

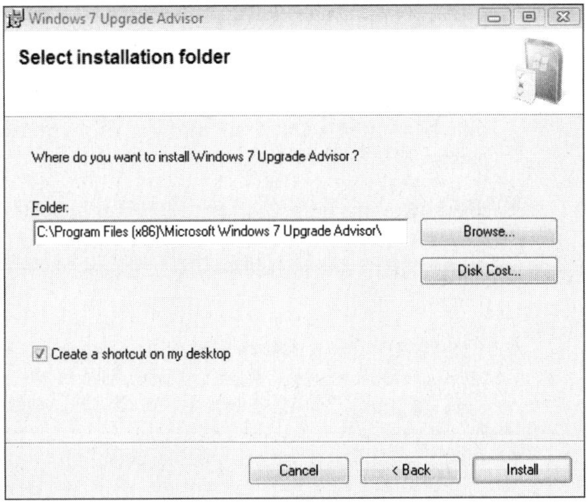

6. At the Installation Complete screen, click the Close button.

7. On the desktop, double-click the Windows 7 Upgrade Advisor icon.

8. When the Windows 7 Upgrade Advisor starts, click the Start Check button to start the scan of the machine.

9. After the system scan is complete, the Upgrade Advisor gives you the results. You can print or save these results. Close the Upgrade Advisor.

AN UPGRADE CHECKLIST

After you make the decision to upgrade, you should develop a plan of attack. The following upgrade checklist (valid for upgrading from Windows Vista) will help you plan and implement a successful upgrade strategy:

♦ Verify that your computer meets the minimum hardware requirements for Windows 7.

♦ Be sure that your hardware is on the HCL.

♦ Make sure you have the Windows 7 drivers for the hardware. You can verify this with the hardware manufacturer.

♦ Run the Windows 7 Upgrade Advisor tool from the Microsoft website, which also includes documentation on using the utility, to audit the current configuration and status of your computer. It will generate a report of any known hardware or software compatibility issues based on your configuration. You should resolve any reported issues before you upgrade to Windows 7.

♦ Make sure that your BIOS is current. Windows 7 requires that your computer has the most current BIOS. If it does not, the computer may not be able to use advanced power-management features or device-configuration features. In addition, your computer may cease to function during or after the upgrade. Use caution when performing BIOS updates, as installing the incorrect BIOS can cause your computer to fail to boot.

♦ Take an inventory of your current configuration. This inventory should include documentation of your current network configuration, the applications that are installed, the hardware items and their configuration, the services that are running, and any profile and policy settings.

♦ Back up your data and configuration files. Before you make any major changes to your computer's configuration, you should back up your data and configuration files and then verify that you can successfully restore your backup. Chances are if you have a valid backup, you won't have any problems.

♦ Delete any unnecessary files or applications, and clean up any program groups or program items you don't use. Theoretically, you want to delete all the junk on your computer before you upgrade. Think of this as the spring-cleaning step.

♦ Verify that there are no existing problems with your drive prior to the upgrade. Perform a disk scan, a current virus scan, and defragmentation. These, too, are spring-cleaning chores. This step just prepares your drive for the upgrade.

♦ Perform the upgrade. In this step, you upgrade from the Windows Vista operating system to Windows 7.

♦ Verify your configuration. After Windows 7 has been installed, use the inventory to compare and test each element that was previously inventoried prior to the upgrade to verify that the upgrade was successful.

HANDLING AN UPGRADE FAILURE

Before you upgrade, you should have a contingency plan in place. Your plan should assume the worst-case scenario. For example, what happens if you upgrade and the computer doesn't work anymore? It is possible that, after checking your upgrade list and verifying that everything should work, your attempt at the actual upgrade might not work. If this happens, you might want to return your computer to the original, working configuration.

Indeed, we have made these plans, created our backups (two, just in case), verified our backups, and then had a failed upgrade anyway — only to discover that we had no clue where to find our original operating system CD. A day later, with the missing CD located, we were able to get up and running again. Our problem was an older BIOS, and the manufacturer of our computer did not have an updated BIOS.

When you install Windows 7, you must decide how you want to partition the disk drive that the Windows 7 operating system will reside on.

Disk Space Partitioning

Disk partitioning is the act of taking the physical hard drive and creating logical partitions. A logical drive is how space is allocated to the drive's primary and logical partitions. For example, if you have a 500 GB hard drive, you might partition it into three logical drives: a C drive, which might be 2000 GB; a D drive, which might be 150 GB; and an E drive, which might be 150 GB.

Some of the major considerations for disk partitioning are as follows:

♦ The amount of space required

♦ The location of the system and boot partition

♦ Any special disk configurations you will use

♦ The utility you will use to set up the partitions

Partition Size   One important consideration in your disk-partitioning scheme is determining the partition size. You need to consider the amount of space taken up by your operating system, the applications that will be installed, and the amount of stored data. It is also important to consider the amount of space required in the future.

Microsoft recommends that you allocate at least 16 GB of disk space for Windows 7. This allows room for the operating system files and for future growth in terms of upgrades and installation files that are placed with the operating system files.

System and Boot Partitions   When you install Windows 7, files will be stored in two locations: the system partition and the boot partition. The system partition and the boot partition can be the same partition.

The system partition contains the files needed to boot the Windows 7 operating system. The system partition contains the Master Boot Record (MBR) and boot sector of the active drive partition. It is often the first physical hard drive in the computer and normally contains the necessary files to boot the computer. The files stored on the system partition do not take any significant disk space. The active partition is the system partition that is used to start your computer. The C drive is usually the active partition.

The boot partition contains the Windows 7 operating system files. By default, the Windows operating system files are located in a folder named Windows.

Special Disk Configurations   Windows 7 supports several disk configurations. Options include simple, spanned, and striped volumes. These configuration options are covered in detail in Chapter 4, "Configuring Disks."

Disk Partition Configuration Utilities   If you are partitioning your disk prior to installation, you can use several utilities, such as the DOS or Windows Fdisk program or a third-party utility such as Norton's Partition Magic. You can also configure the disks during the installation of the Windows 7 operating system.

You might want to create only the first partition where Windows 7 will be installed. You can then use the Disk Management utility in Windows 7 to create any other partitions you need. The Windows 7 Disk Management utility is covered in Chapter 4.

Another configuration option that you must set when you install Windows 7 is the location of where the computer will reside after the install is complete.

Language and Locale

Language and locale settings determine the language the computer will use. Windows 7 supports many languages for the operating system interface and utilities.

Locale settings configure the locality for items such as numbers, currencies, times, and dates. An example of a locality is that English for United States specifies a short date as mm/dd/yyyy, while English for South Africa specifies a short date as yyyy/mm/dd.

After you have planned your installation and you know how you want to install Windows 7, it's time to install the operating system.

Installing Windows 7

You can install Windows 7 either from the bootable DVD or through a network installation using files that have been copied to a network share point. You can also launch the setup.exe file from within the Windows Vista operating system to upgrade your operating system.

The Windows 7 DVD is bootable. To start the installation, simply restart your computer and boot to the DVD. The installation process begins automatically. I will walk you through the steps of installing Windows 7 later in this chapter.

If you are installing Windows 7 from the network, you need a distribution server and a computer with a network connection. A distribution server is a server that has the Windows 7 distribution files copied to a shared folder.

Perform the following steps to install Windows 7 over the network:

1. Boot the target computer.

2. Attach to the distribution server and access the share that has the files copied to it.

3. Launch setup.exe.

4. Complete the Windows 7 installation using either the clean install method or the upgrade method.

These methods are discussed in detail in the following sections.

Performing a Clean Install of Windows 7

On any installation of Windows 7, there are three stages to the installation. First you have the Collecting Information section, then the Installing Windows section, and finally the Setting Up Windows section.

Collecting Information During the collection phase of the installation, Windows 7 gathers the information necessary to complete the installation. This is where Windows 7 gathers your local time, location, keyboard, license agreement, installation type, and installation disk partition.

Installing Windows This section of the installation is where your Windows 7 files are copied to the hard disk and the installation is completed. This phase takes the longest as the files are installed.

Setting Up Windows This phase of the setup is where you set up a username, computer name, password, product key, and security settings, and review your date and time. After this is finished, your installation will be complete.

You can run the installation from the optical media or over a network. The only difference in the installation procedure is your starting point: from your optical drive or from a network share. The steps in the following sections assume you are using the Windows 7 DVD to install Windows 7.

SETTING UP YOUR COMPUTER FOR HANDS-ON EXERCISES

Before you begin any of the procedures, verify that your computer meets the requirements for installing Windows 7 as listed in Table 2.2.

The exercises in this book assume that your computer is configured in a specific manner. Your computer should have at least a 16 GB drive that is configured with at least the minimum space requirements and partitions.

When you boot to the Windows 7 installation media, the Setup program automatically starts the Windows 7 installation.

INSTALLING WINDOWS 7

Before you begin any of the procedures, verify that you have access to Windows 7 Ultimate; other editions might vary slightly. You can also download an evaluation edition of Windows 7 from Microsoft's website at www.microsoft.com/windows7.

Perform the following steps to perform a clean install of Windows 7:

1. Insert the Windows 7 DVD into the machine and start the computer.

2. If you are asked to Hit Any Key to start the DVD, press Enter.

3. The first screen asks you to enter your language, local time, and keyboard. After filling in these fields, click Next, as shown in Figure 2.3.

FIGURE 2.3
Windows 7 Installation screen

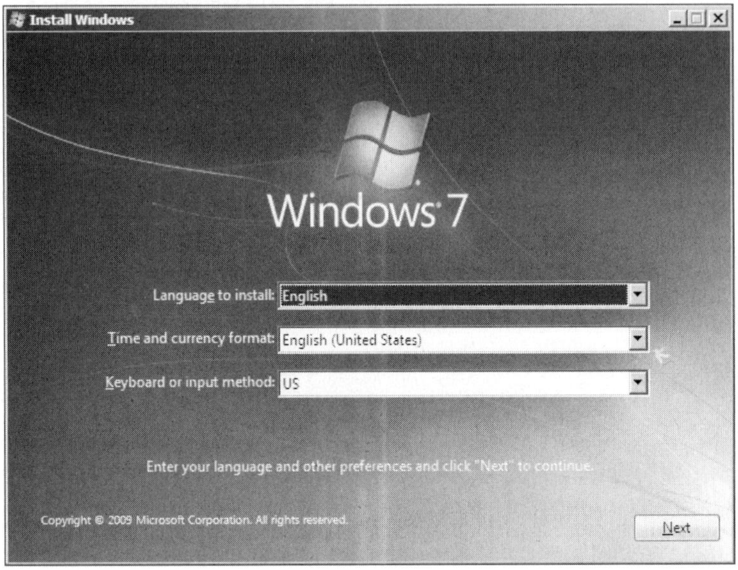

4. At the next screen, click the Install Now button, as shown in Figure 2.4.

5. A message shows you that Setup is starting. The licensing screen will be first. Read the license agreement and then check the "I accept the license term" check box. Click Next.

6. screen asking you "Which type of installation do you want?" is next, as shown in Figure 2.5. Click Custom (Advanced).

7. The next screen asks you where you want to install Windows 7, as shown in Figure 2.6. Choose an unformatted free space or a partition (the partition will be erased) with at least 20 GB available. You can also click the Drive Options (Advanced) link to create your own partition. After you choose your partition, click Next.

8. After your partition is set, the installation starts. You see the progress of the installation during the entire process. After the installation is complete, the machine reboots.

9. After the installation is complete, the username and computer name screen appears, as shown in Figure 2.7. Type in your username and computer name and click Next.

10. Next set your password and password hint, as shown in Figure 2.8. Enter your password twice and enter your hint. Click Next.

FIGURE 2.4
Windows 7 Install
Now screen

FIGURE 2.5
Choosing the Windows
7 installation type

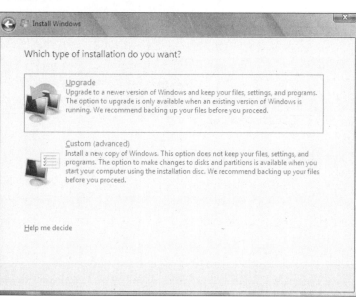

11. The next screen asks you to enter your 25-digit product key. Enter your product key and make sure the check box to automatically register your machine when you're online is selected. Click Next.

12. Settings related to Windows Update and security appear, as shown in Figure 2.9. You can select Use Recommended Settings, Install Important Updates For Windows Only, or have the computer ask you later. If you select the option to use the recommended settings, the following settings are configured:

◆ Windows Update will be enabled and updates will automatically install.

◆ Windows Defender will be installed and any collected information will be sent to Microsoft.

◆ Errors will automatically be sent to Microsoft.

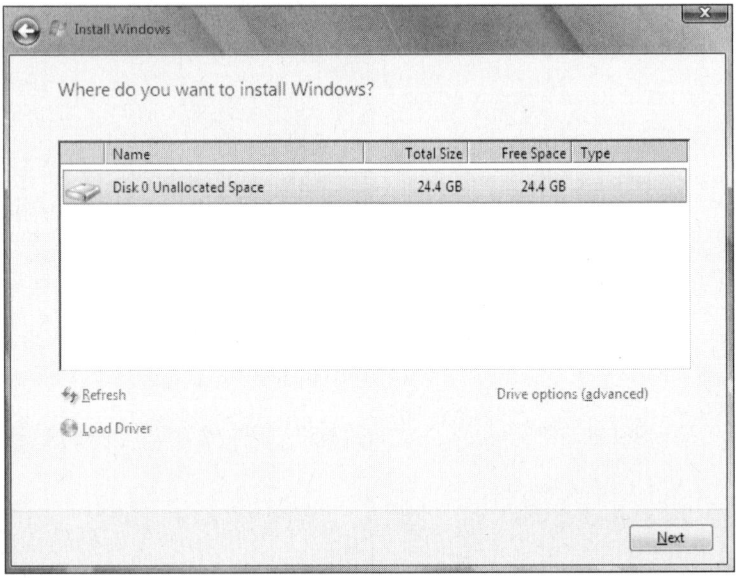

FIGURE 2.6
Specify a location for installing Windows 7.

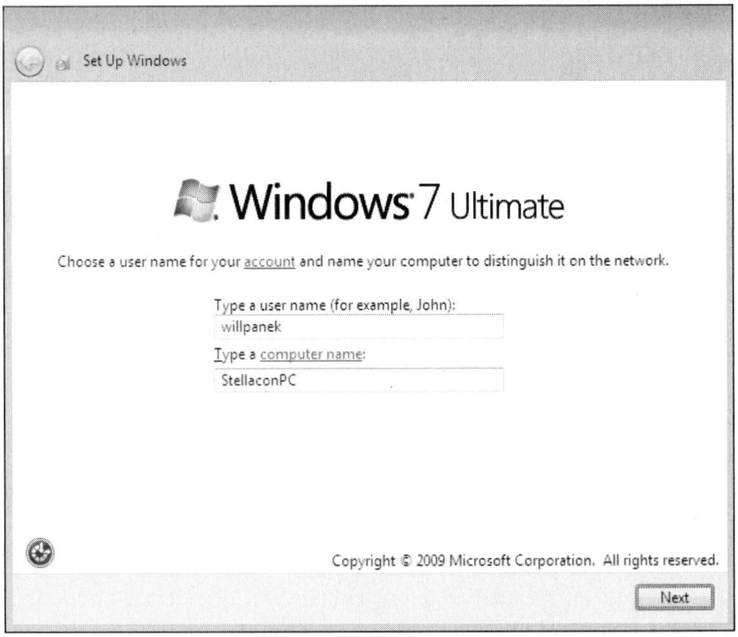

FIGURE 2.7
Adding a username and computer name

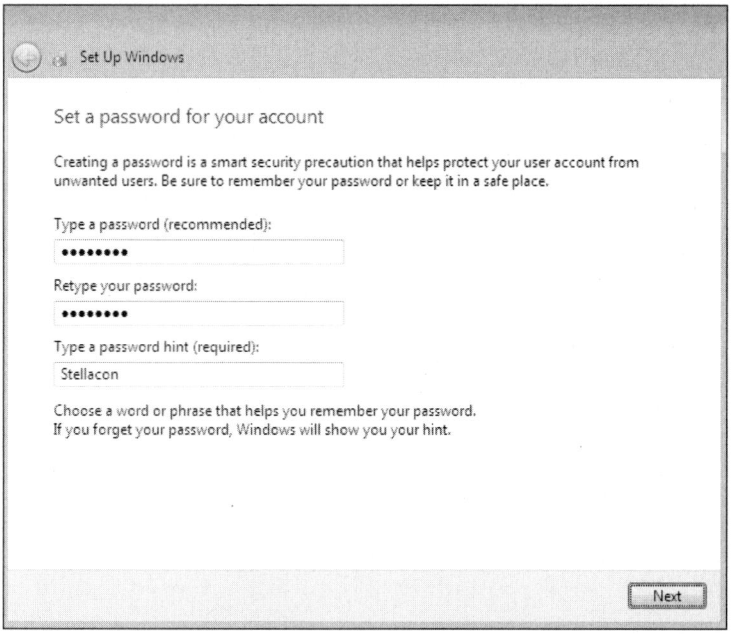

FIGURE 2.8
Password screen

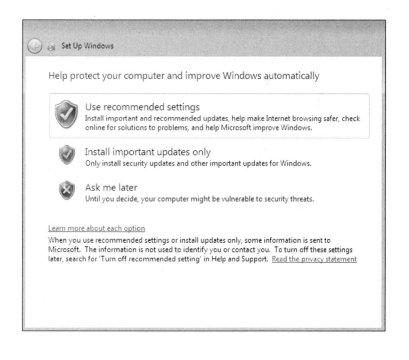

FIGURE 2.9
Specify settings related
to Windows Update
and security.

◆ The latest drivers for your hardware will automatically be downloaded from Windows Update.

13. You are now able to verify your time and date settings. Configure your time, time zone, and date. Click Next.

14. You then set your computer's current location. You have the ability to choose from a home, work, or public location. Choose where your computer is located, as shown in Figure 2.10.

FIGURE 2.10
Choosing a
network location

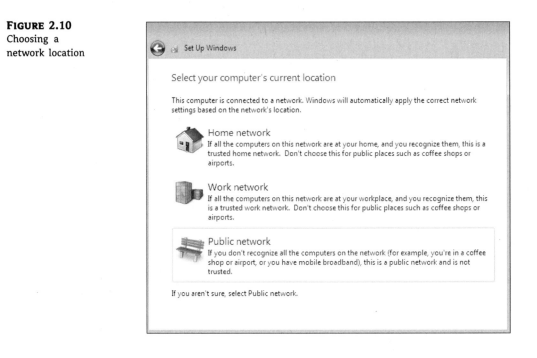

15. Windows will finalize your setup and the installation will be complete.

As you can see, installing Windows 7 is an easy process on a new computer system. But what if the system already has Windows Vista? Let's take a look at how to perform an installation of Windows 7 onto a machine with Windows Vista.

Performing an Upgrade to Windows 7

If your machine has Windows Vista already installed, you have the ability to upgrade the machine to Windows 7.

Similar to a clean install, you can run the installation from the installation DVD or over a network. The only difference in the installation procedure is your starting point: from your optical drive or from a network share. The following steps assume that you are using the Windows 7 DVD to install the Windows 7 operating system.

The three main steps in the Windows 7 upgrade process are similar to the process of a clean install. The three steps of upgrading to Windows 7 are

1. Collecting information

2. Installing Windows

3. Setting up Windows

Perform these steps to go through the process of installing Windows 7 by upgrading Windows Vista:

1. Insert the Windows 7 DVD.

2. If Autorun does not start, go to the DVD drive and click `setup.exe`. After the setup starts (by either method), click Install Windows 7.

3. You are prompted to update your current operating system. If you choose not to update, the installation might fail. You can also choose to send information to Microsoft during this process.

4. The Microsoft Windows 7 license terms will appear. The installation does not allow you to click Next until you have accepted the license terms.

5. You are prompted to select the type of installation you want to perform. Choose the Upgrade link.

6. You will see a compatibility report that alerts you of any applications or drivers that are not supported in Windows 7. Click Next.

The following step occurs in the Installing Windows section of the upgrade:

♦ During the Installing Windows Upgrade phase, all the files required by the Setup program are copied to the hard drive. During the process, the computer automatically reboots. This process takes several minutes and proceeds automatically without user intervention. The following steps appear on the screen along with a completion percentage for each:

1. Copying Windows files

2. Gathering files, settings, and programs

3. Expanding Windows files

4. Installing features and updates

5. Transferring files, settings, and programs

After your computer finishes copying files and reboots, you will be in the Setting Up Windows phase of the installation. Perform the following steps to complete the upgrade:

1. The first screen asks for your Windows product key. Type your 25-digit product key and click Next.

2. Settings related to Windows Update and security appear next. You can use the recommended settings, install important updates only, or have the computer ask you later.

3. On the next screen, you review your time and date settings. Set up your local time and date and choose if you want daylight savings time. Click Next.

4. The installation completes.

When you install Windows 7, you might run into setup problems or errors. Let's take a look at the troubleshooting process involved with Windows 7 installations.

Troubleshooting Installation Problems

The Windows 7 installation process is designed to be as simple as possible. The chances for installation errors are greatly minimized through the use of wizards and the step-by-step process. However, errors may occur.

IDENTIFYING COMMON INSTALLATION PROBLEMS

As most of you are aware, installations seldom go off without a hitch. Some of the possible installation errors that you might encounter are as follows:

Media Errors   Media errors are caused by defective or damaged DVDs. To check the disc, put it into another computer and see if you can read it. Also check your disc for scratches or dirt — it might just need to be cleaned.

Insufficient Disk Space   Windows 7 needs at least 16 GB of free space for the installation program to run properly. If the Setup program cannot verify that this space exists, the program will not let you continue.

Not Enough Memory   Make sure that your computer has the minimum amount of memory required by Windows 7 (1 GB). Having insufficient memory might cause the installation to fail or blue-screen errors to occur after installation.

Not Enough Processing Power   Make sure that your computer has the minimum processing power required by Windows 7 (1 GHz). Having insufficient processing power might cause the installation to fail or blue-screen errors to occur after installation.

Hardware That Is Not on the HCL   If your hardware is not listed on the HCL, Windows 7 might not recognize the hardware or the device might not work properly.

Hardware with No Driver Support   Windows 7 will not recognize hardware without driver support.

Hardware That Is Not Configured Properly   If your hardware is Plug and Play–compatible, Windows 7 should configure it automatically. If your hardware is not Plug and Play–compatible, you need to manually configure the hardware per the manufacturer's instructions.

Incorrect Product Key   Without a valid product key, the installation will not go past the Product Key screen. Make sure that you have not typed an incorrect key (check your Windows 7 installation folder or your computer case for this key).

Failure to Access TCP/IP Network Resources   If you install Windows 7 with typical settings, the computer is configured as a DHCP client. If there is no DHCP server to provide IP configuration information, the client will still generate an autoconfigured IP address but will be unable to access network resources through TCP/IP if the other network clients are using DHCP addresses.

Installing Nonsupported Hard Drives   If your computer is using a hard disk that does not have a driver included on the Windows 7 media, you will receive an error message stating that the hard drive cannot be found. You should verify that the hard drive is properly connected and functional. You will need to obtain a disk driver for Windows 7 from the manufacturer and then specify the driver location by selecting the Load Driver option during partition selection.

TROUBLESHOOTING WITH INSTALLATION LOG FILES

When you install Windows 7, the Setup program creates several log files. You can view these logs files to check for any problems during the installation process. The following two log files are particularly useful for troubleshooting:

♦ The action log includes all of the actions that were performed during the setup process and a description of each action. These actions are listed in chronological order. The action log is stored as \Windows\setupact.log.

♦ The error log includes any errors that occurred during the installation. For each error, there is a description and an indication of the severity of the error. This error log is stored as \Windows\setuperr.log.

In the following steps you will view the Windows 7 setup logs to determine whether there were any problems with your Windows 7 installation.

Follow these steps to troubleshoot failed installations with setup logs:

1. Select Start ➢ Computer.

2. Double-click Local Disk (C:).

3. Double-click Windows.

4. In the Windows folder, double-click the setupact.log file to view your action log in Notepad. When you finish viewing this file, close Notepad.

5. Double-click the setuperr.log file to view your error file in Notepad. If no errors occurred during installation, this file will be empty. When you finish viewing this file, close Notepad.

6. Close the directory window.

After you install Windows 7 and look at the setup logs, it might be necessary to transfer user's data from one system to another or migrate data from the same computer. Let's take a look at the migration process.

Migrating Files and Settings

Rather than perform an in-place upgrade, you can choose to migrate your files and settings from an existing installation. In this case, you can use the User State Migration Tool (USMT) or the Windows Easy Transfer.

USER STATE MIGRATION TOOL

You can download a utility called the User State Migration Tool (USMT) that administrators use to migrate large numbers of users over automated deployments. The USMT for Windows 7 is now part of Windows Automated Installation Kit (Windows AIK). The USMT is similar to Windows Easy Transfer with the following differences:

♦ The USMT is more configurable and can use XML files to specify which files and settings are transferred.

♦ The USMT is scriptable and uses command-line utilities to save and restore user files and settings.

The USMT consists of two executable files: `ScanState.exe` and `LoadState.exe`. In addition, there are three premade migration rule information files: `Migapp.xml`, `Migsys.xml`, and `Miguser.xml`. Finally, you can create a `Config.xml` file that specifies what should and should not be migrated. The purposes of these files are as follows:

♦ `ScanState.exe` collects user data and settings information based on the configuration of the `Migapp.xml`, `Migsys.xml`, and `Miguser.xml` files and stores it as an image file.

♦ `LoadState.exe` then deposits the information that is collected to a computer running a fresh copy of Windows 7.

The information that is migrated includes the following:

♦ From each user:

   ♦ Documents

   ♦ Video

   ♦ Music

   ♦ Pictures

   ♦ Desktop files

   ♦ Start Menu

   ♦ Quick Launch toolbar

   ♦ Internet Explorer Favorites

♦ From the All Users profile:

   ♦ Shared Documents

   ♦ Shared Video

   ♦ Shared Music

   ♦ Shared Desktop files

   ♦ Shared Pictures

   ♦ Shared Start Menu

   ♦ Shared Internet Explorer Favorites

   ♦ Files with certain file types, including `.doc`, `.dot`, `.rtf`, `.txt`, `.wps`, `.wri`, `.xls`, `.csv`, `.wks`, `.ppt`, `.pps`, `.pot`, `.pst`, and more

   ♦ Access control lists (ACLs)

The USMT will not migrate hardware settings, drivers, passwords, application binaries, synchronization files, `.dll` files, or other executables.

USING THE USMT

The USMT is downloadable software from Microsoft's website. In its simplest form, you use the USMT in the following manner:

1. Run ScanState.exe on the source computer. ScanState.exe will copy the user state data to an intermediate store. The intermediate store (for example, a CD-RW) must be large enough to accommodate the data that will be transferred. Scanstate.exe would commonly be executed as a shortcut sent to users that they would deploy in the evening or through a scheduled script.

2. Install a fresh copy of Windows 7 on the target computer.

3. Run LoadState.exe on the target computer. LoadState.exe will access the intermediate store to restore the user settings.

When you use the USMT, you can create a script that can be run manually or can be used as an automated process at a scheduled time. Table 2.4 defines the options for the Scanstate.exe and Loadstate.exe commands.

TABLE 2.4:   Options for Scanstate.exe and Loadstate.exe

OPTION	DESCRIPTION
/config	Specifies the Config.xml file that should be used
/encrypt	Encrypts the store (Scanstate.exe only)
/decrypt	Decrypts the store (Loadstate.exe only)
/nocompress	Disables data compression
/genconfig	Generates a Config.xml file but does not create a store
/targetxp	Optimizes ScanState for use with Windows XP
/all	Migrates all users
/ue	User exclude: excludes the specified user
/ui	User include: includes the specified user
/uel	Excludes user based on last login time
/v verboselevel	Used to identify what verbosity level will be associated with the log file on a scale of 0–13, with 0 the least verbose

WINDOWS EASY TRANSFER

Windows 7 ships with a utility called Windows Easy Transfer that is used to transfer files and settings from one computer to another. You can transfer some or all of the following files and settings from a computer running Windows XP with Service Pack 2 or Windows Vista:

- User accounts
- Folders and files
- Program settings
- Internet settings
- Favorites
- E-mail messages, contacts, and settings

You can transfer the migrated files and settings using the following methods:

- Easy Transfer Cable, which is a USB cable that connects to the source and destination computers
- CD or DVD
- Removable media, such as a USB flash drive or a removable hard drive
- Network share
- Direct network connection

You can password-protect the migrated files and settings if you use CDs, DVDs, removable media, or a network share. Now let's take a look at how to upgrade a Windows XP machine to Windows 7.

Upgrading from Windows XP to Windows 7

Because the upgrade option from Windows XP to Windows 7 is not available, you can use Windows Easy Transfer to integrate settings from Windows XP to Windows 7 on the same computer.

The first step in this migration process is to copy your files to a removable media such as an external hard drive or thumb drive or to a network share. After the installation of the Windows 7 operating system, you can then migrate these files onto the Windows 7 system.

Perform the following steps to migrate from Windows XP to Windows 7:

1. Insert the Windows 7 DVD while running Windows XP. If the Windows 7 installation window opens automatically, close it.

2. Open Windows Explorer by right-clicking the Start menu and then clicking Explore.

3. Browse to the DVD drive on your computer and click `migsetup.exe` in the Support\Migwiz directory.

4. When the Windows Easy Transfer window opens, click Next.

5. Select an external hard disk or USB flash drive.

6. Click This Is My Old Computer. Windows Easy Transfer scans the computer.

7. Click Next. You can also determine which files should be migrated by selecting only the user profiles you want to transfer or by clicking Customize.

8. Enter a password to protect your Easy Transfer file, or leave the box blank, and then click Save.

9. Browse to the external location on the network or to the removable media where you want to save your Easy Transfer file and then click Save.

10. Click Next. Windows Easy Transfer displays the filename and location of the Easy Transfer file you just created.

Perform the following steps to use the Windows 7 DVD to install the operating system:

1. Start Windows 7 Setup by browsing to the root folder of the DVD in Windows Explorer, and then double-clicking `setup.exe`.

2. Click Go Online To Get The Latest Updates (Recommended) to retrieve any important updates for Windows 7. This step is optional. If you choose not to check for updates during Setup, click Do Not Get The Latest Updates.

3. Read and accept the Microsoft Software License Terms. Click "I accept the License Terms (required to use Windows)," and then click Next. If you click "I decline (cancel installation)," Windows 7 Setup will exit.

4. Click Custom to perform an upgrade to your existing Windows installation.

5. Select the partition where you would like to install Windows. To move your existing Windows installation into a `Windows.old` folder and replace the operating system with Windows 7, select the partition where your current Windows installation is located.

6. Click Next and then click OK.

7. Windows 7 Setup will proceed without further interaction.

Now, perform the following steps to migrate files to the destination computer:

1. If you saved your files and settings in an Easy Transfer file on a removable media such as a universal flash device (UFD) rather than on a network share, insert the removable media into the computer.

2. Select Start ➤ All Programs ➤ Accessories ➤ System Tools ➤ Windows Easy Transfer.

3. When the Windows Easy Transfer window opens, click Next.

4. Click An external hard disk or USB flash drive.

5. Click This Is My New Computer.

6. Click Yes, Open The File.

7. Browse to the location where the Easy Transfer file was saved. Click the filename, and then click Open.

8. Click Transfer to transfer all files and settings. You can also determine which files should be migrated by selecting only the user profiles you want to transfer, or by clicking Customize.

9. Click Close after Windows Easy Transfer has completed moving your files.

Once the migration process is complete, you should regain the disk space used by the Windows XP system by using the Disk Cleanup tool to delete the `Windows.old` directory.

Perform the following steps to use the Disk Cleanup tool:

1. Open Disk Cleanup. Select Start ➢ All Programs ➢ Accessories ➢ System Tools ➢ Disk Cleanup.

2. Click Clean Up System Files.

3. Previous installations of Windows are scanned. After they are scanned, select Previous Windows Installation(s) and any other categories of files you want to delete.

4. Click OK and then click Delete Files.

UPGRADING TO WINDOWS VISTA

Another important decision that you should consider is whether to upgrade your Windows XP clients to Windows Vista first and then upgrade the machine to Windows 7.

As you have seen, you can migrate your users' data, but let's say you have software installed and you can't locate the CD/DVD for that software package. It might be beneficial to a user or organization to upgrade the Windows XP machine to Windows Vista. After that installation is complete, upgrade the Vista machine to Windows 7.

This is just another option that is available to you when you migrate your users to the Windows 7 operating system.

Another option you may choose is to run two different operating systems on the same computer system. This gives you the choice of which operating system you want to boot into when the system starts. Installing multiple operating systems onto the same computer is called dual-booting or multibooting.

Supporting Multiboot Options

You might want to install Windows 7 but still be able to run other operating systems. Dual-booting or multibooting allows your computer to boot multiple operating systems. Your computer will be automatically configured for dual-booting if there was a supported operating system on your computer prior to the Windows 7 installation, you didn't upgrade from that operating system, and you installed Windows 7 into a different partition.

One reason for dual-booting is to test various systems. If you have a limited number of computers in your test lab and you want to be able to test multiple configurations, you should dual-boot. For example, you might configure one computer to multi-boot with Windows XP Professional, Windows Vista, and Windows 7.

Here are some keys to successful dual-boot configurations:

◆ Make sure you have plenty of disk space.

◆ Windows 7 must be installed on a separate partition in order to dual-boot with other operating systems.

◆ Install older operating systems before installing newer operating systems.

◆ If you want to support dual-booting with Windows XP and Windows 7, Windows XP must be installed first. If you install Windows 7 first, you cannot install Windows XP without ruining your Windows 7 configuration. This requirement also applies to Windows 9*x*, Windows 2000, and Windows Vista.

◆ Never, ever upgrade to Windows 7 dynamic disks. Dynamic disks are seen only by Windows 2000, Windows XP Professional, Windows Server 2003, Windows Vista, and Windows 7, and are not recognized by any other operating system, including Windows NT and Windows XP Home Edition.

◆ Only Windows NT 4.0 (with Service Pack 4), Windows 2000, Windows XP, Windows Vista, Windows 7, Windows Server 2003, and Windows Server 2008 can recognize NTFS file systems. Other Windows operating systems use FAT16 or FAT32 and cannot recognize NTFS. All Windows-based operating systems can recognize FAT partitions.

◆ If you will dual-boot with Windows 9*x*, you must turn off disk compression or Windows 7 will not be able to read the drive properly.

◆ Do not install Windows 7 on a compressed volume unless the volume was compressed using NTFS compression.

◆ Files that are encrypted with Windows 7 will not be available to Windows NT 4.

WINDOWS NT 4.0 AND WINDOWS 7 DUAL-BOOTING

If you are planning on dual-booting with Windows NT 4, you should upgrade it to NT 4 Service Pack 4 (or higher), which provides NTFS version 5 support.

After you install each operating system, you can choose the operating system that you will boot to during the boot process. You will see a boot selection screen that asks you to choose which operating system you want to boot.

The Boot Configuration Data (BCD) store contains boot information parameters that were previously found in boot.ini in older versions of Windows. To edit the boot options in the BCD store, use the bcdedit utility, which can be launched only from a command prompt.

Perform the following steps to open a command prompt window:

1. Launch \Windows\system32\cmd.exe.

2. Open the Run command by pressing [Windows] key+R.

3. Type **cmd.exe** in the Search Programs And Files box and press Enter.

After the command prompt window is open, type **bcdedit** to launch the bcdedit utility. You can also type **bcdedit /?** to see all the various bcdedit commands.

After the Windows 7 installation is complete, it's time to do some general housekeeping. The first thing we need to do is activate the Windows 7 operating system.

Using Windows Activation

Windows Activation is Microsoft's way of reducing software piracy. Unless you have a corporate license for Windows 7, you will need to perform postinstallation activation. You can do this online or call Microsoft on the telephone. Windows 7 will attempt automatic activation three days after you log on to Windows 7 for the first time. There is a grace period when you will be able to use the operating system without activation. After the grace period expires, you will not be able to create new files or save changes to existing files until Windows 7 is activated. When the grace period runs out, the Windows Activation Wizard automatically starts; it walks you through the activation process.

Using Windows Update

Windows Update, as shown in Figure 2.11, is a utility that connects to Microsoft's website and checks to ensure that you have the most up-to-date version of Microsoft products.

FIGURE 2.11
Windows Update

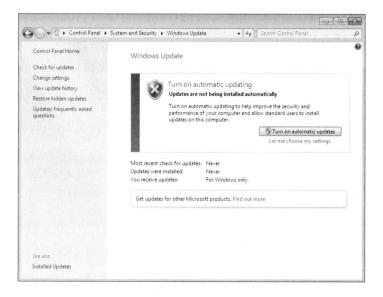

Some of the common update categories associated with Windows Update are as follows:

◆ Critical updates

◆ Service packs

◆ Drivers

Perform the following steps to configure Windows Update:

1. Select Start ➢ Control Panel.

    ◆ From Windows Icons View, select Windows Update.

    ◆ From Windows Category View, select System And Security, Windows Update.

2. Configure the options you want to use for Windows Update, and click OK.

You can access the following options from Windows Update:

◆ Check For Updates

◆ Change Settings

◆ View Update History

- Restore Hidden Updates
- Updates: Frequently Asked Questions
- Installed Updates

CHECK FOR UPDATES

When you click Check For Updates, Windows Update retrieves a list of available updates from the Internet. You can then click View Available Updates to see what updates are available. Updates are marked as Important, Recommended, or Optional. Figure 2.12 shows a sample list of updates.

FIGURE 2.12
Checking for updates

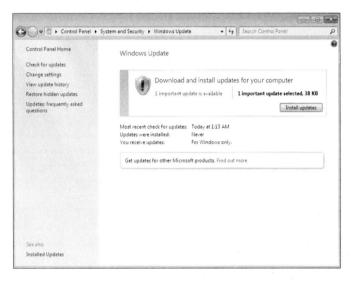

CHANGE SETTINGS

Clicking Change Settings allows you to customize how Windows can install updates. You can configure the following options:

- Install Updates Automatically (Recommended)
- Download Updates But Let Me Choose To Install Them
- Download Updates But Let Me Choose Whether To Download And Install Them
- Never Check For Updates (Not Recommended)

Figure 2.13 shows the settings that you can configure for Windows Update.

VIEW UPDATE HISTORY

View Update History, as shown in Figure 2.14, is used to view a list of all of the installations that have been performed on the computer. You can see the following information for each installation:

- Update Name
- Status (Successful, Unsuccessful, Or Canceled)

- ◆ Importance (Important, Recommended, Or Optional)
- ◆ Date Installed

RESTORE HIDDEN UPDATES

With Restore Hidden Updates you can list any updates that you have hidden from the list of available updates. An administrator might hide updates that they do not want users to install.

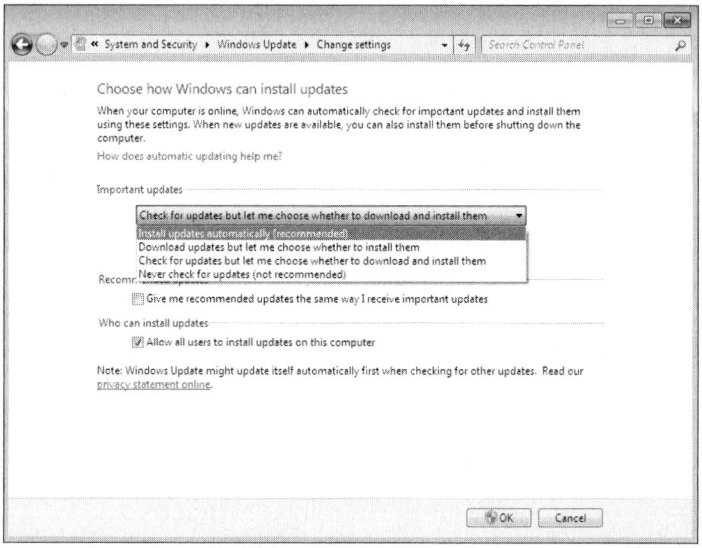

FIGURE 2.13
Changing settings in Windows Update

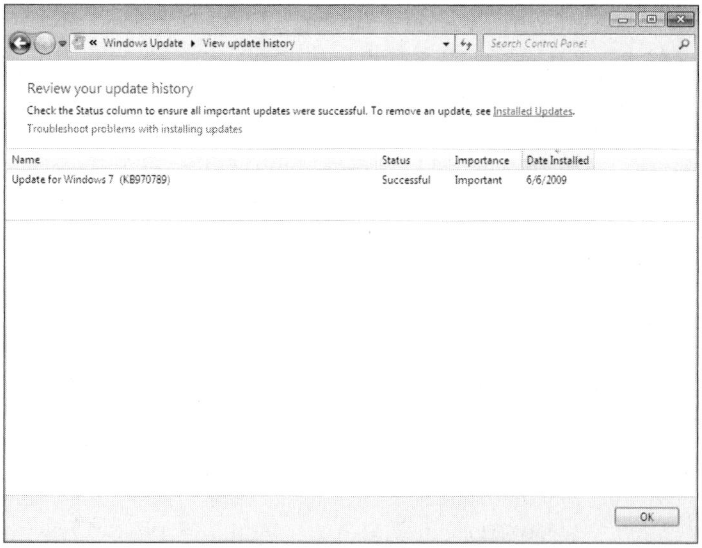

FIGURE 2.14
Windows Update: View Update History

Sometimes it is important for an administrator to test and verify the updates before the users can install the updates. This area allows you to see hidden updates so that they can be tested before deployment.

INSTALLED UPDATES

Installed Updates allows you to see the updates that are installed and to uninstall or change them if necessary. The Installed Updates feature is a part of the Programs and Features applet in Control Panel, which allows you to uninstall, change, and repair programs.

Updates are important to keep your Windows 7 operating system current but when Microsoft has many updates or security patches, they release service packs.

Installing Windows Service Packs

Service packs are updates to the Windows 7 operating system that include bug fixes and product enhancements. Some of the options that might be included in service packs are security fixes or updated versions of software, such as Internet Explorer.

Perform the following steps prior to installing a service pack:

1. Back up your computer.

2. Check your computer to ensure that it is not running any malware or other unwanted software.

3. Check with your computer manufacturer to see whether there are any special instructions for your computer prior to installing the service pack.

You can download service packs from Microsoft.com, receive service packs via Windows Update, or pay for a copy of the service pack to be mailed to you on disc. Before you install a service pack, read the Release Note that is provided for each service pack on Microsoft's website.

The Bottom Line

Determine the hardware requirements for Windows 7.   One of the most important tasks in installing Windows 7 is to verify that the machines that you want to install Windows 7 can handle the installation. The following hardware requirements are for Windows 7:

CPU (processor)	1 GHz 32-bit or 64-bit processor
Memory (RAM)	1 GB of system memory
Hard disk	16 GB of available disk space
Video adapter	Support for DirectX 9 graphics with 128 MB of memory (to enable the Aero theme)
Optional drive	DVD-R/W drive
Network device	Compatible network interface card

Master It You are a consultant who is hired by an organization to migrate the users from Windows Vista and Windows XP to Windows 7. How would you accomplish this?

Determine which version of Windows 7 to install. Microsoft has released six versions of the Windows 7 operating system. It is very important to install the correct version of Windows 7 to match the end user's needs. The six versions are

◆ Windows 7 Starter

◆ Windows 7 Home Basic

◆ Windows 7 Home Premium

◆ Windows 7 Professional

◆ Windows 7 Enterprise

◆ Windows 7 Ultimate

Master It You are an IT manager and you must install a Windows 7 operating system that supports Windows BitLocker. Which edition of Windows 7 could you use?

Install the Windows 7 operating system. Installing Windows 7 is an easy process but it is important to plan the installation before actually installing the operating system.

You can install Windows 7 either from the bootable DVD or through a network installation using files that have been copied to a network share point. You can also launch the `setup.exe` file from within the Windows Vista operating system to upgrade your operating system.

The Windows 7 DVD is bootable. To start the installation, you simply restart your computer and boot to the DVD. The installation process will begin automatically.

Master It Your company has purchased a new computer that meets all the minimum requirements for installing Windows 7. They need Windows 7 installed on the machine. How can you install Windows 7?

Migrate users from Windows XP to Windows 7. Since the upgrade option from Windows XP to Windows 7 is not available, you can use Windows Easy Transfer to integrate settings from Windows XP to Windows 7 on the same computer.

The first step in this migration process is to copy your files to a removable media such as an external hard drive or thumb drive or to a network share. After the installation of the Windows 7 operating system, you can then migrate these files onto the Windows 7 system.

Master It Your organization needs to convert all Windows XP machines to Windows 7. What steps should you take to complete the upgrade?

Chapter 3

Automating the Windows 7 Installation

As you saw in the previous chapter, installing Windows 7 is quick and easy. But as an IT manager and professional, you might have to install hundreds of copies of Windows 7. You wouldn't want to do that one machine at a time.

You can automate the installation of Windows 7 in several ways. You can use the Microsoft Deployment Toolkit (MDT) to deploy Windows 7 in your organization. The MDT will help you automate your desktop and server deployments.

You can also perform an unattended installation by using Windows Deployment Services (WDS) to remotely deploy unattended installations (which requires a Windows Server 2008 machine), or by using the System Preparation Tool for disk imaging.

Another utility that we'll explore is the Windows Automated Installation Kit (Windows AIK), which is a set of utilities and documentation that allows you to configure and deploy Windows operating systems, including Windows 7.

To help customize these tools for automating remote installations, you can take advantage of answer files. Answer files are used with automated installations to provide answers to the questions that are normally asked during the installation process. After you install Windows 7, you can also automate the installation of applications by using Windows Installer packages.

This chapter begins with an overview of the automated deployment tools available with Windows 7. Then, we describe how to access the deployment tools available for Windows 7. Next, we detail the use of unattended installation; discuss WDS; explain how you can use the System Preparation Tool, along with ImageX, to create disk images for automated installation; and explore using Windows System Image Manager (SIM) to create unattended answer files. This chapter will help you build a good foundation for the rest of this book.

In this chapter, you'll learn how to:

◆ Use the Microsoft Deployment Toolkit (MDT) 2010

◆ Take advantage of the Windows Deployment Services (WDS)

◆ Utilize the Windows Automated Installation Kit (Windows AIK)

◆ Make the most of the Microsoft Assessment and Planning (MAP) Toolkit

Choosing Automated Deployment Options

If you need to install Windows 7 on multiple computers, you could manually install the operating system on each computer, as described in Chapter 2, "Installing Windows 7." However, automating the deployment process can make your job easier, more efficient, and more cost-effective if you have a large number of client computers. Windows 7 comes with several tools that you can use for deploying and automating the Windows 7 installation. By using multiple utilities with different functionality, you have increased flexibility in determining how to best deploy Windows 7 within a large corporate environment.

The following sections provide overviews of the automated deployment tools that will help you choose which solution is best for your requirements and environment. Each utility is then covered in more detail throughout this chapter. The tools for automated deployment of Windows 7 are as follows:

- ◆ Microsoft Deployment Toolkit (MDT) 2010

- ◆ Unattended installation, or unattended setup, which uses `Setup.exe`

- ◆ WDS, which requires Windows Server 2008 for deployment

- ◆ System Preparation Tool (`Sysprep.exe`), which is used to create and deploy disk imaging or cloning

- ◆ Windows Automated Installation Kit (Windows AIK)

Later in the chapter, you'll see a table that summarizes the features and requirements of each installation deployment tool.

SYSTEM CENTER CONFIGURATION MANAGER 2007

Another tool that you have to deploy Windows 7 is through System Center Configuration Manager (SCCM) 2007. Because SCCM 2007 is its own application, it is beyond the scope of this book. You can learn more about SMS on the Microsoft website at www.microsoft.com.

Introducing the Microsoft Deployment Toolkit (MDT) 2010

Microsoft has released a new beta program called the Microsoft Deployment Toolkit (MDT) 2010. This toolkit is a way of automating desktop and server deployment. The MDT offers an administrator the following benefits:

- ◆ Administrative tools that allow for the deployment of desktops and servers through the use of a common console, as shown in Figure 3.1

- ◆ Quicker deployments and the capability to have standardized desktop and server images and security

- ◆ "Zero Touch" deployments of Windows 7, Windows Server 2008, Windows Vista, Windows Server 2003, and Windows XP

FIGURE 3.1
The MDT console

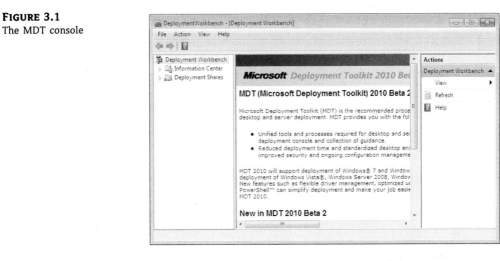

To install the MDT 2010 package onto your computer (regardless of the operating system being deployed), you must first meet the minimum requirements. These requirements need to be met only on the computer where MDT 2010 is being installed:

◆ Microsoft Management Console (MMC) 3.0

◆ Microsoft .NET Framework 2.0 or higher

◆ Windows PowerShell command-line interface, version 1.0 or 2.0

◆ Community Technology Preview (CTP) 3 or higher

◆ Windows AIK for Windows 7 RC (Release Candidate). We describe the installation procedure later in this chapter

---

MDT 2010 INSTALLATION

You can install MDT 2010 without installing Windows AIK first, but you won't be able to use the package fully until Windows AIK is installed.

For Zero Touch deployments, MDT 2010 requires the following components:

◆ If deploying Windows 7 or Windows Server 2008, SCCM 2007 Service Pack 2 (SP2) is required.

◆ If you want to deploy previous versions of Windows using MDT 2010, SCCM 2007 Service Pack 1 (SP1) can be used, but you can't use Deployment Workbench in this configuration to maintain an MDT database. If you're using an MDT database with SCCM, you should use SCCM 2007 SP2.

You can install the MDT 2010 on the Windows 7 operating system machine that we installed in Chapter 2. If you decide to install the MDT onto a server or production machine, we recommend that you perform a full backup before you complete these steps. Installing MDT 2010 will replace any previous version of the MDT that the machine is currently using.

Perform these following steps to download and install MDT 2010:

1. Download the MDT 2010 utility from Microsoft's website.

2. Double-click `MicrosoftDeploymentToolkit_x86.exe` to start the installation. If you downloaded the 64-bit version, click that version.

3. At the Welcome screen, click Next.

4. At the License screen, select the "I accept the terms in the license agreement" radio button and click Next.

5. At the Custom Setup screen, shown in Figure 3.2, click the down arrow next to the Microsoft Deployment Toolkit and choose "Entire feature will be installed on local hard drive." Click Next.

FIGURE 3.2
MDT's Custom
Setup screen

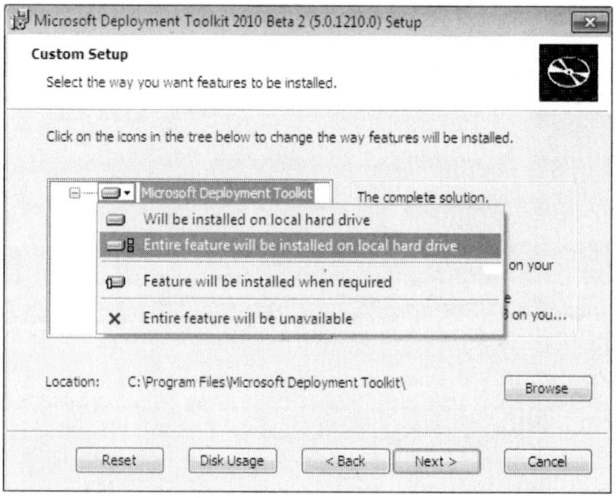

6. At the Ready To Install screen, click Install.

7. When the installation completes, click Finish.

Once you've installed MDT 2010, follow these steps to configure it and set up a distribution share and database:

1. Create a shared folder on your network called **Distribution** and give the Everyone group full control for this exercise.

2. Open the MDT workbench by clicking Start ➤ All Programs ➤ Microsoft Development Toolkit ➤ Deployment Workbench.

3. If the User Account Control box appears, click Yes.

4. In the left-hand pane, right-click Deployment Shares and choose New Deployment Share, as shown in Figure 3.3.

FIGURE 3.3

Select New Deployment Share from this menu.

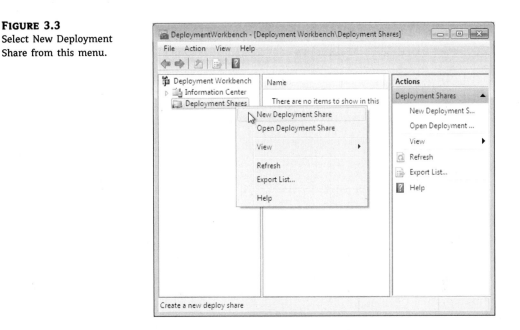

5. The New Deployment Share Wizard begins. At the first screen, choose the directory where the deployments will be stored. Click the Browse button and choose the distribution share that you created in step 1. Then click Next.

6. At the Share Name screen, accept the default, of distribution. Click Next.

7. At the Deployment Share Description screen, accept the default description name and click Next.

8. At the Allow Image Capture screen, make sure the ''Ask if an image should be captured'' check box is selected, as shown in Figure 3.4. Images can be captured after they're deployed to a domain. By checking this box, you have the option to either capture or not capture the image after deployment. Click Next.

9. At the Allow Admin Password screen, check the box that allows the user to set the admin password for the local machine. If the box is not checked, you can preset the password before deployment.

10. At the Allow Product Key screen, select the option ''Ask users to enter a product key at time of installation.'' You also can preset the product key and then the user would not be required to supply the product key. Many organizations have site licenses and the user would not be required to enter a product key. Click Next.

11. At the Summary screen, verify all of your settings and click Next.

12. Once the installation is complete, a confirmation screen appears. Click Finish. Close the MDT Workbench.

Now that you have seen how to install the MDT 2010 utility, let's look at other ways to automatically install Windows 7.

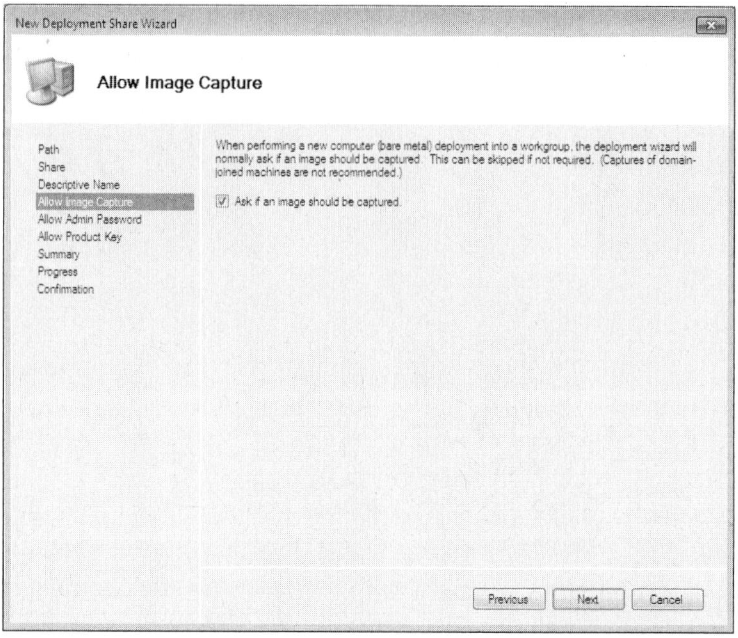

FIGURE 3.4
The Allow Image
Capture screen

Performing an Unattended Installation

Unattended installation is a practical method of automatic deployment when you have a large number of clients to install and the computers require different hardware and software configurations. Unattended installations utilize an answer file called Unattend.xml to provide configuration information during the unattended installation process. Recall the Windows 7 installation from the previous chapter: it asks you for your locale, type of installation, and so forth. The answer file enables these questions to be answered without user intervention.

With an unattended installation, you can use a distribution share to install Windows 7 on the target computers. You can also use a Windows 7 DVD with an answer file located on the root of the DVD, on a floppy disk, or on a universal flash device (UFD), such as an external USB flash drive.

Unattended installations allow you to create customized installations that are specific to your environment. Custom installations can support custom hardware and software installations. Because the answer file for Windows 7 is in XML format, all custom configuration information can be contained within the Unattend.xml file. This is different from past versions of Windows where creating automated installation routines for custom installations required that multiple files be used. In addition to providing standard Windows 7 configuration information, you can use the answer file to provide installation instructions for applications, additional language support, service packs, and device drivers.

If you use a distribution share, it should contain the Windows 7 operating system image and the answer file to respond to installation configuration queries. The target computer must be able to connect to the distribution share over the network. After the distribution share and target computers are connected, you can initiate the installation process. Figure 3.5 illustrates the unattended installation process.

FIGURE 3.5
Unattended installation
with a distribution share
and a target computer

Distribution Share

Target

Stores:
Windows 7 Image File
Answer File (Unattend.xml)

Requires:
Network Connection

ADVANTAGES OF USING AN UNATTENDED INSTALLATION

In a mid-sized or large organization, it just makes sense to use automated setups. As stated earlier, it's impossible to install hundreds of Windows 7 machines one at a time. There are many advantages to using unattended installations as a method for automating Windows 7 installation. Some of the advantages include the following:

◆ An unattended install saves time and money because users do not have to interactively respond to each installation query.

◆ The process can be configured to provide automated query response, while still selectively allowing users to provide specified input during installations.

◆ An unattended install can be used to install clean copies of Windows 7 or upgrade an existing operating system (providing it is on the list of permitted operating systems) to Windows 7.

◆ An unattended install can be expanded to include installation instructions for applications, additional language support, service packs, and device drivers.

◆ The physical media for Windows 7 does not need to be distributed to all computers that will be installed.

DISADVANTAGES OF USING AN UNATTENDED INSTALLATION

A client operating system is one of the most important items that you'll install onto a machine. You probably feel better installing a client operating system when you're physically doing it. That way, if there's a glitch, you can spot it and deal with it immediately.

This method is not practical for mass installations. But one of the biggest disadvantages to using an unattended installation is that an administrator does not physically walk through the installation of Windows 7. If something happens during the install, you might never know it, but the end user might experience small issues throughout the entire lifetime of the machine.

Two other disadvantages to using unattended installations as a method for automating Windows 7 installations include the following:

◆ They require more initial setup than a standard installation of Windows 7.

◆ Someone must have access to each client computer and must initiate the unattended installation process on the client side.

In the next section we'll look at the Windows Deployment Services utility.

Using Windows Deployment Services

Windows Deployment Services (WDS) is an updated version of Remote Installation Services (RIS). WDS is a suite of components that allows you to remotely install Windows 7 on client computers.

A WDS server installs Windows 7 on the client computers, as shown in Figure 3.6. The WDS server must be configured with the Preboot Execution Environment (PXE) boot files, the images to be deployed to the client computers, and the answer file. WDS client computers must be PXE capable. PXE is a technology that's used to boot to the network when no operating system or network configuration has been installed and configured on a client computer.

FIGURE 3.6
WDS uses a WDS server
and WDS clients.

WDS Server

WDS Client

Stores:
PXE Boot Files and Boot Images
Windows 7 Boot Images
Answer File(s)

Requires:
PXE-Compatible Boot

The WDS clients access the network with the help of a Dynamic Host Configuration Protocol (DHCP) server. This allows the WDS client to remotely install the operating system from the WDS server. The network environment must be configured with a DHCP server, a Domain Name System (DNS) server, and an Active Directory to connect to the WDS server. No other client software is required to connect to the WDS server. Remote installation is a good choice for automatic deployment when you need to deploy to large numbers of computers and the client computers are PXE compliant.

ADVANTAGES OF USING WDS

The advantages of using WDS as a method for automating Windows 7 installations are as follows:

♦ You can standardize Windows 7 installations across a group or organization.

♦ You do not need to distribute the physical media for Windows 7 to all computers that will be installed.

♦ You can control end-user installation deployment through the Group Policy utility. For example, you can configure which choices a user can access and which are automatically specified through the end-user Setup Wizard.

Now that we've listed the advantages of WDS, let's take a look at the disadvantages.

DISADVANTAGES OF USING WDS

The disadvantages of using WDS as a method for automating Windows 7 installations include the following:

♦ You can use it only if your network is running Windows Server 2003 or Windows Server 2008 with Active Directory installed.

◆   The clients that use WDS must be PXE capable.

Next let's look at the System Preparation Tool.

Using the System Preparation Tool and Disk Imaging

The System Preparation Tool (Sysprep.exe) is used to prepare a computer for disk imaging, which can then be captured using ImageX (a new imaging management tool included with Windows 7) or third-party imaging software.

Disk imaging is the process of taking a snapshot of a computer and then using that snapshot to create new computers, allowing for automated deployments. The reference, or source, computer has Windows 7 installed and is configured with the settings and applications that should be installed on the target computers. The image (snapshot) is then created and that image can be transferred to other computers, thus installing the operating system, settings, and applications that were defined on the reference computer.

ADVANTAGE OF IMAGING

Using the System Preparation Tool and disk imaging is a good choice (and the most commonly used in the real world) for automatic deployment when you have a large number of computers with similar configuration requirements or machines that need to be rebuilt frequently.

For example, Stellacon Training Center, a Microsoft education center that employs one of the authors, reinstalls the same software every week for new classes. Imaging is a fast and easy way to simplify the deployment process.

Using imaging software can save time and money. It saves time because you do not have to rebuild machines from scratch, and saving time in turn saves an organization money.

 **Real World Scenario**

USING IMAGING SOFTWARE

In the real world, imaging software is the most common way to install or reinstall corporate computers. The reason that most organizations use images is not only to create new machines quickly and easily, but also to re-image end users' machines that crash.

In most companies, end users will have space on a server (home folders) that allow them to store data. The reason we give our end users space on the server is because this way, at night we only need to back up the servers and not the end users' machines. If our end users place all of their important documents on the server, it gets backed up.

Now if we're also using images in our company and an end user's machine crashes, we just reload the image and the user is back up and running in minutes. Because their documents are being saved on the server, users don't lose any of their information.

Many organizations use third-party imaging software instead of using Sysprep.exe and ImageX. This is another good way of imaging your Windows 7 machines. Just make sure that your third-party software supports the Windows 7 operating system.

To perform an unattended install, the System Preparation Tool prepares the reference computer by stripping away any computer-specific data, such as the security identifier (SID), which is used to uniquely identify each computer on the network, any event logs, and any other unique system information. The System Preparation Tool also detects any Plug and Play devices that are installed and can adjust dynamically for any computers that have different hardware installed.

When the client computer starts an installation using a disk image, you can customize what is displayed on the Windows Welcome screen and the options that are displayed through the setup process. You can also fully automate when and how the Windows Welcome screen is displayed during the installation process by using the /oobe (out-of-the-box experience) switch with the System Preparation Tool and an answer file named Oobe.xml.

The System Preparation Tool is a utility that's good only for setting up a new machine. You do not use it to image a computer for upgrading a current machine. There are a few switches that you can use in conjunction with Sysprep.exe to configure the tool for your specific needs. Table 3.1 shows you some of the Sysprep.exe switches and what they can do for you.

TABLE 3.1:   Sysprep.exe Switches

SWITCH	EXPLANATION
/pnp	Forces a mini-setup wizard to start at reboot so that all Plug and Play devices can be recognized.
/generalize	Allows Sysprep to remove all system-specific data from the Sysprep image. If you're running the GUI version of Sysprep, this is a check box.
/oobe	Initiates the Windows Welcome at the next reboot.
/audit	Initiates Sysprep in Audit mode.
/nosidgen	Forces a mini-setup on restart. Sysprep does not generate new SIDs upon restart.
/reboot	Stops and restarts the computer system.
/quiet	Runs without displaying any confirmation dialog messages.
/mini	Tells Sysprep to run the mini-setup on the next reboot.

The Windows System Preparation tool is a free utility that comes on all Windows operating systems. By default, the Sysprep utility can be found on the Windows Server 2008 and Windows 7 operating systems in the \Windows\system32\sysprep directories.

Real World Scenario

THE PROBLEMS WITH DEPLOYMENT SOFTWARE

For many years when we had to create several machines with a Microsoft operating system on them, we'd have to use files to help deploy the multiple systems.

Then multiple third-party companies came out with software that allowed us to take a picture of the Microsoft operating system and then we could deploy that picture to other machines. One advantage to this is that all the software that's installed on the system could also be part of that picture. This was a great way to copy an entire machine's software over to another machine.

However, for years there was one major problem: SID numbers. All computers are assigned a unique number that represents them on a domain network, and that number is called a *security identifier (SID)*. The problem was when we copied one machine to another machine, the SID number was also copied.

Microsoft released Sysprep many years ago and that helped solve this problem. Sysprep allows us to remove the SID number so that a third-party software can image it to another machine. Many third-party image software products now also remove the SID numbers, but Sysprep was one of the first utilities to help solve this problem.

When you decide to use Sysprep to set up your images, you must follow a few rules in order for the utility to work properly:

- ◆ You can use images to restart the Windows activation clock. The Windows activation clock starts to decrease as soon as Windows starts for the first time. You can only restart the Windows activation clock three times using Sysprep.

- ◆ The computer you're running Sysprep on has to be a member of a workgroup. The machine can't be part of a domain. If the computer is a member of the domain, when you run Sysprep the computer is automatically removed from the domain.

- ◆ When you install the image, the system prompts you for a product key. You can use an answer file during the install, which will have all the information needed for the install and you won't be prompted for any information.

- ◆ A third-party utility or ImageX is required to deploy the image that is created from Sysprep.

- ◆ If you're using Sysprep to capture an NTFS partition, any files or folders that are encrypted will become corrupted and unreadable.

One advantage to Sysprep and Windows 7 is that you can use Sysprep to prepare a new machine for duplication. You can use Sysprep to take an image from one machine and then a third-party application can use that image to create another machine. The steps needed to image a new machine are as follows:

1. Install the Windows 7 operating system.

2. Install all components on the OS.

3. Run Sysprep /generalize to create the image.

When you image a computer using the Windows Sysprep utility, a Windows image (.wim) file is created. Most third-party imaging software products can work with the Windows image file.

ADVANTAGES OF USING THE SYSTEM PREPARATION TOOL

The advantages of using the System Preparation Tool as a method for automating Windows 7 installations include the following:

◆ For large numbers of computers with similar hardware, it greatly reduces deployment time by copying the operating system, applications, and Desktop settings from a reference computer to an image, which can then be deployed to multiple computers.

◆ Using disk imaging facilitates the standardization of Desktops, administrative policies, and restrictions throughout an organization.

◆ Reference images can be copied across a network connection or through DVDs that are physically distributed to client computers.

DISADVANTAGES OF USING THE SYSTEM PREPARATION TOOL

The disadvantages of using the System Preparation Tool as a method for automating Windows 7 installations include the following:

◆ You must use ImageX, third-party imaging software, or hardware disk-duplicator devices for an image-based setup.

◆ You must use the version of the System Preparation Tool that shipped with Windows 7. You cannot use an older version of Sysprep on a Windows 7 image.

◆ Sysprep cannot detect any hardware that is non–Plug and Play compliant.

Using the Windows Automated Installation Kit (Windows AIK)

Another way to install Windows 7 is to use the Windows Automated Installation Kit (Windows AIK). The Windows AIK is a set of utilities and documentation that allows an administrator to configure and deploy Windows operating systems. You can use the Windows AIK to

◆ Capture Windows images with ImageX

◆ Configure and edit your images by using the Deployment Image Servicing and Management (DISM) utility

◆ Create Windows PE images

◆ Migrate user data and profiles using the User State Migration Tool (USMT)

◆ Centrally manage volume activations by using the Volume Activation Management Tool (VAMT)

You can install and configure the Windows AIK on the following operating systems:

◆ Windows 7

◆ Windows Server 2008

◆ Windows Server 2003 with SP3

◆ Windows Vista with SP1

The Windows AIK is a good solution for organizations that need to customize the Windows deployment environments. The Windows AIK allows an administrator to have the flexibility needed for mass deployments of Windows operating systems. Because every organization's needs are different, the Windows AIK allows you to use all or just part of the deployment tools available. The Windows AIK allows you to manage deployments by using some additional tools:

Microsoft Deployment Toolkit   The tools included with this part of the Windows AIK allow you to easily deploy and configure Windows operating systems and images.

Application Compatibility Toolkit   When you're installing new Windows operating systems, applications that ran on the previous version of Windows might not work properly. The Application Compatibility Toolkit helps solve these issues before they occur.

Microsoft Assessment and Planning (MAP) Toolkit   The MAP toolkit is a utility that will locate computers on a network and then perform a thorough inventory of these computers. This inventory can then be used to determine which machines can have Windows 7 installed. The MAP utility is explained later in this chapter in the "Microsoft Assessment and Planning" section, and install instructions are also provided.

Summary of Windows 7 Deployment Tools

Table 3.2 summarizes the installation tools for Windows 7 and lists the client hardware and server requirements, and indicates whether the option supports a clean install or an upgrade.

Table 3.3 summarizes the unattended installation tools and files that are used with automated installations of Windows 7, the associated installation method, and a description of each tool.

The Windows 7 installation utilities and resources relating to automated deployment are found in a variety of locations. Table 3.4 provides a quick reference for each utility or resource and its location.

TABLE 3.2:   Summary of Windows 7 Installation Tools

TOOL	REQUIRED CLIENT HARDWARE	REQUIRED SERVER HARDWARE AND SERVICES	CLEAN INSTALL OR UPGRADE ONLY
MDT 2010	PC that meets Windows 7 requirements; access to the network	Network installation, distribution server.	Clean install
Windows AIK	PC that meets Windows 7 requirements	None. Windows AIK can be installed on any compatible machine.	Clean install
Unattended installation	PC that meets Windows 7 requirements; access to the network	None with DVD; if using network installation, distribution server with preconfigured client images.	Clean install or upgrade

TABLE 3.2:   Summary of Windows 7 Installation Tools *(CONTINUED)*

TOOL	REQUIRED CLIENT HARDWARE	REQUIRED SERVER HARDWARE AND SERVICES	CLEAN INSTALL OR UPGRADE ONLY
WDS	PC that meets the Windows 7 requirements and that is PXE compliant	Windows Server 2003 with SP1 or Windows Server 2008 to act as a WDS server with image files, Active Directory, DNS server, and DHCP server.	Clean install
System Preparation Tool	Reference computer with Windows 7 installed and configured; PC that meets the Windows 7 requirements; ImageX, third-party disk imaging software, or hardware disk-duplicator device	None.	Clean install

TABLE 3.3:   Summary of Windows 7 Unattended Deployment Utilities

TOOL OR FILE	AUTOMATED INSTALLATION TOOL	DESCRIPTION
Setup.exe	Unattended installation	Program used to initiate the installation process
Unattend.xml	Unattended installation	Answer file used to customize installation queries
Windows System Image Manager	Unattended installation	Program used to create answer files to be used for unattended installations
ImageX.exe	Sysprep	Command-line utility that works in conjunction with Sysprep to create and manage Windows 7 image files for deployment
Sysprep.exe	Sysprep	System Preparation Tool that prepares a source reference computer that is used in conjunction with a distribution share or with disk duplication through ImageX, third-party software, or hardware disk-duplication devices

TABLE 3.4:   Location of Windows 7 Deployment Utilities and Resources

UTILITY	LOCATION
Sysprep.exe	Included with Windows 7; installed to %WINDIR%\system32\sysprep
ImageX	Installed with the Windows AIK; installed to C:\Program Files\Windows AIK\Tools\x86\imagex.exe
Windows System Image Manager	Installed with Windows AIK; installed to C:\Program Files\Windows AIK\Tools\Image Manager\ImgMgr.exe

Now that you have seen some of the ways you can install Windows 7, let's take a more detailed look at each one.

Deploying Unattended Installations

You can deploy Windows 7 installations or upgrades through a Windows 7 distribution DVD or through a distribution server that contains Windows 7 images and associated files, such as Unattend.xml for unattended installations. Using a DVD can be advantageous if the computer on which you want to install Windows 7 is not connected to the network or is connected via a low-bandwidth network. It is also typically faster to install a Windows 7 image from DVD than to use a network connection.

Unattended installations rely on options configured in an answer file that is deployed with the Windows 7 image. Answer files are XML files that contain the settings that are typically supplied by the installer during attended installations of Windows 7. Answer files can also contain instructions on how programs and applications should be run.

The Windows Setup program is run to install or upgrade to Windows 7 from computers that are running compatible versions of Windows, as discussed in Chapter 2. In fact, Windows Setup is the basis for the other types of installation procedures that we discuss in this chapter, including unattended installations, WDS, and image-based installations.

The Windows Setup program (Setup.exe) replaces Winnt32.exe and Winnt.exe, which are the setup programs used in versions of Windows prior to Windows Vista. Although a graphical tool, Windows Setup can be run from the command line. For example, you can use the following command to initiate an unattended installation of Windows 7:

```
setup.exe /unattend:answerfile
```

The Windows Setup program has several command-line options that can be applied, as you can see in Table 3.5.

Next we'll look at the System Preparation tool (Sysprep), which is one of many ways to install Windows 7 automatically.

Using the System Preparation Tool to Prepare an Installation for Imaging

You can use disk images to install Windows 7 on computers that have similar hardware configurations. Also, if a computer is having technical difficulties, you can use a disk image to quickly restore it to a baseline configuration.

TABLE 3.5: Setup.exe Command-Line Options and Descriptions

Setup.exe OPTION	DESCRIPTION
/1394debug: *channel* [baudrate:*baudrate*]	Enables kernel debugging over a FireWire (IEEE 1394) port for troubleshooting purposes. The [*baudrate*] optional parameter specifies the baud rate for data transfer during the debugging process.
/debug:*port* [*baudrate:baudrate*]	Enables kernel debugging over the specified port for troubleshooting purposes. The [*baudrate*] optional parameter specifies the baud rate for data transfer during the debugging process.
/dudisable	Prevents a dynamic update from running during the installation process.
/emsport:{com1|com2| usebiossettings|off} [/emsbaudrate:*baudrate*]	Configures EMS to be enabled or disabled. The [*baudrate*]optional parameter specifies the baud rate for data transfer during the debugging process.
/m:*folder_name*	Used with Setup to specify that replacement files should be copied from the specified location. If the files are not present, then Setup will use the default location.
/noreboot	Specifies that the computer should not restart so that you can execute another command prior to the restart. Normally, when the down-level phase of Setup.exe is complete, the computer restarts.
/tempdrive:*drive letter*	Specifies the location that will store the temporary files for Windows 7 and the installation partition for Windows 7.
/unattend:[*answerfile*]	Specifies that you'll be using an unattended installation for Windows Vista. The answerfile variable points to the custom answer file you'll use for installation.

To create a disk image, you install Windows 7 on the source computer with the configuration that you want to copy and use the System Preparation Tool to prepare the installation for imaging. The source computer's configuration should also include any applications that should be installed on target computers.

After you prepare the installation for imaging, you can use imaging software such as ImageX to create an image of the installation.

The System Preparation Tool (Sysprep.exe) is included with Windows 7, in the %WINDIR%\system32\sysprep directory. When you run this utility on the source computer, it strips out information from the master copy that must be unique for each computer, such as the SID. Table 3.6 defines the command options that you can use to customize the Sysprep.exe operation.

In the following sections, you'll learn how to create a disk image and how to copy and install from a disk image.

TABLE 3.6:   System Preparation Command-Line Options

SWITCH	DESCRIPTION
/audit	Configures the computer to restart in Audit mode, which allows you to add drivers and applications to Windows or test the installation prior to deployment
/generalize	Removes any unique system information from the image, including the SID and log information
/oobe	Specifies that the Windows Welcome screen should be displayed when the computer reboots
/quiet	Runs the installation with no user interaction
/quit	Specifies that the System Preparation tool should quit after the specified operations have been completed
/reboot	Restarts the target computer after the System Preparation Tool completes
/shutdown	Specifies that the computer should shut down after the specified operations have completed
/unattend	Indicates the name and location of the answer file to use

Preparing a Windows 7 Installation

Follow these steps to run the System Preparation Tool and prepare an installation for imaging:

1. Install Windows 7 on a source computer. The computer should have a similar hardware configuration to the destination computer(s). The source computer should not be a member of a domain. (See Chapter 2 for instructions on installing Windows 7.)

2. Log on to the source computer as an Administrator and, if desired, install and configure any applications, files (such as newer versions of Plug and Play drivers), or custom settings (for example, a custom Desktop) that will be applied to the target computer(s).

3. Verify that your image meets the specified configuration criteria and that all applications are properly installed and working.

4. Select Start ➢ Computer, and navigate to C:\%WINDIR%\System32\sysprep. Double-click the Sysprep application icon.

5. The Windows System Preparation Tool dialog box appears. Select the appropriate options for your configuration.

6. If configured to do so, Windows 7 is rebooted into Setup mode, and you are prompted to enter the appropriate setup information.

7. You are now able to use imaging software to create an image of the computer to deploy to other computers.

Perform the following steps to use the System Preparation Tool to prepare the computer for disk imaging. The Sysprep utility must be run on a machine with a clean version of Windows 7. If you upgraded a Windows Vista machine to Windows 7, you won't be able to run Sysprep.

1. Log on to the source computer as Administrator and, if desired, install and configure any applications that should also be installed on the target computer.

2. Select Start ➢ Computer, and navigate to C:\%WINDIR%\System32\sysprep. Double-click the Sysprep application icon.

3. In the System Preparation Tool dialog box, select the Enter System Out-of-Box Experience (OOBE) in the system cleanup action.

4. Under the Shutdown options, depending on the options selected, you can specify whether the System Preparation Tool will quit, the computer will shut down, or the computer will be rebooted into Setup mode (and you'll need to configure the setup options). Choose the Reboot option. Click OK.

5. Configure the Sysprep utility and name the image **image.wim**.

After creating the Sysprep image, you need to use some type of third-party software to install the image. Windows includes a utility called ImageX for just that purpose.

Using ImageX to Create a Disk Image

After you've run the System Preparation Tool on the source computer, you can create an image from the installation, and you can then install the image on target computers.

To create an image, you can use ImageX, which is a command-line utility that lets you create and manage Windows Image (.wim) files.

Before you can create your disk image using ImageX, you must first build a Windows Preinstallation Environment (PE) disk so you can boot into the Windows PE environment.

WINDOWS AIK

To complete the following steps, you must have the Windows AIK utility installed. If the Windows AIK is not installed, you can install the Windows AIK by following the installation steps in the section "Creating Answer Files with Windows System Image Manager" later in this chapter.

To create the Windows PE boot DVD:

1. Click Start ➢ All Programs ➢ Windows AIK ➢ Deployment Tools Command Prompt.

2. At the command prompt, run

   ```
   Copype.cmd <architecture> <destination>
   ```

   where <architecture> is **x86**, **amd64**, or **ia64**, and <destination> is a path to a local directory.

For example:

```
copype.cmd x86 c:\winpe_x86)
```

will create the following directories:

```
\winpe_x86
\winpe_x86\ISO
\winpe_x86\mount
```

3. On the same computer, create your .iso file using the following command:

```
oscdimg -n -bc:\winpe_x86\etfsboot.com c:\winpe_x86\ISO
c:\winpe_x86\winpe_x86.iso
```

4. Burn the .iso image to a DVD.

Now that you have created the Windows PE disk, you'll run the ImageX utility to create a disk image of a Windows 7 installation:

1. Boot the computer into Windows PE.

2. Type the following command, assuming that your DVD\CD drive is configured as drive D:

```
D:\ImageX.exe /capture C: C:\Images\image.wim "Windows 7" /verify
```

3. Copy the new image to a network share at \\Server\Images by using these commands:

```
net use z: \\Server\Images
copy C:\Images\image.wim z:
```

After you create the disk image, the next step is to install the disk image. In the next section, you'll learn to install the disk image to a new machine.

Installing from a Disk Image

Now that you've run the System Preparation Tool and ImageX on the source computer, you can copy the image and install it on the target computer.

After the image is copied, you should boot the destination computer into Windows PE. If the computer has been used previously, it may be necessary to reformat the hard drive (which you can do using the diskpart utility in Windows PE).

THE DISKPART UTILITY

Diskpart is a command-line utility that allows you to manage and configure your hard disks, volumes, or partitions. To learn more about how to use this utility, check Microsoft's website at www.microsoft.com.

If the image is stored over the network, you should then copy the image to the destination computer by using the `net use [dir] [network share]` and `copy [file] [dir]` commands. Then, use the `/apply` option of the ImageX utility to apply the image to the local computer. If an answer file has not been deployed along with the image, you might have to supply such information as regional settings, the product key, the computer name, and the password to the new computer after the destination computer is rebooted.

Next, you'll install Windows 7 from a disk image. You'll use the stripped image that you created in the previous section to simulate the process of continuing an installation from a disk image.

1. Boot the target computer into the Windows PE environment.

2. Copy the image you created in the previous section to the local computer by using these commands:

```
net use z: \\Server\Images
copy Z:\Images\image.wim C:
```

3. Apply the image to the target computer using the following ImageX command:

```
D:\ImageX.exe /apply C:\Images\image.wim C:
```

When you install Windows 7, the installation wizard asks you questions such as your username and computer name. There is way to answer these questions without actually being in front of the computer. As you'll see in the next section, you can do this by using an answer file.

Using Windows System Image Manager to Create Answer Files

Answer files are automated installation scripts used to answer the questions that appear during a normal Windows 7 installation. You can use answer files with Windows 7 unattended installations, disk image installations, or WDS installations. Setting up answer files allows you to easily deploy Windows 7, with little or no user intervention, to computers that might not be configured in the same manner. Because answer files are associated with image files, you can validate the settings in an answer file against the image file.

You can create answer files by using the Windows System Image Manager (SIM) utility. There are several advantages to using Windows SIM to create answer files:

◆ You can easily create and edit answer files through a graphical interface, which reduces syntax errors.

◆ It simplifies the addition of user-specific or computer-specific configuration information.

◆ You can validate existing answer files against newly created images.

◆ You can include additional application and device drivers to the answer file.

In the following sections, you'll learn about options that you can configure through Windows SIM, how to create answer files with Windows SIM, how to format the answer file, and how to manually edit answer files.

Configuring Components Through Windows SIM

You can use Windows SIM to configure a wide variety of installation options. The following list defines what components you can configure through Windows SIM and gives a short description of each component:

auditSystem   Adds additional device drivers, specifies firewall settings, and applies a name to the system when the image is booted into Audit mode. Audit mode is initiated by using the `sysprep /audit` command.

auditUser   Executes RunSynchronous or RunAsynchronous commands when the image is booted into Audit mode. Audit mode is initiated by using the `sysprep /audit` command.

generalize   Removes system-specific information from an image so that the image can be used as a reference image. The settings specified in the `generalize` component will only be applied if the `sysprep /generalize` command is used.

offlineServicing   Specifies the language packs and packages to apply to an image prior to the image being extracted to the hard disk.

oobeSystem   Specifies the settings to apply to the computer the first time that the computer is booted into the Windows Welcome screen, which is also known as the out-of-the-box experience (OOBE). To boot to the Welcome screen, use the `sysprep /oobe` command.

specialize   Configures the specific settings for the target computer, such as network settings and domain information. This configuration pass is used in conjunction with the `generalize` configuration pass.

Windows PE   Sets the Windows PE–specific configuration settings, as well as several Windows Setup settings, such as partitioning and formatting the hard disk, selecting an image, and applying a product key.

Now let's take a look at how you can create answer files using Windows SIM.

Creating Answer Files with Windows SIM

To create an answer file with Windows SIM, the first thing you must do is install the Windows AIK.

Perform the following steps to download and install the Windows Automated Installation Kit. The Windows AIK is a free download from Microsoft's website.

1. Download the Windows AIK `.iso` file from Microsoft's website.

2. Transfer the `.iso` file to a DVD.

3. Insert the DVD into your Windows 7 machine.

4. When Autoplay starts, select Run StartCD.exe. If Autorun does not appear, open Windows Explorer and click `StartCD.exe` under the DVD drive.

5. At the User Account Control screen, click Yes.

6. The Welcome To Windows Automated Installation Kit screen appears, as shown in Figure 3.7. Click the Windows AIK Setup link on the left.

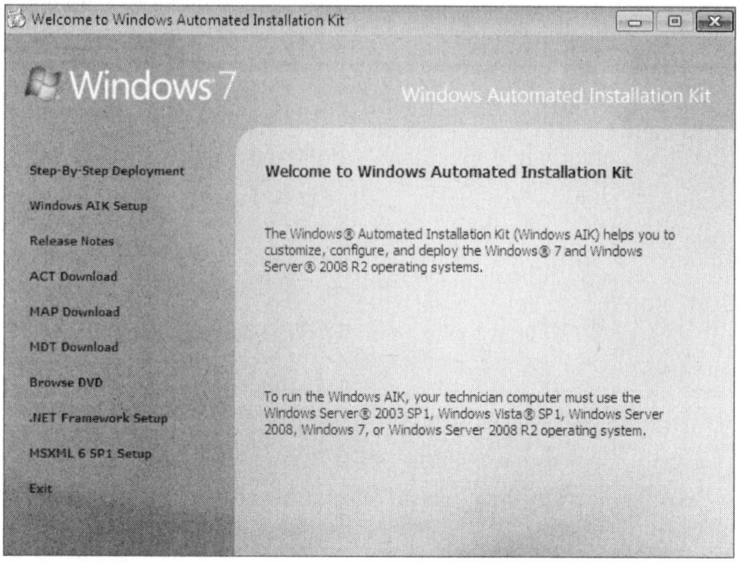

FIGURE 3.7
The Windows AIK
installation screen

7. When you see the Welcome screen, click Next.

8. At the License Terms screen, click the I Agree radio button and click Next.

9. At the Select Installation Folder screen (see Figure 3.8), choose where you want to install the Windows AIK files. You can also choose who has the rights to use the Windows AIK. We are choosing the Everyone radio button. Click Next.

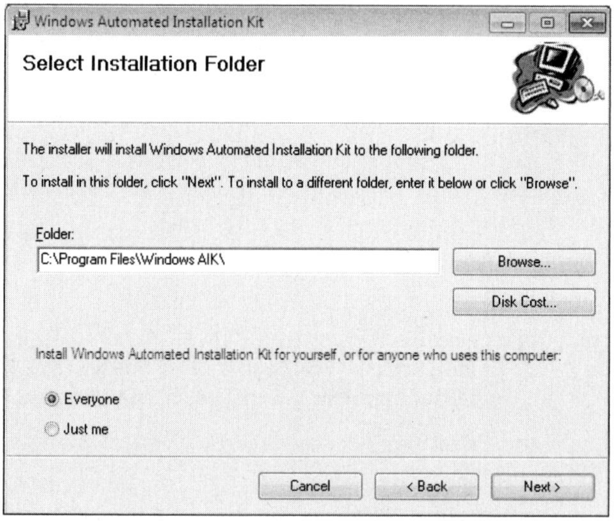

FIGURE 3.8
The Select Installation
Folder screen

10. At the Confirmation screen, verify your settings and click Next.

11. At the installation complete screen, verify that there are no errors and click Close.

12. Close the Windows AIK installation screen.

After you install the Windows AIK, you can run the Windows SIM utility to create a new answer file or edit existing answer files.

Perform the following steps to create a new answer file using Windows SIM:

1. Select Start ➢ All Programs ➢ Microsoft Windows AIK, and click Windows System Image Manager.

2. Windows System Image Manager displays an empty screen with five panes, as shown in Figure 3.9: a pane for selecting distribution shares, a pane for selecting Windows image files, the answer file pane, a properties pane, and a pane for displaying validation messages.

FIGURE 3.9
The Windows SIM screen

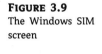

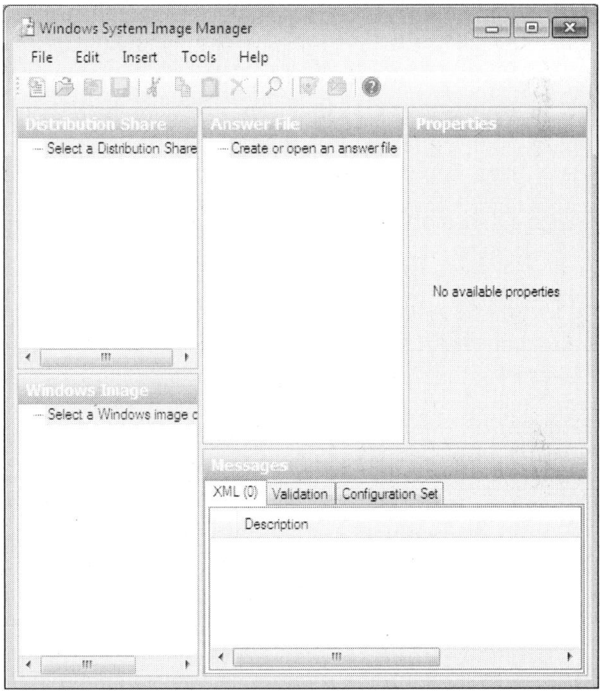

3. Select the Windows 7 image file for which a new answer file should be created by clicking File ➢ Select A Windows Image or catalog file or by right-clicking the Windows Image pane in Windows SIM and clicking Select Windows Image (see Figure 3.10).

4. Select File ➢ New Answer File or right-click the Answer File pane and select New Answer File from the context menu to generate the structure of the new answer file.

5. Right-click each component as desired to modify the configuration pass options that are specific to the new environment. You can drill down within a component to provide specific customizations, or you can modify parent-level components.

6. When you have finished customizing the answer file for the desired environment, click File ➢ Save Answer File to save the answer file.

FIGURE 3.10
Selecting the Windows
Image option

You can use an answer file to provide automated answers for a DVD-based installation. Simply create a new answer file named **Unattend.xml** and copy it to the root of the DVD. Insert the Windows 7 DVD and set the BIOS to boot from the DVD drive. As the installation begins, Windows Setup will implicitly search for answer files in a number of locations, including the root of removable media drives.

In the next section you'll see how to install Windows 7 remotely through the use of Windows Deployment Services.

Using Windows Deployment Services (WDS)

In earlier Windows versions, another method that many IT departments used to deploy operating systems was Remote Installation Services (RIS). RIS was a utility that allowed an administrator to deploy an operating system remotely. On the client machine that was receiving the operating system, you'd use a set of disks (RIS client disks) that would automatically initiate a network card, connect to the RIS server, and download the operating system.

For Windows 7 and Windows Server 2008, a new version of RIS has been developed that's called Windows Deployment Services (WDS). WDS (see Figure 3.11) allows an IT administrator to install a Windows operating system without using a CD or DVD installation disc. Using WDS allows you to deploy the operating system through a network installation. WDS can deploy Windows XP, Windows Server 2003, Microsoft Vista, Windows 7, and Microsoft Windows Server 2008.

FIGURE 3.11
Windows Deployment Services

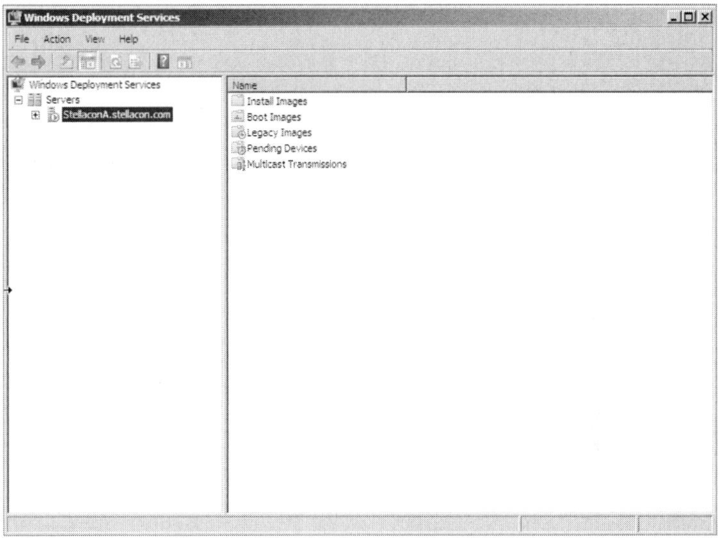

Here are some of the advantages of using WDS for automated installation:

◆ You can remotely install Windows 7.

◆ The procedure simplifies management of the server image by allowing you to access Windows 7 distribution files from a distribution server.

◆ You can quickly recover the operating system in the event of a computer failure.

The basic steps of the WDS process from a PXE-enabled WDS client are as follows:

1. The WDS client initiates a special boot process through the PXE network adapter (and the computer's BIOS configured for a network boot). On a PXE client, the client presses F12 to start the PXE boot process and to indicate that you want to perform a WDS installation.

2. A list of available Windows PE boot images displays. Select the appropriate Windows PE boot image from the menu.

3. The Windows Welcome screen displays. Click Next.

4. Enter your credentials for accessing and installing images from the WDS server.

5. A list of available operating system images displays. Select the appropriate image file to install.

6. At the next screen, enter the product key for the selected image.

7. The Partition And Configure The Disk screen displays. You can install a mass storage device driver, if needed, by pressing F6.

8. The image copy process is initiated, and the selected image is copied to the WDS client computer.

The following sections describe how to set up the WDS server and the WDS clients and how to install Windows 7 through WDS.

Preparing the WDS Server

With the WDS server, you can manage and distribute Windows 7 operating system images to WDS client computers. The WDS server contains any files necessary for PXE booting, Windows PE boot images, and the Windows 7 images to be deployed.

The following steps for preparing the WDS server are discussed in the upcoming sections:

1. Make sure the server meets the requirements for running WDS.

2. Install WDS.

3. Install the WDS Server components.

4. Configure and start WDS.

5. Configure the WDS server to respond to client computers (if this was not configured when WDS was installed).

For WDS to work, the server on which you'll install WDS must meet the requirements for WDS and be able to access the required network services. Now let's take a look at the requirements needed for WDS.

WDS Server Requirements

The WDS server must meet the following requirements:

- The computer must be a domain controller or a member of an Active Directory domain.

- At least one partition on the server must be formatted as NTFS.

- WDS must be installed on the server.

- The computer must be running the Windows Server 2003 or Windows Server 2008 operating system.

- A network adapter must be installed.

Network Services Requirements

The following network services must be running on the WDS server or be accessible to the WDS server from another network server:

- TCP/IP (installed and configured)

- A DHCP server, which is used to assign DHCP addresses to WDS clients (ensure that your DHCP scope has enough addresses to accommodate all the WDS clients that will need IP addresses)

- A DNS server, which is used to locate the Active Directory controller

- Active Directory, which is used to locate WDS servers and WDS clients, as well as to authorize WDS clients and manage WDS configuration settings and client installation options

In the next section you'll see how to install the WDS server components.

INSTALLING THE WDS SERVER COMPONENTS

You can configure WDS on a Windows Server 2003 or Windows Server 2008 computer by using the Windows Deployment Services Configuration Wizard or by using the wdsutil command-line utility. Table 3.7 describes the options for the wdsutil command.

TABLE 3.7:   wdsutil Command-Line Options

OPTION	DESCRIPTION
/initialize	Initializes the configuration of the WDS server
/uninitialize	Undoes any changes made during the initialization of the WDS server
/add	Adds images and devices to the WDS server
/convert	Converts Remote Installation Preparation (RIPrep) images to WIM images
/remove	Removes images from the server
/set	Sets information in images, image groups, WDS servers, and WDS devices
/get	Gets information from images, image groups, WDS servers, and WDS devices
/new	Creates new capture images or discover images
/copy	Copies images from the image store
/export	Exports to WIM files images contained within the image store
/start	Starts WDS services
/stop	Stops WDS services
/disable	Disables WDS services
/enable	Enables WDS services
/approve	Approves Auto-Add devices
/reject	Rejects Auto-Add devices
/delete	Deletes records from the Auto-Add database
/update	Uses a known good resource to update a server resource

The first step in setting up WDS to deploy operating systems to the clients is to install the WDS role. You do this by using Server Manager. You must make sure that DNS, DHCP, and Active Directory are installed before completing the following steps.

NETWORK INFRASTRUCTURE

DNS and DHCP are discussed in detail in *MCTS: Windows Server 2008 Network Infrastructure Configuration Study Guide* by William Panek, Tylor Wentworth, and James Chellis (Sybex, 2008).

To install WDS on Windows Server 2008:

1. Start Server Manager by clicking Start ➤ Administrative Tools ➤ Server Manager.

2. On the left-hand side, click Roles.

3. In the right-hand window pane, click the Add Roles link, which launches the Add Roles Wizard.

4. Click Next at the Before You Begin screen.

5. Click the Windows Deployment Services check box. Click Next.

6. At the Overview screen, click Next.

7. At the Select Role Services screen, make sure both check boxes (Deployment Server and Transport Server) are selected, and then click Next.

8. At the Confirmation screen, verify the installation selections and click Install.

9. At the Installation Results screen, click Close.

10. Close Server Manager.

The next step is to configure the WDS server to respond to the WDS clients.

Configuring the WDS Server to Respond to Client Requests

Perform these steps to configure the WDS server:

1. Start WDS by clicking Start ➤ Administrative Tools ➤ Windows Deployment Services.

2. In the left-hand window pane, expand the Servers link. Click the name of your server, and then right-click it and choose Configure Server.

3. The Welcome screen appears explaining that you need an Active Directory Domain Services, DHCP, DNS, and an NTFS partition. If you meet these minimum requirements, click Next.

4. The Remote Installation Folder Location screen appears. Accept the defaults by clicking Next.

5. When you see the System Volume Warning dialog box, click Yes.

6. The DHCP Option 60 screen is next, as shown in Figure 3.12. Select both check boxes and click Next.

7. The PXE Server Initial Settings screen (see Figure 3.13) asks you to choose how PXE will respond to clients. Choose the "Respond to all (known and unknown) client computers" radio button. Click Finish.

8. At the Configuration Complete screen, make sure the Add Image To The Windows Deployment Server Now check box is deselected. Click Finish.

FIGURE 3.12
The DHCP Option 60 screen

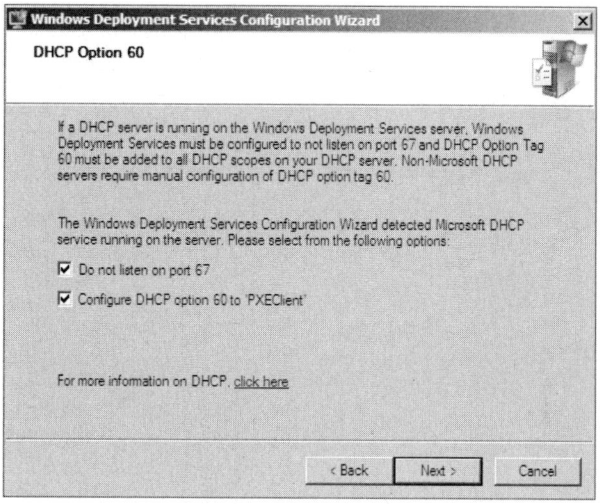

FIGURE 3.13
The PXE Server Initial Settings screen

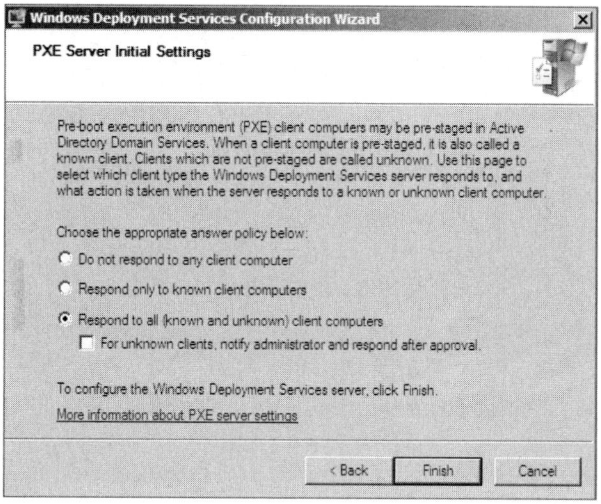

One of the advantages of using WDS is that it can work with Windows image (`.wim`) files. As you learned earlier, you can create Windows image files by using the Windows Sysprep utility.

One component that you need to pay attention to when using WDS is the Preboot Execution Environment (PXE) boot device. PXE boot devices are network interface cards (NICs) that can talk to a network without the need for an operating system because they have a set of preboot commands within the boot firmware.

PXE boot adapters connect to a WDS server and request the data needed to load the operating system remotely. Since most of the machines that you're using WDS for do not have an operating system on the computer, you must have NIC adapters that can connect to a network without an operating system in order for WDS to work properly.

For the same reason, you must set up DHCP to accept PXE machines. Those machines need a valid TCP/IP address so that they can connect to the WDS server.

The WDS server side is now installed and configured. The next step involves setting up the WDS client side.

Preparing the WDS Client

The WDS client is the computer on which Windows 7 will be installed. WDS clients rely on a technology called PXE, which allows the client computer to remotely boot and connect to a WDS server.

To act as a WDS client, the computer must meet all the hardware requirements for Windows 7 (see Chapter 2) and have a PXE-capable network adapter installed. Also, a WDS server must be present on the network. Additionally, the user account used to install the image must be a member of the Domain Users group in Active Directory.

After you install and configure the WDS server, you can install Windows 7 on a WDS client that uses a PXE-compliant network card.

To install Windows 7 on the WDS client:

1. Start the computer. When prompted, press F12 for a network service boot.

2. The Windows PE displays. When you see the Windows Welcome screen, click Next to start the installation process.

3. Enter the username and password of an account that has permissions to access and install images from the WDS server.

4. A list of available operating system images stored on the WDS server appears. Select the image to install and click Next.

5. Enter the product key for the selected Windows 7 image and click Next.

6. At the Partition And Configure the Disk screen, select the desired disk partitioning options, or click OK to use the default options.

7. Click Next to initiate the image-copying process. The Windows Setup process begins after the image is copied to the WDS client computer.

Now you know all the different ways to install Windows 7. Next let's look at a tool that can help you determine which machines can install Windows 7.

Microsoft Assessment and Planning (MAP) Toolkit

This chapter is about installing Windows 7 on multiple computers. One utility that you can use to help design your network is the Microsoft Assessment and Planning (MAP) Toolkit. MAP is a utility that will locate computers on a network and then perform a thorough inventory of these computers. To obtain this inventory, MAP uses multiple utilities like the Windows Management Instrumentation (WMI), the Remote Registry Service, or the Simple Network Management Protocol (SNMP).

Having this information will allow you to determine if the machines on your network will be able to load Windows 7, Windows Vista, Windows Server 2008, Microsoft Office 2007, and Microsoft Application Virtualization. One advantage of using MAP when determining the requirements for Windows 7 is that MAP will also advise you of any hardware upgrades needed for a machine or device driver availability.

Anyone who has been in the industry for a while can see the potential of using MAP. A utility that goes out and discovers your network hardware and then advises you of needed resources to allow the operating system to operate properly is a tool that should be in every administrator's arsenal.

When deciding to locate the computers on your network, you have several approaches. The following list shows your discovery options and how they try to discover the computers:

Use Active Directory Domain Services   Select this check box to find computer objects in Active Directory.

Use The Windows Networking Protocols   Select this check box to find computers in workgroups and Windows NT 4.0 domains.

Import Computer Names From A File   Select this check box to import computer names from a file.

Scan An IP Address Range   Select this check box to find computers within a specified IP address range.

Manually Enter Computer Names And Credentials   Select this check box to enter computer names individually.

You'll probably find it challenging to determine how many servers are needed for Windows 7 end users and where to place them on your network. A useful feature included with MAP is the ability to obtain performance metric data from the computers. MAP will also generate a report that recommends which machines can be used for Windows 7.

MAP generates your report in both Microsoft Excel and Word. These reports can provide information to you in summary and full detail modes. MAP can generate reports for you for some of the following scenarios:

♦   Identify currently installed client operating systems and their requirements for migrating to Windows 7.

♦   Identify currently installed Windows Server systems and their requirements for migrating to Windows Server 2008.

♦   Identify currently installed Microsoft Office software and their requirements for migrating to Office 2007.

♦   Server performance by using the Performance Metrics Wizard.

♦   Hyper-V or Virtual Server 2005 server consolidation and placement.

♦   Assessment of machines (clients, servers) for installation of Microsoft Application Virtualization (formerly known as SoftGrid).

To install MAP, we must first take a look at the system requirements.

MAP System Requirements

MAP is a free utility that you can download from Microsoft. But before you can install MAP, you must verify that the computer that MAP will be installed on meets minimum requirements. The minimum requirements to install MAP are as follows:

Supported Operating Systems   The supported operating systems include Windows 7, Windows Server 2008, Windows Server 2003, Windows Vista with Service Pack 1, and Windows XP Professional Edition.

CPU Architecture   MAP can be installed on both the 32-bit and 64-bit versions of any of the listed operating systems.

Hardware Requirements   Hardware requirements include: 1.6 GHz or faster processor minimum or dual-core for Windows 7; 1.5 GB of RAM minimum, 2 GB recommended for Windows 7 or Windows Vista; minimum of 1 GB of available hard disk space; and a network card that supports 10/100 Mbps.

Additional Requirements   Some additional requirements are Microsoft SQL Server 2005 Express Edition, Microsoft Word (2003 with SP2 or 2007), and Microsoft Excel (2003 with SP2 or 2007).

Follow these steps to install MAP from the Windows AIK installation utility that you downloaded previously in this chapter:

1. Insert the Windows AIK DVD into your machine.

2. When Autoplay starts, click Run StartCD.exe. If Autorun does not display, open Windows Explorer and click StartCD.exe under the DVD drive.

3. At the User Account Control screen, click Yes.

4. The Welcome to Windows Automated Installation Kit screen appears, as shown in Figure 3.14. Click the MAP Download link on the left. This takes you to the Microsoft website where you can download MAP.

5. Scroll down to the bottom of the page and click the download button for Microsoft_Assessment_and_Planning_Solution_Setup.x64.exe or x86.exe.

6. Click Save. Save the file to your hard drive.

7. After the file is downloaded to your hard drive, click Run.

8. The Microsoft Assessment and Planning Solution Accelerator Setup Wizard appears, as shown in Figure 3.15. Make sure the option to automatically check for device compatibility is checked and click Next.

9. The License Agreement screen appears next. Click the "I accept the terms of the license agreement" radio button and click Next.

10. At the Installation Folder screen, accept the default location by clicking Next.

11. A screen appears asking about SQL Server 2005 Express. If you have a previous version of SQL Server 2005 Express on your machine, click the radio button "Install from previous downloaded installation files." If you do not have a previous copy of SQL, make sure that the radio button Download And Install is checked. After your selection, click Next.

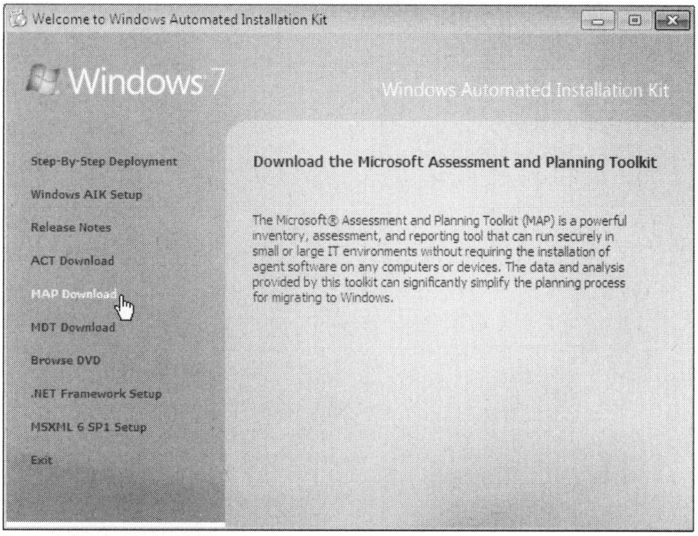

FIGURE 3.14
The Windows AIK
installation screen

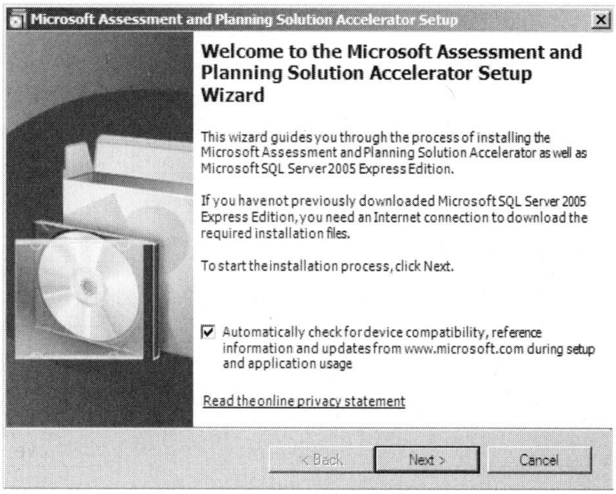

FIGURE 3.15
The MAP setup screen

12. The SQL Server 2005 Express License Agreement screen appears next. Click the "I accept the terms of the license agreement" radio button and click Next.

13. At the Ready To Install screen, click Install. The Installing The Microsoft Assessment And Planning Solution Accelerator status screen appears and shows you the status of the installation process. Once the installation is complete, the Installation Successful screen appears.

Now that you have installed MAP, it's time to configure and test the server. Perform the following steps to create your database for testing:

1. Start MAP by clicking Start ➢ All Programs ➢ Microsoft Planning And Assessment Solution Accelerator, and then clicking Microsoft Planning And Assessment Solution.

2. The first thing you need to do is select your database. You are going to create your database at this time. To accomplish this, click Select A Database in either the center or right window pane, as shown in Figure 3.16.

FIGURE 3.16
Click Select A Database in either the center or right window pane.

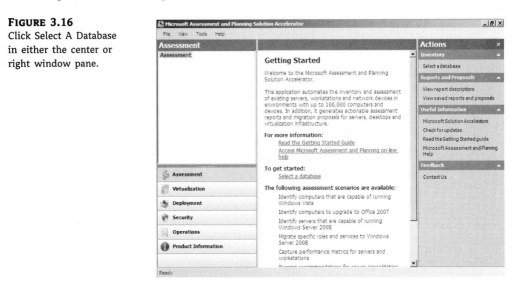

3. The Create Or Select A Database screen appears. Make sure that you click the Create An Inventory Database radio button. In the Name field, type **Windows 7** and click OK.

Once your database is created, you'll have the ability to run the various options to test the machines and servers. At this point, you decide which scenario you'd like to test for your network.

It's useful to have a utility like MAP to help you not only detect your network and its operating systems, but also recommend enhancements.

The Bottom Line

Use the Microsoft Deployment Toolkit (MDT) 2010. Microsoft Deployment Toolkit (MDT) 2010 is a way of automating desktop and server deployment. The MDT gives you tools for deployment of desktops and servers through the use of a common console. It allows for quicker deployments and standardized desktop and server images and security. MDT 2010 also allows for Zero Touch deployments of Windows 7, Windows Server 2008, Windows Vista, Windows Server 2003, and Windows XP.

Master It Your organization has asked you to set up one application that all administrators can use to configure and deploy Windows desktop operating systems. Which utility should you use?

Take advantage of the Windows Deployment Services (WDS). WDS is an updated version of Remote Installation Services (RIS). WDS is a suite of components that allows you to remotely install Windows 7 on client computers.

A WDS server installs Windows 7 on the client computers. The WDS server must be configured with the Preboot Execution Environment (PXE) boot files, the images to be deployed to the client computers, and the answer file. WDS client computers must be PXE capable.

> **Master It** You are hired as a consultant by a large organization with multiple locations. The organization wants to have the ability to deploy Windows 7 remotely. How can you set this up?

Utilize the Windows Automated Installation Kit (Windows AIK). The Windows AIK is a set of utilities and documentation that allows you to configure and deploy Windows operating systems. You can use the Windows AIK to capture Windows Images with ImageX, configure and edit your images by using the Deployment Image Servicing and Management (DISM) utility, create Windows PE images, migrate user data and profiles using the User State Migration Tool (USMT), and centrally manage volume activations by using the Volume Activation Management Tool (VAMT).

> **Master It** You need to configure and deploy Windows operating systems by using images. How can you accomplish this task?

Make the most of the Microsoft Assessment and Planning (MAP) Toolkit. MAP is a utility that will locate computers on a network and then perform a thorough inventory of these computers. To obtain this inventory, MAP uses multiple utilities like the Windows Management Instrumentation (WMI), the Remote Registry Service, or the Simple Network Management Protocol (SNMP).

Having this information will allow you to determine if the machines on your network will be able to load Windows 7, Windows Vista, Server 2008, Microsoft Office 2007, and Microsoft Application Virtualization. One advantage of using MAP when determining the needs for Windows 7 is that MAP will also advise you of any hardware upgrades needed for a machine or device driver availability.

> **Master It** You are a consultant who is hired by an organization to migrate the computers from Windows XP to Windows 7. How would you accomplish this?

Chapter 4

Configuring Disks

When you install Windows 7, you designate the initial configuration for your disks. Through Windows 7's utilities and features, you can change that configuration and perform disk-management tasks. Some of the tasks and decisions that you need to consider when you configure disks are file system configuration and disk type configuration. In this chapter, we'll discuss how to configure these by using Disk Management.

For file system configuration, we recommend that you use NTFS, although you could also format the disk drive as FAT32. You can also update a FAT32 partition to NTFS. This chapter covers the features of each file system and how to use the Convert utility to upgrade to NTFS.

Another task in disk management is choosing the configuration for your physical drives. Windows 7 supports basic, dynamic, and the GUID partition table (GPT) disks. When you install Windows 7 or upgrade from Windows 7 using basic disks, the drives are configured as basic disks.

Dynamic disks are supported by Windows 7, Windows Vista, Windows XP Professional, Windows 2000 (all versions), Windows Server 2003, and Windows Server 2008 and allow you to create simple volumes, spanned volumes, and striped volumes.

After you decide how your disks should be configured, you implement the disk configurations through the Disk Management utility. This utility helps you view and manage your physical disks and volumes. In this chapter, you'll learn how to manage both types of storage and how to upgrade from basic storage to dynamic storage.

This chapter also covers other disk-management features such as data compression, data encryption, disk defragmentation, disk cleanup, and disk error checking.

In this chapter, you'll learn how to:

- ◆ Understand the different file systems
- ◆ Identify disk storage types
- ◆ Understand the benefits of NTFS
- ◆ Use disk-management utilities

Configuring File Systems

Each partition (each logical drive that is created on your hard drive) you create under Windows 7 must have a file system associated with it.

When you select a file system, you can select FAT32 or NTFS. You typically select file systems based on the features you want to use and whether you will need to access the file system using other operating systems. If you have a FAT32 partition and want to update it to NTFS, you can use the Convert utility. The features of each file system and the procedure for converting file systems are covered in the following sections.

Selecting a File System

Your file system is used to store and retrieve the files stored on your hard drive. One of the most fundamental choices associated with file management is the choice of your file system's configuration. Microsoft recommends that you use NTFS with Windows 7, because doing so will allow you to take advantage of features such as local security, file compression, and file encryption. You should choose FAT32 if you want to dual-boot your computer with a version of Windows that does not support NTFS because these file systems are backward compatible with other operating systems.

Table 4.1 summarizes the capabilities of each file system, and they are described in more detail in the following sections.

TABLE 4.1:   File System Capabilities

FEATURE	FAT32	NTFS
Supporting operating systems	Windows 95 OSR2, Windows 98, Windows Me, Windows 2000, Windows XP, Windows Server 2003, Windows Server 2008, Windows Vista, and Windows 7	Windows NT, Windows 2000, Windows XP, Windows Server 2003, Windows Vista, and Windows 7
Long filename support	Yes	Yes
Efficient use of disk space	Yes	Yes
Compression support	No	Yes
Encryption support	No	Yes
Support for local security	No	Yes
Support for network security	Yes	Yes
Maximum volume size	32 GB	16 TB with 4 KB clusters or 256 TB with 64 KB clusters

---

WINDOWS 7 FILE SYSTEM SUPPORT

Windows 7 also supports Compact Disk File System (CDFS). However, CDFS cannot be managed. It is used only to mount and read CDs.

Let's start looking at the supported file systems.

FAT32

FAT32 is an updated version of FAT. FAT32 was first shipped with Windows 95 OSR2 (Operating System Release 2), and can be used by Windows 7.

One of the main advantages of FAT32 is its support for smaller cluster sizes, which results in more efficient space allocation than was possible with FAT16. Files stored on a FAT32 partition can use 20 to 30 percent less disk space than files stored on a FAT16 partition. FAT32 supports drive sizes from 512 MB up to 2 TB, although if you create and format a FAT32 partition through Windows 7, the FAT32 partition can only be up to 32 GB. Because of the smaller cluster sizes, FAT32 can also load programs up to 50 percent faster than programs loaded from FAT16 partitions.

The main disadvantages of FAT32 compared to NTFS are that it does not provide as much support for larger hard drives and it does not provide very robust security options. It also offers no native support for disk compression. Now that you understand FAT32, let's take a look at NTFS.

NTFS

NTFS, which was first used with the NT operating system, offers the highest level of service and features for Windows 7 computers. NTFS partitions can be up to 16 TB with 4 KB clusters or 256 TB with 64 KB clusters.

NTFS offers comprehensive folder- and file-level security. This allows you to set an additional level of security for users who access the files and folders locally or through the network. For example, two users who share the same Windows 7 computer can be assigned different NTFS permissions, so that one user has access to a folder but the other user is denied access to that folder.

NTFS also offers disk-management features — such as compression and encryption services — and data recovery features. The disk-management features are covered later in this chapter. The data-recovery features are covered in Chapter 15, "Maintaining and Optimizing Windows 7."

You should also be aware that there are several different versions of NTFS. Every version of Windows 2000 uses NTFS 3.0. Windows 7, Windows Vista, Windows XP, and Windows Server 2003 use NTFS 3.1. NTFS versions 3.0 and 3.1 use similar disk formats, so Windows 2000 computers can access NTFS 3.1 volumes and Windows 7 computers can access NTFS 3.0 volumes.

NTFS 3.1 includes the following features:

◆ When files are read or written to a disk, they can be automatically encrypted and decrypted.

◆ Reparse points are used with mount points to redirect data as it is written or read from a folder to another volume or physical disk.

♦ There is support for sparse files, which are used by programs that create large files but allocate disk space only as needed.

♦ Remote storage allows you to extend your disk space by making removable media (for example, external tapes) more accessible.

♦ You can use recovery logging on NTFS metadata, which is used for data recovery when a power failure or system problem occurs.

Now that you have seen the differences between FAT32 and NTFS, let's discuss how to change a FAT32 drive to an NTFS drive.

Converting a File System

In Windows 7, you can convert FAT32 partitions to NTFS. File system conversion is the process of converting one file system to another without the loss of data. If you format a drive as another file system, as opposed to converting that drive, all the data on that drive will be lost.

To convert a partition, use the Convert command-line utility. The syntax for the Convert command is as follows:

```
Convert [drive:] /fs:ntfs
```

For example, if you wanted to convert your D drive to NTFS, you'd type the following command from a command prompt:

```
Convert D: /fs:ntfs
```

When the conversion process begins, it will attempt to lock the partition. If the partition cannot be locked — perhaps because the partition contains the Windows 7 operating system files or the system's page file — the conversion won't take place until the computer is restarted.

USING THE Convert COMMAND

You can use the /v switch with the `Convert` command. This switch specifies that you want to use verbose mode, and all messages will be displayed during the conversion process. You can also use the /NoSecurity switch that specifies that all converted files and folders will have no security applied by default so they can be accessed by anyone.

In the following steps, you convert your D drive from FAT32 to NTFS. These steps assume that you have a D drive that is formatted with the FAT32 file system.

Perform the following steps to convert a FAT32 partition to NTFS:

1. Copy some folders to the D drive.

2. Select Start, then type **cmd** into the Search box to open a command prompt.

3. In the Command Prompt dialog box, type **Convert D: /fs:ntfs** and press Enter.

4. After the conversion process is complete, close the Command Prompt dialog box.

5. Verify that the folders you copied in step 1 still exist on the partition.

STOPPING A CONVERSION

If you choose to convert a partition from FAT32 to NTFS, and the conversion has not yet taken place, you can cancel the conversion by editing the Registry with the `regedit` command. The key that needs to be edited is `HKEY_LOCAL_MACHINE\System\CurrentControlSet` `\Control\SessionManager`. The `BootExecute` value should be changed from `autoconv` `\DosDevices\x: /FS:NTFS` to `autocheck autochk*`.

After you decide which file system you want to use, you need to decide what disk storage type you want to configure. Let's take a look at some of the disk storage options that you have.

Configuring Disk Storage

Windows 7 supports three types of disk storage: basic, dynamic, and GUID partition table (GPT). Basic storage is backward compatible with other operating systems and can be configured to support up to four partitions. Dynamic storage is supported by Windows 2000, Windows XP, Windows Server 2003, Windows Server 2008, Windows Vista, and Windows 7, and allows storage to be configured as volumes. GPT storage allows you to configure volume sizes larger than 2 TB and up to 128 primary partitions. The following sections describe the basic storage, dynamic storage, and GPT storage configurations.

Basic Storage

Basic storage consists of primary and extended partitions and logical drives. The first partition that is created on a hard drive is called a primary partition and is usually represented as drive C. Primary partitions use all of the space that is allocated to the partition and use a single drive letter to represent the partition. Each physical drive can have up to four partitions and only four partitions. You can set up four primary partitions, or you can have three primary partitions and one extended partition. With an extended partition, you can allocate the space however you like, and each suballocation of space (called a logical drive) is represented by a different drive letter. For example, a 500 GB extended partition could have a 250 GB D partition and a 250 GB E partition.

At the highest level of disk organization, you have a physical hard drive. You cannot use space on the physical drive until you have logically partitioned the physical drive. A partition is a logical definition of hard drive space.

One of the advantages of using multiple partitions on a single physical hard drive is that each partition can have a different file system. For example, the C drive might be FAT32 and the D drive might be NTFS. Multiple partitions also make it easier to manage security requirements.

Basic storage is the default setting, and this is the type that many users continue to use. But what if you want some additional functionality from your storage type? Let's take a look at some of the more advanced disk storage options.

Dynamic Storage

Dynamic storage is a Windows 7 feature that consists of a dynamic disk divided into dynamic volumes. Dynamic volumes cannot contain partitions or logical drives.

Dynamic storage supports three dynamic volume types: simple volumes, spanned volumes, and striped volumes. Dynamic storage also supports software-based Redundant Array of Inexpensive Disks (RAID).

To set up dynamic storage, you create or upgrade a basic disk to a dynamic disk. When you convert a basic disk to dynamic, you do not lose any of your data. After the disk is converted, you can then create dynamic volumes within the dynamic disk.

You create dynamic storage with the Windows 7 Disk Management utility, which we'll explore following the descriptions of the dynamic volume types. Let's take a closer look at the various types of dynamic volumes.

SIMPLE VOLUMES

A simple volume contains space from a single dynamic drive. The space from the single drive can be contiguous or noncontiguous. Simple volumes are used when you have enough disk space on a single drive to hold your entire volume. Figure 4.1 shows two simple volumes on a physical disk.

FIGURE 4.1
Two simple volumes

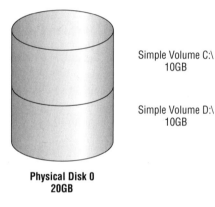

Simple Volume C:\
10GB

Simple Volume D:\
10GB

Physical Disk 0
20GB

SPANNED VOLUMES

A spanned volume consists of disk space on two or more dynamic drives; up to 32 dynamic drives can be used in a spanned volume configuration. Spanned volume sets are used to dynamically increase the size of a dynamic volume. When you create spanned volumes, the data is written sequentially, filling space on one physical drive before writing to space on the next physical drive in the spanned volume set. Typically, administrators use spanned volumes when they are running out of disk space on a volume and want to dynamically extend the volume with space from another hard drive.

You do not need to allocate the same amount of space to the volume set on each physical drive. This means you could combine a 500 GB partition on one physical drive with two 750 GB partitions on other dynamic drives, as shown in Figure 4.2.

Because data is written sequentially, you do not see any performance enhancements with spanned volumes as you do with striped volumes (which we discuss next). The main disadvantage of spanned volumes is that if any drive in the spanned volume set fails, you lose access to all of the data in the spanned set.

FIGURE 4.2
A spanned volume set

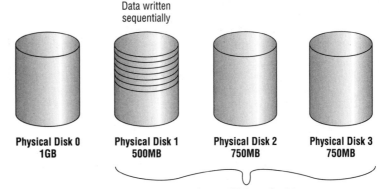

Data written
sequentially

Physical Disk 0	Physical Disk 1	Physical Disk 2	Physical Disk 3
1GB	500MB	750MB	750MB

Spanned Volume Set D:\

STRIPED VOLUMES

A striped volume stores data in equal stripes between two or more (up to 32) dynamic drives, as shown in Figure 4.3. Because the data is written sequentially in the stripes, you can take advantage of multiple I/O performance and increase the speed at which data reads and writes take place. Typically, administrators use striped volumes when they want to combine the space of several physical drives into a single logical volume and increase disk performance.

FIGURE 4.3
A striped volume set

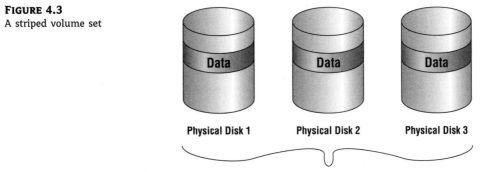

Physical Disk 1	Physical Disk 2	Physical Disk 3
Data	Data	Data

Striped Volume Set D:\

The main disadvantage of striped volumes is that if any drive in the striped volume set fails, you lose access to all of the data in the striped set.

In the last few years a new storage type has emerged in the Microsoft computer world and as with most new technologies, it also has some advantages over the previous technologies. Let's take a look at the newest advantage to storage types.

GUID Partition Table

The GUID partition table (GPT) is available for Windows 7 and was first introduced as part of the Extensible Firmware Interface (EFI) initiative from Intel. Basic and dynamic disks use the Master Boot Record (MBR) partitioning scheme that all operating systems have been using for years. Basic and dynamic disks use Cylinder-Head-Sector (CHS) addressing with the MBR scheme.

The GPT disk partitioning system uses the GUID partition table to configure the disk area. GPT uses a newer addressing scheme called Logical Block Addressing (LBA). Another advantage is that the GPT header and partition table is written to both the front and the back end of the disk, which in turn provides for better redundancy.

The GPT disk partitioning system gives you many benefits over using the MBR system, including the following:

- Allows a volume size larger than 2 TB

- Allows up to 128 primary partitions

- Used for both 32-bit or 64-bit Windows 7 editions

- Includes cyclical redundancy check (CRC) for greater reliability

There is one disadvantage to using the GPT drives. You can only convert a GPT drive if the disk is empty and unpartitioned. We'll show you the steps to creating a GPT disk later in this chapter in the "Upgrading a Basic Disk to a Dynamic or GPT Disk section."

To convert any disk or format any volume or partition, you can use the Disk Management utility. Let's take a look at how to manage your disks using the Disk Management Utility.

Accessing and Managing the Disk Management Utility

The Disk Management utility is a Microsoft Management Console (MMC) snap-in that gives administrators a graphical tool for managing disks and volumes within Windows 7. In this section, you'll learn how to access the Disk Management utility and use it to manage basic tasks, basic storage, and dynamic storage. You will also learn about troubleshooting disks through disk status codes.

But before we dive into the Disk Management utility, let's first take a look at the MMC. It's important to understand the MMC because Disk Management (like many other tools) is actually an MMC snap-in.

Using the MMC

The MMC is the console framework for application management. The MMC provides a common environment for snap-ins. Snap-ins are administrative tools developed by Microsoft or third-party vendors. Some of the MMC snap-ins that you may use are Computer Management, Active Directory Users and Computers, Active Directory Sites and Services, Active Directory Domains and Trusts, and DNS Management.

Knowing how to use and configure the MMC snap-ins allows you to customize your work environment. For example, if you are in charge of Active Directory Users and Computers and DNS, you can add both of these snap-ins into the same window. This would then allow you to just open one application to configure all your tasks.

The MMC offers many other benefits, including the following:

- The MMC is highly customizable — you add only the snap-ins you need.

- Snap-ins use a standard, intuitive interface, so they're easier to use than previous versions of administrative utilities.

- You can save and share MMC consoles with other administrators.

♦ You can configure permissions so that the MMC runs in authoring mode, which an administrator can manage, or in user mode, which limits what users can access.

♦ You can use most snap-ins for remote computer management.

By default, the MMC console contains three panes: a console tree on the left, a details pane in the middle, and an optional Actions pane on the right, as shown in Figure 4.4. The console tree lists the hierarchical structure of all snap-ins that have been loaded into the console. The details pane contains a list of properties or other items that are part of the snap-in that is highlighted in the console tree. The Actions pane provides a list of actions that the user can access depending on the item selected in the details pane.

FIGURE 4.4
The MMC console tree, details pane, and Actions pane

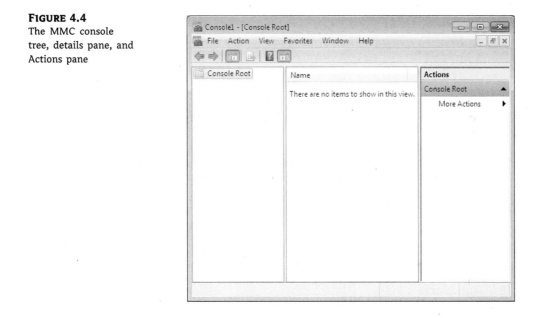

Accessing the MMC

On a Windows 7 computer, to open the MMC, click Start and type **MMC** in the Search dialog box. When you first open the MMC, it contains only the Console Root folder, as shown in Figure 4.4 earlier. The MMC does not have any default administrative functionality. It is simply a framework used to organize administrative tools through the addition of snap-in utilities.

The first thing that you should decide when you use the MMC is which of the different administrative mode types is best suited for your organization.

CONFIGURING MMC MODES

You can configure the MMC to run in author mode, for full access to the MMC functions, or in one of three user modes, which have more limited access to the MMC functions. To set a console mode, while in the MMC editor, select File ➤ Options to open the Options dialog box. In this dialog box, you can select from the console modes listed in Table 4.2.

After you decide which administrative role you are going to run, it's time to start configuring your MMC snap-ins.

TABLE 4.2:   MMC Console Modes

CONSOLE MODE	DESCRIPTION
Author mode	Allows use of all the MMC functions.
User mode — full access	Allows users full access to window management commands, but they cannot add or remove snap-ins or change console properties.
User mode — limited access, multiple window	Allows users to create new windows, but not close any existing windows. Users can access only the areas of the console tree that were visible when the console was last saved.
User mode — limited access, single window	Allows users to access only the areas of the console tree that were visible when the console was last saved, and they cannot create new windows.

ADDING SNAP-INS

The biggest advantage of using the MMC is to add snap-ins the way your organization needs them. Adding snap-ins is a simple and quick procedure.

Perform the following steps to add snap-ins to the MMC console and save it:

1. To start the MMC editor, click Start, type **MMC** in the Search box, and press Enter.

2. From the main console window, select File ➤ Add/Remove Snap-In to open the Add/Remove Snap-In dialog box.

3. Highlight the snap-in you want to add and click Add, as shown in Figure 4.5.

FIGURE 4.5
The MMC Add Or
Remove Snap-ins screen

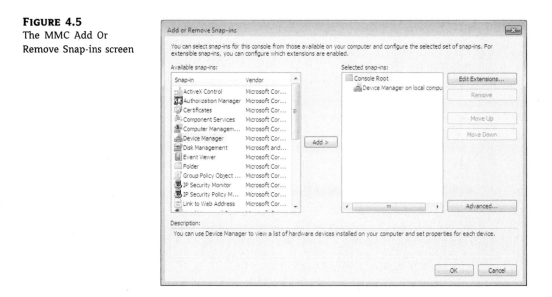

4. If prompted, specify whether the snap-in will be used to manage the local computer or a remote computer, as shown in Figure 4.6. Then click Finish.

FIGURE 4.6
Choose between a local or remote computer.

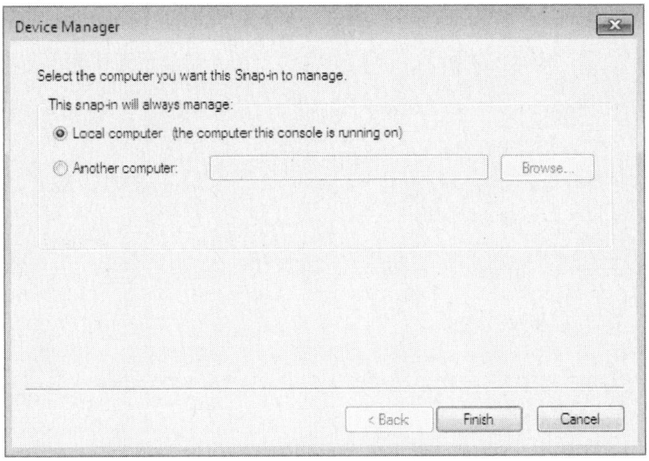

5. Repeat steps 2 and 3 to add each snap-in you want to include in your console.

6. When you finish adding snap-ins, click OK.

7. Click OK to return to the main console screen.

8. After you have added snap-ins to create a console, you can save it by selecting File ➢ Save As and entering a name for your console.

You can save the console to a variety of locations, including a program group or the Desktop. By default, custom consoles have an `.msc` extension.

Many applications that are MMC snap-ins, including Disk Management, are already configured for you under the administrative tools section of Windows 7. Now that we have looked at the MMC editor, let's take a look at the Disk Management utility.

Accessing the Disk Management Utility

The Disk Management utility, located under the Computer Management snap-in by default, is a one-stop shop for configuring your disk options.

First, to have full permissions to use the Disk Management utility, you must be logged on with Administrative privileges. You can access the Disk Management utility a few different ways. You can right-click Computer from the Start menu and select Manage, and then in Computer Management, select Disk Management. You could also choose Start ➢ Control Panel ➢ Administrative Tools ➢ Computer Management.

The Disk Management utility's opening window, shown in Figure 4.7, shows the following information:

◆ The volumes that are recognized by the computer

◆ The type of disk, either basic or dynamic

◆ The type of file system used by each partition

♦ The status of the partition and whether the partition contains the system or boot partition

♦ The capacity (amount of space) allocated to the partition

♦ The amount of free space remaining on the partition

♦ The amount of overhead associated with the partition

FIGURE 4.7
The Disk Management window

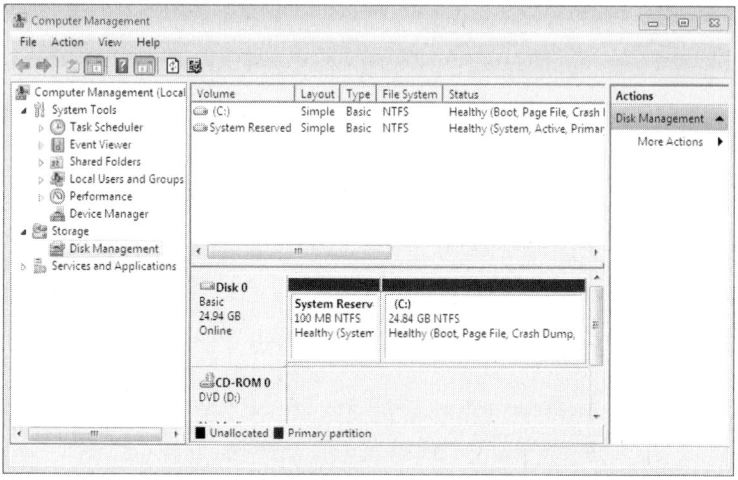

Windows 7 also includes a command-line utility called Diskpart, which you can use as a command-line alternative to the Disk Management utility. You can view all the options associated with the Diskpart utility by typing **Diskpart** at a command prompt, and then typing **?** at the Diskpart prompt.

The Disk Management utility allows you to configure and manage your disks. Let's take a look at some of the tasks that you can perform in Disk Management.

Managing Administrative Hard Disk Tasks

The Disk Management utility allows you to perform a variety of hard drive administrative tasks. These tasks are discussed in the sections that follow:

♦ Viewing disk properties

♦ Viewing volume and local disk properties

♦ Adding a new disk

♦ Creating partitions and volumes

♦ Upgrading a basic disk to a dynamic disk

♦ Changing a drive letter and path

♦ Deleting partitions and volumes

VIEWING DISK PROPERTIES

To view the properties of a disk, right-click the disk number in the lower panel of the Disk Management main window and choose Properties from the context menu. This brings up the disk's Properties dialog box. Click the Volumes tab, as shown in Figure 4.8, to see the volumes associated with the disk, which contains the following disk properties:

◆ The disk number

◆ The type of disk (basic, dynamic, CD-ROM, removable, DVD, or unknown)

◆ The status of the disk (online or offline)

◆ Partition style (MBR)

◆ The capacity of the disk

◆ The amount of unallocated space on the disk

◆ The logical volumes that have been defined on the physical drive

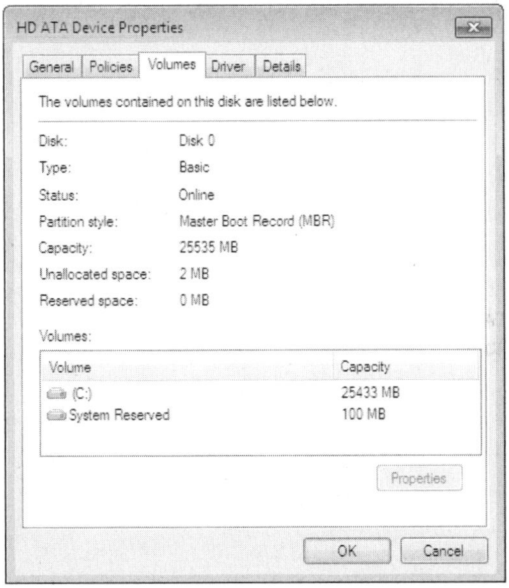

FIGURE 4.8
The Volumes tab of a disk's Properties dialog box

DISK PROPERTIES

If you click the General tab of a disk's Properties dialog box, the hardware device type, the hardware vendor that produced the drive, the physical location of the drive, and the device status are displayed.

VIEWING VOLUME AND LOCAL DISK PROPERTIES

On a dynamic disk, you manage volume properties. On a basic disk, you manage partition properties. Volumes and partitions perform the same function, and the options discussed in the following sections apply to both. (The examples here are based on a dynamic disk using a simple volume. If you're using basic storage, you'll view the local disk properties rather than the volume properties.)

To see the properties of a volume, right-click the volume in the upper panel of the Disk Management main window and choose Properties. This brings up the volume's Properties dialog box. Volume properties are organized on seven tabs: General, Tools, Hardware, Sharing, Security, Quota, and Previous Versions. The Security and Quota tabs appear only for NTFS volumes. Let's explore all these tabs in detail:

General The information on the General tab of the volume's Properties dialog box, as shown in Figure 4.9, gives you an idea of how the volume is configured. This dialog box shows the label, type, file system, used and free space, and capacity of the volume. The label is shown in an editable text box, and you can change it if desired. The space allocated to the volume is shown in a graphical representation as well as in text form.

FIGURE 4.9
General properties for a
volume

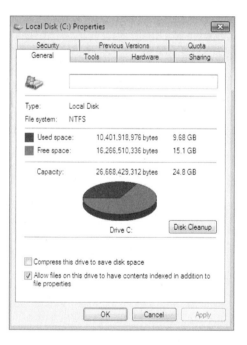

The label on a volume or local disk is for informational purposes only. For example, depending on its use, you might give a volume a label such as APPS or ACCTDB.

The Disk Cleanup button starts the Disk Cleanup utility, with which you can delete unnecessary files and free disk space. This utility is discussed later in this chapter.

This tab also allows you to configure compression for the volume and to indicate whether the volume should be indexed.

Tools   The Tools tab of the volume's Properties dialog box, shown in Figure 4.10, provides access to three tools:

- ◆ Click the Check Now button to run the Error-Checking utility to check the volume for errors. You'd do this if you were experiencing problems accessing the volume or if the volume had been open during a system restart that did not go through a proper shutdown sequence.

- ◆ Click the Defragment Now button to run the Disk Defragmenter utility. This utility defragments files on the volume by storing the files contiguously on the hard drive.

- ◆ Click the Backup Now button to open the Backup Status and Configuration dialog box, which allows you to configure backup procedures.

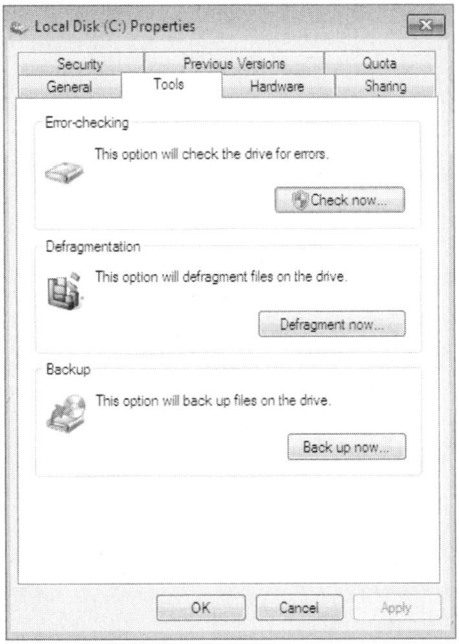

FIGURE 4.10
The Tools tab of the volume's Properties dialog box

Hardware   The Hardware tab of the volume's Properties dialog box, shown in Figure 4.11, lists the hardware associated with the disk drives that are recognized by the Windows 7 operating system. The bottom half of the dialog box shows the properties of the device that's highlighted in the top half of the dialog box.

For more details about a hardware item, highlight it and click the Properties button in the lower-right corner of the dialog box. This brings up a Properties dialog box for the item. Your Device Status field should report that "This device is working properly." If that's not the case, you can click the Troubleshoot button to open a troubleshooting wizard that will help you discover what the problem is.

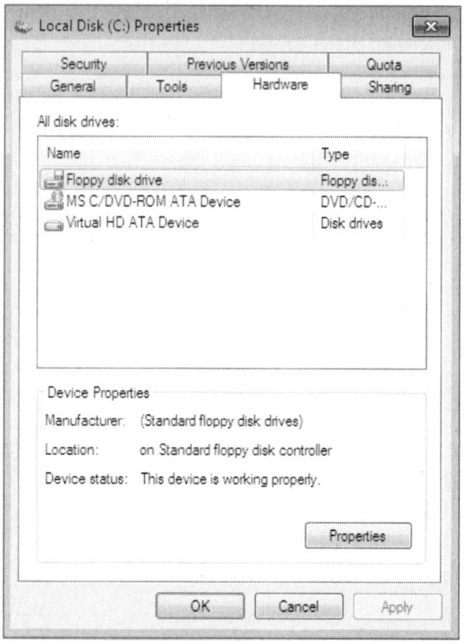

FIGURE 4.11
The Hardware tab of
the volume's Proper-
ties dialog box

Sharing   On the Sharing tab of the volume's Properties dialog box, shown in Figure 4.12, you can specify whether or not the volume is shared. Volumes are not shared by default. To share a volume, click the Advanced Sharing button, which lets you specify whether the volume is shared and, if so, what the name of the share should be. You can also specify who will have access to the shared volume.

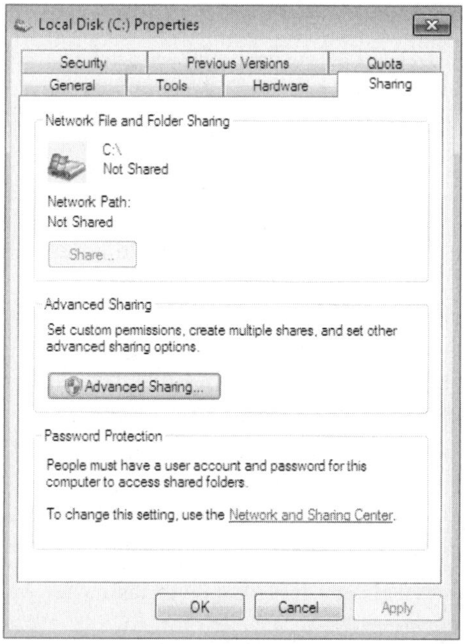

FIGURE 4.12
The Sharing tab of the
volume's Properties dia-
log box

Security   The Security tab of the volume's Properties dialog box, shown in Figure 4.13, appears only for NTFS volumes. Use the Security tab to set the NTFS permissions for the volume.

FIGURE 4.13
The Security tab of the volume's Properties dialog box

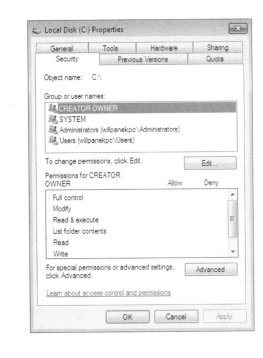

Previous Versions   The Previous Versions tab displays shadow copies of the files that are created by System Restore, as shown in Figure 4.14. Shadow copies of files are backup copies created by Windows in the background in order to enable you to restore the system to a previous state. On the Previous Versions tab, you can select a copy of the volume and either view the contents of the shadow copy or copy the shadow copy to another location. If System Restore is not enabled, then shadow copies of a volume will not be created.

Quota   Quotas give you the advantage to limit the amount of hard disk space that a user can have on a volume or partition, as shown in Figure 4.15. There are a few options that you can configure when you enable quotas. By default, quotas are disabled. To enable quotas, check the Enable Quota Management check box.

The "Deny disk space to users exceeding quota limit" check box is another option. By enabling this box, any user who exceeds their quota limit is denied disk storage. You can choose not to enable this option and this allows you to just monitor the quotas. You also have the ability to set the quota limit and warning size. You can also choose to log all quota events as they happen.

ADDING A NEW DISK

You can add new hard disks to a system in order to increase the amount of disk storage you have. This is a fairly common task that you'll need to perform as your application programs and files grow larger.

FIGURE 4.14
The Previous Versions tab of the volume's Properties dialog box

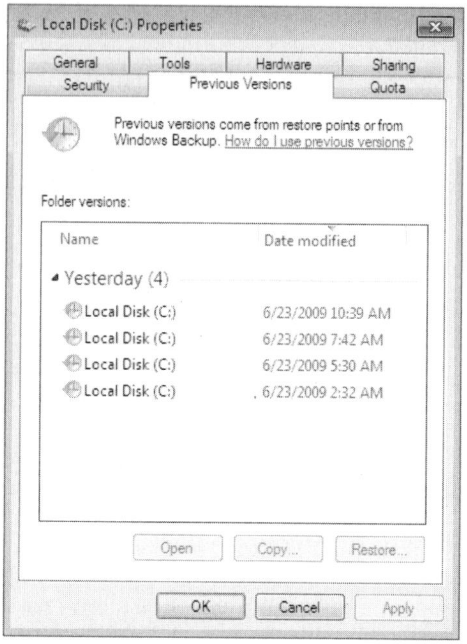

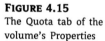

FIGURE 4.15
The Quota tab of the volume's Properties dialog box

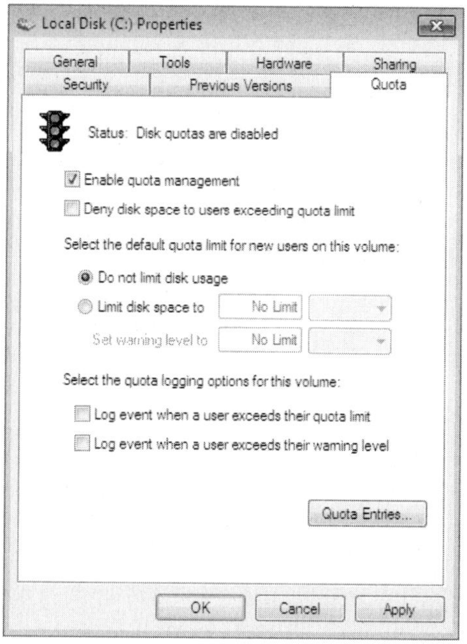

How you add a disk depends on whether your computer supports hot swapping of drives. Hot swapping is the process of adding a new hard drive while the computer is turned on. Most desktop computers do not support this capability. Remember, your user account must be a member of the Administrators group in order to install a new drive. The following list specifies configuration options:

Computer Doesn't Support Hot Swapping   If your computer does not support hot swapping, you must first shut down the computer before you add a new disk. Then add the drive according to the manufacturer's directions. When you finish, restart the computer. You should find the new drive listed in the Disk Management utility.

Computer Supports Hot Swapping   If your computer does support hot swapping, you don't need to turn off your computer first. Just add the drive according to the manufacturer's directions. Then open the Disk Management utility and select Action ➢ Rescan Disks. You should find the new drive listed in the Disk Management utility.

Creating Partitions and Volumes   After you add a new disk, the next step is to create a partition (on a basic disk) or a volume (on a dynamic disk). Partitions and volumes fill similar roles in the storage of data on disks, and the processes for creating them are the same.

CREATING A VOLUME OR A PARTITION

Creating a volume or partition is a fairly easy process. To do so, right-click the unformatted free space and start the wizard. The New Volume Wizard guides you through the process of creating a new volume, as follows:

1. In the Disk Management utility, right-click an area of free storage space and choose the type of volume to create. If only one drive is installed, you'll only be able to create a simple volume. You can click New Simple Volume to create a new simple volume.

2. The Welcome to the New Simple Volume Wizard appears. Click Next.

3. The Select Volume Size screen appears. Select the size of the volume that you want to create and then click Next.

4. Next you see the Assign Drive Letter or Path screen, as shown in Figure 4.16. You can specify a drive letter, mount the volume as an empty folder, or choose not to assign a drive letter or drive path. If you choose to mount the volume as an empty folder, you can have an unlimited number of volumes, negating the drive-letter limitation. If you choose not to assign a drive letter or path, users will not be able to access the volume. Make your selections and click Next.

5. The Format Partition screen appears, as shown in Figure 4.17. This screen allows you to choose whether you will format the volume. If you choose to format the volume, you can format it as FAT32 or NTFS. You can also select the allocation block size, enter a volume label (for information only), specify a quick format, or choose to enable file and folder compression. After you've made your choices, click Next.

6. The Completing the New Volume Wizard screen appears next. Verify your selections. If you need to change any of them, click the Back button to reach the appropriate screen. When everything is correctly set, click Finish.

Now that we created a new volume or partition, let's take a look at how to convert a basic disk to dynamic or GPT.

FIGURE 4.16
The Assign Drive Letter
or Path screen

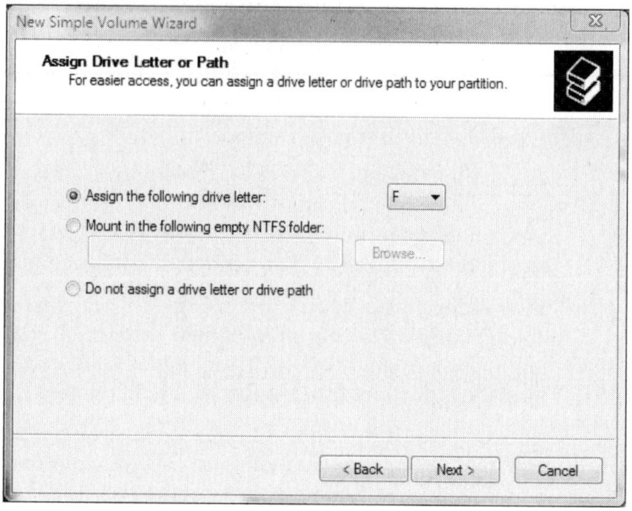

FIGURE 4.17
The Format Partition
screen

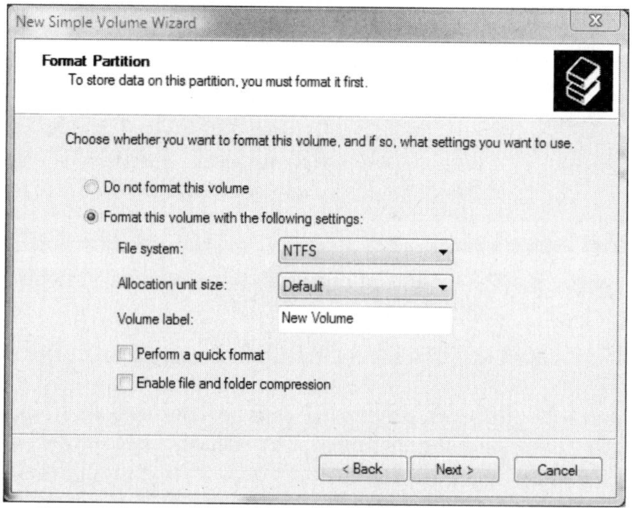

UPGRADING A BASIC DISK TO A DYNAMIC OR GPT DISK

When you install a fresh installation of Windows 7, your drives are configured as basic disks. To take advantage of the features offered by Windows 7 dynamic or GPT disks, you must upgrade your basic disks to either dynamic or GPT disks.

UPGRADING DISKS

Upgrading basic disks to dynamic disks is a one-way process as far as preserving data is concerned and a potentially dangerous operation. Before you perform this upgrade (or make any major change to your drives or volumes), create a new backup of the drive or volume and verify that you can successfully restore the backup.

You can convert any basic partition to a dynamic disk, but you can only convert unformatted free space to a GPT disk.

Perform the following steps to convert a drive to a GPT:

1. If the volume or partition that you want to convert has data, first delete the partition or volume.

2. Open the Disk Management utility by clicking the Start button, right-click Computers, and choose Manage.

3. Click Disk Management in the lower-left section.

4. Right-click the drive letter and choose Convert To GPT Disk, as shown in Figure 4.18.

FIGURE 4.18
Choosing Convert To GPT Disk

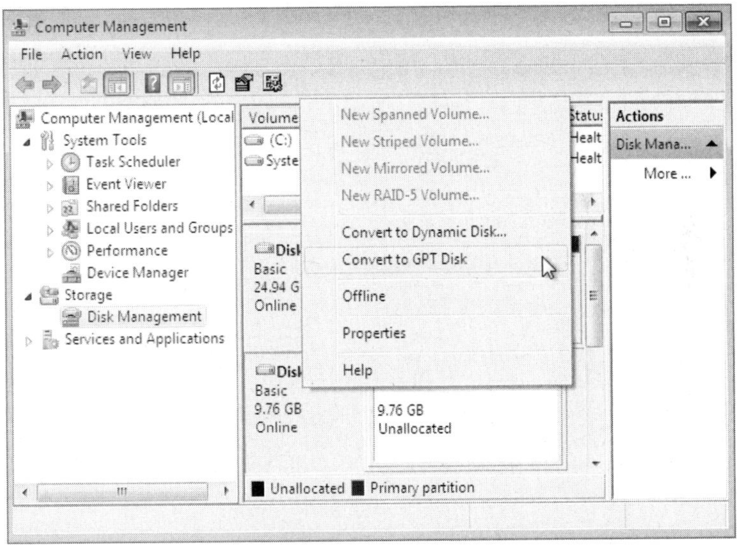

5. After the disk converts, you can right-click the disk and see that the Convert To MBR Disk is now available.

CONVERTING TO A GPT DISK

There are a few other methods for converting a basic disk to a GPT disk. You can use the Diskpart utility and type in the **Convert GPT** command. You can also create a GPT disk when you first install a new hard drive. After you install the new hard drive, during the initialization phase, you can choose GPT Disk.

Another type of conversion that you might need to perform is converting a basic disk to a dynamic disk.

Follow these steps to convert a basic disk to a dynamic disk:

1. In the Disk Management utility, right-click the disk you want to convert and select the Convert To Dynamic Disk option.

2. In the Convert To Dynamic Disk dialog box, check the disk that you want to upgrade and click OK.

3. In the Disks To Convert dialog box, click Convert.

4. confirmation dialog box warns you that you will no longer be able to boot previous versions of Windows from this disk. Click Yes to continue to convert the disk.

🌐 **Real World Scenario**

BENEFITS OF CONVERTING DISKS

For many years as IT managers we used just basic disks. There's a huge disadvantage to just using basic disks. Basic disks can't be extended without the use of a third-party utility. One problem that many IT managers ran into related to home folder storage. Home folders are storage areas on the server for your users. Users store data on the home folders and that data can then be backed up.

The main issue with home folders is that the space you give your users is never enough. The home folders tend to fill up your hard drive or partition. With basic disks, you could not extend the partition. But one of the advantages of dynamic disks is that they can be extended (as long as they are formatted with NTFS). Now if the hard disk or volume fills up, just extend the volume to a free area on the hard disk or add another hard drive. This is a huge advantage to anyone who has dealt with hard drives or partitions filling up.

As you are configuring the volumes or partitions on the hard drive, another thing that you might need to configure is the drive letter and paths.

CHANGING THE DRIVE LETTER AND PATH

There might be times when you need to change drive letters and paths when you add new equipment. Let's suppose that you have a hard drive with two partitions; drive C assigned as your first partition and drive D assigned as your second partition. Your DVD-ROM is assigned the drive letter of E. You add a new hard drive and partition it as a new volume. By default, the new partition is assigned as drive F. If you want your logical drives to appear listed before the DVD-ROM drive, you can use the Disk Management utility's Change Drive Letter And Paths option to rearrange your drive letters.

When you need to reassign drive letters, right-click the volume for which you want to change the drive letter and choose Change Drive Letter And Paths. This brings up the dialog box shown in Figure 4.19. Click the Change button to access the Change Drive Letter Or Path dialog box, as shown in Figure 4.20. Use the drop-down list next to the Assign The Following Drive Letter option to select the drive letter you want to assign to the volume.

FIGURE 4.19
The dialog box for changing a drive letter or path

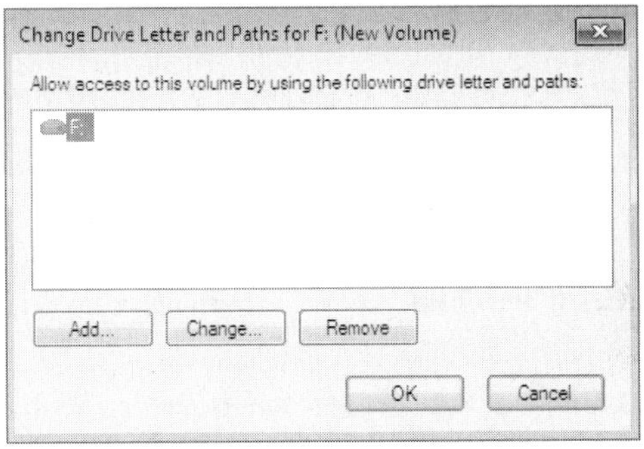

FIGURE 4.20
Editing the drive letter

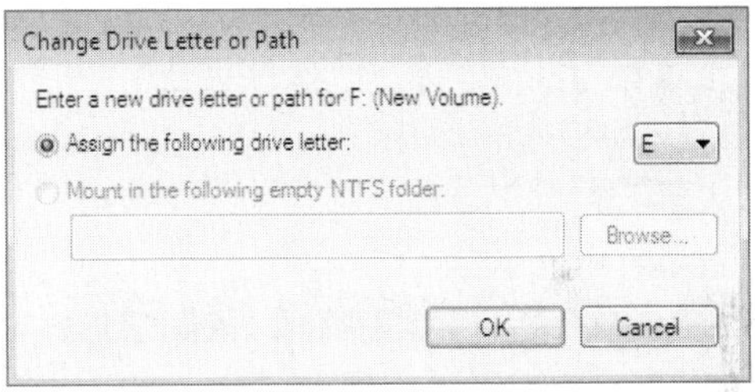

Perform the following steps to edit the drive letter of the partition you created:

1. Select Start ➤ Control Panel ➤ System And Maintenance ➤ Administrative Tools. Double-click Computer Management; then expand Storage and then Disk Management.

2. Right-click a drive that you have created and select Change Drive Letter And Paths.

3. In the Change Drive Letter And Paths dialog box, click Change.

4. In the Change Drive Letter Or Path dialog box, select a new drive letter and click OK.

5. In the dialog box that appears, click Yes to confirm that you want to change the drive letter.

Another task that you might need to perform is deleting a partition or volume that you have created. The next section looks at these tasks.

DELETING PARTITIONS AND VOLUMES

When you configure your hard disks, there may be a time that you want to reconfigure your drive by deleting the partitions or volumes on the hard drive. You may also want to delete a volume so that you can extend another volume. You can configure these tasks in Disk Management.

When you delete a volume or partition, you see a warning that all the data on the partition or volume will be lost. You have to click yes to confirm that you want to delete the volume or partition. This confirmation is important because after you delete a partition or volume, it's gone for good.

DELETING SYSTEM VOLUMES

The system volume, the boot volume, or any volume that contains the active paging (swap) file can't be deleted through the Disk Management utility. If you are trying to remove these partitions because you want to delete Windows 7, you can use a third-party disk-management utility.

In the following steps, you will delete a partition that you have created. When you delete a partition or volume, make sure that it's an empty partition or volume or back up all the data before the deletion.

1. In the Disk Management utility, right-click the volume or partition that you want to remove and choose Delete Volume.

2. A warning box appears stating that after this volume is deleted, all data will be lost. Click Yes. The volume will be removed and the area will be returned as unformatted free space.

Now that we've looked at some of the basic tasks of Disk Management, let's explore how to manage storage.

Managing Dynamic Storage

The Disk Management utility offers support for managing storage. You can create, delete, and format partitions or volumes on your hard drives. You can also extend or shrink volumes on dynamic disks. Additionally, you can delete volume sets and striped sets. The first topic we'll cover is dynamic storage and volumes.

As noted previously in this chapter, a dynamic disk can contain simple, spanned, or striped volumes. With the Disk Management utility you can create volumes of each type. You can also create an extended volume, which is the process of adding disk space to a single simple volume. The following sections describe these disk-management tasks.

Creating Simple, Spanned, and Striped Volumes

As explained previously in "Creating Partitions and Volumes," you use the New Volume Wizard to create a new volume. To start the New Volume Wizard, in the Disk Management utility right-click an area of free space where you want to create the volume. Then you can choose the type of volume you want to create: Simple, Spanned, or Striped.

When you choose to create a spanned volume, you are creating a new volume from scratch that includes space from two or more physical drives, up to a maximum of 32 drives.

When you choose to create a striped volume, you are creating a new volume that combines free space from two to 32 drives into a single logical partition. The free space on all drives must be equal in size. Data in the striped volume is written across all drives in 64 KB stripes. (Data in spanned and extended volumes is written sequentially.)

Striped volumes are RAID 0 because stripped volumes do not offer any type of redundancy. Striped volumes offer you better performance and are normally used for temporary files or folder. The problem with a striped volume is if you lose one of the drives in the volume, the entire striped volume is lost.

Another option that you have with volumes is extending the volumes to create a larger storage area, which we discuss in the next section.

Creating Extended Volumes

When you create an extended volume, you are taking a single, simple volume (maybe one that is almost out of disk space) and adding more disk space to it, using free space that exists on the same physical hard drive. When the volume is extended, it is seen as a single drive letter. To extend a volume, the simple volume must be formatted as NTFS. You cannot extend a system or boot partition.

An extended volume assumes that you are using only one physical drive. A spanned volume assumes that you are using two or more physical drives.

Perform the following steps to create an extended volume:

1. In the Disk Management utility, right-click the volume you want to extend and choose Extend Volume.

2. The Extend Volume Wizard starts. Click Next.

3. The Select Disks screen appears, as shown in Figure 4.21. You can specify the maximum size of the extended volume. The maximum size you can specify is determined by the amount of free space that exists in all of the dynamic drives on your computer. Click Next.

FIGURE 4.21
The Select Disks screen

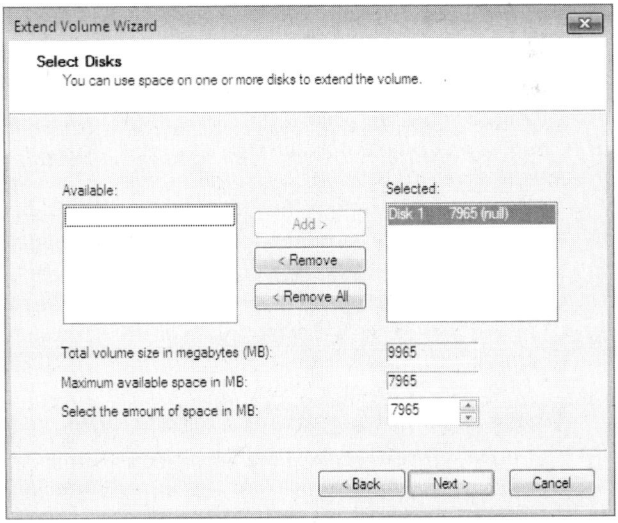

4. The Completing The Extend Volume Wizard screen appears. Click Finish.

After a volume is extended, no portion of the volume can be deleted without losing data on the entire set. (However, you can shrink a volume without losing data by using the Shrink Volume option in Disk Management.)

🌐 **Real World Scenario**

YOU'RE RUNNING OUT OF DISK SPACE

Crystal, a user on your network, is running out of disk space. The situation needs to be corrected so she can be brought back up and running as quickly as possible. Crystal has a 250 GB drive (C) that runs a very large customer database. She needs additional space added to the C drive so the database will recognize the data, because it must be stored on a single drive letter. Crystal's computer has a single IDE drive with nothing attached to the second IDE channel.

You have two basic options for managing space in these circumstances. One is to upgrade the disk to a larger disk, but this will necessitate reinstalling the OS and the applications and restoring the user's data. The other choice is to add a temporary second drive and extend the volume. This will at least allow Crystal to be up and running — but it should not be considered a permanent solution. If you do choose to extend the volume, and then either drive within the volume set fails, the user will lose access to both drives. When Crystal's workload allows time for maintenance, you can replace the volume set with a single drive.

One issue that you might run into with hard drives is that they go bad from time to time. In case you have never heard a hard drive fail, it is a distinct clicking. Once you experience it, you will never forget it. When drives go bad, Disk Management can help determine which drive and what the issue may be. In the next section, we'll look at hard disk errors.

Troubleshooting Disk Management

You can use the Disk Management utility to troubleshoot disk errors through a set of status codes; however, if a disk will not initialize, no status code is displayed. Disks will not initialize if there is no valid disk signature.

The problem with disk errors is that you don't know when a disk fails or which disk failed. Disk Management can help you with this. When disks have problems or errors, status codes are assigned. Knowing what these codes mean will help you determine what the problem is, but more importantly, what steps you need to take to fix the problem.

In this section we'll discuss many of the error codes that Disk Management can issue to the disk, volume, or partition.

Using Disk Management Status Codes

The main window of the Disk Management utility displays the status of disks and volumes. The following list contains the possible status codes and a description of each code; these are very useful in troubleshooting disk problems.

Online Indicates that the disk is accessible and that it is functioning properly. This is the normal disk status.

Online (Errors)   Indicates that I/O errors have been detected on the dynamic disk. Only used with dynamic disks. One possible fix for this error is to right-click the disk and select Reactivate Disk to attempt to return the disk to Online status. This fix will work only if the I/O errors were temporary. You should immediately back up your data if you see this error and suspect that the I/O errors are not temporary.

Healthy   Specifies that the volume is accessible and functioning properly.

Healthy (At Risk)   Indicates that a dynamic volume is currently accessible, but I/O errors have been detected on the underlying dynamic disk. This option is usually associated with Online (Errors) for the underlying disk.

Offline or Missing   Indicates that the disk is not accessible. Used only with dynamic disks This error can occur if the disk is corrupted or the hardware has failed. If the error is not caused by hardware failure or major corruption, you may be able to re-access the disk by using the Reactivate Disk option to return the disk to Online status. If the disk was originally offline and then the status changed to Missing, it indicates that the disk has become corrupted, has been powered down, or was disconnected.

Unreadable   Indicates that the disk is inaccessible and might have encountered hardware errors, corruption, or I/O errors or that the system disk configuration database is corrupted. This can occur on basic or dynamic disks. This message may also appear when a disk is spinning up while the Disk Management utility is rescanning the disks on the computer.

Failed   Specifies that the volume can't be started. Can be seen with basic or dynamic volumes. This error can occur because the disk is damaged or the file system is corrupted. If this message occurs with a basic volume, you should check the underlying disk hardware. If the error occurs on a dynamic volume, verify that the underlying disks are Online.

Unknown   Occurs if the boot sector for the volume becomes corrupted — for example, from a virus. Used with basic and dynamic volumes. This error can also occur if no disk signature is created for the volume.

Incomplete   Occurs when you move some, but not all, of the disks from a multidisk volume. If you do not complete the multivolume set, then the data will be inaccessible.

Foreign   Occurs if you move a dynamic disk from a computer running Windows 2000 (any version), Windows XP Professional, Windows Vista, Windows Server 2003, or Windows Server 2008 to a Windows 7 computer. This error is caused because configuration data is unique to computers where the dynamic disk was created. You can correct this error by right-clicking the disk and selecting the option Import Foreign Disks. Any existing volume information will then be visible and accessible.

Besides knowing the error codes, you might face other issues that can arise when installing or configuring disks. One issue that might occur is that a disk fails to initialize when installed.

Troubleshooting Disks That Fail to Initialize

When you add a new disk to your computer in Windows 7, the disk does not initially contain a disk signature, which is required for the disk to be recognized by Windows. Disk signatures are at the end of the sector marker on the Master Boot Record (MBR) of the drive.

When you install a new drive and run the Disk Management utility, a wizard starts and lists all new disks that have been detected. The disk signature is written through this process. If you cancel the wizard before the disk signature is written, you see the disk status Not Initial-ized. To initialize a disk, right-click the disk you want to initialize and select the Initialize Disk option.

As you have seen, Disk Management can be a useful tool in your computer management arsenal. If you decide to format your partition or volume using NTFS, you then receive added benefits like compression, encryption, quotas, and security. In the next section, we'll explore some of these benefits.

Managing Data Compression

One of the advantages of using NTFS over FAT32 is the ability to compress data. There's a well-known infomercial where people put all of their blankets into a large bag and then they hook a vacuum to the bag and suck all the air out. This is a great example of how compres-sion works. Data compression is the process of storing data in a form that takes less space than uncompressed data.

If you have ever "zipped" or "packed" a file, you have used a form of data compression. The compression algorithms support cluster sizes only up to 4 KB, so if you are using larger cluster sizes, NTFS compression support is not available. If you have the Modify permission on an NTFS volume, you can manage data compression through Windows Explorer or the Compact command-line utility.

Files as well as folders in the NTFS file system can be either compressed or uncompressed. Files and folders are managed independently, which means that a compressed folder can contain uncompressed files, and an uncompressed folder can contain compressed files.

Access to compressed files by applications is transparent. For example, if you access a compressed file through Microsoft Word, the file will be uncompressed automatically when it is opened and then automatically compressed again when it is closed.

Compression happens quickly, but if, for example, you compress a 500 GB hard drive, we can't guarantee that there won't be any lag time on your machine or server.

Data compression is available only on NTFS partitions. Because of this, if you copy or move a compressed folder or file to a FAT32 partition, Windows 7 automatically uncompresses the folder or file.

Certain system files (for example, Pagefile.sys) can't be compressed. You also have the ability to show compressed files and folders with an alternate color.

Perform the following steps to compress and uncompress folders and files:

1. Select Start ➤ Run, type **Explorer**, and click OK.

2. In Windows Explorer, find and select Computer, the Local Disk (C), and then a folder on the C drive. The folder you select should contain files.

3. Right-click the folder and select Properties. In the General tab of the folder's Properties dialog box, note the value listed for Size On Disk. Then click Advanced.

4. In the Advanced Attributes dialog box, check the Compress Contents To Save Disk Space option, as shown in Figure 4.22. Then click OK.

5. In the Confirm Attribute Changes dialog box, select the option Apply Changes To This Folder, Subfolders and Files. (If this confirmation dialog box does not appear, you can display it by clicking the Apply button in the Properties dialog box.) Click OK to confirm your changes.

FIGURE 4.22
Advanced Attributes
screen

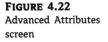

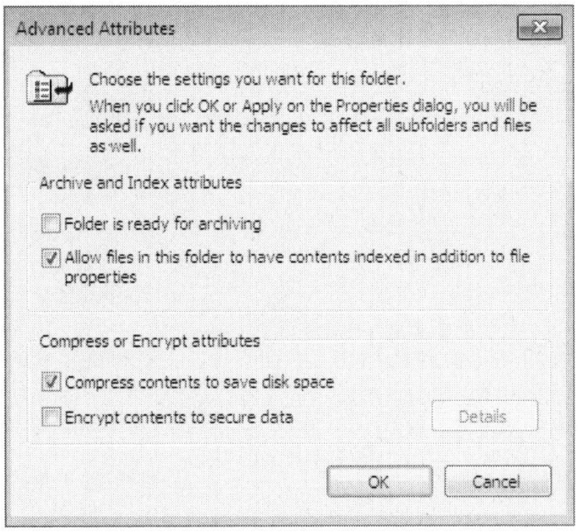

6. On the General tab of the folder's Properties dialog box, note the value that now appears for Size On Disk. This size should have decreased because you compressed the folder.

To uncompress folders and files, repeat the steps of this exercise and uncheck the Compress Contents To Save Disk Space option in the Advanced Attributes dialog box.

As I said previously, you can specify that compressed files be displayed in a different color from the uncompressed files. To do so, in Windows Explorer, select Organize ➢ Folder And Search Options ➢ View. Under Files And Folders, check the Show Encrypted Or Compressed NTFS Files In Color option.

Besides compressing files and folders in Windows Explorer, you can also compress the files and folders using the Compact command-line utility.

Using the Compact Command-Line Utility

The command-line options for managing file and folder compression are Compact and Expand. You can access these commands from a command prompt. Using the Compact utility offers you more control over file and folder compression than Windows Explorer. For example, you can use the Compact command with a batch script or to compress only files that meet a specific criterion (for example, all the .doc files in a specific folder). Some of the options that you can use with the Compact command are shown in Table 4.3.

Another way that you can save disk space is by zipping folders. In the following section we'll discuss how to save space using zipped folders.

Using Compressed (Zipped) Folders

Windows 7 also supports compressed (zipped) folders. This feature is different from NTFS compressed folders. The advantage of using compressed (zipped) folders is that they are supported on FAT32 or NTFS volumes. In addition, you can use compressed (zipped) folders to share data with other programs that use zipped files. The downside to using compressed (zipped) folders is that it is slower than using NTFS compression.

Within Windows Explorer you create a zipped folder (or file) by right-clicking a folder and selecting Send To ➢ Compressed (Zipped) Folder. You create a zipped file by right-clicking a file and selecting New ➢ Compressed (Zipped) Folder. When you create a compressed folder, it displays as a folder with a zipper.

TABLE 4.3:   Compact and Expand Commands

OPTION	PURPOSE
/C	Compresses the specified file or folder
/U	Uncompresses the specified file or folder
/S:dir	Specifies which folder should be compressed or uncompressed
/A	Displays any files that have hidden or system file attributes
/I	Indicates that any errors should be ignored
/F	Forces a file to be compressed
/Q	Reports only critical information, when used with reporting
/?	Displays help

Compression is a nice advantage to using NTFS; another advantage is data encryption. In the following section you'll learn the benefits of using data encryption.

Managing Data Encryption with EFS

Data encryption is a way to increase data security. Encryption is the process of translating data into code that is not easily accessible to users other than the person who encrypted the data. After data has been encrypted, you must have the correct key (SID number) to decrypt the data. Unencrypted data is known as plain text, and encrypted data is known as cipher text.

The Encrypting File System (EFS) is the Windows 7 technology that is used to store encrypted files on NTFS partitions. Encrypted files add an extra layer of security to your file system. A user with the proper key can transparently access encrypted files. A user without the proper key is denied access. If the user who encrypted the files is unavailable, you can use the data recovery agent (DRA) to provide the proper key to decrypt folders or files.

The EFS features included with Windows 7 include some of the following:

◆ The ability to automatically color-code encrypted files in green text, so you can easily identify files that have been encrypted

◆ Support so that offline folders can also be encrypted

◆ A shell user interface (UI) that is used to support encrypted files for multiple users

◆ Control over who can read the encrypted files

In the following sections you'll learn how to encrypt and decrypt data, create and manage DRAs, recover encrypted files, share encrypted files, and use the Cipher utility.

Encrypting and Decrypting Folders and Files

To use EFS, a user specifies that a folder or file on an NTFS partition should be encrypted. The encryption is transparent to users. However, when other users try to access the file, they will not be able to unencrypt the file — even if those users have Full Control NTFS permissions. Instead, they receive an error message.

COMPRESSION AND ENCRYPTION

Windows 7 does not allow you to have a folder or file compressed and encrypted at the same time. A feature included with Windows Server 2003 and Windows Server 2008 is support for concurrent compression and encryption.

Perform the following steps to use EFS to encrypt a folder. Before you encrypt any data, first you must create a new user.

1. To create a new user, select Start ➤ Control Panel ➤ System And Maintenance ➤ Administrative Tools. Under System Tools, expand Local Users And Groups and right-click the Users folder. Choose New User.

2. Create a new user named Paige and make her password **P@ssw0rd**. Deselect the User Must Change Password At Next Logon option for this user. Click Create.

3. Close Computer Management.

4. Select Start and type **Explorer** in the Search box.

5. In Windows Explorer, find and select a folder on the C drive. The folder you select should contain files. Right-click the folder and select Properties.

6. On the General tab of the folder's Properties dialog box, click Advanced.

7. In the Advanced Attributes dialog box, check the Encrypt Contents To Secure Data option. Then click OK.

8. In the Confirm Attribute Changes dialog box (if this dialog box does not appear, click the Apply button in the Properties dialog box to display it), select Apply Changes To This Folder, Subfolders And Files. Then click OK.

9. Log off as Administrator and log on as Paige.

10. Open Windows Explorer and attempt to access one of the files in the folder you encrypted. You should receive an error message stating that the file is not accessible.

11. Log off as Paige and log on as Administrator.

To decrypt folders and files, repeat these steps, but uncheck the Encrypt Contents To Secure Data option in the Advanced Attributes dialog box.

The problem with encryption is that no one but the user who encrypts the data is the only one who can open the files. But the owner of the data can share the encrypted files with other users. In the next section, we'll look at how to share your encrypted data with other users.

Managing EFS File Sharing

In Windows 7, it is possible to share encrypted files with another person or between two computers. To share encrypted files, you must have a valid EFS certificate for the user who should have access to the file. By implementing EFS file sharing, you provide an additional level of recovery in the event that the person who encrypted the files is unavailable.

Perform the following steps to implement EFS file sharing:

1. Encrypt the file if it is not already encrypted (see the previous section for the steps involved).

2. Through Windows Explorer, access the encrypted file's properties. At the bottom of the dialog box, click Advanced.

3. The Advanced Attributes dialog box appears. In the Compress Or Encrypt Attributes section of the Advanced Attributes dialog box, click the Details button, which brings up the Encryption Details dialog box.

4. In the Encryption Details dialog box, click the Add button to add any additional users (provided they have a valid certificate for EFS in Active Directory or that you have imported a valid certificate onto the local computer) who should have access to the encrypted file.

5. Close the Properties box for the folder.

One issue that you might run into is if someone has encrypted files or folders and then they leave the company. There are a few ways to unencrypt the data. In the next section we'll show you how to recover encrypted data.

Using the DRA to Recover Encrypted Data

If the user who encrypted the folders or files is unavailable or no longer with the company and they can't decrypt the folders or files, you can use the data recovery agent (DRA) to access the encrypted files. DRAs are implemented differently depending on the version of your operating system and the configuration of your computer.

◆ For Windows 7 computers that are a part of a Windows Server 2008 Active Directory domain, the domain Administrator user account is automatically assigned the role of DRA.

◆ For Windows 7 computers that are installed as stand-alone computers or if the computer is a part of a workgroup, no default DRA is assigned.

You should use extreme caution when using EFS on a stand-alone Windows 7 computer. If the key used to encrypt the files is lost, there is no default recovery process, and all access to the files will be lost.

Creating a DRA on a Stand-Alone Windows 7 Computer

If you install Windows 7 on a stand-alone computer or on a computer that is part of a workgroup, then no DRA is created by default. To manually create a DRA, use the Cipher command-line utility as follows:

```
Cipher /R:filename
```

The /R switch is used to generate two files, one with a .pfx extension and one with a .cer extension. The .pfx file is used for data recovery, and the .cer file includes a self-signed EFS recovery agent certificate.

The .cer file (self-signed public key certificate) can then be imported by an administrator into the local security policy, and the .pfx file (private key) can be stored by an administrator in a secure location. Cipher is explained further in the next section.

After you create the public and private keys to be used with EFS, perform the following steps to specify the DRA through Local Security Policy:

1. Through Local Security Policy, which you can access through Administrative Tools or the Local Computer Policy MMC snap-in, expand Public Key Policies and then Encrypting File System, as shown in Figure 4.23.

FIGURE 4.23

Encrypting File System in Local Policies

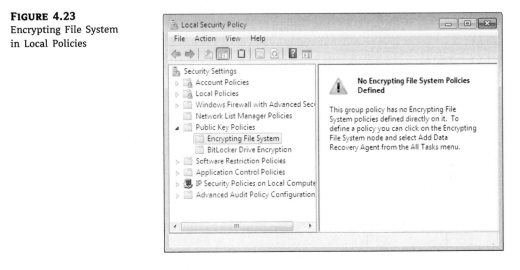

2. Right-click Encrypting File System and select Add Data Recovery Agent.

3. The Add Recovery Agent Wizard starts. Click Next to continue.

4. The Select Recovery Agents screen appears, as shown in Figure 4.24. Click the Browse Folders button to access the .cer file you created with the Cipher /R:*filename* command. Select the certificate and click Next.

FIGURE 4.24

The Select Recovery Agents screen of the Add Recovery Agent Wizard

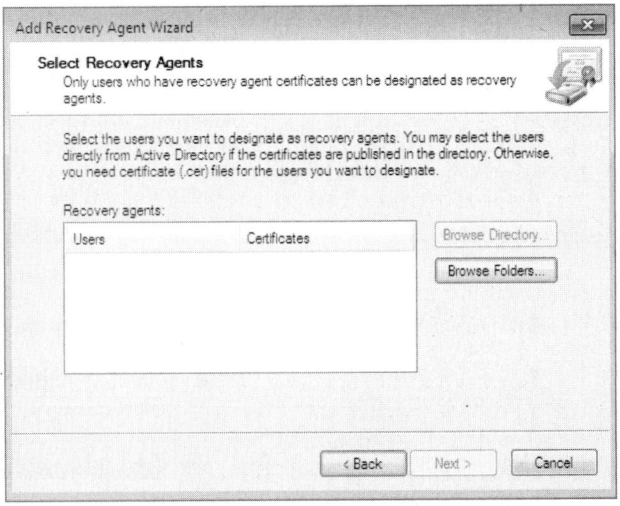

5. The Completing The Add Recovery Agent Wizard screen appears. Confirm that the settings are correct and click Finish.

You will see the data recovery agent listed in the Local Security Settings dialog box, under Encrypting File System. Let's continue encryption with recovering encrypted files in the next section.

Recovering Encrypted Files

If the DRA has the private key to the DRA certificate (that was created through `Cipher /R:filename`), the DRA can decrypt files in the same manner as the user who originally encrypted the file. After the encrypted files are opened by a DRA, they are available as unencrypted files and can be stored as either encrypted or unencrypted files.

Using the Cipher Utility

Cipher is a command-line utility that you can use to encrypt files on NTFS volumes. The syntax for the Cipher command is as follows:

```
Cipher /[command parameter] [filename]
```

Table 4.4 lists common command parameters associated with the `Cipher` command. This list is only a partial representation of all the `Cipher` commands.

TABLE 4.4:   `Cipher` Command Parameters

PARAMETER	DESCRIPTION
/E	Specifies that files or folders should be encrypted. Any files that are subsequently added to the folder will be encrypted.
/D	Specifies that files or folders should be decrypted. Any files that are subsequently added to the folder will not be encrypted.
/S:dir	Specifies that subfolders of the target folder should also be encrypted or decrypted based on the option specified.
/I	Causes any errors that occur to be ignored. By default, the Cipher utility stops whenever an error occurs.
/H	Specifies that hidden and system files should be displayed. By default, files with hidden or system attributes are omitted from display.
/K	Creates a new certificate file and certificate key.
/R	Generates a recovery agent key and certificate for use with EFS.
/X	Backs up the EFS certificate and keys into the specified file name.

Perform the following steps to use the Cipher utility to encrypt files. Make sure that you have encrypted a folder on the C drive before you complete these steps.

1. Select Start ➢ All Programs ➢ Accessories ➢ Command Prompt.

2. In the Command Prompt dialog box, type **C:** and press Enter to access the C drive.

3. At the C:\> prompt, type **cipher**. You'll see a list of folders and files and the state of encryption. The folder you encrypted should be indicated by an E.

4. Type **MD TEST** and press Enter to create a new folder named Test.

5. Type **cipher /e test** and press Enter. You'll see a message verifying that the folder was encrypted.

By now you have seen many of the advantages of using NTFS to format your volumes and partitions. Next we'll look at how to keep these volumes and partitions running at peak performance.

Using Disk Maintenance Tools

As an IT professional, part of our job is to keep our systems running the best way that they can. Most of us have seen machines running quickly when they are new but then they start to slow down over time — even when we do not install any new software.

Microsoft Windows 7 includes a few utilities that you can run to help keep your system running efficiently. In the next sections we'll discuss three of these utilities: Disk Defragment, Disk Cleanup, and Check Disk.

Running the Disk Defragment Utility

Data is normally stored sequentially on the disk as space is available. Fragmentation naturally occurs as users create, delete, and modify files. The access of noncontiguous data is transparent to the user; however, when data is stored in this manner, the operating system must search through the disk to access all the pieces of a file. This slows down data access.

Disk defragmentation rearranges the existing files so they are stored contiguously, which optimizes access to those files. In Windows 7, you use the Disk Defragmenter utility to defragment your disk.

The Disk Defragmenter window displays, as shown in Figure 4.25; you can schedule when the Disk Defragmenter should run or run the Disk Defragmenter tool immediately.

You can also defragment disks through the command-line utility, Defrag. The disk needs to have at least 15 percent free space for Defrag to run properly. You can analyze the state of the disk by using Defrag VolumeName /a.

🌐 **Real World Scenario**

DISK DEFRAGMENT ISSUES

One issue that we have run into with Disk Defragment is the amount of time the process might take to complete. When a client asks us to make their machine quicker, one thing we always do is run the Disk Defragment utility, but the problem is that most users have never run it before.

Because most users haven't run the utility before, it could take hours to defrag a machine. It is important to inform your users to run this utility on a regular basis or set it to run automatically.

Another issue with Disk Defragment is your antivirus programs. Make sure that all programs are closed (including antivirus software) before running the Disk Defragment utility.

If applications are open when the Disk Defragment utility runs, it could cause the Disk Defragment utility to stop working or run even slower than normal.

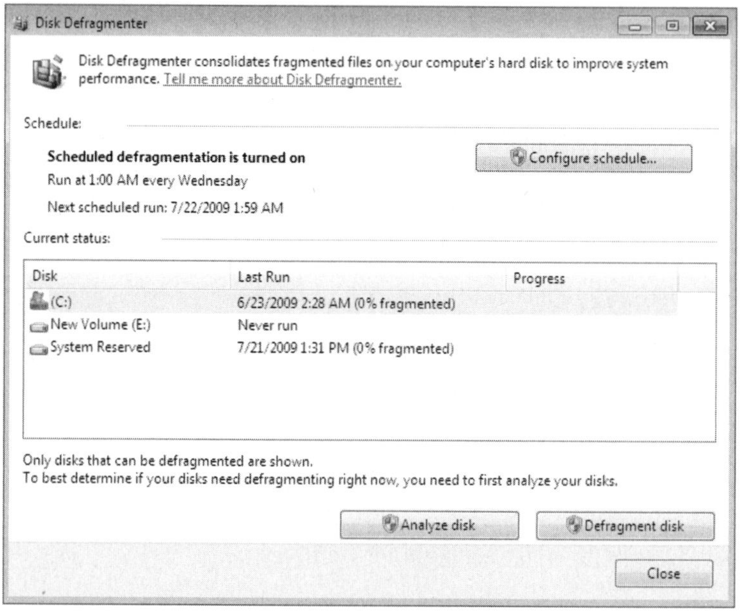

FIGURE 4.25

The Disk Defragmenter window

Perform the following steps to defragment your Windows 7 machine:

1. Start the Disk Defragmenter utility by opening Computer Management.

2. Right-click the C drive and choose Properties.

3. Click the Tools tab.

4. Click the Defragment Now button.

5. Either schedule a defragment or click the Defragment Disk button to start the defragment immediately.

It is a good practice to run the disk defragmenter at least once a week on a Windows 7 machine that is constantly being used. If the machine is not used that often, you can space out how often you defrag the machine.

In the next section we'll discuss another tool that is included with Windows 7: the Disk Cleanup utility.

Running the Disk Cleanup Utility

One concern that most IT professionals face is how to conserve hard disk space for users. Hard drives continue to get larger and larger but so do applications. This is where the Disk Cleanup utility can help.

When the Disk Cleanup utility runs, it calculates the amount of disk space you can free up. Perform the following steps to run the Disk Cleanup utility:

1. Select Start ➢ Control Panel ➢ System And Maintenance ➢ Administrative Tools ➢ Computer Management.

2. Right-click the drive and choose Properties.

3. On the General tab, click the Disk Cleanup button. The Disk Cleanup utility will start to calculate the system data.

4. After the analysis is complete, you will see the Disk Cleanup dialog box, as shown in Figure 4.26, which lists files that are suggested for deletion and shows how much space will be gained by deleting those files. Click OK.

FIGURE 4.26
The Disk Cleanup utility

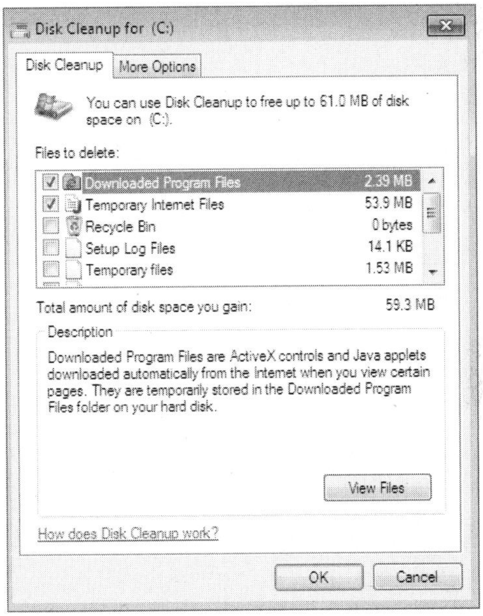

5. When you are asked to confirm that you want to delete the files, click Yes. The Disk Cleanup utility deletes the files and automatically closes the Disk Cleanup dialog box.

Another issue that you might run into is bad sectors on your hard disk. Windows 7 also includes a utility to help you troubleshoot disk devices and volumes.

Running the Check Disk Utility

If you are having trouble with your disk devices or volumes, you can use the Windows 7 Check Disk utility. This utility detects bad sectors, attempts to fix errors in the file system, and scans for and attempts to recover bad sectors. In order to use Check Disk you must be logged in as a member of the Administrators group.

File system errors can be caused by a corrupted file system or by hardware errors. If you have software errors, the Check Disk utility might help you find them. There is no way to fix hardware errors through software, however. If you have excessive hardware errors, you should replace your disk drive.

Perform the following steps to run the Check Disk utility:

1. Select Start ➤ Control Panel ➤ System And Maintenance ➤ Administrative Tools.

2. Double-click Computer Management and then expand Storage and select Disk Management.

3. Right-click the C drive and choose Properties.

4. Click the Tools tab and then click the Check Now button.

5. In the Check Disk dialog box, you can choose one or both of the options to automatically fix file system errors and to scan for and attempt recovery of bad sectors, as shown in Figure 4.27. For this exercise, check both of the disk options check boxes. Then click Start.

FIGURE 4.27
The Check Disk utility

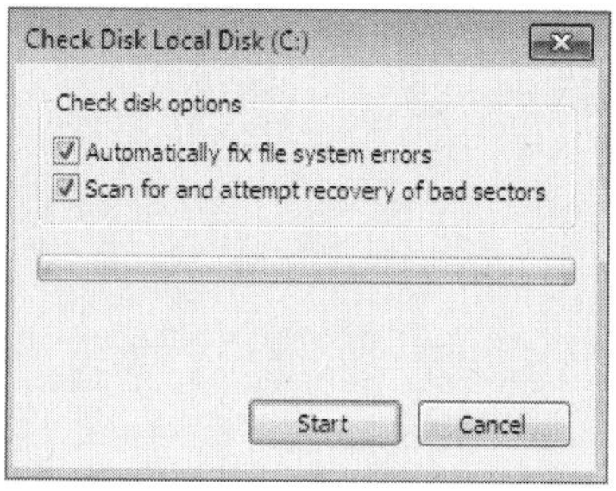

Another way to run the Check Disk utility is from the command line, using the command Chkdsk. Chkdsk is used to create and display a status report, which is based on the file system you are using.

The Bottom Line

Understand the different file systems.   When you select a file system, you can select FAT32 or NTFS. You typically select file systems based on the features you want to use and whether you will need to access the file system using other operating systems. If you have a FAT32 partition and want to update it to NTFS, you can use the Convert or Disk Management utility.

Master It   You are the system administrator for your organization and you have to install a new Windows 7 laptop for a salesperson who goes on the road. Data protection and hard drive space are important features that must be included on the Windows 7 laptop. How would you configure the file system?

Identify disk storage types.   Windows 7 supports three types of disk storage: basic, dynamic, and GUID partition table (GPT). Basic storage is backward compatible with other operating systems and can be configured to support up to four partitions. Dynamic storage is supported by Windows 2000, Windows XP, Windows Server 2003, Windows Server 2008, Windows Vista, and Windows 7, and allows storage to be configured as volumes. GPT storage allows you to configure volume sizes larger than 2 TB and up to 128 primary partitions.

Master It   Your organization has asked you to configure a Windows 7 Desktop. The Desktop was already installed but the company would like you to reconfigure the disks so that some of the storage areas can be extended. How would you set up the disk storage?

Understand the benefits of NTFS.   NTFS offers comprehensive folder and file-level security. This allows you to set an additional level of security for users who access the files and folders locally or through the network. NTFS also offers disk management features such as compression, encryption, quotas, and data recovery features.

Master It   You have a Windows 7 machine in your organization that multiple users operate. The users keep complaining that other users are using too much hard disk space. Your organization has asked you to set up disk space limits for the Windows 7 machine. How would you configure this?

Use disk-management utilities.   Microsoft Windows 7 includes a few utilities that you can run to help keep your system running efficiently. Two utilities that continue to allow the machine to run at its peak performance are Disk Defragment and Disk Cleanup.

Master It   You have users on your network who are complaining that their Windows 7 machines are starting to show slower response times when opening or managing files and applications. What are some of the ways you can help speed up the machines?

Chapter 5

Managing the Windows 7 Desktop

Windows 7 allows a user to configure their Desktop to suit their personal preferences. These options include customizing the Taskbar and Start menu, creating shortcuts, setting display properties for their themes, and configuring Windows gadgets.

Because of Windows 7's modular architecture, support for multiple languages and regional settings is improved over previous versions. The support that comes with localized editions of Windows 7 allows users to view, edit, and print multilingual documents, which can include documents that are written in almost any language.

You can also specify locale settings for the Desktop to customize items such as the date format and currency for your geographical location.

The accessibility options support users with limited sight. You can configure the Desktop and use Windows 7 utilities to provide a higher degree of accessibility.

You can also configure the Power button to make it easier for your users. Its default setting is Shut Down, but you can change that. Finally, we'll look at using a machine with multiple users and how to configure the options to customize these users.

In this chapter, you'll learn how to:

◆ Understand the Start menu shortcuts

◆ Customize the Start menu and Taskbar

◆ Work with regional settings

◆ Use accessibility features

Configuring Desktop Settings

Before you begin configuring, let's discuss what the Windows 7 Desktop actually is. The Windows 7 Desktop is the visual settings that appear when a user logs into the operating system. The Desktop includes the wallpaper, Start menu, and icons, as shown in Figure 5.1.

The Windows 7 Desktop default settings also include the default All Programs section, as shown in Figure 5.2. One of the advantages to the Windows 7 Desktop is that administrators can configure the Desktop the way they like it.

Microsoft includes premade Desktops called themes. Administrators can set Windows 7 to use the Windows 7 Aero theme, the Windows 7 Standard theme, the Windows 7 Basic theme, the Windows Classic theme, or any customized theme that the administrator wants.

FIGURE 5.1
Default Windows 7
Desktop from a clean
install

FIGURE 5.2
Default All Programs
section

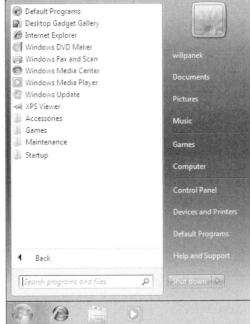

The Windows 7 Default Desktop appears (on a clean install only) after a user has logged on to a Windows 7 computer for the first time. Users can then configure their Desktops to suit their personal preferences and to work more efficiently.

When an administrator installs Windows 7 from a clean install, they will notice that the Desktop contains no icons except for the Recycle Bin. The following list shows the common default options that appear on the Start menu and All Programs section.

Getting Started Use Getting Started to access preset tasks, as shown in Figure 5.3. Some of these tasks include Discover Windows 7, Personalize Windows, Transfer Your Files, Back Up Your Files, and Add New Users.

FIGURE 5.3
Getting Started tasks

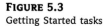

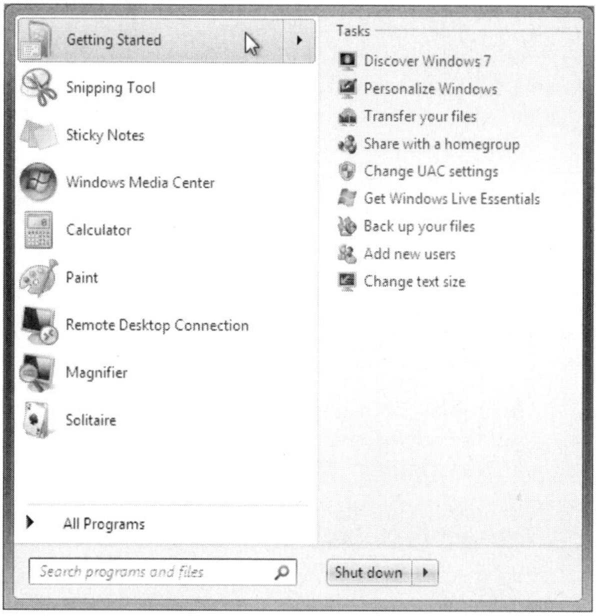

Windows Media Center This shortcut starts the Windows Media Center that is used to play the multimedia files.

Calculator This shortcut starts the Calculator program.

Sticky Notes This application places a Sticky Note on the Desktop, like the one shown in Figure 5.4. You can then type a message or reminder onto the Sticky Note. The note remains on the Desktop until you remove it.

Snipping Tool This tool allows a user to capture an item on the Desktop, as shown in Figure 5.5. The user clicks the Snipping Tool and then drags the cursor around an area that will then be captured. The captured area can be drawn on, highlighted, or saved as a file.

Paint This shortcut starts the Paint program, an application that allows you to change or manipulate graphic files.

Remote Desktop Connection This program allows a user to connect remotely to another machine. To connect to another computer, the Remote Desktop Connection must be enabled on the receiving computer.

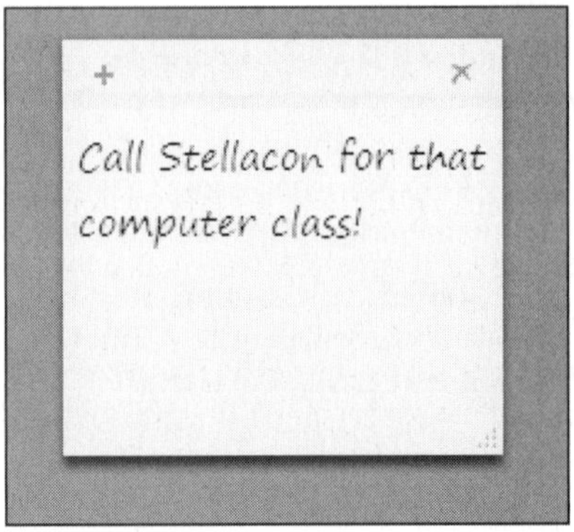

FIGURE 5.4
Sticky Notes

FIGURE 5.5
Snipping Tool

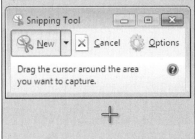

Magnifier   The Magnifier utility is one of the Ease Of Access utilities. The Ease Of Access utilities are included with Windows 7 to allow limited-sight users to experience Windows 7 more easily. Some of these tools include the Magnifier, Narrator, and On-Screen Keyboard.

Solitaire   This shortcut starts the Solitaire game. You can also access this game from the Games section of the Start menu.

Default Programs   When choosing the Default Programs shortcut, you can access four different configuration items: Set Your Default Programs, Associate A File Type Or Protocol With A Program, Change Autoplay Settings, and Set Program Access And Computer Defaults.

Default Gadget Gallery   This shortcut opens the default Gadget Gallery. Gadgets are mini-applications that can be placed on the Desktop. Gadgets are explained in detail later in this chapter in the section "Configuring Windows Gadgets."

Internet (Internet Explorer 8)   This shortcut starts the built-in web browser. When used with an Internet connection, Internet Explorer 8 provides an interface for accessing the Internet or a local intranet.

Windows DVD Maker   This application is used to view and edit photo and video files to create your own personal DVDs.

Windows Fax And Scan   This application allows the user to create and manage scans and faxes. Windows Fax And Scan allows users to send or receive faxes from their workstation.

Windows Media Center   Windows Media Center lets you watch TV on your computer or laptop. When you start the Media Center for the first time, a wizard walks you through the TV setup. Windows Media Center also allows you to play DVD movies and music.

Windows Media Player   The Windows Media Player allows a user to play all your media files. Windows Media Player allows you to play videos, music, pictures, and recorded TV.

Windows Update   This shortcut allows users to receive updates from either Microsoft's web server or from a Windows Server Update Services (WSUS) machine. Windows Updates allows you to receive updates and security patches for the Windows 7 operating system.

XPS Viewer   The XPS viewer is a new application that allows you to view Microsoft XML Paper Specification (XPS) files. The XPS viewer also allows you to print these files.

Accessories   The Accessories section includes many Windows 7 tools such as Calculator, Command Prompt, Windows PowerShell, Ease Of Use, Run, Paint, Notepad, and so forth, as shown in Figure 5.6.

FIGURE 5.6
Accessories section of
Start menu

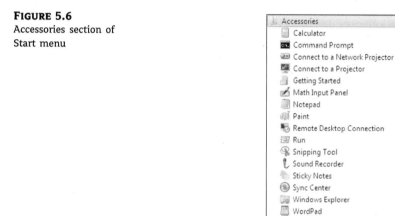

Games   This section opens up the games that are included with Windows 7, among them Chess Titans, FreeCell, Games Explorer, Hearts, Internet Backgammon, Internet Checkers, Internet Spades, Mahjong Titans, Minesweeper, Purble Place, Solitaire, and Spider Solitaire.

Maintenance   The Maintenance section includes important maintenance utilities like Backup And Restore, Create A System Repair Disk, Help And Support, and Windows Remote Assistance.

Startup   The Startup section allows administrators to place application shortcuts within the Startup section. After these shortcuts are placed in the Startup section, the application automatically starts when the system user logs in.

User Documents   This shortcut (shown as willpanek in Figure 5.2 earlier) opens the user's personnel folders.

Documents   By default, the Documents folder stores the documents that the user creates. Each user has a unique Documents folder, so even if a computer is shared, individual users have unique personal folders.

Pictures   This application displays any pictures that are in the user's Pictures folder.

Music   This shortcut displays any music that is in the My Music folder.

Computer   This shortcut allows users to centrally manage your computer's files, hard drives, and devices with removable storage. Also allows you to manage system tasks and other places (such as other computers on the network) and to view details about your computer.

Control Panel   Control Panel holds many utilities and tools that allow you to configure your computer. We discuss Control Panel in greater detail in Chapter 6, ''Managing the Interface.''

Devices And Printers   This shortcut opens the Devices And Printers section. Here you can add or configure any of your hardware devices or printers.

Help And Support   This shortcut is used to access the Windows 7 Help And Support resources. Users can also access Windows 7 online help from this utility.

Search   This feature searches for pictures, music, video, documents, files and folders, computers, or people.

Shut Down Button   This button is used to shut down the computer. There is an arrow next to the button that allows your machine to Switch User, Log Off, Lock, Restart, or Sleep.

REMOTE MANAGEMENT TOOLS

If you use any kind of remote management tools, you might want to rename the Computer icon to the actual computer's name. This allows you to easily identify which computer you're accessing.

When you configure the Desktop, you have the ability to switch between background and Desktop themes. To switch between these different themes, right-click an area of open space on the Desktop and select Personalize. In the Theme Settings section, you can then select the theme you want to use.

The Desktop also includes the Recycle Bin. The Recycle Bin is a special folder that holds the files and folders that have been deleted, assuming that your hard drive has enough free space to hold the deleted files. If the hard drive is running out of disk space, the files that were deleted first will be copied over. You can retrieve and clear files (for permanent deletion) from the Recycle Bin.

Administrators or users can configure the Desktop by customizing the taskbar and Start menu, adding shortcuts, and setting display properties. You'll learn about these configurations in the following sections. Let's start with the Desktop themes.

Configuring Windows Aero

Windows Aero is the user interface component of Windows 7. When the Windows Aero theme is configured, open windows are displayed with a transparent glass effect and subtle animations.

MINIMUM REQUIREMENTS

Enabling Windows Aero on a computer that has less than 1 GB of RAM and less than 128 MB of video RAM could adversely affect the performance of the computer. Ensure that your computer meets the minimum requirements before you enable Windows Aero. We discuss Windows 7 minimum requirements in detail in Chapter 2, "Installing Windows 7."

To enable Windows Aero, you must first ensure that the Windows 7 theme is selected. This can be accomplished through the Personalization Control Panel option. You can open this Control Panel option by right-clicking the Desktop, selecting Personalize, and then choosing the Windows 7 theme by clicking the theme you want in the Aero Theme (7) section.

After you choose the Windows 7 theme, you can configure the theme's background picture, color, sounds, and screen savers. To configure the theme's background picture, click the Background link on the bottom and then choose the picture you like. To configure the Windows Aero color scheme, just click the Color link below and then select the color you want from the Color Scheme list.

You do the same for sounds and screen saver. Just click the link below the Themes box and select the sounds and screen saver that you want to use with your theme.

After you specify your Desktop theme, it's time to configure your Taskbar and Start menu. Perform the following steps to configure your Windows 7 themes:

1. Right-click an open area of the desktop and choose Personalize.

2. Scroll down to the Aero Themes (7) section and choose a theme.

The Personalization dialog box also includes several configurable options that control various aspects of your theme:

Desktop Background   This option lets you pick your Desktop background, which uses a picture or an HTML document as wallpaper.

Windows Color And Appearance   This option allows you to fine-tune the color and style of your windows.

Sounds   This option lets you choose the sounds that will be played based on the action taken. Each action can have its own sound.

Screen Saver   This option lets you select a screen saver that starts after the system has been idle for a specified amount of time. You can also specify a password that must be used to re-access the system after it has been idle. When the idle time has been reached, the computer will be locked, and the password of the user who is currently logged on must be entered to access the computer. You can also adjust monitor power settings.

Windows 7 includes many different screen saver options that can be used and configured. Some of these screen saver options are:

◆   None

◆   3D Text

◆   Blank

- Bubbles
- Mystify
- Photos
- Ribbons

Change Desktop Icons   This option allows users to customize the Desktop icons. Users also have the ability to change shortcut icons.

Change Mouse Pointers   This option allows users to customize the appearance of the mouse pointers.

Change Your Account Picture   This option lets users change their account picture. The account picture is the picture next to your account name when you log on.

Perform the following steps to configure your theme options:

1. Right-click an unoccupied area on the Desktop and select Personalize to open the Personalization dialog box.

2. Select Desktop Background and then select the Picture Library option from the pull-down menu. Click the Clear All box. Then put a check in the picture that you want to use for your Desktop background. In the Picture Position box, choose Fill. Click Save Changes.

3. Click Screen Saver, select the 3d Text, and specify a wait of five minutes. Click OK.

⊕ Real World Scenario

CONFIGURING PERSONAL PREFERENCES

One thing that we noticed as IT managers is that the most common configuration changes that users make is to configure their Desktop. This lets them use the computer more efficiently, and the customization makes them more comfortable with their computer.

To help users work more efficiently with their computers, we would determine which applications or files are frequently and commonly used and add shortcuts or Start menu items for those elements. You can also remove shortcuts or Start menu items for elements that are used seldom or not at all, helping to make the work area less cluttered and confusing.

Less-experienced users will feel more comfortable with their computer if they have a Desktop personalized to their preferences. This might include their choice of Desktop theme (for example, Windows 7 Aero or Windows Classic themes) and screen saver.

Perform the following steps to change your account picture:

1. Right-click your Desktop and choose Personalize.

2. Click the Change Your Account Picture link in the upper-left corner.

3. Choose a new picture for your account.

4. Click the Change Picture button.

ACCOUNT PICTURES

You also have the ability to add more pictures to your choices by browsing the pictures on your computer system. Users can also download pictures that can be used for the account picture.

Now that you have seen how to configure your Desktop theme, let's take a look at how to configure your Taskbar and Start menu.

Customizing the Taskbar and Start Menu

Users can customize the Taskbar and Start menu using the Properties dialog box shown in Figure 5.7. The easiest way to access this dialog box is to right-click a blank area in the Taskbar and choose Properties from the context menu.

FIGURE 5.7

The Taskbar tab of the Taskbar And Start Menu Properties dialog box

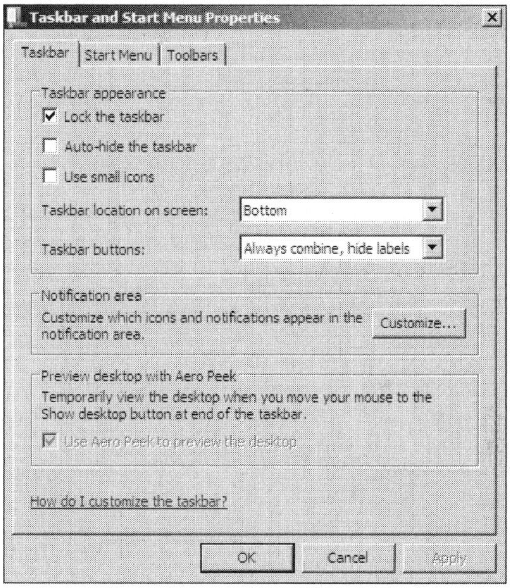

The Taskbar And Start Menu Properties dialog box has three tabs: Taskbar, Start Menu, and Toolbars. Let's look at each one.

CONFIGURING TASKBAR PROPERTIES

On the Taskbar tab of the Taskbar And Start Menu Properties dialog box, you can specify Taskbar features, such as whether the Taskbar is always visible and its location on the screen. Table 5.1 lists the properties on the Taskbar tab.

Next let's look at the second tab and see how to configure the Start menu properties.

CONFIGURING START MENU PROPERTIES

The Start menu tab of the Taskbar And Start Menu Properties dialog box allows you to customize your Start menu. By selecting the Start Menu tab, you can customize many of the Windows 7 Start menu options and even configure the Power button.

TABLE 5.1:   Taskbar Properties

PROPERTY	DESCRIPTION
Lock The Taskbar	Locks the taskbar into the current position so it cannot be moved around the Desktop and locks the size of the Taskbar. This option is enabled by default.
Auto-Hide The Taskbar	Hides the Taskbar. This option is disabled by default. When it is enabled, you show the Taskbar by clicking the area of the screen where the Taskbar appears.
Use Small Icons	Allows the use of small icons on the desktop. This is disabled by default.
Taskbar Location On Screen	Allows you to choose where the Taskbar location will be on your Desktop. The four choices are Bottom, Left, Right, and Top.
Taskbar Buttons	Allows an administrator to decide what to do with the Taskbar buttons. There are three choices: Always Combine And Hide Labels, Combine When Taskbar Is Full, and Never Combine.
Notification Area	Allows you to customize which icons and notifications appear in the notification area.
Preview Desktop With Aero Peek	Allows you to temporarily view the Desktop when you move your mouse to show desktop buttons at the end of the Taskbar.

Users or administrators can add or remove items from the Start menu, remove records of recently accessed items, and specify which Start menu options are configured by clicking the Customize button. Figure 5.8 shows the options for customizing the Start menu for Windows 7.

FIGURE 5.8
Customize Start Menu
dialog box

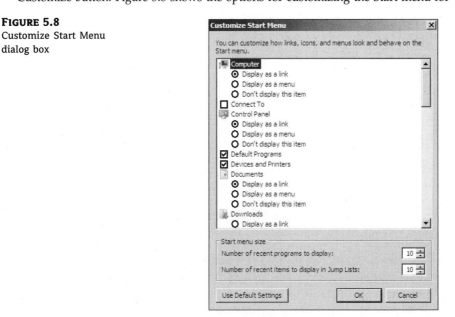

The Customize Start Menu dialog box shows a list of options that administrators or users can enable or disable to change the look and feel of the Start menu. Table 5.2 lists the options that you can configure using the Customize Start Menu dialog box.

TABLE 5.2: The Start Menu Customizable Options

OPTION	SETTINGS
Computer	The Computer icon can be configured to be displayed as a link, as a menu, or not displayed at all.
Connect To	The Connect To option can be enabled or disabled.
Control Panel	The Control Panel icon can be configured to be displayed as a link, as a menu, or not displayed at all.
Default Programs	The Default Programs option can be enabled or disabled.
Devices And Printers	Enabled by default. Shows the Devices And Printers shortcut on the Start menu.
Documents	The Documents icon can be configured to be displayed as a link, as a menu, or not displayed at all.
Downloads	This option shows the Downloads folder on the Start menu. The three choices are Display As Link, Display As A Menu, and Don't Display This Item (the default setting).
Enable Context Menus And Dragging And Dropping	The Enable Context Menus And Dragging And Dropping option can be enabled or disabled.
Favorites Menu	The Favorites menu can be enabled or disabled.
Games	The Games icon can be configured to be displayed as a link, as a menu, or not displayed at all.
Help	The Help option can be enabled or disabled.
Highlight Newly Installed Programs	The Highlight Newly Installed Programs option can be enabled or disabled.
Homegroup	This option displays the Homegroup shortcut on the Start menu. It is not enabled by default.
Music	The Music icon can be configured to be displayed as a link, as a menu, or not displayed at all.
Network	The Network option can be enabled or disabled.
Open Submenus When I Pause On Them With The Mouse Pointer	The Open Submenus When I Pause on Them with the Mouse Pointer option can be enabled or disabled.

TABLE 5.2: The Start Menu Customizable Options (*CONTINUED*)

OPTION	SETTINGS
Personal Folder	The Personal Folder icon can be configured to be displayed as a link, as a menu, or not displayed at all.
Pictures	The Pictures icon can be configured to be displayed as a link, as a menu, or not displayed at all.
Printers	The Printers option can be enabled or disabled.
Recent Items	This option shows Recent Items on the Start menu. It is not enabled by default.
Recorded TV	This option shows the Recorded TV folder on the Start menu. The three choices are Display As Link, Display As A Menu, and Don't Display This Item (the default setting).
Run Command	The Run Command option can be enabled or disabled.
Search	The Search option can be enabled or disabled.
Search Communications	The Search Communications option can be enabled or disabled.
Search Favorites And History	The Search Favorites And History option can be enabled or disabled.
Search Files	The Search Files icon can be configured to search the user's files, search the entire index, or to not search for files.
Search Programs	The Search Programs option can be enabled or disabled.
Sort All Programs Menu By Name	The Sort All Programs Menu By Name option can be enabled or disabled.
System Administrative Tools	The System Administrative Tools icon can be configured to be displayed on the All Programs menu, on the All Programs menu and the Start menu, or not displayed at all.
Use Large Icons	The Use Large Icons option can be enabled or disabled.
Videos	This option shows the Videos folder on the Start menu. The three choices are Display As Link, Display As A Menu, and Don't Display This Item (the default setting).

The final tab in Taskbar And Start Menu Properties dialog box is Toolbars. Let's take a look.

CONFIGURING TOOLBAR OPTIONS

The Toolbars tab of the Taskbar And Start Menu Properties dialog box allows you to configure which toolbars will be displayed on the Taskbar, as shown in Figure 5.9. The toolbars that can be displayed include the Address, Links, Tablet PC Input Panel, and Desktop toolbars. None of the toolbars are enabled by default.

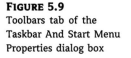

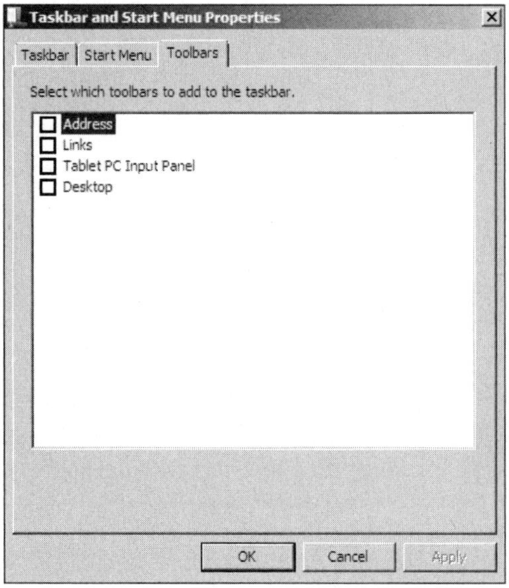

FIGURE 5.9
Toolbars tab of the
Taskbar And Start Menu
Properties dialog box

Perform the following steps to check your current Taskbar and Start menu configuration and then configure Taskbar and Start menu properties:

1. Select Start ➤ All Programs. Note the size of the icons in the Start menu. There is no Programs menu item for Administrative Tools.

2. Right-click an empty space on the Taskbar and choose Properties.

3. Click the Start Menu tab and then click the Customize button.

4. In the Customize Start Menu dialog box, scroll down to System Administrative Tools, click Display On The All Programs Menu And Start Menu, and then click OK twice.

5. Select Start ➤ All Programs and note that the All Programs menu lists Administrative Tools.

6. Edit the Taskbar and Start Menu properties as you like or return them to their default settings.

Knowing how to configure your Start menu allows you to customize the user's environment. Now let's look at how to set up and configure shortcuts.

Configuring Shortcuts

As you know, shortcuts are links to objects that are easily accessible from your computer. You can use a shortcut to quickly access a file, program, folder, printer, or computer from your Desktop. Shortcuts can exist in various locations, including on the Desktop, on the Start menu, and within folders.

To create a shortcut from Windows Explorer, just right-click the item for which you want to create a shortcut, and select Send To ➢ Desktop (Create Shortcut) from the context menu. Then you can click the shortcut and drag it where you want it to appear.

Perform the following steps to create a shortcut and place it on the Desktop:

1. Select Start ➢ All Programs ➢ Accessories ➢ Windows Explorer to start Windows Explorer.

2. Expand Computer, then Local Disk, then Windows, and then System32. Right-click System32 and choose Send To ➢ Desktop (Create Shortcut).

3. In the System32 folder, scroll down until you see Calc. Right-click Calc and select Send To ➢ Desktop (Create Shortcut). A shortcut to `calc.exe` will be placed on the Desktop.

4. View the Desktop and verify that both shortcuts are present.

After you set up your shortcuts, you can configure how your display will look by adding gadgets. Let's look at how to set up and configure gadgets.

Configuring Windows Gadgets

Windows gadgets were first introduced in Windows Vista Sidebar. Windows 7 has removed the Sidebar but still allows you to add gadgets. Windows gadgets are programs that provide quick, visual representations of information, such as the weather, RSS (web) feeds, your calendar, and the current time.

Windows gadgets are installed by default on Windows 7, but they have to be added to the Windows 7 Desktop, as shown in Figure 5.10.

FIGURE 5.10
Windows gadgets

Administrators or users can add or remove gadgets to the Windows desktop. To remove a gadget, click the gadget and choosing Remove.

To add a gadget, right-click the desktop and choose Gadgets, choose the gadget that you want by right-clicking the gadget and choosing the Add link.

Perform the following steps to add the Windows 7 gadgets to your desktop:

1. Right-click the desktop and choose Gadgets to open the Add Gadgets screen.

2. Right-click the gadget that you would like to install and choose Add.

3. Close the Add Gadgets screen.

After you have added the gadget to the desktop, you can configure the gadget. To do so, mouse over the gadget and a small picture of a wrench appears, as shown in Figure 5.11. Click the wrench to configure the gadget.

FIGURE 5.11
Configuring the gadget

Administrators or users can also remove gadgets at any time by closing the gadget. Again when you mouse over the gadget, you can click the X above the wrench to close the gadget (see Figure 5.11). You can also add other gadgets by going to the Internet and viewing and adding other gadgets.

Perform the following steps to add other gadgets from the Internet:

1. Right-click the desktop and choose Gadgets.

2. Click the Get More Gadgets Online link.

3. Find the gadget you want to install and choose Download, as shown in Figure 5.12.

4. After you click the Download link, it will take you to another website where you click the Download link again.

5. The File Download box appears. Click the Save button.

6. Save the file to a folder on your machine.

7. After the download is complete, click the Open button.

8. On the Desktop Gadgets screen, click the Install button.

   After the installation is complete, the new gadget appears on the Desktop.

FIGURE 5.12
Installing a new gadget
from the Internet

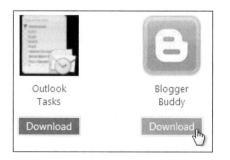

Now that you know how to add and configure gadgets to your desktop, you'll learn how to set your regional settings and multiple language settings.

Managing Multiple Languages and Regional Settings

In addition to configuring your Desktop, you can configure the language and regional settings that are used on your computer Desktop. Windows 7 supports multiple languages through the use of multilanguage technology. Multilanguage technology is designed to meet the following needs:

♦ Provide support for multilingual editing of documents.

♦ Provide support for various language interfaces in your environment.

♦ Allow users who speak various languages to share the same computer.

In the following sections, you will learn about multilingual technology, what options are available for Windows 7 multilingual support, and how to enable and configure multilingual support.

Configuring Multilingual Technology

Windows 7 is built on Multilanguage User Interface (MUI) technology and thus supports user options to view, edit, and process documents in a variety of languages. These options are provided through Unicode support, the National Language Support API, the Multilingual API, language files, and Multilingual Developer Support. Let's discuss each in turn:

Unicode   This is an international standard that allows character support for the common characters used in the world's most common languages.

National Language Support API   This is used to provide information for locale, character mapping, and keyboard layout. Locale settings are used to set local information such as date and time format, currency format, and country names. Character mapping arranges the mapping of local character encodings to Unicode. Keyboard layout settings include character typing information and sorting information.

Multilingual API   This is used to set up applications to support keyboard input and fonts from various language versions of applications. For example, Japanese users will see vertical text, and Arabic users will see right-to-left ligatures. This technology allows users to create mixed-language documents.

Language Files   These are files in which Windows 7 stores all language-specific information, such as text for help files and dialog boxes. They are separate from the operating system files.

System code can thus be shared by all language versions of Windows 7, which allows modular support for different languages.

Multilingual Developer Support   This is a special set of APIs that enables developers to create generic code and then provide support for multiple languages.

Configuring Windows 7 Multilanguage Support

Multilanguage support is implemented using Multilanguage User Interface (MUI) technology, which allows the Windows 7 user interface to be presented in different languages and for applications to be viewed and edited in different languages based on the language file selected.

Depending on the level of language support required by your environment, you may use either a localized version of Windows 7 or install language files to support multiple languages. In this section we'll describe these versions and show you how to configure multilanguage support.

USING LOCALIZED VERSIONS OF WINDOWS 7

Microsoft provides localized editions of Windows 7. For example, users in the United States will most likely use the English version, and users in Japan will most likely use the Japanese version. Localized versions of Windows 7 include fully localized user interfaces for the language that was selected. In addition, localized versions allow users to view, edit, and print documents in many different languages.

 **Real World Scenario**

MULTILANGUAGE ORGANIZATIONS

We are IT managers for an organization that has locations around the world, so we must know what country our computers are being shipped to. We have to ensure that the appropriate Windows 7 language is installed on those computers.

Often we are setting up multiple computers at the same time. Most of us use a third-party imaging tool to create our computer operating system images. We must be sure to install the proper image for the country. A few times we had to ship machines back from other countries because we failed to install the appropriate localized version of Windows.

Installing the localized version of Windows 7 is important, but what if you have users who speak multiple languages? Let's take a look at Windows 7 language packs.

INSTALLING WINDOWS 7 LANGUAGE PACKS

Windows 7 MUI support provides user interfaces in several languages. This is useful in multinational corporations where users speak several languages and must share computers. It is also appropriate when administrators want to deploy a single image of Windows 7 worldwide. You can manage multiple users who share a single computer and speak different languages through user profiles (covered in Chapter 8, "Configuring Users and Groups") or through Group Policies (covered in Chapter 9, "Managing Security").

To implement multilanguage support, the appropriate language files to be implemented must be installed on the computer. There are two types of languages files in Windows 7:

Multilingual User Interface Pack (MUI)   This type of language file provides a translated version of the majority of the user interface. A license is required to use MUIs.

Language Interface Pack (LIP)   LIP language files consist of freely available files that provide a translated version of the most popular aspects of the user interface. LIPs require a parent language because LIP files do not translate all components of the user interface.

Now that you have seen what the multilanguage options are, let's take a look at how to configure and enable multilingual support.

Enabling and Configuring Multilingual Support

On the Windows 7 operating system, you can enable and configure multilingual editing and viewing by choosing Start ➢ Control Panel ➢ Regional And Language Options. This opens the Region And Language dialog box, as shown in Figure 5.13.

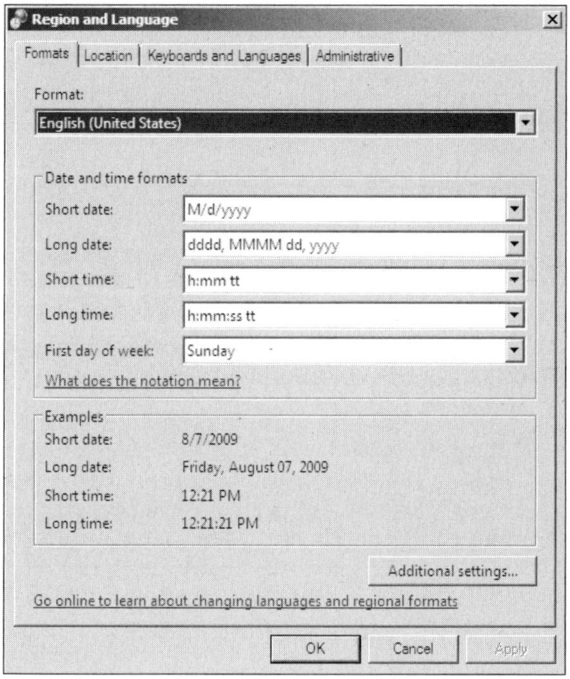

FIGURE 5.13
The Region And
Language dialog box

Here you can configure options on the following tabs:

Formats Tab   The Formats tab of the Region And Language dialog box enables you to configure how numbers, currencies, dates, and times are displayed on the screen. You can change the current format using the Current Format drop-down list, which provides many different format options such as English (United States), German (Germany), and Chinese (Singapore).

The Customize This Format button provides the ability to customize how numbers, currencies, times, and dates are displayed based on user or corporate preferences.

On the Formats tab, you can click the Additional Settings button to configure the rest of your options, as shown in Figure 5.14.

FIGURE 5.14
Additional Settings screen

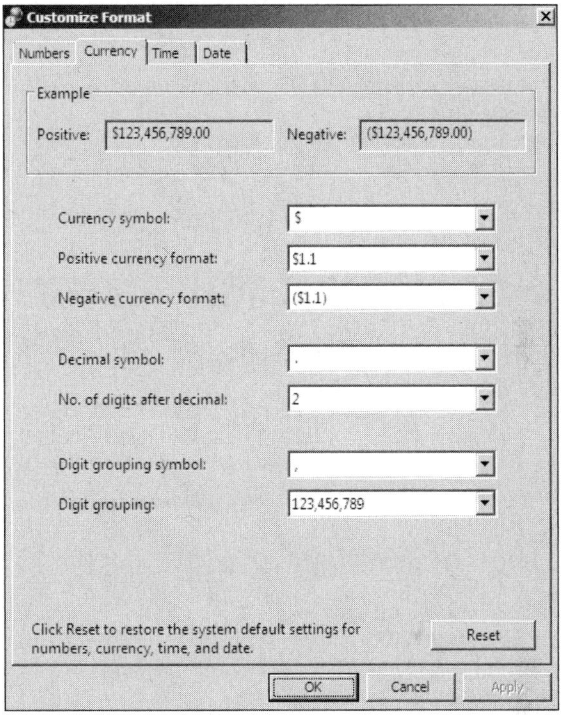

Location Tab The Location tab of the Region And Language dialog box, as shown in Figure 5.15, enables you to specify the current location to use in software that provides localized information, such as news and weather information. The Current Location drop-down list provides you with a list of locations that can be selected.

Keyboards And Languages Tab The Keyboards And Languages tab of the Region And Language dialog box enables you to configure the input and keyboard language, and allows you to install or uninstall language packs, as shown in Figure 5.16. This tab also provides the ability to configure the language bar options and advanced keyboard settings. Click the Install/Uninstall Languages button to open the Install Or Uninstall Display Languages Wizard, which lets you select the languages to install or uninstall on your computer.

Administrative Tab The Administrative tab, as shown in Figure 5.17, allows you to support languages for non-Unicode programs. This enables non-Unicode programs to display menus and dialog boxes in the user's native language. This tab also allows you to copy the current settings to reserved accounts, such as the default user account or to system accounts.

FIGURE 5.15
Location tab

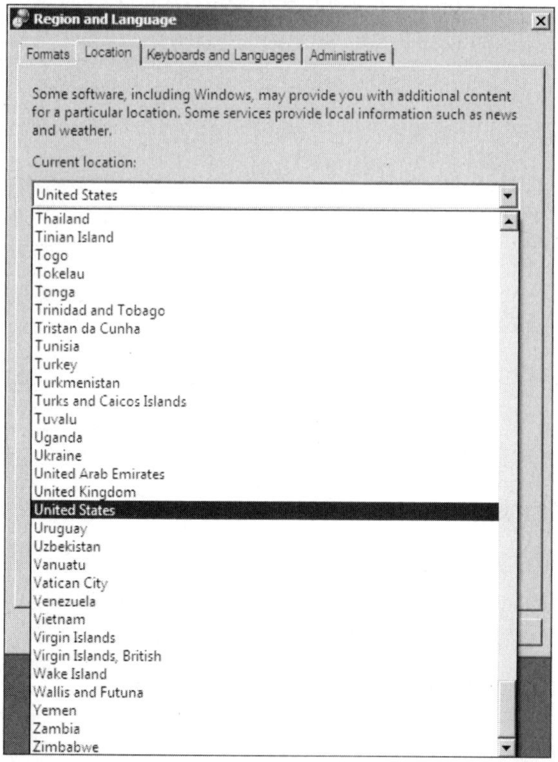

FIGURE 5.16
Keyboards And
Languages tab

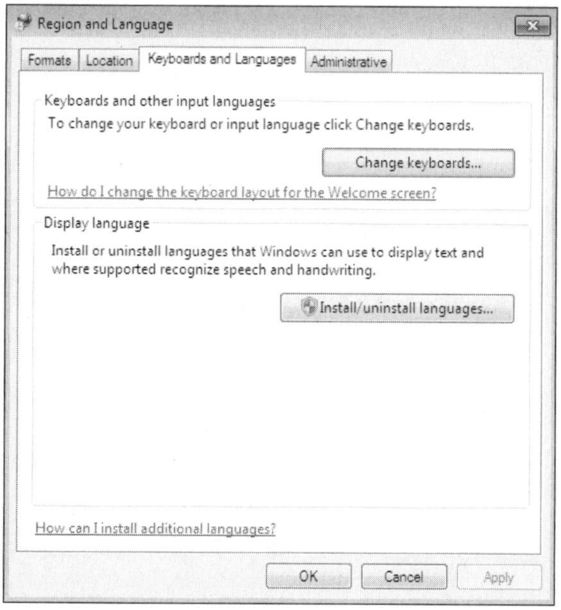

FIGURE 5.17
Administrative tab

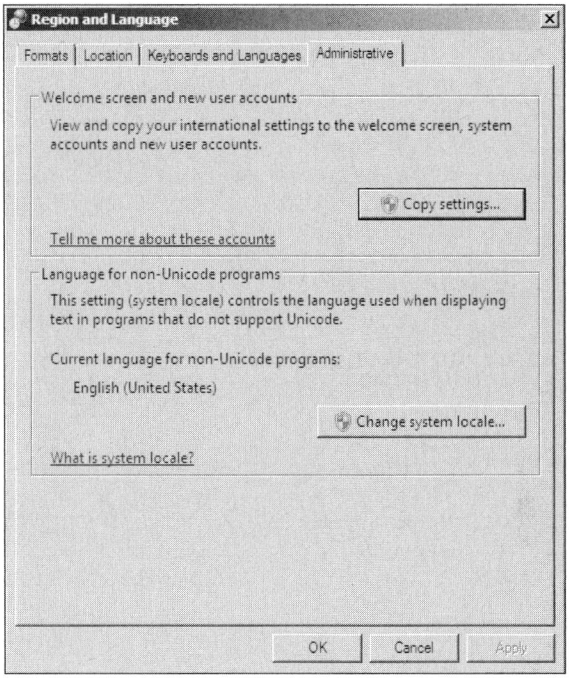

Perform the following steps to configure the locale settings on your computer:

1. Select Start ➢ Control Panel ➢ Regional And Language Options.

2. One by one, click the Formats, Location, Keyboards And Languages, and Administrative tabs and note the configurations on each tab.

3. Click the Formats tab and select the Danish (Denmark) option from the Current Format drop-down list. Then click the Apply button.

4. In the Number, Currency, Time, and Date fields, note the changed configurations.

5. Reset your locale to the original configuration and click Apply.

SUPPORTING MULTILINGUAL ENVIRONMENTS

Your company has an office in Tokyo. Computers are shared by users there who require both English and Japanese language support, for document management as well as the UI. Your CIO has asked you to set up a system that lets users in the Tokyo office use Windows 7 in any language.

To do this, you must install each language file to use. Each computer user can select the preferred UI and specify locale information. This is stored as part of the user's profile. When you log on as a specific user, you see the linguistic and locale information that has been configured.

After configuring your multilingual support, another feature that can be configured is your accessibility features. The next section focuses on configuring the accessibility options.

Configuring Accessibility Features

Windows 7 allows you to configure the Desktop so those users with special accessibility needs can use the Desktop more easily. Through its accessibility options and accessibility utilities, Windows 7 supports users with limited sight, hearing, or mobility. This section describes how to use these accessibility features.

Setting Accessibility Options

Through the Ease Of Access Center available in Control Panel, you can configure keyboard, sound, display, mouse, and general properties of Windows 7 for users with special needs. To access the accessibility options screen, as shown in Figure 5.18, select Control Panel ➢ Ease Of Access Center.

FIGURE 5.18

The Ease Of Access Center

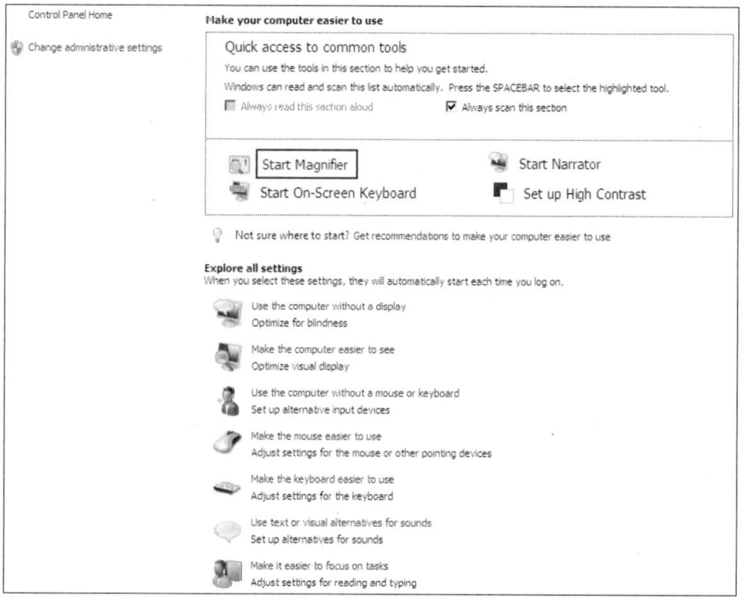

The Ease Of Access Center provides several options for customizing the computer to make it easier to use. Some commonly configured accessibility options include magnifying the text on the screen, configuring the text on the screen to be narrated, configuring an on-screen keyboard, and configuring a high-contrast desktop environment. Here are some other settings that can be modified for improved accessibility:

Use The Computer Without A Display   This option allows the computer to be optimized for visually impaired users, as shown in Figure 5.19. You can turn on the narrator, turn on audio descriptions, and turn off animations.

Make The Computer Easier To See   This option allows the display to be optimized for users with sight impairments, as shown in Figure 5.20. You can select a high-contrast color scheme, turn on the narrator and audio descriptions, turn on the screen magnifier, and fine-tune display effects.

FIGURE 5.19
Use The Computer
Without A Display
option

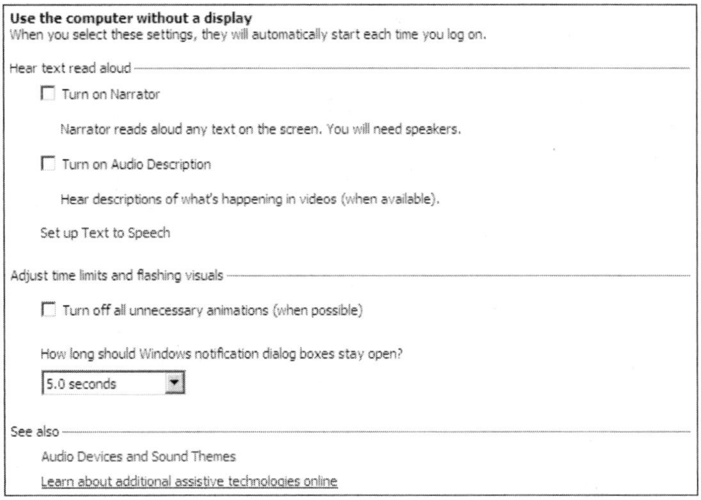

Use the computer without a display
When you select these settings, they will automatically start each time you log on.

Hear text read aloud ──────────────────────────────────────

☐ Turn on Narrator

Narrator reads aloud any text on the screen. You will need speakers.

☐ Turn on Audio Description

Hear descriptions of what's happening in videos (when available).

Set up Text to Speech

Adjust time limits and flashing visuals ──────────────────────

☐ Turn off all unnecessary animations (when possible)

How long should Windows notification dialog boxes stay open?

[5.0 seconds ▼]

See also ───

Audio Devices and Sound Themes

Learn about additional assistive technologies online

FIGURE 5.20
Make The Computer
Easier To See options

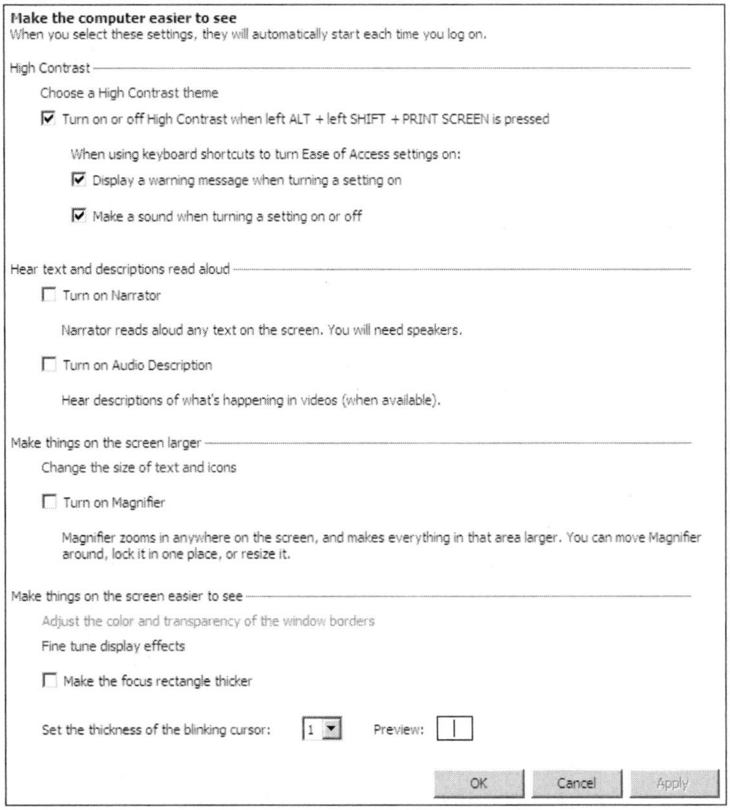

Make the computer easier to see
When you select these settings, they will automatically start each time you log on.

High Contrast ──

Choose a High Contrast theme

☑ Turn on or off High Contrast when left ALT + left SHIFT + PRINT SCREEN is pressed

When using keyboard shortcuts to turn Ease of Access settings on:

☑ Display a warning message when turning a setting on

☑ Make a sound when turning a setting on or off

Hear text and descriptions read aloud ────────────────────────

☐ Turn on Narrator

Narrator reads aloud any text on the screen. You will need speakers.

☐ Turn on Audio Description

Hear descriptions of what's happening in videos (when available).

Make things on the screen larger ─────────────────────────────

Change the size of text and icons

☐ Turn on Magnifier

Magnifier zooms in anywhere on the screen, and makes everything in that area larger. You can move Magnifier around, lock it in one place, or resize it.

Make things on the screen easier to see ──────────────────────

Adjust the color and transparency of the window borders

Fine tune display effects

☐ Make the focus rectangle thicker

Set the thickness of the blinking cursor: [1 ▼]   Preview: [|]

[OK]   [Cancel]   [Apply]

Use The Computer Without A Mouse Or Keyboard This option allows the computer to use an alternative input device. You can configure the on-screen keyboard to be displayed, or you can configure speech recognition.

Make The Mouse Easier To Use This option adjusts the appearance of the mouse pointer, whether the keyboard should be used to move the mouse around, and whether hovering over a window will activate the window, as shown in Figure 5.21.

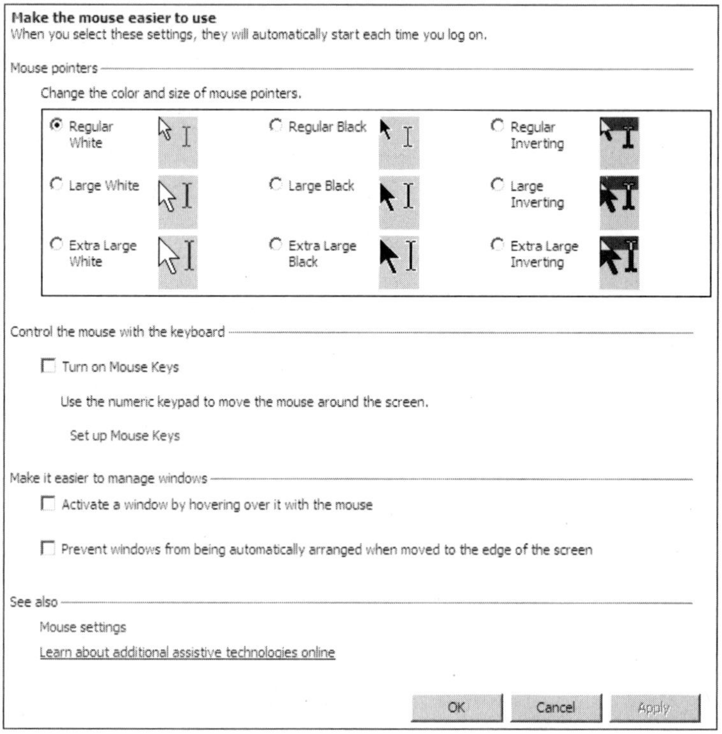

FIGURE 5.21
Mouse options

Make The Keyboard Easier To Use This option optimizes the keyboard configuration, as shown in Figure 5.22. This contains settings for using Sticky Keys, Filter Keys, and Toggle Keys. Sticky Keys allows the Shift, Ctrl, Alt, or Windows key to be used in conjunction with another key by pressing the keys separately rather than simultaneously. Filter Keys ignores brief or repeated keystrokes and slows the repeat rate. Toggle Keys makes a noise whenever you press the Caps Lock, Num Lock, or Scroll Lock key.

Use Text Of Visual Alternatives For Sounds This option allows you to specify whether you want to use Sound Sentry, which generates a visual warning whenever the computer makes a sound, and whether to display captions for speech and sounds on your computer.

Make It Easier To Focus On Tasks This option allows you to configure settings for optimizing reading and typing settings, and animations. Some of the settings are Turn On Narrator, Turn On Sticky Keys, Turn On Toggle Keys, and Turn On Filter Keys.

FIGURE 5.22

Keyboard accessibility options

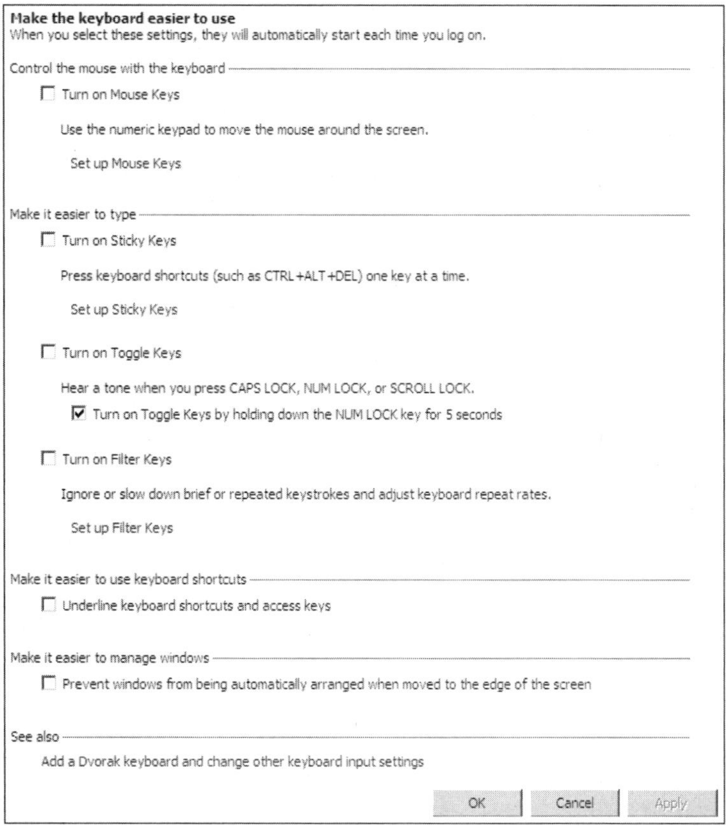

> **Make the keyboard easier to use**
> When you select these settings, they will automatically start each time you log on.
>
> Control the mouse with the keyboard ─────────────────────────────
>   ☐ Turn on Mouse Keys
>
>   Use the numeric keypad to move the mouse around the screen.
>
>   Set up Mouse Keys
>
> Make it easier to type ───
>   ☐ Turn on Sticky Keys
>
>   Press keyboard shortcuts (such as CTRL+ALT+DEL) one key at a time.
>
>   Set up Sticky Keys
>
>   ☐ Turn on Toggle Keys
>
>   Hear a tone when you press CAPS LOCK, NUM LOCK, or SCROLL LOCK.
>   ☑ Turn on Toggle Keys by holding down the NUM LOCK key for 5 seconds
>
>   ☐ Turn on Filter Keys
>
>   Ignore or slow down brief or repeated keystrokes and adjust keyboard repeat rates.
>
>   Set up Filter Keys
>
> Make it easier to use keyboard shortcuts ───────────────────────
>   ☐ Underline keyboard shortcuts and access keys
>
> Make it easier to manage windows ──────────────────────────────
>   ☐ Prevent windows from being automatically arranged when moved to the edge of the screen
>
> See also ──
>   Add a Dvorak keyboard and change other keyboard input settings
>
>   [OK] [Cancel] [Apply]

⊕ Real World Scenario

USING STICKY KEYS

You can access the sticky keys by clicking the Shift key 5 times. As an IT Manager, I would always disable this feature. The reason for this is that a common hacking trick is to change the 5 Shift keys from the sticky keys to use the command prompt.

So if they change the 5 Shifts keys to the Command prompt, what can that do, Right? Well that can give a hacker full access to your computer. At the Logon screen, click the Shift key 5 times and if the sticky keys are enabled, they will appear. If you change the 5 Shift keys to use the Command prompt, then the command prompt will appear.

At the command prompt, if the hacker types **System**, the System account will open, bypassing the Logon screen. For 5 minutes, the hacker will be logged on as the System account.

Windows 2008 Server and Windows 7 have made this hack much harder to pull off. They have changed the permissions on the Sethc.exe file (this is the file that is started when the Shift key is hit five times) to make it harder to hack this file.

Now that you have an understanding of the different accessibility options, let's take a look at how to use some of the Accessibility utilities.

Configuring Accessibility Utilities

Windows 7 provides several accessibility utilities, including the Magnifier, Narrator, and the On-Screen Keyboard. Let's take a look at these options in more detail.

Using the Magnifier Utility   The Magnifier utility creates a separate window to magnify a portion of your screen, as shown in Figure 5.23. This option is useful for users who have poor vision. To access Magnifier, select Start ➤ All Programs ➤ Accessories ➤ Ease Of Access ➤ Magnifier. As you can see in Figure 5.23, when you place your mouse over an object, it magnifies the object.

FIGURE 5.23
The Magnifier utility

Using the Narrator Utility   The Narrator utility can read aloud on-screen text, dialog boxes, menus, and buttons. This utility requires that you have some type of sound output device installed and configured. To access Narrator, select Start ➤ All Programs ➤ Accessories ➤ Ease Of Access ➤ Narrator. This brings up the dialog box shown in Figure 5.24.

FIGURE 5.24
The Microsoft Narrator
dialog box

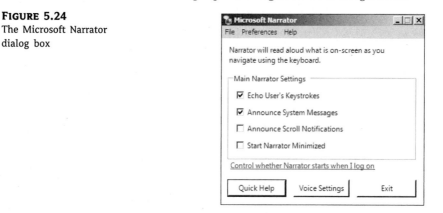

Using the On-Screen Keyboard The On-Screen Keyboard displays a keyboard on the screen, as shown in Figure 5.25. Users can use the On-Screen Keyboard keys through a mouse or another input device as an alternative to the keys on the regular keyboard. To access the On-Screen Keyboard, select Start ➤ All Programs ➤ Accessories ➤ Ease Of Access ➤ On-Screen Keyboard.

FIGURE 5.25

The On-Screen Keyboard

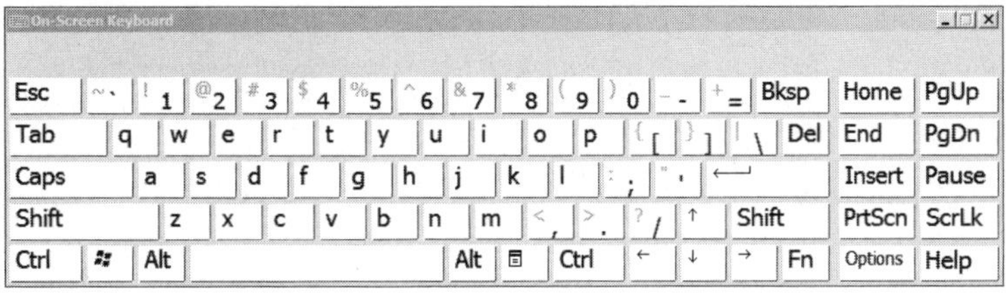

Perform these steps to configure the Windows 7 accessibility features:

1. Select Start ➤ All Programs ➤ Accessories ➤ Ease Of Access ➤ Magnifier.

2. Experiment with the Magnifier utility. When you finish, click the Exit button in the Magnifier Settings dialog box.

3. Select Start ➤ All Programs ➤ Accessories ➤ Ease Of Access ➤ On-Screen Keyboard.

4. Select Start ➤ All Programs ➤ Accessories ➤ Notepad to open Notepad.

5. Create a text document using the On-Screen Keyboard. When you finish, close the Notepad document without saving it.

6. Close the On-Screen Keyboard.

Two other Desktop options that you can use are Shut Down and Switch Users. Let's take a look at these features.

Configuring the Power Button

Unless you decide to run your computer 24 hours a day, you will eventually want to shut down. By default on the Start menu, you have a Shut Down button (this is called the power button). By clicking this button, your machine will power off. But the power button does not have to be set to the Shut Down option. You can configure this button to Switch User, Log Off, Lock, Restart, or Shut Down, as shown in Figure 5.26.

You may have a machine that is shared by multiple users, and it may be better for you to have the Switch User button on the Start menu instead of the Shut Down button. Configuring the Switch User option would make it easier on your users.

Perform the following steps to configure the power button to Switch User:

1. Right-click the Shut Down button and choose Properties.

2. The Taskbar And Start Menu Properties dialog box appears. Make sure that you are working on the Start Menu tab.

3. From the Power Button Action drop-down list, choose Switch User.

4. Click OK.

5. Click the Start menu and verify that the power button is now set to Switch User.

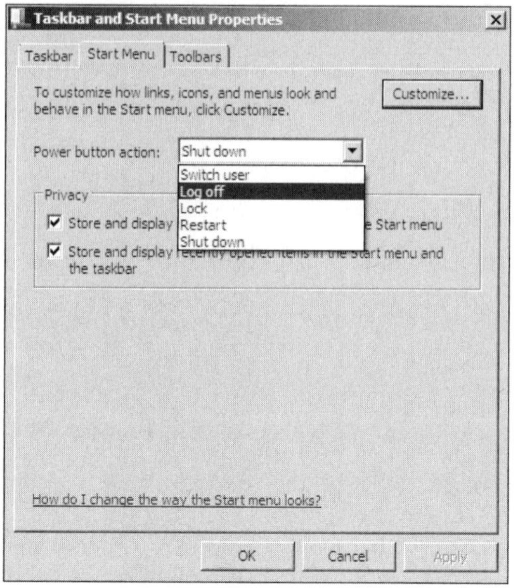

FIGURE 5.26
Shut Down button
options

If you have a machine that has multiple users, these users might be working on the machine at different times. Let's talk about how to configure your machine for multiple users.

Managing a Multiple-User Environment

Many organizations have machines that multiple users must work on. As an administrator, you can configure a Windows 7 machine for multiple users.

When a user first logs onto a Windows 7 computer, the user will have a generic default Desktop and generic default settings. An administrator can configure the machine so that a preset Desktop and preset configuration takes effect, as shown in Figure 5.27.

As you can see in Figure 5.27, there are two check boxes in the Copy Your Current Settings To section. These two check boxes allow an administrator to copy their current settings to the Welcome screen, system accounts, and a new user.

Perform the following steps to make your administrative account the default settings for all new users:

1. Click Start ➤ Control Panel ➤ Region And Language.

2. Click the Administrative tab.

3. Click the Copy Settings button.

4. Check the New User Accounts check box.

5. Click OK.

Another task that an administrator can complete is to allow the users' Desktop to follow them anywhere on the network. Let's now look at roaming profiles.

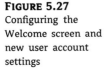

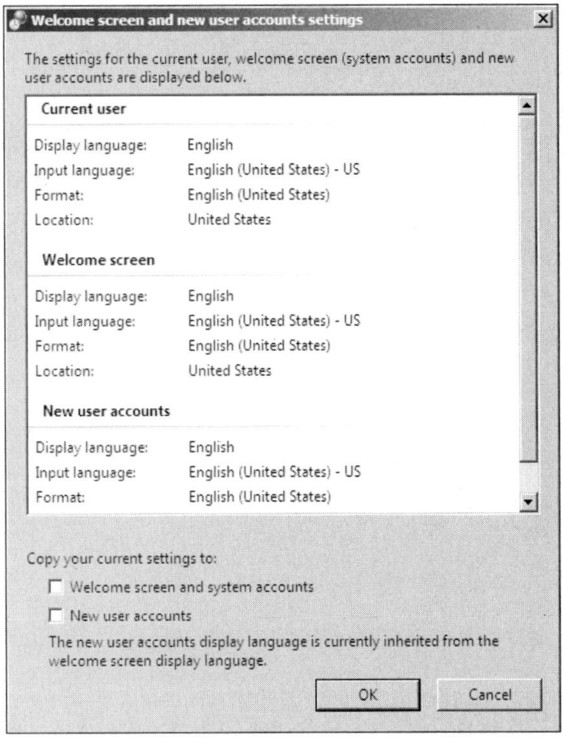

FIGURE 5.27
Configuring the Welcome screen and new user account settings

Managing User Profiles

User profiles are the Desktop settings that a user currently uses. When a user logs onto Windows 7 and sets up their Desktop, this is called a local user profile.

As an administrator, you can set it up so that the user's local profile can become a roaming profile. A roaming profile is a user profile that follows the user to any machine that they log into.

To set up a roaming profile, you must first be connected to a domain (domains are explained in detail in Chapter 12, "Networking with Windows Server 2008"). Then the administrator needs to set up a shared folder on a server and copy the user's profile to that folder. The user's domain account properties would need to point to the roaming profile, and you are all set.

Perform the following steps to copy the Windows 7 user's profile to a server location. Your Windows 7 computer must be part of a domain to complete these steps. On the domain you must have a shared folder that you can place the profile into.

1. Click Start ➢ Control Panel ➢ System.

2. Click the Advance System Settings link in the upper-left corner.

3. In the System Properties dialog box, click the Advanced tab.

4. On the Advanced tab, click the Settings button in the User Profiles section, as shown in Figure 5.28.

5. Choose a profile and click the Copy To button.

6. Copy the profile to one of your servers.

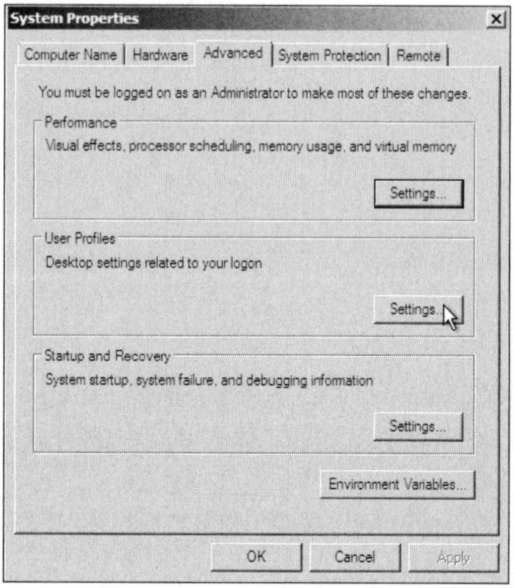

FIGURE 5.28
Click Settings in the
User Profiles section.

You'll learn how to turn this account into a roaming profile through Active Directory in Chapter 12. The steps that you just completed are the client-side steps to the process; we'll discuss the server-side steps in Chapter 12.

Real World Scenario

ROAMING PROFILES

As an IT Manager, I like to set up roaming profiles for my network users. Many users are not computer savvy. You can give a good salesperson a calling list and a phone, and they can sell. But we ask them to do everything on a computer.

When you set up roaming profiles, it does not matter where the user logs on; their Desktop will follow them from place to place. This enables a user to feel more comfortable when they see a Desktop that they are accustomed to seeing. Because a user knows their own Desktop and icons, it will help with their productivity.

User profiles are an easy way to make your users feel better no matter what computer they log onto. Knowing how to configure your Desktop from start to finish is a great way to personalize any Windows 7 computer.

The Bottom Line

Understand the Start menu shortcuts.   The Start menu has many default shortcuts that are preloaded when the Windows 7 operating system is created. Some of the default shortcuts are Getting Started, Windows Media Center, Calculator, Sticky Notes, Snipping Tool, Remote Desktop Connection, Startup, and Internet.

Master It   You are the system administrator for your organization, and you have salespeople who need an application to start every time they log into the Windows 7 system. How would you configure the application so that it starts when the salespeople log into their machine?

Customize the Start menu and Taskbar.   Users can customize the Taskbar and Start menu using the Taskbar And Start Menu Properties dialog box. This dialog box has three tabs: Taskbar, Start Menu, and Toolbars. The easiest way to access the dialog box is to right-click a blank area in the Taskbar and choose Properties from the context menu.

Master It   You are the system administrator for your organization, and you have a user who has received a computer that was previously used by another user. The machine was not formatted, but the new user's data was migrated over. The user complains because the Taskbar disappears on its own. The user gets the Taskbar back when the mouse is moved over the bottom of the screen. How can you stop the Taskbar from disappearing?

Work with regional settings.   Multilanguage and regional support is available with Windows 7 that allows the user interface to be presented in different languages and that allows applications to be viewed and edited in different languages. Depending on the level of language support required by your environment, you may use either a localized version of Window Windows 7 or install language files to support multiple languages.

Master It   You are the system administrator for an organization that has multiple sites all over the world. You are responsible for rolling out Windows 7 client machines to users in all offices. You have to set up a Windows 7 machine for a user overseas. How do you configure the Windows 7 machine?

Use accessibility features.   Windows 7 allows you to configure the Desktop so those users with special accessibility needs can use the Windows 7 Desktop more easily. Through its accessibility options and accessibility utilities, Windows 7 supports users with limited sight, hearing, or mobility.

Master It   You are the administrator for a mid-sized computer training company. You have a user that has difficulty seeing the Desktop clearly. You have already made the icons larger, but the user is still having issues. What other steps can you show the user so that the Desktop and applications are easier to see?

Chapter 6

Managing the Interface

After you install Windows 7, you need to install and configure the system. In this chapter, we examine the process of configuring the Windows 7 environment, beginning with an overview of the main configuration utilities.

Control Panel is one of the most important configuration areas of Windows 7. The Control Panel includes many icons that can help us optimize, maintain, and personalize the operating system. One of the most important icons in the Control Panel is the System icon. not only has operating system information but you can configure Devices, Remote Settings, and System Protection in the System icon

Another important component that we need to manipulate and configure is the video adapter. Many users have moved to multiple adapters to make their working environment more customizable. The user may have an application running on one monitor and their email open on another.

If you use Windows 7 on a laptop computer, it is important to properly configure your power options. Configuring the power options on a laptop will allow you to get the most life from your laptop batteries. You can choose among many power options to customize laptops for each of your users.

We'll examine how services operate and how to configure your services to start manually or automatically. We'll also explore how to configure services in the event of a service error.

In this chapter, you will learn to

◆ Understand Control Panel

◆ Use the System Icon

◆ Configure mobile computers

◆ Configure services

Configuring Windows 7

Windows 7 includes several utilities for managing various aspects of the operating system configuration. In the following sections, you will learn how to configure your operating system using Control Panel and the Registry Editor.

Let's start with Control Panel and the various utilities included within it.

What's in Control Panel?

Control Panel is a set of GUI utilities that allow you to configure Registry settings without using a Registry editor. The Registry is a database used by the operating system to store configuration information.

Let's take a closer look at the utilities that are available through Control Panel:

Action Center The Action Center has two configurable sections: Security and Maintenance. The Security section allows you to configure four options:

◆ Virus Protection, which allows you to install and configure virus protection

◆ Windows Update, which allows you to update Windows 7

◆ Check For Solutions To Unreported Problems, which allows you to report and check for unreported problems

◆ Set Up Backup, which allows you to configure a backup

The Maintenance section allows you to set up a backup. Backups and Windows Update are explained later in this section.

Administrative Tools By clicking this icon, you can access multiple administrative tools that can help you configure and monitor the Windows 7 operating system. These tools include

◆ Computer Services

◆ Computer Management

◆ Data Sources (ODBC)

◆ Event Viewer

◆ iSCSI Initiator

◆ Local Security Policy

◆ Performance Monitor

◆ Print Management

◆ Services

◆ System Configuration

◆ Task Scheduler

◆ Windows Firewall with Advanced Security

◆ Windows Memory Diagnostics

◆ Windows PowerShell Modules

AutoPlay AutoPlay lets you configure media disks that will automatically start when inserted into the Media Player, as shown in Figure 6.1. Each of the media you use has different configuration settings, but the basic choices are as follows:

◆ Play Media Using The Windows Media Player

◆ Open The Folder To View Files Using Windows Explorer

◆   Take No Action

◆   Ask Me Every Time

FIGURE 6.1
AutoPlay options

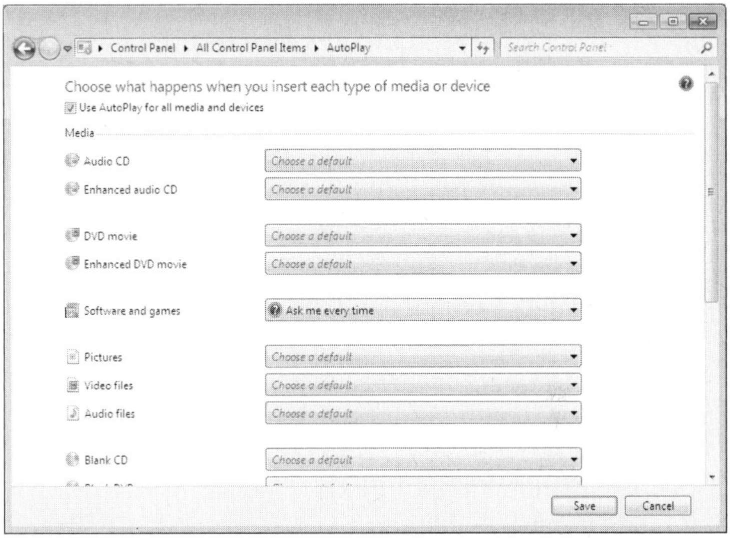

Backup And Restore   Backup And Restore allows you to install and configure your backup media. Backups allow a user to make a copy of all important data on their machine in the event of a hardware failure or disaster. Chapter 15, ''Maintaining and Optimizing Windows 7,'' goes into greater detail about backups.

BitLocker Drive Encryption   BitLocker Drive Encryption helps prevent unauthorized users from accessing files stored on the hard drives. The user is able to use the computer as normal but unauthorized users cannot read or use any of their files. Chapter 9, ''Managing Security,'' discusses BitLocker Drive Encryption.

Color Management   Color Management allows you to configure some of the video adapter settings, as shown in Figure 6.2. You can configure the Windows Color System Defaults, ICC Rendering Intent To WCS Gamut Mapping, and Display Calibration, as well as change the system defaults.

Credential Manager   You use Credential Manager to store credentials such as usernames and passwords. These usernames and passwords are stored in vaults so that you can easily log on to computers or websites.

There are three credential sections: Windows Credentials, Certificate-Based Credentials, and Generic Credentials. You can add credentials by just clicking the Add Credentials link next to each of the three sections, as shown in Figure 6.3.

Date And Time   Click the Date And Time icon to configure the local date and time for your Windows 7 machine. You also have the ability to synchronize your clock with the Internet, as shown in Figure 6.4.

Default Programs   Click the Default Programs icon to choose the programs that Windows uses by default. For example, you can set Internet Explorer 8 (IE8) to be the default Internet browser, as shown in Figure 6.5.

FIGURE 6.2
Color Management

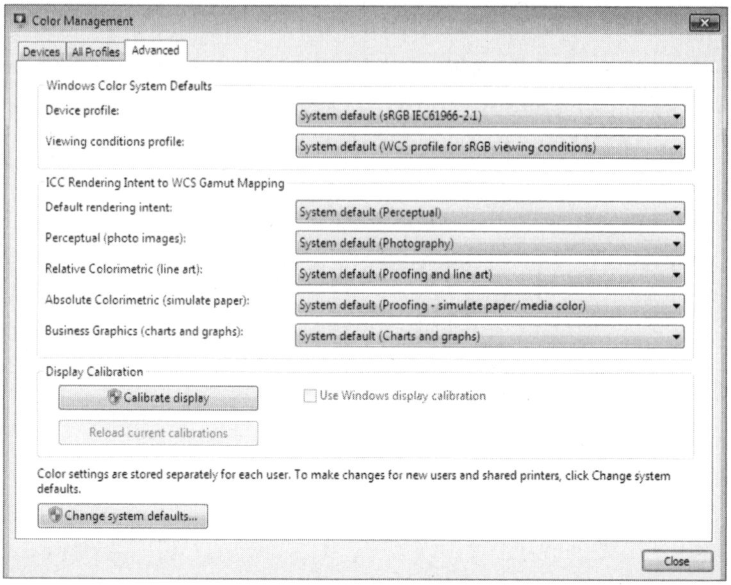

FIGURE 6.3
Credential Manager

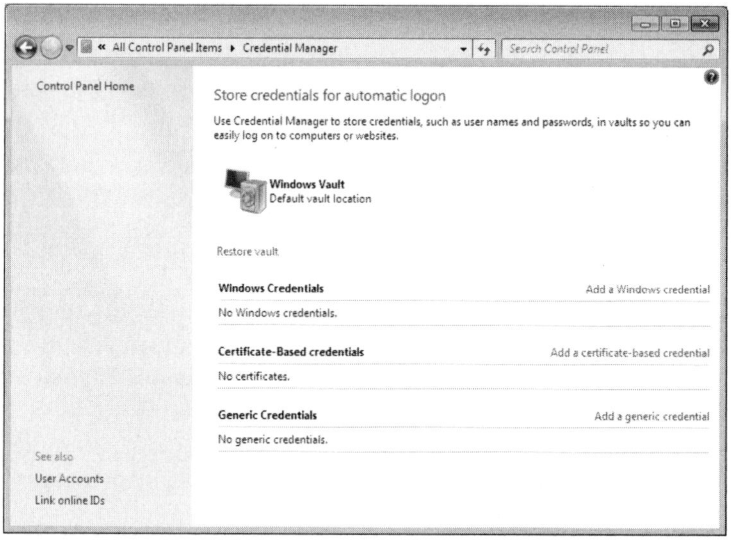

Desktop Gadgets Click the Desktop Gadgets icon to set up various gadgets for your Windows 7 Desktop. To learn more about gadgets, refer to Chapter 5, "Managing the Windows 7 Desktop."

Device Manager Click the Device Manager icon to configure the devices on your Windows 7 machine. You can configure such devices as disk drives, display adapters, DVD/CD-ROM drives, monitors, and network adapters. Chapter 10, "Configuring Hardware and Printing," gives more details about Device Manager.

FIGURE 6.4
Time synchronization

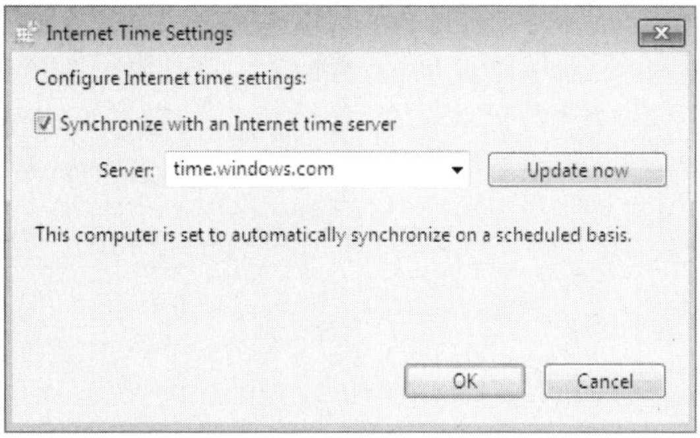

FIGURE 6.5
Setting default programs

Devices And Printers   Click the Devices And Printers icon to add or configure the devices on your machine and your printers. Chapter 10, "Configuring Hardware and Printing," discusses in detail devices and printers.

Display   Click the Display icon to configure your display properties, as shown in Figure 6.6. You can change the size of the text and other items on your screen. You also have the ability to change the resolution, calibrate colors, change display settings, adjust ClearType text, and change custom text size.

Ease Of Access Center   The Ease Of Access Center enables you to set up your accessibility options. Chapter 5, "Managing the Windows 7 Desktop," explains in detail the Ease Of Access Center.

Folder Options   Click the Folder Options icon to configure how you can view the folders on your Windows 7 machine by default. You can configure how you browse and navigate folders, which files and folders you can view, and how folders are searched, as shown in Figure 6.7.

FIGURE 6.6
Display options

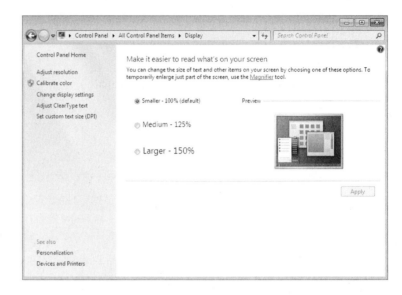

FIGURE 6.7
View Folder options

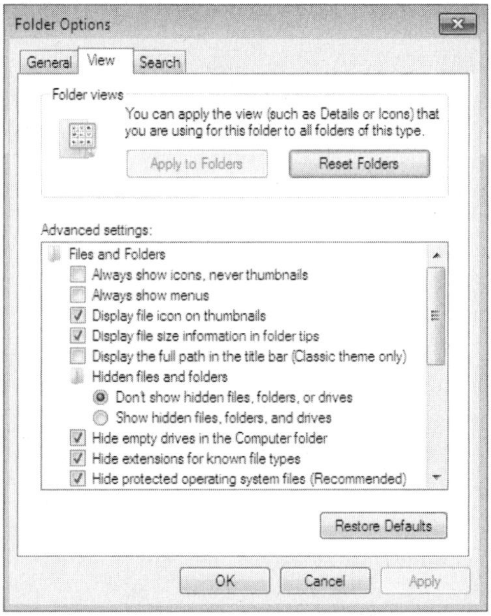

Fonts   Click the Fonts icon to install, preview, delete, show, hide, and configure the fonts that the applications on your Windows 7 operating system can use. get fonts online, adjust ClearType text, find a character, and change font size.

Getting Started   The Getting Started icon allows you to learn about and configure your Windows 7 operating system. By clicking this icon, you can do the following:

◆   Go online to find out what's new in Windows 7.

◆   Personalize Windows.

- Transfer files and settings from another computer.

- Use a HomeGroup to share with other computers in your home.

- Choose when to be notified about changes to your computer.

- Go online to get Windows Live Essentials.

- Back up your files.

- Add new users to your computer.

- Change the size of the text on your screen.

HomeGroup   The HomeGroups icon gives you the ability to create and configure your HomeGroup. HomeGroups are small local networks that you can easily configure at home and work.

When you install HomeGroups on your first computer, a password is assigned so that you can connect other computers to this HomeGroup. You can change the password by clicking the HomeGroup icon. Chapter 11, "Configuring Network Connectivity," discusses HomeGroups in detail.

Indexing Options   Windows uses the Indexing feature to perform very fast searches of common files on your computer. Index Settings give you the ability to configure which files and applications are indexed, as shown in Figure 6.8.

FIGURE 6.8
The Index Settings tab
of Advanced Options

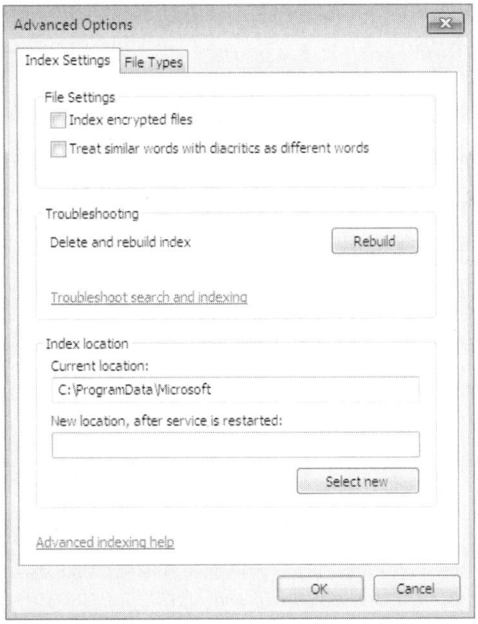

Internet Properties   Click the Internet Properties icon to configure how the Internet will operate, as shown in Figure 6.9. From this icon you can configure your Home page, Browsing history, Tabs, Security, Privacy, Content, Connections, and Programs. Chapter 13, "Configuring Internet Explorer," discusses Internet Explorer 8 in detail.

FIGURE 6.9
Internet Properties

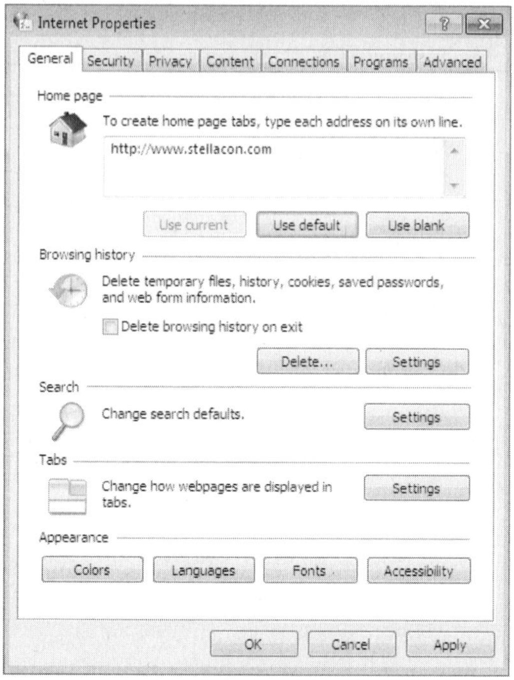

Keyboard In Keyboard Properties, you configure how the keyboard will react when used. You can set the character repeat speed (how fast the keyboard will repeat what you are typing) and the cursor speed. You can also configure the keyboard drivers in this properties window.

Location And Other Sensors Sensors are either software or hardware devices that pick up information from the surrounding area for your computer. Windows 7 supports both hardware and software sensors.

Examples of hardware sensors are motion detectors, and an example of a software sensor is your computer reacting from a network packet. Windows 7 supports the following list of the sensors:

◆ GPS

◆ Accelerometer

◆ Proximity

◆ Light

◆ RFID (radio frequency identification)

◆ Compass

◆ Camera

◆ Microphone

◆ Temperature

◆   Moisture

◆   Motion detector

◆   Traffic

◆   Weather station

Mail   Setting the Mail properties allows you to set up your client side mail settings. In the Mail properties window, you can set up different user profiles (mailboxes) and specify which local mail servers or Internet mail servers they connect to.

Mouse   The Mouse icon gives you the ability to configure how the mouse will operate, as shown in Figure 6.10. You can configure the buttons, click speed, clicklock, pointer type, pointer options, center wheel, and hardware properties.

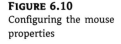

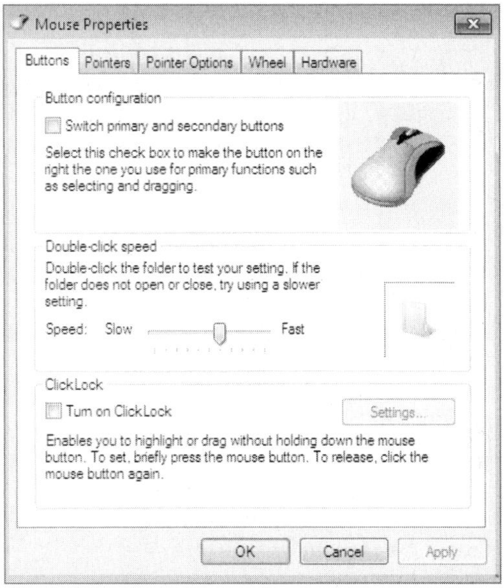

FIGURE 6.10
Configuring the mouse
properties

Network And Sharing Center   The Network And Sharing Center allows you to configure your Windows 7 machine to connect to a local network or the Internet. You can configure TCP/IP, set up a new network, connect to a network, choose a HomeGroup, and configure the network adapter. See Chapter 11, "Configuring Network Connectivity," gives more details about the Network And Sharing Center.

Notification Area   The Notification Area is the icon in the lower-right hand window of Windows 7 (next to the time) taskbar. The Notification Area icon in Control Panel allows you to configure which icons appear on the Taskbar and which notifications are shown.

Parental Controls   Parental Controls allow you to manage how children can use your Windows 7 computer. With Parental Controls, you can set the hours that children can use the computer, the programs that they can access, and the type of games that they can play.

When children try to access an application or game that they are not allowed to use, a notification will let them know that the application or game is restricted. The child can click a link that will then ask for access to the application or game, and the parent can accept or decline the request. Chapter 9, "Managing Security," discusses Parental Controls in detail.

Performance Information And Tools   The Performance Information and Tools icon gives you the ability to run a Windows Experience Index measurement, as shown in Figure 6.11. The Windows Experience Index measures the performance of the computer system.

The results will be issued as a base score. The higher the base score, the better your machine will perform. The Performance Information and Tools icon also shows you how you can improve the performance of your machine.

FIGURE 6.11
Performance
Information And Tools

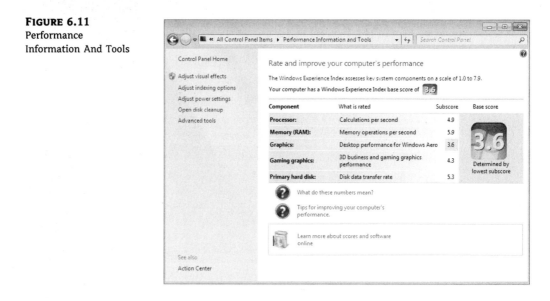

Personalization   Personalization allows you to set up your desktop environment. We discussed Personalization in Chapter 5, "Managing the Windows 7 Desktop," gives more details about the Personalization icon.

Phone And Modem   The Phone And Modem properties window allows you to set up your local dialing properties and modem options, as shown in Figure 6.12. You can specify your dialing location, modem properties, and telephone providers.

Power Options   Power plans allow a user to maximize their Windows 7 machine's performance and/or conserve energy. You have the ability to enter your own power restrictions to customize your machine. Power options are important settings when dealing with laptops. Because many users of laptops use batteries, power options allow you to get the most time from their batteries. There is more information later in this chapter about Power management.

Programs And Features   The Programs and Features icon is the old Add/Remove Programs icon in Windows XP. The Programs and Features icon allows you to uninstall, change, or repair programs and features, as shown in Figure 6.13.

Programs And Features also allows you to choose which Windows 7 features you want installed on your machine, as shown in Figure 6.14. Some of the features that you can enable are games, Indexing Services, Telnet Client, and Telnet Server.

FIGURE 6.12
Phone And Modem
properties window

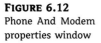

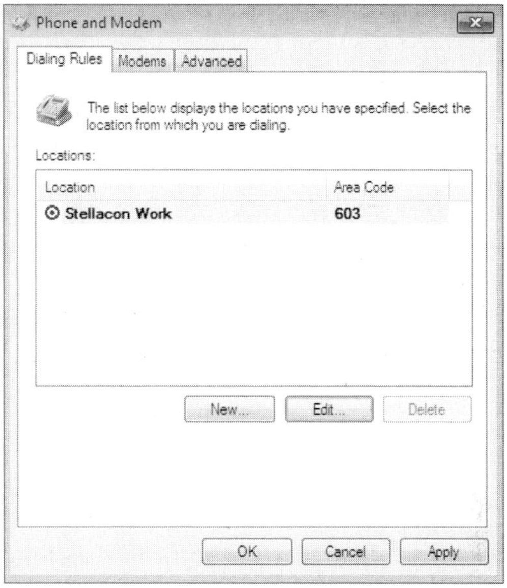

FIGURE 6.13
Programs and
Features Icon

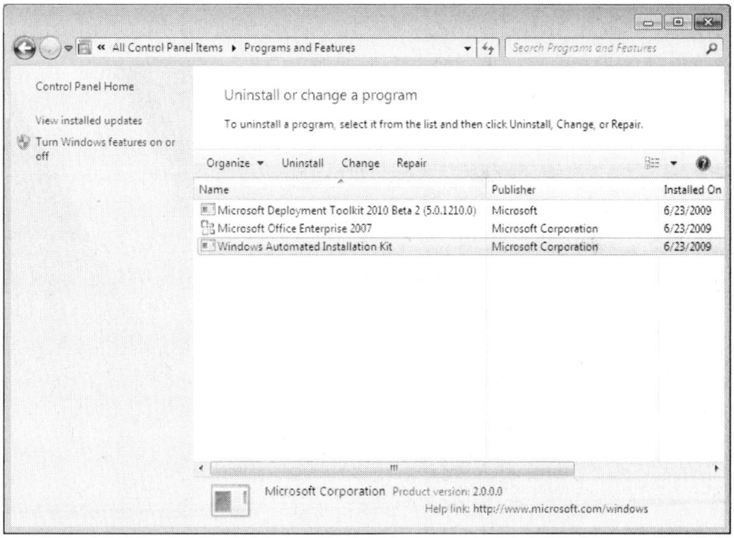

Recovery   The Recovery icon allows a user or administrator to recover the Windows 7 system to a previously captured restore point. System Restore is one of the first recovery options when your Windows 7 system experiences problems. Chapter 15 discusses Recovery in detail.

Region And Language   The Region and Language icon allows you to configure your local regional settings. Chapter 5, "Managing the Desktop," discusses in detail the Region and Language icon.

FIGURE 6.14
Features Icon

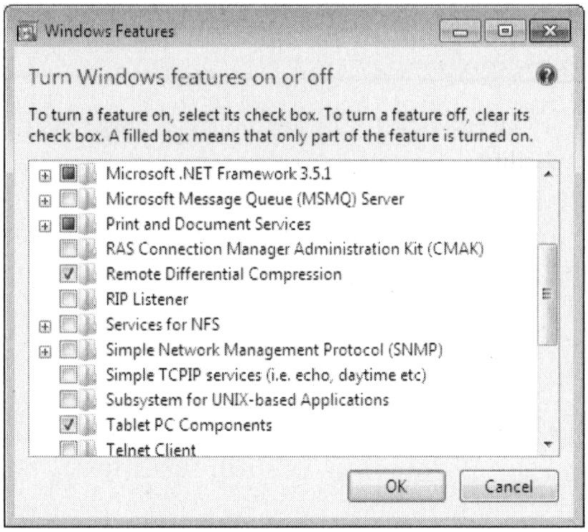

RemoteApp And Desktop Connections   Click the RemoteApp And Desktop Connections icon to access programs and desktops on your network. To connect to these resources (Remote Applications and Desktops), you must have the proper permissions to access these resources.

The RemoteApp and Desktop Connections allows you to connect to either a remote computer or a virtual computer. To create a new connection, use the Set Up A New Connection Wizard included with the RemoteApp And Desktop Connections icon.

Sound   The Sound icon allows you to configure your machine's audio. You can configure output (speakers and audio drivers) and you can configure your input devices (microphones).

Speech Recognition   The Speech Recognition icon allows you to configure your speech properties. Speech Recognition allows you to speak into the computer and that speech is displayed on the system. Many programs like Microsoft Office can type in the words as you speak them into the system. In the Speech Recognition icon, you can complete the following items:

◆ Start Speech Recognition.

◆ Set Up Microphone.

◆ Take Speech Tutorials.

◆ Train Your Computer To Better Understand You.

◆ Open The Speech Reference Card.

Sync Center   The Sync Center allows you to configure synchronization between the Windows 7 machine and a network server. The Sync Center also enables you to see when the synchronization occurred, if the synchronization was successful, and if there were any errors.

System   The System icon is one of the most important icons in Control Panel. The System icon allows you to view which operating system your machine is using, check system resources (Processor, RAM), change the computer name/domain/workgroup, and activate your Windows 7. From the System icon you can also configure the following:

◆ Device Manager

◆ Remote Settings

- ◆ System Protection

- ◆ Advanced Settings

We'll discuss the System utility in detail in the following section, "Using the System Utility."

Taskbar And Start Menu   The Taskbar and Start Menu icon allows you to configure how the Taskbar, Start Menu, and Toolbars will operate. Chapter 5, "Managing the Windows 7 Desktop," discusses in detail the Taskbar and Start Menu icon.

Troubleshooting   The Troubleshooting utility in Control Panel allows you to troubleshoot common Windows 7 problems, as shown in Figure 6.15. You can troubleshoot the following:

- ◆ Programs

- ◆ Hardware And Sound

- ◆ Network And Internet

- ◆ Appearance And Personalization

- ◆ System And Security

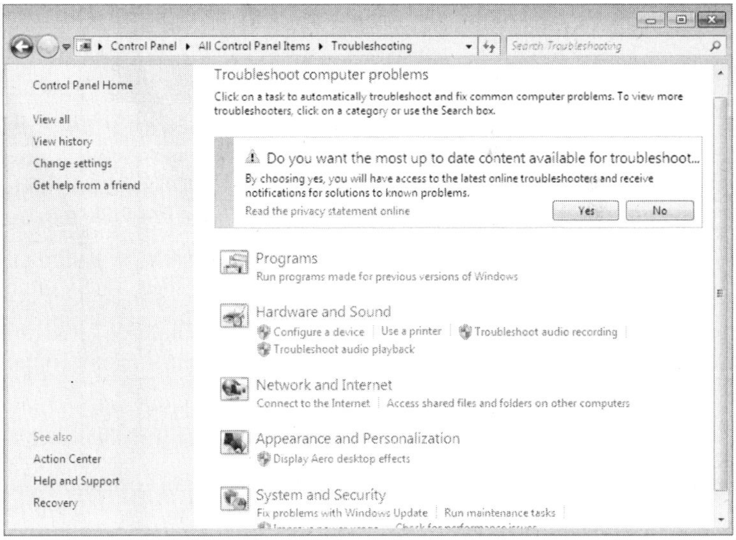

FIGURE 6.15
Troubleshooting options

We discuss troubleshooting common Windows 7 issues in detail in Chapter 15.

User Accounts   The User Accounts icon allows you to create and modify user accounts. In the User Account icon, you can do the following:

- ◆ Change user passwords.

- ◆ Remove passwords.

◆ Change the account picture.

◆ Change the account name.

◆ Change the account type.

◆ Manage accounts.

◆ Change User Account Control settings.

We discuss user accounts in detail in Chapter 8, "Configuring Users and Groups."

Windows CardSpace Windows CardSpace is a new way for you to interact with websites and online services. Windows CardSpace allows you to replace the username and passwords that you currently use with online services. Using Windows CardSpace allows you to do the following:

◆ Review the identity of the site.

◆ Manage your information by using information cards.

◆ Review card information before you send it to a site.

◆ Allow sites to request information from you.

Windows Defender Windows Defender is a built-in Windows 7 Spyware protector. It is included free with the operating system and starts automatically protecting your system after you turn it on. Windows Defender can operate in the following two modes:

Real-Time Protection Real-Time Protection allows Windows Defender to run in the background and protect your system as you are working live on the Internet or network.

Scanning Options The Scanning Options mode allows you to run a system scan at any time to check for Spyware. This mode does not require the Windows Defender to always be running.

Windows Firewall Windows Firewall, as shown in Figure 6.16, helps prevent unauthorized users or hackers from accessing your Windows 7 machine from the Internet or the local network. Chapter 9, "Managing Security," explains in detail the Windows Firewall.

Windows Update Windows Update allows you to configure how the Windows 7 operating system receives updates from Microsoft's website. Chapter 2, "Installing Windows 7," explains Windows Update.

Perform the following steps to install the Telnet client on the Windows 7 operating system:

1. Open the Programs And Features utility by clicking Start ➢ Control Panel ➢ Programs And Features.

2. Click the Turn Windows Features On Or Off link in the upper-left corner.

3. Scroll down the features list and check the Telnet Client check box.

4. Click OK.

FIGURE 6.16
Windows Firewall

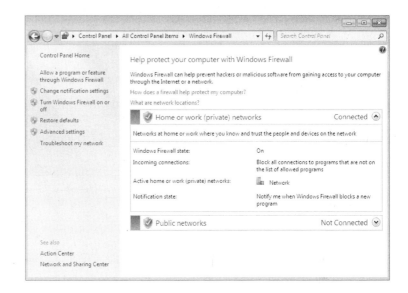

Real World Scenario

USING TELNET

As an IT manager, my job did not just consist of working on Windows machines. It was almost my responsibility to work on routers. This is why it is important to also have an understanding of routers.

When working with most routers, you can use the Telnet client to connect to the router. You can configure the router to operate the way your organization needs.

In the previous section, we talked about the Windows Firewall. We do not recommend that you use the Windows Firewall as your main line of defense against hackers. You should purchase a good router and firewall to complete this task. Knowing how to configure this router using the Telnet client will help you accomplish your networking needs.

It is fine to use the Windows Firewall on all the clients as an added line of defense, but do not make it your main defense.

Perform the following steps to run Performance Information And Tools to receive your baseline performance score:

1. Open the Performance Information And Tools utility by clicking Start ➤ Control Panel ➤ Performance Information And Tools.

2. If the computer has not been rated yet, click the Rate This Computer button. If the computer has a rating, click the Update My Score link.

3. The computer will take a few minutes and test your hardware. After your score appears, close the Performance Information And Tools window.

Now let's take a look at how to work with the Windows Defender. Perform the following steps to configure the Windows Defender:

1. Open Windows Defender by clicking Start ➤ Control Panel ➤ Windows Defender.

2. Click the Check For Updates Now button, as shown in Figure 6.17.

FIGURE 6.17
Windows Defender

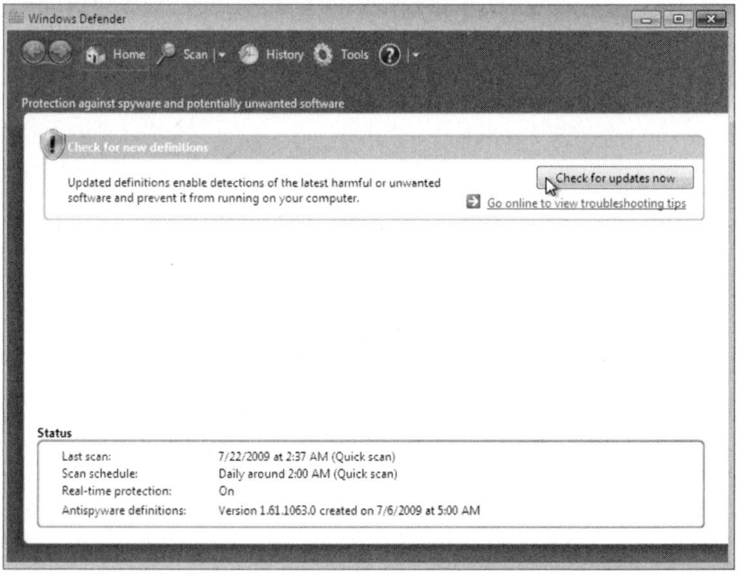

3. The Checking For Updates screen appears. This process may take a few minutes. After the update is complete, a message should state the status of the machine. If no unwanted software is detected, close Windows Defender. If unwanted software is detected, remove the unwanted software and then close Windows Defender.

Now that we have looked at all the icons in Control Panel, let's now look at the System utility in greater detail.

Understanding the System Icon

The System utility in Control Panel is a useful set of utilities and tasks that allow you to configure remote access, system devices, system protection, and the computer name, just to name a few.

Let's look at the tasks that can be configured in Control Panel:

Windows Edition The Windows Edition section shows you which edition of Windows the machine is currently using. The Windows Edition section also shows whether service packs are installed.

System The System section shows information about the system hardware. The System sections also shows:

◆ Rating

◆ Processor

◆ Installed Memory (RAM)

◆ System Type

◆ Pen and Touch

Computer Name/Domain Changes In the Computer Name, Domain, and Workgroup setting section you can change the name of the computer system and also change the workgroup or domain, as shown in Figure 6.18.

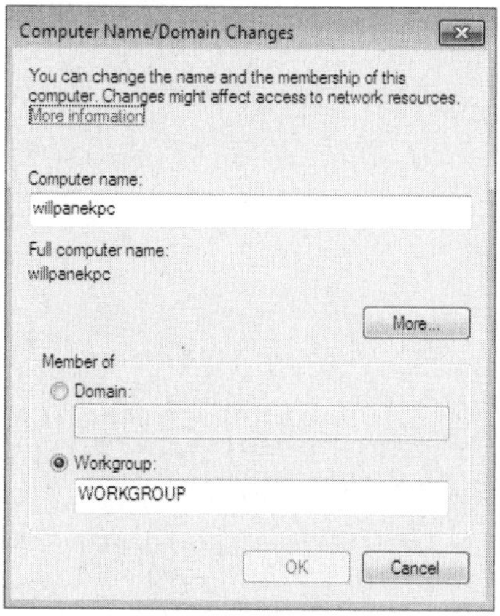

FIGURE 6.18
Change Computer Name,
Domain, or Workgroup

Windows Activation The Windows Activation section allows you to activate your Windows 7 operating system. The Windows Activation section also allows you to change your product key before activating.

Remote Settings The Remote Settings section allows you to set the Remote Assistance and Remote Desktop settings for the Windows 7 system, as shown in Figure 6.19. Windows Remote Assistance allows you to connect to a machine and control the mouse and keyboard while the user is on with you. This option can be enabled or disabled.

Remote Desktop allows you to have your own session on the Windows 7 operating system. While you are logged on to the Windows 7 operating system through Remote Desktop, the user of the machine can't view the session. You can choose from the following three Remote Desktop options:

Don't Allow Connections From This Machine Choosing this option prevents anyone from connecting to this machine through Remote Desktop.

Allow Connections From Computers Running Any Version Of Remote Desktop (Less Secure) This setting allows any computer running Remote Desktop to connect to this Windows 7 machine. These machines do not need to use network-level authentication, and that's makes this connection type less secure.

FIGURE 6.19
Remote Settings Screen

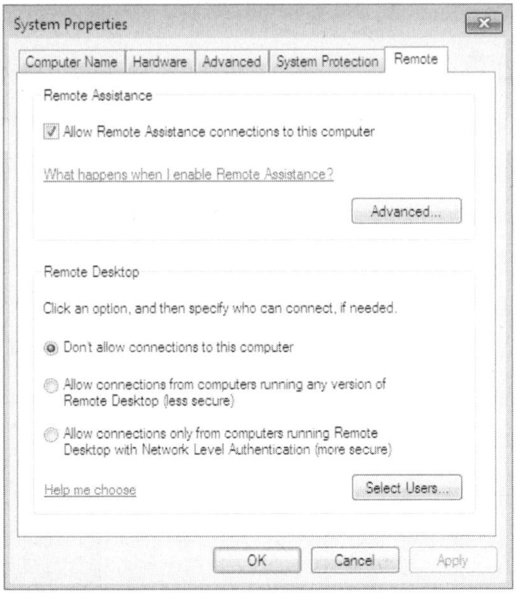

Allow Connections Only From Computers Running Remote Desktop With Network Level Authentication (More Secure) Network-level authentication is a new method used for Remote Desktop (Windows Vista and higher). It allows Remote Desktop users to connect to the Windows 7 operating system securely.

You also have the ability in Remote Desktop to specify which users have access to the Windows 7 machine through the use of Remote Desktop.

System Protection The System Protection section allows you to configure restore points and recoverability for the Windows 7 operating system, as shown in Figure 6.20. You can also manage disk space and manage all of your restore points in the System Protection section.

Advanced System Settings The Advanced System Settings section allows you to set up such items as visual effects, processor scheduling, memory usage, virtual memory, desktop settings, system startup, and recoverability, as shown in Figure 6.21.

There are three main sections within the Advanced System Settings section.

Performance The Performance section allows you to configure the Visual Effects, the virtual memory, processor scheduling, and data execution prevention for the Windows 7 operating system.

The virtual memory is a section of the hard drive that is used by the system and RAM. Think of RAM as a pitcher of water. As the water fills up the pitcher, the pitcher fills. Once full, the water would overflow. The virtual memory is the overflow for RAM. When RAM fills up, the oldest data in the RAM gets put into the virtual memory. This way, the system does not need to look at an entire hard drive for that data. It finds it in the virtual memory.

The Data Execution Prevention section helps protect against damage from viruses and other security threats.

FIGURE 6.20
System Protection
Screen

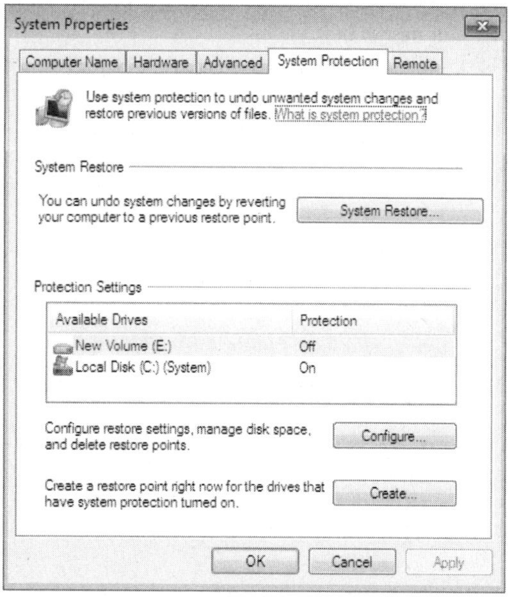

FIGURE 6.21
Advanced System
Settings

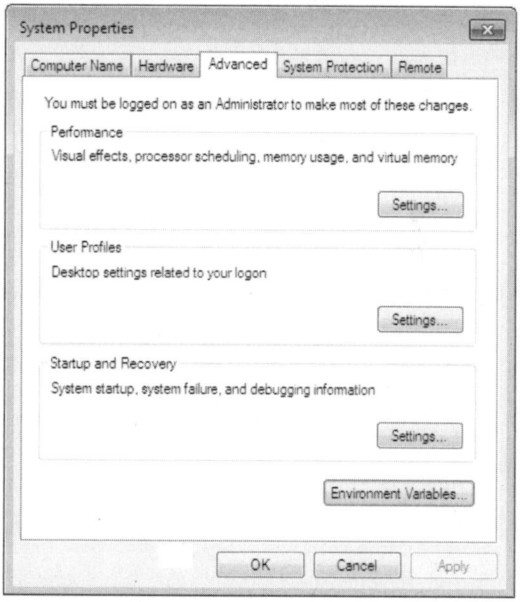

User Profiles   The User Profiles section allows you to copy, delete, or move a user's desktop profile to another location or user account. Chapter 5 discusses user profiles in detail.

Startup And Recovery   The Startup And Recovery section, as shown in Figure 6.22, allows you to configure which operating system will be booted by default (important for dual-booting machines) and what should happen when the system gets a startup error.

FIGURE 6.22
Startup And Recovery
options

FIGURE 6.22
Startup And Recovery
options

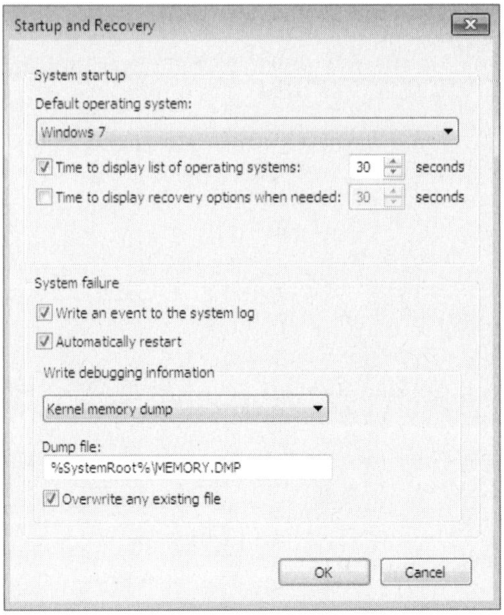

You can also configure Device Manager from the System utility. Chapter 10 discusses Device Manager in detail.

Let's now take a look at configuring some of the options using the System utility.

Perform the following steps to change the computer name:

1. Open the System utility by clicking Start ➢ Control Panel ➢ System.

2. In the resulting window, in the Computer Name, Domain and Workgroup section, click the Change Settings link.

3. Click the Change button in the To Rename This Computer section.

4. In the Computer Name field, enter a new name for your computer. Click OK.

5. A dialog box asking to reboot the machine appears. Click OK.

6. Click Close. Click the Restart Now button.

Now that we have renamed the computer, let's take a look at how to configure performance options.

Perform the following steps to manipulate your system's virtual memory:

1. Open the System utility by clicking Start ➢ Control Panel ➢ System.

2. In the left-hand side, click the Advanced System Settings link.

3. In the Performance section, click the Settings button.

4. When the Performance screen appears, click the Advanced tab.

5. In the Virtual Memory section, click the Change button.

6. Uncheck the check box that states Automatically Manage Paging File Size For All Drives check box.

7. Click the Custom Size radio button.

8. Set the Minimum and Maximum settings to one and half times RAM. For example, if your RAM is 1024 MB, change both settings to 1536 MB.

9. Click the Set button.

10. Click OK. Click OK at the Performance screen.

11. Close the System Properties window.

VIRTUAL MEMORY

Microsoft Windows 7 handles the virtual memory requirements by default, but I would recommend increasing the virtual memory on your machine if hard drive space is available. I use the rule of thumb of one and a half to two times the size of RAM. You want to make sure that the virtual memory is at least the same size as RAM as a minimum.

Now let's see how to set up some recoverability options for your operating system. Perform the following steps to create a restore point:

1. Open the System utility by clicking Start ➢ Control Panel ➢ System.

2. In the left-hand side, click the System Protection link.

3. When the System Protection screen appears, click the Create button in the Create A Restore Point Right Now section.

4. A dialog box asks you to type in a description to help identify which restore point it is. Type in today's date and click the Create button.

5. After it finishes, a dialog box stating that the restore was created successfully appears. Click the Close button.

6. Click the System Restore button.

7. At the System Restore screen, click Next.

   At the "Restore your computer to the state it was in before the selected event" screen, you should see the restore point that you just created.

8. If the restore that you created is there, click Cancel. If the restore is not there, repeat steps 2 through 5.

Another task that we will complete is allowing Remote Desktop connections. Perform the following steps to enable Remote Desktop connections:

1. Open the System utility by clicking Start ➢ Control Panel ➢ System.

2. In the left-hand side, click the Remote Settings link.

3. In the Remote Desktop section, click the Allow Connections From Computers Running Any Version Of Remote Desktop (Less Secure) radio button.

4. Make sure that the Allow Remote Assistance Connections To This Computer check box is selected.

5. Click OK.

6. Close the System Properties window.

Another way to configure options within the Windows 7 operating system is to configure the settings directly in the Registry. In the next section you'll learn how to use the Registry Editor.

Using the Registry Editor

You use the Registry Editor program to edit the Registry. This utility is designed for advanced configuration of the system. Usually, when you make changes to your configuration, you use other utilities, such as those available in Control Panel, which we discussed in the previous section.

ADMINISTERING THE REGISTRY

Only experienced administrators should use the Registry Editor. It is intended for making configuration changes that can be made directly through the Registry only. For example, you might edit the Registry to specify an alternate location for a print spool folder. Improper changes to the Registry can cause the computer to fail to boot. Use the Registry Editor with extreme caution.

Windows 7 uses the REGEDIT program as the primary utility for Registry editing in Windows 7. This program supports full editing of the Registry. To use REGEDIT, select Start and type **REGEDIT** in the Search dialog box.

The Registry is organized in a hierarchical tree format of keys and subkeys that represent logical areas of computer configuration. By default, when you open the Registry Editor, you see five Registry key listings, as shown in Figure 6.23 and described in Table 6.1.

FIGURE 6.23
The Registry Editor window

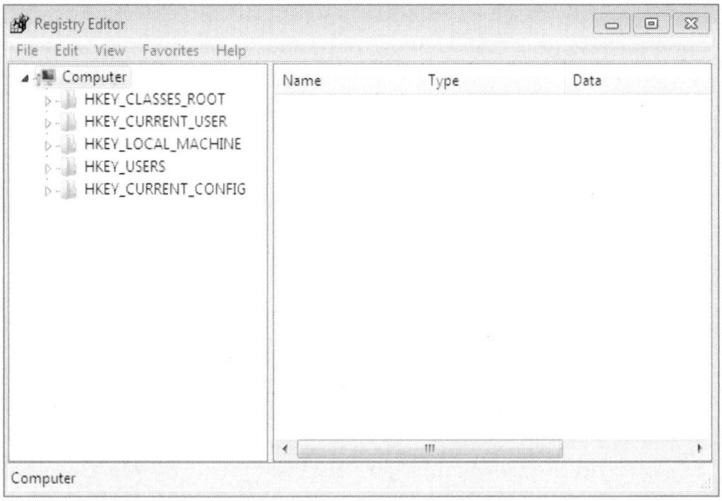

TABLE 6.1:   Registry Keys

REGISTRY KEY	DESCRIPTION
HKEY_CLASSES_ROOT	Configuration information that Windows Explorer uses to properly associate file types with applications.
HKEY_CURRENT_USER	Configuration information for the user who is currently logged on to the computer. This key is a subkey of the HKEY_USERS key.
HKEY_LOCAL_MACHINE	Computer hardware configuration information. This computer configuration is used regardless of the user who is logged on.
HKEY_USERS	Configuration information for all users of the computer.
HKEY_CURRENT_CONFIG	Configuration of the hardware profile that is used during system startup.

 **Real World Scenario**

USING THE REGISTRY EDITORS

As IT Manager we have used Registry Editor many times in our career. One change that I like to make to my servers is the **ShutDownWithoutLogon** entry.

If you start your Registry Editor and do a search on **ShutDownW** (it's the only one, so you do not need to type it out completely), a value of 0 will be shown. We change this value to 1. Now what does this do?

When you log on to a server, by default at the logon screen, the Shutdown button is grayed out. The reason this is set this way by default is that you might not want just anyone shutting down the server. So you want them to log in before shutting down.

If our servers are locked in a secure computer room, we change the Shutdown button so that it is active. We do this so that if we need to use the Last Known Good option to recover the Registry, we can shut down at the logon screen.

Another configuration that you can set is the display devices. Let's take a look at how to configure them.

Managing Display Devices

When we configure display devices, most users think we are speaking of just the monitors. But the display device is attached to a video adapter and that is actually what we are configuring.

A video adapter is the device that outputs the display to your monitor. You install a video adapter in the same way that you install other hardware. If it is a Plug and Play device, all you need to do is shut down your computer, add the video adapter, and turn on your computer. Windows 7 automatically recognizes the new device.

You can configure several options for your video adapters, and if you have multiple monitors with their own video adapters, you can configure multiple-display support. The following sections describe video adapter configuration and how to configure your computer to support multiple monitors.

VIDEO ADAPTER INSTALLATION

You install video adapters as you would any Plug and Play or non–Plug and Play device. We discussed how to install Plug and Play and non–Plug and Play devices earlier in the chapter.

Configuring Video Adapters

The options for video settings are on the Monitor tab of the Display Settings dialog box, as shown in Figure 6.24. To access this dialog box, select Control Panel ➢ Appearance and Personalization ➢ Personalization ➢ Display Settings. Alternatively, you could right-click an empty area on your Desktop, select Personalize from the pop-up menu, and then select Display.

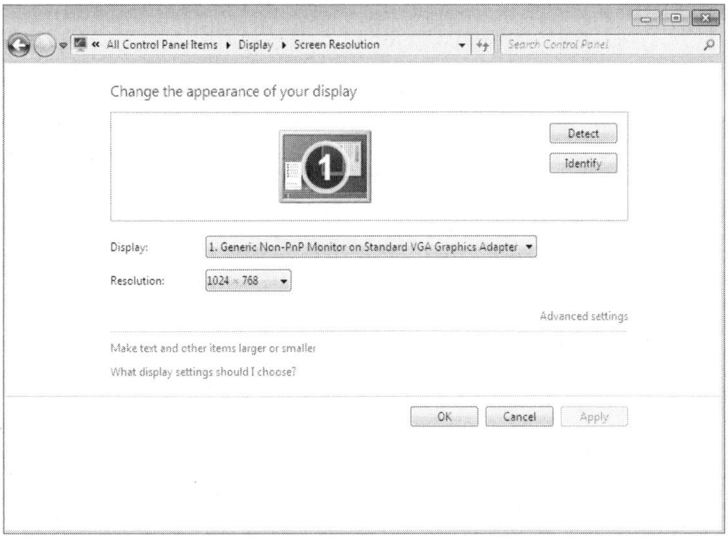

FIGURE 6.24
The Monitor tab of the Display Settings dialog box

Within the Display properties you can configure the resolution, calibrate the colors, change display settings, adjust ClearType text, and set the custom DPI.

To configure advanced settings for your video adapter, click the Advanced button in the lower-right corner of the Display properties. This button opens the Properties dialog box for the display monitor, as shown in Figure 6.25.

You'll see the following four tabs with options for your video adapter and monitor:

Adapter Allows you to view and configure the properties of your video adapter. In the Adapter section, there is a Properties button. The Properties button allows you to configure the graphic adapter properties, including drivers.

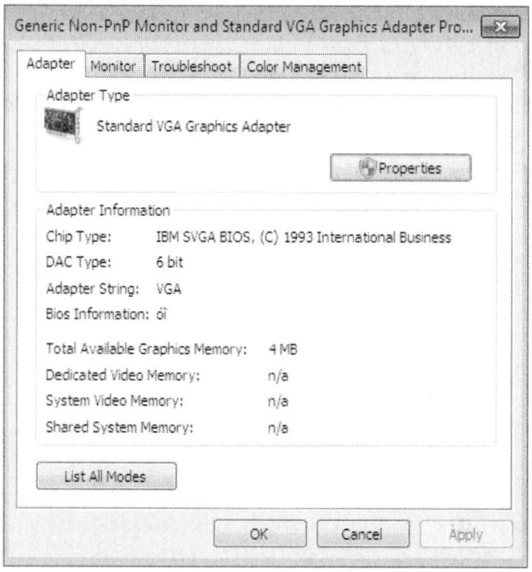

FIGURE 6.25
The Properties dialog box for a display monitor

Monitor   Allows you to view and configure the properties of your monitor, including the refresh frequency (how often the screen is redrawn) and colors shown (High Color 16 or True Color 32).

LOWER REFRESH FREQUENCY

A lower refresh frequency setting can cause your screen to flicker. Setting the refresh frequency too high can damage some hardware.

Troubleshooter   Allows you to configure how Windows 7 uses your graphics hardware. For example, you can configure hardware acceleration settings, as shown in Figure 6.26.

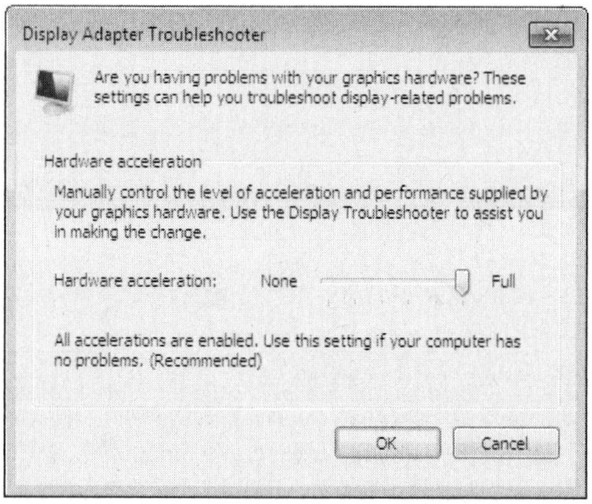

FIGURE 6.26
Display Adapter Troubleshooter

Color Management   Allows you to select color profiles (the colors that are displayed on your monitor), calibrate your display, and change system setting default, as shown in Figure 6.27.

FIGURE 6.27
Color Management,
Advanced tab

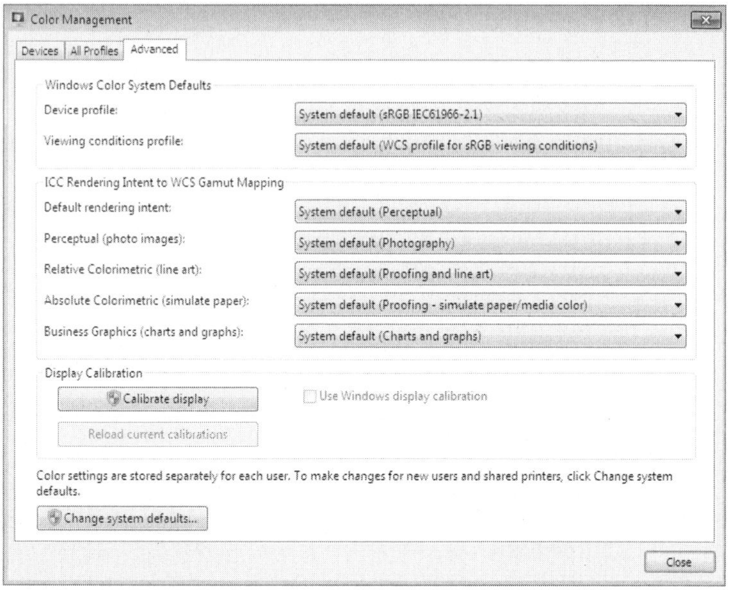

VIDEO ADAPTER SETTINGS

Usually, the video adapter is configured for typical use. Be careful if you change these settings because improper settings may cause your display to be unreadable.

Perform the followings steps for viewing and documenting your video adapter settings:

1. Right-click an empty area on the Desktop, choose Personalize, and select Display Settings.

2. Click the Change Display Settings link.

3. Click the Advanced Settings link.

4. Click the Monitor tab. Make a note of your current settings.

5. Click the Troubleshoot tab. Make a note of your current settings.

6. Click OK to close the monitor Properties dialog box.

7. Click OK to close the Display Settings dialog box.

SETTING THE VIDEO'S RESOLUTION, COLOR SELECTION, AND REFRESH RATE

Depending on your video adapter, you can configure a monitor's resolution, color selection, and refresh rate. Resolution specifies how densely packed the pixels are. The more pixels or dots per inch (dpi), the clearer is the image. The Super Video Graphics Adapter

(SVGA) standard is 1024/768, but many current models can display higher resolution, such as 1600/1200. The color selection specifies how many colors are supported by your video adapter. Refresh rate indicates how many times per second the screen is refreshed (redrawn). To avoid flickering, this rate should be set to at least 72 Hz.

Certain applications require specific configurations based on the graphics used. If you run across an application that requires a specific resolution, color selection, or refresh rate, or if a user makes a request based on personal preferences, you can then easily configure the options that are supported by the video adapter.

Using Multiple-Display Support

Windows 7 allows you to extend your Desktop across multiple monitors. This means you can spread your applications across multiple monitors.

Using multiple monitors are becoming a more common practice in the corporate environment. Many programmers use multiple monitors while coding, and many like to have multiple monitors so that they can work and monitor email at the same time.

SETTING UP MULTIPLE-DISPLAY SUPPORT

To set up multiple-display support, you must have a video adapter installed that supports multiple monitors or a separate video adapter installed for each monitor.

If your computer has the video adapter built into the system board, you should install Windows 7 before you install the second video adapter because Windows 7 will disable the video adapter that is built into the system board if it detects a second video adapter. When you add a second video adapter after Windows 7 is installed, it automatically becomes the primary video adapter.

Perform the followings steps to configure multiple-display support:

1. Turn off your computer and install the new video adapters, if needed. Plug your monitors into the video adapters and turn on your computer. Assuming that the adapters are Plug and Play–compatible, Windows 7 automatically recognizes your new adapters and load the correct drivers.

2. Open the Display Settings dialog box (right-click an empty area on your Desktop, select Personalize, and click Display Settings). You should see an icon for each of the monitors.

3. Click the number of the monitor that will act as your additional display. Then select the Extend the Desktop Onto This Monitor check box. Repeat this step for each additional monitor you want to configure. You can arrange the order in which the displays are arranged by dragging and dropping the monitor icons in the Monitor tab of the Display Settings dialog box.

4. When you finish configuring the monitors, click OK to close the dialog box.

TROUBLESHOOTING MULTIPLE-DISPLAY SUPPORT

If you are having problems with multiple-display support, use the following troubleshooting guidelines:

The Extend The Desktop Onto This Monitor option isn't available. If the Monitor tab of the Display Settings dialog box doesn't give you the option Extend The Desktop Onto This

Monitor, confirm that your secondary adapter is supported for multiple-display support. Confirm that you have the most current drivers (that are Windows 7–compliant and support dual-mode capabilities) loaded. Confirm that Windows 7 is able to detect the secondary video adapter. Try selecting the secondary adapter rather than the primary adapter in the Display Settings dialog box.

No output appears on the secondary display.   Confirm that your secondary adapter is supported for multiple-display support, especially if you are using a built-in motherboard video adapter. Confirm that the correct video driver has been installed for the secondary display. Restart the computer to see if the secondary video driver is initialized. Check the status of the video adapter in Device Manager. Try switching the order of the video adapters in the computer's slots. See if the system will recognize the device as the primary display.

An application is not properly displayed.   Disable the secondary display to determine if the problem is specific to multiple-display support. Run the application on the primary display. If you are running MS-DOS applications, try running the application in full-screen mode. For Windows applications, try running the application in a maximized window.

Now that we have configured Control Panel and the display adapters, let's look at how to configure your power options for mobile computers.

Power Management for Mobile Computer Hardware

Windows 7 includes several features that are particularly useful for laptop computers. For example, through Power Options in Control Panel, you can select a power plan and enable power-management features with Windows 7.

POWER OPTIONS

To see many of these power options, you must be using Windows 7 on a laptop computer. If you are running Windows 7 on a desktop, you will see many but not all of the following features.

Recognizing the Improvements to Power Management

Windows 7 builds upon the power-management features that were introduced with Windows XP with some the following enhancements:

◆ Battery meter, which provides a notification icon in the system tray that details the computer's battery power

◆ Power plans, which are collections of hardware and software settings optimized for a specific function

◆ Sleep power state, which combines the speed of standby with the features of hibernate mode

◆ ReadyDrive, which provides faster booting and resume times when used in conjunction with ReadyDrive-capable hard drives

---

POWER ENHANCEMENTS

These power enhancements were present with Windows Vista but we listed them here because we understand that many users and administrators did not switch to Windows Vista.

After looking at some of the features of Windows 7 Power Management, let's look at managing the various power options.

Managing Power States

In Windows 7, the Advanced Configuration Power Interface (ACPI) specifies the following different levels of power states:

- Fully active PC

- Sleep

- Hibernation

- Complete shutdown of PC

The sleep power state is a new power state introduced with Windows 7 that combines the features of hibernate and standby. When a computer enters the sleep power state, data including window locations and running applications is saved to the hard disk, and that session is available within seconds when the computer wakes. This allows the computer to be put into a power-saving state when not in use but allows quick access to the in-process user session, thus enabling the user to begin working more quickly than if the computer were shut down or put into hibernation.

Hibernation falls short of a complete shutdown of the computer. With hibernation, the computer saves all of your Desktop state as well as any open files. To use the computer again, press the power button. The computer should start more quickly than from a complete shutdown because it does not have to go through the complete startup process. You will have to again log on to the computer. Similar to when the computer is put into Sleep mode, all the documents that were open when the computer went into hibernation are still available. With hibernation you can easily resume work where you left off. You can configure your computer to hibernate through Power Options or by choosing Start, and then clicking the arrow and selecting Hibernate from the drop-down menu. This option appears only if hibernation has been enabled through Power Options.

SLEEP MODE

Unless you want to completely shut down the computer, configuring the computer to enter Sleep mode is typically the best power-saving option. You might need to upgrade your computer's BIOS in order to use advanced power modes, such as Sleep.

The Hibernation mode might not be available on your Windows 7 laptop by default. You must make sure that your firmware can support Hibernation.

If the Hibernation mode does not appear by default and your system can support Hibernation, perform the following steps to enable the Hibernate function:

1. Open an elevated command prompt. (Right-click the command prompt and choose Run As Administrator, as shown in Figure 6.28.)

FIGURE 6.28
Running an elevated
command prompt

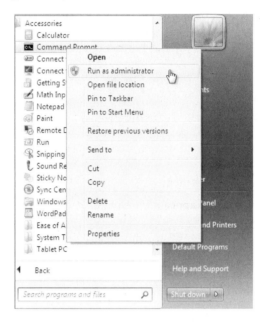

2. Click Yes at the dialog box.

3. At the prompt, type **powercfg -h on** and press Enter. Entering the same command and using the off switch would disable Hibernate on the machine.

4. Close the command prompt.

Now let's look at the different types of power options that we can configure.

Managing Power Options

You configure power options through the Power Options Properties dialog box. To access this dialog box, open Control Panel and click Power Options. The Power Options dialog box provides the ability to manage power plans and to control power options, such as when the display is turned off, when the computer sleeps, and what the power button does.

Configuring Power Plans

Windows 7 includes three configurable power plans: Balanced, Power Saver, and High Performance. Power plans control the trade-off between quick access to an existing computer session and energy savings. In Windows 7, each power plan contains default options that you can customize to meet the needs of various scenarios.

The Balanced power plan, as its name suggests, provides a balance between power savings and performance. By default, this plan is configured to turn off the display after 20 minutes, and to put the computer to sleep after one hour of idle time. These times can be modified as needed. Other power options that can be modified include Wireless Adapter settings and Multimedia settings. You can configure wireless adapters for maximum power saving or maximum performance. By default, the Balanced power plan configures wireless adapters for maximum performance. You can configure the Multimedia settings so that the computer will not be put into Sleep mode when sharing media from the computer. For example, if the computer is acting as a Media Center device, you can configure the computer to remain on by setting the Prevent Idling To Sleep option so that other computers can connect to it and stream media from it even when the computer is not being used for other purposes.

The Power Saver power plan is optimized for power savings. By default, the display is configured to be turned off after 20 minutes of inactivity, and the computer is put into Sleep mode after one hour of inactivity. Additionally, this power plan configures hard disks to be turned off after 20 minutes of inactivity.

The High Performance power plan is configured to provide the maximum performance for portable computers. By default, the computer will never enter Sleep mode, but the display will be turned off after 20 minutes. When this setting is configured, by default, the Multimedia settings are configured with the Allow The Computer To Enter Away Mode option, which allows the computer to enter into a new power state called Away mode. Away mode configures the computer to appear off to users but remain accessible for media sharing. For example, the computer can record television shows when in Away mode.

You can modify the existing power plans to suit your needs by clicking Change Plan Settings, or you can use the preconfigured power plans listed in Table 6.2.

TABLE 6.2:   Windows 7 Power Plans

POWER PLAN	TURN OFF DISPLAY	PUT THE COMPUTER TO SLEEP
Balanced	After 20 minutes	1 hour
Power Saver	After 20 minutes	1 hour
High Performance	After 20 minutes	Never

After you decide which power plan is going to be used, you might want to configure some of the advanced power options. In the next section we'll discuss the various power options.

Configuring Advanced Power Settings

Each power plan contains advanced settings that can be configured, such as when the hard disks will be turned off and whether a password is required on wakeup. To configure these advanced settings, open Control Panel, click Power Options, and select the power plan you want to use. Then click Change Advanced Power Settings to open the Advanced Settings tab of the Power Options dialog box, as shown in Figure 6.29.

You can then modify the settings as desired or restore the plan defaults. For example, one option that you might want to change if you are using a mobile computer is the Power Buttons And Lid option, which configures what happens when you press the power button or close the lid of the mobile computer. When either of these actions occurs, the computer can be configured to do nothing, shut down, go into Sleep mode, or go into Hibernate mode.

FIGURE 6.29
Advanced power settings

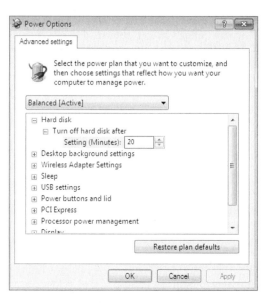

Configuring Hibernation

Although Sleep is the preferred power-saving mode in Windows 7, Hibernation mode is still available for use. Hibernation for a computer means that anything stored in memory is also stored on your hard disk. This ensures that when your computer is shut down, you do not lose any of the information that is stored in memory. When you take your computer out of hibernation, it returns to its previous state.

To configure your computer to hibernate, access the Advanced Settings tab of the Power Options dialog box. The Hibernate option appears under the Sleep option.

Perform the following steps to configure a power plan for your computer. If the Hibernate option is not present, perform the steps in the previous section to enable hibernation.

1. Select Start ➢ Control Panel and click the Power Options icon.

2. Select a power plan to modify from the Preferred Plans list and click Change Plan Settings.

3. Configure the power plan options for your computer based on your personal preferences. Click Change Advanced Power Settings to modify advanced power settings. When all changes are made, click Save Changes.

4. Close Control Panel.

One advantage when you use a laptop on the battery is that you can see how much time you have left until the battery dies. Let's take a look at the battery meter.

Managing Power Consumption Using the Battery Meter

Windows 7 includes a battery meter that you can use to monitor the battery power consumption on your computer. The battery meter also provides notification on what power plan is being used.

The battery meter appears in the notification area of the Windows Taskbar and indicates the status of the battery, including the percentage of battery charge. As the battery charge gets lower, the battery meter provides a visual indication of the amount of charge left. For example, when the battery charge reaches the low-battery level, a red circle with a white X is displayed.

The battery meter also provides a quick method for changing the power plan in use on the computer. By clicking the battery meter icon, you can select between the three preferred power plans available with Windows 7.

Using Windows ReadyBoost and Windows 7

With Windows Vista, Microsoft had introduced several new technologies to help boost operating system performance. Windows ReadyBoost is a new technology introduced with Windows Vista but is also available in Windows 7.

Windows ReadyBoost allows for the use of multiple nonvolatile flash memory devices as an additional memory cache. When the physical memory devices become full on a computer with Windows ReadyBoost configured, data is written to the flash device instead of to the hard drive. This improves performance because data can be read more quickly from the flash drive than from the hard drive.

When a compatible device is installed on a Windows 7 computer, a ReadyBoost tab is displayed on the device's properties page that can be used to configure Windows ReadyBoost.

To use a flash memory device with Windows ReadyBoost, the device must meet the following specifications:

◆ The device must have a storage capacity of at least 256 MB.

◆ The device must support USB 2.0.

◆ The device must support a throughput of 2.5 MB/sec for 4 K random reads and 1.75 MB/sec for 512 K random writes.

Configuring Advanced Settings

ReadyDrive is also a technology included with Windows 7 that you can use to speed up the boot process, resume from a hibernation state faster, and conserve battery power for mobile computers. ReadyDrive relies on new hybrid hard disks, which use flash memory technology in conjunction with mechanical hard disk technology.

When you use ReadyDrive, data is written to flash memory instead of to the mechanical hard disk. This saves battery power because the mechanical hard disk does not need to perform as many read/write actions. Additionally, read/write times with flash memory is quicker than with traditional hard disk media, so resuming from hibernation occurs faster.

Configuring the power options on a laptop can help save energy and extend battery life. Another important item to take into account when configuring Windows 7 is how we are managing our Windows services.

Managing Windows 7 Services

A service is a program, routine, or process that performs a specific function within the Windows 7 operating system. You can manage services through the Services window, as shown in Figure 6.30, which can be accessed in a variety of ways. If you go through the Computer Management utility, right-click Computer, select Manage, expand Services And Applications, and then expand Services. You can also go through Administrative Tools or set up Services as a Microsoft Management Console (MMC) snap-in.

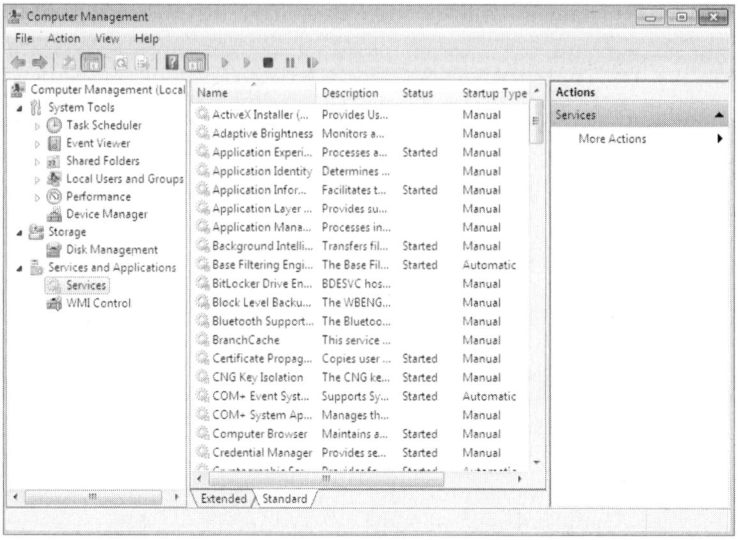

FIGURE 6.30
The Services window

For each service, the Services window lists the name, a short description, the status, the startup type, and the logon account that is used to start the service. To configure the properties of a service, double-click it to open its Properties dialog box, as shown in Figure 6.31. This dialog box contains the following four tabs of options for services: General, Log On, Recovery, and Dependencies.

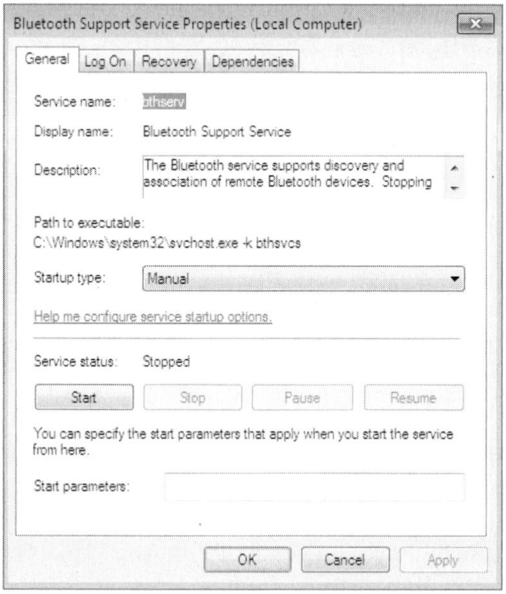

FIGURE 6.31
The Properties dialog
box for a service

General Allows you to view and configure the following options:

◆ The service display name

◆ Display name

◆ A description of the service

◆ The path to the service executable

◆ The startup type, which can be Automatic, Manual, or Disabled

◆ The current service status

◆ Start parameters that can be applied when the service is started

In addition, the buttons across the lower part of the dialog box allow you change the service status to start, stop, pause, or resume the service.

Log On The Log On tab, as shown in Figure 6.32, allows you to configure the logon account that is used to start the service. Choose the local system account or specify another logon account.

FIGURE 6.32
The Log On tab of a service's Properties dialog box

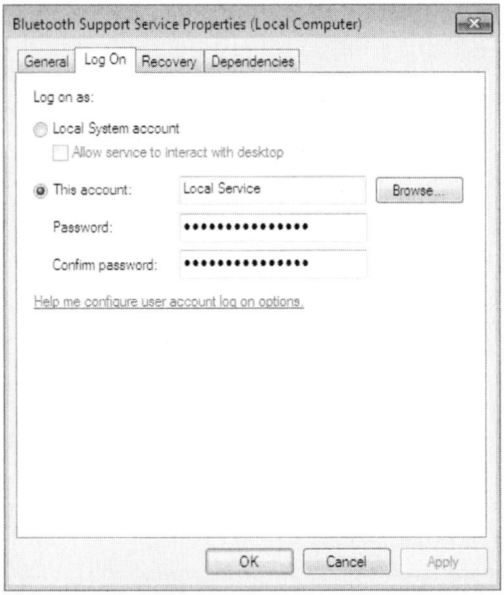

Recovery The Recovery tab, as shown in Figure 6.33, allows you to designate what action will be taken if the service fails to load. For the first, second, and subsequent failures, you can select from the following actions:

◆ Take No Action

◆ Restart The Service

◆   Run A Program

◆   Restart The Computer

If you choose Run A Program, specify it along with any command-line parameters. If you choose Restart The Computer, you can configure a message that will be sent to users who are connected to the computer before it is restarted. You can also specify how long until a machine is restarted if an error occurs.

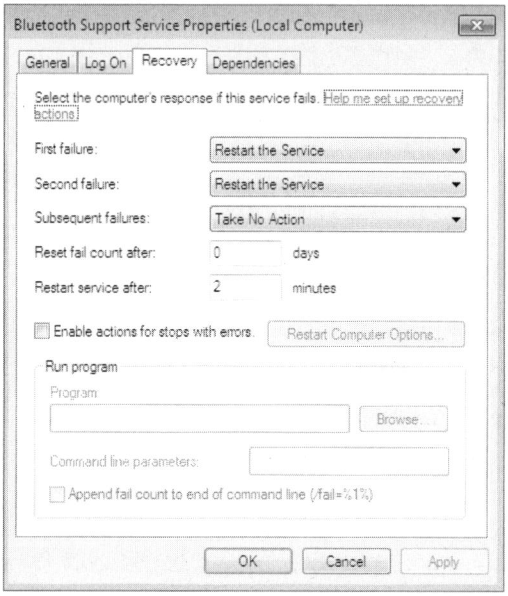

FIGURE 6.33
The Recovery tab of a service's Properties dialog box

Dependencies   The Dependencies tab, shown in Figure 6.34, lists any services that must be running in order for the specified service to start. If a service fails to start, you can use this information to examine the dependencies and then make sure each one is running. In the bottom panel, you can verify whether any other services depend on this service before you decide to stop it.

Perform the following steps to configure services in the Windows 7 operating system:

1. Start Computer Management by clicking Start and then right-clicking Computer. Choose Manage from the context menu.

2. In the Computer Management MMC, expand the Services And Applications section.

3. Click the Services link.

4. Scroll down the list and double-click Remote Desktop Configuration.

5. Under the Startup Type, choose Automatic.

6. Under the Logon tab, click the This Account radio button.

7. Click the Browse button and choose the local administrator account, as shown in Figure 6.35. Click OK.

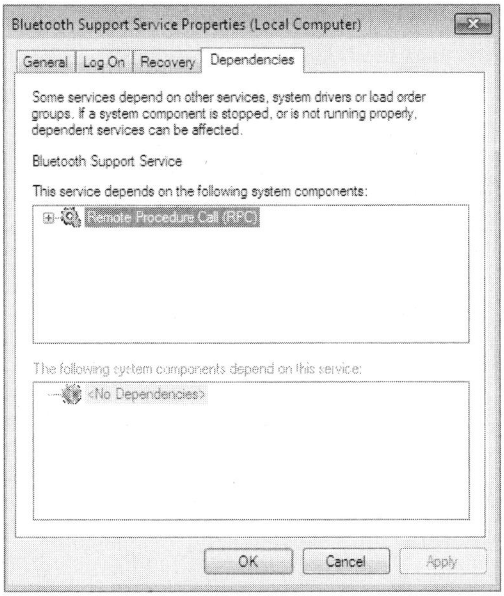

FIGURE 6.34
The Dependencies tab of a service's Properties dialog box

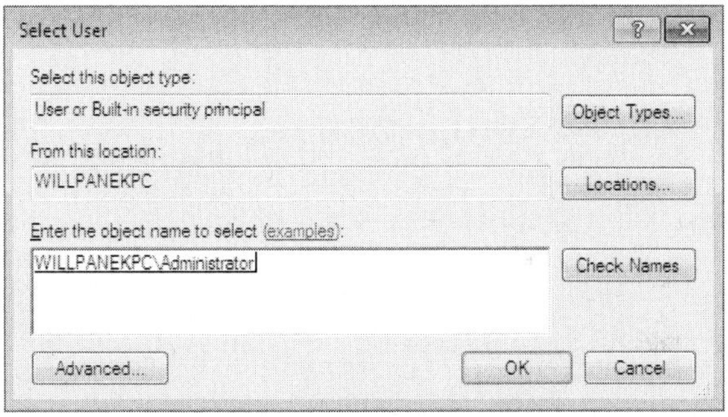

FIGURE 6.35
Select User screen

8. In the Password boxes, type and verify the Administrator password.

9. In the Recovery tab, make sure the following settings are configured, as shown in Table 6.3.

TABLE 6.3: Recovery Tab Options

ACTION	RESPONSE
First Failure	Restart The Service
Second Failure	Restart The Service
Subsequent Failures	Take No Action
Reset Fail Count After	1 Day
Restart Service After	10 Minutes

10. Click OK.

11. Close the Computer Management MMC.

 **Real World Scenario**

SERVICES

As IT professionals, we have had to troubleshoot many problems while doing our job. One of the very first things we always check when encountering an error with an application is the services for that application. Many times you need to just set the service from Manual to Automatic to solve the problem.

If the service is set to Automatic and it is still not starting properly, check the Dependencies tab. The Dependencies tab shows you whether all the other services that are required to start this service are configured and running properly.

Services are just another troubleshooting and configuring tool that is part of your arsenal of troubleshooting techniques. Properly working services allow your Windows 7 operating system to work properly.

The Bottom Line

Understand Control Panel. Windows 7 uses the Registry when the operating system starts. The Registry is the database used by the operating system to store configuration information. Control Panel is a set of GUI utilities that allow you to configure Registry settings without using a Registry editor.

> **Master It** You are the administrator for a large computer company. One of your salespeople calls and asks you if they can remove an old application from their machine. How would you instruct them to remove the old application properly from the Windows 7 machine?

Use the System utility. The System icon is one of the most important icons in Control Panel. The System icon allows you to view which operating system your machine is using; check system resources (processor, RAM); change the computer name, domain, or workgroup; and activate your Windows 7. From the System icon you can also configure the Device Manager, Remote Settings, System Protection, and Advanced settings.

> **Master It** You are the system administrator for your organization and you have a salesperson who has been trying to activate his legal company version of Windows 7. He gets an error message stating that the product key is invalid. What can you do to help activate the Windows 7 machine?

Configure mobile computers. Windows 7 includes several features that are useful for laptop computers. One of the best features for laptops is configuring the power options. Power options allow you to select a power plan and enable power-management features with Windows 7. By selecting the proper power plan, users can increase the life of their battery.

Master It You are the administrator for a small company that uses only laptops for their end users. You need to configure the laptops to extend the life of the battery. How would you configure the power options on their laptops?

Configure services. A service is a program, routine, or process that performs a specific function within the Windows 7 operating system. Most applications and features use services to help make that application run properly.

Master It You are the system administrator for your organization and you have a salesperson who needs a service to start every time she turns on the Windows 7 system. How would you configure the service so that it starts when the salesperson starts her machine?

Chapter 7

Using Remote Assistance and Remote Desktop

End-user support for most IT departments is a major concern and a time-consuming endeavor. As administrators, anything we can do to provide an efficient solution to user problems is a major benefit. Basic telephone or chat support works in many cases, but what if you could see what the end users see, or even interface with them...Enter Remote Assistance and Remote Desktop. If you've been using these features with Windows XP and Vista, you're really going to be pleased with Windows 7.

Remote Assistance in Windows Vista provided many enhancements over previous versions, including improvements in security, performance, and usability. Windows 7 goes even further by adding Easy Connect, which makes it even easier for novice users to request help from expert users. Group Policy support has been enhanced as well. There's also command-line functionality (meaning we can add scripting), bandwidth optimization, logging, and even more.

Remote Desktop is a tool that allows you to take control of a remote computer's keyboard, video, and mouse. This tool does not require someone collaborating with you on the remote computer. Remote Desktop is used to access a remote machine's applications, troubleshoot issues, and meet end-user needs when you want complete control of the remote machine.

In this chapter, we'll explain some of the new features and benefits to using Remote Assistance and Remote Desktop in Windows 7. We'll describe how to support end users, and implement Group Policy and scripting. We'll explain the integration of the previous operating system Remote Assistance and Remote Desktop with Windows 7 as well as highlight the Windows 7 to Windows 7 functionality.

In this chapter, you'll learn how to:

◆ Assist novice users with Windows 7

◆ Provide help from Windows 7 to older operating systems

◆ Access a machine from a remote location

◆ Script a session for automated connection

Using Remote Assistance

Windows 7's Remote Assistance provides a method for inviting help by instant message, email, a file, or an Easy Connect option. To use Remote Assistance, the computer requesting help and the computer providing help must have Remote Assistance capabilities, and both computers must have network connectivity.

Remote Assistance is designed to have an expert user provide assistance to a novice user. The terms *expert* and *novice* describe the assistor (expert) and the user needing help (novice). When you assist a novice user, you can use the text-based chat built into Remote Assistance. You can also take control of a novice user's desktop (with the user's permission, of course). Common examples of when you would use Remote Assistance include the following:

◆ Diagnosing problems that are difficult to explain or reproduce. Remote Assistance can allow you to remotely view the computer and the novice user can show you an error or problem.

◆ Guiding a novice user to perform a complex set of instructions. You can also take control of the computer and complete the tasks if necessary.

New and Updated Features in Remote Assistance

The Windows 7 Remote Assistance feature builds on the implementations in previous versions of Windows. Multiple sessions over a shared network are now reliable using the connectivity improvement of network address translation (NAT) traversal using IPv6 and Teredo tunneling. (We'll cover the specifics of TCP/IP [IPv4 and IPv6] in Chapter 11, "Configuring Network Connectivity.") A stand-alone executable (`msra.exe`) accepts several options, thus making script options available as well. Performance enhancements that optimize bandwidth, shorten connect time, and improve startup times have also been added. Group Policy settings have been added for improved manageability. The new Easy Connect feature for soliciting Remote Assistance will provide one more level of simplicity for the end users — always a huge benefit to any IT department.

Using Easy Connect

The Easy Connect method for getting Remote Assistance is new for Windows 7. Easy Connect uses the Peer Name Resolution Protocol (PNRP) to set up direct peer-to-peer transfer using a central machine in the Internet to establish the connection. PNRP uses IPv6 and Teredo tunneling to register a machine as globally unique. You're not using IPv6? You are with PNRP; Windows 7 (as well as Vista and Server 2008) has IPv6 turned on natively as well as the currently used standard of IPv4. You will, however, only be able to use Easy Connect with Windows 7 and beyond. To establish a Remote Assistance session with a user using Easy Connect, open the Windows Remote Assistance screen by selecting Start ➤ All Programs ➤ Maintenance ➤ Windows Remote Assistance, as shown in Figure 7.1.

You can also access the Remote Assistance feature by clicking the Start button and choosing Help And Support, then selecting More Support Options in the lower left of the Windows Help And Support window. Some users might be accustomed to opening the Windows Help And Support window in previous operating system versions. The window looks different, but it's still there. You can also launch the Windows Remote Assistance screen by typing **msra** in the Start menu's search box, as shown in Figure 7.2.

Whichever way you and the novice user launch the feature, the Windows Remote Assistance screen opens. To get started using Easy Connect, the novice user should select Invite Someone

You Trust To Help You. The initial Remote Assistance window where the novice user initiates an invitation is shown in Figure 7.3.

FIGURE 7.1
Accessing Remote
Assistance via the Start
menu

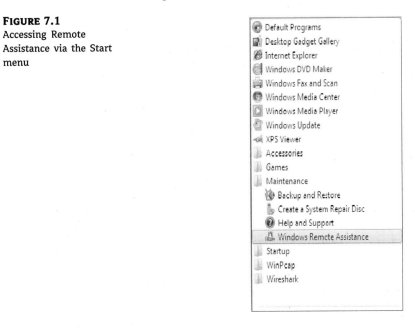

FIGURE 7.2
Accessing Remote
Assistance via the search
box

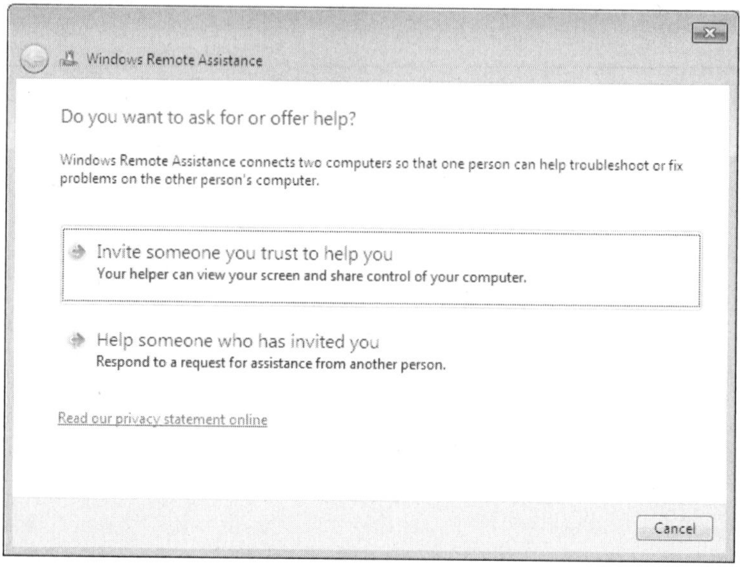

FIGURE 7.3
The Remote Assistance
initial screen

ALLOWING REMOTE ASSISTANCE

The Windows 7 machine is configured by default to allow Remote Assistance. If this feature has been disabled in the configuration, an error will be generated at this point and you must enable Remote Assistance. To enable a remote computer to allow Remote Desktop access, select Start ➤ Control Panel ➤ System And Security ➤ System. Click Remote Settings in the left pane. Select the "Allow Remote Assistance connection to this computer" check box and click OK. This creates an exception in the Windows Firewall to allow Remote Assistance.

The Windows Remote Assistance screen, as shown in Figure 7.4, asks How Do You Want To Invite Your Trusted Helper? and offers the user the option Use Easy Connect.

REMOTE ASSISTANCE INVITATION METHODS

We are using the Easy Connect request method here. The Remote Assistance session is the same regardless of which request method is used. The options Save This Invitation As A File and Use E-mail to Send An Invitation are covered later in this chapter in the section, "Requesting an Invitation as a File."

One nice feature of Easy Connect is that if the novice user has already established an Easy Connect session previously with an expert user, the screen after selecting Use Easy Connect offers the novice the ability to connect to the same expert user. The novice user can also choose to invite someone new and/or delete the old contact if necessary, as shown in Figure 7.5. The expert user has the same option after choosing Use Easy Connect from the machine used in a previous Easy Connect session.

FIGURE 7.4
The Remote Assistance
invite screen

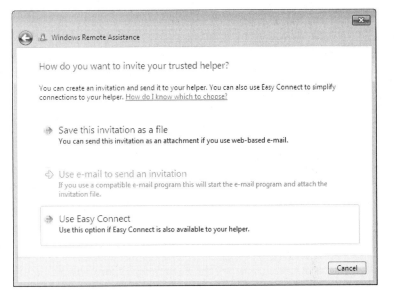

FIGURE 7.5
Remote Assistance
makes it easy to
reconnect.

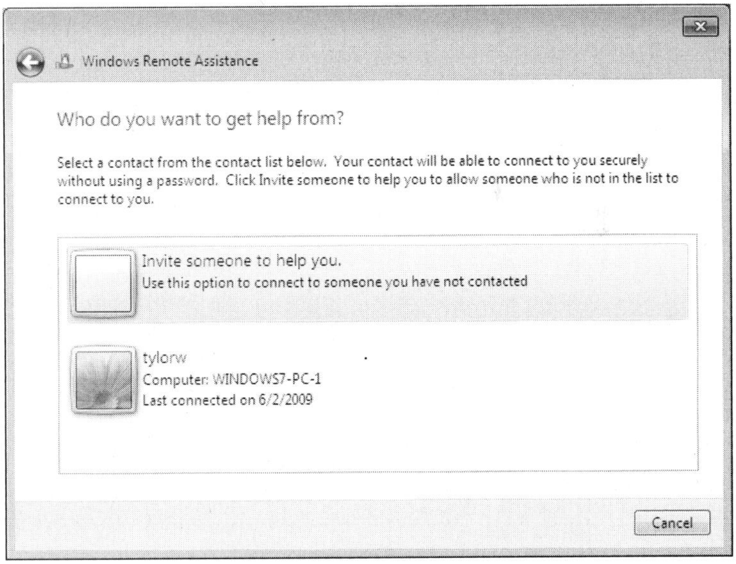

After the novice user selects the Use Easy Connect option, Windows 7 verifies network connectivity briefly. This is the point at which the PNRP actions take place and the novice user's information is added to a *cloud* in the Internet space. The cloud is the group of machines holding little pieces of information (the identifiers of users needing connectivity), set up in a peer-to-peer sharing environment. PNRP uses this distributed infrastructure for its peer-to-peer name resolution. The novice user's contact information is entered in the PNRP cloud; then an associated password is created, as shown in Figure 7.6, and displayed to the novice user.

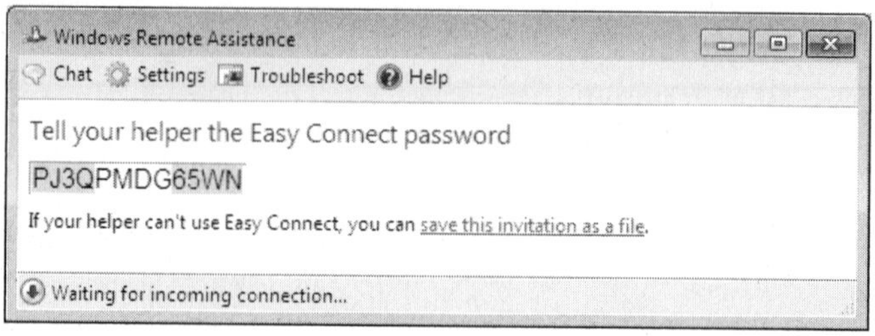

FIGURE 7.6
The Remote Assistance password is displayed to the user.

At this point, the novice user relays the password to you (the expert user) by text message, telephone, or any convenient conversation method. The novice will simply have to wait for you to initiate your part; they will still have to accept the connection after you start the Remote Assistance session.

You must start a Remote Assistance session in much the same way the novice did, but you instead choose Help Someone Who Has Invited You from the Windows Remote Assistance screen.

As shown in Figure 7.7, a dialog box prompts you to enter the password given by the novice user who is initiating the Remote Assistance session.

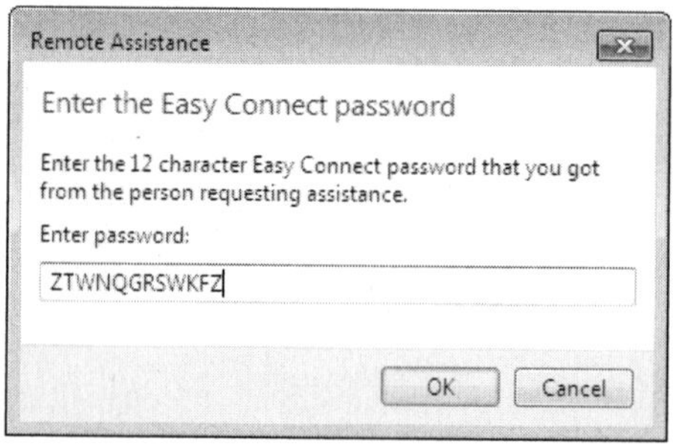

FIGURE 7.7
Enter the password supplied by the novice user who is initiating the Remote Assistance session.

After a few moments of querying the PNRP cloud and finding the connection path back to the novice user, Remote Assistance presents the novice user with a confirmation box, as shown in Figure 7.8, that verifies that they want to allow help from you.

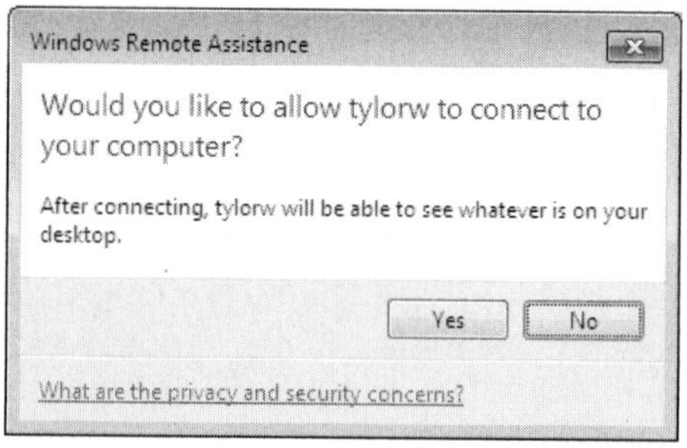

FIGURE 7.8
This screen asks the novice user to verify that they want to allow help from the expert user.

Once the novice user clicks Yes, they will have a control bar on their screen that indicates the Remote Assistance session is active, as shown in Figure 7.9. From this control bar the novice can initiate a chat session with you, the expert user, and modify general session settings (bandwidth, logging, contact information exchange, and sharing control) if necessary to improve the performance of the Remote Assistance session.

FIGURE 7.9
The Remote Assistance control bar for the novice user

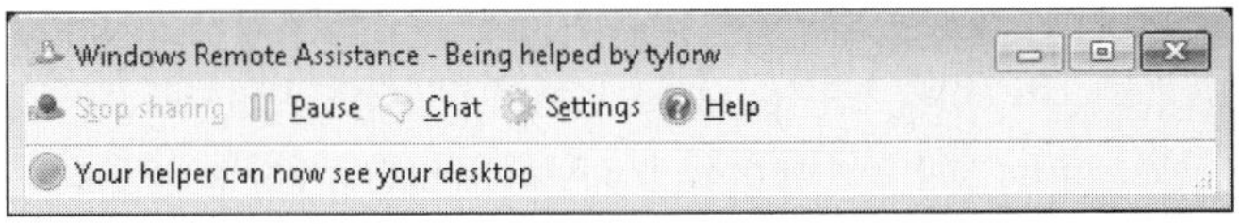

You are shown the novice user's desktop within a separate Remote Assistance window. You'll also have general configuration setting capabilities as well as an option to request control of the novice user's desktop, as shown in Figure 7.10. The novice user will, of course, be allowed to accept or reject your request.

FIGURE 7.10
The Remote Assistance control bar for the expert user

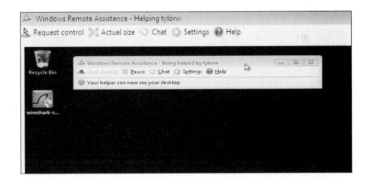

You and the novice user can now have an interactive session in which you can provide the necessary assistance. This method of help takes out the "Can you tell me what you see on your screen?" issues between two users. Remember, only Windows 7 and later versions of Windows can connect using this feature.

Requesting an Invitation as a File

Requesting Remote Assistance from Windows7 and other operating systems can also be initiated by using an invitation as a file. As the expert user, you must ask the novice user to send a file to you. The novice user also has to provide the password for the connection to you.

REMOTE ASSISTANCE SETUP

Most procedures presented in this section require two machines (real or virtual) to be connected to provide Remote Assistance novice and Remote Assistance expert functionality.

In the following example, a novice user generates an invitation file to be sent to you to initiate a Remote Assistance session. You then accept the invitation, and the novice user allows you to complete the connection.

Perform the following steps to use an invitation by file:

1. Ask the novice user to generate an invitation file and password by selecting Start ➢ All Programs ➢ Maintenance ➢ Windows Remote Assistance.

2. Instruct the novice user to choose Invite Someone You Trust To Help You.

3. Instruct the novice user to choose Save This Invitation To A File.

4. The novice user is given the option to save the invitation file. The default location is Libraries/Documents with a filename of Invitation.msrcIncident. Ask the novice user to accept the default location by clicking the Save button, as shown in Figure 7.11.

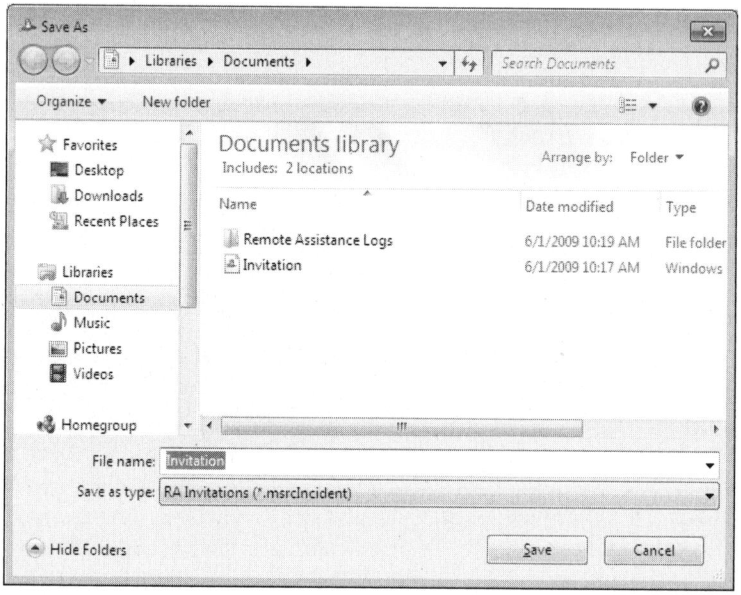

FIGURE 7.11
Saving the Remote Assistance invitation as a file

5. The novice user sees the Windows Remote Assistance window, as shown in Figure 7.12, with a password and the instructions Give Your Helper The Invitation File And Password. The invitation file must now be delivered to you, and you must also be given the password to complete the Remote Assistance connection.

FIGURE 7.12
The Remote Assistance Password window

6. Save the invitation file received from the novice user to the machine being used for Remote Assistance. You can use the default location or Documents/Libraries. You should also have the password that the novice user generated.

7. Continue the establishment of the Remote Assistance session by selecting Start ➢ All Programs ➢ Maintenance ➢ Windows Remote Assistance.

8. Choose Help Someone Who Has Invited You.

9. Select Use An Invitation File.

10. Select the saved invitation file and choose Open.

11. You'll be presented with a Remote Assistance password dialog box. Enter the password supplied by the novice user. Your machine now establishes a connection to that of the novice user. Once the novice user accepts the connection, the Remote Assistance session continues.

Administrators, desktop support personnel, knowledgeable users in the working environment, as well as folks in their home environment are often asked a "quick question" and can use the Remote Assistance feature to work with users to provide answers.

🌐 Real World Scenario

HELPING NOVICE USERS WITHOUT BEING THERE

Many times it is far easier to guide a novice user through the process of fixing a problem by looking at their machine. But most of the time it's extremely inconvenient to travel to the user's machine, and therefore Remote Assistance is a valuable tool.

Recently, one of the authors was traveling to a customer site when he received a telephone call from his cousin. When the cousin had opened his Internet browser, it had opened to a page he wasn't comfortable with. Someone had changed the home page as a joke and the cousin didn't know how to change it back. The author explained to his cousin how to use Help And Support on his Windows XP machine to email him a Remote Assistance invitation. The author then pulled into a local shop providing Internet access, and using web-based email, opened the invitation file, provided the password, and walked his cousin through the process of changing his home page back. This potentially saved lots of time and anxiety for both of them.

Requesting an Invitation as Email

Requesting Remote Assistance from Windows 7 and other operating systems can also be initiated by using an invitation sent by the default email program on the novice user's machine. You must instruct the novice user to email the invitation to you as well as provide the password for the connection.

Perform the following steps to have a novice user create an email invitation and send it to you to request Remote Assistance:

1. Ask the user needing assistance to generate an email invitation file and password by selecting Start ➢ All Programs ➢ Maintenance ➢ Windows Remote Assistance.

2. Ask the novice user to choose Invite Someone You Trust To Help You.

3. Ask the novice user to choose Use E-mail To Send An Invitation As A File. If the user does not have a default email program setup, this option will be unavailable.

4. The novice user's default email application launches with the invitation file as an attachment and a generic message that requests help (see Figure 7.13). Ask the novice user to enter your email address and then send the email.

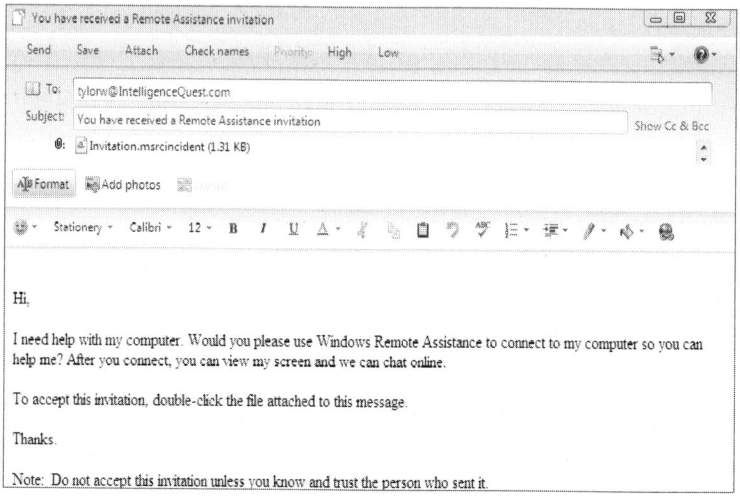

FIGURE 7.13
An email invitation for
Remote Assistance

5. When the novice user sees the Windows Remote Assistance window with a password and the instructions Tell Your Helper The Connection Password, ask the user to tell you the password.

6. When you receive the email, open the attachment to initiate the connection to the novice user. You should also have the password that the novice user generated.

7. You'll be presented with a Remote Assistance password dialog box. Enter the password supplied by the novice user. Your machine establishes a connection to that of the novice user. Once the novice user accepts the connection, the Remote Assistance session continues.

LIVE MESSENGER REMOTE ASSISTANCE

Remote Assistance can also be initiated by using Windows Live Messenger. Although you can share an invitation file through Live Messenger, a menu item is available (as an Action item from the chat window) that allows a simplified Remote Assistance invitation offer. This could be a useful function for users who participate in the Windows Live Messenger experience.

Using Command-Line Remote Assistance

Windows Remote Assistance is also available from the command line using the Microsoft Remote Assistance executable (`msra.exe`) in both Windows 7 and Vista. This feature allows you to launch any of the functions of Remote Assistance from the command line. It also allows you to set up a scripted environment for novice users. Type **msra.exe** without any switches at the command line to open the initial Windows Remote Assistance screen shown in Figure 7.14.

FIGURE 7.14
Accessing the initial
Windows Remote
Assistance screen via
the command line

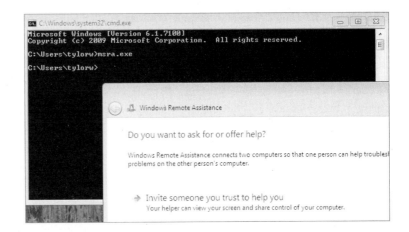

You can also incorporate Remote Assistance in Group Policy in an enterprise environment by configuring yourself as a helper for users in the enterprise (by domain or organizational unit). Once configured as a helper, you can initiate a Remote Assistance session by issuing the command **msra/offerra**. This brings up the Who Do You Want to Help? Remote Assistance screen, as shown in Figure 7.15. You can also include the novice user's IP address or computer name as an option to the /offerRA switch to initiate the Remote Assistance session in one stop (for example, msra /offerra *ipaddress | computername*).

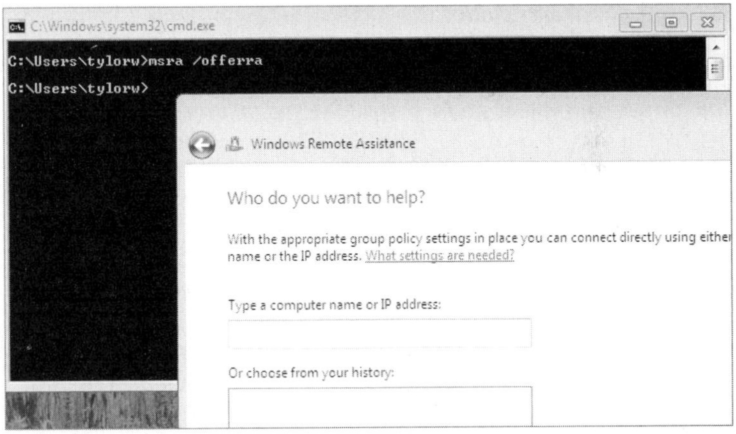

FIGURE 7.15
The Who Do You
Want to Help? Remote
Assistance screen

Several switches are available to further control the establishment of the Remote Assistance session for both the novice and expert user. Table 7.1 highlights many of the switches.

Being able to run Windows Remote Assistance from the command line has many benefits to an IT team. Scripting is one benefit of msra.exe in addition to simplicity for administrators who are comfortable with using the command line. Let's go through the process of establishing an Easy Connect session and a reestablishment of the session using msra.exe. The following two examples use the command line.

TABLE 7.1:   MSRA Command-Line Switches

SWITCH	OS AVAILABILITY	FUNCTIONALITY
/?	Vista and Windows 7	Displays the help options.
/novice	Vista and Windows 7	Starts Remote Assistance at the Invite screen.
/expert	Vista and Windows 7	Starts Remote Assistance at the Help Someone screen.
/offerRA ip | computer	Vista and Windows 7	Starts Remote Assistance at the Expert Initiated screen or with the options, by automatically initiating with the novice user (used with Group Policy configured in an enterprise environment).
/email password	Vista and Windows 7	Creates an email invitation to be sent to an expert user to request assistance using the novice user's default email program; a random password is generated and needs to be conveyed to the expert user, or a password can be specified with the password option and conveyed to the expert user.
/saveasfile path password	Vista and Windows 7	Creates a file invitation to be given to an expert user to request assistance; a random password is generated or optionally a password can be specified with the password option and conveyed to the expert user.
/openfile path	Vista and Windows 7	Used to open the invitation file sent to the expert user; can be local or on a shared network drive; the expert user enters the password given to the user when the session was initiated.
/geteasyhelp	Windows 7 only	Starts a novice user's Remote Assistance session using Easy Connect; presents the novice user with the password to convey to the expert user.
/offereasyhelp	Windows 7 only	Starts an expert user's Remote Assistance session using Easy Connect; presents the expert user with the screen to enter the password from the novice user.
/getcontacthelp address	Windows 7 only	Reestablishes a Remote Assistance session from a novice user's machine to the address from the previous session. The address is in the RAContactHistory.xml file as a 20 byte hexadecimal string with an .RAContact extension.
/offercontacthelp address	Windows 7 only	Reestablishes a Remote Assistance session from an expert user's machine to the address from the previous session. The address is in the RAContactHistory.xml file as a 20 byte hexadecimal string with an .RAContact extension.

CONNECTING WITH THE COMMAND LINE, FIRST-TIME ESTABLISHMENT

Perform the following steps to initiate a first-time Remote Assistance connection establishment:

1. Ask the novice user to launch Easy Connect from the command line by select Start ➢ All Programs ➢ Accessories ➢ Command Prompt and then typing **msra/geteasyhelp**.

2. Ask the novice user to give you the Easy Connect password.

3. Launch Easy Connect from the command line: select Start ➢ All Programs ➢ Accessories ➢ Command Prompt and type **msra/offereasyhelp**.

4. Enter the Easy Connect password generated from the novice user's machine for this session.

5. The novice user's machine displays the screen to accept help from the expert user; instruct the novice user to choose Yes to establish this session.

The Remote Assistance session is established and you can help the novice user.

USING msra.exe TO REESTABLISH AN EASY CONNECT SESSION

Perform the following steps to reconnect to the same party:

1. Acquire the Remote Assistance address for the session that is going to be reestablished from the novice user's machine; this is in the \users*user*\appdata\local directory on the novice user's machine in the file RAContactHistory.xml (see Figure 7.16). The entry is in the ADDRESS= line near the bottom of the file and is 20 bytes in length.

FIGURE 7.16
RAContactHistory.xml
text

2. Ask the novice user to launch Easy Connect from the command line by selecting Start ➢ All Programs ➢ Accessories ➢ Command Prompt and typing **msra/getcontacthelp** *address*.

The novice user's machine is now waiting for you to establish the connection.

3. On your machine, acquire the Remote Assistance address for the session that is going to be reestablished to the novice user's machine; this is in the \users*user*\appdata\local directory on your machine in the file RAContactHistory.xml. The entry is in the ADDRESS= line near the bottom of the file and is 20 bytes in length.

4. Launch Easy Connect from the command line: select Start ➤ All Programs ➤ Accessories ➤ Command Prompt and type **msra/offercontact help** *address*.

5. The novice user's machine displays the screen to accept help from the expert user; instruct the novice user to choose Yes (if this Remote Assistance session is to be reestablished).

The Remote Assistance session is established, and you can help the novice user.

The `msra.exe` command-line options for saving as a file and emailing an invitation can also be valuable to the IT staff. Scripting to the command line for creating an email invitation can be a time-saver for IT personnel. Remember that a password can be defined or it can be randomly generated if the `password` parameter is not included in the `msra.exe` command.

CREATING AN EMAIL INVITATION WITH A PASSWORD DEFINED BY THE NOVICE USER

Perform the following steps to create an email invitation with a specific password:

1. Ask the novice user to select Start ➤ All Programs ➤ Accessories ➤ Command Prompt and type **msra /email ratylorW** (the password is case sensitive). If the `password` parameter is not entered, a random password will be generated.

2. The default email program on the novice user's machine launches with a message stating help is desired. The message includes an attachment: the invitation file `Invitation.msraincident`. Ask the novice user to enter your email address and send the invitation. The novice user must provide you with the password so that you can establish the Remote Assistance session.

3. When you receive the email that the novice user sent, open the attachment, which launches the Remote Assistance program and requests the password for the novice user's session.

4. Enter the password (this is case sensitive) and click OK. The novice user will accept, and the Remote Assistance session continues normally.

You might want to create a scripted invitation using `msra.exe` that chooses a random password rather than a predefined one. You might do this for security reasons or just to achieve consistency in policy. An IT staff creating a Remote Assistance request script will probably use the same password over and over again. If the password is generally known, a nonadministrative person could ultimately discover the password (from a past session), and the possibility of someone establishing a Remote Assistance session inappropriately becomes a possibility. To avoid this, you should let `msra.exe` create the password dynamically. Doing so will force the novice user to be involved and convey the password back to the expert user. If you chose the password when you created the invitation file, the novice user would see the password, but you would not have to ask for it; this is a security flaw.

CREATING A REMOTE ASSISTANCE INVITATION AS A FILE USING A RANDOM PASSWORD

Perform the following steps to create an invitation file using a random password:

1. Ask the novice user to select Start ➤ All Programs ➤ Accessories ➤ Command Prompt and type **msra /saveasfile** *path* (the *path* is an accessible directory and filename for the invitation). The file will be saved with the `.msraincident` extension. A password can optionally be added to the command to specify a password to be used (it is case sensitive).

2. The novice user's machine displays the password to be conveyed to you, the expert user. Ask the novice user to give you the file in the **path** location.

3. When you receive the file from the novice user, open the file by selecting Start ➢ All Programs ➢ Accessories ➢ Command Prompt and typing `msra /openfile path` (the **path** is an accessible directory and filename for the invitation).

4. Enter the password (it is case sensitive) and click OK. The novice user accepts and the Remote Assistance session continues normally.

Using Remote Desktop

Remote Desktop is a tool in Windows 7 that allows you to take control of a remote computer's keyboard, video, and mouse. This tool does not require that someone be available to collaborate with you on the remote computer. While the remote computer is being accessed, it remains locked and any actions that are performed remotely will not be visible via the monitor that is attached to the remote computer.

Remote Desktop has been available for several releases of Windows. With each release, improvements are made and new features added. Windows 7 is no different.

New and Updated Features in Remote Desktop

Windows 7 Remote Desktop is again an enhanced version of remote desktop functionality that has been with us for many of the previous versions of Windows, both client and server operating systems. Remote Desktop uses the Remote Desktop Protocol (RDP) to provide the data between a host and a client machine. Windows 7 uses the latest version, RDP 7.0. Windows 7 Remote Desktop enhancements include:

◆ RDP core performance enhancements

◆ True multimonitor support

◆ Direct 2D and Direct 3D 10.1 application support

◆ Windows 7 Aero support

◆ Bi-directional audio support

◆ Multimedia and Media Foundation support

There are many uses for Remote Desktop. The most popular use is an administrator attempting to perform a task on an end-user machine (or server). This is a valid use, but you can take it further and make it an end-user function as well. Previous versions of RDP gave users a workable experience, but the new enhancements to the core of RDP make keyboard input and mouse movements even more responsive. RDP's enhanced performance gives users a seamless integration of a home and office environment. Along with the RDP core enhancements, the addition of Direct 2D and Direct 3D 10.1 application support means more program video is supported and applications will look the same from the local machine as well as from a Remote Desktop session. Multimedia and Media Foundation support as well as bi-directional audio support add to the functionality and allow more applications that run on a local machine to be available to a Remote Desktop session.

The one caveat is that the end user expects the same functionality and performance regardless of which keyboard they're sitting at (home or office). If you notice the enhancements to

Remote Desktop (which are enhancements to RDP), you can see that the main goal of enhancing Remote Desktop is to make the user experience as comfortable and seamless as possible. Let's look at true multimonitor support, one of Remote Desktop's enhancements. In the previous version of Remote Desktop, we could span multiple monitors. This did not give us the multiple-monitor functionality we would have at the local machine (in the case of a laptop with an external monitor). The Windows 7 implementation allows independent multiple-monitor functionality. The end-user experience is also enhanced with the new audio functionality. This becomes a better environment for the administrator as well.

🌐 Real World Scenario

USING REMOTE DESKTOP FUNCTIONALITY

We speak many times about using Remote Desktop for troubleshooting client computers. As administrators, we like to take control of an end-user machine and fix it. Although this can be done with Remote Assistance, the end user is required to allow us access and then can watch what we do. With Remote Desktop, we just take control and close the interactive session at the remote machine (yes, the remote end user can block us or take over the session, but not if they want their problem solved). We also refer to Remote Desktop as a Terminal Service client (in fact, Microsoft is calling the Terminal Services client from the legacy functionality Remote Desktop now).

There are other uses for Remote Desktop as well. At our company, we provide our clients a server with resources that need to be changed or updated on a regular basis (sometimes a couple of changes in a day). The clients access the files on the provided server using a proprietary client program. As administrators, we might have to make changes at any time to the clients server. Remote Desktop allows us to maintain their server and database from wherever we are without affecting our clients or other administrators. Where Remote Desktop takes over an active session on the remote server, every once in a while when we log in to perform maintenance, it seems as though someone locally was right in the middle of doing something (and they were). The other admin can simply retake over the session (my screen disconnects). No problem, I wait a few minutes and reconnect and complete my tasks. This allows me to save time by not having to go back to the office and also not trying to direct someone to make a change for me.

A few steps are involved to make sure that you can connect to a Windows 7 machine using Remote Desktop.

Configuring a Computer for Remote Desktop

To enable a remote computer to allow Remote Desktop access, select Start ➢ Control Panel ➢ System And Security ➢ System. Click Remote Settings in the left pane. On the Remote tab of System Properties, choose either Allow Connections From Computers Running Any Version Of Remote Desktop (Less Secure) or Allow Connections Only From Computers Running Remote Desktop With Network Level Authentication (More Secure). The option Don't Allow Connections To This Computer is the default selection. The Allow selections create an exception in Windows Firewall to permit Remote Desktop sessions. Figure 7.17 shows the Remote tab of the System Properties dialog box where Remote Desktop access is configured.

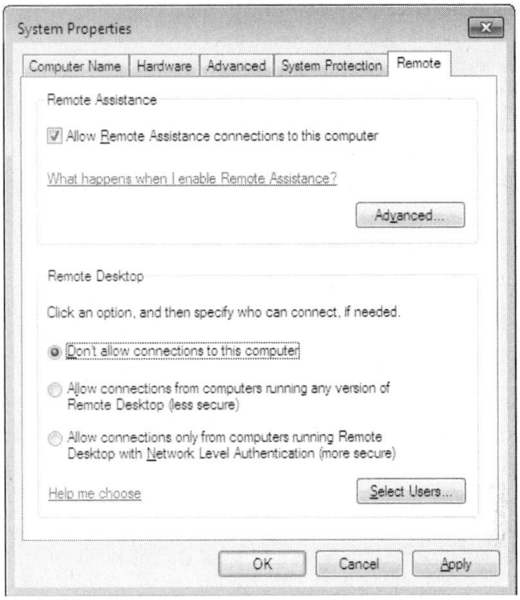

FIGURE 7.17
The Remote tab of
System Properties

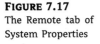

By default, only members of the Administrators group can access a computer that has been
configured to use Remote Desktop. To enable other users to access the computer remotely,
choose Select Users. You'll add users in the Remote Desktop Users dialog box, shown in
Figure 7.18, and users are added to the Remote Desktop Users group on the machine.

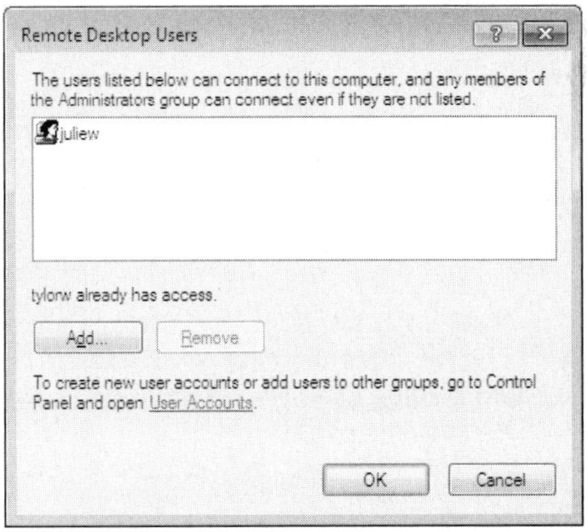

FIGURE 7.18
The Remote Desktop
Users dialog box

You can verify the exceptions in Windows Firewall by choosing Start ➤ Control Panel ➤
System And Security ➤ Windows Firewall. Select Allow A Program Or Feature Through Win-
dows Firewall in the left pane. Remote Desktop should be selected in the Allowed Programs
And Features box.

REMOTE DESKTOP SETUP

Most procedures presented in this section require two machines (real or virtual) to be connected to provide Remote Desktop host and Remote Desktop client functionality.

After you complete the configuration that allows a Remote Desktop session on the computer being accessed remotely (the host) and permissions have been granted for the user to access the machine, then a Remote Desktop session can be started.

INITIATING A REMOTE DESKTOP SESSION

Perform the following steps to set up a Remote Desktop session to a remote machine:

1. From the machine where the Remote Desktop session is being initiated (the client), choose Start ➤ All Programs ➤ Accessories ➤ Remote Desktop Connection. This opens the Remote Desktop Connection window, as shown in Figure 7.19.

REMOTE DESKTOP LAUNCH OPTION

You can also type **mstsc.exe** at the command line to initiate the Remote Desktop session.

FIGURE 7.19
The Remote Desktop
Connection window

2. Enter the computer name or IP address of the host machine where the Remote Desktop session is going to be established. This is a machine that has been configured to accept Remote Desktop connections.

3. Click the Connect button.

4. Enter user credentials with permission to establish a Remote Desktop session on the remote machine, as shown in Figure 7.20, and click OK.

5. You might be asked to continue with a certificate that cannot be verified. If you are confident you are connecting to the correct machine, you can choose Yes to continue.

FIGURE 7.20
Remote Desktop
Credentials Window

> **CONNECTION CERTIFICATE WARNING**
>
> When a connection is attempted, the host machine sends a certificate to the client to allow a secure connection to be made. If the client machine cannot validate the certificate as coming from an entity it trusts, the user will be notified. Initially, the host machine will use a self-signed certificate and will not be trusted — hence the warning, as shown here:

6. If a user was logged on to the remote machine, you may continue by clicking OK, as shown in Figure 7.21, but the user will be disconnected from the terminal. The user will remain logged in to the machine, but will not have access while the Remote Desktop session is active. The user at the remote machine will be given the opportunity to cancel the connection, but the connection will be established if no intervention occurs.

FIGURE 7.21
Clicking OK disconnects
the local user.

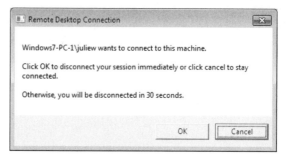

7. The client machine now displays the Desktop of the host machine. Administrative and/or user functions can be carried out as if the administrator or user is sitting at the host machine.

8. When the session is complete, end the terminal session by closing the Remote Desktop window or by choosing Start ≻ Logoff ≻ Disconnect, as shown in Figure 7.22. This ends the interactive session; however, the logon session will remain active on the host machine. To disconnect and log off the Remote Desktop session, choose Start ≻ Logoff.

FIGURE 7.22
Choosing Start ≻ Logoff
≻ Disconnect

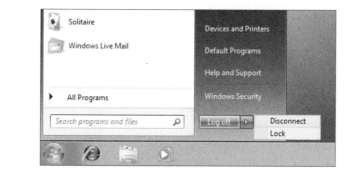

IDENTIFYING REMOTE DESKTOP CONNECTION OPTIONS

When you connect to a Remote Desktop host machine, there are several options available to enhance the client user session. The options allow configuration for general settings, display options, local resource access, programs to be executed on startup, the user experience, and advanced options for security and Remote Desktop gateway access. Access these options by clicking the Options button in the lower left of the initial Remote Desktop Connection screen. Figure 7.23 shows the options window both hidden and displayed.

On the General tab, you select the host computer and username. You can choose and save user credentials on this tab as well. You can save the connection settings to a file or open an existing RDP file on the General tab.

On the Display tab, shown in Figure 7.24, you can choose the size of the display screen. This is also where you can select the option to use multiple monitors. You select the color depth (color quality) on the Display tab. The option to display the connection bar when using full-screen display is available here as well.

FIGURE 7.23
Remote Desktop options

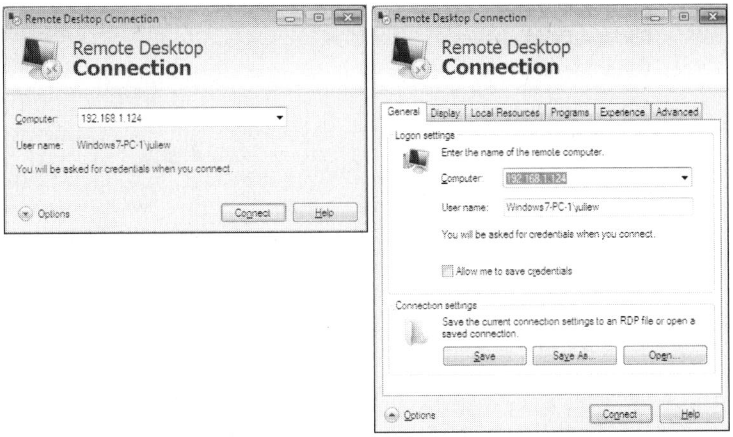

FIGURE 7.24
Remote Desktop Display
tab

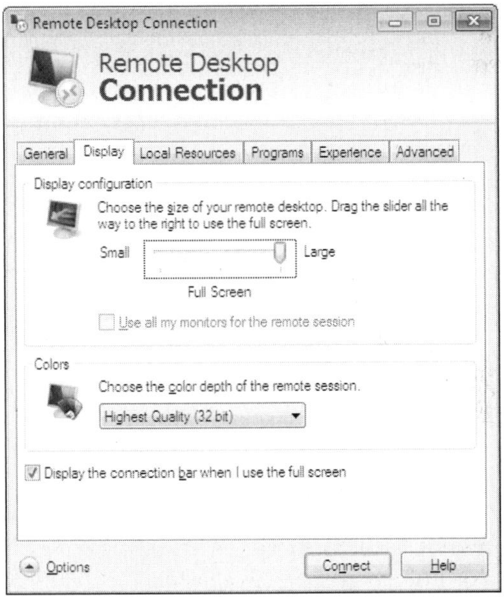

On the Local Resources tab, shown in Figure 7.25, you configure remote audio settings, keyboard settings, and local device and resources access.

The Programs tab, shown in Figure 7.26, lets you specify a program to run at connection startup. The program name and path are specified as well as a startup folder if necessary.

The end-user experience is important to the overall success of using Remote Desktop in the user environment. Remember that Remote Desktop can be used to give a user the ability to connect to their machine and "remote in." The most seamless environment from the work to the remote location is desirable, but is dependent on the bandwidth available. The more bandwidth, the more high-end features can be made available to the end user. This is also nice for the administrator who is working on an end-user machine. The Experience tab (Figure 7.27) allows you to configure options related to the end-user experience.

FIGURE 7.25
Remote Desktop Local
Resources tab

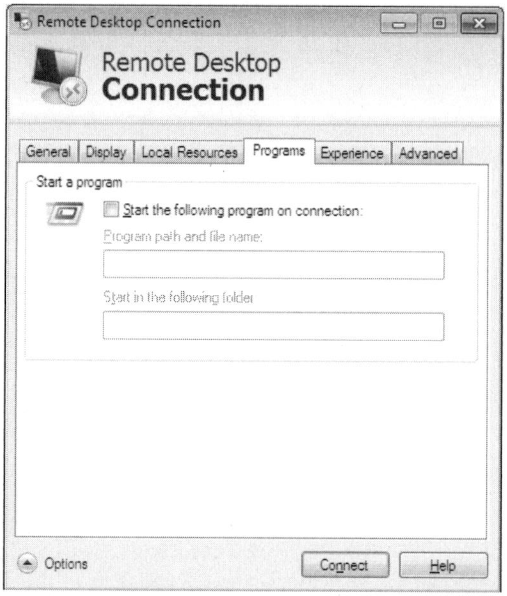

FIGURE 7.26
Remote Desktop
Programs tab

To control the behavior of the Remote Desktop connection with regard to security, you configure the connection properties on the Advanced tab, as shown in Figure 7.28. The Advanced tab also lets you configure a Remote Desktop Gateway to allow Remote Desktop connections to be established from any Internet location through SSL. The user must still be authorized and the Remote Desktop client must still be available.

FIGURE 7.27
Remote Desktop
Experience tab

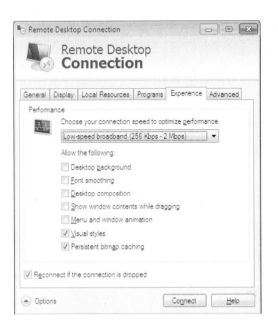

FIGURE 7.28
Remote Desktop
Advanced tab

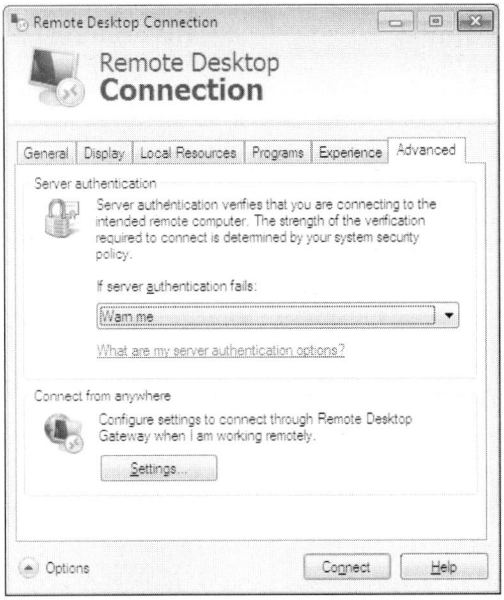

USING REMOTE DESKTOP CONNECTION OPTIONS

A nice feature of Remote Desktop is the ability to save your RDP connection parameters as a file that can then be opened (as simply as double-clicking the file on a machine with a Remote Desktop client available).

SAVING A REMOTE DESKTOP RDP FILE

Perform the following steps to save an RDP file used to supply preconfigured parameters to a Remote Desktop session establishment:

1. Ensure that the user's host machine is configured to allow Remote Desktop connections. The user should be a member of the Remote Desktop Users group, as shown in Figure 7.29.

FIGURE 7.29
The user must be a member of the Remote Desktop Users group.

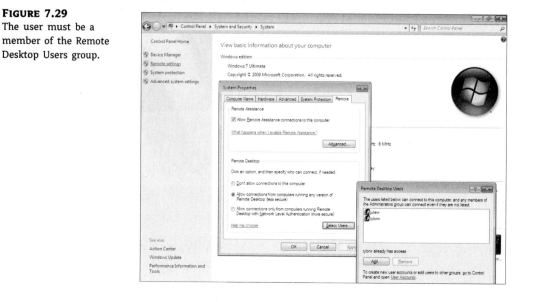

2. Launch the Remote Desktop Connection dialog box by selecting Start ➢ All Programs ➢ Accessories ➢ Remote Desktop Connection.

3. Click Options in the lower left of the Remote Desktop Connection dialog box to expand to the options.

4. Ensure the computer name or IP address and username are entered for the desired connection.

5. Optionally, configure other options if desired.

6. Click Save As on the General tab.

7. Enter a filename for the RDP connection file, as shown in Figure 7.30, and click Save to save the file. Note the default location is Documents from the Libraries parent. You might want to access this file later; it does not need to be run from this directory.

The perfect ending to using an RDP Remote Desktop file is to reestablish a Remote Desktop session using the saved file.

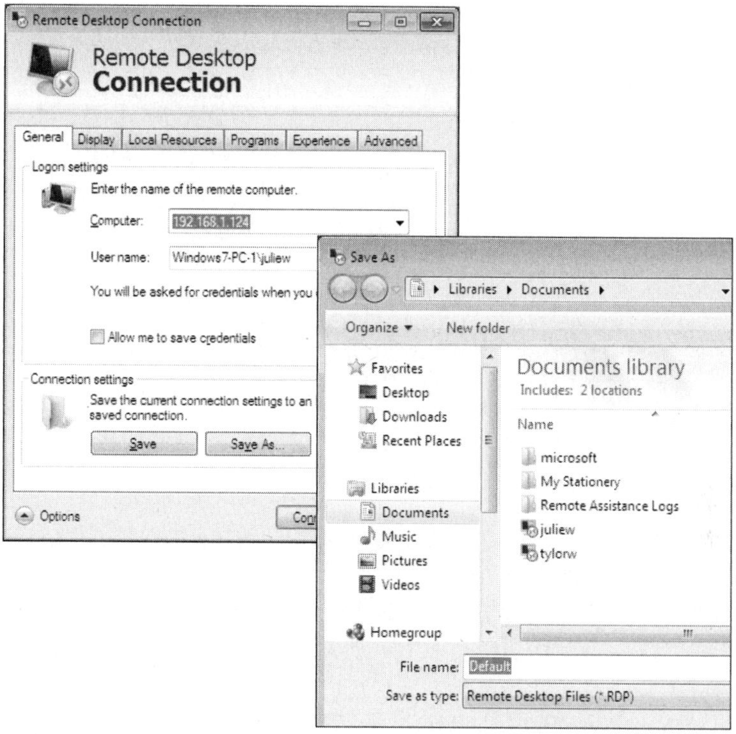

FIGURE 7.30
Saving the RDP
connection file

USING A SAVED RDP REMOTE DESKTOP FILE

Perform the following steps to reestablish a Remote Desktop session using a saved RDP file:

1. Launch the Remote Desktop Connection dialog box by selecting Start ➤ All Programs ➤ Accessories ➤ Remote Desktop Connection.

2. Click Options in the lower left of the Remote Desktop Connection dialog box to expand to the options.

3. On the General tab of the Remote Desktop Connection screen, with the Options screen expanded, click Open.

ACCESSING A SAVED RDP CONNECTION FILE

You can also browse to a previously saved RDP connection file and double-click the file. The file is a standard configuration file and can be moved to a more convenient location if desired as well as to another machine as long as the other machine has the Remote Desktop client available.

4. The RDP file opens. As you can see, the connection parameters appear on the Remote Desktop Connection screen. Click Connect to establish the Remote Desktop session using the configured parameters. A warning message might appear (Figure 7.31) stating that the publisher of the remote connections cannot be verified. You can continue if you are confident this is the correct file. From this warning box, you can also open options to allow or prohibit resource access for this connection.

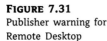

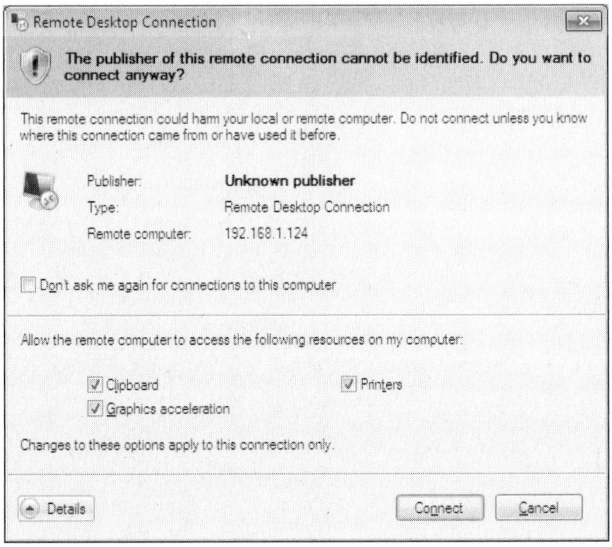

FIGURE 7.31
Publisher warning for
Remote Desktop

5. The Remote Desktop session will now begin.

One of the added features of Remote Desktop in Windows 7 is the ability to handle the Windows Aero interface. The Aero interface uses opaque window borders as well as the flip functionality available since Vista. This experience was not available in previous versions of Remote Desktop. To have the full Windows Aero experience, you must select the Desktop Composition option in the Remote Desktop Connection window on the Experience tab.

SETTING THE USER EXPERIENCE OPTION OF REMOTE DESKTOP

Perform the following steps to go through the process of enabling Desktop Composition:

1. Launch the Remote Desktop Connection dialog box by selecting Start ➢ All Programs ➢ Accessories ➢ Remote Desktop Connection.

2. Click Options in the lower left of the Remote Desktop Connection window.

3. Select the Experience tab.

4. Specify the appropriate bandwidth or type of connection between the client and the host (choose the slowest link between them). Bandwidth-based experience parameters, as shown in Figure 7.32, are suggestions and they can be modified by choosing the desired (or undesired) experience item. Remember, Desktop Composition is going to present the client user with the Windows Aero experience.

FIGURE 7.32
Choose the appropriate bandwidth or type of connection.

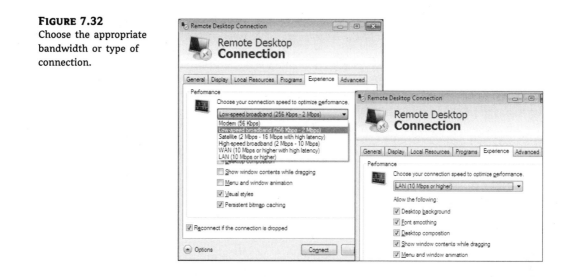

ADVANCED REMOTE DESKTOP GATEWAY OPTIONS

Windows Server 2008 has the ability to be a Remote Desktop Gateway when you add the TS Gateway role. Once installed, a client can connect to (or through as the case may be) the host via the Terminal Server. This can be accomplished via Internet Explorer and an HTTPS session (the Remote Desktop client can be automatically installed when connecting) or by configuring a Remote Desktop Gateway on the Advanced tab of the Remote Desktop Connection dialog box.

VIEWING THE ADVANCED REMOTE DESKTOP GATEWAY OPTIONS

Follow these steps to view the advanced Remote Desktop gateway options:

1. Open the Remote Desktop Connection dialog box by selecting Start ➤ All Programs ➤ Accessories ➤ Remote Desktop Connection.

2. Click Options in the lower left of the Remote Desktop Connection window.

3. Choose the Advanced tab.

4. In the Connect From Anywhere section, click the Settings button.

5. Review the Remote Desktop Gateway configuration items, as shown in Figure 7.33.

Providing Command-Line Remote Desktop

It is possible to initiate a Remote Desktop session using command-line functionality. This provides an administrator with scripting capabilities for Remote Desktop. The command line uses the `mstsc.exe` (Microsoft Terminal Server Client) application with optional switches for configuration. Several switches can be included on the same command line if appropriate (screen width and screen height, for example). The command-line options are shown in Table 7.2.

FIGURE 7.33
Advanced configuration
for Remote Desktop

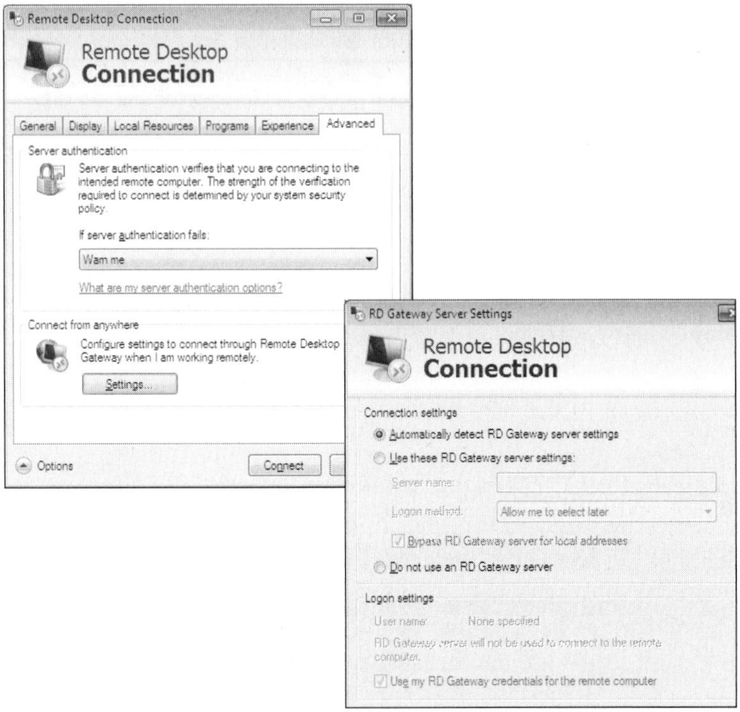

Rather than use the menu structure to launch the Remote Desktop Connection screen, you can launch it through the command prompt or from the Start menu's search.

USING MSTSC TO INITIATE A REMOTE DESKTOP SESSION

To launch Remote Desktop from the command prompt:

1. On the client machine, launch Remote Desktop from the command line: select Start ➢ All Programs ➢ Accessories ➢ Command Prompt and type **mstsc**.

2. Enter the name or IP address of the host machine where the Remote Desktop session is to be established. The host machine must be configured to allow Remote Desktop sessions and the user connecting will need to have authorization to establish a Remote Desktop session.

3. On the client machine, enter credentials and the Remote Desktop session continues normally.

4. When the session is complete, end the terminal session by closing the Remote Desktop window or choosing Start ➢ Logoff ➢ Disconnect. This ends the interactive session, but the logon session remains active on the host machine. To disconnect and log off the Remote Desktop session, choose Start ➢ Logoff.

If you know the IP address (or name) of the machine you want to establish a Remote Desktop session with, you can include the IP or name as a parameter to the mstsc.exe command.

TABLE 7.2:   MSTSC Command-Line Switches

SWITCH	FUNCTIONALITY
/?	Displays the help options.
/v:<server[:port]>	Starts Remote Desktop, specifying the host machine to connect to and a port if the default is not used.
/admin	Starts Remote Desktop in admin mode bypassing TS Cal (Terminal Server Client Access License) requirements and disabling several functions not required for administration services.
/f	Starts Remote Desktop in full-screen mode.
/w:<width>	Specifies the width of the Remote Desktop connection window.
/h:<height>	Specifies the height of the Remote Desktop connection window.
/public	Starts Remote Desktop in public mode; passwords and bitmaps will not be cached.
/span	Matches the Remote Desktop width and height with the local virtual desktop. This can span multiple monitors if necessary; monitors must be arranged to form a rectangle.
/multimon	Configures the Remote Desktop session to match the client-side configuration for multiple monitors. The layout does not have to be rectangular and can consist of various size monitors.
/edit	Opens a previously defined RDP file for editing. The opens the file in the Remote Desktop Connection window with Options selected, allowing you to edit the existing parameters in the RDP file.
/migrate	Migrates legacy connection files created with the previous Client Connection Manager to the new .rdp connection file format.

USING MSTSC TO INITIATE A REMOTE DESKTOP SESSION BY IP ADDRESS

To initiate a Remote Desktop session by IP address:

1. On the client machine, launch Remote Desktop from the command line: select Start ➤ All Programs ➤ Accessories ➤ Command Prompt and type **mstsc /v:*ip-address*** (use the IP address of the host machine). The host machine must be configured to allow Remote Desktop sessions and the user connecting needs to have authorization to establish a Remote Desktop session.

2. On the client machine, enter credentials and the Remote Desktop session continues normally.

3. When the session is complete, end the terminal session by closing the Remote Desktop window or choosing Start ➤ Logoff ➤ Disconnect. This ends the interactive session, but the

logon session remains active on the host machine. To disconnect and log off the Remote Desktop session, choose Start ➢ Logoff.

If you have previously configured a Remote Desktop connection and saved the file, you can open the file for editing by using `mstsc.exe`. When you open the file for editing, the file is loaded into the Remote Desktop Connection dialog box without attempting to establish the connection. The Remote Desktop Connection window is opened with the Option screen expanded (you don't have to click the Options button).

USING MSTSC TO EDIT A PREVIOUSLY SAVE RDP CONFIGURATION FILE

Perform the following steps to use `mstsc.exe` to edit an `.rdp` configuration file that has been previously saved:

1. On the client machine, launch Remote Desktop from the command line: select Start ➢ All Programs ➢ Accessories ➢ Command Prompt and type **mstsc /edit *filename*** (where *filename* is the path and filename for a previously defined RDP connection file).

2. The Remote Desktop Connection window opens with the Options window expanded and the parameter from the previously defined RDP file loaded for editing.

3. Make changes (or verify parameters) by viewing the configuration of the various option tabs.

4. Save any changes made to the RDP file by clicking Save As on the General tab.

5. Use the existing filename or enter a new filename for the RDP connection file and click Save to save the file.

You can specify other parameters when launching a Remote Desktop session from the command line as well. Two more options for `mstsc.exe` are the width and height of the display window on the local machine. Next, you'll configure the IP address of the machine you are connecting to as well as set the local machine's display size to 640×480 for Remote Desktop.

USING MSTSC TO SPECIFY AN IP ADDRESS AND DEFINE WIDTH AND HEIGHT FOR THE DISPLAY

To use `mstsc.exe` to specify an IP address as well as define the local machine's display width and height for Remote Desktop:

1. On the client machine, launch Remote Desktop from the command line: select Start ➢ All Programs ➢ Accessories ➢ Command Prompt and type **mstsc /v:*ip-address* /w:640 /h:480**. The host machine must be configured to allow Remote Desktop sessions and the user connecting to it needs to have authorization to establish a Remote Desktop session.

2. On the client machine, enter credentials and the Remote Desktop session continues normally.

3. When the session is complete, end the terminal session by closing the Remote Desktop window or choosing Start ➢ Logoff ➢ Disconnect. This ends the interactive session, but the logon session remains active on the host machine. To disconnect and log off the Remote Desktop session, choose Start ➢ Logoff.

The Bottom Line

Assist novice users with Windows 7. Remote Assistance is a great collaboration tool used between an expert and a novice user that allows the expert to help the novice by watching the novice user's actions on another machine. If desired, the expert can even request control (which has to be granted by the novice user) to perform an action. Remote Assistance can be used as a teaching tool or simply to fix a problem for a novice user.

> **Master It** You are an administrator on your local network, and one of your users is try-ing to find their IP address. You know it's easiest to open the command prompt and type `ipconfig`, but you're not sure if the user can follow your instructions and you would like to watch them so they don't get lost while you give the instructions. You know you've said too many times, "Tell me what you see." You have decided to use Remote Assistance to help the user. Both you and the user needing assistance are using Windows 7. How can you assist your novice user to get the IP address of their machine?

Provide help from Windows 7 to older operating systems. Remote Assistance is available on legacy operating systems as well as Windows 7. It works the same way on most current oper-ating systems, except that the Easy Connect option (available in Windows 7) is not available on previous operating system versions. To integrate a Windows 7 Remote Assistance session with a previous version, an invitation file or email invitation is a solution. The Remote Assis-tance established by a file or email invitation will allow an expert user to assist a novice user interactively (both can see what's happening).

> **Master It** You are the network administrator for your company and you have taken a phone call from a novice user asking for help changing the default printer they are on from one device to another. You know this is a fairly simple operation but would like to be look-ing over the user's shoulder as the changes are made to avoid any problems that may be created by the change. The novice user is running Windows Vista and you are running Win-dows 7. How can you have the user request a Remote Assistance session with you so you won't have to physically go to the novice user's location?

Access a machine from a remote location. Remote Desktop is another form of remote access that allows a user to connect to a machine and have access to that machine's resources. The host machine is the machine being connected to; the client machine is where the user accessing the remote resources is located. The host machine can be the end users in the case of telecommut-ing or even that of the end user if the user is in a different office for the day.

> **Master It** You are currently working in a remote office and realize you have left an impor-tant document on your home office machine. You thought you'd put it on your stick, but alas, it's not there and you don't think asking someone to log into your machine and retrieve it is a good idea (good thinking, by the way). You need to access your machine remotely to get the file. How will you do it?

Script a session for automated connection. As the network administrator, you need to log in to a server machine on a regular basis to check on its performance and make minor changes. You have been going down to the server room and physically logging in every time you have to make changes or log data. You now know you can use Remote Desktop to access the server and would like to start using the application.

Master It   You know you can launch Remote Desktop from the menu structure of Windows 7, but you would like to be able to have an icon on your Desktop to launch a Remote Desktop session with one of the servers you are responsible for. You know that down the road you will have to manage more machines this way, and if you create an icon for one now it will be pretty easy to create more icons later so you can simply double-click any one of the individual icons to initiate the Remote Desktop session to any of several individual servers. You want to create a Notepad file with the appropriate command line to launch a Remote Desktop session to a server at 192.168.1.62 and make it so double-clicking it will initiate the Remote Desktop session.

Chapter 8

Configuring Users and Groups

One of the most fundamental tasks in network management is creating user and group accounts. Without a user account, a user cannot log on to a computer, server, or network.

When users log on, they supply a username and password. Then their user accounts are validated by a security mechanism. In Windows 7, users can log on to a computer locally, or they can log on through Active Directory.

When you first create users, you assign them usernames, passwords, and password settings. After a user is created, you can change these settings and select other options for that user through the User Accounts utility in Control Panel.

Group accounts are used to ease network administration by grouping together users who have similar permission requirements. Groups are an important part of network management. Many administrators are able to accomplish the majority of their management tasks through the use of groups; they rarely assign permissions to individual users. Windows 7 includes built-in local groups, such as Administrators and Backup Operators. These groups already have all the permissions needed to accomplish specific tasks. Windows 7 also uses default special groups, which are managed by the system. Users become members of special groups based on their requirements for computer and network access.

You create and manage local groups through the Local Users and Groups utility. With this utility, you can add groups, change group membership, rename groups, and delete groups.

In this chapter, you'll learn how to:

◆ Understand user account types

◆ Create accounts

◆ Configure accounts

◆ Understand local groups

Understanding Windows 7 User Accounts

When you install Windows 7, several user accounts are created automatically. You can then create new user accounts. As you already know, these accounts allow users to access resources.

On Windows 7 computers, you can create local user accounts. If your network has a Windows Server 2008, Windows Server 2003, or Windows Server 2000 domain controller, your network can have domain user accounts as well.

One of the features included with Windows 7 is User Account Control (UAC). UAC provides an additional level of security by limiting the level of access that users have when performing normal, everyday tasks. When needed, users can gain elevated access for specific administrative tasks.

In the following sections, you will learn about the default user accounts that are created by Windows 7 and the difference between local and domain user accounts.

Account Types

Windows 7 supports two basic types of user accounts: Administrator and Standard User, as shown in Figure 8.1. Each one of these accounts has a specific purpose:

FIGURE 8.1
User Types screen

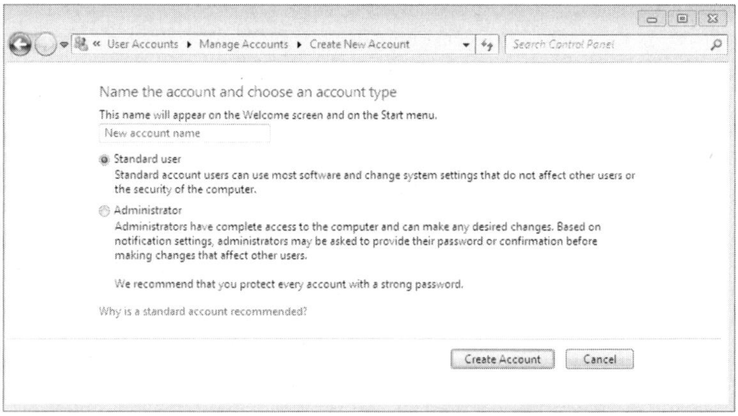

Administrator   The Administrator account provides unrestricted access to performing administrative tasks. As a result, Administrator accounts should be used only for performing administrative tasks and should not be used for normal computing tasks.

Only Administrator accounts can change the Registry. This is important to know because when you install most software onto a Windows 7 machine, the Registry gets changed. This is why you need administrator rights to install most software.

Standard User   You should apply the Standard User account for every user of the computer. Standard User accounts can perform most day-to-day tasks, such as running Microsoft Word, accessing e-mail, using Internet Explorer, and so on. Running as a Standard User increases security by limiting the possibility of a virus or other malicious code from infecting the computer and making systemwide changes, because Standard User accounts are unable to make systemwide changes.

When you install Windows 7, by default premade accounts called built-in accounts are established. Let's look at these account types.

Built-in Accounts

Built-in accounts are accounts that are created at the time you install the Windows 7 operating system. Windows 7, when installed into a workgroup environment, has four user accounts, as shown in Figure 8.2:

Administrator   The Administrator account is a special account that has full control over the computer. The Administrator account can perform all tasks, such as creating users and groups, managing the file system, and setting up printing. Note that the Administrator account is disabled by default.

Guest   The Guest account allows users to access the computer even if they do not have a unique username and password. Because of the inherent security risks associated with this type of user, the Guest account is disabled by default. When this account is enabled, it is usually given limited privileges.

HomeGroup User   The HomeGroup user is created by default to allow this machine to connect to other machines within the same HomeGroup network. This account is enabled by default.

Initial User   The initial user account uses the name of the registered user. By default, the initial user is a member of the Administrators group.

ADMINISTRATOR ACCOUNT

By default, the name Administrator is given to a user account that is a member of the Administrators group. However, in Windows 7 this user account is disabled by default. You can increase the computer's security by leaving this account disabled and assigning other members to the Administrators group. This way, a malicious user is unable to log on to the computer using the Administrator user account.

These users are considered local users and their permissions are contained to the Windows 7 machine. You can also have users logging into the Windows 7 computer that are considered domain users. Let's look at the difference between these account types.

Local and Domain User Accounts

Windows 7 supports two kinds of users: local users and domain users. A computer that is running Windows 7 has the ability to store its own user accounts database. The users stored at the local computer are known as local user accounts.

Active Directory is a directory service that is available with the Windows Server 2008, Windows Server 2003, and Windows 2000 Server platforms. It stores information in a central database called Active Directory that allows users to have a single user account for the network. The users stored in Active Directory's central database are called domain user accounts.

If you use local user accounts, they must be configured on each computer that the user needs access to within the network. For this reason, domain user accounts are commonly used to manage users on any network with more than 10 users.

On Windows 7, Windows Server 2008, Windows Server 2003, Windows XP, and Windows 7 computers you can create local users through the Local Users and Groups utility, as described in the section "Working with User Accounts," later in this chapter. On Windows Server 2008, Windows Server 2003, and Windows 2000 Server domain controllers, you manage users with the Microsoft Active Directory Users and Computers utility.

WINDOWS SERVER 2008

Active Directory is covered in more detail in Chapter 12, "Networking with Windows Server 2008." But if you are looking for a book that covers Active Directory in detail, refer to *MCTS: Windows Server 2008 Active Directory Configuration Study Guide*, by William Panek and James Chellis (Sybex, 2008).

Now that we've looked at the different types of users, let's see how to use accounts to log on and log off the local machine or domain.

Logging On and Logging Off

Users and administrators must log on to a Windows 7 computer before they can use that computer. When you create user accounts, you set up the computer to accept the logon information provided by the Windows 7 user. You can log on locally to a Windows 7 computer using a local computer account, or you can log on to a domain using an Active Directory account.

When you install the computer, you specify that it will be a part of a workgroup, which implies a local logon, or that the computer will be a part of a domain, which implies a domain logon.

When users are ready to stop working on a Windows 7 computer, they should log off. Users can log off using the Windows Security dialog box.

In the following sections, you will learn about local user authentication and how a user logs out of a Windows 7 computer.

Local User Logon Authentication Process

Depending on whether you are logging on to a computer locally or are logging into a domain, Windows 7 uses two different logon procedures. When you log on to a Windows 7 computer locally, you must present a valid username and password (ones that exist within the local accounts database). As part of a successful authentication, the following steps take place:

1. At system startup, the user is prompted to click their username from a list of users who have been created locally. This is significantly different from the Ctrl+Alt+Del logon sequence that was used by earlier versions of Windows. The Ctrl+Alt+Del sequence is still used when you log on to a domain environment. You can also configure the Ctrl+Alt+Del logon sequence as an option in a local environment.

2. The local computer compares the user's logon credentials with the information in the local security database.

3. If the information presented matches the account database, an access token is created. Access tokens are used to identify the user and the groups of which that user is a member.

ACCESS TOKENS

Access tokens are created only when you log on. If you change group memberships, you need to log off and log on again to update the access token.

Other actions that take place as part of the logon process include the following list:

◆ The system reads the part of the Registry that contains user configuration information.

◆ The user's profile is loaded. (User profiles are discussed in the section "Setting Up User Profiles, Logon Scripts, and Home Folders," later in this chapter.)

◆ Any policies that have been assigned to the user through a user or Group Policy are enforced. (Policies for users are discussed later in Chapter 9, "Managing Security.")

◆ Any logon scripts that have been assigned are executed. (We discuss assigning logon scripts to users in the "Setting Up User Profiles, Logon Scripts, and Home Folders" section.)

◆ Persistent network and printer connections are restored.

PERMISSIONS

Through the logon process, you can control what resources a user can access by assigning permissions. Permissions are granted to either users or groups. Permissions also determine what actions a user can perform on a computer. In Chapter 9, "Managing Security," you will learn more about assigning resource permissions.

Now that we've seen how a local logon process works, let's explore logging off a Windows 7 machine.

Logging Off Windows 7

To log off Windows 7, click Start, point to the arrow next to the Shutdown button, and then click Logoff. Pressing Ctrl+Alt+Del also presents you with a screen that allows you to select whether to lock the computer, switch user, log off, change the password, or start Task Manager.

 **Real World Scenario**

LOGGING OFF COMPUTERS

As network administrator, we made it a practice to teach our users to log off their computers every night. What happens in many companies is that users come in on Monday, turn on their computers, and then leave them on and logged in until Friday night.

Having computers logged on to a local machine or to a network all week long is a dangerous practice. This makes it easy for any other user in the company to sit down at their machine and cause trouble. Have your users get into the practice of logging off at night and locking their keyboard when stepping away for break or lunch.

At this point, you should have a good grasp of the various types of accounts on a Windows 7 computer. Next let's see how to manage these accounts.

Working with User Accounts

To set up and manage your local user accounts, use the Local Users and Groups utility or the User Accounts utility in Control Panel. With either option, you can create, disable, delete, and rename user accounts, as well as change user passwords.

Utilizing the Local Users and Groups Utility

Here are the two common methods for accessing the Local Users and Groups utility:

◆ You can load Local Users and Groups as a Microsoft Management Console (MMC) snap-in. (See Chapter 4, "Configuring Disks," for details on the MMC and the purpose of snap-ins.)

◆ You can access the Local Users and Groups utility through the Computer Management utility.

Perform the following steps for accessing the Local Users and Groups utility. The steps first add the Local Users and Groups snap-in MMC to the desktop.

1. Select Start. In the search box, type **MMC**, and then press Enter.

2. If a warning box appears, click Yes.

3. Select File ➢ Add/Remove Snap-in.

4. Scroll down the list, highlight Local Users and Groups, and then click the Add button, as shown in Figure 8.3.

5. In the Choose Target Machine dialog box, click the Finish button to accept the default selection of Local Computer.

6. Click OK in the Add Or Remove Snap-in dialog box.

7. In the MMC window, right-click the Local Users and Groups folder and choose New Window From Here. You will see that Local Users and Groups is now the main window.

8. Click File ➤ Save As. Name the console **Local Users and Groups** and make sure you save it to the Desktop using the Save In drop-down box, as shown in Figure 8.4. Click the Save button.

9. Close the MMC Snap-in.

FIGURE 8.3
Local Users and Groups snap-in

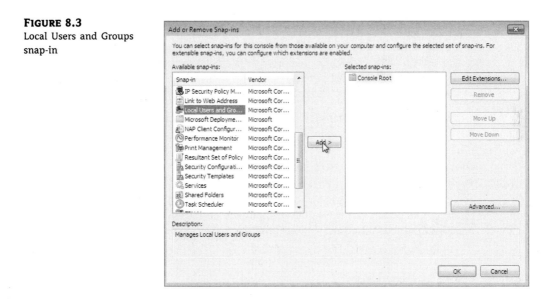

FIGURE 8.4
Saving the Local Users and Groups console

You should now see the Local Users and Groups snap-in on your Desktop. You can also open the Local Users and Groups MMC from the Computer Management utility.

Perform the following steps for opening the Local Users and Groups utility from the Computer Management utility:

1. Select Start and then right-click My Computer and select Manage.

2. In the Computer Management window, expand the System Tools folder and then the Local Users and Groups folder.

COMPUTER MANAGEMENT UTILITY

If your computer doesn't have the MMC configured, the quickest way to access the Local Users and Groups utility is through the Computer Management utility.

Now let's look at another way to configure users and groups: using the User Accounts utility in Control Panel.

Using the User Accounts Utility in Control Panel

The User Accounts utility in Control Panel provides the ability to manage user accounts, in addition to configuring parental controls. To access this utility, click Start ➢ Control Panel ➢ User Accounts. Table 8.1 shows the configurable options in User Accounts.

After you install Windows 7, you must create user accounts for users who will be accessing the machine. Let's take a look at this process.

Creating New Users

To create users on a Windows 7 computer, you must be logged on as a user with permissions to create a new user, or you must be a member of the Administrators group. In the following sections, you will learn about username rules and conventions, usernames, and security identifiers in more detail.

USERNAME RULES AND CONVENTIONS

The only requirement for creating a new user is that you must provide a valid username. "Valid" means that the name must follow the Windows 7 rules for usernames. However, it's also a good idea to have your own rules for usernames, which form your naming convention.

The following rules apply to Windows 7 usernames:

◆ A username must be from 1 to 20 characters.

◆ The username must be unique to all other user and group names stored on that specified computer.

◆ The username cannot contain the following characters:

  $* / \setminus [ ] : ; | = , + ? < > " @$

◆ A username cannot consist exclusively of periods or spaces.

TABLE 8.1:   Configurable User Account Options

OPTION	EXPLANATION
Change Your Password	This allows a user to change their password.
Remove Your Password	Allows you to remove a password from a user's account.
Change Your Picture	Allows you to change the account picture.
Change Your Account Name	Allows you to rename the account.
Change Your Account Type	Allows you to change your account type from Standard User to Administrator, or vice versa.
Manage Another Account	Allows you to configure other accounts on the Windows 7 machine.
Change UUAC Settings	Allows you to set the level of notification when changes are made to a user's computer. These notifications can prevent potentially hazardous programs from being loaded onto the operating system.
Manage Your Credentials	Allows you to set up credentials that easily enable you to connect to websites that require usernames and passwords or computers that require certificates.
Create A Password Reset Disk	Allows you to create a disk that users can use when they forget their password.
Link Online IDs	Allows you to link an Online ID with your Windows account. This makes it easier to share files with other computers.
Manage Your File Encryption Certificates	Allows you to manage your file encryption certificates.
Configure Advanced User Profile Properties	This link brings you directly to the User's Profile dialog box in Control Panel ➤ System ➤ Advanced ➤ System Settings.
Change My Environment Variables	Allows you to access the Environment Variables dialog box directly.

Keeping these rules in mind, you should choose a naming convention (a consistent naming format). For example, consider a user named William Panek. One naming convention might use the last name and first initial, for the username WillP or WilliamP. Another naming convention might use the first initial and last name, for the username WPanek.

Other user-naming conventions are based on the naming convention defined for email names, so that the logon name and email name match. You should also provide a mechanism that would accommodate duplicate names. For example, if you had a user named Jane Smith and a user named John Smith, you might use a middle initial for usernames, such as JDSmith and JRSmith.

It is also a good practice to come up with a naming convention for groups, printers, and computers.

NAMING CONVENTIONS

It's not a good practice to use the first name, first letter of the user's last name, as in WilliamP. In a mid-sized to large company, there are greater chances of having two WilliamP users' accounts, but the odds that you will have two WPaneks are rare.

If you choose to use the first name, first letter of the last name option, it can be a lot of work to go back and change this format later if the company grows larger. Choose a naming convention that can grow with the company.

Now let's look at how usernames get a special ID number associated with the account and how that number affects your accounts.

USERNAMES AND SECURITY IDENTIFIERS

When you create a new user, a security identifier (SID) is automatically created on the computer for the user account. The username is a property of the SID. For example, a user SID might look like this:

```
S-1-5-21-823518204-746137067-120266-629-500
```

It's apparent that using SIDs for user identification would make administration a nightmare. Fortunately, for your administrative tasks, you see and use the username instead of the SID.

SIDs have several advantages. Because Windows 7 uses the SID as the user object, you can easily rename a user while still retaining all the properties of that user. The reason is that all security settings get associated with the SID and not the user account.

SIDs also ensure that if you delete and re-create a user account with the same username, the new user account will not have any of the properties of the old account because it is based on a new, unique SID. Every time you create a new user, a unique SID gets associated. Even if the username is the same as a previously deleted account, the system still sees the username as a new user.

Because every user account gets a unique SID number, it is a good practice to disable accounts for users who leave the company instead of deleting the accounts. If you ever need to access the disabled account again, you can do so. Disabling user accounts and deleting user accounts are discussed in detail in the next two sections.

When you create a new user, there are many options that you have to configure for that user. Table 8.2 describes all the options available in the New User dialog box.

TABLE 8.2:   User Account Options Available in the New User Dialog Box

OPTION	DESCRIPTION
User Name	Defines the username for the new account. Choose a name that is consistent with your naming convention (for example, WPanek). This is the only required field. Usernames are not case sensitive.

TABLE 8.2:   User Account Options Available in the New User Dialog Box (*CONTINUED*)

OPTION	DESCRIPTION
Full Name	Allows you to provide more detailed name information. This is typically the user's first and last names (for example, Will Panek). By default, this field contains the same name as the User Name field.
Description	Typically used to specify a title and/or location (for example, Sales-Nashville) for the account, but it can be used to provide any additional information about the user.
Password	Assigns the initial password for the user. For security purposes, avoid using readily available information about the user. Passwords are case sensitive.
Confirm Password	Confirms that you typed the password the same way two times to verify that you entered the password correctly.
User Must Change Password at Next Logon	If enabled, forces the user to change the password the first time they log on. This is done to increase security. By default, this option is selected.
User Cannot Change Password	If enabled, prevents a user from changing their password. It is useful for accounts such as Guest and accounts that are shared by more than one user. By default, this option is not selected.
Password Never Expires	If enabled, specifies that the password will never expire, even if a password policy has been specified. For example, you might enable this option if this is a service account and you do not want the administrative overhead of managing password changes. By default, this option is not selected.
Account Is Disabled	If enabled, specifies that this account cannot be used for logon purposes. For example, you might select this option for template accounts or if an account is not currently being used. It helps keep inactive accounts from posing security threats. By default, this option is not selected.

Perform the following steps to create a new local user account. Before you complete these steps, make sure you are logged on as a user with permissions to create new users and have already added the Local Users and Groups snap-in to the MMC.

1. Open the Admin Console MMC desktop shortcut that was created in the previous steps and expand the Local Users and Groups snap-in. If a dialog box appears, click Yes.

2. Highlight the Users folder and select Action ➢ New User. The New User dialog box appears, as shown in Figure 8.5.

3. In the User Name text box, type **CPanek**.

4. In the Full Name text box, type **Crystal Panek**.

5. In the Description text box, type **Operations Manager**.

6. Leave the Password and Confirm Password text boxes empty and accept the defaults for the check boxes. Make sure you deselect the User Must Change Password At Next Logon option. Click the Create button to add the user.

FIGURE 8.5
New User dialog box

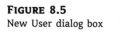

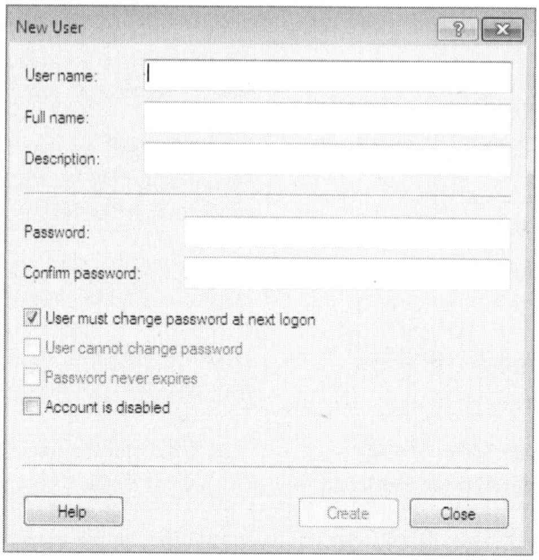

7. Use the New User dialog box to create six more users, filling out the fields as follows:

   ◆ Name: **WPanek**; Full Name: **Will Panek**; Description: **IT Admin**; Password: (blank)

   ◆ Name: **TWentworth**; Full Name: **Tylor Wentworth**; Description: **Cisco Admin**; Password: (blank)

   ◆ Name: **GWashington**; Full Name: **George Washington**; Description: **President**; Password: **P@ssw0rD**

   ◆ Name: **JAdams**; Full Name: **John Adams**; Description: **Vice President**; Password: **v!$t@**

   ◆ Name: **BFranklin**; Full Name: *Ben Franklin*; Description: **NH Sales Manager**; Password: **P3@ch** (with a capital P)

   ◆ Name: **ALincoln**; Full Name: **Abe Lincoln**; Description: **Tech Support**; Password: **Bearded1** (capital B)

8. After you finish creating all the users, click the Close button to exit the New User dialog box.

COMMAND-LINE UTILITY

You can also create users through the command-line utility NET USER. For more information about this command, type **NET USER /?** at a command prompt.

As we stated earlier, it's a good practice to disable accounts for users who leave the company. Let's look at that process.

Disabling User Accounts

When a user account is no longer needed, the account should be disabled or deleted. After you've disabled an account, you can later enable it again to restore it with all of its associated user properties. An account that is deleted, however, can never be recovered.

SECURITY THREATS

User accounts not in use pose a security threat because an intruder could access your network through an inactive account. User accounts that are no longer needed should be disabled immediately.

You might disable an account because a user will not be using it for a period of time, perhaps because that employee is going on vacation or taking a leave of absence. Another reason to disable an account is that you're planning to put another user in that same function.

For example, suppose that Gary, the engineering manager, quits. If you disable his account, when your company hires a new engineering manager, you can simply rename Gary's user account (to the username for the new manager) and enable that account. This ensures that the user who takes over Gary's position will have all the same user properties and own all the same resources.

Disabling accounts also provides a security mechanism for special situations. For example, if your company were laying off a group of people, a security measure would be to disable their accounts at the same time the layoff notices were given out. This prevents those users from inflicting any damage to the company's files after they receive their layoff notice.

Perform the following steps to disable a user account. Before you complete these steps, you should have already created new users, as shown in the previous section.

1. Open the Admin Console MMC desktop shortcut and expand the Local Users and Groups snap-in.

2. Open the Users folder. Double-click user WPanek to open his Properties dialog box.

3. In the General tab, check the Account Is Disabled box. Click OK.

4. Close the Local Users and Groups MMC.

5. Log off and attempt to log on as WPanek. This should fail because the account is now disabled.

6. Log back on using your user account.

PROPERTIES SHORTCUT

Another option for accessing a user's properties is to highlight the user, right-click, and select Properties.

Now when users have left a company for a long period of time and you know you no longer need the user account, you can delete the account. Let's look at how to delete user accounts.

Deleting User Accounts

As noted in the preceding section, you should disable a user account if you are not sure that the account will ever be needed again. But if the account has been disabled and you know that the user account will never need access again, you should then delete the account.

To delete a user, open the Local Users and Groups utility, highlight the user account you want to delete, and click Action to bring up the menu, as shown in Figure 8.6. Then select Delete. You can also delete an account by clicking the account and pressing the Delete key on the keyboard.

FIGURE 8.6
Deleting a user account

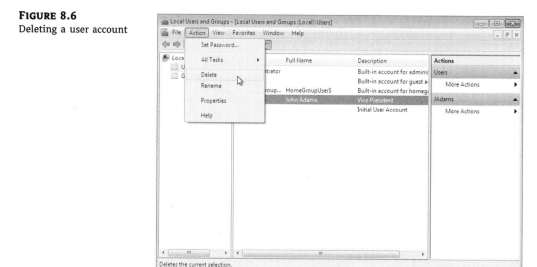

Because user deletion is a permanent action, you see the dialog box shown in Figure 8.7 that asks you to confirm that you really want to delete the account. After you click the Yes button, you will not be able to re-create or reaccess the account (unless you restore your local user accounts database from a backup).

FIGURE 8.7
Confirming user deletion

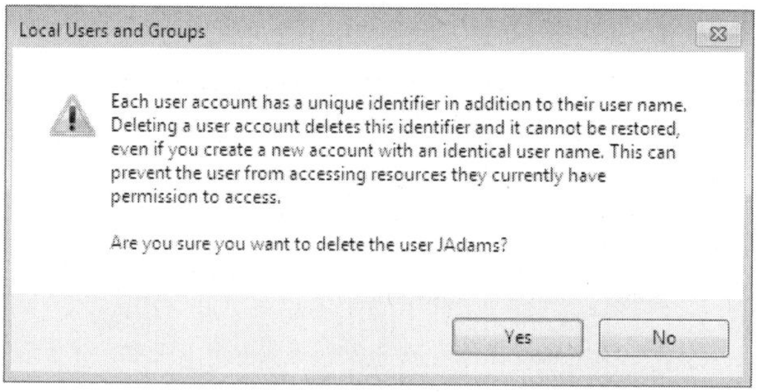

Perform the following steps to delete a user account. These steps assume you have completed the previous steps in this chapter.

1. Open the Admin Console MMC Desktop shortcut and expand the Local Users and Groups snap-in.

2. Expand the Users folder and single-click on user JAdams to select his user account.

3. Select Action ➤ Delete. The dialog box for confirming user deletion appears.

4. Click Yes to confirm that you want to delete this user.

5. Close the Local Users and Groups MMC.

Now that we have disabled and deleted accounts, let's see how to rename a user's account.

Renaming User Accounts

After you have created an account, you can rename the account at any time. Renaming a user account allows the user to retain all the associated user properties of the previous username. As noted previously in the chapter, the name is a property of the SID.

You might want to rename a user account because the user's name has changed (for example, the user got married) or because the name was spelled incorrectly. Also, as explained in the "Disabling User Accounts" section, you can rename an existing user's account for a new user, such as someone hired to take an ex-employee's position, when you want the new user to have the same properties.

Perform the following steps to rename a user account. These steps assume you have completed all of the previous steps in this chapter.

1. Open the Admin Console MMC shortcut and expand the Local Users and Groups snap-in.

2. Open the Users folder and highlight user ALincoln.

3. Select Action ➤ Rename.

4. Type the username **RReagan** and press Enter. Notice that the Full Name retained the original property of Abe Lincoln in the Local Users and Groups utility.

5. Double-click RReagan to open their properties and change the user's full name to **Ronald Reagan**.

6. Click the User Must Change Password At Next Logon checkbox.

7. Click OK.

8. Close the Local Users and Groups MMC.

RENAMED USER'S PROPERTIES

Renaming a user does not change any "hard-coded" names, such as the user's home folder. If you want to change these names as well, you need to modify them manually, for example, through Windows Explorer.

Another common task that we must deal with is resetting the user's password. You'll learn how next.

Changing a User's Password

What should you do if a user forgets his password and can't log on? You can't just open a dialog box and see the old password. However, as the administrator, you can change the user's password and then the user can use the new one.

It is important as IT managers and IT administrators to teach your users the proper security measures that go along with password protection. As you have all probably seen before, the users who tape their password to their monitors or under the keyboards need to be taught the correct methods for protecting their passwords.

It's our job as IT professionals to teach our users proper security and it always amazes me when I do consulting how many IT departments don't teach their users properly.

IT personnel should give classes to their users at least once a month on different topics. One of these topics should be proper password security. Teach your users how to protect their passwords and what to do if their passwords get compromised.

Perform the following steps to change a user's password. This exercise assumes you have completed all the previous steps in this chapter.

1. Open the Admin Console MMC Desktop shortcut and expand the Local Users and Groups snap-in.

2. Open the Users folder and highlight user CPanek.

3. Select Action ➤ Set Password. The Set Password dialog box appears.

4. A warning appears that indicates risks are involved in changing the password. Select Proceed.

5. Type the new password and then confirm the password. Click OK.

6. Close the Local Users and Groups MMC.

Now that you have seen how to create users in Windows 7, let's look at configuring and managing your user's properties.

Managing User Properties

For more control over user accounts, you can configure user properties. Through the user's Properties dialog box, you can change the original password options, add the users to existing groups, and specify user profile information.

To open a user's Properties dialog box, access the Local Users and Groups utility, open the Users folder, and double-click the user account. The user's Properties dialog box has tabs for the three main categories of properties: General, Member Of, and Profile.

The General tab contains the information you supplied when you set up the new user account, including any Full Name and Description information, the password options you selected, and whether the account is disabled. If you want to modify any of these properties after you've created the user, simply open the user's Properties dialog box and make the changes on the General tab.

You can use the Member Of tab to manage the user's membership in groups. The Profile tab lets you set properties to customize the user's environment. The following sections discuss the Member Of and Profile tabs in detail.

Managing User Group Membership

The Member Of tab of the user's Properties dialog box displays all the groups that the user belongs to, as shown in Figure 8.8. On this tab, you can add the user to an existing group or remove that user from a group. To add a user to a group, click the Add button and select the group that the user should belong to. If you want to remove the user from a group, highlight the group and click the Remove button.

FIGURE 8.8
The Member Of tab of
the user's Properties
dialog box

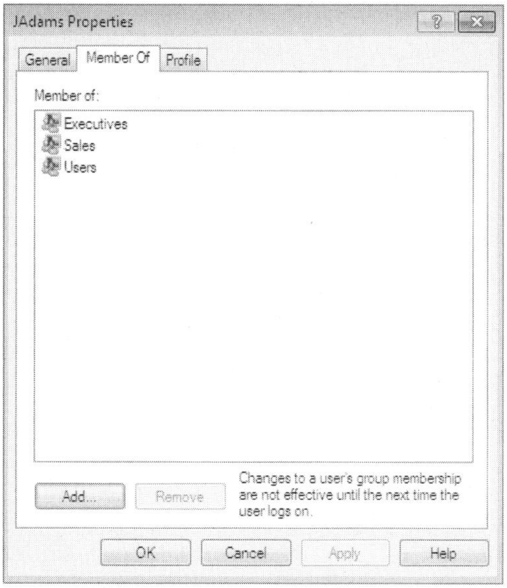

Perform the following steps to add a user to an existing group. These steps assume you have completed all the previous steps in this chapter.

1. Open the Local Users and Groups MMC Desktop snap-in that you created in the previous steps.

2. Open the Users folder and double-click user WPanek. The WPanek Properties dialog box appears.

3. Select the Member Of tab and click the Add button. The Select Groups dialog box appears.

4. Under Enter The Object Names To Select, type **Backup Operators** and click the Check Names button. After the name is confirmed, click OK.

5. Click OK to close the WPanek Properties dialog box.

The final tab in the user's properties is called the Profile tab. Now let's look at that Profile tab and the options that you can configure within that tab.

Setting Up User Profiles, Logon Scripts, and Home Folders

The Profile tab of the user's Properties dialog box, shown in Figure 8.9, allows you to customize the user's environment. Here, you can specify the following items for the user:

◆ User profile path

◆ Logon script

◆ Home folder

FIGURE 8.9
The Profile tab of
the user's Properties
dialog box

The following sections describe how these properties work and when you might want to use them.

SETTING A PROFILE PATH

User profiles contain information about the Windows 7 environment for a specific user. For example, profile settings include the Desktop arrangement, program groups, and screen colors that users see when they log on.

Each time you log on to a Windows 7 computer, the system checks to see if you have a local user profile in the Users folder, which was created on the boot partition when you installed Windows 7.

USERS PROFILES

The default location for user profiles is `systemdrive:\Users\UserName`.

If you need to reapply the default user profile for a user, you can delete the user's profile by opening the Control Panel ➤ click System ➤ click Advanced system settings ➤ click Settings in the User Profiles area of the Advanced tab ➤ select the user profile to delete ➤ and click Delete.

The first time users log on, they receive a default user profile. A folder that matches the user's logon name is created for the user in the Users folder. The user profile folder that is created holds a file called `NTUSER.DAT`, as well as subfolders that contain directory links to the user's Desktop items.

Perform the following steps to create two new users and set up local user profiles:

1. Using the Local Users and Groups utility, create two new users: APanek and PPanek. Deselect the User Must Change Password At Next Logon option for each user.

2. Select Start ➢ All Programs ➢ Accessories ➢ Windows Explorer. Expand Computer, then Local Disk (C:), and then Users. Notice that the Users folder does not contain user profile folders for the new users.

3. Log off and log on as APanek.

4. Right-click an open area on the Desktop and select Personalize. In the Personalization dialog box, select a color scheme and click Apply, and then click OK.

5. Right-click an open area on the Desktop and select New ➢ Shortcut. In the Create Shortcut dialog box, type **CALC**. Accept CALC as the name for the shortcut and click Finish.

6. Log off as APanek and log on as PPanek. Notice that user PPanek sees the Desktop configuration stored in the default user profile.

7. Log off as PPanek and log on as APanek. Notice that APanek sees the Desktop configuration you set up in steps 3, 4, and 5.

8. Log off as APanek and log on as your user account. Select Start ➢ All Programs ➢ Accessories ➢ Windows Explorer. Expand Computer, then Local Disk (C:), and then Users. Notice that this folder now contains user profile folders for APanek and PPanek.

The drawback of local user profiles is that they are available only on the computer where they were created. For example, suppose all of your Windows 7 computers are a part of a domain and you use only local user profiles.

User Rick logs on at Computer A and creates a customized user profile. When he logs on to Computer B for the first time, he will receive the default user profile rather than the customized user profile he created on Computer A. For users to access their user profile from any computer they log on to, you need to use roaming profiles; however, these require the use of a network server and they can't be stored on a local Windows 7 computer.

In the next sections, you will learn about how roaming profiles and mandatory profiles can be used. In order to have a roaming profile or a mandatory profile, your computer must be a part of a network with server access.

Using Roaming Profiles

A roaming profile is stored on a network server and allows users to access their user profile, regardless of the client computer to which they're logged on. Roaming profiles provide a consistent Desktop for users who move around, no matter which computer they access. Even if the server that stores the roaming profile is unavailable, the user can still log on using a local profile.

If you are using roaming profiles, the contents of the user's systemdrive:\Users\UserName folder will be copied to the local computer each time the roaming profile is accessed. If you have stored large files in any subfolders of your user profile folder, you might notice a significant delay when accessing your profile remotely as opposed to locally.

If this problem occurs, you can reduce the amount of time the roaming profile takes to load by moving the subfolder to another location, such as the user's home directory, or you can use

Group Policy Objects within Active Directory to specify that specific folders should be excluded when the roaming profile is loaded.

Using Mandatory Profiles

A mandatory profile is a profile that can't be modified by the user. Only members of the Administrators group can manage mandatory profiles. You might consider creating mandatory profiles for users who should maintain consistent Desktops.

For example, suppose you have a group of 20 salespeople who know enough about system configuration to make changes but not enough to fix any problems they create. For ease of support, you could use mandatory profiles. This way, all of the salespeople will always have the same profile and will not be able to change their profiles.

You can create mandatory profiles for a single user or a group of users. The mandatory profile is stored in a file named NTUSER.MAN. A user with a mandatory profile can set different Desktop preferences while logged on, but those settings will not be saved when the user logs off.

MANDATORY PROFILES

You can use only roaming profiles as mandatory profiles. Mandatory profiles do not work for local user profiles.

There is a second type of mandatory profile called Super Mandatory Profile. Let's look at this other type of profile.

Using Super Mandatory Profiles

A super mandatory profile is a mandatory user profile with an additional layer of security. With mandatory profiles, a temporary profile is created if the mandatory profile is not available when a user logs on. However, when super mandatory profiles are configured, temporary profiles are not created if the mandatory profile is not available over the network, and the user is unable to log on to the computer.

The process for creating super mandatory profiles is similar to creating mandatory profiles, except that instead of renaming the user folder to Username.v2, you name the folder Username.man.v2.

🌐 Real World Scenario

COPYING USER PROFILES

Within your company you have a user, Paige, who logs in with two different user accounts. One account is a regular user account and the other is an Administrator account used for administrative tasks only.

When Paige established all her Desktop preferences and installed the computer's applications, she used the Administrator account. Now when she logs in with the regular user account, she can't access the Desktop and profile settings that were created for her as an administrative user.

> To solve this problem, you can copy a local user profile from one user to another (for example, from Paige's Administrator account to her regular user account). Choose Control Panel ➤ System, click Advanced System Settings, and click the User Profiles Settings button. When you copy a user profile, the following items are copied: Favorites, Cookies, Documents, Start menu items, and other unique user Registry settings.

Another configurable item on the Profile tab of the user's properties is using logon scripts. Let's see how to configure these scripts.

CONFIGURING LOGON SCRIPTS

Logon scripts are files that run every time a user logs on to the network. They are usually batch files, but they can be any type of executable file.

You might use logon scripts to set up drive mappings or to run a specific executable file each time a user logs on to the computer. For example, you could run an inventory management file that collects information about the computer's configuration and sends that data to a central management database. Logon scripts are also useful for compatibility with non–Windows 7 clients who want to log on but still maintain consistent settings with their native operating system.

To run a logon script for a user, enter the script name in the Logon Script text box on the Profile tab of the user's Properties dialog box.

Next we'll look at another item that you can configure on the Profile tab: home folders.

SETTING UP HOME FOLDERS

Users usually store their personal files and information in a private folder called a home folder. In the Profile tab of the user's Properties dialog box, you can specify the location of a home folder as a local folder or a network folder.

To specify a local path folder, choose the Local Path option and type the path in the text box next to that option. To specify a network path for a folder, choose the Connect option and specify a network path using a Universal Naming Convention (UNC) path.

A UNC consists of the computer name and the share that has been created on the computer. In this case, a network folder should already be created and shared. For example, if you wanted to connect to a folder called \Users\Will on a server called SALES, you'd choose the Connect option, select a drive letter that would be mapped to the home directory, and then type **\\SALES\Users\Will** in the To box.

If the home folder you are specifying does not exist, Windows 7 attempts to create the folder for you. You can also use the variable %username% in place of a specific user's name.

Perform the following steps to assign a home folder to a user. These steps assume you have completed all the previous steps in this chapter.

1. Open the Admin Console MMC desktop shortcut and expand the Local Users and Groups snap-in.

2. Open the Users folder and double-click user WPanek. The WPanek Properties dialog box appears.

3. Select the Profile tab and click the Local Path radio button to select it.

4. Specify the home folder path by typing **C:\HomeFolders\WPanek** in the text box for the Local Path option. Then click OK.

5. Use Windows Explorer to verify that this folder was created.

6. Close the Local Users and Groups MMC.

🌐 Real World Scenario

MANAGING HOME FOLDERS

As an administrator for a large network, one of my primary responsibilities is to make sure that all data is backed up daily. This practice can be difficult because making daily backups of each user's local hard drive is impractical. You can also have problems with employees deleting important corporate information as they are leaving the company.

After examining the contents of a typical user's local drive, you will realize that most of the local disk space is taken by the operating system and the user's stored applications. This information does not change and does not need to be backed up. What we are primarily concerned with is backing up the user's data.

To more effectively manage this data and accommodate the necessary backup, you should create home folders for each user, stored on a network share. This allows the data to be backed up daily, to be readily accessible should a local computer fail, and to be easily retrieved if the user leaves the company.

Here are the steps to create a home folder that resides on the network. Decide which server will store the users' home folders, create a directory structure that will store the home folders efficiently (for example, C:\HOME), and create a single share to the home folder. Then use NTFS and share permissions to ensure that only the specified user has permissions to their home folder. Setting permissions is covered in Chapter 9, "Managing Security." After you create the share and assign permissions, you can specify the location of the home folder on the Profile tab of the user's Properties dialog box.

After you create your users' accounts, there is a possibility that you can run into errors or issues with the user's accounts. In the next section we look at how to troubleshoot user account issues.

Troubleshooting User Accounts Authentication

When a user attempts to log on through Windows 7 and is unable to be authenticated, you need to track down the reason for the problem.

The following sections offer some suggestions that can help you troubleshoot logon authentication errors for local and domain user accounts.

Troubleshooting Local User Account Authentication

If a local user is having trouble logging on, the problem might be with the username, with the password, or with the user account itself. The following list gives some common causes of local logon errors:

Incorrect Username You can verify that the username is correct by checking the Local Users and Groups utility. Verify that the name was spelled correctly.

Incorrect Password   Remember that passwords are case sensitive. Is the Caps Lock key on? If you see any messages that relate to an expired password or locked-out account, the reason for the problem is obvious. If necessary, you can assign a new password through the Local Users and Groups utility.

Prohibitive User Rights   Does the user have permission to log on locally at the computer? By default, the Log On Locally user right is granted to the Users group, so all users can log on to Windows 7 computers.

However, if this user's right was modified, you will see an error message stating that the local policy of this computer does not allow interactive logon. The terms *interactive logon* and *local logon* are synonymous and mean that the user is logging on at the computer where the user account is stored on the computer's local database.

A Disabled or Deleted Account   You can verify whether an account has been disabled or deleted by checking the account properties using the Local Users and Groups utility.

A Domain Account Logon at the Local Computer   If a computer is part of a domain, the logon dialog box has options for logging on to the domain or to the local computer. Make sure that the user has chosen the correct option.

You might also have issues with logging onto the domain. In the next section we look at how to troubleshoot domain accounts.

Troubleshooting Domain User Accounts Authentication

Troubleshooting a logon problem for a user with a domain account involves checking the same areas as you do for local account logon problems, as well as a few others.

We cover domain accounts in detail in Chapter 12, but let's cover some of the issues you might encounter with domain accounts authentication.

The following list gives some common causes of domain logon errors:

Incorrect Password   As with local accounts, check that the password was entered in the proper case (and the Caps Lock key isn't on), the password hasn't expired, and the account has not been locked out. If the password still doesn't work, you can assign a new password using the Active Directory Users and Computers utility.

Incorrect Username   You can verify that the username is correct by checking the Active Directory Users and Computers utility to verify that the name was spelled correctly.

Prohibitive User Rights   Does the user have permission to log on locally at the computer? This assumes that the user is attempting to log on to the domain controller. Regular users do not have permission to log on locally at the domain controller. The assumption is that users will log on to the domain from network workstations. If the user has a legitimate reason to log on locally at the domain controller, that user should be assigned the Log On Locally user right.

A Disabled or Deleted Account   You can verify whether an account has been disabled or deleted by checking the account properties using the Active Directory Users and Computers utility.

A Local Account Logon at a Domain Computer   Is the user trying to log on with a local user account name instead of a domain account? Make sure that the user has selected to log on to a domain in the Logon dialog box.

The Computer Being Used Is Not Part of the Domain Is the user sitting at a computer that is part of the domain to which the user is trying to log on? If the Windows 7 computer is not part of the domain that contains the user account or does not have a trust relationship defined with the domain that contains the user account, the user will be unable to log on.

Unavailable Domain Controller, DNS Server, or Global Catalog Is the domain controller available to authenticate the user's request? If the domain controller is down for some reason, the user will be unable to log on until it comes back up (unless the user logs on using a local user account). A DNS server and the Global Catalog for Active Directory are also required.

When a user login is successful, the logon credentials are saved to local cache. The next time the user attempts to log on, the cached credentials can be used to log on in the event that they can't be authenticated by a domain controller.

If Group Policies have been updated and a user is using cached credentials, the new Group Policy updates will not be applied. If you want to force a user to log on using noncached credentials, you can set the number of cached credentials to 0 using a Group Policy. Group Policy is covered in detail in Chapter 9.

After creating user accounts, normally we place these user accounts into groups, which we discuss in the next section.

Creating and Managing Groups

Groups are an important part of network management. Many administrators are able to accomplish the majority of their management tasks through the use of groups; they rarely assign permissions to individual users.

Windows 7 includes built-in local groups, such as Administrators and Backup Operators. These groups already have all the permissions needed to accomplish specific tasks. Windows 7 also uses default special groups, which are managed by the system. Users become members of special groups based on their requirements for computer and network access.

You can create and manage local groups through the Local Users and Groups utility. With this utility, you can add groups, change group membership, rename groups, and delete groups.

One misconception with groups is that they have to work with Group Policy Objects (GPOs). This is not correct. GPOs are a set of rules that allow you to set computer configuration and user configuration options that apply to users or computers. Group Policies are typically used with Active Directory and are applied as GPOs. GPOs are discussed in detail in Chapter 9, "Managing Security."

In the following sections, you will learn about groups and all the built-in groups. Then you will learn how to create and manage these groups.

Using Built-in Groups

On a Windows 7 computer, default local groups have already been created and assigned all necessary permissions to accomplish basic tasks. In addition, there are built-in special groups that the Windows 7 system handles automatically. These groups are described in the following sections.

Using Default Local Groups A local group is a group that is stored on the local computer's accounts database. These are the groups you can add users to and can manage directly on a Windows 7 computer. By default, the following local groups are created on Windows 7 computers:

- ◆ Administrators

- ◆ Backup Operators

- ◆ Cryptographic Operators

- ◆ Distributed COM Users

- ◆ Event Log Readers

- ◆ Guests

- ◆ IIS_IUSRS

- ◆ Network Configuration Operators

- ◆ Performance Log Users

- ◆ Performance Monitor Users

- ◆ Power Users

- ◆ Remote Desktop Users

- ◆ Replicator

- ◆ Users

We briefly describe each group, its default permissions, and the users assigned to the group by default.

BUILT-IN GROUPS

If possible, you should add users to the built-in local groups rather than creating new groups from scratch. This simplifies administration because the built-in groups already have the appropriate permissions. All you need to do is add the users whom you want to be members of the group.

The Administrators Group   The Administrators group has full permissions and privileges. Its members can grant themselves any permissions they do not have by default to manage all the objects on the computer. (Objects include the file system, printers, and account management.) By default, the Administrator account, which is disabled by default, and the initial user account are members of the Administrators local group.

ADMINISTRATORS GROUP

Assign users to the Administrators group with caution because they will have full permissions to manage the computer.

Members of the Administrators group can perform the following tasks:

- Install the operating system.
- Install and configure hardware device drivers.
- Install system services.
- Install service packs, hot fixes, and Windows updates.
- Upgrade the operating system.
- Repair the operating system.
- Install applications that modify the Windows system files.
- Configure password policies.
- Configure audit policies.
- Manage security logs.
- Create administrative shares.
- Create administrative accounts.
- Modify groups and accounts that have been created by other users.
- Remotely access the Registry.
- Stop or start any service.
- Configure services.
- Increase and manage disk quotas.
- Increase and manage execution priorities.
- Remotely shut down the system.
- Assign and manage user rights.
- Reenable locked-out and disabled accounts.
- Manage disk properties, including formatting hard drives.
- Modify systemwide environment variables.
- Access any data on the computer.
- Back up and restore all data.

The Backup Operators Group   Members of the Backup Operators group have permissions to back up and restore the file system, even if the file system is NTFS and they have not been assigned permissions to access the file system. However, the members of Backup Operators can access the file system only using the Backup utility. To access the file system directly, Backup Operators must have explicit permissions assigned. There are no default members of the Backup Operators local group.

The Cryptographic Operators Group   The Cryptographic Operators group has access to perform cryptographic operations on the computer. There are no default members of the Cryptographic Operators local group.

The Distributed COM Users Group   The Distributed COM Users group has the ability to launch and run Distributed COM objects on the computer. There are no default members of the Distributed COM Users local group.

The Event Log Readers Group   The Event Log Readers group has access to read the event log on the local computer. There are no default members of the Event Log Readers local group.

The Guests Group   The Guests group has limited access to the computer. This group is provided so that you can allow people who are not regular users to access specific network resources. As a general rule, most administrators do not allow Guest access because it poses a potential security risk. By default, the Guest user account is a member of the Guests local group.

The IIS_IUSRS Group   The IIS_IUSRS group is used by Internet Information Services (IIS). The NT AUTHORITY\IUSR user account is a member of the IIS_IUSRS group by default.

The Network Configuration Operators Group   Members of the Network Configuration Operators group have some administrative rights to manage the computer's network configuration — for example, editing the computer's TCP/IP settings.

The Performance Log Users Group   The Performance Log Users group has the ability to access and schedule logging of performance counters and can create and manage trace counters on the computer.

The Performance Monitor Users Group   The Performance Monitor Users group has the ability to access and view performance counter information on the computer. Users who are members of this group can access performance counters both locally and remotely.

The Power Users Group   The Power Users group is included in Windows 7 for backward compatibility. The Power Users group is included to ensure that computers upgraded from Windows XP function as before with regard to folders that allow access to members of the Power Users group. Otherwise, the Power Users group has limited administrative rights.

The Remote Desktop Users Group   The Remote Desktop Users group allows members of the group to log on remotely for the purpose of using the Remote Desktop service.

The Replicator Group   The Replicator group is intended to support directory replication, which is a feature that domain servers use. Only domain users who will start the replication service should be assigned to this group. The Replicator local group has no default members.

The Users Group   The Users group is intended for end users who should have very limited system access. If you have installed a fresh copy of Windows 7, the default settings for the Users group prohibit its members from compromising the operating system or program files. By default, all users who have been created on the computer, except Guest, are members of the Users local group.

Another type of group that is used by Windows 7 is special groups. In the next section we will look at special groups and how they work.

Using Special Groups

Special groups can be used by the system or by administrators. Membership in these groups is automatic if certain criteria are met. You cannot manage special groups through the Local Users and Groups utility, but an administrator can add these special groups to resources. Table 8.3 describes several of the special groups that are built into Windows 7.

TABLE 8.3:   Special Groups in Windows 7

GROUP	DESCRIPTION
Anonymous Logon	This group includes users who access the computer through anonymous logons. When users gain access through special accounts created for anonymous access to Windows 7 services, they become members of the Anonymous Logon group.
Authenticated Users	This group includes users who access the Windows 7 operating system through a valid username and password. Users who can log on belong to the Authenticated Users group.
Batch	This group includes users who log on as a user account that is used only to run a batch job. Batch job accounts are members of the Batch group.
Creator Owner	This is the account that created or took ownership of the object and is typically a user account. Each object (files, folders, printers, and print jobs) has an owner. Members of the Creator Owner group have special permissions to resources. For example, if you are a regular user who has submitted 12 print jobs to a printer, you can manipulate your print jobs as Creator Owner, but you can't manage any print jobs submitted by other users.
Dialup	This group includes users who log on to the network from a dial-up connection. Dial-up users are members of the Dialup group.
Everyone	This group includes anyone who could possibly access the computer. The Everyone group includes all users who have been defined on the computer (including Guest), plus (if your computer is a part of a domain) all users within the domain. If the domain has trust relationships with other domains, all users in the trusted domains are part of the Everyone group as well. The exception to automatic group membership with the Everyone group is that members of the Anonymous Logon group are not included as a part of the Everyone group.
Interactive	This group includes all users who use the computer's resources locally. Local users belong to the Interactive group.
Network	This group includes users who access the computer's resources over a network connection. Network users belong to the Network group.
Service	This group includes users who log on as a user account that is used only to run a service. You can configure the use of user accounts for logon through the Services program, and these accounts become members of the Service group.
System	When the system accesses specific functions as a user, that process becomes a member of the System group.
Terminal Server User	This group includes users who log on through Terminal Services. These users become members of the Terminal Server User group.

Now that we have looked at the different types of groups, let's explore at how to manage and work with these groups.

Working with Groups

Groups are used to logically organize users with similar rights requirements. Groups simplify administration because you can manage a few groups rather than many user accounts. For the same reason, groups simplify troubleshooting. Users can belong to as many groups as needed, so it's not difficult to put users into groups that make sense for your organization.

For example, suppose Jane is hired as a data analyst to join the four other data analysts who work for your company. You sit down with Jane and create an account for her, assigning her the network permissions for the access you think she needs. Later, however, you find that the four other data analysts (who have similar job functions) sometimes have network access Jane doesn't have, and sometimes she has access they don't have. This is happening because all their permissions were assigned individually and months apart.

To avoid such problems and reduce your administrative workload, you can assign all the company's data analysts to a group and then assign the appropriate permissions to that group. Then, as data analysts join or leave the department, you can simply add them to or remove them from the group.

You can create new groups for your users, and you can use the Windows 7 default local built-in groups that were described in the previous section. In both cases, your planning should include checking to see if an existing local group meets your requirements before you decide to create a new group.

For example, if all the users need to access a particular application, it makes sense to use the default Users group rather than creating a new group and adding all the users to that group.

To work with groups, you can use the Local Users and Groups utility. Let's see how to create new groups.

CREATING NEW GROUPS

To create a group, you must be logged on as a member of the Administrators group. The Administrators group has full permissions to manage users and groups.

As you do in your choices for usernames, keep your naming conventions in mind when assigning names to groups. When you create a local group, consider the following guidelines:

◆ The group name should be descriptive (for example, Accounting Data Users).

◆ The group name must be unique to the computer, different from all other group names and usernames that exist on that computer.

◆ Group names can be up to 256 characters. It is best to use alphanumeric characters for ease of administration. Most special characters — for example, backslash (\) — are not allowed.

Creating groups is similar to creating users, and it is a fairly easy process. After you've added the Local Users and Groups MMC or use the Local Users and Groups through Computer Management, expand it to see the Users and Groups folders. Right-click the Groups folder and select New Group from the context menu. This brings up the New Group dialog box, as shown in Figure 8.10.

The only required entry in the New Group dialog box is the group name. If appropriate, you can enter a description for the group, and you can add (or remove) group members. When you're ready to create the new group, click the Create button.

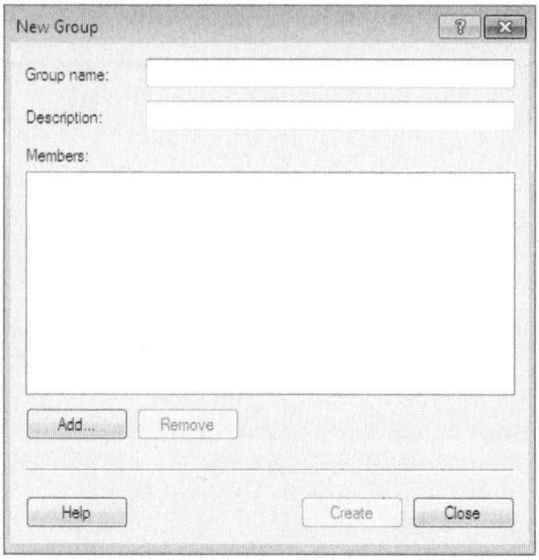

FIGURE 8.10
The New Group dialog
box

Perform the following steps to create two new local groups:

1. Open the Admin Console MMC Desktop shortcut you created and expand the Local Users and Groups snap-in.

2. Right-click the Groups folder and select New Group.

3. In the New Group dialog box, type **Data Users** in the Group Name text box. Click the Create button.

4. In the New Group dialog box, type **Application Users** in the Group Name text box. Click the Create button.

After the groups are created, you have to manage the groups and its membership. In the next section we look at managing groups.

MANAGING GROUP MEMBERSHIP

After you've created a group, you can add members to it. As mentioned earlier, you can put the same user in multiple groups. You can easily add and remove users through a group's Properties dialog box, as shown in Figure 8.11. To access this dialog box from the Groups folder in the Local Users and Groups utility, double-click the group you want to manage.

From the group's Properties dialog box, you can change the group's description and add or remove group members. When you click the Add button to add members, the Select Users dialog box appears, as shown in Figure 8.12.

In the Select Users dialog box, enter the object names of the users you want to add. You can use the Check Names button to validate the users against the database. Select the user accounts you want to add and click Add. Click OK to add the selected users to the group.

SPECIAL GROUPS

Although the special groups that were covered earlier in the chapter are listed in this dialog box, you cannot manage the membership of these special groups.

FIGURE 8.11
A group's Properties
dialog box

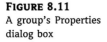

FIGURE 8.12
The Select Users
dialog box

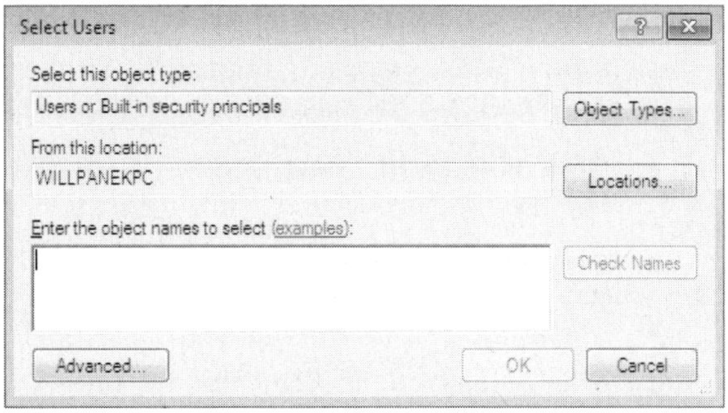

To remove a member from the group, select the member in the Members list of the Properties dialog box and click the Remove button.

Perform the following steps to create new user accounts and then add these users to one of the groups you created in the previous steps:

1. Open the Admin Console MMC shortcut you created and expand the Local Users and Groups snap-in.

2. Create two new users: JDoe and DDoe. Deselect the User Must Change Password At Next Logon option for each user.

3. Expand the Groups folder.

4. Double-click the Data Users group.

5. In the Data Users Properties dialog box, click the Add button.

6. In the Select Users dialog box, type the username **JDoe**, then click OK. Click Add and type the username **DDoe**, then click OK.

7. In the Data Users Properties dialog box, you will see that the users have all been added to the group. Click OK to close the group's Properties dialog box.

Another task that might need to be completed is changing the name of a group, and we discuss this in the next section.

RENAMING GROUPS

Windows 7 provides an easy mechanism for changing a group's name. For example, you might want to rename a group because its current name does not conform to existing naming conventions, or you may need to rename a group because the group task or location may change.

For example, let's say we have a group called Sales but as the company grows, so do the office locations. We now might have to rename the group NHSales and then create other groups for the other locations.

GROUPS

As happens when you rename a user account, a renamed group keeps all of its properties, including its members and permissions.

To rename a group, right-click the group and choose Rename from the context menu. Enter a new name for the group and press Enter.

Perform the following steps to rename one of the groups you created in the previous steps:

1. Open the Admin Console MMC Desktop shortcut and expand the Local Users and Groups snap-in.

2. Expand the Groups folder.

3. Right-click the Data Users group and select Rename.

4. Rename the group to **App Users** and press Enter.

There might come a point when a specific group is no longer needed. In the next section we look at how to delete a group from the Local Users and Groups utility.

DELETING GROUPS

If you are sure that you will never again want to use a particular group, you can delete it. Once a group is deleted, you lose all permissions assignments that have been specified for the group.

To delete a group, right-click the group and choose Delete from the context menu. You will see a warning that after a group is deleted, it is gone for good. Click the Yes button if you're sure you want to delete the group.

If you delete a group and give another group the same name, the new group won't be created with the same properties as the deleted group because as with users, groups are assigned unique SIDs at the time of creation.

Perform the following steps to delete the group that you created in the previous steps:

1. Open the Admin Console MMC shortcut you created and expand the Local Users and Groups snap-in.

2. Expand the Groups folder.

3. Right-click the App Users group and choose Delete.

4. In the dialog box that appears, click Yes to confirm that you want to delete the group.

Creating users and groups is one of the most important tasks that we as IT members can do. On a Windows 7 machine, creating users and groups is an easy and straightforward process.

Because most of the Windows 7 machines that you deal with will be part of a domain, you might need to create these users and groups as domain users. This process is discussed in detail in Chapter 12, "Networking with Windows Server 2008."

The Bottom Line

Understand user account types. Windows 7 uses two basic account types: Administrator and Standard User. The Administrator account type provides unrestricted access to performing administrative tasks. Administrator accounts should be used only for performing administrative tasks and should not be used for normal computing tasks.

The Standard User type is the account type that should be applied for every user of the computer. Standard User accounts can perform most day-to-day tasks on the Windows 7 machine.

> **Master It**   You are the administrator for a large computer company. You need to set up 20 Windows 7 machines and 20 local user accounts on those machines. When setting up the user accounts, what type of user account should these users have?

Create accounts. To create user accounts for your Windows 7 users, you have multiple options. To create local user accounts you can use the Local Users and Groups MMC snap-in, or you can use the User Accounts option in Control Panel. To create domain users accounts, you use Active Directory Users and Computers (see Chapter 12 for more information).

> **Master It**   You are the administrator for a large computer company. You need to create 20 local users accounts for the 20 new Windows 7 machines that your company has just purchased. How would you accomplish this task?

Configure accounts. When you're configuring users' accounts, you deal with three main categories of properties: General, Member Of, and Profile.

The General tab contains the information you supplied when you set up the new user account, including any Full Name and Description information, the password options you selected, and whether the account is disabled.

The Member Of tab allows you to place this account into local groups on this Windows 7 machine. The Profile tab enables you to configure a user's Profile data, including user profile path, logon scripts, and home folder locations.

Master It   You are the administrator for a small pottery company. Your users are complaining that when they work on any machine that is not their own, the desktop settings are different. This is causing an issue for your users. What can you do to make sure that all users have their own desktop settings no matter which machine they are working on?

Understand local groups.   Groups are a way to make sure that similar users get access to similar resources without having to add individual user accounts to each resource. Groups are an important part of network management.

Windows 7 includes built-in local groups, such as Administrators and Backup Operators. These groups already have all the permissions needed to accomplish specific tasks. Windows 7 also uses default special groups, which the system manages. Users become members of special groups based on their requirements for computer and network access.

You can create and manage local groups through the Local Users and Groups utility. The Local users and Groups snap-in allows you to add groups, change group membership, rename groups, and delete groups.

Master It   You are the administrator for a large organization. You have decided to set up local groups on all the Windows 7 machines so that all salespeople have access to the same resources. How do you accomplish this goal?

Chapter 9

Managing Security

Windows 7 offers a wide variety of security options. If the Windows 7 computer is part of a domain, you can apply security through a Group Policy Object using the Group Policy Management Console. If the Windows 7 computer is not part of a domain, you use Local Group Policy Objects to manage local security.

In the first part of this chapter, you will learn about the different Windows 7 environments and the utilities that you can use to manage security.

You can use policies to help manage user accounts. Account policies control the logon environment for the computer, such as password and logon restrictions. Local policies specify what users can do after they log on and include auditing, user rights, and security options. You can also manage critical security features through the Windows Security Center.

We continue the chapter with NTFS security and shared permissions and how they work independently and how they work together.

In this chapter, you'll learn how to:

◆ Understand Local Group Policy Objects

◆ Understand User Account Control (UAC)

◆ Configure NTFS security

◆ Manage shared permissions

Managing Security Configurations

The tools you use to manage Windows 7 computer security configurations depend on whether the Windows 7 computer is part of a Windows 2000, Windows 2003, or Windows 2008 domain environment.

If the Windows 7 client is not part of a domain, you apply security settings through Local Group Policy Objects (LGPOs). LGPOs are a set of security configuration settings that are applied to users and computers. LGPOs are created and stored on the Windows 7 computer.

If your Windows 7 computer is part of a domain, which uses the services of Active Directory, you typically manage and configure security through Group Policy Objects (GPOs). Active Directory is the database that contains all your domain user and group accounts together with all other domain objects.

GPOs are policies that can be placed on either users or computers in the domain. The Group Policy Management Console (GPMC) is a Microsoft Management Console (MMC) snap-in that is used to configure and manage GPOs for users and computers via Active Directory.

Windows 7 computers that are part of a domain still have LGPOs, and you can use LGPOs in conjunction with the Active Directory group policies.

GROUP POLICY OBJECTS

Use of GPOs is covered in detail in *MCTS: Windows Server 2008 Active Directory Configuration*, by William Panek and James Chellis (Sybex, 2008).

The settings you can apply through the Group Policy Management Console (GPMC) utility are more comprehensive than the settings you can apply through LGPOs.

By default, LGPOs are stored in %systemroot% System32\GroupPolicyUsers. Table 9.1 lists some of the options that you can set for GPOs within Active Directory and which of those options you can apply through LGPOs.

TABLE 9.1:   Group Policy and LGPO Setting Options

GROUP POLICY SETTING	AVAILABLE FOR LGPO?
Software Installation	No
Remote Installation Services	Yes
Scripts	Yes
Printers	Yes
Security Settings	Yes
Policy-Based QOS	Yes
Administrative Templates	Yes
Folder Redirection	No
Internet Explorer Configuration	Yes

In the next section, we look at how GPOs work within an Active Directory domain.

Understanding Group Policy Objects and Active Directory

Most Windows 7 computers reside within a Windows Server 2000, Windows Server 2003, or Windows Server 2008 domain. GPOs are applied through Active Directory by using the Group Policy Management Console (GPMC). It is much easier to globally manage GPOs through the GPMC than applying LGPOs at local levels of each Windows 7 machine.

To help you understand how GPOs and LGPOs work together, the following sections first provide an overview of Active Directory and then show you how GPOs and LGPOs are applied based on predefined inheritance rules.

Active Directory Overview

First, the easiest way to explain Active Directory is to state that Active Directory is a database. That's it. Active Directory is just a database — but it's the most important database in your domain because the Active Directory database contains all your usernames and passwords, groups, and other objects within the domain.

Within that Active Directory database, you have several levels of a hierarchical structure. A typical structure consists of domains and Organizational Units (OUs). Other levels exist within Active Directory, but this overview focuses on domains and OUs in the context of using GPOs.

The domain (for example, Panek.com) is the main unit of organization within Active Directory, as shown in Figure 9.1. Within a domain are many domain objects, including security objects such as user and group accounts. Each domain security object can then have permissions applied that specify what rights that security object can have when it accesses resources within the domain.

FIGURE 9.1

Active Directory hierarchical structure

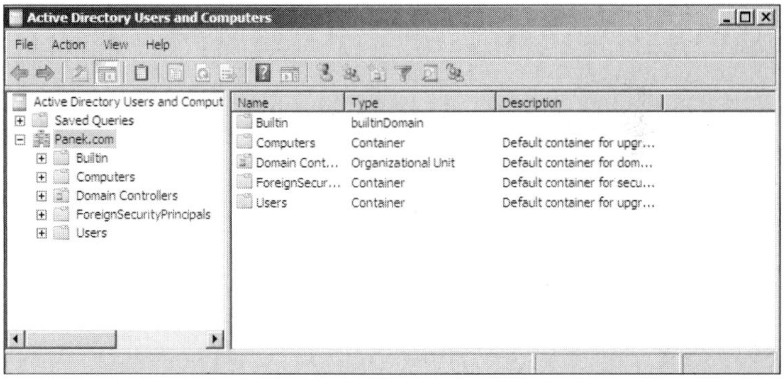

Within a domain, you can further subdivide and organize domain objects through the use of Organizational Units (OUs). This is one of the key differences between Windows NT 4 domains and Windows 2000, 2003, and 2008 domains. The NT domains were not able to store information hierarchically. Windows 2000, 2003, and 2008 domains, through the use of OUs, allow you to store objects hierarchically, typically based on function or geography.

For example, assume that your company is called Stellacon. You have locations in New York, San Jose, and Belfast. You might create a domain called Stellacon.Com with OUs called NY, SJ, and Belfast. In a large corporation, you might also organize the OUs based on function. For example, the domain could be Stellacon.Com and the OUs might be Sales, Accounting, and R&D. Based on the size and security needs of your organization, you might also have OUs nested within OUs. As a general rule, however, you want to keep your Active Directory structure as simple as possible.

Domains are logical grouping of objects. If we had the Stellacon.com domain, we would expect that everyone in the domain would belong to the company named Stellacon.

A domain does not have to be in one geographical location. Microsoft is a worldwide company and the Microsoft.com domain has locations all over the world.

If you need to set up physical locations, you would set up *sites*. Sites are physical representations of the domain. For example, let's say that we have a company with two buildings next to each other. You might want all the users in one building to access resources within that building and the same for the other building.

You can set up two sites, one for each building. Then users will always try to find resources in their own site first. If the resource in the site is not available, the user will automatically leave the site and try to find the resource in another site. Sites are an excellent way to keep your users local to their location.

SITES

Usage of sites is covered in detail in *MCTS: Windows Server 2008 Active Directory Configuration,* by William Panek and James Chellis (Sybex, 2008).

Now we'll explain how GPO inheritance works and what happens when multiple GPOs conflict with each other.

Understanding GPO Inheritance

When GPOs are created within Active Directory using the GPMC, there is a specific order of inheritance. That is, the policies are applied in a specific order within the hierarchical structure of Active Directory. When a user logs onto Active Directory, depending on where within the hierarchy GPOs have been applied, the order of application is as follows:

1. Local

2. Site

3. Domain

4. OU

Each level of the hierarchy is called a container. Containers higher in the hierarchy are called parent containers; containers lower in the hierarchy are called child containers. Settings from these containers are inherited from parent container to child container. By default, child container policy settings override any conflicting settings applied by parent containers.

For example, if you set the wallpaper at the site level to be red and set the wallpaper at the OU level to be blue, if a user who belongs to both the site and the OU logs on, their wallpaper would be blue.

The local policy is, by default, applied first when a user logs on. Then the site policies are applied, and if the site policy contains settings that the local policy doesn't have, they are added to the local policy. If any conflicts exist, the site policy overrides the local policy. Then the domain policies are defined.

Again, if the domain policy contains additional settings, they are incorporated. The domain policy overrides the site policy or the local policy when settings conflict. Finally, the OU policies are applied. Any additional settings are incorporated; for conflicts, the OU policy overrides the domain, site, and local policies. If any child OUs exist, their GPOs are applied after the parent OU GPOs.

So as we have just stated, the child policy overrides the parent policy by default, but this can be changed. As with any child/parent relationship, the parent can force the child to accept the policy that is being issued. The Enforce option allows you to override a child option. There is also the ability to block inheritance. Let's look at these two options:

Enforce (No Override) The Enforce option is used to specify that child containers can't override the policy settings of higher-level containers. For example, if a site policy is marked as

Enforce, it will not be overridden by conflicting domain or OU policies. If multiple Enforced policies are set, the one from the highest container would take precedence.

The Enforce option would be used if you wanted to set corporate-wide policies without allowing administrators of lower-level containers to override your settings. This option can be set per container, as needed.

The Enforce option used to be known as the No Override option. When you created a GPO in Active Directory Users and Computers, this option was called No Override. Now that we use the Group Policy Management Console (GPMC), it's called Enforce.

Block Inheritance   The Block Inheritance option is used to allow a child container to block GPO inheritance from parent containers. Use this option if you do not want to inherit GPO settings from parent containers and want only the GPO you have set for your container to be applied. For example, if you set Block Inheritance on an OU policy, only the OU policy would be applied; no parent container policies would be inherited.

If a conflict exists between the Enforce and the Block Inheritance settings, the Enforce option is applied.

APPLYING GPOs

You manage a network that consists of 500 computers all running Windows 7. You are already using Active Directory and have logically defined your OUs based on function. One OU, called Sales, has 50 users. Your task is to configure the Sales computers so they all have a consistent Desktop that can't be modified. You also need to add the new Sales Management software to each computer.

It would take days for you to manually configure each computer with a Local Group Policy and then add the software. In this case, GPOs are a real benefit. As the administrator of the Sales OU, you can create a single GPO that will be applied to all users of the container. You can specify the Desktop settings and publish any applications that you want to install. Next time the Sales users log on, the Group Policies are applied, and the users' Registries are updated to reflect the changes. In addition, through the automated publishing applications, the GPO can be configured to be automatically loaded on each of the Sales users' computers.

By using GPOs, you can add new software, configure computers, and accomplish other tasks from your computer that would normally require you to physically visit each machine.

Now that we have looked at GPOs, let's explore some of the tools available for creating and managing GPOs.

Using the Group Policy Result Tool

When a user logs on to a computer or domain, a resulting set of policies to be applied is generated based on the LGPOs, site GPOs, domain GPOs, and OU GPOs. The overlapping nature of Group Policies can make it difficult to determine what Group Policies will be applied to a computer or user.

To help determine what policies will actually be applied, Windows 7 includes a tool called the Group Policy Result Tool, also known as the Resultant Set of Policy (RSoP). You can access this tool through the GPResult command-line utility. The gpresult command displays the resulting set of policies that were enforced on the computer and the specified user during the logon process.

The gpresult command displays the RSoP for the computer and the user who is currently logged in. You can use several options with this command. Table 9.2 shows the different switches that you can use for the gpresult command.

TABLE 9.2: gpresult Switches

SWITCH	EXPLANATION
/F	Forces gpresult to override the filename specified in the /X or /H command
/H	Saves the report in an HTML format
/P	Specifies the password for a given user context
/R	Displays RSoP summary data
/S	Specifies the remote system to connect to
/U	Specifies which user context under which the command should be executed
/V	Specifies that verbose information should be displayed
/X	Saves the report in XML format
/Z	Specifies that the super verbose information should be displayed
/?	Shows all the gpresult command switches
/scope	Specifies whether the user or the computer settings need to be displayed
/User	Specifies the username for which the RSoP data is to be displayed

In the next section, you'll learn how to create and apply LGPOs to the Windows 7 machine.

Creating and Applying LGPOs

As we discussed previously, policies that have been linked through Active Directory will, by default, take precedence over any established Local Group Policies. Local Group Policies are typically applied to computers that are not part of a network or are in a network that does not have a domain controller, and thus do not use Active Directory.

Previous versions of Windows (before Vista) only contained one LGPO that applied to all the computer's users unless NTFS permissions were applied to the LGPO. However, Windows 7 and Windows Vista changed that with the addition of Multiple Local Group Policy

Objects (MLGPOs). Like Active Directory GPOs, MLGPOs are applied in a certain hierarchical order, as follows:

1. Local Computer Policy

2. Administrators and Non-Administrators Local Group Policy

3. User-Specific Group Policy

The Local Computer Policy is the only LGPO that includes computer and user settings; the other LGPOs only contain user settings. Settings applied here apply to all users of the computer.

The Administrators and Non-Administrators LGPOs were new to Windows Vista and are still included with Windows 7. The Administrators LGPO is applied to users who are members of the built-in local Administrators group. As you might guess, the Non-Administrators LGPO is applied to users who are not members of the local Administrators group. Because each user of a computer can be classified as an administrator or a non-administrator, either one policy or the other will apply.

User-Specific LGPOs are also included with Windows 7. These LGPOs make it possible for specific policy settings to apply to a single user.

Like Active Directory GPOs, any GPO settings applied lower in the hierarchy will override GPO settings applied higher in the hierarchy by default. For example, any user-specific GPO settings will override any conflicting administrator/non-administrator GPO settings or Local Computer Policy settings. And, of course, any AD GPO settings will still override any conflicting LGPO settings.

DISABLING THE LOCAL GROUP POLICY OBJECT

Domain administrators can disable LGPOs on Windows 7 computers by enabling the Turn Off LGPOs Processing domain GPO setting, which you can find under Computer Configuration\ Administrative Templates\System\Group Policy.

You apply an LGPO to a Windows 7 computer through the GPO Editor snap-in within the MMC. Figure 9.2 shows the Local Computer Policy dialog box for a Windows 7 computer. Perform the following steps to add the Local Computer Policy snap-in to the MMC:

1. Open the Admin Console MMC shortcut by typing **MMC** in the Search Programs And Files box.

2. A User Account Control dialog box appears. Click Yes.

3. Select File ➤ Add/Remove Snap-in.

4. Highlight the Group Policy Object Editor Snap-in and click the Add button.

5. The Group Policy Object specifies Local Computer by default. Click the Finish button.

6. In the Add Or Remove Snap-ins dialog box, click OK.

7. In the left-hand pane, right-click the Local Computer Policy and choose New Windows From Here.

8. Choose File ➤ Save As and name the console **LGPO**. Make sure you save it to the Desktop. Click Save.

9. Close the MMC Admin console.

FIGURE 9.2
Local Computer Policy
dialog box

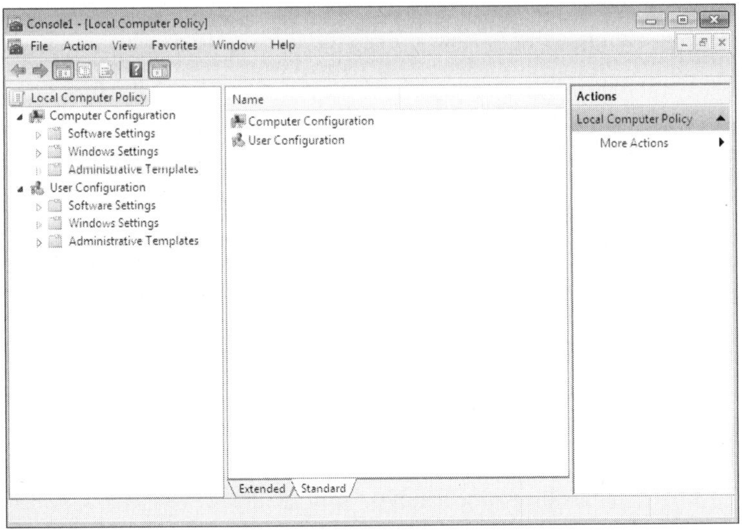

Now let's see how to open an LGPO for a specific user account on a Windows 7 machine. Perform the following steps to access the Administrators, Non-Administrators, and User-Specific LGPOs. The previous steps must be completed to use this procedure.

1. Open the Admin Console MMC shortcut by typing **MMC** in the Search Programs And Files box.

2. Select File ➤ Add/Remove Snap-in.

3. Highlight the Group Policy Object Editor Snap-in and click Add.

4. Click Browse to look for a different GPO.

5. Click the Users tab.

6. Select the user that you want to access and click OK.

7. In the Select Group Policy Object dialog box, click Finish.

8. In the Add Or Remove Snap-ins dialog box, click OK. You can close the console when you are finished looking at the LGPO settings for the user you chose.

USER CONFIGURATION SETTINGS ONLY

Notice that the Administrators, Non-Administrators, and User-Specific LGPOs contain only User Configuration settings, not Computer Configuration settings.

Now let's examine the various security settings that you can configure in the LGPO.

Configuring Local Security Policies

Through the use of the Local Computer Policy, you can set a wide range of security options under Computer Configuration\Windows Settings\Security Settings.

This portion of the Local Computer Policy is also known as the Local Security Policy. The following list describes in detail how to apply security settings through LGPOs, as shown in Figure 9.3.

FIGURE 9.3
Security settings of the LGPO

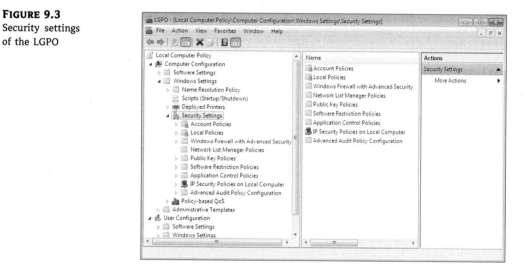

The main areas of security configuration of the LGPO are as follows:

Account Policies   You can use Account policies to configure password and account lockout features. Some of these settings include Password History, Maximum Password Age, Minimum Password Age, Minimum Password Length, Password Complexity, Account Lockout Duration, Account Lockout Threshold, and Reset Account Lockout Counter After.

Local Policies   You can use Local Policies to configure auditing, user rights, and security options.

Windows Firewall with Advanced Security   Windows Firewall with Advanced Security provides network security for Windows computers. Through this LGPO, you can set Domain, Private, and Public Profiles. You can also set this LGPO to authenticate communications between computers and inbound/outbound rules.

Network List Manager Policies   This section allows you to set the network name, icon, and location Group Policies. Administrators can set Unidentified Networks, Identifying Networks, and All Networks.

Public Key Policies   You can use the Public Key Policies settings to specify how to manage certificates and certificate life cycles.

Software Restriction Policies   Software Restriction Policies allow you to identify malicious software and control that software's ability to run on the Windows 7 machine. These policies allow an administrator to protect the Windows 7 operating system against security threats such as viruses and Trojan horse programs.

Application Control Policies   You can use these policies to set up AppLocker. AppLocker allows you to configure a Denied list and an Accepted list for applications. Applications that are configured on the Denied list will not run on the system, and applications on the Accepted list will operate properly.

IP Security Policies on Local Computer   You can use these policies to configure the IPSec policies. IPSec is a way to secure data packets at the IP level of the message.

Advanced Audit Policy Configuration   You can use Advanced Audit Policy configuration settings to provide detailed control over audit policies. This section also allows you to configure auditing to help show administrators either successful or unsuccessful attacks on their network.

ACCESSING THE LOCAL SECURITY POLICY

You can also access the Local Security Policy by running `secpol.msc` or by opening Control Panel and selecting Administrative Tools ➤ Local Security Policy.

Now that we have seen all the options in the security section of the LGPO, let's look at account policies and local policies in more detail in the following sections.

Using Account Policies

You use account policies to specify the user account properties that relate to the logon process. They allow you to configure computer security settings for passwords and account lockout specifications.

If security is not an issue — perhaps because you are using your Windows 7 computer at home — you don't need to bother with account policies. If, on the other hand, security is important — for example, because your computer provides access to payroll information — you should set very restrictive account policies.

ACCOUNT POLICIES

Account policies at the LGPO level apply only to local user accounts, not domain accounts. To ensure that user account security is configured for domain user accounts, you need to configure these policies at the Domain GPO level.

To access the Account Policies folder from the MMC, follow this path: Local Computer Policy ➤ Computer Configuration ➤ Windows Settings ➤ Security Settings ➤ Account Policies. We look at all these folders and how to use them throughout the rest of this chapter.

In the following sections you will learn about the password policies and account lockout policies that define how security is applied to account policies.

SETTING PASSWORD POLICIES

Password policies ensure that security requirements are enforced on the computer. It is important to understand that the password policy is set on a per-computer basis; it cannot be configured for specific users. Figure 9.4 shows the password policies that Table 9.3 describes.

FIGURE 9.4
The password policies

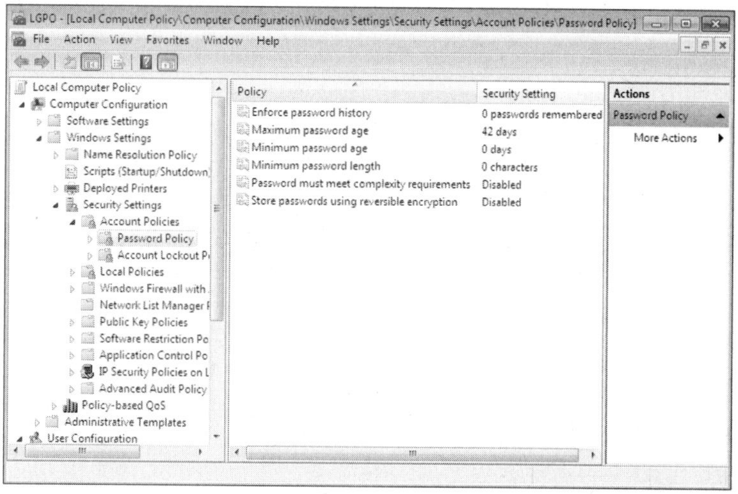

You can use the password policies shown in Table 9.3 as follows:

Enforce Password History   Prevents users from repeatedly using the same passwords. Users must create a new password when their password expires or is changed.

Maximum Password Age   Forces users to change their password after the maximum password age is exceeded. Setting this value to 0 will specify that the password will never expire.

Minimum Password Age   Prevents users from changing their password several times in rapid succession in order to defeat the purpose of the Enforce Password History policy.

Minimum Password Length   Ensures that users create a password and specifies the length requirement for that password. If this option isn't set, users are not required to create a password at all.

Password Must Meet Complexity Requirements   Passwords must be six characters or longer and cannot contain the user's account name or any part of the user's full name. In addition, passwords must contain three of the following character types:

♦   English uppercase characters (A through Z)

♦   English lowercase characters (a through z)

♦   Decimal digits (0 through 9)

♦   Symbols (such as !, @, #, $, and %)

Store Passwords Using Reversible Encryption   Provides a higher level of security for user passwords. This is required for Challenge Handshake Authentication Protocol (CHAP) authentication through remote access or Internet Authentication Services (IAS) and for Digest Authentication with Internet Information Services (IIS).

TABLE 9.3:   Password Policy Options

POLICY	DESCRIPTION	DEFAULT	MINIMUM	MAXIMUM
Enforce Password History	Keeps track of user's password history	Remember 0 passwords	Same as default	Remember 24 passwords
Maximum Password Age	Determines maximum number of days user can keep valid password	Keep password for 42 days	Keep password for 1 day	Keep password for up to 999 days
Minimum Password Age	Specifies how long password must be kept before it can be changed	0 days (password can be changed immediately)	Same as default	998 days
Minimum Password Length	Specifies minimum number of characters password must contain	0 characters (no password required)	Same as default	14 characters
Password Must Meet Complexity Requirements	Requires that passwords meet minimum levels of complexity	Disabled		
Store Passwords Using Reversible Encryption	Specifies higher level of encryption for stored user passwords	Disabled		

Perform the following steps to configure password policies for your computer. These steps assume that you have added the Local Computer Policy snap-in to the MMC completed in earlier steps.

1. Open the LGPO MMC shortcut that you created earlier.

2. Expand the Local Computer Policy snap-in.

3. Expand the folders as follows: Computer Configuration ➢ Windows Settings ➢ Security Settings ➢ Account Policies ➢ Password Policy.

4. Open the Enforce Password History policy. On the Local Security Setting tab, specify that 5 passwords will be remembered. Click OK.

5. Open the Maximum Password Age policy. On the Local Security Setting tab, specify that the password expires in 60 days. Click OK.

Let's look at how to set and manage the Account Lockout Policies section.

SETTING ACCOUNT LOCKOUT POLICIES

The account lockout policies specify how many invalid logon attempts should be tolerated. You configure the account lockout policies so that after x number of unsuccessful logon attempts within y number of minutes, the account will be locked for a specified amount of time or until the administrator unlocks the account.

Account lockout policies are similar to a bank's arrangements for ATM access code security. You have a certain number of chances to enter the correct PIN. That way, anyone who steals your card can't just keep guessing your access code until they get it right. Typically, after three unsuccessful attempts, the ATM takes the card. Then you need to request a new card from the bank. Figure 9.5 shows the account lockout policies that Table 9.4 describes.

FIGURE 9.5

The account lockout policies

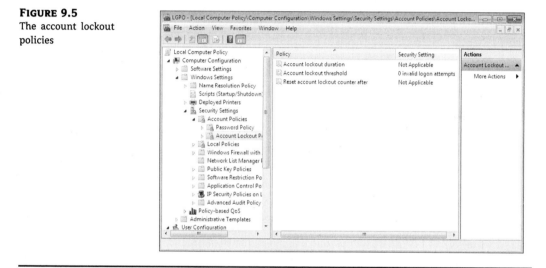

TABLE 9.4:   Account Lockout Policy Options

POLICY	DESCRIPTION	DEFAULT	MINIMUM	MAXIMUM
Account Lockout Duration	Specifies how long account will remain locked if Account Lockout Threshold is reached	Disabled, but if Account Lockout Threshold is enabled, 30 minutes	Same as default	99,999 minutes
Account Lockout Threshold	Specifies number of invalid attempts allowed before account is locked out	0 (disabled; account will not be locked out)	Same as default	999 attempts
Reset Account Lockout Counter After	Specifies how long counter will remember unsuccessful logon attempts	Disabled, but if Account Lockout Threshold is enabled, 30 minutes	Same as default	99,999 minutes

The Account Lockout Duration and Reset Account Lockout Counter After policies will be disabled until a value is specified for the Account Lockout Threshold. After the Account Lockout Threshold is set, the Account Lockout Duration and Reset Account Lockout Counter After policies will be set to 30 minutes. If you set the Account Lockout Duration to 0, the account will remain locked out until an administrator unlocks it.

RESET ACCOUNT LOCKOUT COUNTER

The Reset Account Lockout Counter After value must be equal to or less than the Account Lockout Duration value.

Perform the following steps to configure account lockout policies and test their effects. Make sure that you completed all previous procedures before you perform these steps.

1. Open the LGPO MMC shortcut.

2. Expand the Local Computer Policy snap-in.

3. Expand the folders as follows: Computer Configuration ➢ Windows Settings ➢ Security Settings ➢ Account Policies ➢ Account Lockout Policy.

4. Open the Account Lockout Threshold policy. On the Local Security Setting tab, specify that the account will lock after three invalid logon attempts. Click OK.

5. Accept the "Suggested Value Changes for the Account Lockout Duration and Reset Account Lockout Counter After" policies by clicking OK.

6. Open the Account Lockout Duration policy. On the Local Security Setting tab, specify that the account will remain locked for 5 minutes. Click OK.

7. Accept the "Suggested Value Changes for the Reset Account Lockout Counter After" policy by clicking OK.

8. Log off your administrator account. Try to log on as one of the accounts that were created on this Windows 7 machine and enter an incorrect password four times.

9. After you see the error message that states that the referenced account has been locked out, log on as an administrator.

10. To unlock the account, open the Local Users and Groups snap-in in the MMC, expand the Users folder, and double-click the user.

11. On the General tab of the users Properties dialog box, click to remove the check from the Account Is Locked Out check box. Then click OK.

In the next section we discuss how to control a user or computer after the user has logged into the Windows 7 machine.

Using Local Policies

As you learned in the preceding section, account policies are used to control logon procedures. When you want to control what a user can do after logging on, you use local policies. With local policies, you can implement auditing, specify user rights, and set security options.

To use local policies, first add the Local Computer Policy snap-in to the MMC. Then, from the MMC, follow this path to access the Local Policies folders: Local Computer Policy ➢ Computer Configuration ➢ Windows Settings ➢ Security Settings ➢ Local Policies. Figure 9.6 shows the three Local Policies folders: Audit Policy, User Rights Assignment, and Security Options. We look at each of these in the following sections.

FIGURE 9.6
Accessing the Local
Policies folders

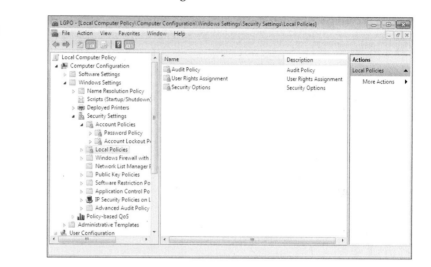

SETTING AUDIT POLICIES

You can implement audit policies to track success or failure of specified user actions. You audit events that pertain to user management through the audit policies. By tracking certain events, you can create a history of specific tasks, such as user creation and successful or unsuccessful logon attempts. You can also identify security violations that arise when users attempt to access system management tasks for which they do not have permissions.

AUDITING FAILED ATTEMPTS

As an IT manager, you have to make sure that you monitor failed attempts to resources. A failed attempt to a resource usually means that someone tried to access a resource and they were denied due to insufficient privileges.

Users who try to go to areas for which they do not have permissions usually fall into two categories: hackers and people who are just curious to see what they can get away with. Both are very dangerous.

If a user is trying to access an area that they do not belong to, be sure to warn the user about the attacks. This is very common on a network and needs to be nipped in the bud immediately.

When you define an audit policy, you can choose to audit success or failure of specific events. The success of an event means that the task was successfully accomplished. The failure of an event means that the task was not successfully accomplished.

By default, auditing is not enabled, and it must be manually configured. After you have configured auditing, you can see the results of the audit in the Security log by using the Event Viewer utility.

Figure 9.7 shows the audit policies that Table 9.5 describes.

FIGURE 9.7
The audit policies

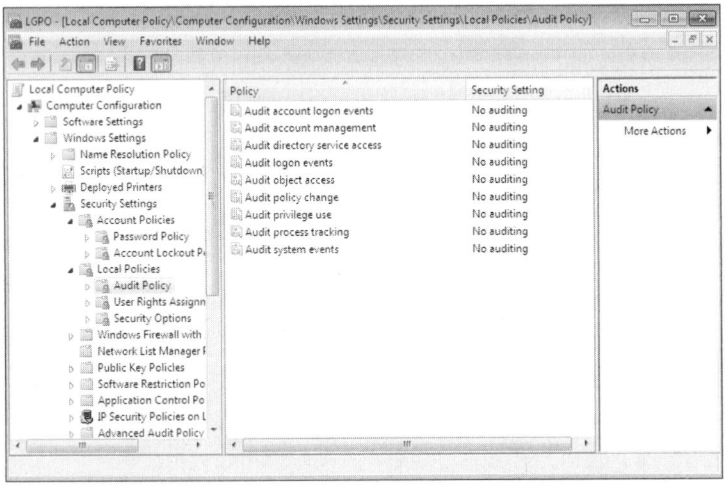

After you set the Audit Object Access policy to enable auditing of object access, you must enable file auditing through NTFS security or print auditing through printer security.

Perform the following steps to configure audit policies and view their results. These steps assume that you have added the Local Group Object Policy snap-in to the MMC completed in earlier steps.

1. Open the LGOP MMC shortcut.

2. Expand the Local Computer Policy Snap-in.

3. Expand the folders as follows: Computer Configuration ➢ Windows Settings ➢ Security Settings ➢ Local Policies ➢ Audit Policy.

4. Open the Audit Account Logon Events policy. Check the boxes for Success and Failure. Click OK.

5. Open the Audit Account Management policy. Check the boxes for Success and Failure. Click OK.

6. Log off your administrator account. Attempt to log back on as your administrator account with an incorrect password. The logon should fail (because the password is incorrect).

7. Log on as an administrator.

8. Select Start, right-click Computer, and select Manage to open Computer Management. Click Event Viewer.

9. From Event Viewer, open the Security log by selecting Windows Logs ➢ Security. You should see the audited events listed with a Task Category of Credential Validation.

TABLE 9.5:   Audit Policy Options

POLICY	DESCRIPTION
Audit Account Logon Events	Tracks when a user logs on or logs off either their local machine or the domain (if domain auditing is enabled)
Audit Account Management	Tracks user and group account creation, deletion, and management actions, such as password changes
Audit Directory Service Access	Tracks directory service accesses
Audit Logon Events	Audits events related to logon, such as running a logon script or accessing a roaming profile or accessing a server
Audit Object Access	Enables auditing of access to files, folders, and printers
Audit Policy Change	Tracks any changes to the audit policies, trust policies, or user rights assignment policies
Audit Privilege Use	Tracks users exercising a user right
Audit Process Tracking	Tracks events such as activating a program, accessing an object, and exiting a process
Audit System Events	Tracks system events such as shutting down or restarting the computer, as well as events that relate to the Security log in Event Viewer

AUDITING

You might want to limit the number of events that are audited. If you audit excessive events on a busy computer, the log file can grow quickly. In the event that the log file becomes full, you can configure the computer to shut down through a security option policy, Audit: Shut Down System Immediately If Unable To Log Security Audits. If this option is triggered, the only user who will be able to log on to the computer will be an administrator until the log is cleared. If this option is not enabled and the log file becomes full, you have the option of overwriting older log events.

In the next section, we look at how to configure the user rights on the Windows 7 machine.

ASSIGNING USER RIGHTS

The user right policies determine what rights a user or group has on the computer. User rights apply to the system. They are not the same as permissions, which apply to a specific object (permissions are discussed later in this chapter, in the section "Managing File and Folder Security").

An example of a user right is the Back Up Files And Directories right. This right allows a user to back up files and folders, even if the user does not have permissions that have been defined through NTFS file system permissions. The other user rights are similar because they deal with system access as opposed to resource access.

Figure 9.8 shows the user right policies that Table 9.6 describes.

FIGURE 9.8
The user right policies

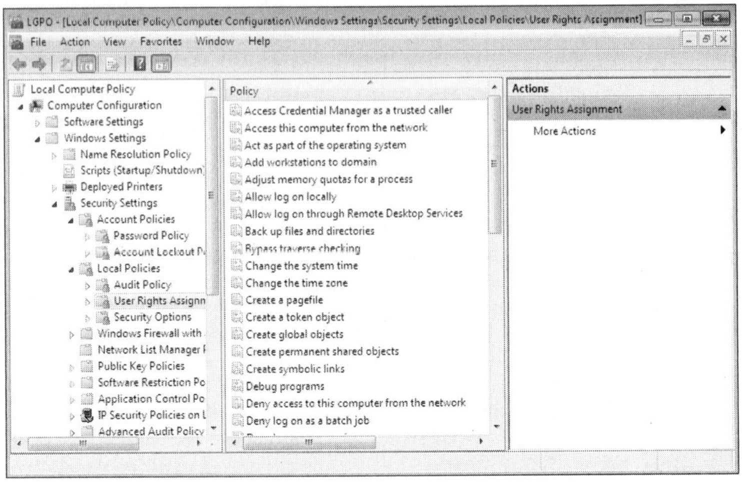

TABLE 9.6: User Rights Assignment Policy Options

RIGHT	DESCRIPTION
Access Credential Manager As A Trusted Caller	Used to back up and restore Credential Manager.
Access This Computer From The Network	Allows a user to access the computer from the network.
Act As Part Of The Operating System	Allows low-level authentication services to authenticate as any user.
Add Workstations To Domain	Allows a user to create a computer account on the domain.
Adjust Memory Quotas For A Process	Allows you to configure how much memory can be used by a specific process.
Allow Log On Locally	Allows a user to log on at the physical computer.
Allow Log On Through Terminal Services	Gives a user permission to log on through Terminal Services. Does not affect Windows 2000 computers prior to SP2.
Back Up Files And Directories	Allows a user to back up all files and directories, regardless of how the file and directory permissions have been set.
Bypass Traverse Checking	Allows a user to pass through and traverse the directory structure, even if that user does not have permissions to list the contents of the directory.
Change The System Time	Allows a user to change the internal time and date on the computer.
Change The Time Zone	Allows a user to change the time zone.

TABLE 9.6:   User Rights Assignment Policy Options (*CONTINUED*)

RIGHT	DESCRIPTION
Create A Pagefile	Allows a user to create or change the size of a page file.
Create A Token Object	Allows a process to create a token if the process uses an internal API to create the token.
Create Global Objects	Allows a user to create global objects when connected using Terminal Server.
Create Permanent Shared Objects	Allows a process to create directory objects through the Object Manager.
Create Symbolic Links	Allows a user to create a symbolic link.
Debug Programs	Allows a user to attach a debugging program to any process.
Deny Access To This Computer From The Network	Allows you to deny specific users or groups access to this computer from the network. Overrides the Access This Computer from the Network policy for accounts present in both policies.
Deny Log On As A Batch Job	Allows you to prevent specific users or groups from logging on as a batch file. Overrides the Log On as a Batch Job policy for accounts present in both policies.
Deny Log On As A Service	Allows you to prevent specific users or groups from logging on as a service. Overrides the Log On as a Service policy for accounts present in both policies.
Deny Log On Locally	Allows you to deny specific users or groups access to the computer locally. Overrides the Log On Locally policy for accounts present in both policies.
Deny Log On Through Terminal Services	Specifies that a user is not able to log on through Terminal Services. Does not affect Windows 2000 computers prior to SP2.
Enable Computer And User Accounts To Be Trusted For Delegation	Allows a user or group to set the Trusted For Delegation setting for a user or computer object.
Force Shutdown From A Remote System	Allows the system to be shut down by a user at a remote location on the network.
Generate Security Audits	Allows a user, group, or process to make entries in the Security log.
Impersonate A Client After Authentication	Enables programs running on behalf of a user to impersonate a client.
Increase A Process Working Set	Allows the size of a process working set to be increased.
Increase Scheduling Priority	Specifies that a process can increase or decrease the priority that is assigned to another process.

TABLE 9.6:   User Rights Assignment Policy Options (*CONTINUED*)

RIGHT	DESCRIPTION
Load And Unload Device Drivers	Allows a user to dynamically unload and load device drivers. This right does not apply to Plug and Play drivers.
Lock Pages In Memory	Allows an account to create a process that runs only in physical RAM, preventing it from being paged.
Log On As A Batch Job	Allows a process to log on to the system and run a file that contains one or more operating system commands.
Log On As A Service	Allows a service to log on in order to run the specific service.
Manage Auditing And Security Log	Allows a user to enable object access auditing for files and other Active Directory objects. This right does not allow a user to enable general object access auditing in the Local Security Policy.
Modify An Object Label	Allows a user to change the integrity level of files, folders, or other objects.
Modify Firmware Environment Variables	Allows a user to install or upgrade Windows. It also allows a user or process to modify the firmware environment variables stored in NVRAM of non-x86-based computers. This right does *not* affect the modification of system environment variables or user environment variables.
Perform Volume Maintenance Tasks	Allows a user to perform volume maintenance tasks such as defragmentation and error checking.
Profile Single Process	Allows a user to monitor nonsystem processes through performance-monitoring tools.
Profile System Performance	Allows a user to monitor system processes through performance-monitoring tools.
Remove Computer From Docking Station	Allows a user to undock a laptop through the Windows 7 user interface.
Replace A Process Level Token	Allows a process, such as Task Scheduler, to call an API to start another service.
Restore Files And Directories	Allows a user to restore files and directories, regardless of file and directory permissions.
Shut Down The System	Allows a user to shut down the Windows 7 computer locally.
Synchronize Directory Service Data	Allows a user to synchronize Active Directory data.
Take Ownership Of Files Or Other Objects	Allows a user to take ownership of system objects, such as files, folders, printers, and processes.

Perform the following steps to apply a user right policy. These steps assume that you added the Local Group Object Policy snap-in to the MMC completed in earlier steps.

1. Open the LGPO MMC shortcut.

2. Expand the Local Computer Policy Snap-in.

3. Expand the folders as follows: Computer Configuration ➤ Windows Settings ➤ Security Settings ➤ Local Policies ➤ User Rights Assignment.

4. Open the Log On As A Service user right.

5. Click the Add User Or Group button. The Select Users Or Groups dialog box appears.

6. Click the Advanced button and then select Find Now.

7. Select a user. Click OK.

8. Click OK in the Select Users Or Groups dialog box.

9. In the Log On As A Service Properties dialog box, click OK.

Now we look at how to define security options within the LGPO.

DEFINING SECURITY OPTIONS

You can use security option policies to configure security for the computer. Unlike user right policies, which are applied to a user, security option policies apply to the computer. Figure 9.9 shows the security option policies that Table 9.7 describes.

FIGURE 9.9
The security option policies

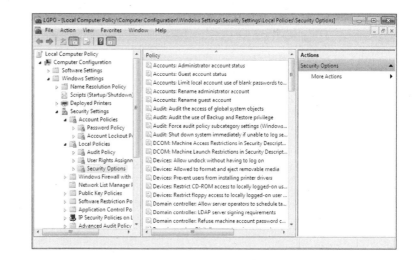

TABLE 9.7:   Security Options

OPTION	DESCRIPTION	DEFAULT
Accounts: Administrator Account Status	Specifies whether the Administrator account is enabled or disabled under normal operation. Booting under Safe Mode, the Administrator account is enabled, regardless of this setting.	Disabled
Accounts: Guest Account Status	Determines whether the Guest account is enabled or disabled.	Disabled
Accounts: Limit Local Account Use Of Blank Passwords To Console Logon Only	Determines whether a local user with a blank password will be able to log on remotely. If this policy is enabled, users with blank passwords will only be able to log on locally. This setting does not apply to domain logon accounts.	Enabled
Accounts: Rename Administrator Account	Allows the Administrator account to be renamed.	Administrator account is named Administrator.
Accounts: Rename Guest Account	Allows the Guest account to be renamed.	Guest account is named Guest.
Audit: Audit The Access Of Global System Objects	Allows access of global system objects to be audited.	Disabled
Audit: Audit The Use Of Backup And Restore Privilege	Allows the use of backup and restore privileges to be audited.	Disabled
Audit: Force Audit Policy Subcategory Settings (Windows 7 Or Later) To Override Audit Policy Category Settings	Allows audit policy subcategory settings to override audit policy category settings at the category level.	Not defined
Audit: Shut Down System Immediately If Unable To Log Security Audits	Specifies that the system shuts down immediately if it is unable to log security audits.	Disabled
DCOM: Machine Access Restrictions In Security Descriptor Definition Language (SDDL) Syntax	Specifies the users who can access DCOM applications.	Not defined
DCOM: Machine Launch Restrictions In Security Descriptor Definition Language (SDDL) Syntax	Specifies the users who can launch DCOM applications.	Not defined

TABLE 9.7: Security Options (*CONTINUED*)

OPTION	DESCRIPTION	DEFAULT
Devices: Allow Undock Without Having To Log On	Allows a user to undock a laptop computer from a docking station by pushing the computer's eject button without first having to log on.	Enabled
Devices: Allowed to Format and Eject Removable Media	Specifies which users can format and eject removable NTFS media.	Not defined
Devices: Prevent Users From Installing Printer Drivers	If enabled, allows only Administrators to install print drivers for a network printer.	Disabled
Devices: Restrict CD-ROM Access To Locally Logged-On User Only	Specifies whether the CD-ROM is accessible to local users and network users. If enabled, only the local user can access the CD-ROM, but if no local user is logged in, then the CD-ROM can be accessed over the network. If disabled or not defined, access is not restricted.	Not defined
Devices: Restrict Floppy Access To Locally Logged-On User Only	Specifies whether the floppy drive is accessible to local users and network users. If enabled, only the local user can access the floppy, but if no local user is logged in, then the floppy can be accessed over the network. If disabled or not defined, access is not restricted.	Not defined
Domain Controller: Allow Server Operators To Schedule Tasks	Allows server operators to schedule specific tasks to occur at specific times or intervals. Applies only to tasks scheduled through the AT command and does not affect tasks scheduled through Task Scheduler.	Not defined
Domain Controller: LDAP Server Signing Requirements	Specifies whether a Lightweight Directory Access Protocol server requires server signing with an LDAP client.	Not defined
Domain Controller: Refuse Machine Account Password Changes	Specifies whether a domain controller will accept password changes for computer accounts.	Not defined
Domain Member: Digitally Encrypt Or Sign Secure Channel Data (Always)	Specifies whether a secure channel must be created with the domain controller before secure channel traffic is generated.	Enabled
Domain Member: Digitally Encrypt Secure Channel Data (When Possible)	Specifies that if a secure channel can be created between the domain controller and the domain controller partner, it will be.	Enabled

TABLE 9.7:   Security Options (*CONTINUED*)

OPTION	DESCRIPTION	DEFAULT
Domain Member: Digitally Sign Secure Channel Data (When Possible)	Specifies that all secure channel traffic be signed if both domain controller partners who are transferring data are capable of signing secure data.	Enabled
Domain Member: Disable Machine Account Password Changes	Specifies whether a domain member must periodically change its computer account password as defined in the Domain Member: Maximum Machine Account Password Age setting.	Disabled
Domain Member: Maximum Machine Account Password Age	Specifies the maximum age of a computer account password.	30 days
Domain Member: Require Strong (Windows 2000 Or Later) Session Key	If enabled, the domain controller must encrypt data with a 128-bit session key; if not enabled, 64-bit session keys can be used.	Disabled
Interactive Logon: Do Not Display Last User Name	Prevents the last username in the logon screen from being displayed.	Disabled
Interactive Logon: Do Not Require Ctrl+Alt+Del	Allows the Ctrl+Alt+Del requirement for logon to be disabled.	Not defined, but it is automatically used on standalone workstations, meaning users who log on to the workstation see a start screen with icons for all users who have been created on the computer.
Interactive Logon: Message Text For Users Attempting To Log On	Displays message text for users trying to log on, usually configured for displaying legal text messages.	Not defined
Interactive Logon: Message Title For Users Attempting to Log On	Displays a message title for users trying to log on.	Not defined
Interactive Logon: Number Of Previous Logon Attempts To Cache (In Case Domain Controller Is Not Available)	Specifies the number of previous logon attempts stored in the cache. This option is useful if a domain controller is not available.	10

TABLE 9.7:   Security Options (*CONTINUED*)

OPTION	DESCRIPTION	DEFAULT
Interactive Logon: Prompt User To Change Password Before Expiration	Prompts the user to change the password before expiration.	14 days before password expiration
Interactive Logon: Require Domain Controller Authentication To Unlock	Specifies that a user name and password be required to unlock a locked computer. When this is disabled, a user can unlock a computer with cached credentials. When this is enabled, a user is required to authenticate to a domain controller to unlock the computer.	Disabled
Interactive Logon: Require Smart Card	Specifies that a smart card is required to log on to the computer.	Disabled
Interactive Logon: Smart Card Removal Behavior	Specifies what happens if a user who is logged on with a smart card removes the smart card.	No action
Microsoft Network Client: Digitally Sign Communications (Always)	Specifies that the server should always digitally sign client communication.	Disabled
Microsoft Network Client: Digitally Sign Communications (If Server Agrees)	Specifies that the server should digitally sign client communication when possible.	Enabled
Microsoft Network Client: Send Unencrypted Password To Third-Party SMB Servers	Allows third-party Server Message Block servers to use unencrypted passwords for authentication.	Disabled
Microsoft Network Client: Amount Of Idle Time Required: Before Suspending Session	Allows sessions to be disconnected when they are idle.	15 minutes
Microsoft Network Server: Digitally Sign Communications (Always)	Ensures that server communications will always be digitally signed.	Disabled
Microsoft Network Server: Digitally Sign Communications (If Client Agrees)	Specifies that server communications should be signed when possible.	Disabled
Microsoft Network Server: Disconnect Clients When Logon Hours Expire	If a user logs on and then their logon hours expire, specifies whether an existing connection will remain connected or be disconnected.	Enabled

TABLE 9.7: Security Options (*CONTINUED*)

OPTION	DESCRIPTION	DEFAULT
Network Access: Allow Anonymous SID/Name Translation	Specifies whether an anonymous user can request the security identifier (SID) attributes for another user.	Disabled
Network Access: Do Not Allow Anonymous Enumeration Of SAM Accounts	If enabled, prevents an anonymous connection from enumerating Security Account Manager (SAM) accounts.	Enabled
Network Access: Do Not Allow Anonymous Enumeration Of SAM Accounts And Shares	If enabled, prevents an anonymous connection from enumerating Security Account Manager (SAM) accounts and network shares.	Disabled
Network Access: Do Not Allow Storage Of Credentials Or .NET Passports for Network Authentication	Specifies whether passwords, credentials, and .NET Passports are stored and available for use after a user is authenticated to a domain.	Disabled
Network Access: Let Everyone Permissions Apply To Anonymous Users	Specifies whether Everyone permission will apply to anonymous users.	Disabled
Network Access: Named Pipes That Can Be Accessed Anonymously	Specifies which communication sessions are allowed to anonymous users.	Defined
Network Access: Remotely Accessible Registry Paths	Determines which Registry paths will be accessible when the winreg key is accessed for remote Registry access, regardless of the ACL setting.	Defined
Network Access: Remotely Accessible Registry Paths And Sub-Paths	Determines which Registry paths and subpaths will be accessible when the winreg key is accessed for remote Registry access, regardless of the ACL setting.	Defined
Network Access: Restrict Anonymous Access To Named Pipes And Shares	Specifies whether anonymous access is allowed to shares and pipes for the Network Access: Named Pipes That Can Be Accessed Anonymously and Network Access: Shares That Can Be Accessed Anonymously policies	Enabled
Network Access: Shares That Can Be Accessed Anonymously	Specifies which network shares can be accessed by anonymous users.	Not defined
Network Access: Sharing And Security Model For Local Accounts	Specifies how local accounts will be authenticated over the network.	Classic – Local Users Authenticate As Themselves

TABLE 9.7:   Security Options (*CONTINUED*)

OPTION	DESCRIPTION	DEFAULT
Network Security: Do Not Store LAN Manager Hash Value On Next Password Change	Specifies whether LAN Manager will store hash values from password changes.	Enabled
Network Security: Force Logoff When Logon Hours Expire	Specifies whether a user with a current connection will be automatically logged off when the user's logon hours expire.	Disabled
Network Security: LAN Manager Authentication Level	Specifies the LAN Manager Authentication Level.	Send NTLMv2 Response Only
Network Security: LDAP Client Signing Requirements	Specifies the client signing requirements that will be enforced for LDAP clients.	Negotiate Signing
Network Security: Minimum Session Security For NTLM SSP Based (Including Secure RPC) Clients	Specifies the minimum security standards for application-to-application client communications.	No minimum
Network Security: Minimum Session Security For NTLM SSP Based (Including Secure RPC) Servers	Specifies the minimum security standards for application-to-application server communications.	No minimum
Recovery Console: Allow Automatic Administrative Logon	Specifies whether a password is required for Administrative logon when the Recovery Console is loaded. If Enabled, the password is not required.	Disabled
Recovery Console: Allow Floppy Copy and Access To All Drives And All Folders	Allows you to copy files from all drives and folders when the Recovery Console is loaded.	Disabled
Shutdown: Allow System To Be Shut Down Without Having To Log On	Allows the user to shut down the system without logging on.	Enabled
Shutdown: Clear Virtual Memory Pagefile	Specifies whether the virtual memory pagefile will be cleared when the system is shut down.	Disabled
System Cryptography: Force Strong Key Protection For User Keys Stored On The Computer	Specifies whether a password is required to use a private key.	Not defined
System Cryptography: Use FIPS Compliant Algorithms For Encryption, Hashing and Signing	Specifies which encryption algorithms should be supported for encrypting, hashing, and signing file data.	Disabled

TABLE 9.7:   Security Options (*CONTINUED*)

OPTION	DESCRIPTION	DEFAULT
System Objects: Default Owner For Objects Created By Members Of The Administrators Group	Determines whether, when an object is created by a member of the Administrators group, the owner will be the Administrators group or the user who created the object.	Object Creator
System Objects: Require Case Insensitivity For Non-Windows Subsystems	By default, Windows 7 does not specify case insensitivity for file subsystems. However, subsystems such as POSIX use case-sensitive file systems, so this option allows you to configure case sensitivity.	Enabled
System Objects: Strengthen Default Permissions Of Internal System Objects (for example, Symbolic Links)	Specifies the default discretionary access control list for objects.	Enabled
System Settings: Optional Subsystems	Specifies the subsystems that are used to support applications in your environment.	POSIX
System Settings: Use Certificate Rules On Windows Executables For Software Restriction Policies	Specifies whether digital certificates are required when a user or process runs an EXE file.	Disabled
User Account Control: Admin Approval Mode For The Built-in Administrator Account	If Enabled, the built-in Administrator account will require approval for any operation that requires privilege elevation. If Disabled, the built-in Administrator account will use XP-compatible mode with full administrative privileges.	Disabled
User Account Control: Behavior Of The Elevation Prompt For Administrators In Admin Approval Mode	Specifies the method for approval of privilege elevation for administrators.	Prompt For Consent
User Account Control: Behavior Of The Elevation Prompt For Standard Users	Specifies the method for approval of privilege elevation for standard users.	Prompt For Credentials
User Account Control: Detect Application Installations And Prompt For Elevation	Specifies how applications are installed and whether approval is required.	Enabled
User Account Control: Only Elevate Executables That Are Signed And Validated	Specifies whether PKI signature checks are required for applications that request privilege elevation.	Disabled

TABLE 9.7:   Security Options (*CONTINUED*)

OPTION	DESCRIPTION	DEFAULT
User Account Control: Only Elevate UIAccess Applications That Are Installed In Secure Locations	Requires that applications executing with a UIAccess integrity level reside in a secure file system location.	Enabled
User Account Control: Run All Administrators In Admin Approval Mode	Enforces UAC policy for all users, including administrators.	Enabled
User Account Control: Switch To The Secure Desktop When Prompting For Elevation	If Enabled, elevation requests will go to the Secure Desktop. If Disabled, elevation requests will appear on the users' desktop.	Enabled
User Account Control: Virtualize File And Registry Write Failures To Per-User Locations	Allows standard users to run pre-Windows 7 applications that formerly required administrator-level access to write to protected locations.	Enabled

Perform the following steps to define some security option policies and see how they work. These steps assume that you added the Local Group Object Policy snap-in to the MMC completed in earlier steps.

1. Open the LGPO MMC shortcut.

2. Expand the Local Computer Policy Snap-in.

3. Expand the folders as follows: Computer Configuration ➤ Windows Settings ➤ Security Settings ➤ Local Policies ➤ Security Options.

4. Open the policy Interactive Logon: Message Text For Users Attempting To Log On. On the Local Policy Setting tab, type **Welcome to all authorized users**. Click OK.

5. Open the policy Interactive Logon: Message Title For Users Attempting To Log On. On the Local Security Setting tab, type **Welcome Message**. Click OK.

6. Open the policy Interactive Logon: Prompt User To Change Password Before Expiration. On the Local Security Setting tab, type **3 days**. Click OK.

7. Log off your administrator account and see the Welcome Message text appear. Click OK.

8. Log on as an administrator.

In the next section we look at how users can install resources on Windows 7 without being an administrator by using the User Account Control.

Configuring User Account Control

Most administrators have had to wrestle with the balance between security and enabling applications to run correctly. In the past, some applications simply would not run correctly under Windows unless the user running the application was a local administrator.

Unfortunately, granting local administrator permissions to a user also allows the user to install software and hardware, change configuration settings, modify local user accounts, and delete critical files. Even more troubling is the fact that malware that infects a computer while an administrator is logged in is also able to perform those same functions.

Limited user accounts in Windows XP were supposed to allow applications to run correctly and allow users to perform necessary tasks. However, in practical application, it did not work as advertised. Many applications require that users have permissions to write to protected folders and to the Registry, and limited user accounts did not allow users to do so.

Windows 7's answer to the problem is User Account Control (UAC). UAC enables nonadministrator users to perform standard tasks, such as install a printer, configure a VPN or wireless connection, and install updates, while preventing them from performing tasks that require administrative privileges, such as installing applications.

Managing Privilege Elevation

UAC protects computers by requiring privilege elevation for all users, even users who are members of the local Administrators group. As you have no doubt seen by now, UAC prompts you for permission when you perform a task that requires privilege elevation. This prevents malware from silently launching processes without your knowledge.

Privilege elevation is required for any feature that contains the four-color security shield. For example, the small shield shown on the Change Date And Time button in the Date And Time dialog box in Figure 9.10 indicates an action that requires privilege elevation.

FIGURE 9.10
Date And Time
dialog box

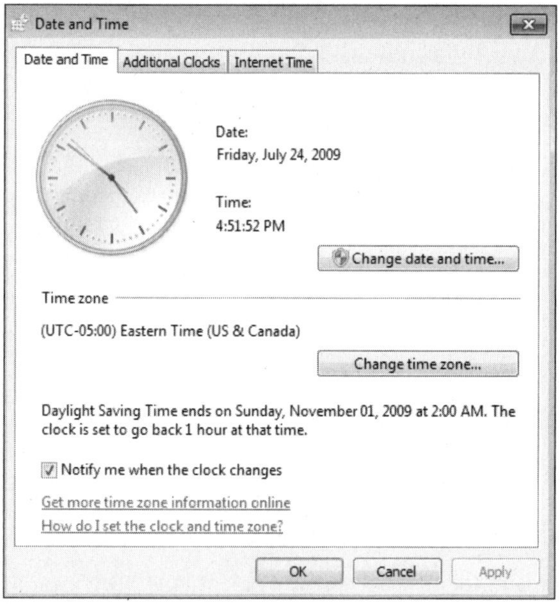

Now let's look at how to elevate privileges for users.

ELEVATED PRIVILEGES FOR USERS

By default, local administrators are logged on as standard users. When administrators attempt to perform a task that requires privilege escalation, they are prompted for confirmation by default. You can require administrators to authenticate when performing a task that requires privilege escalation by changing the User Account Control: Behavior Of The Elevation Prompt For Administrators In Admin Approval Mode policy setting to Prompt For Credentials. On the other hand, if you don't want UAC to prompt administrators for confirmation when elevating privileges, you can change the policy setting to Elevate Without Prompting.

Nonadministrator accounts are called standard users. When standard users attempt to perform a task that requires privilege elevation, they are prompted for a password of a user account that has administrative privileges. You cannot configure UAC to automatically allow standard users to perform administrative tasks, nor can you configure UAC to prompt a standard user for confirmation before performing administrative tasks. If you do not want standard users to be prompted for credentials when attempting to perform administrative tasks, you can automatically deny elevation requests by changing the User Account Control: Behavior Of The Elevation Prompt For Standard Users policy setting to Automatically Deny Elevation Requests.

The built-in Administrator account, though disabled by default, is not affected by UAC. UAC will not prompt the Administrator account for elevation of privileges. Thus, it is important to use a normal user account whenever possible and use the built-in Administrator account only when absolutely necessary.

Perform the following steps to see how UAC affects administrator and nonadministrator accounts differently:

1. Log on to Windows 7 as a nonadministrator account.

2. Select Start ➢ Control Panel ➢ Large Icons View ➢ Windows Firewall.

3. Click the Turn Windows Firewall On Or Off link on the left side. The UAC box should prompt you for permission to continue, as shown in Figure 9.11. Click Yes. You should not be allowed access to the Windows Firewall Settings dialog box.

FIGURE 9.11
UAC dialog box

4. Log off and log on as the administrator account.

5. Select Start ➢ Control Panel ➢ Large Icons View ➢ Windows Firewall.

6. Click the Turn Windows Firewall On Or Off link.

7. You should automatically go to the Windows Firewall screen. Close the Windows Firewall screen

Now instead of just elevating privileges for users, let's look at elevating privileges for executable applications.

ELEVATED PRIVILEGES FOR EXECUTABLES

You can also enable an executable file to run with elevated privileges. To do so on a one-time basis, you can right-click a shortcut or executable and select Run As Administrator.

But what if you need to configure an application to always run with elevated privileges for a user? To do so, log in as an administrator, right-click a shortcut or executable, and select Properties. On the Compatibility tab, click the Run This Program As An Administrator check box. If the Run This Program As An Administrator check box is unavailable, the program is blocked from permanently running as an administrator, the program doesn't need administrative privileges, or you are not logged on as an administrator.

Many applications that are installed on a Windows 7 machine need to have access to the Registry. Windows 7 protects the Registry from nonadministrator accounts. Let's look at how this works.

Registry and File Virtualization

Windows 7 uses a feature called Registry and file virtualization to enable nonadministrator users to run applications that previously required administrative privileges to run correctly. As discussed previously, some applications write to the Registry and to protected folders, such as C:\Windows and C:\Program Files. For nonadministrator users, Windows 7 redirects any attempts to write to protected locations to a per-user location. By doing so, Windows 7 enables users to use the application successfully while it protects critical areas of the system.

In the next section, we look at other areas of security such as Windows Firewall and the Action Center.

Using Advanced Security Options

In this section, we look at some of the advanced security options that you can configure to protect a Windows 7 machine. The first section discusses Windows Firewall and how to use the firewall to protect against intruders.

We then look at the Action Center, shown in Figure 9.12. The Action Center is designed to allow you to monitor and configure critical settings through a centralized dialog box. Critical settings include Automatic Updating, Malware Protection, and Other Security Settings. Malware Protection includes virus protection and spyware protection (included through Windows Defender).

Let's start by looking at how to configure and maintain Windows Firewall.

Configuring Windows Firewall

Windows Firewall, which is included with Windows 7, helps to prevent unauthorized users or malicious software from accessing your computer. Windows Firewall does not allow unsolicited traffic (traffic that was not sent in response to a request) to pass through the firewall.

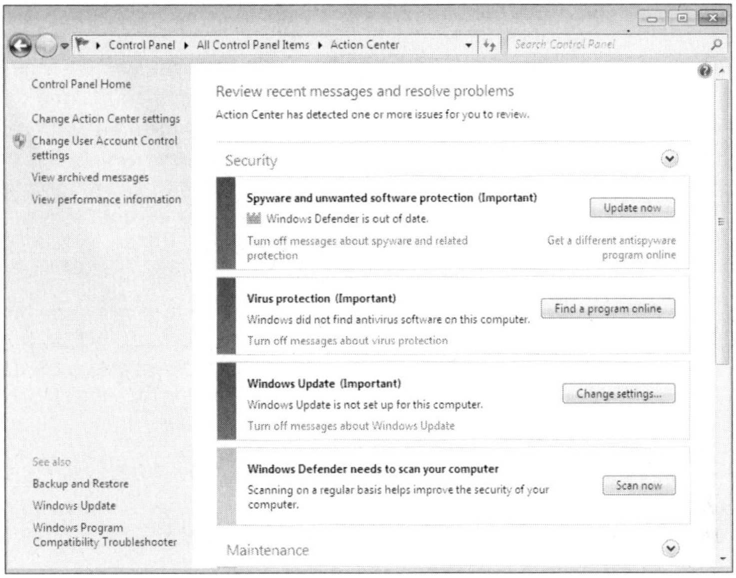

FIGURE 9.12
Windows Security
Center dialog box

FIGURE 9.12
Windows Security
Center dialog box

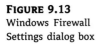

To configure Windows Firewall, select Start ➢ Control Panel ➢ Large Icons View ➢ Windows Firewall, then click Turn Windows Firewall On Or Off. The Windows Firewall Settings dialog box appears, as shown in Figure 9.13.

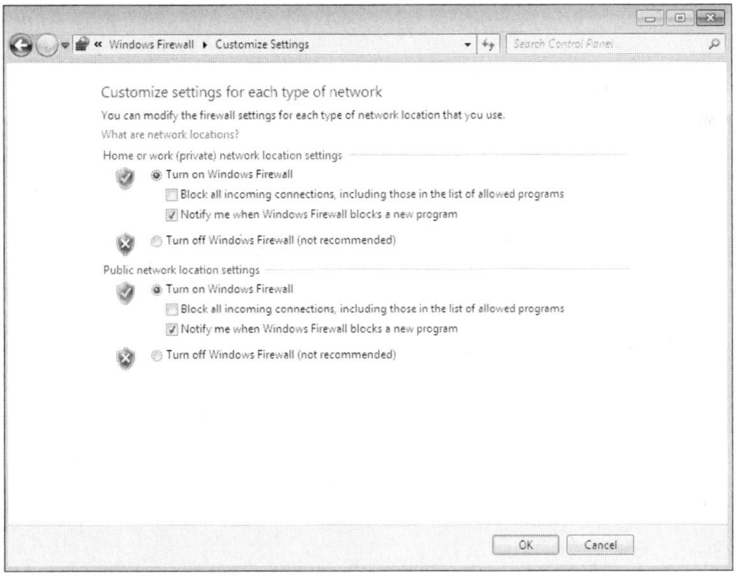

FIGURE 9.13
Windows Firewall
Settings dialog box

The Windows Firewall Settings dialog box allows you to turn Windows Firewall on or off for both private and public networks. The On setting blocks external sources except those that are specified on the Exceptions tab. The Off setting allows external sources to connect.

There is also a check box for Block All Incoming Connections. This feature allows you to connect to networks that are not secure. When Block All Incoming Connections is enabled, exceptions are ignored and no notification is given when an application is blocked by Windows Firewall.

The exceptions section of the Windows Firewall Settings dialog box, shown in Figure 9.14, allows you to define which programs and services should be allowed to pass through Windows Firewall. You can select from a defined list of programs and services, or you can use the Add Another Program button to customize your exceptions.

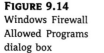

FIGURE 9.14
Windows Firewall
Allowed Programs
dialog box

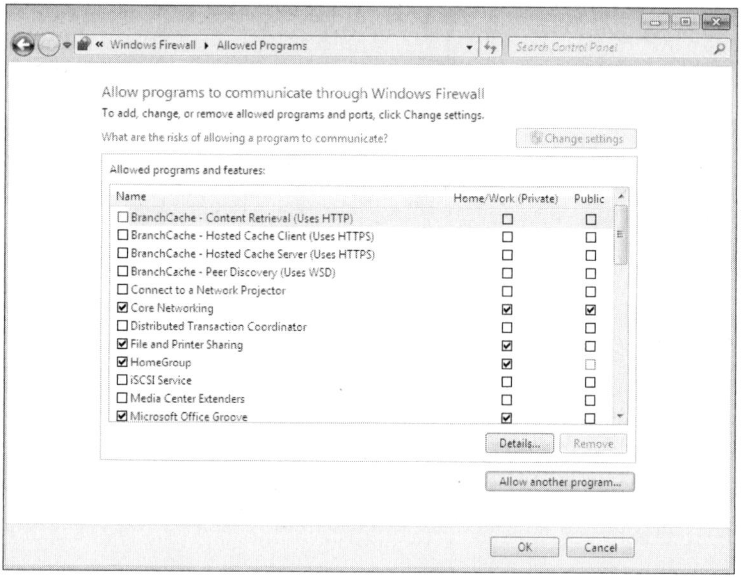

Take great care in enabling exceptions. Exceptions allow traffic to pass through the firewall, which could expose your computer to risk. Remember that the Block All Incoming Connections setting ignores all exceptions.

Now that we have looked at the basic Windows Firewall settings, let's discuss Windows Firewall with Advanced Security.

Windows Firewall with Advanced Security

You can configure more advanced settings by configuring Windows Firewall with Advanced Security (WFAS). To access Windows Firewall with Advanced Security, click Start ➤ Control Panel ➤ Large Icons View ➤ Windows Firewall and then click the Advanced Settings link. The Windows Firewall With Advanced Security On Local Computer dialog box appears, as shown in Figure 9.15.

The scope pane to the left shows that you can set up specific inbound and outbound rules, connection security rules, and monitoring rules. The central area shows an overview of the firewall's status, as well as the current profile settings. Let's look at these in detail.

INBOUND AND OUTBOUND RULES

Inbound and outbound rules consist of many preconfigured rules that can be enabled or disabled. Obviously, inbound rules monitor inbound traffic, and outbound rules monitor outbound traffic, as shown in Figure 9.16. By default, many are disabled. Double-clicking a rule brings up its Properties dialog box, as shown in Figure 9.17.

FIGURE 9.15
Windows Firewall With Advanced Security On Local Computer dialog box

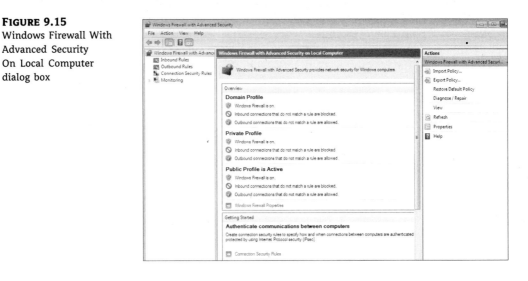

FIGURE 9.16
Inbound Rules dialog box

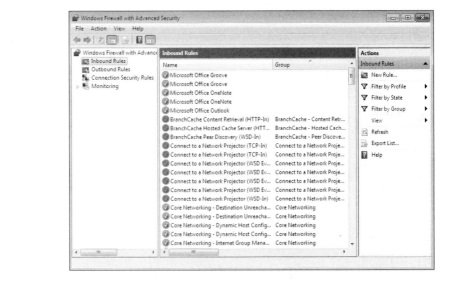

You can filter the rules to make them easier to view. Filtering can be performed based on the profile the rule affects, whether the rule is enabled or disabled, or based on the rule group.

If you can't find a rule that is appropriate for your needs, you can create a new rule by right-clicking Inbound Rules or Outbound Rules in the scope pane and then selecting New Rule. The New Inbound (or Outbound) Rule Wizard launches, and you are asked whether you want to create a rule based on a particular program, protocol or port, predefined category, or custom settings.

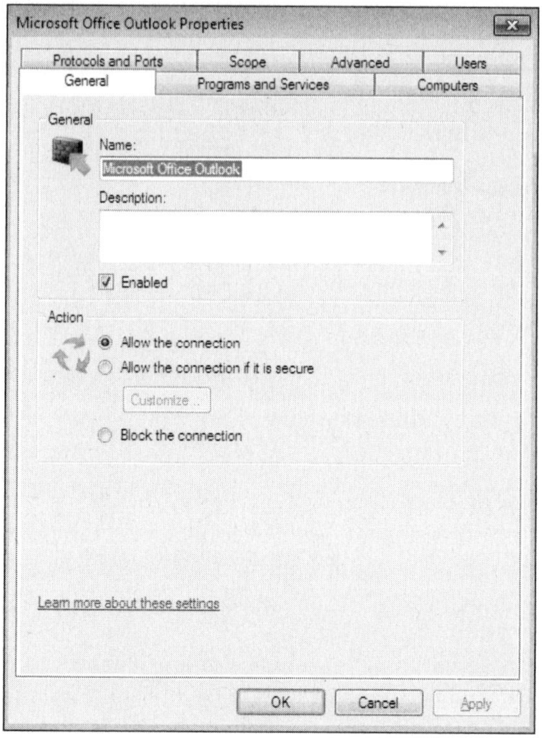

FIGURE 9.17
An inbound rule's
Properties dialog box

Perform the following steps to create a new inbound rule that will allow only encrypted TCP traffic:

1. Select Start ➤ Control Panel ➤ Large Icon View ➤ Windows Firewall.

2. Click Advanced Settings on the left-hand side.

3. Right-click Inbound Rules and select New Rule.

4. Choose a Rule Type. For this exercise, let's choose Custom so that we can see all the options available to us; then click Next.

5. Choose the programs or services that are affected by this rule. For this exercise, let's choose All Programs; then click Next.

6. Choose the protocol type, as well as the local and remote port numbers that are affected by this rule. For this exercise, let's choose TCP, and ensure that All Ports is selected for both Local Port and Remote Port. Click Next to continue.

7. Choose the local and remote IP addresses that are affected by this rule. Let's choose Any IP Address for both local and remote, and then click Next.

8. Specify whether this rule will allow the connection, allow the connection only if it is secure, or block the connection. Let's select the option Allow The Connection If It Is Secure and then click Next.

9. Specify whether connections should be allowed only from certain users. You can experiment with these options if you want; then click Next to continue.

10. Specify whether connections should be allowed only from certain computers. Again you can experiment with these options if you want; then click Next to continue

11. Choose which profiles will be affected by this rule. Select one or more profiles and click Next to continue.

12. Give your profile a name and description and then click Finish. Your custom rule appears in the list of Inbound Rules and the rule is enabled.

13. Double-click your newly created rule. Notice that you can change the options that you previously configured.

14. Disable the rule by deselecting the Enabled check box. Click OK.

Now let's look at setting up Connection Security Rules through Windows Firewall with Advanced Security.

CONNECTION SECURITY RULES

You can use Connection Security Rules to configure how and when authentication occurs. These rules do not specifically allow connections; that's the job of inbound and outbound rules. You can configure the following connection security rules, as shown in Figure 9.18:

Isolation   To restrict a connection based on authentication criteria

Authentication Exemption   To specify computers that are exempt from authentication requirements

Server-to-Server   To authenticate connections between computers

Tunnel   To authenticate connections between gateway computers

Custom   Allows you to provide a custom connection security rule.

The final section of Windows Firewall with Advanced Security we'll discuss is the Monitoring section.

MONITORING

The Monitoring section shows detailed information about the firewall configurations for the Domain Profile, Private Profile, and Public Profile settings, as shown in Figure 9.19. These network location profiles determine what settings are enforced for private networks, public networks, and networks connected to a domain.

 **Real World Scenario**

FIREWALLS

When doing consulting, it always make me laugh when I see small to mid-size companies using Microsoft Windows Firewalls and no other protection.

Microsoft Windows Firewalls should be your *last* line of defense. You need to make sure that you have good hardware firewalls that separate your network from the world.

Also watch Windows Firewalls when it comes to printing. I have run into many situations where a printer that needs to talk to the operating system has issues when the Windows Firewall is enabled. If this happens, make sure that the printer is allowed in the allowed programs section.

FIGURE 9.18
Connection security rules

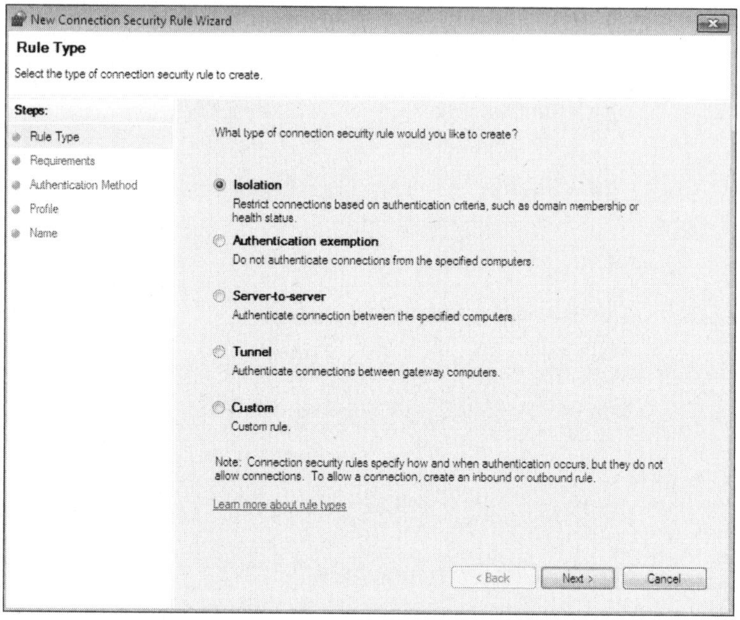

FIGURE 9.19
Monitoring section

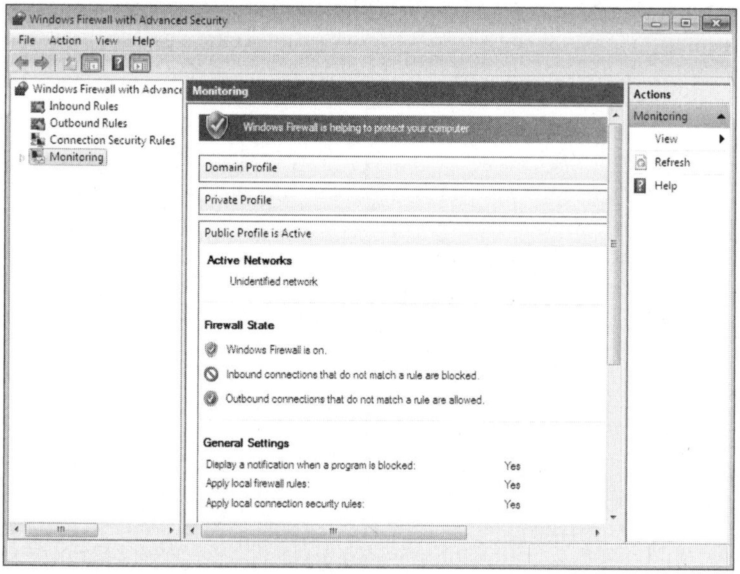

In the next section we look at the Action Center and some of the functions that you can perform from the Action Center.

Configuring the Action Center

These days, having a firewall just isn't enough. Spyware and viruses are becoming more widespread, more sophisticated, and more dangerous. Users can unintentionally pick up spyware and viruses by visiting websites, or by installing an application in which spyware and viruses are bundled.

Even worse, malicious software cannot typically be uninstalled. Thus, antispyware and virus protection applications are also required to ensure that your computer remains protected. Let's take a look at some of the ways you can protect your Windows 7 computers using the Action Center.

Using Windows Defender

Windows 7 comes with an antispyware application called Windows Defender. Windows Defender offers real-time protection from spyware and other unwanted software. You can also configure Windows Defender to scan for spyware on a regular basis.

Like antivirus programs, Windows Defender relies on definitions, which are used to determine whether a file contains spyware. Out-of-date definitions can cause Windows Defender to fail to detect some spyware. Windows Update is used to regularly update the definitions used by Windows Defender so that the latest spyware can be detected. You can also configure Windows Defender to manually check for updates using Windows Update.

To access Windows Defender, as shown in Figure 9.20, click Start ➢ Control Panel ➢ Large Icons View ➢ Action Center ➢ Windows Defender. status appears at the bottom of the screen, which includes time of the last scan, the scan schedule, the real-time protection status, and the definition version.

FIGURE 9.20
Windows Defender
dialog box

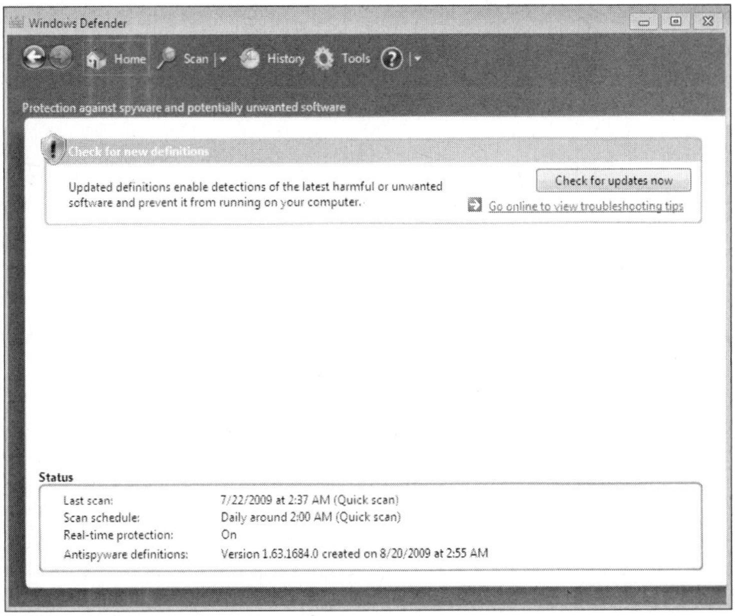

Let's look at how we can scan the system for spyware using Windows Defender.

Performing a Manual Scan

You can configure Windows Defender to perform a manual scan of your computer at any time. You can perform the following three types of scans:

◆ Quick Scan checks only where spyware is most likely to be found.

◆ Full Scan checks all memory, running processes, and folders.

◆ Custom Scan checks only the drives and folders that you select.

By default, Windows Defender performs a Quick Scan daily at 2 a.m. You can change this setting by using the Tools menu option, as shown in Figure 9.21.

FIGURE 9.21
Windows Defender Tools menu dialog box

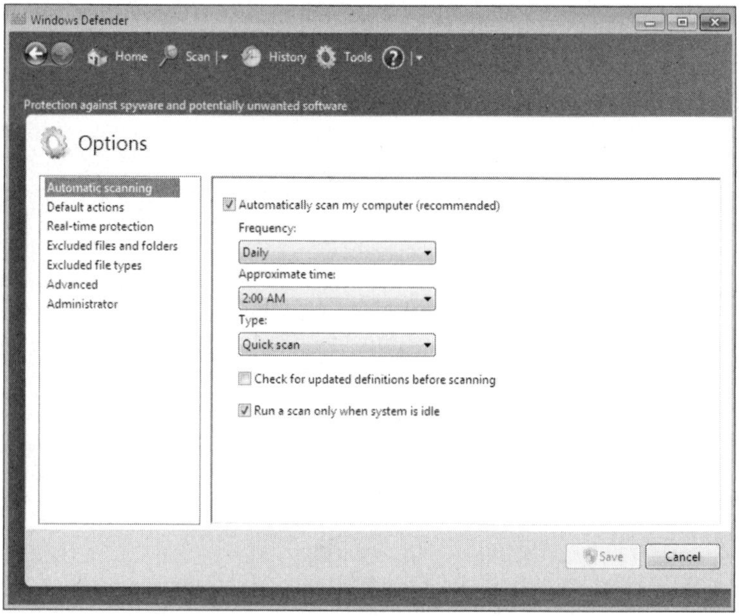

Programs are classified into four spyware alert levels, as shown in Figure 9.22:

◆ Severe

◆ High

◆ Medium

◆ Low

Depending on the alert level, you can choose to have Windows Defender ignore, quarantine, remove, or always allow software.

FIGURE 9.22
Spyware alert levels

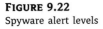

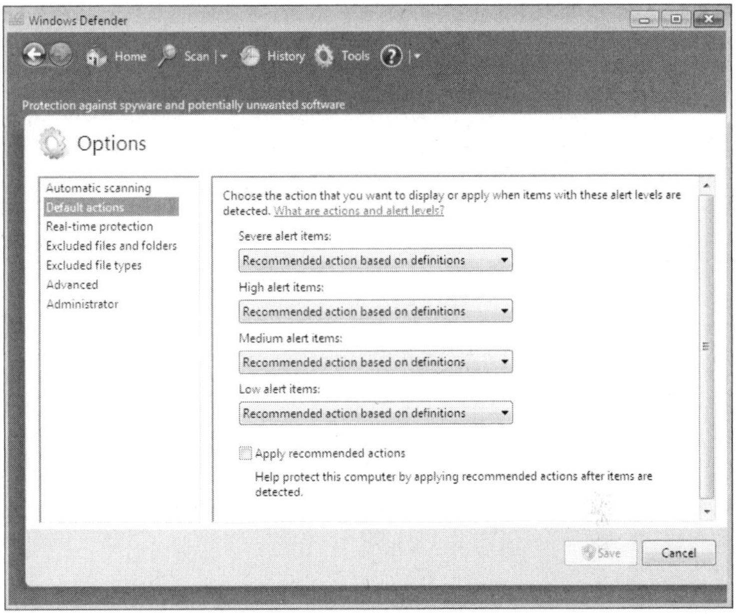

In the next section, you will learn how to configure the many options of Windows Defender.

Configuring Windows Defender

Use the Tools and Settings menu to configure Windows Defender. As shown in Figure 9.23, you can access the following items through this menu:

◆ Options

◆ Microsoft SpyNet

◆ Quarantined Items

◆ Allowed Items

◆ Windows Defender Website

◆ Microsoft Malware Protection Center

Let's look at each one of these Windows Defender options in greater detail.

OPTIONS

Click Options on the Tools and Settings menu to enable you to configure the default behavior of Windows Defender. You can configure the following options:

Automatic Scanning You can configure Windows Defender to scan automatically, how often automatic scans should occur, the time that scans will occur, and the type of scan to perform.

You can also configure whether definitions should be updated before scanning, and whether the default actions should be taken on any spyware that is found.

Default Actions   You can configure the actions Windows Defender should take on High, Medium, and Low Alert items. You can set each level so that Windows Defender can take the default action for that level, always remove the item, or always ignore the item.

Real-Time Protection   You can configure whether real-time protection is enabled, which security agents you want to run, how you should be notified about threats, and whether a Windows Defender icon is displayed in the notification area.

Excluded Files And Folders   You can set up files and folders that are to be excluded during a scan.

Excluded File Types   You can specify certain file types that will be excluded from a scan, as shown in Figure 9.24. For example, you can exclude all .doc files if needed.

Advanced   These options let you configure whether to:

◆   Archived files and folders are scanned.

◆   Email is scanned.

◆   Removable drives.

◆   Heuristics are used to detect unanalyzed software.

◆   A restore point is created before removing spyware.

You can also specify file locations that are exempt from scanning.

FIGURE 9.23
Windows Defender Tools
and Settings menu

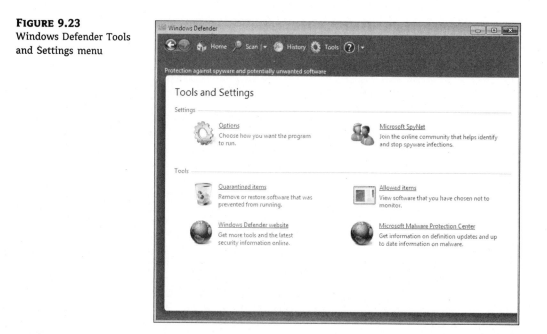

Administrator   These options let you configure whether Windows Defender is enabled, and whether you display items from all users on this computer.

FIGURE 9.24
Excluded File Types

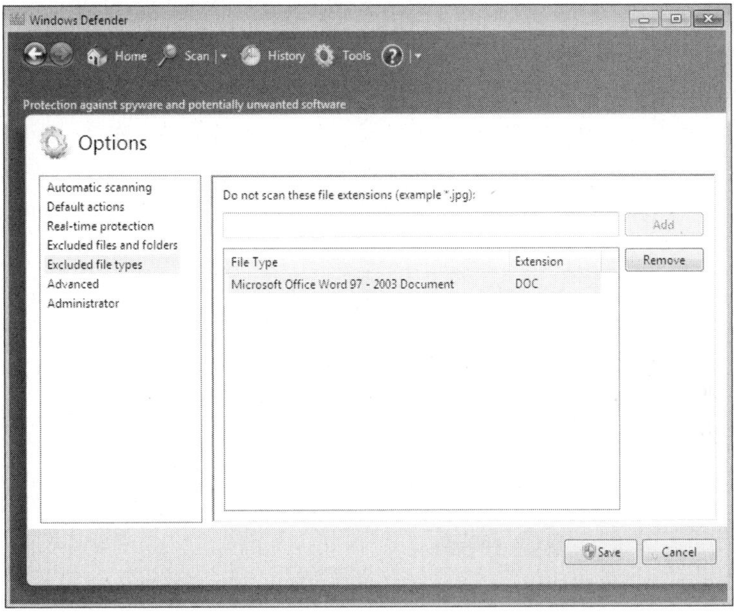

The next option that we look at from the Windows Defenders Tools is Microsoft SpyNet.

MICROSOFT SPYNET

Microsoft SpyNet is an online community that can help you know how others respond to software that has not yet been classified by Microsoft. Participation in SpyNet is voluntary, as shown in Figure 9.25, and subscription to SpyNet is free. If you choose to volunteer, your choices will be added to the community so that others can learn from your experiences.

To join the SpyNet community, click Microsoft SpyNet on the Tools menu, and then choose either a basic or advanced membership. The level of membership will specify how much information is sent to Microsoft when potentially unwanted software is found on your computer.

By default, I Do Not Want To join Microsoft SpyNet At This Time is selected, but you can choose to participate in SpyNet by selecting the appropriate radio button. If you choose not to participate, no information is sent to Microsoft, and Windows Defender does not alert you regarding unanalyzed software.

QUARANTINED ITEMS

Software that has been quarantined by Windows Defender is placed in Quarantined Items. Quarantined software will remain here until you remove it. If you find that a legitimate application is accidentally removed by Windows Defender, you can restore the application from Quarantined Items.

FIGURE 9.25
Microsoft SpyNet
participation options

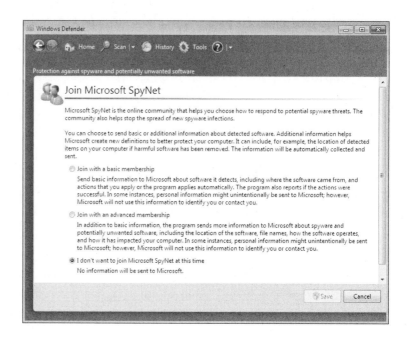

ALLOWED ITEMS

Software that has been marked as allowed is added to the Allowed Items list. Only trusted software should be added to this list. Windows Defender will not alert you regarding any software found on the Allowed Items list. If you find that a potentially dangerous application has been added to the Allowed Items list, you can remove it from the list so that Windows Defender can detect it.

WINDOWS DEFENDER WEBSITE

Clicking Windows Defender Website opens Internet Explorer and takes you to the Windows Defender website. Here you can find information on Windows Defender, spyware, and security.

MICROSOFT MALWARE PROTECTION CENTER

Clicking Microsoft Malware Protection Center opens Internet Explorer and takes you to the Malware Protection Center website. Here, you can find information on antimalware research and responses.

HISTORY MENU OPTION

There is also a History menu option next to the tools option. You can use the History menu option to see what actions have been taken by Windows Defender. Information is included about each application, the alert level, the action taken, the date, and the status. Information is retained until you click the Clear History button.

In the next section, we look at using Windows BitLocker Drive Encryption and how it can help you protect your hard drive.

Using BitLocker Drive Encryption

To prevent individuals from stealing your computer and viewing personal and sensitive data found on your hard disk, some editions of Windows 7 come with a new feature called Bit-Locker Drive Encryption. BitLocker encrypts the entire system drive. New files added to this drive are encrypted automatically, and files moved from this drive to another drive or computers are decrypted automatically.

Only Windows 7 Enterprise and Ultimate include BitLocker Drive Encryption and only the operating system drive (usually C:) or internal hard drives can be encrypted with BitLocker. Files on other types of drives must be encrypted using BitLocker To Go.

BitLocker uses a Trusted Platform Module (TPM) version 1.2 or higher to store the security key. A TPM is a chip that is found in newer computers. If you do not have a computer with a TPM, you can store the key on a removable USB drive. The USB drive will be required each time you start the computer so that the system drive can be decrypted.

If the TPM discovers a potential security risk, such as a disk error, or changes made to BIOS, hardware, system files, or startup components, the system drive will not be unlocked until you enter the 48-digit BitLocker recovery password or use a USB drive with a recovery key.

BITLOCKER RECOVERY PASSWORD

The BitLocker recovery password is very important. Do not lose it, or you may not be able to unlock the drive. Even if you do not have a TPM, be sure to keep your recovery password in case your USB drive becomes lost or corrupted.

BitLocker requires that you have a hard disk with at least two partitions, both formatted with NTFS. One partition will be the system partition that will be encrypted. The other partition will be the active partition that is used to start the computer; this partition will remain unencrypted.

In the next section, we look at two of the most important security features available: proper permissions and file and folder security.

Managing File and Folder Security

Setting up proper file and folder security is one of the most important tasks that an IT professional can perform. If permissions and security are not properly configured, users will be able to access resources that they shouldn't.

File and folder security defines what access a user has to local resources. You can limit access by applying security for files and folders. You should know what NTFS security permissions are and how they are applied.

A powerful feature of networking is the ability to allow network access to local folders. In Windows 7, it is easy to share folders. You can also apply security to shared folders in a manner that is similar to applying NTFS permissions. After you share a folder, users with appropriate access rights can access the folders through a variety of methods.

Before diving into the security section of folders, let's first look at some folder options.

Folder Options

The Windows 7 Folder Options dialog box allows you to configure many properties associated with files and folders, such as what you see when you access folders and how Windows searches through files and folders. To open the Folder Options dialog box, click Start ➢ Computer, and then select Folder And Search Options under the Organize drop-down list. You can also access Folder Options by clicking its icon in Control Panel, selecting Large Icons View, and clicking Folder Options. The Folder Options dialog box has three tabs: General, View, and Search. The options on each of these tabs are described in the following sections.

FOLDER GENERAL OPTIONS

The General tab of the Folder Options dialog box, shown in Figure 9.26, includes the following options:

♦ Whether folders are opened all in the same window when a user is browsing folders or each folder is opened in a separate window

♦ Whether a user opens items with a single mouse click or a double-click

♦ A navigation pane that allows you to show all folders or automatically expand to the current folder

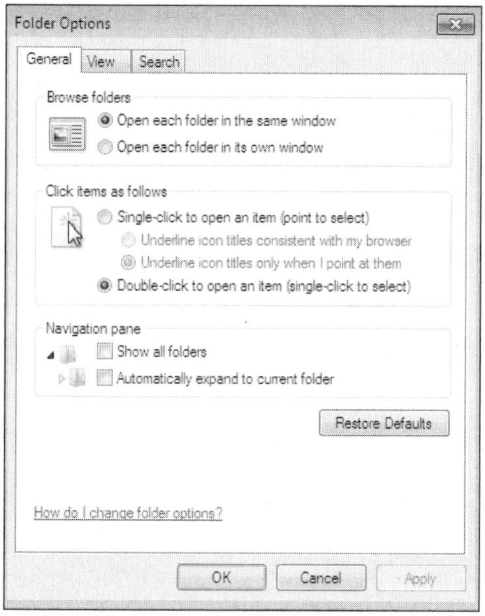

FIGURE 9.26
The General tab of the Folder Options dialog box

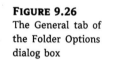

FOLDER VIEW OPTIONS

The options on the View tab of the Folder Options dialog box, shown in Figure 9.27, are used to configure what users see when they open files and folders. For example, you can change the default setting so that hidden files and folders are displayed. Table 9.8 describes the View tab options.

TABLE 9.8:   Folder View Options

OPTION	DESCRIPTION	DEFAULT VALUE
Always Show Icons, Never Thumbnails	Shows icons for files instead of thumbnail previews.	Not selected
Always Show Menus	Shows the File, Edit, View, Tools, and Help menus when browsing for files.	Not selected
Display File Icon On Thumbnails	Displays the file icon on thumbnails.	Enabled
Display File Size Information In Folder Tips	Specifies whether the file size is automatically displayed when you hover your mouse over a folder.	Enabled
Display The Full Path In The Title Bar (Classic Theme Only)	Specifies whether the title bar shows an abbreviated path of your location. Enabling this option displays the full path, such as C:\Word Documents\Sybex\Windows 7 Book\Chapter 9 as opposed to showing an abbreviated path, such as Chapter 9.	Not selected
Hidden Files And Folders	Specifies whether files and folders with the Hidden attribute are listed. Choosing Show Hidden Files And Folders displays these items.	Do Not Show Hidden Files And Folders
Hide Empty Drives In The Computer Folder	This option will not display drives that are empty in the computer folder.	Enabled

TABLE 9.8:   Folder View Options (*CONTINUED*)

OPTION	DESCRIPTION	DEFAULT VALUE
Hide Extensions For Known File Types	By default, filename extensions, which identify known file types (such as .doc for Word files and .xls for Excel files) are not shown. Disabling this option displays all filename extensions.	Enabled
Hide Protected Operating System Files (Recommended)	By default, operating system files are not shown, which protects operating system files from being modified or deleted by a user. Disabling this option displays the operating system files.	Enabled
Launch Folder Windows In A Separate Process	By default, when you open a folder, it shares memory with the previous folders that were opened. Enabling this option opens folders in separate parts of memory, which increases the stability of Windows 7 but can slightly decrease the performance of the computer.	Not selected
Show Drive Letters	Specifies whether drive letters are shown in the Computer folder. When disabled, only the name of the disk or device will be shown.	Enabled
Show Encrypted Or Compressed NTFS Files In Color	Displays encrypted or compressed files in an alternate color when they are displayed in a folder window.	Enabled
Show Pop-up Description For Folder And Desktop Items	Displays whether a pop-up tooltip is displayed when you hover your mouse over files and folders.	Enabled
Show Preview Handlers In Preview Pane	Shows the contents of files in the Preview pane.	Enabled
Use Check Boxes To Select Items	Adds a check box to each file and folder so that one or more of them may be selected. Actions can then be performed on selected items.	Not selected
Use Sharing Wizard (Recommended)	This option allows you to share a folder using a simplified sharing method.	Enabled
When Typing Into List View	Selects whether text is automatically typed into the search box or whether the typed item is selected in the view.	Select The Typed Item In The View

SEARCH OPTIONS

You can use the Search tab of the Folder Options dialog box, shown in Figure 9.28, to configure how Windows 7 searches for files. You can choose for Windows 7 to search by filename only, by filenames and contents, or a combination of the two, depending on whether indexing is enabled. You can also select from the following options:

- Include Subfolders

- Find Partial Matches

- Use Natural Language Search

- Don't Use The Index When Searching the File System

- Include System Directories (in nonindexed locations)

- Include Compressed Files in Non-indexed Locations

FIGURE 9.28
The Search tab of the Folder Options dialog box

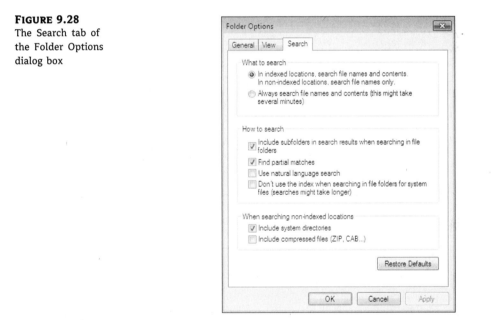

To search for files and folders, click Start ➢ Search and type your query in the search box. In the next section we look at how to secure these folders and files.

Securing Access to Files and Folders

On NTFS partitions, you can specify the access each user has to specific folders or files on the partition, based on the user's logon name and group associations. Access control consists of rights and permissions. A right (also referred to as a privilege) is an authorization to perform a specific action.

Permissions are authorizations to perform specific operations on specific objects. The owner of an object or any user who has the necessary rights to modify permissions can apply permissions to NTFS objects. If permissions are not explicitly granted within NTFS, they are implicitly denied. Permissions can also be explicitly denied, which then overrides explicitly granted permissions.

The following sections describe design goals for access control, as well as how to apply NTFS permissions and some techniques for optimizing local access. Let's look at design goals for setting up security.

DESIGN GOALS FOR ACCESS CONTROL

Before you start applying NTFS permissions to resources, you should develop design goals for access control as a part of your overall security strategy. Basic security strategy suggests that you provide each user and group with the minimum level of permissions needed for job functionality. Some of the considerations when planning access control include the following:

- ◆ Defining the resources that are included within your network — in this case, the files and folders residing on the file system

- ◆ Defining which resources will put your organization at risk; this includes defining the resources and defining the risk of damage if the resource was compromised

- ◆ Developing security strategies that address possible threats and minimize security risks

- ◆ Defining groups that security can be applied to based on users within the group membership who have common access requirements, and applying permissions to groups, as opposed to users

- ◆ Applying additional security settings through Group Policy, if your Windows 7 clients are part of an Active Directory network

- ◆ Using additional security features, such as EFS, to provide additional levels of security or file auditing to track access to critical files and folders

After you have decided what your design goals are, you can start applying your NTFS permissions.

APPLYING NTFS PERMISSIONS

NTFS permissions control access to NTFS files and folders. This is based on the technology that was originally developed for Windows NT. Ultimately, the person who owns the object has complete control over the object. You configure access by allowing or denying NTFS permissions to users and groups.

Normally, NTFS permissions are cumulative, based on group memberships if the user has been allowed access. This means that the user gets the highest level of security from all the different groups they belong to. However, if the user had been denied access through user or group membership, those permissions override the allowed permissions. Windows 7 offers the following six levels of NTFS permissions:

Full Control   This permission allows the following rights:

- ◆ Traverse folders and execute files (programs) in the folders. The ability to traverse folders allows you to access files and folders in lower subdirectories, even if you do not have permissions to access specific portions of the directory path.

- ◆ List the contents of a folder and read the data in a folder's files.

- See a folder's or file's attributes.

- Change a folder's or file's attributes.

- Create new files and write data to the files.

- Create new folders and append data to the files.

- Delete subfolders and files.

- Delete files.

- Compress files.

- Change permissions for files and folders.

- Take ownership of files and folders.

If you select the Full Control permission, all permissions will be checked by default and can't be unchecked.

Modify   This permission allows the following rights:

- Traverse folders and execute files in the folders.

- List the contents of a folder and read the data in a folder's files.

- See a file's or folder's attributes.

- Change a file's or folder's attributes.

- Create new files and write data to the files.

- Create new folders and append data to the files.

- Delete files.

If you select the Modify permission, the Read & Execute, List Folder Contents, Read, and Write permissions will be checked by default and can't be unchecked.

Read & Execute   This permission allows the following rights:

- Traverse folders and execute files in the folders.

- List the contents of a folder and read the data in a folder's files.

- See a file's or folder's attributes.

If you select the Read & Execute permission, the List Folder Contents and Read permissions will be checked by default and can't be unchecked.

List Folder Contents   This permission allows the following rights:

- Traverse folders.

- List the contents of a folder.

- See a file's or folder's attributes.

Read   This permission allows the following rights:

◆ List the contents of a folder and read the data in a folder's files.

◆ See a file's or folder's attributes.

◆ View ownership.

Write   This permission allows the following rights:

◆ Overwrite a file.

◆ View file ownership and permissions.

◆ Change a file's or folder's attributes.

◆ Create new files and write data to the files.

◆ Create new folders and append data to the files.

Special Permissions   This permission allows you to configure auditing, take ownership, and permissions beyond the normal permissions (for example, List or Traverse Folder).

Any user with Full Control access can manage the security of a folder. However, to access folders, a user must have physical access to the computer as well as a valid logon name and password. By default, regular users can't access folders over the network unless the folders have been shared. Sharing folders is covered in the "Creating Shared Folders" section later in this chapter.

To apply NTFS permissions, right-click the file or folder to which you want to control access, select Properties from the context menu, and then select the Security tab. The Security tab lists the users and groups that have been assigned permissions to the file or folder. When you click a user or group in the top half of the dialog box, you see the permissions that have been allowed or denied for that user or group in the bottom half.

Perform the following steps to manage NTFS permission:

1. Right-click the file or folder to which you want to control access, select Properties from the context menu, and click the Security tab.

2. Click the Edit button to modify permissions.

3. Click the Add button to open the Select Users Or Groups dialog box, as shown in Figure 9.29. You can select users from the computer's local database or from the domain you are in (or trusted domains) by typing the user or group name in the Enter The Object Names To Select portion of the dialog box and clicking OK.

4. You return to the Security tab of the folder's Properties dialog box. Highlight a user or group in the top list box, and in the Permissions list, specify the NTFS permissions to be allowed or denied. When you have finished, click OK.

By clicking the Advanced button on the Security tab, you can configure more granular NTFS permissions, such as Traverse Folder and Read Attributes permissions.

To remove the NTFS permissions for a user, computer, or group, highlight that entity in the Security tab and click the Remove button. Be careful when you remove NTFS permissions. You won't be asked to confirm their removal, as you are when deleting most other types of items in Windows 7.

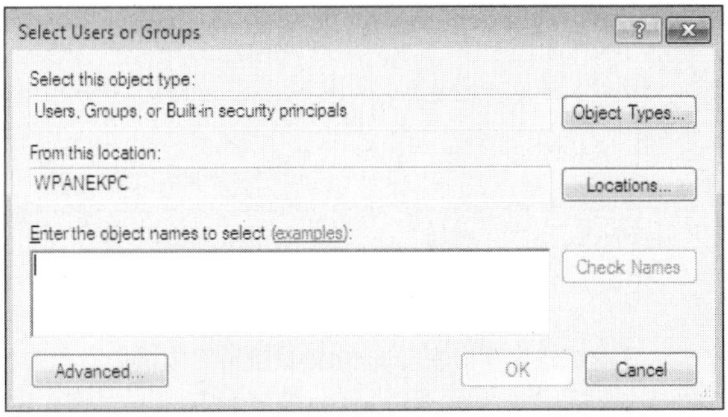

FIGURE 9.29
The Select Users Or
Groups dialog box

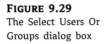

CONTROLLING PERMISSION INHERITANCE

Normally, the directory structure is organized in a hierarchical manner. This means you are likely to have subfolders in the folders to which you apply permissions. In Windows 7, by default, the parent folder's permissions are applied to any files or subfolders in that folder, as well as any subsequently created objects. These are called inherited permissions.

You can specify how permissions are inherited by subfolders and files through the Advanced options from the Security tab of a folder's Properties dialog box by clicking the Advanced button. This calls up the Permissions tab of the Advanced Security Settings dialog box. To edit these options, click the Change Permissions button. The options can include the following:

◆ Include Inheritable Permissions From This Object's Parent

◆ Replace All Existing Inheritable Permissions On All Descendants With Inheritable Permissions From This Object

If an Allow or a Deny check box in the Permissions list on the Security tab has a shaded check mark, this indicates that the permission was inherited from an upper-level folder.

If the check mark is not shaded, it means the permission was applied at the selected folder. This is known as an explicitly assigned permission. Knowing which permissions are inherited and which are explicitly assigned is useful when you need to troubleshoot permissions.

UNDERSTANDING OWNERSHIP AND SECURITY DESCRIPTORS

When an object is initially created on an NTFS partition, an associated security descriptor is created. A security descriptor contains the following information:

◆ The user or group that owns the object

◆ The users and groups that are allowed or denied access to the object

◆ The users and groups whose access to the object will be audited

After an object is created, the Creator owner of the object has full permissions to change the information in the security descriptor, even for members of the Administrators group. You can view the owner of an object from the Security tab of the specified folder's Properties and click the Advanced button. Then click the Owner tab to see who the owner of the object is. From this dialog box, you can change the owner of the object.

Although the owner of an object can set the permissions of an object so that the Administrator can't access the object, the Administrator or any member of the Administrators group can take ownership of an object and thus manage the object's permissions. When you take ownership of an object, you can specify whether you want to replace the owner on subdirectories and objects of the object. If you would like to see who owns a directory from the command prompt, type **dir /q**.

Real World Scenario

USING THE TAKE OWNERSHIP OPTION

You are the administrator of a large network. The manager of the accounting department, Will, set up a series of files and folders with a high level of security. Will was the owner of these and all of the associated files and folders. When he set up NTFS security for his files and folders, he removed access for everyone, including the Administrators group. Will recently left the company, and Kevin has been hired to take over the accounting manager's job. When Kevin tries to access Will's files, he can't. When you log on as Administrator, you also can't access any of the files.

In this case, you should access the Owner tab of the parent folder for the files and folders and change the owner to Kevin. You should ensure that you check Replace Owner On Subcontainers And Objects, and Kevin will then have Full Control permissions to the resources.

In the next section, we discuss how to determine the effective permission of a file or folder.

Determining Effective Permissions

To determine a user's effective rights (the rights the user actually has to a file or folder), add all the permissions that have been allowed through the user's assignments based on that user's username and group associations. After you determine what the user is allowed, you subtract any permissions that have been denied the user through the username or group associations.

As an example, suppose that user Marilyn is a member of both the Accounting and Execs groups. The following assignments have been made to the Accounting group permissions:

Permission	Allow	Deny
Full Control		
Modify	X	
Read & Execute	X	
List Folder Contents		
Read		
Write		

The following assignments have been made to the Execs group permissions:

Permission	Allow	Deny
Full Control		
Modify		
Read & Execute		
List Folder Contents		
Read	X	
Write		

To determine Marilyn's effective rights, you combine the permissions that have been assigned. The result is that Marilyn's effective rights are Modify, Read & Execute, and Read so she basically has Modify (the highest right).

As another example, suppose that user Dan is a member of both the Sales and Temps groups. The following assignments have been made to the Sales group permissions:

Permission	Allow	Deny
Full Control		
Modify	X	
Read & Execute	X	
Permission	Allow	Deny
List Folder Contents	X	
Read	X	
Write	X	

The following assignments have been made to the Temps group permissions:

Permission	Allow	Deny
Full Control		
Modify		X
Read & Execute		
List Folder Contents		
Read		
Write		X

To determine Dan's effective rights, you start by seeing what Dan has been allowed: Modify, Read & Execute, List Folder Contents, Read, and Write permissions. You then remove anything that he is denied: Modify and Write permissions. In this case, Dan's effective rights are Read & Execute, List Folder Contents, and Read. Now let's see what rights users have.

Viewing Effective Permissions

If permissions have been applied at the user and group levels, and inheritance is involved, it can sometimes be confusing to determine what the effective permissions are. To help identify which effective permissions will actually be applied, you can view them from the Effective Permissions tab of Advanced Security Settings, or you can use the ICACLS command-line utility.

To see what the effective permissions are for a user or group, click the Select button and then type the user or group name. Then click OK. If a box is checked and not shaded, that means explicit permissions have been applied at that level. If the box is shaded, the permissions to that object were inherited.

The ICACLS command-line utility can also be used to display or modify user access rights. The options associated with the ICACLS command are as follows:

- /grant grants permissions.

- /remove revokes permissions.

- /deny denies permissions.

- /setintegritylevel sets an integrity level of Low, Medium, or High.

One issue that IT people run into is what happens to the security when you move or copy a file or folder. Let's look at NTFS permissions when moved or copied.

Determining NTFS Permissions for Copied or Moved Files

When you copy or move NTFS files, the permissions that have been set for those files might change. The following guidelines can be used to predict what will happen:

- If you move a file from one folder to another folder on the same volume, the file will retain the original NTFS permissions.

- If you move a file from one folder to another folder between different NTFS volumes, the file is treated as a copy and will have the same permissions as the destination folder.

- If you copy a file from one folder to another folder on the same volume or on a different volume, the file will have the same permissions as the destination folder.

- If you copy or move a file or folder to a FAT partition, it will not retain any NTFS permissions.

Now that we know how to deal with the NTFS security, let's look at shared permissions.

Managing Network Access

In every network, there are resources that the users need to gain access to. As IT professionals, we share these resources so that our users can do their jobs.

Sharing is the process of allowing network users access to a resource located on a computer. A network share provides a single location to manage shared data used by many users. Sharing also allows an administrator to install an application once, as opposed to installing it locally at each computer, and to manage the application from a single location.

The following sections describe how to create and manage shared folders, configure share permissions, and provide access to shared resources.

Creating Shared Folders

You can share a folder in two ways. Right-click a folder and select Share to use the Sharing Wizard. If the Sharing Wizard feature is enabled, you will see the File Sharing screen. Here, you can add local users.

However, you cannot use the Sharing Wizard to share resources with domain users. To share a folder with domain users, you should right-click the folder and select Properties, and then select the Sharing tab, as shown in Figure 9.30.

FIGURE 9.30
The Sharing tab of a folder's PerfLogs Properties dialog box

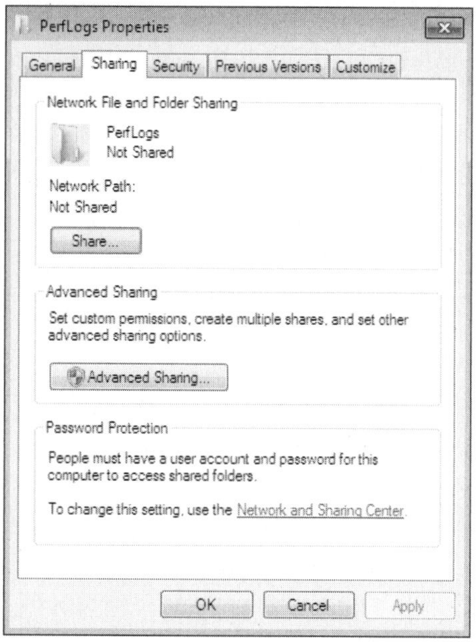

Clicking the Share button takes you to the Sharing Wizard. To configure Advanced Sharing, click the Advanced Sharing button, which opens the Advanced Sharing dialog box. When you share a folder, you can configure the options listed in Table 9.9.

If you share a folder and then decide that you do not want to share it, just deselect the Share This Folder check box. You can easily tell that a folder has been shared by the group icon located at the bottom left of the folder icon. The following statements also hold true:

♦ Only folders, not files, can be shared.

♦ Share permissions can be applied only to folders and not to files.

♦ If a folder is shared over the network and a user is accessing it locally, then share permissions will not apply to the local user; only NTFS permissions will apply.

♦ If a shared folder is copied, the original folder will still be shared but not the copy.

♦ If a shared folder is moved, the folder will no longer be shared.

♦ If the shared folder will be accessed by a mixed environment of clients, including some that do not support long filenames, you should use the 8.3 naming format for files.

♦ Folders can be shared through the Net Share command-line utility.

TABLE 9.9:   Share Folder Options

OPTION	DESCRIPTION
Share This Folder	Makes the folder available through local access and network access
Share Name	A descriptive name by which users will access the folder
Comments	Additional descriptive information about the share (optional)
Limit The Number Of Simultaneous Users To	The maximum number of connections to the share at any one time (no more than 10 users can simultaneously access a share on a Windows 7 computer)
Permissions	How users will access the folder over the network
Caching	How folders are cached when the folder is offline

Now let's look at configuring share permissions for your users.

Configuring Share Permissions

You can control users' access to shared folders by assigning share permissions. Share permissions are less complex than NTFS permissions and can be applied only to folders (unlike NTFS permissions, which can be applied to files and folders).

To assign share permissions, click the Permissions button in the Advanced Sharing dialog box. This brings up the Permissions For PerfLogs dialog box, as shown in Figure 9.31.

FIGURE 9.31
The Permissions For
PerfLogs dialog box

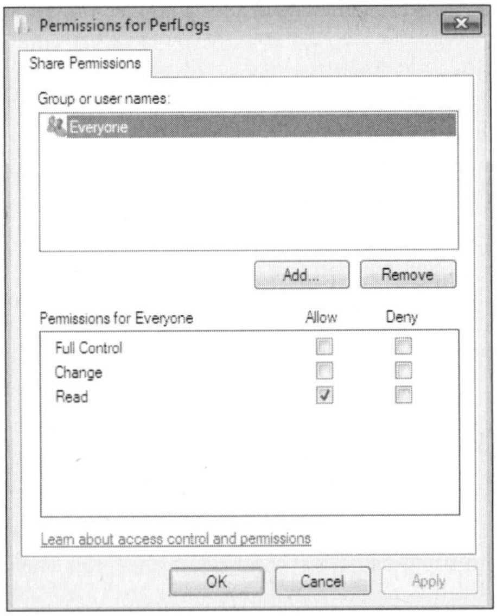

You can assign the following three types of share permissions:

Full Control   Allows full access to the shared folder.

Change   Allows users to change data within a file or to delete files.

Read   Allows a user to view and execute files in the shared folder. Read is the default permission on shared folders for the Everyone group.

Shared folders do not use the same concept of inheritance as NTFS folders. If you share a folder, there is no way to block access to lower-level resources through share permissions.

Combining Share and NTFS

When Share and NTFS permissions conflict, the most restrictive permissions apply. Remember that Share and NTFS permissions are both applied only when a user is accessing a shared resource over a network. Only NTFS permissions apply to a user accessing a resource locally.

So for example, if a user's NTFS security settings were Read Only on a resource and the Share permission was Full Control on that same resource, the user would have Read Only when they connect to that resource. The most restrictive set of permissions wins.

The Bottom Line

Understand Local Group Policy Objects.   Local Group Policy Objects (LGPOs) are a set of security configuration settings that are applied to users and computers. LGPOs are created and stored on the Windows 7 computer.

If your Windows 7 computer is a part of a domain, which uses the services of Active Directory, then you typically manage and configure security through Group Policy Objects (GPOs). LGPOs are rules that can be placed on either users or computers.

Master It   You are the administrator for a large computer company. You need to make sure that all of the Windows 7 machines reset their passwords every 45 days. How can you accomplish this?

Understand User Account Control (UAC).   User Account Control (UAC) enables nonadministrator users to perform standard tasks, such as install a printer, configure a VPN or wireless connection, and install updates, while preventing them from performing tasks that require administrative privileges, such as installing applications.

Master It   You are the administrator for a small plumbing company. You need to set 20 Windows 7 machines so that the users can always run applications with elevated privileges. How do you accomplish this goal?

Configure NTFS security.   NTFS permissions control access to NTFS files and folders. The person who owns the object has complete control over the object. You configure access by allowing or denying NTFS permissions to users and groups.

NTFS permissions are cumulative, based on group memberships if the user has been allowed access. This means that the user gets the highest level of security from all the different groups they belong to. However, if the user had been denied access through user or group membership, those permissions override the allowed permissions.

Master It   You are the administrator for a small organization that has decided to use NTFS on each Windows 7 machine. The company needs to make sure that all files and folders are secure. How do you make sure that all files and folders are secure on the Windows 7 NTFS drives?

Manage shared permissions.   Sharing is the process of allowing network users access to a resource located on a computer. A network share provides a single location to manage shared data used by many users. Sharing also allows an administrator to install an application once, as opposed to installing it locally at each computer, and to manage the application from a single location.

Master It   You are the administrator for a large computer company. You need everyone in the company to have access to the reports folder on Server A. How should you give everyone enough access to change and create reports?

Chapter 10

Configuring Hardware and Printers

Getting hardware up and running in today's operating systems is not usually a problem. With Plug and Play technology, the initial installation and configuration will typically go smoothly. However, most of the time the software controlling the hardware (drivers) will need to be updated over time and might have to be rolled back in case of an issue in a new package. There will also be times when the drivers need to be installed manually for legacy hardware. You might also have to verify hardware configuration and make adjustments. The utility provided to perform these functions is Device Manager.

Device Manager displays all installed hardware, including input/output (I/O) devices like your mouse, keyboard, and monitor. It also displays information on storage, both removable and fixed, and communication devices like network interface cards and wireless and Bluetooth devices. What you won't see for hardware in Device Manager are printers (unless they're USB; in that case, you'll see the USB port and thus the printer will be identified, but you won't be able to configure the printer from here). You'll use the Devices And Printers applet for configuring and troubleshooting printers. New functionality in Windows 7 integrates some Device Manager functionality into Devices And Printers. This new functionality is known as Device Stage.

In this chapter, you'll learn how to:

◆ Use Device Manager

◆ Manage and update device drivers

◆ Install, uninstall, and disable hardware

◆ Manage I/O and removable storage devices

◆ Install and configure printers

Configuring Hardware

Device Manager in Windows 7 works the same way as it did in Vista and XP. Device Manager is designed to display information about the hardware installed on your computer, provides an interface to add new hardware, and lets you configure the hardware. Hardware today follows the Plug and Play standard, so simply connecting most hardware will allow Device Manager (well, the OS processes controlling devices that are displayed to you) to automatically configure them. If you have devices that are not Plug and Play, you can install them manually from Device Manager as well. Windows 7 introduces a new functionality known as Device Stage, which is an enhanced graphic output that gives better details and functionality to installed devices such as cameras.

You can use Device Manager to ensure that all devices are working properly and to troubleshoot misbehaving devices. For each device installed, you can view specific properties of each device down to the resources being used, such as the input/output (I/O) port and interrupt requests (IRQs). The specific actions that you can take with Device Manager include the following:

- Viewing a list of all hardware installed on your computer

- Determining which device driver is installed for each device

- Managing and updating device drivers

- Installing new devices

- Disabling, enabling, and uninstalling devices

- Using driver rollback returning to a previous version of a driver

- Troubleshooting device problems

Although many of the features of Device Manager in Windows 7 work similarly to Device Manager in older versions of Windows, a new feature has been added to make configuration and use of some devices easier: Device Stage.

Introducing Device Stage

Throughout the evolution of technologies and PCs, one of the greatest features is how PCs let us use such a wide array of devices. Device Manager lets us see all the hardware connected and make configuration changes, but utilizing the features of the devices themselves has been left up to alternate programs outside the Windows interface. Windows 7 introduces a new specification for hardware vendors (knowing that most hardware comes with software for the user to interface with) that allows them to provide user access within Windows. The new feature and specification is known as Device Stage. Windows 7 Devices And Printers is the interface for displaying and accessing hardware that supports Device Stage. The Windows 7 Devices And Printers screen is shown in Figure 10.1.

Take the example of a digital camera. When you connect the camera to the PC, the PC recognizes the device (which is Plug and Play) and typically displays the camera as a mass storage device. The user wanting advanced features like downloading or editing the photos uses another program. When you plug in a device like a camera supporting Device Stage technology, Device Stage displays a single window that gives you easy access to common device tasks, such as importing pictures, launching the vendor-supplied editing program, or simply browsing all from one interface. With Windows 7, you'll be able to access all of your connected and wireless devices from the single Devices And Printers screen as well as the clicking the device that displays in the Windows 7 enhanced Taskbar and using the menu as shown in Figure 10.2. From this device menu, you can work with your devices, browse files on them, or manage device settings.

Device Stage–supported devices also include wireless and Bluetooth devices that make managing these resources for the end user more efficient than ever. As portable devices are disconnected and reconnected, the Device Stage–driven Devices And Printers screen updates in real time.

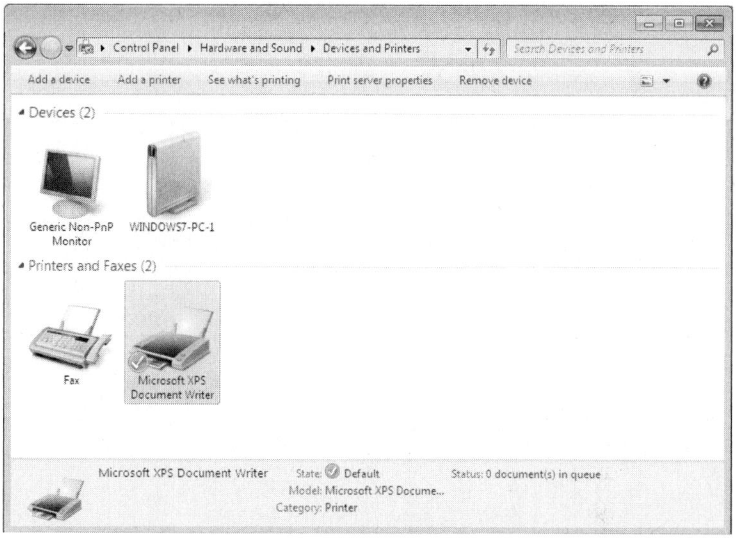

FIGURE 10.1
Devices And Printers

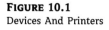

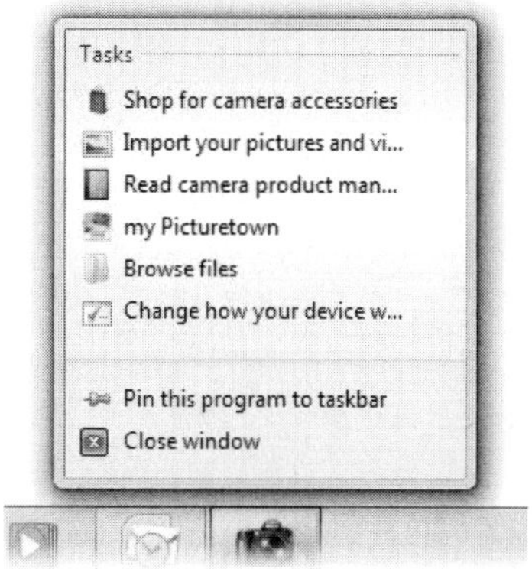

FIGURE 10.2
Device options appear in
the Taskbar.

The following procedures will guide you through opening and viewing devices recognized on your Windows 7 machine.

Perform the following steps to find Devices And Printers in Control Panel:

1. Choose Start ➤ Control Panel ➤ Hardware And Sound.

2. Choose Devices And Printers from the main window.

3. Right-click a device to see functions specific to that device.

Perform the following steps to open Devices And Printers from the Start menu:

1. Click Start ➤ Control Panel ➤ Devices And Printers.

2. Right-click a device to see functions specific to that device.

Or you can do the following:

◆ Click the Start button and type **device** in the Start menu's search box, as shown in Figure 10.3, to launch Devices And Printers, the first applet in the search list.

FIGURE 10.3
Type the word *device* in the Start menu's search box.

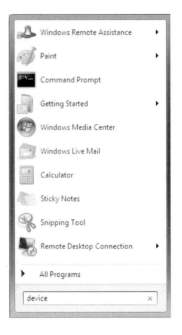

Using Device Manager

Device Manager is this first-line component in Windows 7 to display which devices are connected to your machine. More appropriately (and importantly) is the ability to see which devices Windows 7 has recognized. If you install or connect a new piece of hardware, you won't see it in Device Manager if Windows 7 doesn't recognize it. This would be an unusual occurrence given the sophistication of today's hardware vendors and the standards like Plug and Play that have been implemented. However, this is an important step in seeing just which devices are known to Windows 7.

In some cases, Windows 7 doesn't recognize a device but can tell what *type* of device it is. Device Manager adds an Unknown Device item with as much information about the device that it can present. Hopefully, this will give you enough information about the hardware so that you can manually install the device driver. Keep in mind that we've been using Device Manager for many versions of Windows, so what we're discussing is applicable to legacy versions as well. Device Manager has a fairly simple opening screen but a lot of functionality behind it. Open Device Manager in Windows 7 quickly by typing **Device Manager** in the Start menu's search bar and view the opening screen as shown in Figure 10.4.

On the opening screen, you get a good first feeling for the hardware installed and recognized, as well as a glimpse at any major issues such as a device that's recognized but does not have its drivers installed or working correctly. How do you see that? A warning symbol is displayed over the misbehaving device. For example, say you have just installed a new network adapter but the device does not seem to be working. You can open Device Manager and click the Network Adapters option to start the troubleshooting.

FIGURE 10.4
Device Manager opening
screen

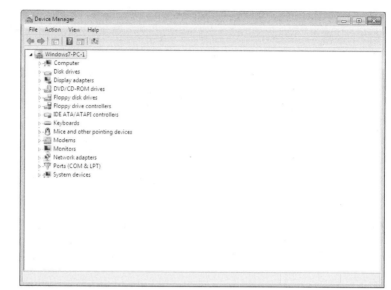

NOTIFICATION ICONS

When something occurs that's outside the normal functionality in a Windows interface, an additional notification icon appears. As shown in the following graphic, the yellow triangle with the exclamation point icon is the indicator that a device is experiencing difficulty. Informational notifications consist of a blue circle with a question mark. A critical error displays as a red circle with an X through it.

To continue troubleshooting a network adapter in Device Manager, you right-click the misbehaving adapter and select Properties to open the dialog box shown in Figure 10.5. This is just the start to the functionality within Device Manager.

FIGURE 10.5
Device Manager network
adapter properties
window

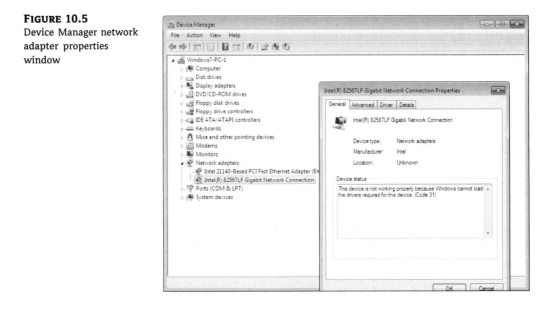

LAUNCHING DEVICE MANAGER AND VIEWING NETWORK ADAPTERS

There are many reasons to view the devices installed and configured on a machine. One reason is to verify hardware type and status. Suppose someone in your organization has given you documentation for a user's machine with the machine's hardware specifications. You're concerned that the stated network adapter for the machine may not be the one installed.

Follow these steps if you want Device Manager on the machine in question to show you the recognized network adapters in the machine:

1. Choose Start ➢ Control Panel ➢ Hardware And Sound ➢ Device Manager (under Devices And Printers).

2. Click the triangle next to Network Adapters (or double-click Network Adapters) to expand Network Adapters, as shown here:

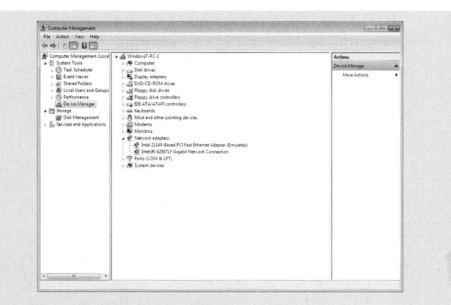

Here's another way to launch Device Manager:

1. Click Start.

2. Type **Device Manager** in the Start menu's search box.

3. Press Enter.

Or you can:

1. Click Start and then right-click Computer.

2. Select Manage.

3. In the navigation pane of the Microsoft Management Console (MMC), select Device Manager.

The latter method puts Device Manager into a functional interface, MMC, that allows access to several administrative tools from one location.

Device Properties Available Within Device Manager

After you open Device Manager and have access to the installed devices on your machine, you might want to view the properties for the hardware. The properties dialog box lets you view and change configuration parameters if necessary. The tabs in the dialog box vary from device to device.

Many device properties dialog boxes include an Advanced tab, as shown in Figure 10.6.

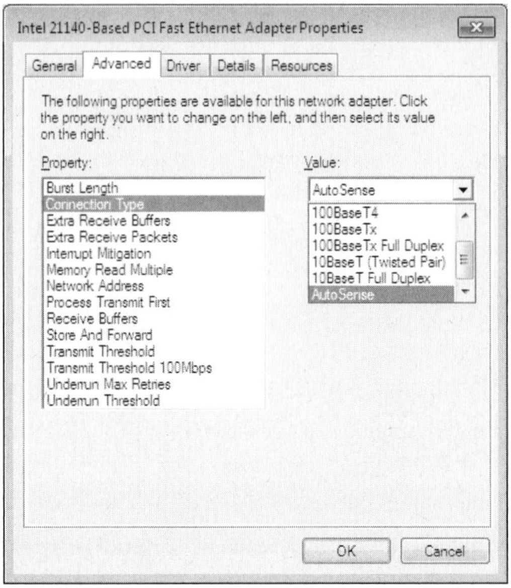

FIGURE 10.6
You can click the
Advanced tab to see
additional properties
specific to the device.

Configuring Network Adapter Advanced Properties

If you need to change the hardware configuration properties, Device Manager is the best way
to access the parameters.

Perform the following steps to access the advanced properties of your network adapter
where you can make configuration changes if necessary:

1. Choose Start ➢ Control Panel ➢ Hardware And Sound ➢ Device Manager (under Devices
    and Printers).

2. Click the triangle next to Network Adapters (or double-click Network Adapters) to expand
    Network Adapters.

3. Right-click your network adapter and select Properties.

4. Choose the Advanced tab.

5. Select various properties and view the parameters.

After installing a new piece of hardware, you might need to update the drivers to a later
version than those shipped with the hardware.

Installing and Updating Device Drivers

Device drivers are the controlling code that interfaces the hardware components with the
operating system. The commands issued to a piece of hardware are specific to each piece of
hardware and might be different commands, memory locations, or actions even within the
same type of hardware. A network interface card (NIC) from one vendor might have a different set of instructions necessary for its operation than a NIC from a different manufacturer.

This doesn't work well for an operating system or software vendor who would like to be able to issue a standard command and have the same functionality across the hardware, regardless of the vendor. This is where the driver comes in; the driver takes a standard instruction from the operating system and issues the command to the hardware to perform the desired function.

Why do we update drivers? There are cases where a command set for the driver might perform a function incorrectly. This might produce errors in some cases and has to be fixed. The hardware vendor will update the driver to fix the problem. It might also be the case that new or better functionality is desired and the hardware vendor needs to change the driver code to allow added functionality or provide better performance; this will also lead to an update.

⊕ Real World Scenario

DRIVER CODE CAUSING AN ARBITRARY NONREPRODUCIBLE ERROR

While working on a consulting job for a company where we were installing a new program and hardware that provided bar-code scanning for a company, we were plagued with random failures of the bar-code readers connected to PCs. The bar-code readers seemed to install correctly and they showed as functioning properly within Device Manager. However, periodically, the hardware readers would fail to input data into the application we were using. We could reboot the affected machine and the bar-code reader would work fine again (for a while).

It was easy to blame the operating system because the reboot seemed to fix the problem, but this was not the case. After several days of troubleshooting and working with the manufacturer, we determined that the driver interfacing the operating system with the hardware was not releasing memory resources correctly and was causing the driver to fail. We received an updated driver, applied the update to the machines, and the problem was resolved.

Be careful not to blame the operating system prematurely and investigate other areas for possible problems.

Typical first-time installation of drivers today happens automatically, thanks to the Plug and Play specification. After installation of the hardware, Windows 7 will recognize the new hardware and will launch the driver installation program. Take, for example, the connection of a digital camera to the USB port of your computer. Windows 7 will recognize that a device has been plugged in and will gather the information about the USB device. Windows 7 will then install the best driver it knows about (and if it doesn't know about the device, it will ask you how to proceed). Figure 10.7 shows the message that indicates the operating system found a driver and is installing it automatically.

The installation completes and the device is now available in Device Manager. Figure 10.8 shows the digital camera as a hardware item you can now access as you did previously with the network adaptor.

If you need to review the driver details for your newly installed device — the digital camera in our example — you can right-click the device in Device Manager and choose Properties. Figure 10.9 shows the right-click menu (also known as the context menu); note the top choice in this menu is a faster way to access the Update Driver Software command — rather than selecting Properties and clicking the Update Driver button — if that's what you're trying to do.

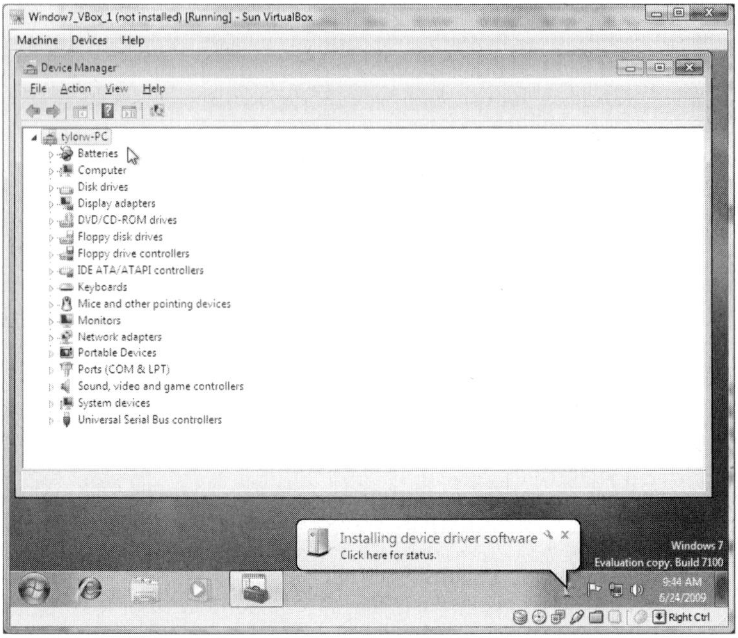

FIGURE 10.7
Automatic driver
installation

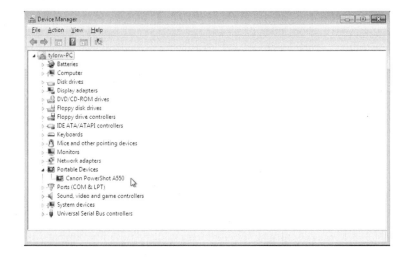

FIGURE 10.8
New device availability
in Device Manager

You might want to verify the driver general information such as the driver provider or version; you can see that information on the Driver tab of the Properties window. You can also choose to view the driver details, which are the supporting files and associated paths. Figure 10.10 shows our digital camera's Properties window with the Driver tab selected, along with the Driver File Details dialog box that opened when we clicked the Driver Details button.

FIGURE 10.9
The right-click menu for a device in Device Manager

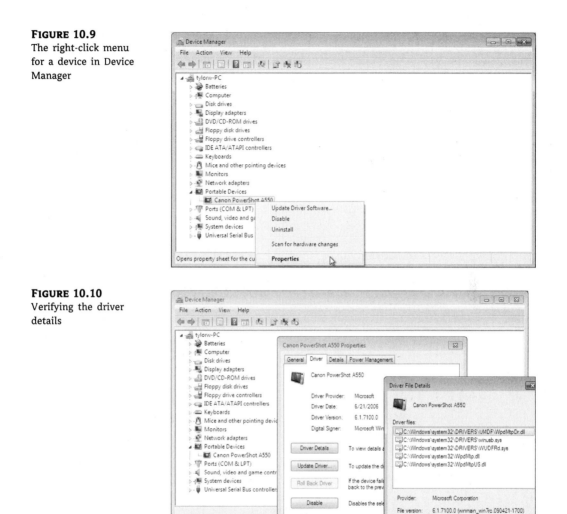

FIGURE 10.10
Verifying the driver details

VIEWING DRIVER DETAILS

When you're having issues with a hardware device, you can go online and read forums or query search engines for ideas. A lot of the time someone will say, "We had a terrible time with driver version 2.1.1 but version 2.1.2 fixed it," referencing your exact problem.

Perform the following steps to see your device driver information:

1. Choose Start ➢ Control Panel ➢ Hardware And Sound ➢ Device Manager (or type **device manager** in the Start menu's search box).

2. Click the triangle next to the category you're interested in to expand the item list; you can also double-click the category name (for example, double-click the Portable Devices category to see the portable devices connected to the machine).

3. Right-click the hardware item and select Properties.

4. Select the Driver tab and view the Driver Version setting.

5. Click the Driver Details button to see the files associated with the hardware.

UPDATING DRIVERS

Perform the following steps to update drivers:

1. Choose Start ➤ Control Panel ➤ Hardware And Sound ➤ Device Manager (or type **device manager** in the Start menu's search box).

2. Click the triangle next to the category you're interested in to expand the item list.

3. Right-click the hardware item and select Properties.

4. Select the Driver tab.

5. Click the Update Driver button; a window launches and asks how you want to update the driver.

6. Choose Search Automatically For Updated Driver Software to have Windows 7 search for you, or you can choose Browse My Computer For Driver Software if you already have the new drivers. Windows 7 searches for and updates the drivers or reports back that you have the most current version.

WHY UPDATE A DEVICE DRIVER?

You might install a new driver for new or updated functionality even if you're not having issues. You can receive notification from the manufacturer if you have let them know you're interested by registering your hardware. Otherwise, visit the manufacturer's website periodically to see if updates are available.

Occasionally an update breaks a piece of functioning hardware or doesn't solve a problem. In that case, you'll want to go back to the previous version, or "roll back" the driver.

ROLLING BACK TO A PREVIOUS VERSION OF A DEVICE DRIVER

Perform the following steps to roll back to a previous version of an updated driver:

1. Choose Start ➤ Control Panel ➤ Hardware And Sound ➤ Device Manager (or type **device manager** in the Start menu's search box).

2. Click the triangle next to the category you're interested in to expand the item list.

3. Right-click the hardware item and select Properties.

4. Select the Driver tab.

5. Click the Roll Back Driver button. The previous driver will be installed and the hardware will return to its previous state of functionality.

THE ROLLBACK OPTION MAY NOT BE AVAILABLE

If the Roll Back Driver button is grayed out, there isn't a previous version available to roll back to.

The Driver tab for a piece of installed hardware in Device Manager also provides functionality for disabling and uninstalling a driver. Why would you want to disable a driver? There are several possibilities, but troubleshooting is in the forefront. Disabling the driver effectively disables the hardware; it will no longer function as designed. Uninstalling the device driver also has a similar effect, but if the hardware is still installed, you can uninstall it, perform a hardware scan to ensure the hardware is still recognized, and then reinstall.

Many times we have disabled a device from Device Manager to eliminate one piece of a problem we are having with a system. If we're confident the problem exists with the hardware, we'll uninstall the driver and let the operating system reinstall it as part of the troubleshooting procedure. This works much of the time.

DISABLING A DEVICE

Perform the following steps to disable a device:

1. Choose Start ➢ Control Panel ➢ Hardware And Sound ➢ Device Manager (or type **device manager** in the Start menu's search box).

2. Click the triangle next to the category you're interested in to expand the item list.

3. Right-click the hardware item and select Properties.

You can select Disable directly from the context menu if you want.

4. Select the Driver tab.

5. Click the Disable button (this is a toggle button; it will say Disable if the device is enabled, or Enable if the device is disabled).

The device driver and thus the device will be disabled and will no longer function. A down arrow appears on the item in Device Manager, as shown in Figure 10.11, and the General tab will show the device as disabled.

FIGURE 10.11
The down arrow indicates the device is disabled.

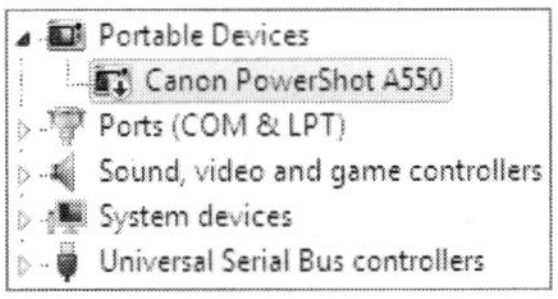

ENABLING A DEVICE

Perform the following steps to enable a device:

1. Choose Start ➢ Control Panel ➢ Hardware And Sound ➢ Device Manager (or type **device manager** in the Start menu's search box).

2. Click the triangle next to the category you're interested in to expand the item list.

3. Right-click the hardware item and select Properties. (Alternatively, select Enable from the context menu.)

4. Choose the Driver tab. (Alternatively, click Enable Device on the General tab).

5. Click the Enable button (Figure 10.12). This is a toggle button; it will say Enable if the device is disabled, or Disable if the device is enabled.

The device driver will become enabled and the hardware will work as designed (barring any other issues).

FIGURE 10.12
Enabling a device

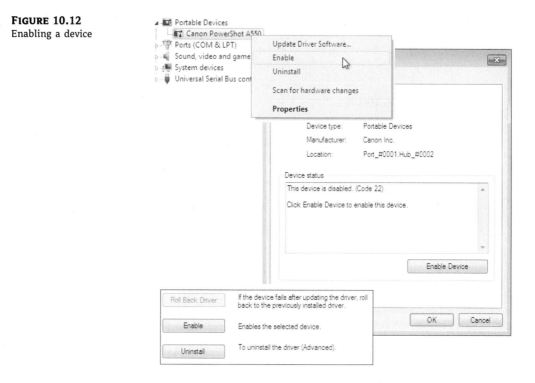

It might be beneficial at times to uninstall and reinstall a device driver. By uninstalling and reinstalling a device driver, many times the default configuration parameters will be reset to their original specifications. Therefore, any changes you have made will need to be reconfigured. You might also consider using a different device driver than Windows 7 is set up to use via Plug and Play. Uninstalling the device driver and manually installing a different version might be a solution as well. Keep in mind that uninstalling a device driver does not delete the driver files from the machine; uninstalling the device drivers removes the operating system configuration for the hardware. You might want to find the files and delete them manually in some cases. Remember, you can find the files (and thus the filenames) by clicking the Driver Details button on the Driver tab of the hardware device's Properties pages.

UNINSTALLING A DEVICE DRIVE

If you have determined the device driver for a misbehaving hardware is potentially the problem you are having, you can uninstall the device driver. Windows 7 will detect the device again (assuming that it found the device the first time) and reinstall the driver. You have the option of letting Windows 7 search and install the driver, or you can manually choose where to install it from.

Perform the following steps to uninstall a device driver:

1. Choose Start ➢ Control Panel ➢ Hardware And Sound ➢ Device Manager (or type **device manager** in the Start menu's search box).

2. Click the triangle next to the category you're interested in to expand the item list.

3. Right-click the hardware item and select Properties. (You can select Uninstall directly from the context menu if you want.)

4. Select the Driver tab.

5. Click the Uninstall button.

6. Click OK in the Confirm Device Uninstall dialog box. A progress box will appear as the device driver is uninstalled. Device Manager will no longer show the hardware.

REINSTALLING A DEVICE DRIVER AUTOMATICALLY

You can have Windows 7 automatically reinstall an uninstalled driver. To begin, from the Device Manager click Action ➢ Scan For Hardware Changes. Alternatively, you can right-click the machine name in Device Manager and select Scan For Hardware Changes from the context menu.

Windows 7 initiates the process of discovering the Plug and Play device and reinstalls the device driver configuration into the operating system. The hardware will be available again within Device Manager.

Some hardware manufacturers would like you to install the driver files and some software for their device before the operating system has a chance to discover it. This might be just so the software program controlling some of the hardware functionality will be installed first; that way, its configuration file can accurately reference the installed drivers. Another reason might be to add the driver files to the driver configuration directories of the operating system before the OS discovers the device. This is usually done by inserting and running a setup program from a provided CD or DVD. Following the manufacturer's recommendations will most often produce a better result.

🌐 Real World Scenario

FOLLOW THE HARDWARE VENDOR'S RECOMMENDATION

We once installed a new wireless USB adaptor into a machine by just plugging it in despite the big red sticker that said "Run the setup on the CD first!" Sure enough, Windows found the adapter and proceeded to install the drivers. The hardware showed up in Device Manager but would not work. We decided to run the setup program on the CD. It turns out the driver files on the CD were a different version (actually older) than the installed files and Windows would not replace the installed drivers. Even after manually uninstalling them, we had to go back and find five different files in numerous locations and delete each one. Finding those files was not the simplest operation; a lot of online research went into solving this problem and several hours of our time was wasted.

Simply following the hardware vendor instructions would have been much easier. We did the same installation on another machine following the vendor recommendations, and everything worked perfectly.

There are also situations we run into that require a manual installation of hardware. This might be for legacy hardware you are using, for drivers not supplied in the operating system distribution files, or drivers that might perform different functions from the default drivers available. You can also perform a manual driver installation in Windows 7 by using the Add Hardware Wizard.

In the manual installation process, you can have Windows 7 access a Microsoft online database with available drivers to find a current driver, or you can specify a location of your choosing locally.

From Device Manager, launch the Add Hardware Wizard by choosing Add Legacy Hardware from either the Action menu or the context menu of the machine. The next step is to tell Windows 7 where to look for the driver. The next screen of the Add Hardware Wizard shows the default selection, as shown in Figure 10.13.

FIGURE 10.13
Select this option to have the wizard install the hardware for you.

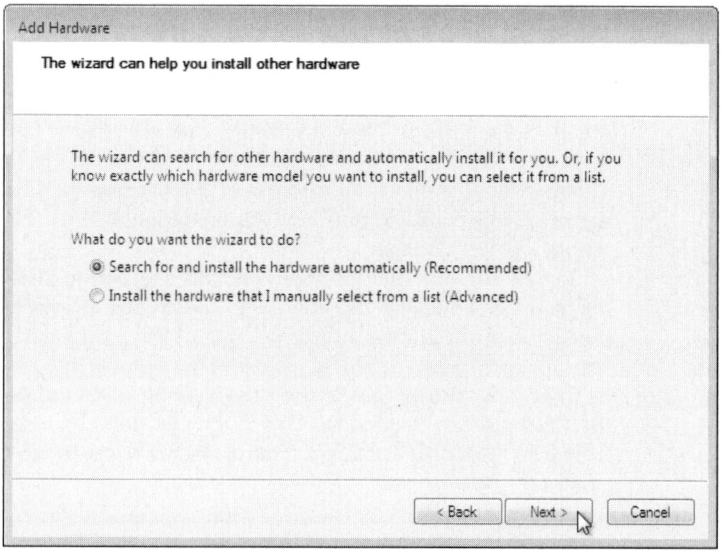

In order to choose a piece of hardware from a list of supplied drivers, or more importantly, to choose a specific path, you select the option Install The Hardware That I Manually Select For A List (Advanced) and click Next. This allows you to select a device or choose Show All Devices; if you choose Show All Devices, click Next to choose a location.

If you have a disk or have the appropriate drivers stored in an accessible location, click the Have Disk button, as shown in Figure 10.14, and browse to the driver files you need to install. If all goes as planned, the hardware device drivers will be installed and Device Manager will display the newly installed hardware.

The devices you use to get information into and out of your Windows 7 machine are your I/O devices. I/O devices include your keyboard, mouse, scanner, and printer. These devices are also configurable through Device Manager, as you'll learn in the next section.

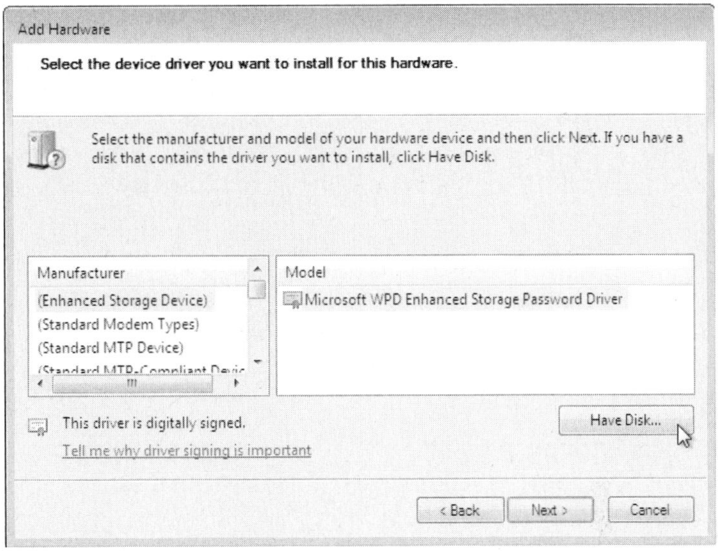

FIGURE 10.14
Click the Have Disk
button.

Managing I/O Devices

Your I/O devices might be connected to your computer by standard cabling or via USB, or you might use a wireless technology such as IrDA (infrared) or RF (radio frequency). Most of the time you will not have to (or want to) change the configuration of these devices. However, doing so is possible, and in this section we'll show you how to make changes.

Configuring the Keyboard

Most of the time you can leave the keyboard settings at their default values. There are ease-of-access properties as well as advanced keyboard options you can configure if desired. Accessing the ease-of-access features for the keyboard by choosing Start ➢ Control Panel ➢ Ease Of Access and clicking the Change How Your Keyboard Works link, as shown in Figure 10.15. You can also click the Ease Of Access Center link (from Ease of Access) and then choose Make The Keyboard Easier To Use. Either way, you get to the same window and can access the advanced properties from this window by selecting Keyboard Settings in the See Also section.

The advanced properties for the keyboard allow you to change the character repeat delay and the character repeat rate. The delay is how long Windows 7 waits before repeating characters when a key is held down, and the repeat rate is how quickly the characters repeat after the delay interval has expired. The keyboard properties also include a setting for the cursor blink rate. Figure 10.16 shows the Keyboard Properties window. The Hardware tab allows you to access the device driver properties (as found in Device Manager).

If you have an issue where your typing style has you hold down a key on your keyboard a little too long sometimes and the characters start to repeat, you can change the amount of time Windows 7 waits before repeating the character.

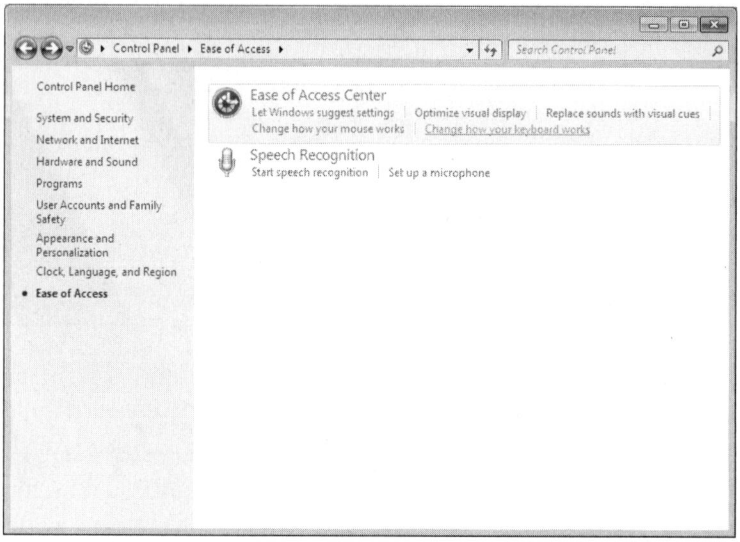

FIGURE 10.15
Keyboard Ease of Access
Center

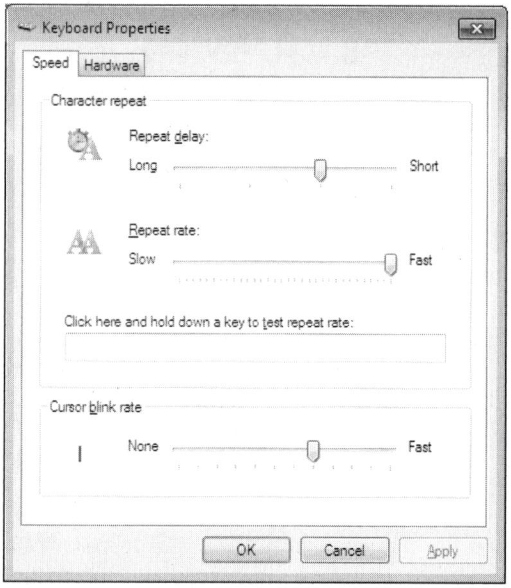

FIGURE 10.16
Keyboard Properties
window

Changing the Repeat Delay for Your Keyboard

Perform the following steps to modify the repeat delay for your keyboard:

1. Choose Start ➤ Control Panel ➤ Ease Of Access.

2. Click Change How Your Keyboard Works.

3. Scroll down to the See Also section and choose Keyboard Settings to open the Keyboard Properties window.

4. Select the Repeat Delay slider and adjust the repeat delay to a longer value.

Configuring the Mouse

As with many I/O devices, you probably won't need to change your mouse configuration. Once you know you can, you might try out a few different options, just because you are able to. To check out the mouse options, open Control Panel, select Ease Of Access, and click Change How Your Mouse Works, as shown in Figure 10.17.

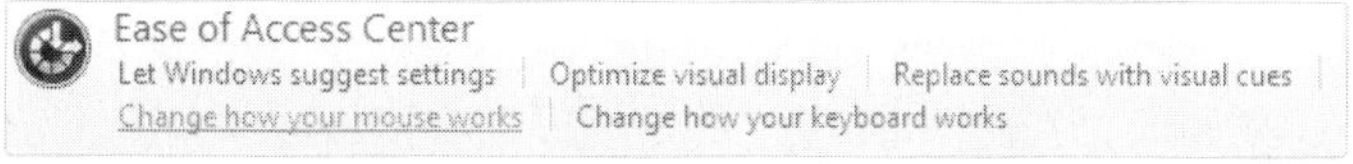

FIGURE 10.17
In Ease Of Access,
click Change How Your
Mouse Works.

Ease of Access Center
Let Windows suggest settings | Optimize visual display | Replace sounds with visual cues
Change how your mouse works | Change how your keyboard works

The Make The Mouse Easier To Use window opens, displaying several options we used to refer to as Accessibility options in previous versions of Windows. The Ease Of Access options include changing the color or size of the mouse pointer, controlling the mouse with the keyboard, managing windows with the mouse, as well as having access to the mouse properties dialog box. You access the mouse properties by choosing Mouse Settings in the See Also section at the bottom of the Make The Mouse Easier To Use window, as shown in Figure 10.18.

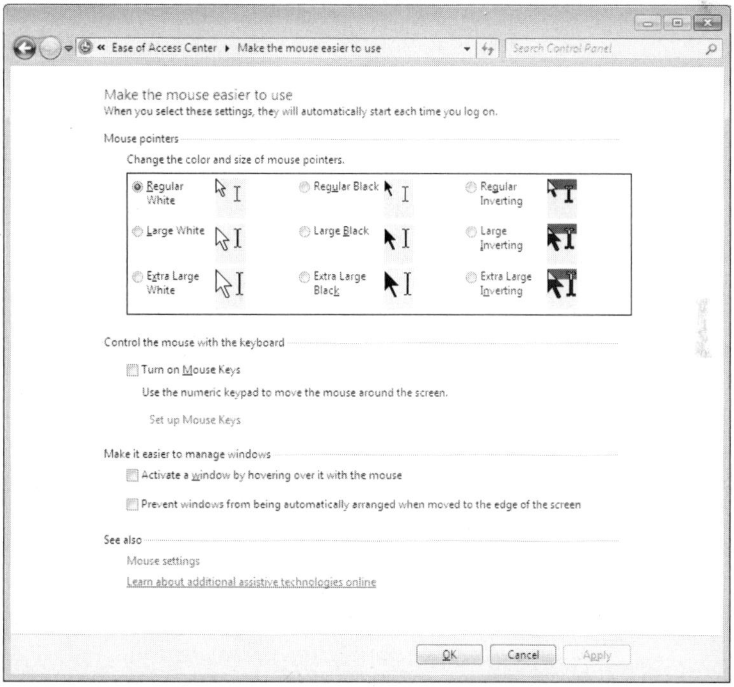

FIGURE 10.18
The Make The Mouse
Easier To Use window

After you select Mouse Settings, the Mouse Properties window opens, where you can configure more of your mouse functionality and display options. The Mouse Properties window provides five tabs of options for you work with. The first tab on the left, as shown in Figure 10.19, is labeled Buttons.

This tab allows you to switch the primary and secondary buttons. These are what we refer to as the left and right mouse buttons; the left is the primary and the right is the secondary. This is the default setup the way a person using the mouse on the right side (physically "right side" in lieu of the "correct side") would normally and intuitively think of the functions. If a user uses their mouse on the left side of the keyboard, it would be more reasonable to have the right and left (primary and secondary) functions reversed. The Buttons tab also allows you to change the double-click speed and set up a function called ClickLock. With ClickLock enabled, a single click acts as a click and hold — like when you want to drag a window, you "click and hold" and then drag, releasing to drop. ClickLock has you click and release on a window, drag it to where you want it, and click a second time to drop it. You can modify the setting for the length of time you hold the initial click before the window is grabbed; that way, a casual click to change cursor position will not attach the window to the mouse pointer.

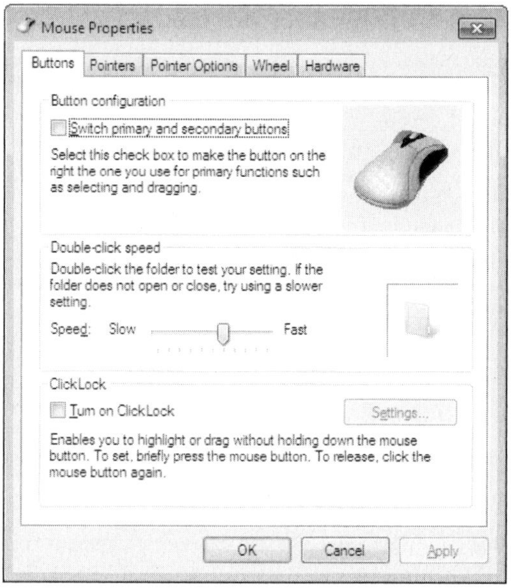

FIGURE 10.19
The Buttons tab of the Mouse Properties window

The Pointers tab of the Mouse Properties window, as shown in Figure 10.20, allows you to change the pointer properties. The pointer is the image we normally just refer to as the mouse.

You might not have considered the importance of the mouse pointer; it gives us feedback to what is going on within the operating system. You can check out the Customize section of the Pointers tab to get an idea of just how many different feedback pointers there are. The pointers available do (or can) change with the user interface (UI) scheme, and you have the option to change them as a whole on the Pointers tab as well.

Figure 10.21 shows the Pointer Options tab of the Mouse Properties window. These options allow you to change the Motion parameters and Visibility options. There's an option to set up Snap To, which will automatically move the mouse to the default button in a dialog box.

Depending on the style of mouse you are using, you might have a scroll wheel. This wheel allows vertical scrolling as well as horizontal scrolling. The Mouse Properties dialog box's Wheel tab allows you to change the Vertical Scrolling and Horizontal Scrolling configuration, as you can see in Figure 10.22.

As a network administrator, you need to provide the best environment for your users to be productive. Sometimes this involves changing a user's I/O environment. There are cases where the user will use their mouse on the left side of their keyboard instead of the right and might need to have the primary and secondary functions reversed. The user may also use a more condensed screen and need the mouse pointers to be a larger size so they can see them better. Because of the type of work being done on the machine, the user would also be better served having the scroll wheel scroll pages (screens) instead of lines for each roll of the wheel.

FIGURE 10.20
The Pointers tab of the Mouse Properties window

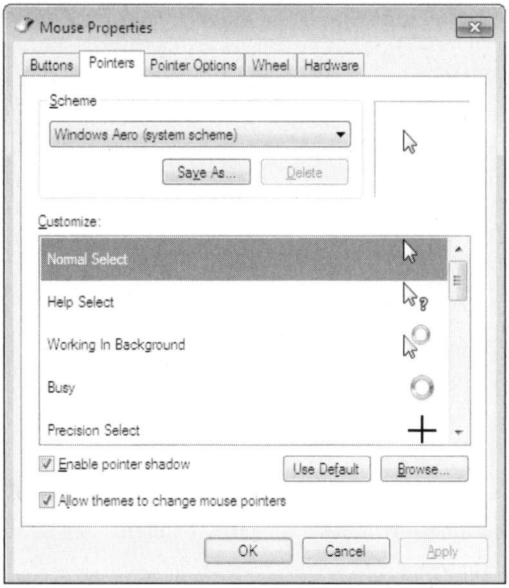

FIGURE 10.21
The Pointer Options tab of the Mouse Properties window

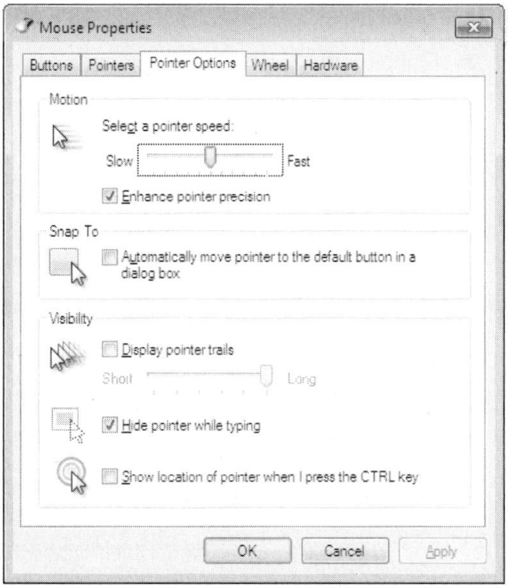

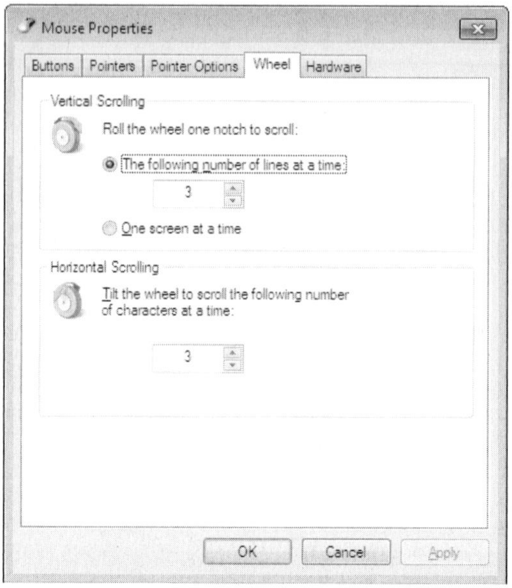

FIGURE 10.22
The Wheel tab of
the Mouse Properties
window

REVERSING THE PRIMARY AND SECONDARY BUTTONS FROM THE DEFAULT

Perform the following steps to change the primary and secondary buttons to a keyboard left-style mouse:

1. Choose Start ➢ Control Panel ➢ Ease Of Access.

2. Click Change How Your Mouse Works.

3. Select Mouse Settings in the See Also section.

4. On the Buttons tab, click the Switch Primary And Secondary Buttons check box.

5. Click OK to close the Mouse Properties window.

6. Click OK to close the Change How Your Mouse Works window.

7. Close the Ease Of Access Center window.

CHANGING THE POINTER TO THE LARGE-SIZED WINDOWS AERO SCHEME

Perform the following steps to change the mouse pointer and Windows Aero scheme:

1. Choose Start ➢ Control Panel ➢ Ease Of Access.

2. Click Change How Your Mouse Works.

3. Click Mouse Settings in the See Also section.

4. On the Pointers tab, open the Scheme drop-down list, as shown in Figure 10.23.

FIGURE 10.23
The Scheme drop-down
list

5. Select the Windows Aero (Large) (System Scheme) option from the Scheme drop-down list.

6. Click OK to close the Mouse Properties window.

7. Click OK to close the Change How Your Mouse Works window.

8. Close the Ease Of Access Center window.

CHANGING THE MOUSE WHEEL FUNCTION TO SCROLL SCREENS RATHER THAN LINES

Follow these steps to change the mouse wheel functionality to scroll screens as opposed to lines:

1. Choose Start ➢ Control Panel ➢ Ease Of Access.

2. Click Change How Your Mouse Works.

3. Click Mouse Settings in the See Also section.

4. On the Wheel tab, select the One Screen At A Time radio button in the Vertical Scrolling section.

5. Click OK to close the Mouse Properties window.

6. Click OK to close the Change How Your Mouse Works window.

7. Close the Ease of Access Center window.

Today we have to deal with removable storage devices being connected to our machines; it's rare to have a user on our Windows machine who doesn't want to save something to a memory stick. Next, you'll learn how to configure removable storage devices.

Configuring Removable Storage Devices

Removable storage devices have been part of our computing world since the beginning. CDs, DVDs, and floppy disks are examples of removable storage. Today, we're using other types of removable storage as well, including flash-based electronics such as USB sticks, memory cards, USB or FireWire external rotating hard drives, cameras, phones, and so on. These devices (or media) are discovered automatically as the devices are connected.

CONNECTING REMOVABLE DEVICES

We'll concentrate on dynamically connected devices in this section utilizing the USB/FireWire connectivity and memory cards. These devices present challenges to the administrative team because end users utilizing the technology might not follow the guidelines (loss as well as security guidelines) for protecting their data.

Windows 7 includes improvements to the Safely Remove Hardware (Eject) menu. For example, it's now possible to eject just one memory card at a time and physically remove it, whereas previously ejecting one card removed all the memory cards from the software interface. You have to physically reinstall any cards you still want to access (from a single hub) and keep the ports available for future use. Removable media is now listed under its own label through Devices And Printers, as shown in Figure 10.24, rather than just its drive letter, as it was in previous versions of Windows. This is also part of the new Device Stage functionality of Windows 7, where the hardware vendors can include configuration information about portable devices and give users more resources from one location.

FIGURE 10.24
Devices And Printers
with USB stick installed

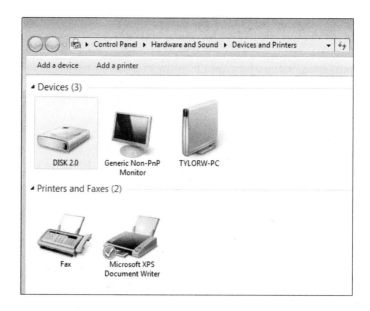

You must consider certain factors related to data access performance with the portable devices as well. To improve data access and make saves faster, it's possible to have the operating system cache the data and write it to the portable device later (when there's free processor time). However, this increases the possibility of a user removing the portable device before the write is made; this would mean a loss of data. Windows 7 defaults to writing the data immediately, which minimizes the chance of data loss and the cost of performance. The configuration for optimizing the portable device for Quick Removal or Better Performance is found on the Policies tab for the hardware in Device Manager.

Depending on how your portable storage device is used, you might want to change the write cache policy for better operating system performance.

MODIFYING THE WRITE CACHE POLICY FOR A PORTABLE STORAGE DEVICE

Perform these steps to change the write cache policy for a USB memory stick attached to a Windows 7 machine:

1. Choose Start ≻ Control Panel ≻ Hardware And Sound ≻ Device Manager (under Devices And Printers) or type **Device Manager** in the Start menu's search box.

2. Click the triangle next to Disk Drives (or double-click Disk Drives) to expand that item.

3. Right-click USB Disk Hardware and select Properties.

4. Choose the Policies tab.

5. Select the Better Performance radio button, as shown in Figure 10.25, and then click OK.

FIGURE 10.25
Click the Better Performance radio button.

REMOVING A PORTABLE HARDWARE DEVICE

In our next example, we've changed the USB portable storage device write cache policy for better performance; this means writes to the portable device may be saved and written at a later time (when the processor has clock cycles available). To ensure no loss of data, it is fairly important to eject the device through Windows 7 before physically removing the device.

Click the icon in the Taskbar to eject the device, as shown in Figure 10.26, which initiates a stop for the hardware, forcing any cached writes in memory to be written to the device.

Stopping the portable hardware device can also be done from the Devices And Printers window by choosing Eject from the context menu of the device. The device will close, meaning the writes have been made, and you are presented with a window saying it's safe to remove the hardware.

FIGURE 10.26
Clicking the Taskbar
icon to eject the device

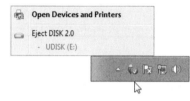

Another device that administrators have to deal with on a regular basis is the corporate printer. Next, we'll explore printer management.

Managing Printers

Printers have long been an issue for IT teams. Every new version of an operating system has new software intelligence to make the installation and maintenance easier, but printer technology continues to grow and hardware vendors continue to make changes. The driver base for all the different printers out there is huge, and even for the same printer, there are numerous variations. Each printer itself might have lots of options that can be made available, and this all has to be controlled by the operating system through the printer drivers.

MICROSOFT DEFINITIONS IN THE PRINTER WORLD

When we use the term *printer*, we're referring to the physical piece of hardware and the functions of that hardware. In the Windows world, we need to distinguish between the functionality of the hardware and of the software (both the driver software and the controlling software). In the Windows world, the physical device that has paper in it is the *print device*, not the printer. The *printer* is the software application on the local machine controlling the print device. The printer driver is the software shim between the operating system and the locally installed software (the printer).

You will find in most organizations that a print device is not attached to every computer. We share the print devices between users. This is cost effective on many levels, but it tends to cause issues. We don't know very many users who do not have a need to print something once in a while, and so we send our documents or web pages to be printed to the print device. The print device might be connected to someone's machine and shared for others to use, or it might be a stand-alone. You might have a server on your network to which one or more print devices are attached and everyone sends their documents to a central location. Each user machine has a printer installed and the appropriate drivers to allow Windows 7 to send the document to the print device through the printer with the appropriate instructions.

Do you think the print device can physically print a document at the same speed the printer can send to the data to it? No, of course not. This is where a software component called the spool (spooler or print spool) comes in. You need a software component that can buffer the print job until the print device can complete it. In fact, there might be more than one user sending documents to be printed to the same print device at the same time — and yes, the spool handles this as well.

 **Real World Scenario**

WHAT, NO SPOOL?

We were working on a networking problem for a local veterinary clinic. They were complaining about issues they were having with their PCs being extremely slow at times but normal other times, and they were sure the network hardware was causing them issues.

We asked about any recent hardware or software changes, and they said they had upgraded a piece of their software package to allow more functionality, which included having a couple of centralized printers for the doctors and technicians to use. It seems as though every time someone printed, the network bogged down to a point of uselessness. Casual discussions ensued, and we determined that the network bog-down only affected the machine (or machines) actively sending a print job. Hmmm! Looking into the problem a little further showed the vendor installation defaulted to printing directly to the print device, with no spooling. Each machine had to wait for the print job to complete before releasing any local resources (yes, that's right — not even background printing), and the other machines on the network ended up waiting as well. Allowing the machines to spool their print jobs solved the problem of slow networking (clearly not a networking issue in the end).

Installing Printers

You install printers to a machine in two distinct ways; one where the print device is physically connected to the machine and one where it is not (it's connected over the network). There has to be software drivers in either case, and these can be located on a CD/DVD, on a network share, or even in the Windows distribution files. Printers in Windows 7 will be located in the Devices And Printers window and will allow the Device Stage configuration to accommodate a full range of functionality from this one location. To add a printer to a machine locally, you'll usually run the setup program on the CD/DVD (following the manufacturer's instructions). The manufacturer's setup program in a wizard format asks the appropriate questions. You can set up the printer through Windows 7 as well by using the Add Printer functionality of Devices And Printers. To add a printer using the Windows 7 functionality, choose Start ➢ Devices And Printers and then choose Add Printer. USB printers will be automatically detected and have their drivers installed (or at least searched for automatically).

Choosing Add Printer launches the Add Printer Wizard and brings up the screen where you make the choice of installing the printer and print device locally or installing the printer locally to access a print device remotely.

From the opening screen, you can follow the next example to install the printer for a physically connected print device to a machine. We're going on the premise that the setup program on the CD/DVD (if one existed) was not run and we're installing the printer from the wizard associated with Windows.

Installing a Printer for a Locally Connected Print Device

Perform the following steps to install a printer to your local machine's parallel port (lpt1):

1. Choose Start ➢ Devices And Printers.

2. Choose Add Printers.

3. Select the Add A Local Printer option.

4. In the Add Printer window, choose the Use An Existing Port radio button and use the drop-down window to select LPT1: (Printer Port); then click Next.

5. Select the manufacturer of your print device and the printer model you want to install in the Install A Printer Driver window, as shown in Figure 10.27.

FIGURE 10.27
The Install The Printer Driver window

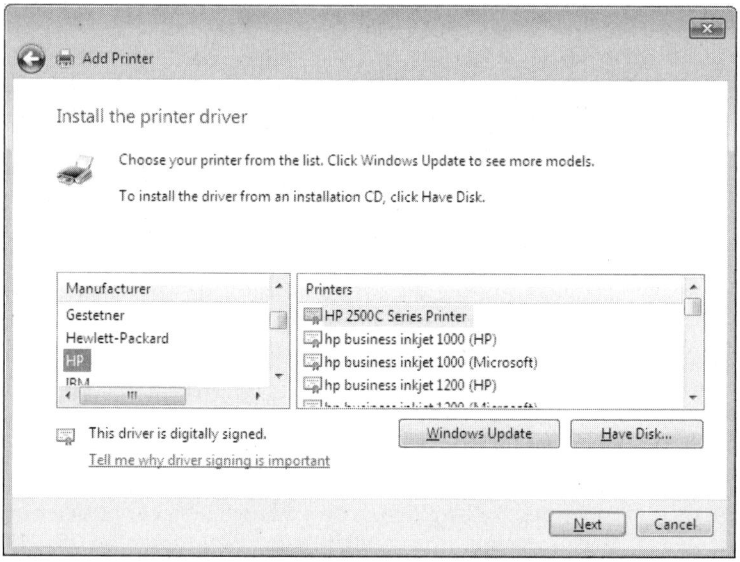

WHAT IF YOUR DEVICE IS NOT AVAILABLE?

If you don't find your model in list, it wasn't included in the distribution files; you can select the Windows Update button to get more choices from Microsoft. If you still don't have your model available and you have the original disk, you can choose Have Disk and browse to the driver files. (OK, if you had the disk, wouldn't you have just run the setup? Ah, you didn't have the disk — you went onto the Internet and downloaded the drivers ...) Use the Have Disk option to browse to the folder with the .inf file for the printer drivers.

6. If there was a driver previously installed, you will be given the option to use the existing driver or replace it.

7. After choosing the appropriate device driver or using the existing driver and clicking Next, you choose the name of the printer. An intuitive name is always a good choice here. Enter the name and click Next.

8. You can make the print device available on the network by sharing it. The next page of the Add Printer Wizard gives you the opportunity to share it. For most of the options

within the wizard, you can change the values or function from the properties pages (if, for example, you change your mind later). After making your choice, click Next.

9. On the final page of the Add Printer Wizard, select the Set As The Default Printer check box (to make this the default printer for any application on the machine) and click Print A Test Page. After the test page prints, click Finish and the wizard completes. The locally connected print device has its printer installed on the local machine.

SAVE THE PRINTER

Do not remove this printer; we'll use it in a later example.

After you complete the Add Printer Wizard (or let the hardware vendor's setup program install your printer), you can open the Devices And Printers window and see the printer(s) available. The context menu gives you access to the properties pages as well as some of the standard printing functions we've had in Windows past. As hardware vendors start implementing functionality for Windows 7, you'll have a full array of access to software components from the Devices And Printers window, at least for the vendors who are going to participate in the Device Stage specification.

What about installing a printer on a machine that needs to access a print device connected to another machine? That's fine — that is the functionality we want. You launch the Add Printer Wizard and go through the process of installing the printer, but point to a share or stand-alone network printer. Knowing that not all machines on any company's network are going to have print devices physically attached, there is functionality to allow sharing of networked devices and printers (software) to be installed on client machines.

Installing a Printer to Connect to a Shared Network Print Device

Perform the following steps to install printer client software (and drivers) for a network printer:

1. Choose Start ➤ Devices And Printers.

2. Click Add Printers.

3. Click Add A Network, Wireless Or Bluetooth Printer.

4. The Add Printers Wizard searches the locally available network for print devices that are available.

5. Select the networked print device from the Select A Printer section. If the device is not listed, you can choose The Printer That I Want Is Not Listed and enter the parameters for the networked print device.

6. The print device is detected, the driver is discovered and installed, and you are able to use the printer. Open Devices And Printers and you'll see this print device is available.

Once the printer is installed for a print device physically connected on the local machine (or if it's a network-connected printer), you can view the configuration parameters and modify them if necessary from the properties dialog box. Access the properties dialog box from Devices And Printers. Right-click the printer, as shown in Figure 10.28, and select Properties for the hardware properties and Printer Properties for the software components.

FIGURE 10.28
Printer context menu from Devices And Printers

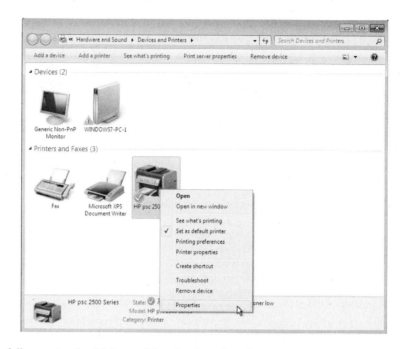

Printer properties follow a standard Microsoft has in place, but the content is up to the manufacturer. Some vendors supply more information than others. Most printers provide a basic set of tabs, as follows:

General Tab   The printer name, location, and comment are displayed here. The model is typically shown as well as the features of the specific print device and available paper. The Printer Preferences page is available by clicking the Preferences button, and you can print a test page by clicking the Print Test Page button.

Sharing Tab   The Sharing tab allows you to share a printer if it wasn't shared during its installation, or to stop sharing it if it were previously shared. You can also add drivers for other flavors of operating systems so the printer installed locally and shared can supply drivers for other machines attempting to connect and use the locally connected printer.

Ports Tab   You can view available ports and print devices connected to them on the Ports tab. You can add a port, delete a port, and configure ports on this tab as well. You can also configure bidirectional support for print devices supporting this functionality (sending codes back from the print device to the printer for control) on the Ports tab. Printer pooling is also available here; printer pooling is the ability of the IT staff to configure multiple print devices (using identical drivers) to appear as one printer to connected users. The print jobs are printed on one of the devices in the pool (the first available prints the job). If a print device fails, the others keep working, which makes life better for the users.

Security Tab   Group or user access permissions are controlled on the Security tab. You can specify advanced permissions here as well.

Advanced Tab   The Advanced tab provides various configuration parameters to control the printer and print device functions. The time period a printer is available is a configuration parameter on the Advanced tab. You can install drivers for the print device as well as add a new driver (by launching an Add Printer Driver Wizard). Spool options include whether or not to spool, and whether to start printing immediately upon job submission or start printing after the last page is spooled.

The following buttons are available on the Advanced tab:

Printing Defaults Button   Launches the Printer Properties window for the vendor as it applies to the documents.

Print Processor Button   Lets you choose whether to use the vendor-supplied print processor or the built-in Windows print processor and to choose the default data type to be sent to the print device.

Separator Page Button   Allows a specific page to be inserted between print jobs, making the separation of different documents easier.

Device Settings   Specific parameters for each print device are set up on the Device Settings tab. Items like form to tray assignment, font substitution, or other installable options for the print device are configurable here.

After the configuration is complete and the printer and print device are working in harmony, life is good. You can see the status of the document currently being printed as well as documents waiting to be printed (the print queue).The queue was previously viewed by selecting the Queue option from the context menu for the printer; Windows 7 now calls it See What's Printing, as shown in Figure 10.29.

FIGURE 10.29
See What's Printing

Selecting See What's Printing opens the window that shows you what's going on with your printer (as far as document/job control).

To take a look at the better functionality of Device Stage, you can select the context menu from Devices And Printers. To observe a graphical view of Device Stage, double-click the printer in Devices And Printers and get a consolidated view and the popular (as decided by the vendor) menu choices. Figure 10.30 shows a popular printer and its options when you double-click Devices And Printers.

We've installed printers in previous examples for both a locally connected and a network connected printer. Let's take a look at sending a print job to the locally connected printer from a previous example and view the document properties.

FIGURE 10.30
Printer window from
Devices And Printers

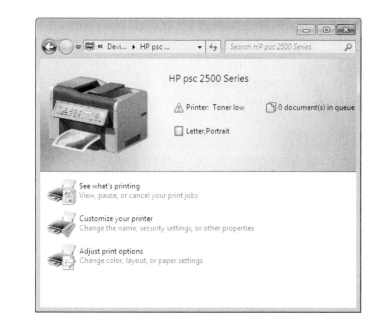

First, you might not actually have the print device available and the printer won't be able to send the job anywhere. We'll go to the Printer window and pause printing so the job will simply stay in the queue and not attempt to be sent to the print device. We'll use the Device Stage interface to perform our tasks.

Pausing Printing for the Locally Connected Printer

Follow these steps to pause printing for a locally connected printer:

1. Choose Start ➢ Devices And Printers.

2. Double-click the printer previously installed as the locally connected printer. You will have a window similar to Figure 10.30. If you haven't installed the printer yet, you can return and complete the previous steps in the section "Installing a Printer for a Locally Connected Print Device."

3. To pause printing, open the Printer window; double-click the See What's Printing area in the body of the window or single-click the Printer item in the top of the window.

4. Choose Printer ➢ Pause Printing.

5. View the status bar of the printer to verify the printer is paused; there will also be a check mark next to Pause Printing in the menu.

Sending a Test Document to the Paused Locally Connected Printer

Perform the following steps to send a document to a locally connected printer:

1. In the Printer window, select Printer ➢ Properties.

2. On the General tab of the Properties dialog box, click the Print Test Page button.

3. An information box appears stating a test page was sent to the printer; click the Close button.

4. Click OK in the printer's Properties window.

5. The Printer window displays the print job in the queue.

Viewing Document Properties from a Job in the Print Queue

Follow these steps to view a document's properties from the print queue:

1. In the Printer window, click the specific document you want to view.

2. Choose Document ➢ Properties to view the document properties; you can also right-click the print job and select Properties from the context menu. The General tab shows you the document properties; the other tabs are vendor supplied to control additional printer functionality for the document.

3. Click OK or Cancel to close the Properties window. OK saves any changes made and closes the window; Cancel closes the window without saving any changes. If you have made any configuration changes, the Apply button becomes available; selecting Apply saves any changes that you made but it does not close the window.

There might be times when managing a printer that you will need to delete a document from the print queue. Let's take a look.

Deleting a Document from the Queue

Perform the following steps to delete a document from the printer:

1. In the Printer window, click the specific job you want to delete from the queue.

2. Choose Document ➢ Cancel from the Printer window menu structure to delete the document. You can also right-click the document and select Cancel to delete the print job. Either method prompts a confirmation message box that asks Are You Sure You Want To Cancel The Document? Click Yes. The document will no longer appear in the queue in the Printer window.

3. Choose Printer ➢ Close to close the Printer window.

There might also be times when you want to delete a printer, either locally connected or a network printer, from your Windows 7 machine. This might be due to a replacement of an older print device, or perhaps you're moving a user to a new print device and the old one is no longer needed.

Removing a Printer from Windows 7

Follow these steps to remove a printer (to remove the software configuration in the operating system) from Windows 7:

1. Choose Start ➢ Devices And Printers.

2. Right-click the printer you want to remove and select Remove Device from the context menu; alternatively, choose Remove Device from the Devices And Printers menu to unpair the printer from the machine.

3. Click Yes when you see the prompt Are You Sure You Want To Remove This Device? You are presented with a status box during the removal process, and then the device is no longer available in Devices And Printers.

The Bottom Line

Use Device Manager.   Device Manager is the primary management tool for installing, configuring, troubleshooting, and updating hardware devices and their associated driver components.

> **Master It**   You recently updated a piece of hardware on one of your servers; you have added a video capture card that will be tied in to the security system in the server room. You did all the necessary due diligence before installing the hardware and verifying prerequisites successfully. The card seems to have installed correctly from the manufacturer's setup program. Now that you're trying to use the connected camera to capture video, you cannot get it to work correctly. You need to verify that Windows 7 sees the device and believes the status is good. How will you do it?

Manage and update device drivers.   Device Manager shows you the driver status as seen by Windows 7 for the hardware installed in your machine. If there is a problem, you should be able to see that a problem exists.

> **Master It**   After installing a video capture card into one of your servers, you find that it is misbehaving. You see in Device Manager that the device driver is not communicating with the device. Researching the manufacturer's website, you find they have identified a bug in the driver code and offer an updated device driver. How will you install the new device driver on your server?

Install, uninstall, and disable hardware.   Device Manager in Windows 7 gives you the ability to install, uninstall, and disable hardware installed in your machines. Troubleshooting hardware issues many times requires actions to be performed from Device Manager.

> **Master It**   You have recently changed a piece of hardware you had installed to a device with more functionality from a different vendor. You physically disconnected the old device and installed the new device. You are using a server health program that monitors your servers, including the one with the new hardware. Your health program is now showing the old hardware as failed (although it does not even exist in the machine now). You must uninstall the old device's software components so Windows will not try to report its status.

Manage I/O and removable storage devices.   Device Manager is the central application for controlling hardware installed in your machines, which includes I/O devices such as your keyboard and mouse. Ease Of Access features allow you to control keyboard and mouse behavior.

> **Master It**   Managing I/O devices for users is not normally a concern, but you are now opening an office and have inexperienced users who are having problems following the mouse they are learning to use. You need to turn on the option to have mouse trailers available and would also like the users to be able to find the mouse on the screen easily. How will you do it?

Install and configure printers.   Printers and print devices can be one of the most problematic areas for IT staff to handle. Every user will need to have at least one printer installed on their machine. Although many times this is an automated process, it is possible to manually install the software printer on the end user's machine.

Master It   You are completing the installation of several new machines in a remote office. The last Windows 7 machine you are setting up has a specific requirement to connect to a network printer in the main office, which is not part of your automated installation. How do you install the network printer in the local machine?

Chapter 11

Configuring Network Connectivity

To successfully establish network connectivity, you must have a properly installed and configured network interface card (NIC) and network protocol. The first step is to physically install and configure the network adapter that you will use and verify that Windows 7 recognizes the hardware. The installation of the hardware might go smoothly, but you need to be able to troubleshoot any issues that arise. Today, a big part of most networks is wireless connectivity that presents a whole new and interesting set of challenges. Not only does wireless connectivity present challenges in physical connectivity, but it requires a more thorough understanding of the physical connectivity to ensure a secure network.

The second step is to install, configure, and test the network protocol you have installed. In most home networks, network protocol connectivity seems automatic, but as an administrator, you need to understand the protocols like TCP/IPv4 as well as TCP/IPv6.

From here, you need to connect to other resources you have on your network, including shared resources on other machines, whether it's servers or other users' machines. You might also need to connect to printers, cameras, or other data-supplying devices needed for you or your users' productivity or pleasure. Setting up peer-to-peer networking is a big part of connecting to other devices as most users will want to be able to browse to the resources.

In this chapter, you'll learn how to:

- ◆ Set up hardware to provide network connectivity

- ◆ Connect to network devices

- ◆ Set up peer-to-peer networking

- ◆ Configure network protocols

Connecting Network Devices

NICs are hardware components used to connect computers or other devices to the network. NICs are responsible for providing the physical connection that recognizes the physical address of the device where they are installed.

PHYSICAL ADDRESSES VS. LOGICAL ADDRESSES

The Open System Interconnect (OSI) model defines the encapsulation technique that builds the basic data structure for data transport across an internetwork. The OSI model provides interoperability between hardware vendors, network protocols, and applications. The physical address is the OSI address, or for Ethernet technologies, the Media Access Control address (MAC address). This is not the IP address, which is the OSI Layer 3 or Network Layer address, also generically defined as the Logical Address. We'll discuss logical addressing later in this chapter in the section, "Basics of IP Addressing and Configuration."

The most common place you see network adapters installed are computers, but you also see NICs installed in network printers and specialized devices like intrusion detection systems (IDSs) and firewalls. We generically refer to the interface between our network devices and the software components of the machines as network adapters. Network adapters do not need to be separate cards; they can be built in as in the case of most PCs today or other network-ready devices such as network cameras or network media players. These adapters (and all other hardware devices) need a driver to communicate with the Windows 7 operating system.

Installing a Network Adapter

Before you physically install a NIC or network adapter, it's important to read the vendor's instructions that come with the hardware. Most network adapters you get today should be self-configuring using Plug and Play capabilities. After you install a network adapter that supports Plug and Play, it should work following the installation procedure (which should be automated if the vendor says it is). You might have to restart, but our operating systems are getting much better with this, and you might just get lucky and be all right immediately.

If you happen to have a network adapter that is not Plug and Play, the operating system should detect the new piece of hardware and start a wizard that leads you through the process of loading the adapter's driver and sets initial configuration parameters. You can see your network connection and manage the network connection properties through the Network And Sharing Center. We'll explore this applet in the "Connecting Wireless Devices" section later in this chapter.

Configuring a Network Adapter

After you have installed the network adapter, you configure it through its Properties dialog box. There are several ways to access the properties: by using the Network And Sharing Center, through the Computer Management MMC, or via Device Manager. We'll look at the Network And Sharing Center later in the section, "Viewing the Network And Sharing Center." Let's use the Device Manager applet for the network adapter configuration here. To access the Properties dialog box, choose Start and type **Device Manager** in the Start menu's search box to launch Device Manager. Alternatively, you can right-click Computer on the Start menu and choose Manage from the context menu to access Computer Management, which lets you access Device Manager, as shown in Figure 11.1.

Figure 11.1 shows the Network Adapters item expanded. Having Computer Management open is a great way to open Device Manager; this MMC has numerous other installed plug-ins available that might be helpful as you work with your machines.

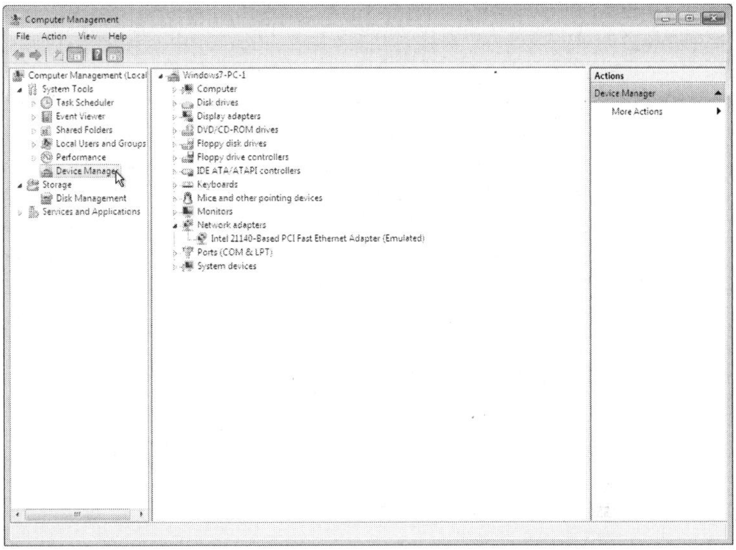

FIGURE 11.1
Accessing Device
Manager from the
Computer Management
MMC

NETWORK ADAPTER PROPERTIES

Accessing the network adapter properties allows you to view and change configuration parameters of the adapter. You do this by right-clicking the adapter in Device Manager and selecting Properties from the context menu. Figure 11.2 shows the Properties dialog box and the tabs available for a network adapter. The available tabs depend on the hardware manufacturer:

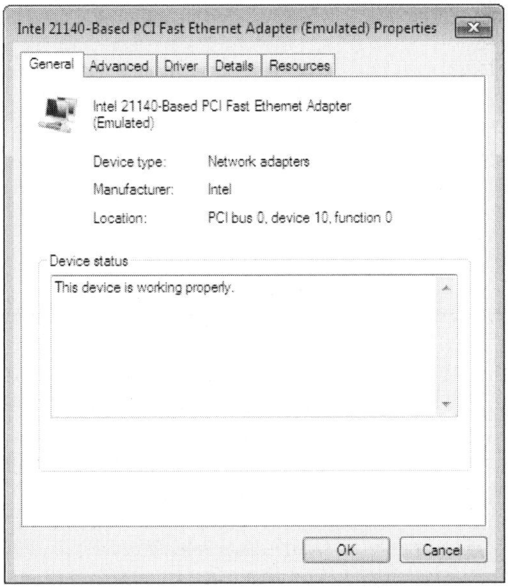

FIGURE 11.2
Network adapter
Properties dialog box

The General Tab The General tab of the network adapter Properties dialog box (the tab open in Figure 11.2) shows the name of the adapter, the device type, the manufacturer, and the location. The Device Status box reports whether or not the device is working properly. If a device is not working, the Device Status box gives you an error code and a brief description of what Windows 7 identifies as the issue. You can perform an Internet search for the error code(s) if the text is not sufficient.

The Advanced Tab The contents of the Advanced tab of a network adapter's Properties dialog box vary depending on the network adapter and driver that you are using. Figure 11.3 shows an example of the Advanced tab for a Fast Ethernet adapter. To configure options in this dialog box, choose the property you want to modify in the Property list box and specify the desired value for the property in the Value box on the right. We have selected the Connection Type property and opened the Value drop-down list to show you the options for this network adapter.

FIGURE 11.3
The Advanced tab of
a network adapter's
Properties dialog box

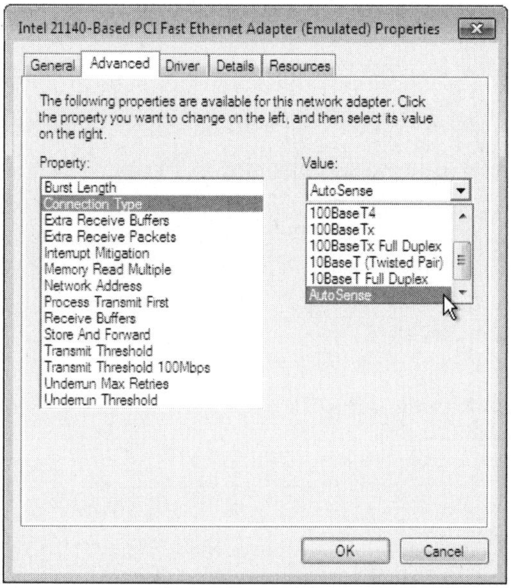

The Driver Tab The Driver tab of the network adapter's Properties dialog box provides the following information about your driver:

◆ The driver provider

◆ The date the driver was released

◆ The driver version (useful in determining whether you have the latest driver installed)

◆ The digital signer (the company that provides the digital signature for driver signing)

The Driver tab for our adapter is shown in Figure 11.4. The information here varies from driver to driver and even from vendor to vendor.

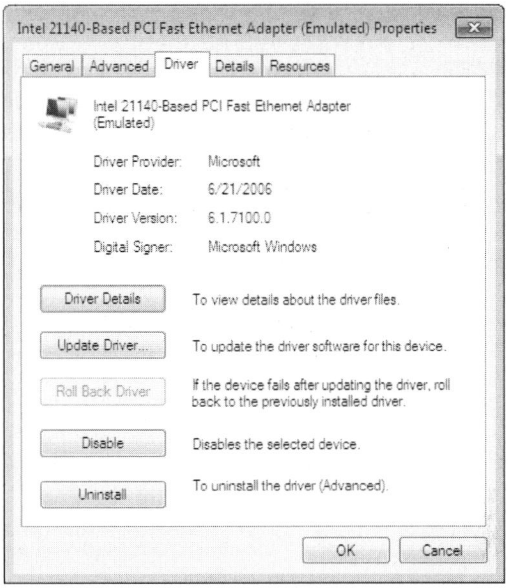

FIGURE 11.4
The Driver tab of a
network adapter's
Properties dialog box

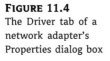

Intel 21140-Based PCI Fast Ethernet Adapter (Emulated) Properties

| General | Advanced | Driver | Details | Resources |

Intel 21140-Based PCI Fast Ethernet Adapter
(Emulated)

Driver Provider:	Microsoft
Driver Date:	6/21/2006
Driver Version:	6.1.7100.0
Digital Signer:	Microsoft Windows

Driver Details — To view details about the driver files.

Update Driver... — To update the driver software for this device.

Roll Back Driver — If the device fails after updating the driver, roll
back to the previously installed driver.

Disable — Disables the selected device.

Uninstall — To uninstall the driver (Advanced).

OK | Cancel

Clicking the Driver Details button on the Driver tab opens the Driver File Details dialog box, which provides the following details about the driver:

◆ The location of the driver file (useful for troubleshooting)

◆ The original provider of the driver

◆ The file version (useful for troubleshooting)

◆ Copyright information about the driver

◆ The digital signer for the driver

The Update Driver button starts a wizard to step you through upgrading the driver for an existing device.

The Roll Back Driver button allows you to roll back to the previously installed driver if you update your network driver and encounter problems. In Figure 11.4, the Roll Back Driver button is unavailable because we have not updated the driver or a previous driver is not available.

The Disable button is used to disable the device. After you disable the device, the Disable button changes into an Enable button, which you can use to enable the device.

The Uninstall button removes the driver from your computer's configuration. You would uninstall the driver if you were going to remove the device from your system or if you wanted to completely remove the driver configuration from your system so that you could reinstall it from scratch either automatically or manually.

The Details Tab The Details tab of the network adapter's Properties dialog box lists the resource settings for your network adapter. Information found on the Details tab varies by hardware device. Figure 11.5 shows the Details tab for our adapter in Figure 11.5 with the Property drop-down list open to show the options.

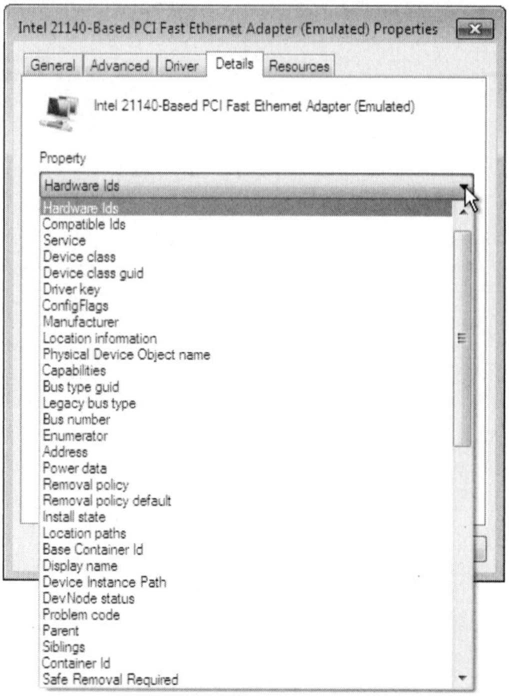

FIGURE 11.5
The Details tab of
a network adapter's
Properties dialog box

FIGURE 11.5
The Details tab of
a network adapter's
Properties dialog box

The Resources Tab   The Resources tab of a network adapter's Properties dialog box lists the resource settings for your network adapter. Resources include interrupt request (IRQ), memory, and input/output (I/O) resources. This information can be important for troubleshooting if other devices are trying to use the same resource settings. This is not normally the case as Windows 7 and the Plug and Play specification should set up nonconflicting parameters. If there are issues, the Conflicting Device list box at the bottom of the Resources tab shows the conflicts.

NAVIGATING TO THE ADVANCED TAB AND ASSIGNING A CONNECTION TYPE

There might be times when you, as a network administrator, need to manually assign a connection type for one of your servers' NICs. For example, suppose the hardware switch to which you are connecting does not seem to negotiate with the NIC in your server and you want to set up the best connection. When you view the NIC parameters, it seems to be set up for half duplex and you know the switch is set to full duplex.

Perform the following steps to navigate to the Advanced tab and assign the connection type to 100 Mbps and Full Duplex for the most efficient connection for your server and switch connection:

1. Click Start and type **Device Manager** in the Start menu's search box.

2. Double-click Network Adapters in Device Manager to expand the Network Adapters item.

3. Right-click your NIC in the Network Adapters list and select Properties from the context menu.

4. Click the Advanced tab of your NIC's Properties dialog box.

5. Choose Connection Type in the Property list box.

6. Click the drop-down list box and select the choice that allows you to have Full Duplex at 100 Mbps. This item will probably be set at Auto Sense by default, which is not working in this scenario.

7. Click OK to save your changes and close your NIC's Properties dialog box.

8. Close Device Manager.

Troubleshooting a Network Adapter

If your network adapter is not working, the problem might be with the hardware, the driver software, or the network protocols. We discuss the Layer 3 (network protocol) issues later in this chapter in the section, "Basics of IP Addressing and Configuration." The following list gives some common causes for network adapter problems related to Layer 1 and Layer 2:

Network Adapter Not on the HCL   If the device is not on the Hardware Compatibility List (HCL), use Internet resources to see if others have discovered a solution or contact the hardware vendor for advice.

Outdated Driver   Make sure that you have the most current driver for your adapter. You can check for an updated driver by selecting the Driver tab of the adapter's Properties dialog box and clicking the Update Driver button. Windows 7 searches for a better driver or checks for the latest driver on the hardware vendor's website.

Network Adapter Not Recognized by Windows 7   Check Device Manager to see if Windows 7 recognizes the adapter. If you don't see your adapter, you can try to manually install it.

Improperly Configured Network Card   Verify that the settings for the network card are correct for the parameters known within your network and the hardware device the machine is connected to.

Cabling Problem   Make sure that all network cables are functioning and are the correct type. This includes making sure the connector is properly seated, the cable is straight or crossed (depending on where it's plugged into), and the cable is not broken. You can do this by looking at the little green light (LGL) for the link and activity on the NIC. This does not guarantee a good connection even if the LGLs are illuminated. A single conductor failure in a cable can still have a link light on but that doesn't mean data is passing.

Bad Network Connection Device   Verify that all network connectivity hardware is properly working. For example, on a Fast Ethernet network, make sure the switch and port being used are functioning properly.

⊕ Real World Scenario

CABLING ISSUES CAN BE A PAIN TO DISCOVER

Today, cabling issues should not be nearly as hard to deal with as they were in the past. We have so much autosensing now in our hardware that just about any cable should work. We have been in many situations where we were using the latest hardware but still ran into issues.

Autosensing covers the speed the hardware communicates with, whether it's 10 Mbps, 100 Mbps, or in the Gigabit range. Some IT departments choose to hard-code or define the speed at which communication occurs. If both sides are not set to the same value, problems will exist. We have seen several instances where autospeed settings have the devices swapping between transfer speeds intermittently, thus causing random failures and periodic problems on the network. We have set the speed parameters manually and have found this to be the solution (and actually the troubleshooting step that identified the issue).

When we use autosensing, the hardware negotiates half or full duplex, which is either only transmitting data or receiving data (half duplex) or allowing the hardware to transmit and receive at the same time (full duplex). The original Ethernet specification was based on a contention-based system using a single coaxial cable for data distribution, where all devices connected shared the same distribution wire; only one device could talk at a time. Every device had to listen for data to know if two devices tried to communicate at the same time. When two devices did attempt to transmit data at the same time, a collision occurred and all data had to stop; all devices had to regroup and attempt to communicate again following the one-at-a-time method. With the implementation of twisted-pair wiring and the use of switches, we have hardware (the switch) that controls which devices hear what and can effectively eliminate the potential for collisions. If there are no collisions, there is no need to listen to the media to see if someone else is talking, so talking and listening (transmitting and receiving) at the same time is all right (full duplex). Both devices at the end of the cable must be set up to allow transmitting and receiving at the same time, or intermittent problems will exist. We have run into this many times as well; a switch port was set up as full duplex and the autosensing NIC of our server decided half duplex was the choice. We started seeing collisions increasing within the switch!

One of the more bothersome issues we had to address was the use of either straight-through or cross-over cabling. Autosensing now uses auto MDI/MDX to determine straight (I) or crossed (X), the port type, and lets us always use a straight-through cable. Before, you could go with the old LGL trick for link status and just change the cable if the LED didn't come on. Now, the autosensing takes care of it, but we still seem to have issues with some devices and need to disable auto MDI/MDX and use the correct cable.

Let autosensing be your friend, but don't assume everything is going to just work because all your hardware is new. We find cabling still accounts for a large percentage of our issues, even when just changing a network adapter. Moving a cable in and out of a jack might be just enough to fracture a conductor and cause grief. Start with Layer 1 and verify physical connections before going crazy with the software components.

Connecting to a Network Projector

Windows 7 includes network projector support. We use a projector to display presentations, and it's normally connected with a video cable. Today many projectors come with a network interface, wireless or wired, to provide a convenient way to get video output to the projector. If the projector is configured properly for the network, you can use Windows 7 to provide the video to it as a networked display. The projector functionality is designed to use the Remote

Desktop Protocol (RDP) to send the video stream of a machine to a remote device via the network.

Select Start and then type **Network Projector** into the Start menu's search box (you can also choose Start ➤ All Programs ➤ Accessories ➤ Connect To A Network Projector) to initiate the connection process. The Connect To A Network Projector Wizard launches, as shown in Figure 11.6.

FIGURE 11.6

The Connect To A
Network Projector
Wizard

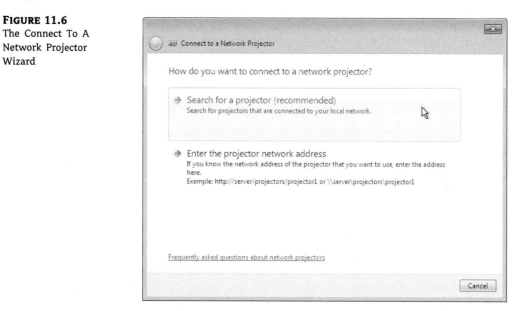

Click Search For A Projector to locate a projector connected to your wired or wireless network. If no projectors are found, you can go back and enter the name or IP address of a projector. If you know the name or IP address, you can simply choose Enter The Projector Address during the initial wizard screens. You might also need the password of the projector if a password has been configured, as shown in Figure 11.7.

Connecting to a Network Printer

Adding a network printer to Windows 7 is even easier than it was in Vista (which was much easier than previous versions). There is new functionality in Windows 7 for devices and printers known as Device Stage (discussed in Chapter 10). To add a network printer, select Start ➤ Devices And Printers. When the Devices And Printers applet launches, choose the Add A Printer menu item.

Next, select Add A Network, Wireless Or Bluetooth Printer. Windows 7 searches for available printers and allows you to install them. If your printer isn't found, you can select The Printer That I Want Isn't Listed and browse for a printer, or you can select a printer by name or IP address. Chapter 10 has more details and examples about printers.

We have been using wired connections since the beginning of networking. Today, we are transitioning to a wireless network infrastructure, and Windows 7 is well versed to integrate into the wireless world.

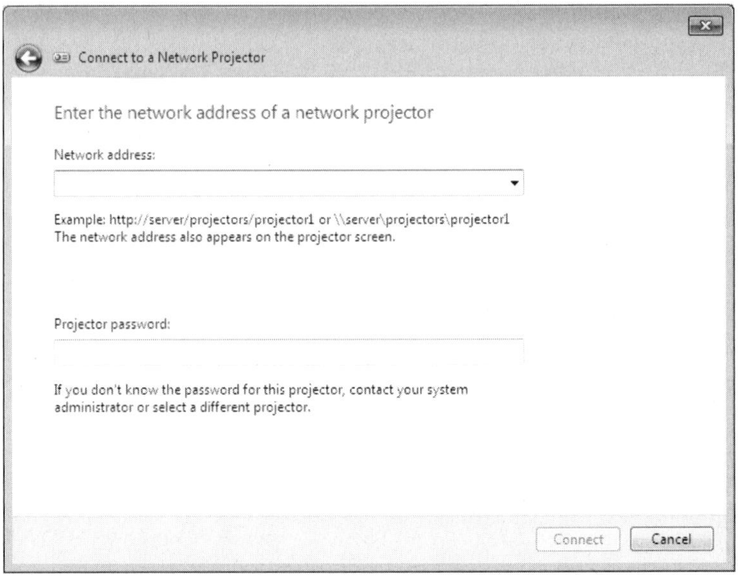

FIGURE 11.7
You might have to enter
a projector password.

Connecting Wireless Devices

Wireless technology has matured to the point of becoming cost-effective and secure. The use of wireless network adapters is increasingly popular, scaling well out of the home and into the workplace. Windows 7 supports wireless autoconfiguration, which makes wireless network connections easy to use. Windows 7 will automatically discover the wireless networks available and connect your machine to the preferred network. Although this connection is convenient, you must still take certain considerations into account, such as security.

Configuring Wireless Network Settings

If you have a wireless network adapter compatible with Windows 7, it will be automatically recognized by the operating system. This can be a built-in adapter (which most modern laptops come with), a wireless card you install in the machine, or even a wireless USB adapter. After it is installed, it is recognized and shown in Device Manager as well as the Network And Sharing Center in the View Your Active Networks section. We used Device Manager in the previous section for the network adapter configuration, so let's use the Network And Sharing Center for the wireless network configuration. Figure 11.8 shows the Network And Sharing Center with two active networks: the wireless network connection and the wired local area connection.

VIEWING THE NETWORK AND SHARING CENTER

Perform the following step to access the Network and Sharing Center:

♦ Choose Start and type **Network and Sharing Center** into the Start menu's search box.

or

♦ Choose Start ➤ Control Panel ➤ Network And Internet ➤ Network And Sharing Center.

or

♦ Choose Start, and then right-click Network and select Properties from the context menu.

FIGURE 11.8
Network And Sharing
Center

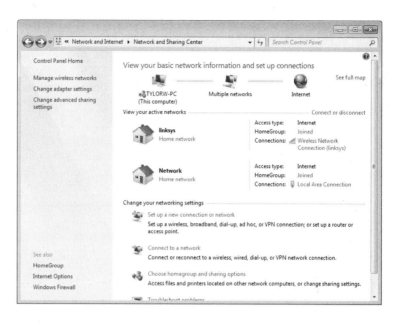

THE NETWORK OPTION IN THE START MENU

The caveat to this choice is the Network option on the Start menu is not available by default in Windows 7 (the same as in previous Windows versions) and must be added as a customized option to your Start menu using its properties dialog box. You can see all three windows open showing the Network option selected in the following graphic:

VIEWING THE WIRELESS NETWORK CONNECTION STATUS

From the Network And Sharing Center you have easy access to the Wireless Network Connection Status window. This window gives you an initial look at the status by providing the Layer 3 connectivity status (IPv4 and IPv6), media state, Service Set Identifier (SSID) being used, how long the connection has been active (Duration), the negotiated speed of the connection, and the signal quality. The Wireless Network Connection Status window is shown in Figure 11.9.

FIGURE 11.9

The Wireless Network Connection Status window

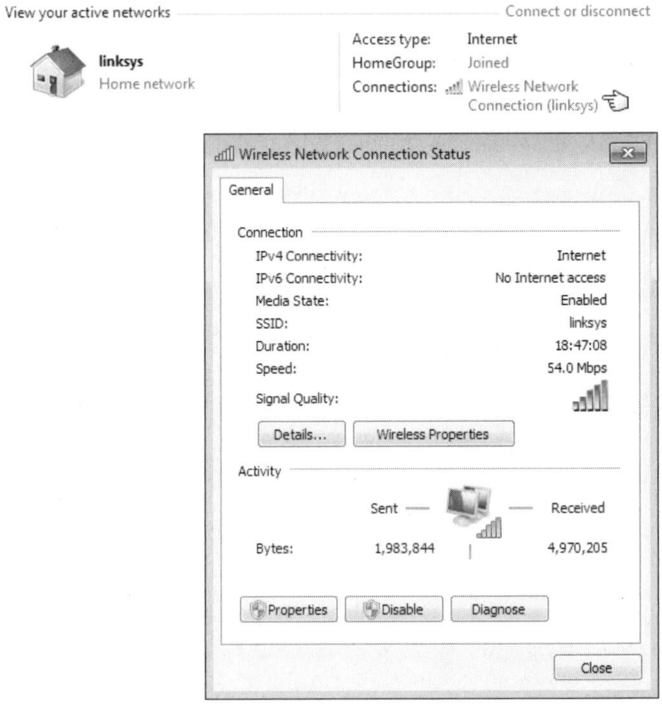

The Details button in the Wireless Network Connection Status window provides detailed information, including the physical address (Layer 2), logical address (Layer 3), dynamic addressing parameters (DHCP), name resolution items, and more. After you verify physical layer parameters, this area of properties and status is a great place to verify and troubleshoot logical (driver and software) issues.

VIEWING WIRELESS NETWORK CONNECTION DETAILS

If you have a wireless adapter in your machine, perform the following steps to view the network connection details for your wireless network connection:

1. Choose Start and type **Network and Sharing Center** into the Start menu's search box; press Enter.

2. Select the Wireless Network Connection option in the View Your Active Networks section.

3. Click the Details button.

4. Review the network connection details for this connection.

The Wireless Network Connection Status window has an Activity section showing real-time traffic (in bytes) being sent from and received by the wireless network. In this window, you also have access to the wireless network connection properties, which includes access to the wireless adapter configuration pages. You access the Properties dialog box by clicking the Properties button in the Activity section (not the Wireless Properties button in the Connection section; you can identify these buttons, as shown previously in Figure 11.9). The Wireless Network Connection Properties window is shown in Figure 11.10.

FIGURE 11.10
Wireless Network
Connection Properties
window

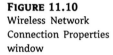

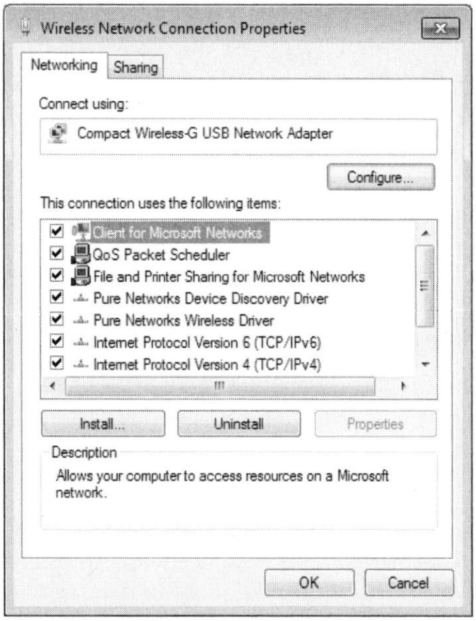

The Wireless Network Connection Properties window has a Networking tab that shows which network adapter is being used for this connection (which you can change if you have more than one available). There is also a tab to allow you to configure Internet Connection Sharing (ICS), which allows other users on your network to access resources through this machine's connection. The This Connection Uses The Following Items section displays the various client, service, and protocols that are currently available for this connection. You can install or uninstall network clients, network services, and network protocols by choosing the appropriate button. You can also view the client, service, or protocol properties if they are available by clicking the Properties button for the selected item (if the Properties button is gray, a properties window is not available for the item). From the Wireless Network Connection Properties window, you have access to the network adapters' hardware configuration properties pages. These would be the same pages you have access to from Device Manager.

ACCESSING THE WIRELESS NETWORK ADAPTER PROPERTIES PAGE FROM THE NETWORK AND SHARING CENTER

Perform the following steps to access the network adapter properties from the Wireless Network Connection Properties window:

1. Choose Start and type **Network and Sharing Center** into the Start menu's search box; press Enter.

2. Select Wireless Network Connection in the View Your Active Networks section.

3. Click the Properties button in the Activity section.

4. Click the Configure button.

5. View the various tabs regarding the network adapter properties.

6. Choose Cancel to return to the Wireless Network Connection Status window.

Configuring Wireless Network Security

Wireless network security is a very large part of setting up our wireless networks. The focal point for this is the wireless access point or wireless router to which we connect.

WIRELESS CONNECTION: INFRASTRUCTURE OR AD HOC?

You might not always be connecting to an access point or router; these connections are considered infrastructure mode connections. Infrastructure mode connections are similar to our wired connection of a PC to a switch. You might connect in an ad hoc fashion that could be a computer-to-computer connection to share information with other wireless network devices without another wireless device acting as an intermediary. Ad hoc connections exist in our wired environment as well where we would connect two PCs' NICs together using an Ethernet crossover cable. Securing data transfer in an ad hoc setup is equally important as it is in infrastructure mode where the data is still traversing between devices using radio frequency (RF). Network sniffers today running the wireless adapter promiscuously (in monitor mode) have no problem viewing the RF data stream. If the data stream is not encrypted, the sniffers will have access to it.

Whether you are using a small wireless network or large wireless infrastructure, you should have a plan for ensuring secure communications and configuring wireless network security. There are several basic parameters you can configure on your network access devices that you should increase the security of your wireless network:

◆ Disable broadcast of the SSID, which is the name of the wireless network. When SSID broadcast is disabled, the wireless network cannot be detected automatically until you manually configure your wireless network card to connect to that SSID.

◆ Create a Media Access Control (MAC) address filter list so only specifically allowed wireless devices are allowed to connect to the wireless network, or require users attempting to connect to supply connection credentials.

◆ Enable encryption such as Wi-Fi Protected Access (WPA) or WPA2.

For large implementations, there are several vendors supplying wireless access points under the control of a wireless director, offering software-based controllers that allow access points on the network, providing user access control, and enforcing encryption policies. For smaller implementations, this control functionality is done manually when the wireless routers or access points are set up. The security policies put in place are configured on the wireless access device and the wireless client. The Windows 7 client components in our case must be set up to match the security settings of the wireless network access devices.

During the setup of the most wireless access devices that the hardware vendor provides, the administrator will configure the security parameters. Configuring can be done during the setup program and/or when accessing the wireless access device configuration pages through a web browser. Most of our current devices have a built-in web server to allow the HTTP connection from a web browser. Windows 7 also has the ability to configure the wireless access device if the hardware vendor makes it available. If there is no specific component written, you can launch the web browser–based configuration from a convenient location: the Network And Sharing Center.

CONFIGURING A NETWORK AND SHARING CENTER WIRELESS ACCESS DEVICE

Perform the following steps to see how to initiate a Windows 7 wireless access point configuration:

1. Choose Start and type **Network and Sharing Center** into the Start menu's search box; press Enter.

2. Choose the Set Up A New Connection Or Network option.

3. Choose Set Up A New Network to configure a new router or access point, as shown in Figure 11.11, and then click Next.

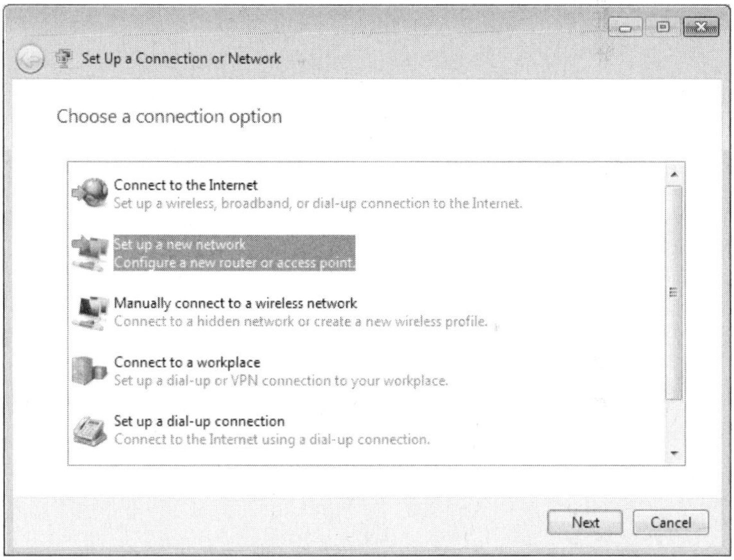

FIGURE 11.11
Setting up a new network

4. Select the wireless access device you want to configure, as shown in Figure 11.12, from the Set Up A Network window and click Next.

5. Depending on your device, you might be asked to enter a PIN or other identifying parameter to access the device. Enter the PIN and click Next.

6. On the next screen, as shown in Figure 11.13, you will be able to configure the security settings dictated by the wireless security policy to be implemented. The settings defined here need to be configured for each client machine connecting to the wireless network. After making the setting choices, click Next.

7. The configuration of the wireless network device completes and you are shown a confirmation window. Click Finish to close the window.

FIGURE 11.12
Choosing the wireless router

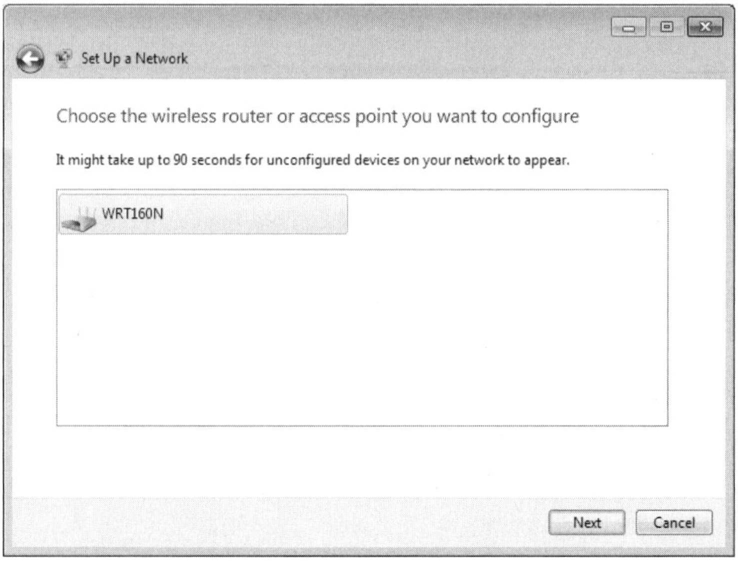

FIGURE 11.13
Wireless security configuration

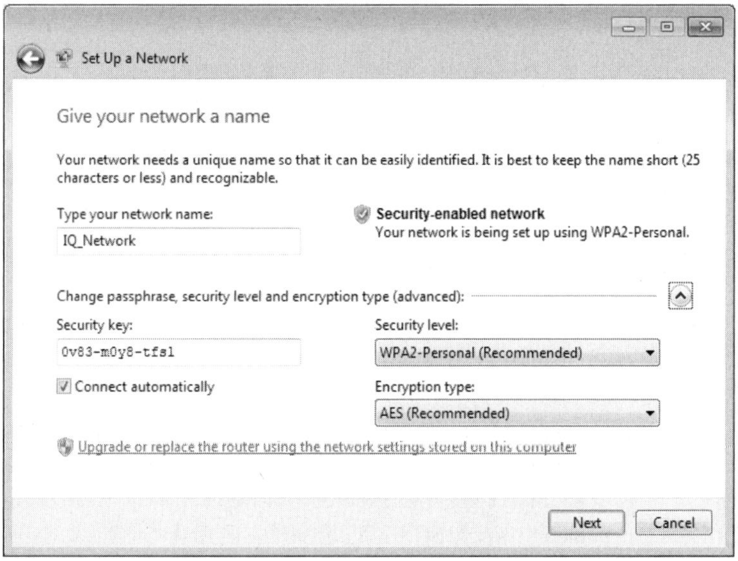

Whether you had Windows 7 configure the wireless network connection or you performed the setup through the manufacturer's process, you still need to configure your Windows 7 client access. If you have performed the simplest configuration, and there are no security parameters configured (bad idea, by the way), Windows 7 will connect automatically with a quick window showing the wireless network it's connecting to and providing access without much user intervention. Even canceling through the screens will produce a successful (non-secure) connection. This simple configuration process makes connecting a home or small network easy and straightforward for nontechnical users, but this is not a good solution.

If you have configured wireless network security (a good idea), then you need to configure the Windows 7 client with the correct settings. Once again, the configuration screens are available from a convenient location known as the Network And Sharing Center.

CONFIGURING THE NETWORK AND SHARING CENTER WIRELESS NETWORK CLIENT

Perform the following steps to access the Windows 7 client wireless network properties:

1. Choose Start and type **Network and Sharing Center** into the Start menu's search box; then press Enter.

2. Choose Wireless Network Connection item in the View Your Active Networks section of the Network And Sharing Center.

3. Click the Wireless Properties button in the Connection area of the Wireless Network Connection Status window, as shown in Figure 11.14.

FIGURE 11.14
Click Wireless
Properties.

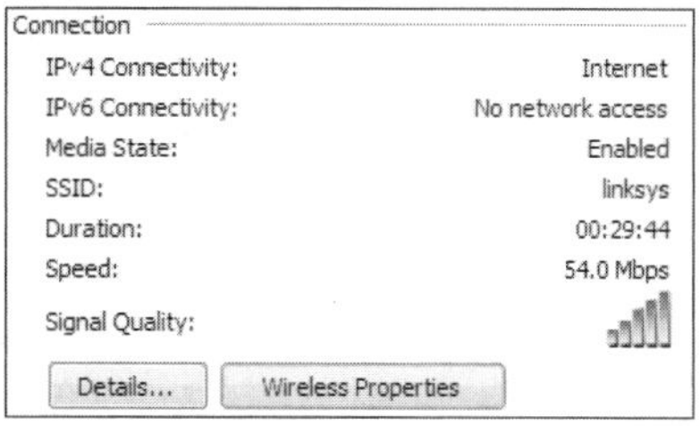

Connection	
IPv4 Connectivity:	Internet
IPv6 Connectivity:	No network access
Media State:	Enabled
SSID:	linksys
Duration:	00:29:44
Speed:	54.0 Mbps
Signal Quality:	.ooll

Details...   Wireless Properties

The Wireless Network Properties dialog box opens, displaying the current setup for the wireless network.

Figure 11.15 shows the Connection tab of the Wireless Network Properties dialog box. Here, you have the ability to set or change the Windows 7 client configuration.

The Connection tab displays the following information:

Name The name assigned to the wireless network.

SSID The Service Set Identifier (SSID) of the wireless connection. This defines a friendly name for the wireless network. This is normally an ASCII string and is usually broadcast by default, allowing a machine or users to select a wireless network with which to connect. Some wireless access devices will allow more than one SSID to be available (or broadcast) at the same time, thus creating more than one wireless network within the same device.

Network Type Displays the mode in which the wireless network is operating. If the wireless network is in infrastructure mode, this parameter will be Access Point. If the wireless network is ad hoc, this field will display Computer-To-Computer.

Network Availability Displays to whom the wireless network is available — All Users or Me Only, for example.

You can configure the following information:

Connect Automatically When This Network Is In Range This option, when checked, allows automatic connection for this wireless network. If this option is deselected, the user has to select this wireless network for connection.

FIGURE 11.15

The Connection tab of the Wireless Network Properties dialog box

Connect To A More Preferred Network If Available   Windows 7 will attempt to connect to a preferred network (if the Connect Automatically option is selected). If there is more than one preferred network, Windows 7 might switch back and forth if they are both available at the same time. Clearing this option allows the currently connected network to stay connected until it is no longer available, possibly preventing the dropping of data or even dropped connections.

Connect Even If The Network Is Not Broadcasting Its Name (SSID)   If the wireless network you are attempting to connect to is not broadcasting its SSID, you must select this option to allow Windows 7 to automatically connect.

There is one more option on the Connection tab of the Wireless Network Properties tab: Copy This Network Profile To A USB Flash Drive. Selecting this link launches the Copy Network Settings Wizard, as shown in Figure 11.16. After you insert a USB flash drive, Windows 7 saves the currently configured wireless network configuration in the form of a setupSNK.exe program and a folder named SMRTNTKY with the configuration parameters. Exercise caution to protect this information as all the configuration parameters (including security keys) are stored in clear text.

After the files and folder are created and saved, you are presented with a confirmation screen with simple instructions and a link for the detailed information about wireless network configuration. The confirmation page is shown in Figure 11.17.

The second tab of the Wireless Network Properties dialog box is the Security tab. This tab allows you to configure the security parameters as defined in your security policy and configured on your wireless network access devices. Figure 11.18 shows the Security tab with the Security Type and Encryption Type drop-down lists open. You can also see the Network Security Key entry as clear text as the Show Characters option is enabled.

FIGURE 11.16
Copy Network Settings Wizard for the wireless connection

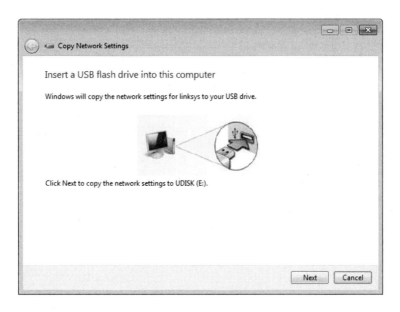

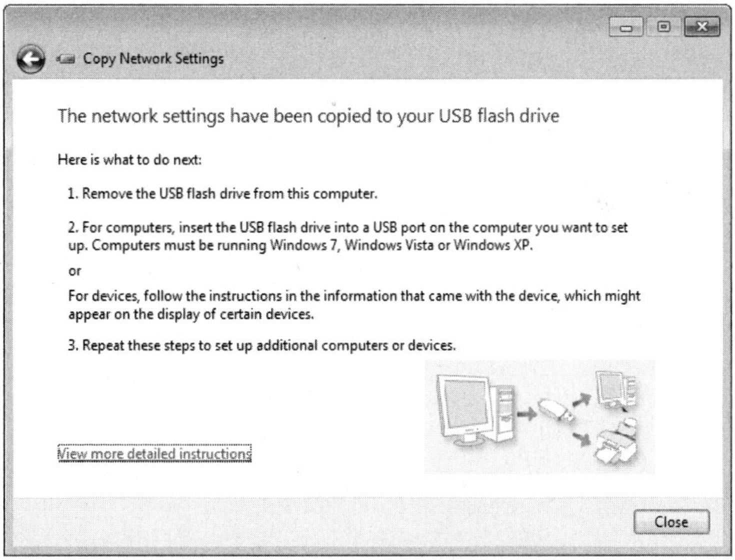

FIGURE 11.17
Wireless connection copy confirmation window

FIGURE 11.18
Wireless Network
Properties, Security tab

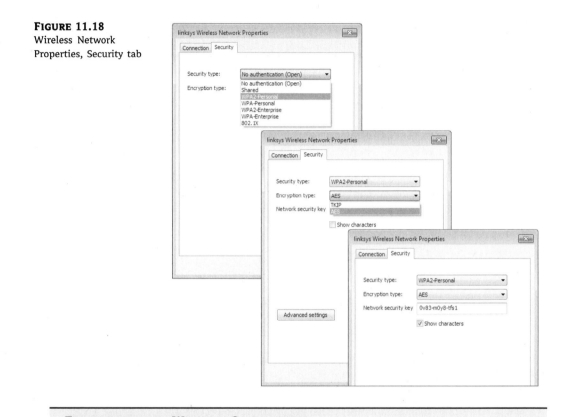

TROUBLESHOOTING WIRELESS CONNECTIVITY

If you're having problems connecting to your wireless network, check this list:

Ensure that your wireless card and the access device are compatible.   Cards that are compatible with the 802.11b standard can only connect to 802.11b or an 802.11b/g access device configured to accept 802.11b. Cards using 802.11a can only connect to 802.11a or 802.11 a/b/g access devices configured to accept 802,11a. An 802.11n card needs to connect to an 802.11n access device for efficiency (although most will auto-negotiate to the best spec available). The specification you're using on the card has to be available and turned on in the wireless access device.

Ensure that your wireless network card is enabled.   Many newer laptops and tablets have either a switch or a hotkey setting that enables and disables the wireless device. A laptop switch may be turned off, or the user has unintentionally pressed the key sequence to shut off the PC's wireless radio. The Physical layer always seems to be a good place to start looking.

Ensure that the access point signal is available.   The output power of the signal might be fine, but the radio frequency (RF) power is attenuated as it goes through walls, insulation, or water. You need to make sure there is nothing that might be causing interference of the wireless signal.

Ensure the security parameters are configured alike.   The SSID, encryption type, encryption algorithm, and passphrase/security key have to be set the same on both the wireless access device as well as the wireless client. In the desire to make the initial setup and the secure setup easier for end users, some hardware vendors have an "easy" button to allow the network access device to negotiate a secure set of parameters with the client. After the wireless network has been working correctly for a while, a failure shows the parameters to now be incompatible, thanks in large part to someone pressing the easy button just before the failure.

Ensure automatic connections if the SSID is not being broadcast.   If you are having trouble connecting to a network that does not broadcast its SSID, select the Connect Even If The Network Is Not Broadcasting check box in the Wireless Network Properties dialog box.

One final thought on troubleshooting in the wireless world: wireless routers are quite technologically sophisticated. They have switch ports for connecting hard-wired devices on the private network as well as an Internet port to connect to the outside world. The wireless portion of the device is like another switch port on the private side, thus allowing the wireless devices to interact with the hard-wires. When you troubleshoot, start with the hard-wired devices and see if they can communicate with one another and the outside (the other side of your wireless router). Try to communicate between the hard-wired and wireless as well to eliminate the router components. Also, never use the wireless network to configure the wireless devices. If you do, you will undoubtedly lose connectivity in the middle of a configuration and be forced to connect with the cable, leaving the access point unusable until you complete the task you started wirelessly.

Joining and Sharing HomeGroups in Windows 7

Have you ever wanted to share your music or pictures and found it difficult? HomeGroup is a new functionality of Windows 7 that simplifies the sharing of music, pictures, and documents in your small office or home network between Windows 7 PCs. HomeGroup allows you to share USB connected printers, too. If you have a printer installed on a Windows 7 computer and it's shared by HomeGroup, it is automatically installed onto the other HomeGroup-enabled Windows 7 PCs. This even extends to domain-joined computers; they can be part of a HomeGroup as well.

The first step in the process of using HomeGroup for sharing is to create a new HomeGroup or join an existing one. If the Windows 7 Network Discovery feature is not enabled, you will be asked to create a HomeGroup. In the Network And Sharing Center select Choose Homegroup And Sharing Options and then click the Create A Homegroup button (both items are shown in Figure 11.19).

With Windows 7 Network Discovery turned on (the default), HomeGroup is created automatically. You still need to join the HomeGroup to make use of the other shared resources and to share yours. In the Network And Sharing Center, you can join an existing HomeGroup by clicking the Join Now button, as shown in Figure 11.20.

Part of joining a HomeGroup setup is to define the resources that you want to make available to the other members of HomeGroup. The next screen in the setup, as shown in Figure 11.21, lets you choose which resources you want to share.

The next step is to enter the HomeGroup password. Windows 7, by default, will recognize a HomeGroup on the network. However, the other Windows 7 machines will not have access to the resources. Allowing any Windows 7 machine connecting to the network to automatically have shared resource access would be a huge security hole. To protect the Windows 7 user resources, a password must be entered to join HomeGroup. Figure 11.22 shows the screen where you enter the password.

FIGURE 11.19
Creating a HomeGroup

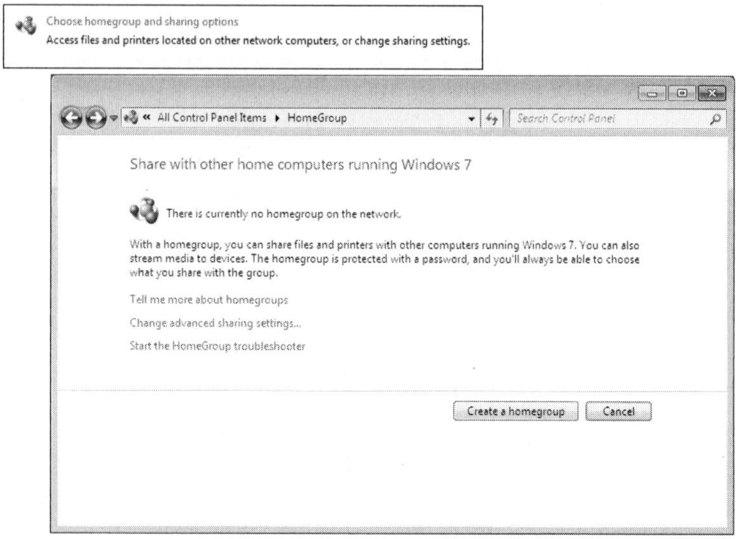

FIGURE 11.20
Joining an existing
HomeGroup

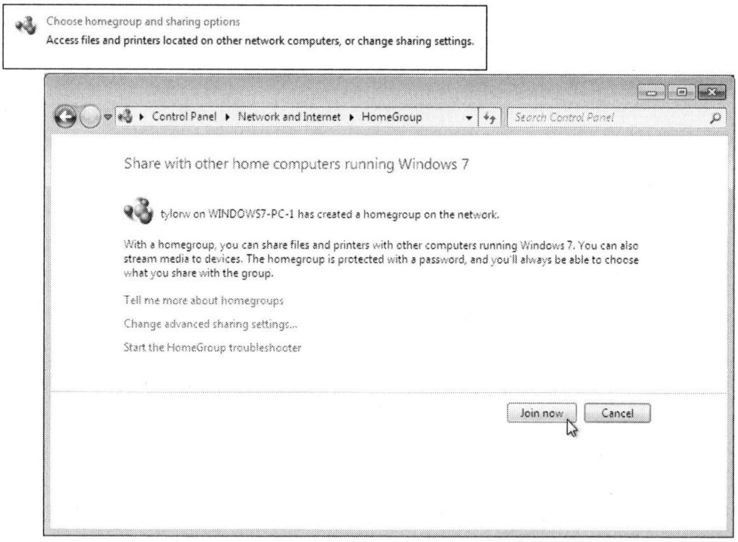

FIGURE 11.21
HomeGroup sharing
selections

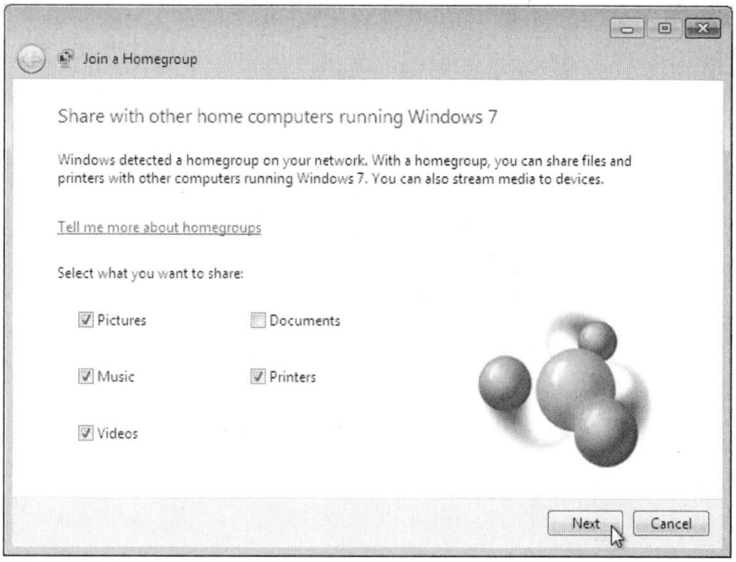

FIGURE 11.22
HomeGroup password
screen

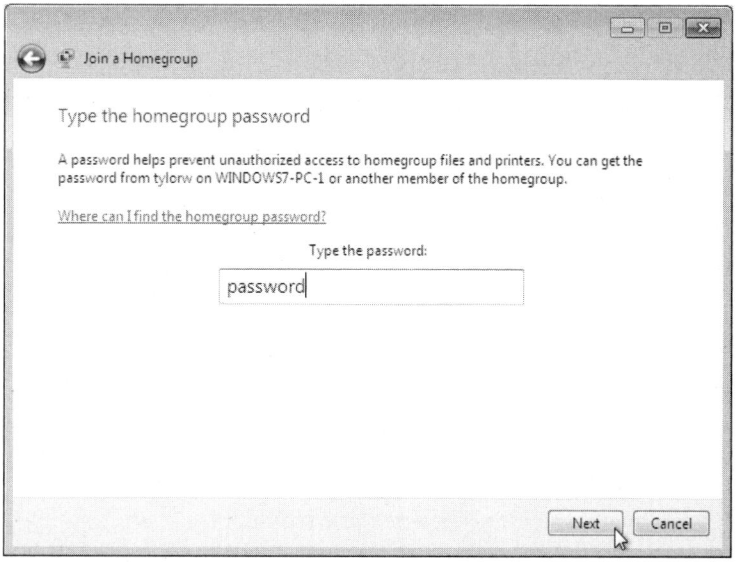

The password for the HomeGroup can be found or changed on the machine that established the HomeGroup. After other machines have joined, each machine has the ability to view or change the password, but they must join the HomeGroup first. The initial machine in the HomeGroup will create a random secure password. To view and/or print the HomeGroup password, select Choose Homegroup And Sharing Options in the Network And Sharing Center and then choose View Or Print The Homegroup Password, as shown in Figure 11.23. Again, this can be done from any Windows 7 machine that is already a member of the HomeGroup, but not from one that wants to join.

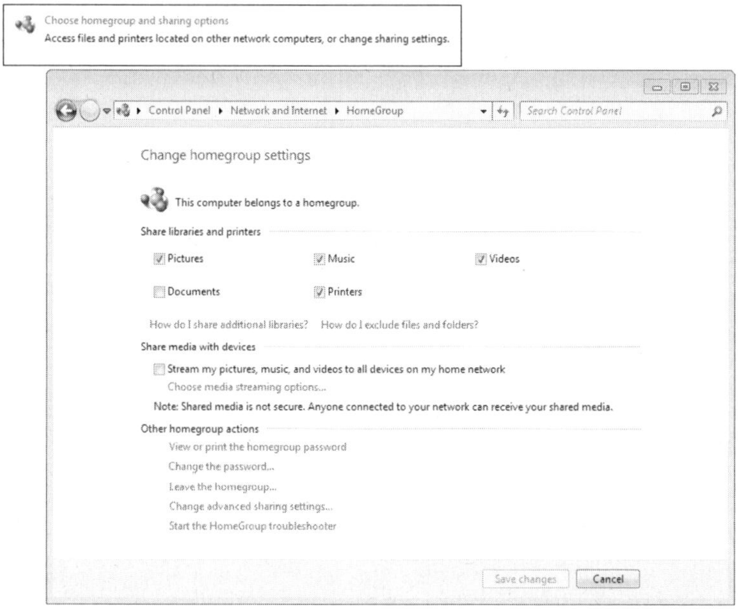

FIGURE 11.23
Changing the
HomeGroup settings

Figure 11.24 shows the View And Print Your Homegroup Password screen. We have changed the password to "password" (not recommended for your network).

Remember that Windows 7 will initially create a random secure password for the Home-Group, and you need to visit the View And Print Your Homegroup Password screen to find out what it is. You will probably want to change it. To change the password, choose the Change The Password option on the Change Homegroup Settings screen and then select Change The Password on the Change Your Homegroup Password screen, as shown in Figure 11.25. When you change the HomeGroup password, you need to go to each of the other Windows 7 machines that are members of the HomeGroup and change the password if you still want the others to share resources.

After the HomeGroup is set up, you can see the other members' resources by choosing the HomeGroup option in Windows Explorer. You can also add the HomeGroup option to your Start menu, as shown in Figure 11.26.

Choosing the HomeGroup option from the Start menu (or choosing Computer and selecting HomeGroup in the Explorer window) allows you to access the other members of your Home-Group. Figure 11.27 shows the HomeGroup item expanded and another Windows 7 machine's resources that has joined the HomeGroup.

FIGURE 11.24
View And Print Your
Homegroup Password
screen

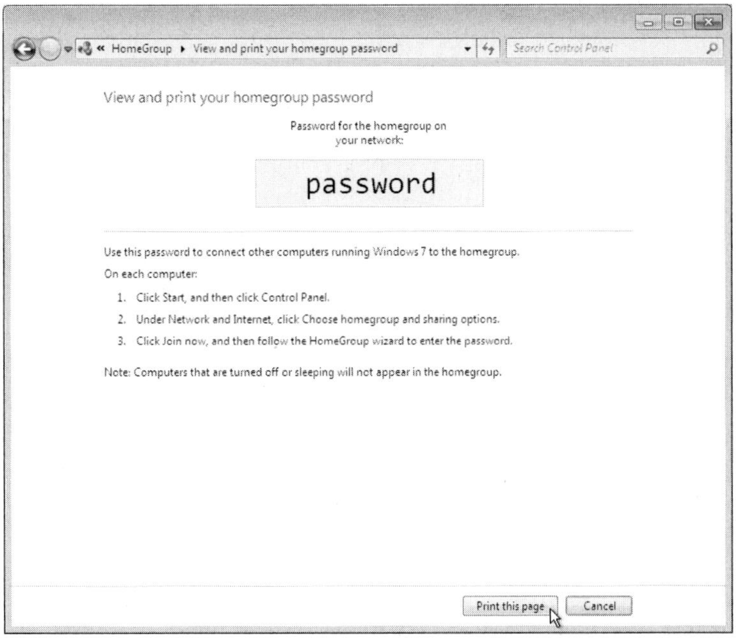

FIGURE 11.25
Changing the
HomeGroup password

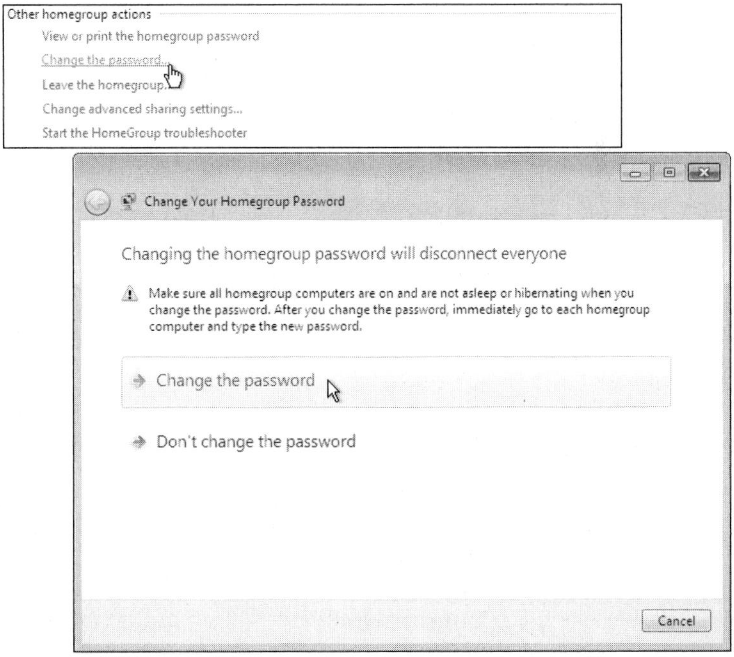

FIGURE 11.26
HomeGroup in the Start
menu

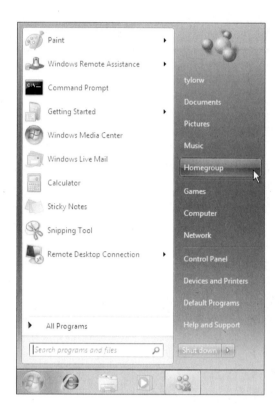

FIGURE 11.27
Viewing HomeGroup
resources from Explorer

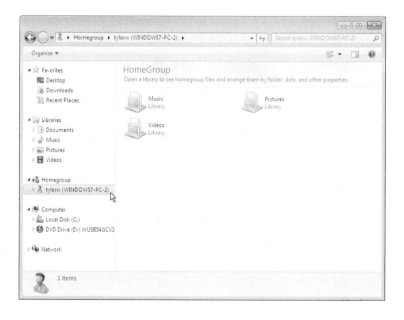

HomeGroups are a great option for users in the Windows 7 environment for sharing resources. But what if you still have non–Windows 7 machines? The legacy function of simply sharing resources and setting permissions still works for Windows 7 and will allow older operating systems to have access to resources shared on Windows 7 machines. It also allows users running Windows 7 to have access to the shared resources on Vista and XP.

To connect to other network devices, having a network protocol configured correctly is a key process. TCP/IP is the default network protocol for Windows 7.

Understanding Network Protocols

Network protocols function at the OSI model Layer 3 (the Network layer) and Layer 4 (the Transport layer). Network protocols are responsible for transporting data across an internetwork. They are responsible for reliable communication as well. The only network protocol installed by default in Windows 7 is TCP/IP, both version 4 and version 6 (called IPv4 and IPv6).

A solid understanding of TCP/IP and the configuration required for network communication is a substantial piece of the Windows 7 setup.

Overview of TCP/IP

Transmission Control Protocol/Internet Protocol (TCP/IP) is the most commonly used network protocol. It is a suite of protocols that have evolved into the industry standard for network, internetwork, and Internet connectivity. The main protocols providing basic TCP/IP services include Internet Protocol (IP), Transmission Control Protocol (TCP), User Datagram Protocol (UDP), Address Resolution Protocol (ARP), Internet Control Message Protocol (ICMP), and Internet Group Management Protocol (IGMP).

BENEFITS OF USING TCP/IP

TCP/IP as a protocol suite was accepted as an industry standard in the 1980s and continues to be the primary internetworking protocol today. For a default installation of Windows 7, IPv4 and IPv6 are both installed by default. TCP/IP has the following benefits:

◆ TCP/IP is the most common protocol and is supported by almost all network operating systems. It is the required protocol for Internet access.

◆ TCP/IP is dependable and scalable for use in small and large networks.

◆ Support is provided for connectivity across interconnected networks, independent of the operating systems being used at the upper end of the OSI model or the physical components at the lower end of the OSI model.

◆ TCP/IP provides standard routing services for moving packets over interconnected network segments. Dividing networks into multiple subnetworks (or subnets) optimizes network traffic and facilitates network management.

◆ TCP/IP is designed to provide data reliability by providing a connection at the transport layer and verifying each data segment is received and passed to the application requiring the data by retransmitting lost information.

◆ TCP/IP allows for the classification of data in regard to its importance (quality of service). This allows important time-sensitive streams of data to get preferential treatment (like Voice over IP).

◆ TCP/IP is designed to be fault tolerant. It is able to dynamically reroute packets if network links become unavailable (assuming alternate paths exist).

◆ Protocol applications can provide services such as *Dynamic Host Configuration Protocol (DHCP)* for TCP/IP configuration and Domain Name System (DNS) for hostname-to-IP address resolution.

◆ Windows 7 continues to support *Automatic Private IP Addressing (APIPA)* used by small local connection–only networks without a DHCP server to allow Windows 7 to automatically assign an IP address to itself.

◆ Support for *NetBIOS* over TCP/IP (NetBT) is included in Windows 7. NetBIOS is a software specification used for identifying computer resources by name as opposed to IP address. We still use TCP/IP as the network protocol, so we map the NetBIOS name to an IP address.

◆ The inclusion of *Alternate IP Configuration* allows users to have a static and a DHCP-assigned IP address mapped to a single network adapter, which is used to support mobile users who roam between different network segments.

◆ IPv6 incorporates a much larger address space and, more importantly, incorporates many of the additional features of TCP/IP into a standardized protocol. This is important because if a vendor says they support TCP/IP, they only have to support the 1980s version and may not support additional features like the Internet protocol security features of IPSec. IPv6 as a standard includes these features and is thus a more robust network protocol.

FEATURES OF TCP/IP

One of the main features of TCP/IP is that it allows a common structure for network communications across a wide variety of diverse hardware and operating systems and a lot of applications, specifically written to configure and control it. Several of the features of TCP/IP included with Windows 7 are:

◆ TCP/IP connectivity tools allowing access to a variety of hosts across a TCP/IP network. TCP/IP tools in Windows 7 include clients for HTTP, FTP, TFTP, Telnet, and finger, among others. Server components for the tools are available.

◆ Inclusion of a Simple Network Management Protocol (SNMP) agent that can be used to monitor performance and resource use of a TCP/IP host, server, or network hardware devices.

◆ TCP/IP management and diagnostic tools are provided for maintenance and diagnostic support. TCP/IP management and diagnostic commands include `ipconfig`, `arp`, `ping`, `nbtstat`, `netsh`, `route`, `nslookup`, `tracert`, and `pathping`.

◆ Support for TCP/IP network printing, allowing you to print to networked print devices.

◆ Logical and physical multihoming, allowing multiple IP addresses on a single computer for single or multiple network adapters. Multiple network adapters installed on a single computer are normally associated with routing for internetwork connectivity.

♦ Support for internal IP routing, which allows a Windows 7 computer to route packets between multiple network adapters installed in one machine.

♦ Support for virtual private networks, which allows you to transmit data securely across a public network via encapsulated and encrypted packets.

BASICS OF IP ADDRESSING AND CONFIGURATION

Before you can configure TCP/IP, you should have a basic understanding of TCP/IP configuration and addressing. Let's review TCP/IP addressing. To configure a TCP/IP client, you must specify an IP address (also known as the logical address), subnet mask, and default gateway (if you're going to communicate outside your local network). Depending on your network, you might want to configure a DNS server, domain name, or maybe even a WINS server.

You can see the Windows 7 TCP/IP version 4 properties window in Figure 11.28. We will go through the configuration steps and show you how to access this window later in this section.

FIGURE 11.28

Windows 7 TCP/IP version 4 properties

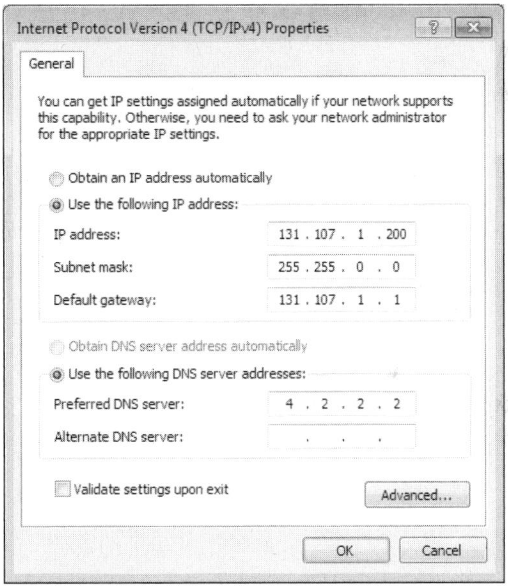

IPv4 Address Types

There are three types of IPv4 addresses: broadcast, multicast, and unicast.

A broadcast address is read by all hosts that hear it (the broadcast will not go across a router, so only local devices hear the broadcast). The IPv4 broadcast address is 255.255.255.255; every single bit is a one.

A multicast address is a special address that one or more devices will listen for by joining a multicast group. Not all the local devices respond and process the data in the multicast packet; only the devices configured to listen for it respond. A multicast address will have a value between 224 and 239 in the first octet (the leftmost number in the dotted decimal representation). A multicast example is 224.0.0.5.

A unicast IP address uniquely identifies a computer or device on the network. An IPv4 unicast address is a four-octet, 32-bit address represented as dotted decimal (an example is 131.107.1.200). Each number in the dotted decimal notation is a decimal representation of 8 bits, and the value of each is going to be between 0 and 255 (255 is the numerically largest value that 8 bits can represent). A portion of the IPv4 unicast address is used to identify the network the device is on (or the network of a destination device), and part is used to identify the individual host on the local network or the unique host on a remote network. The IPv4 address scheme is the only address space that the Internet uses today, and TCP/IP is the only network protocol that the Internet uses today.

IPv4 Address Classes

When the TCP/IP suite was accepted as a standard in the 1980s, three classes of unicast IP addresses were defined. Depending on the class you use, different parts of the address show the default network portion of the address and the host address. We still refer to these addresses by class, but we no longer really utilize this class structure; we'll explain shortly.

Table 11.1 shows the three classes of network addresses and the number of networks and hosts available for each network class as defined by the original TCP/IP version 4 standard.

TABLE 11.1:   IPv4 Class Assignments

NETWORK CLASS	ADDRESS RANGE OF FIRST OCTET	NUMBER OF UNIQUE NETWORKS AVAILABLE	NUMBER OF UNIQUE HOSTS PER NETWORK
A	1–126	126	16,777,214
B	128–191	16,384	65,534
C	192–223	2,097,152	254

The values are based on the number of bits that can be changed (or used) by the network portion for the number of networks available or by the host portion for the number of hosts available. A quick example: if you have 8 bits to work with, 2 raised to the 8th power are the total number of different combination (of 8 bits) you can make. 2 raised to the 8th power is 256. So, if you have 8 bits available to you in the host portion of an IP address, you can have 256 possible addresses. The catch here is that the first address in the range is not assignable to a host (we use the first address to define the network ID) and the last address is not assignable to a host (we use the last address as the subnetwork broadcast address). If you have 8 bits to use, you can only assign 254 to unique unicast IPv4 addresses to devices. It just so happens that the original IPv4 specification for a Class C address space allocated 24 bits to the network portion and 8 bits for the host portion. How many unique addresses are available? Yes: 254.

IPv4 Subnet Mask

The *subnet mask* is used to specify which portion of the unicast IPv4 address defines the network value and which portion of the unicast IPv4 address defines the unique host value. The subnet mask can be shown as dotted decimal, as with 255.255.255.0, or as slash notation, as in /24. The 1980s standard for classful network addressing defined subnet masks for each class, as shown in Table 11.2.

TABLE 11.2: IPv4 Classful Subnet Masks

CLASS	DEFAULT MASK	SLASH NOTATION
Class A	255.0.0.0	Slash 8 (/8)
Class B	255.255.0.0	Slash 16 (/16)
Class C	255.255.255.0	Slash 24 (/24)

The slash notation is easier to use as it defines the same information in a more convenient format. If you look at the Class A default (or natural) mask or 255.0.0.0, you can say that 255 is 8 ones (converting a decimal 255 to binary yields 1111 1111). Slash 8 simply means there are 8 ones in the subnet mask (or 255.0.0.0). By using 255, you are selecting the octet or octets (or, in some cases, the piece of an octet) used to identify the network address. For example, in the Class B network address 192.168.2.1, with the default subnet mask for a Class B space being 255.255.0.0, then 192.168 is the network address and 2.1 is the unicast host address.

IPv4 Default Gateway

For each machine to communicate to other devices, the machine evaluates the network portion of the IP address it desires to communicate with (the destination device) and the network portion of its IP address. If the two network values are the same, the machine attempts to communicate directly with the destination machine. If the network portions of the two IP addresses are different, then the local machine sends the packet to the default gateway. The default gateway will then decide where the destination is by evaluating the network portion of the IP address and send it to the next device. You configure a *default gateway* if the network contains routers (the default gateway is a router). A *router* is a device that connects two or more network segments (IP subnetworks) together. Routers function at the Network layer of the OSI model.

You can configure a Windows 7 computer or Windows Server 2008 to act as a router by installing two or more network cards in the server, attaching each network card to a different network segment, and then configuring each network card for the segment to which it will attach. You can also use third-party routers, which typically offer more features than Windows 7 computers or Windows Server 2008 configured as a router. Many times in our network we use the first available IP address as the address of our default gateway (for example, 131.107.1.1). You do not send packets to the default gateway; the network protocol does by getting the physical address (MAC) or the default gateway and inserting it as the destination MAC address with the actual destination IP or the remote device.

DNS Servers

Domain Name System (DNS) servers are used to resolve hostnames to IP addresses. Name resolution makes it easier for people to access other IP hosts. For example, do you know what the IP address is for Google? No? Do you know the hostname of Google server? Yes, you would use www.google.com. From your computer, pinging www.google.com actually sends the request to 66.102.1.147, the IP address returned by your DNS server. You can understand why many people might not know the IP address but would know the domain hostname. Windows 7 asks the DNS server configured on the machine for the resolution of the hostname to an IP address. Most companies and Internet service providers (ISPs) have their own DNS servers that know how to resolve any valid request. There are public DNS servers that can be used as well.

FULLY QUALIFIED DOMAIN NAME

The name you use to access the Google server, www.google.com, is an example of a fully qualified domain name (FQDN). This notation has a domain component, which is google.com. The "dot com" is the top-level domain that parents most company names. You will see "dot gov" for government agencies and "dot edu" for educational institutions, along with a lot more. The "google" of the google.com domain is the organization who is logically responsible for the resource. Finally, the "www" is the unique identifier within the organization for the resource. We have become very familiar with this notation, but it is not guaranteed to be the name (nor does it have to be). You might well have seen your browser go to www1.acme.com or even bob.jester.edu. As long as the name resolves to the correct IP address, all is good.

If you do not have access to a properly configured DNS server or simply don't want your machine to resolve an IP address dynamically, you can statically configure a hostname to an IP address by editing the HOSTS file on your Windows 7 machine. Why would you do this? Perhaps there is more than one server available with the same name (do you think there is only one Google server?), and you want to use one of the addresses specifically. You can edit your local host's file, as shown in Figure 11.29, with a FQDN and the configured IP address will be used.

FIGURE 11.29
HOSTS file location in
Windows 7

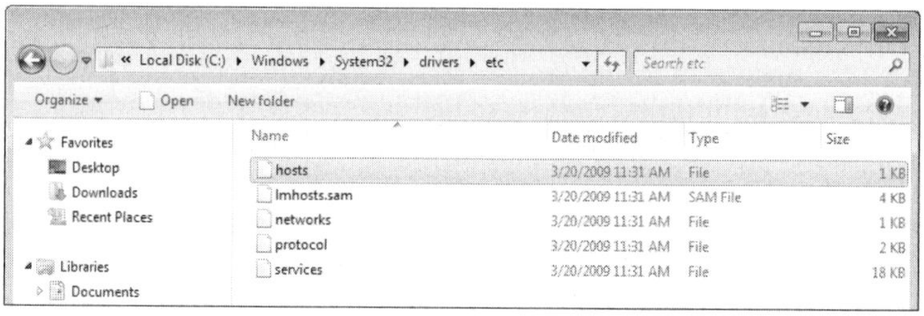

WINS Servers

Windows Internet Name Service (WINS) servers are used to resolve NetBIOS (Network Basic Input/Output System) names to IP addresses. Windows 7 uses NetBIOS names in addition to hostnames to identify network computers. This is mainly for backward compatibility with legacy Windows operating systems, which used this addressing scheme extensively. When you attempt to access a computer using the NetBIOS name, the computer must be able to resolve the NetBIOS name to an IP address. This address resolution can be accomplished by using one of the following methods:

◆ Through a broadcast (if the computer you are trying to reach is on the same network segment)

◆ Through a WINS server

◆ Through an LMHOSTS (LAN Manager HOSTS) file, which is a static mapping of IP addresses to NetBIOS computer names

Dynamic Host Configuration Protocol (DHCP)

Each device that will use TCP/IP on your network must have a valid, unique IP address. This address can be manually configured or better yet can be automated through *Dynamic Host Configuration Protocol (DHCP)*. DHCP is implemented as a client/server application. The server is configured with a pool of IP addresses and other IP-related configuration settings, such as subnet mask, default gateway, DNS server address, and WINS server address. The client is configured to automatically request IP configuration information from the DHCP server and use it for a given period of time (the lease length). Figure 11.30 shows the TCP/IP version 4 properties pages set up to use DHCP.

FIGURE 11.30
TCP/IP properties using DHCP

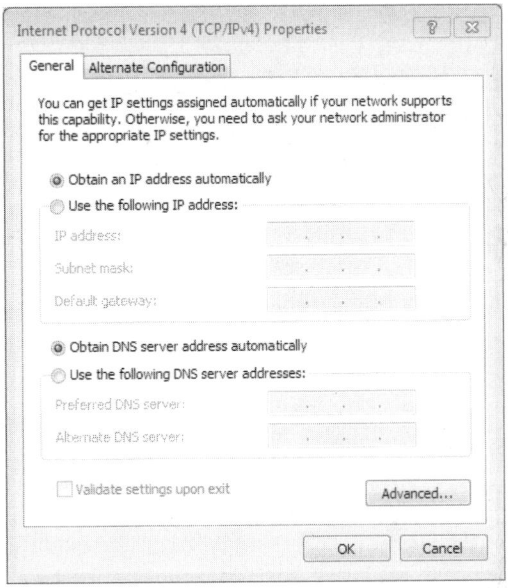

DHCP works in the following manner:

1. When the client computer starts up, it sends a broadcast DHCPDISCOVER message, requesting a DHCP server. The request includes the hardware address of the client computer.

2. Any DHCP server receiving the broadcast that has available IP addresses will send a DHCPOFFER message to the client. This message offers an IP address for a set period of time (called a *lease*), a subnet mask, and a server identifier (the IP address of the DHCP server). The address that is offered by the server is marked as unavailable and will not be offered to any other clients during the DHCP negotiation period.

3. The client selects one of the offers and broadcasts a DHCPREQUEST message, indicating its selection. This allows any DHCP offers that were not accepted to be returned to the pool of available IP addresses.

4. The DHCP server that was selected sends back a DHCPACK message as an acknowledgment, indicating the IP address, subnet mask, and duration of the lease that the client computer will use. It might also send additional configuration information, such as the address of the default gateway and the DNS server address.

Using Deployment Options for TCP/IP Configurations

Windows 7 has four methods available for configuring TCP/IP:

◆ Static IP addressing

◆ Dynamic Host Configuration Protocol (DHCP)

◆ Automatic Private IP Addressing (APIPA)

◆ Alternate IP configuration

Although DHCP is the most common method for configuring an IP address on the machines in a network, the other methods are used as well.

CONFIGURING STATIC IP ADDRESSING

You can manually configure IP addressing if you know your IP address and subnet mask. If you are using optional components such as a default gateway or a DNS server, you will need to know the IP addresses of the computers that host these services as well. This option is not typically used in large networks because it is time consuming and prone to user error.

Statically Configuring a Windows 7 IPv4 address and DNS Server

Perform the following steps to manually configure a static IP address for a Windows 7 machine:

1. Select Start and type **Network and Sharing Center** into the Start menu's search box.

2. In the Network And Sharing Center window, click Local Area Connection in the View Your Active Networks section.

3. Click the Properties button in the Activity section of the Local Area Connection Status box.

4. In the Local Area Connection Properties dialog box, select Internet Protocol Version 4 (TCP/IPv4), as shown in Figure 11.31, and click the Properties button.

FIGURE 11.31
Select Internet Protocol
Version 4 (TCP/IPv4).

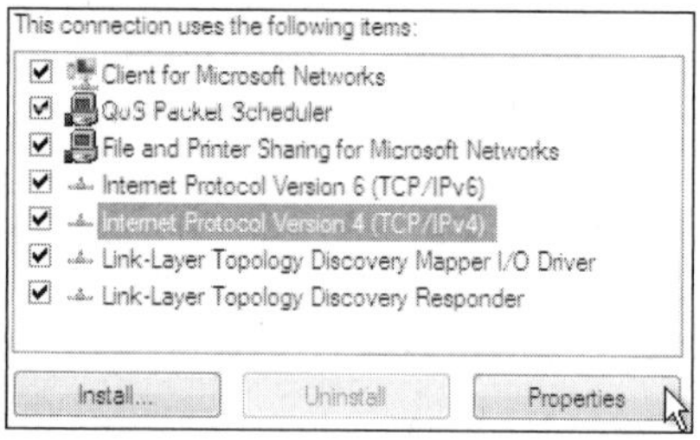

5. Choose Use The Following IP Address in the Internet Protocol Version 4 (TCP/IPv4) Properties dialog box.

6. In the IP Address box, enter **131.200.1.200**; in the Subnet Mask box, enter **255.255.0.0**; and in the Default Gateway box, enter **131.107.1.1**.

USE A VALID ADDRESS FOR YOUR NETWORK

The example in step 6 is likely not a valid IP address on your network. You can substitute a valid address, subnet mask, and default gateway if you know them. If you click OK and see this is not a valid IP address for your network, you will lose connectivity!

7. Choose Use The Following DNS Server Addresses in the Internet Protocol Version 4 (TCP/IPv4) Properties dialog box.

8. Enter **4.2.2.2** in the Preferred DNS Server box. You can leave the Alternate DNS Server box blank.

9. If you have entered valid information in steps 6 and 8, you can click OK to save your settings and close the dialog box; otherwise, click Cancel to revoke your changes.

Access Advanced Configuration TCP/IPv4 Properties

Clicking the Advanced button in the Internet Protocol Version 4 (TCP/IPv4) dialog box opens the Advanced TCP/IP Settings dialog box, as shown in Figure 11.32. In this dialog box, you can configure advanced IP, DNS, and WINS settings.

FIGURE 11.32
Advanced TCP/IPv4
Properties dialog box

You can edit or add multiple addresses to the same machine in the Advanced TCP/IP Settings windows as well as edit or add default gateways here. You also have access to the advanced DNS and WINS tabs, where you can modify specific parameters for both hostname resolution (DNS) and NetBIOS name resolution (WINS). Figure 11.33 shows both the DNS and WINS tabs of the Advanced TCP/IP Settings dialog box.

Table 11.3 shows the DNS advanced configuration properties and outlines the functionality.

FIGURE 11.33
Advanced DNS and
WINS properties tabs

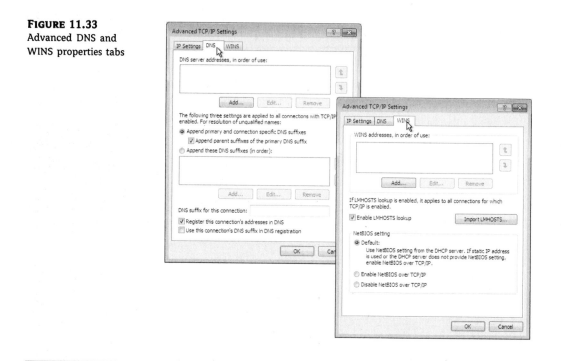

TABLE 11.3: Advanced DNS TCP/IP Settings Options

OPTION	DESCRIPTION
DNS Server Addresses, In Order Of Use	Specifies the DNS servers that are used to resolve DNS queries. Use the arrow buttons on the right side of the list box to move a server up or down in the list.
Append Primary And Connection Specific DNS Suffixes	Specifies how unqualified domain names are resolved by DNS. For example, if your primary DNS suffix is iq.com and you type **ping bob**, DNS will try to resolve the address as bob.iq.com.
Append Parent Suffixes Of The Primary DNS Suffix	Specifies whether name resolution includes the parent suffix for the primary domain DNS suffix, up to the second level of the domain name. For example, if your primary DNS suffix is maine.iq.com and you type **ping bob**, DNS will try to resolve the address as bob.maine.iq.com. If this doesn't work, DNS will try to resolve the address as bob.iq.com.
Append These DNS Suffixes (In Order):	Specifies the DNS suffixes that will be used to attempt to resolve unqualified name resolution. For example, if your primary DNS suffix is iq.com and you type **ping bob**, DNS will try to resolve the address as bob.iq.com. If you append the additional DNS suffix Corp.com and type **ping bob**, DNS will try to resolve the address as bob.iq.com and bob.Corp.com.

TABLE 11.3:   Advanced DNS TCP/IP Settings Options (*CONTINUED*)

OPTION	DESCRIPTION
DNS Suffix For This Connection:	Specifies the DNS suffix for the computer. If this value is configured by a DHCP server and you specify a DNS suffix, it will override the value set by DHCP.
Register This Connection's Addresses In DNS	Specifies that the connection will try to register its addresses dynamically using the computer name that was specified through the System Properties dialog box (accessed through the System icon in Control Panel).
Use This Connection's DNS Suffix In DNS Registration	Specifies that when the computer registers automatically with the DNS server, it should use the combination of the computer name and the DNS suffix.

Table 11.4 shows the WINS advanced configuration properties and outlines the functionality.

TABLE 11.4:   Advanced WINS TCP/IP Settings Options

OPTION	DESCRIPTION
WINS Addresses, In Order Of Use	Specifies the WINS servers that are used to resolve WINS queries. You can use the arrow buttons on the right side of the list box to move a server up or down in the list.
Enable LMHOSTS Lookup	Specifies whether an LMHOSTS file can be used for name resolution. If you configure this option, you can use the Import LMHOSTS button to import an LMHOSTS file to the computer.
Default: Use NetBIOS Setting From The DHCP Server	Specifies that the computer should obtain its NetBIOS-over-TCP/IP and WINS settings from the DHCP server.
Enable NetBIOS Over TCP/IP	Allows you to use statically configured IP addresses so that the computer is able to communicate with pre–Windows XP computers (NetBIOS was discontinued with XP).
Disable NetBIOS Over TCP/IP	Allows you to disable NetBIOS over TCP/IP. Use this option only if your network includes only Windows XP clients, Windows Vista clients, or DNS-enabled clients.

SETTING UP DHCP

Dynamic IP configuration assumes that you have a DHCP server on your network that is reachable by the DHCP clients. DHCP servers are configured to automatically provide DHCP clients with all their IP configuration information, including IP address, subnet mask, and DNS server. For large networks, DHCP is the easiest and most reliable way of managing IP configurations. By default, a Windows 7 machine is configured as a DHCP client for dynamic IP configuration.

Perform the following steps if your computer is configured for manual IP configuration and you want to use dynamic IP configuration:

1. Select Start and type **Network and Sharing Center** into the Start menu's search box.

2. In the Network And Sharing Center window, click Local Area Connection in the View Your Active Networks section.

3. Click the Properties button in the Activity section of the Local Area Connection Status box.

4. In the Local Area Connection Properties dialog box, select Internet Protocol Version 4 (TCP/IPv4) and click the Properties button.

5. Choose Obtain An IP Address Automatically on the General tab of the Internet Protocol Version 4 (TCP/IPv4) Properties dialog box.

6. Choose Obtain DNS Server Address Automatically on the General tab.

7. To use this configuration, click OK to accept the selection and close the dialog box. To exit without saving (if you had a valid static configuration), click Cancel.

USING APIPA

Automatic Private IP Addressing (APIPA) is used to automatically assign private IP addresses for home or small business networks that contain a single subnet, have no DHCP server, and are not using static IP addressing. If APIPA is being used, clients will be able to communicate only with other clients on the same subnet that are also using APIPA. The benefit of using APIPA in small networks is that it is less tedious and has less chance of configuration errors than statically assigning IP addresses and configuration.

APIPA is used with Windows 7 under the following conditions:

♦ When the client is configured as a DHCP client, but no DHCP server is available to service the DHCP request.

♦ When the client originally obtained a DHCP lease from a DHCP server, but when the client tried to renew the DHCP lease, the DHCP server was unavailable and the lease period expired.

APIPA uses a Class B network addresses space that has been reserved for its use. The address space is the 169.254.0.0 network where the range of 169.254.0.1–169.254.255.254 is available for host to assign to themselves.

The steps that APIPA uses are as follows:

1. The Windows 7 client attempts to use a DHCP server for its configuration, but no DHCP servers respond.

2. The Windows 7 client selects a random address from the 169.254.0.1–169.254.255.254 range of addresses and uses a subnet mask of 255.255.0.0.

   The client uses a duplicate-address detection method to verify the address it selected is not already in use on the network.

3. If the address is already in use, the client repeats steps 1 and 2. If the address is not already in use, the client configures its network interface with the address it randomly selected. If you note the number of the address the APIPA client can select from (65536 addresses), the odds of selecting a duplicate is very slim.

4. The Windows 7 network client continues to search for a DHCP server every five minutes. If a DHCP server replies to the request, the APIPA configuration is dropped and the client receives new IP configuration settings from the DHCP server.

You can determine if your network interface has been configured using APIPA by looking at your IP address. You can do this easily from the command interpreter using the `ipconfig /all` command.

Perform the following steps to view your IP address this way:

1. Click Start and enter **cmd** into the Start menu's search box.

2. Type **ipconfig /all** into the command interpreter.

3. Look at the Local Area Connection IP address. If your IP address is in the range of 169.254.0.1–169.254.255.254 and the text Autoconfiguration Enabled is present, as shown in Figure 11.34, your machine is using APIPA.

FIGURE 11.34
Autoconfigured IP
address

USING MULTIPLE IP ADDRESSES

Windows 7 allows you to configure more than one network adapter in a single computer, an approach known as *multihoming*. You can also configure multiple IP addresses on the same network adapter in Windows 7, an approach known as logical multihoming. You would use logical multihoming if you had a single physical network logically divided into subnets and you wanted your computer to be connected with more than one subnet.

Perform the following steps to configure multiple IP addresses for a single network adapter:

1. Select Start and type **Network and Sharing Center** in the Start menu's search box.

2. In the Network and Sharing Center window, click Local Area Connection in the View Your Active Networks section.

3. Click the Properties button in the Activity section of the Local Area Connection Status box.

4. In the Local Area Connection Properties dialog box, select Internet Protocol Version 4 (TCP/IPv4) and click the Properties button.

5. You will need to have a static IP address to use multihoming. Choose Use The Following IP Address in the Internet Protocol Version 4 (TCP/IPv4) Properties dialog box.

6. In the IP Address box, enter **131.200.1.200**; in the Subnet Mask box, enter **255.255.0.0**; and in the Default Gateway box, enter **131.107.1.1**.

USE A VALID ADDRESS FOR YOUR NETWORK

The example in step 6 is likely not a valid IP address on your network. You can substitute a valid address, subnet mask, and default gateway if you know them. If you click OK and see this is not a valid IP address for your network, you will lose connectivity!

---

7. Click the Advanced button to access the Advanced TCP/IP Settings dialog box. On the IP Settings tab in the IP Addresses section, click the Add button, as shown in Figure 11.35.

FIGURE 11.35
Advanced TCP/IP
Settings dialog box

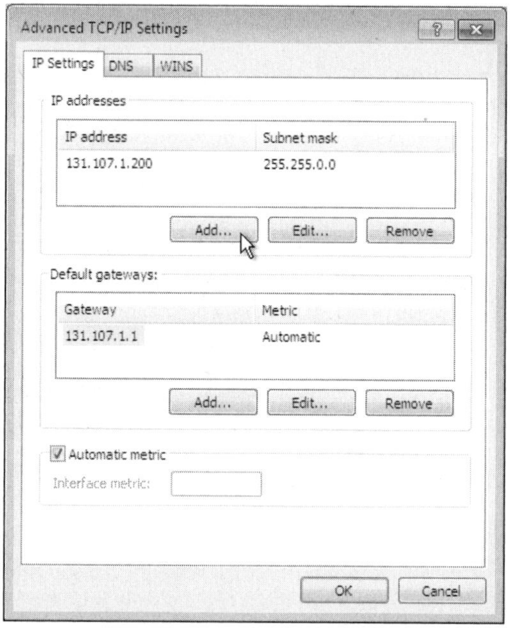

8. You add additional IP addresses by entering them into the TCP/IP address window launched in step 5 along with their subnet mask and then clicking Add. You can repeat this step to add additional IP addresses.

9. If you need to assign more than one default gateway to your IP configuration, use the Default Gateways section of Advanced IP Settings.

USING ALTERNATE CONFIGURATION

Alternate Configuration is designed to be used by laptops and other mobile computers to manage IP configurations when the computer is used in multiple locations and one location requires a static IP address and the other location(s) require dynamic IP addressing. For example, a user with a laptop might need a static IP address to connect to their broadband ISP at home, and then use DHCP when connected to the corporate network.

Alternate Configuration works by allowing the user to configure the computer so that it will initially try to connect to a network using DHCP; if the DHCP attempt fails (for example, when the user is at home), the alternate static IP configuration is used. The alternate IP address can be an APIPA or a manually configured IP address.

Perform the following steps to configure Alternate Configuration:

1. Select Start and type **Network and Sharing Center** in the Start menu's search box.

2. In the Network and Sharing Center window, click Local Area Connection in the View Your Active Networks section.

3. Click the Properties button in the Activity section of the Local Area Connection Status box.

4. In the Local Area Connection Properties dialog box, select Internet Protocol Version 4 (TCP/IPv4) and click the Properties button.

5. Select the Alternate Configuration tab in the Internet Protocol Version 4 (TCP/IPv4) Properties dialog box.

6. The Automatic Private IP address radio button is selected by default. To create a static configuration if the DHCP server is unavailable, choose the User Configured radio button and enter the values for your Alternate Configuration.

7. Click OK to save your Alternate Configuration or reset to the default Automatic Private IP Address radio button and click OK, or click Cancel to abandon your changes and close the window.

USING IPV6 ADDRESSES

Though most of this section we've been referencing TCP/IP as the network protocol, but you should remember that it is really a suite of protocols running in Layer 3 and Layer 4 of the OSI model. Internet Protocol (IP) is the Layer 3 protocol responsible for assigning end devices globally unique addresses (and we mean the whole company for private addresses to the whole Internet for public addresses). Back in the 1980s, it was unimaginable that we would ever need more than 4 billion addresses, but we do. They (the keepers of the Internet) realized in the 1990s that we were going to have a problem and decided that a new Layer 3 would be needed. This was not an easy task, and integration into the existing infrastructure was going to be long as well. They (the keepers of the Internet) came up with an interim solution while the new Layer 3 protocol became standardized. The interim solution is known as NAT and PAT. NAT/PAT allowed more than one device to use the same IP address on a private network as long as there was one Internet address available. Cool enough, but this is not the real solution.

IPv6 is the solution to the IPv4 address depletion. As time has progressed from the IPv4 standard acceptance in the 1980s, we have needed new and better functionality. However, given the way the standards process works around the world, you can add functionality but it may or may not be supported in any vendor's TCP/IPv4 network stack. What happened in IPv6 is not only did the address space increase in size, but the additional functionality that may or may not have been included before has become part of the IPv6 standard. For example, IPv4 is defined as having a variable-length header, which is cumbersome as we need to read an additional piece of data to see how big the header is. Most of the time it stays the same, so why not just fix its length and add perhaps an extension to the header if we need to carry more information? IPv6 uses a fixed-length IP header with the capability of carrying more information in an extension to the header known as an "extension header."

What about the Layer 4 piece, TCP and UDP? Those don't need to change; we're only changing Layer 3. What about the MAC address and the Ethernet specification? Those don't need to change, either; we're only changing Layer 3 (We'll have to add a new identifier for the Layer 2 header so we know to hand the data to IPv6.).

Microsoft has been including IPv6 in its operating systems since NT 4.0; it just has not been enabled by default. Windows 7 (as did Vista) natively supports both IPv4 and IPv6. The main differences you will notice between IPv4 and IPv6 is the format and size of the IP address. IPv6 addresses are 128 bits (IPv4 is 32 bits) and typically written as eight groups of four hex characters. IPv4 as you saw earlier is four decimal representations of 8 bits. Each of the eight groups of characters is separated by a colon. An example of a valid IPv6 address is 2001:4860:0000:0000:0012:10FF:FECD:00EF.

Leading zeroes can be omitted, so we can write our example address as 2001:4860:0:0:12:10FF:FECD:EF. Additionally, a double colon can be used to compress a set of consecutive zeroes, so we can write our example address as 2001:4860::12:10FF:FECD:EF. The IPv6 address is 128 bits; when you see a double colon, it's a variable that says fill enough zeros within the colons to make the address 128 bits. You can only have one set of double colon — two variables in one address is not going to work.

Will we see IPv6 take over the Global Address space soon? Even with IPv4's lack of address space, we are going to continue to use it for many years. The integration of IPv6 into the infrastructure is going to happen as a joint venture, with IPv4 and IPv6 running at the same time in the devices and on some networks.

There are many mechanisms for enabling IPv6 communications over an IPv4 network, including the following:

♦ Dual Stack, which involves a computer or device running both the IPv4 and IPv6 protocol stacks at the same time

♦ ISATAP (Intra-Site Automatic Tunnel Addressing Protocol)

♦ 6to4, which is an encapsulation technique for putting IPv6 addresses inside IPv4 addresses

♦ Toredo Tunneling, which is another encapsulation technique for putting IPv6 traffic inside an IPv4 packet

Some IPv6-to-IPv4 dynamic translation techniques require that a computer's IPv4 address be used as the last 32 bits of the IPv6 address. When these translation techniques are used, it is common to write the last 32 bits as you would typically write an IPv4 address, such as 2001:4850::F8:192.168.122.26.

TESTING IP CONFIGURATION

After you have installed and configured the TCP/IP settings, you can test the IP configuration using the `ipconfig`, `ping`, and `nbtstat` commands. These commands are also useful in troubleshooting IP configuration errors. You can graphically view connection details through the Local Area Connection Status of the Network And Sharing Center.

Using the `ipconfig` Command

The `ipconfig` command displays your IP configuration. Table 11.5 lists the command switches that you can use with the `ipconfig` command.

TABLE 11.5:   ipconfig Switches

SWITCH	DESCRIPTION
/?	Shows all of the help options for ipconfig
/all	Shows verbose information about your IP configuration, including your computer's physical address, the DNS server you are using, and whether you are using DHCP
/allcompartments	Shows IP information for all compartments
/release	Releases an IPv4 address that has been assigned through DHCP
/release6	Releases an IPv6 address that has been assigned through DHCP
/renew	Renews an IPv4 address through DHCP
/renew6	Renews an IPv6 address through DHCP
/flushdns	Purges the DNS Resolver cache
/registerdns	Refreshes DHCP leases and re-registers DNS names
/displaydns	Displays the contents of the DNS Resolver Cache
/showclassid	Lists the DHCP class IDs allowed by the computer
/setclassID	Allows you to modify the DHCP class ID

Perform the following steps to use ipconfig to view your IP address configuration:

1. Select Start and type **cmd** into the Start menu's search box or choose Start ➤ All Programs ➤ Accessories ➤ Command Prompt.

2. In the Command Prompt dialog window, type **ipconfig** and press Enter. Note the IPv4 address as well as the IPv6 address.

3. In the Command Prompt dialog box, type **ipconfig /all** and press Enter. You now see more information such as the Ethernet address, IPv6 tunnel parameters, and their interface identifiers. Close the Command Prompt window when you have finished viewing the information by typing **exit** or closing the window.

Using the ping Command

The ping command is useful for verifying connectivity between two IP devices. The command sends an Internet Control Message Protocol (ICMP) Echo Request message to a remote machine and receives an ICMP Echo Reply message back if the remote device is able to respond.

You can ping a computer based on the computer's IPv4 address, IPv6 address, hostname (DNS resolves), or NetBIOS name (WINS resolves). The following list shows examples of `ping`:

- `ping 131.107.1.200`
- `ping 2001:4860::12:10FF:FECD:EF`
- `ping www.google.com`
- `ping windows7-pc-1`

If you are having trouble connecting to a host on another network, `ping` could help you verify that a valid communication path exists. You might ping the following addresses:

- The IPv4 loopback address, 127.0.0.1
- The IPv6 loopback address, ::1
- The local computer's IP address
- The local router's (default gateway's) IP address
- The remote computer's IP address

If `ping` failed to get a reply from any of these addresses, you would have a starting point for troubleshooting the connection error. The error messages that can be returned from a ping request include the following:

Request Timed Out   Means that the Echo Reply message was not received from the destination computer within the time allotted. By default, destination computers have 4 seconds to respond.

TTL Expired In Transit   Means the packet exceeded the number of hops specified to reach the destination device. Each time a packet passes through a router, the Time To Live (TTL) counter is decremented and reflects the pass through the router as a hop. If the TTL reaches 0, this message is returned.

Destination Host Unreachable   Generated when a local or remote route path does not exist between the sending host and the specified destination computer. This error could occur because the router is misconfigured or the target computer is not available.

Ping Request Could Not Find Host   Indicates the destination hostname couldn't be resolved. You should verify the destination hostname was properly specified, that all DNS and WINS settings are correct, and that the DNS and WINS servers are available.

Using the nbtstat Command

NBT is NetBIOS over TCP/IP, and the `nbtstat` command is used to display TCP/IP connection protocol statistics over NBT. Table 11.6 lists the command-line options that you can use.

TCP/IP Troubleshooting

If you are having trouble connecting to network resources, you might want to check the following:

- If you can access resources on your local subnet but not on a remote subnet, you should check the default gateway settings on your computer. Pinging a remote host and receiving a Destination Unreachable message is also related to default gateway misconfiguration.

◆ If you can access some but not all resources on your local subnet or remote subnet, you should check your subnet mask settings, the wiring to those resources, or the devices between your computer and those resources.

◆ Use the `ipconfig` command to ensure you are not configured with an APIPA address. If so, determine why you are not receiving IP settings from your DHCP server.

◆ If you can access a resource (for example, by pinging a computer) by IP address, but not by name, you should check the DNS settings on your computer.

TABLE 11.6:   `nbtstat` Command-Line Options

SWITCH	OPTION	DESCRIPTION
`/?`	Help	Shows all of the help options for `nbtstat`
`-a`	adapter Status	Shows adapter status and lists the remote computer's name, based on the hostname you specify
`-A`	Adapter Status	Shows adapter status and lists the remote computer's name, based on the IP address you specify
`-c`	cache	Displays the NBT cache of remote computers through their names and IP addresses
`-n`	names	Shows a list of the local computer's NetBIOS names
`-r`	resolved	Shows a list of computer names that have been resolved through either broadcast or WINS
`-R`	Reload	Causes the NBT remote cache name table to be purged and reloaded (must be logged on as an administrator with privilege elevation)
`-S`	Sessions	Shows the current sessions table with the destination IP addresses
`-s`	sessions	Shows the current sessions table and the converted destination IP address to the computer's NetBIOS name
`-RR`	Release Refresh	Sends a Name Release packet to the WINS server and then starts a refresh

The Bottom Line

Set up hardware to provide network connectivity.   After installing a new piece of hardware into Windows 7, the operating system goes through a process of discovery and installation. This goes smoothly most of the time, although occasionally, you must step in as the administrator and correct an issue.

    Master It   You have just installed a new network adapter into one of your Windows 7 machines. The operating system discovered the new device and installed the driver, but the adapter doesn't work. You checked Device Manager and the network adapter appears to have been installed with a generic network adapter driver. You have a disk with the correct driver for Windows 7. How do you install a network adapter driver from a disk supplied by the hardware vendor to allow Windows 7 to use the NIC to connect to the network?

Connect to network devices. Windows 7 offers many enhancements for administrators to connect to network devices. One option that can make implementation easier is to connect to a network capable projector.

Master It One of your training rooms has a new overhead projector that has the capability of being connected to the network and displaying information from the connection. Tim, the instructor, just received a new machine in the classroom running Windows 7 and has asked you to configure the machine to use the network projector to present his PowerPoint presentations. The projector has an IP address of 172.25.2.100. How will you set up a network projector option in Windows 7 to allow PowerPoint to display using the current network infrastructure rather than a video cable in your classroom?

Set up peer-to-peer networking. Having the ability to share resources has been one of Windows' main features since network capability was added to the operating system. Each release of Windows has added new or enhanced functionality to peer-to-peer networking and Windows 7 is no exception with the addition of HomeGroups.

Master It How can you use the HomeGroup functionality in Windows 7 to allow users in the remote office to share file and printer resources with each other.

Configure network protocols. In order to allow machines to communicate through a network, network protocols must be installed and configured on each device. As administrators, we can use dynamic methods to configure our users machines, but sometimes we may need to manually configure the network protocol.

Master It As a network administrator, you are responsible for ensuring users have a proper network configuration to access the network. Your network is setup for DHCP for the client machines. One of your users currently set up as a DHCP client needs to have a static IP address due to the use of a specific application. How do you configure a Windows 7 client machine that is set up as a DHCP client to have a Static IPv4 address of 172.16.1.50 with a subnet mask of 255.255.255.0 and a default gateway of 172.16.1.1?

Chapter 12

Networking with Windows Server 2008

In most organizations, Windows 7 will be a member of a domain, so it is important to know how to properly configure it in a domain environment.

In this chapter we discuss peer-to-peer networks and the advantages and disadvantages of this network model. We will also look at Windows Server 2008 domain-based networks using Active Directory and how to configure Windows 7 to work within the Windows Server 2008 domain environment.

Another technology that we will discuss is Windows Server 2008 Hyper-V, Microsoft's newest version of virtualization. Virtualization, one of the fastest-growing and hottest technologies to hit the market in the past few years, has started to make an impact due to its vast economic advantages. Virtualization gives an organization the ability to run multiple operating systems, called virtual machines, on a single machine. The ability to run multiple operating systems on a single machine can help an organization reduce their hardware costs and allow an organization to reduce their IT department overhead. We show you how to turn Windows 7 into a virtual machine that can run on Hyper-V or Microsoft Virtual PC.

In this chapter, you'll learn how to:

♦ Connect Windows 7 to the domain

♦ Configure Hyper-V

♦ Use Microsoft Virtual PC

Understanding Networking

The first thing that we have to discuss is Microsoft's network model types. Because this book is geared toward administrators, this might be a refresher for some, but many administrators do not do work on servers. So this chapter will be useful either way.

The way you design your network determines how you set up the rest of the computers and servers on your network. The choice you make here is going to be determined by many factors. The number of users on your network or the amount of money you can spend helps determine your network design. Microsoft uses two networking models: peer-to-peer networks and domain-based networks.

The Windows Peer-to-Peer Network Model

Let's begin with the peer-to-peer model. When you set up a Windows peer-to-peer network (also referred to as a workgroup network), it is important to understand that all computers on the network are equal. All of the peer-to-peer computers, also referred to as nodes, simultaneously act as both clients and servers.

This can be an advantage for small networks that have 10 or fewer users. It allows a small network to share resources without the need of a costly server. In addition, it enables a small company to have a network setup without hiring an internal IT department.

Peer-to-peer networks are no more than Windows XP, Windows Vista, and Windows 7 machines connected by a centralized connection like a router or hub, as shown in Figure 12.1.

FIGURE 12.1

The peer-to-peer model

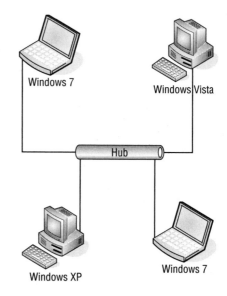

Windows 7

Windows Vista

Hub

Windows XP

Windows 7

WINDOWS NETWORKING

To learn more about Windows peer-to-peer networks, see *MCTS: Windows Server 2008 Network Infrastructure Configuration Study Guide: Exam 70-642*, by William Panek, Tylor Wentworth, and James Chellis (Sybex, 2008).

One of the biggest debates among IT professionals is when to use a peer-to-peer network. These types of networks have their place in the networking world. Most of you at home use this type of network. All computers connect using a small Internet router.

Well, it's the same for companies. You would use this network in a small environment with 10 or fewer users. This allows small organizations to share resources without the need of expensive equipment or server software.

But just like everything that is good, there is a downside to peer-to-peer networks. The biggest downside is manageability. Many new IT people like working on a small peer-to-peer network because of its size, but in fact a network with 10 users and 10 computers can be difficult to manage.

Because there is no server to centralize user accounts, each Microsoft Windows XP or Vista computer must have a user account and a password. So if you have 10 users with 10 computers and all 10 users must be able to access all 10 computers, you end up creating 100 accounts.

Another disadvantage to peer-to-peer networks is backups. Most IT departments do not back up individual user machines, and because there is no centralized server for data storage, data recoverability can be an issue.

So now that you have seen the advantages and disadvantages of a peer-to-peer network, let's discuss the pros and cons of a domain-based network.

Windows Server 2008 Active Directory Network

A domain-based network is a network that uses Microsoft's *Active Directory*. Active Directory is a single, distributed database that contains all the objects within your network. Some of these objects are user accounts, group accounts, and published objects (folders and printers).

The first of many advantages to Active Directory is centralized management. As we just stated, the Active Directory database contains all the network information within a single, distributed data repository. Because these objects are all located in the same database, an administrator can easily manage the domain from one location.

Another major advantage to using Active Directory is domain security. An administrator has the advantage of creating a single username and password for all users within the domain. This password can be used to access all resources that an individual has the proper rights to access. An administrator can determine, based on job function or position, which files or folders a user can obtain. In our peer-to-peer example, you needed to create 100 accounts. Now with a domain, you need to create only 10 accounts.

An Active Directory structure is made up of one or more *domains*. A domain is a logical grouping of objects within your organization. For example, if we had the Stellacon.com domain, all users in that domain should be members of the Stellacon.com organization. The objects that are contained within a domain do not need to be in the same physical location. Domains can span the entire globe even though they are part of the same organization.

One of the advantages to using domains is the ability to have child domains. A child domain is a subdomain of another domain. You can build child domains based on physical locations, departments, and so forth. Figure 12.2 shows the hierarchy structure of Stellacon.com with its child domains (based on geographic location).

FIGURE 12.2
Domain structure

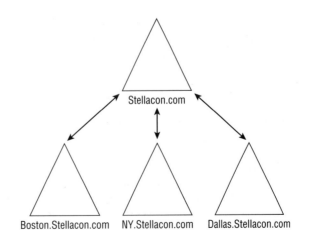

Stellacon.com

Boston.Stellacon.com   NY.Stellacon.com   Dallas.Stellacon.com

---

MICROSOFT DOMAINS

Microsoft domains are represented as triangles. It is important to remember that when looking at any Microsoft websites or white papers.

One of the benefits of creating child domains is scalability. Active Directory has the ability to store millions of objects within a single domain, but child domains give you the flexibility to design a structure layout that meets your organizational needs.

When setting up child domains, the parent and child domains already establish a *trust* relationship. *Trusts* allow users to be granted access to resources in a domain even when their accounts reside in a different domain. To make administration of trust relationships easier, Microsoft has made transitive two-way trusts the default relationship between domains. This means that, by default, all domains within the same forest automatically trust one another. As shown in Figure 12.2, Stellacon.com automatically trusts Boston.Stellacon.com, NY.Stellacon.com, and Dallas.Stellacon.com. This means that all child domains implicitly trust one another.

The last Active Directory advantage that we discuss is an extensible schema. The Active Directory schema is the attributes of the database. For example, when you create a new user using the Active Directory Users and Computers snap-in, the system asks you to fill in the user's first name, last name, username, password, and so forth. These fields are the attributes of Active Directory and that is the schema. An administrator has the ability to change or expand these fields based on organizational needs.

Real World Scenario

CHANGING THE SCHEMA

You may be asking yourself why an organization needs to change the schema. Many years ago, when I got out of the military and before I got into the computer industry, I used to cast toilets for American Standard. I made 50 toilets a day. When working for American Standard, I had an employee number of 343. All of my toilets used to get stamped 343 (so the company knew who made the product) on the bottom base of the toilet. My time card did not even have my name, just my number.

This would be an example of a field that would need to be added to your Active Directory schema. I would have an account in Active Directory with my name but there would need to be a field that showed my employee number. You might have to adjust your Active Directory schema based on your organizational requirements.

The major disadvantage to an Active Directory model is cost. When setting up an Active Directory domain, an organization needs a powerful enough machine to handle the Windows Server 2008 operating system. Also, most companies that decide to use a domain-based organization will require the IT personnel to manage and maintain the network infrastructure.

In the next section we look at some of the server terminology that we use in the remainder of this chapter.

Microsoft Networking Terms and Roles

The following are some networking terms and roles. You will be familiar with some of these terms, but it's always good to get a refresher.

Server   A server is a machine that users connect to so that they can access resources located on that machine. These resources can be files, printers, applications, and so forth. Usually the type of server is dependent on the resource that the user needs. For example, a print server is a server that controls printers. A file server is a server that contains files. Application servers can run applications for the users. Sometimes you will hear a server referred to by the specific application that it may be running, such as "That's our SQL server" or "That's our Exchange server."

Domain Controller   This server contains a replica of Active Directory. Active Directory is your database that contains all the objects in your network. A domain controller is a server that contains this database. Years ago (when we were using NT 3.51 and NT 4.0), we had to have a Primary Domain Controller (PDC) as well as Backup Domain Controllers (BDC), but that's not true today. All domain controllers are equal in a Windows Server 2008 network. Some domain controllers may contain extra roles, but they all have the same copy of Active Directory.

Member Server   A member server is a server that is a member of a domain-based network, but it does not contain a copy of Active Directory. For example, it is recommended that Exchange be loaded on a member server instead of a domain controller. Both domain controllers and member servers can act as file, print, or application servers. It just depends on whether or not you need that server to have a replica of Active Directory.

Stand Alone Server   A stand alone server is a server that is not a member of a domain. Many organizations might use this type of server for virtualization. For example, you load Windows Server 2008 with Microsoft's version of virtualization (Hyper-V) on a stand alone server. You can then create virtual machines that act as domain controllers to run the network.

Client Machine   A client machine is a computer that normally is used for your end users in a company. The most common operating systems for a client machine are Windows XP, Windows Vista, and Windows 7.

DNS Server   The *Domain Name Service (DNS)* server is a server that has the DNS service running on it. DNS is a name resolution service. DNS turns a host name into a TCP/IP address (forward lookup). DNS also has the ability to turn a TCP/IP address into a name (reverse lookup). When you install an operating system onto a computer, you assign that computer a hostname. The problem is that computers talk to each other using the TCP/IP protocol (example: 192.168.1.100). It would be difficult for most users to remember all the different TCP/IP addresses on a network. So normally you connect to a machine by using its hostname. DNS does the conversion of hostname to TCP/IP address for you.

The easiest way to understand how this works is to think of your phone number. If someone wants to call you and they don't have your telephone number, they call information. They give information your name and they get your phone number. Well, this is how a network works. DNS is information on your network. You give DNS a hostname and it returns a network telephone number (TCP/IP address). DNS is a requirement if you want to install Active Directory. You can install DNS before or during the Active Directory installation.

DHCP Server   A *Dynamic Host Configuration Protocol (DHCP)* server is the server that runs the DHCP service. DHCP is the server on the network that assigns TCP/IP information to your computers dynamically. Every computer needs three settings to operate properly (with the Internet and intranet): a TCP/IP number, a subnet mask, and a default gateway (router number). Your computers can get this minimum information two ways: manually (someone assigns the TCP/IP information) or dynamically (automatically installed). DHCP can assign more than just these three settings. DHCP can assign any TCP/IP configuration information (DNS server, WINS server, time servers, etc.).

In the previous section on DNS, we said that DNS was information on your network. Well, following this example, DHCP would be the phone company. DHCP is the component that assigns the telephone number (TCP/IP address).

Global Catalog   The Global Catalog is a database of all Active Directory objects without all the attributes. The Global Catalog is a partial representation of the Active Directory objects. Think of the Global Catalog as an index. If you needed to look something up in this Windows 7 book, you would go to the index and find what page you need to turn to. You would not just randomly look through the book for the information. This is what the Global Catalog does on your Active Directory domain. When you need to find a resource in the domain (user, published printer, and so forth), you can search the Global Catalog to find its location.

Domain controllers need to use a Global Catalog to help with user authentication. Global Catalogs are a requirement on an Active Directory domain. All domain controllers can be Global Catalogs, but this is not always a good practice. Your network should have at least two Global Catalogs for redundancy, but too many can cause too much Global Catalog replication traffic.

ACTIVE DIRECTORY NETWORK

To learn more about Microsoft Active Directory networks, see *MCTS: Windows Server 2008 Active Directory Configuration Study Guide: Exam 70-640*, by William Panek and James Chellis (Sybex, 2008).

In the next section, we'll discuss the Windows Server 2008 operating system.

New Microsoft Windows 2008 Server Features

Microsoft Windows Server 2008 is the latest release of Microsoft's server operating systems. It is important to understand Windows Server 2008 and also how to install the operating system. There are many new and upgraded features in Windows Server 2008. In this section, we will show you the different versions of Microsoft Windows Server 2008 and some of the new features of Windows Server 2008.

Hyper-V   Hyper-V allows an organization to create and manage virtualized server environments. This is a new feature of Windows Server 2008 64-bit edition. We discuss Hyper-V in detail in the section "Understanding Virtualization," later in this chapter.

AD Rights Management Services (AD RMS)   Active Directory Rights Management Service (AD RMS) is included with Windows Server 2008. AD RMS gives network users or administrators the ability to determine the access level (open, read, modify, and so forth) they would like to assign to other users in an organization. By using Microsoft Office 2003 Professional or Microsoft Office 2007, users can secure email messages, internal websites, and documents.

The advantage to AD RMS is that any user can secure confidential or critical company information. To use AD RMS, an AD RMS client is required. The AD RMS client is included with Windows Vista and Windows 7 by default.

Server Manager Windows Server 2008 has included a new single-source utility for installing, configuring, and managing roles on a server, as shown in Figure 12.3. *Server Manager* displays server status and system information, and also identifies problems with server roles.

FIGURE 12.3
Server Manager

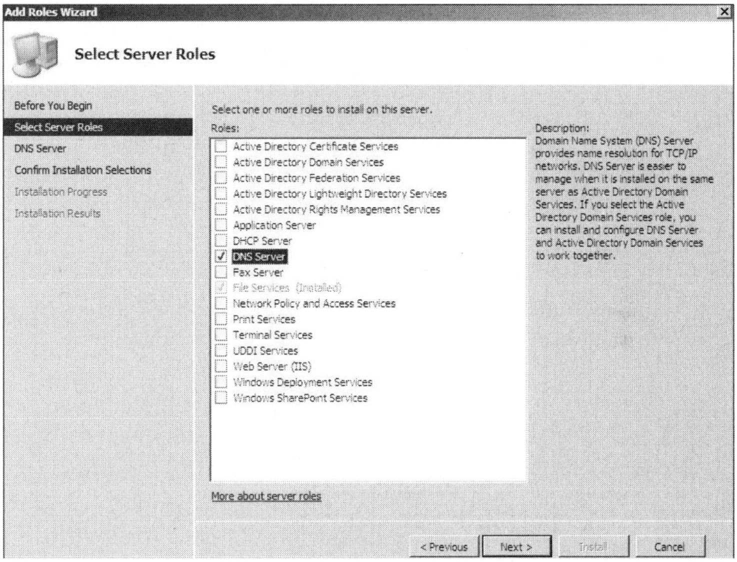

Server Manager has replaced several features that had been included with Windows Server 2003. These replaced features include Manage Your Server, Configure Your Server, and Add or Remove Windows Components.

An issue that you face when deploying servers is the need to run the Security Configuration Wizard. Server Manager, by default, allows you to deploy servers without running the Security Configuration Wizard because Server Manager server roles are configured with Microsoft-recommended security settings.

Network Access Protection (NAP) Windows Server 2008 has a new security feature called Network Access Protection (NAP). You can use NAP to define network access, based on client requirements. The advantage of using NAP is that you can define this access at the granular level. NAP also gives you the ability to allow network access based on compliancy with corporate governance policies. Here's a list of some of the new features associated with NAP:

◆ Network layer protection

◆ DHCP enforcement

◆ VPN enforcement

◆ IPSec enforcement

◆ 802.1X enforcement

◆ Flexible host isolation

Read-Only Domain Controllers (RODC) Windows Server 2008 introduced a new type of secure domain controller called a *read-only domain controller (RODC)*. A read-only domain controller is a noneditable copy of Active Directory. This allows an organization to place a domain controller in an area or off-site location that does not have much physical security.

All domain controllers are equal. They all have the same version of Active Directory. This is also true with a read-only domain controller. Replication between domain controllers is bidirectional (replication happens both ways) except for the use of read-only domain controllers. Replication traffic between domain controllers and RODCs is unidirectional. Other domain controllers have the ability to talk to the RODC but the RODC does not have the ability to talk to other domain controllers.

An advantage to using an RODC in a nonsecure location is that an organization can give a normal user the right to administer and maintain the RODC. This user would not require domain administrator rights. They would be allowed to have the administrator role for the one RODC only. This concept is known as Administrator role separation.

Server Core Installation Another feature new to Microsoft servers is the Server Core installation, which allows you to install Windows Server 2008 with minimal options. Server Core is a low-maintenance version of Windows Server 2008 and has limited functionality.

Windows Server 2008 Server Core has no graphical user interface (GUI) utilities. All commands have to be issued through the use of a command prompt. If you have been in the industry long enough, think of UNIX or Cisco. You must know the command-line utilities to maintain the server. This is a great security feature.

Think of a normal server. If you want to add or modify a user, you go to Active Directory Users and Computers (domain based) or Computer Management for workstations or nondomain servers. Once in the application, you can do what's needed. The problem with this is that it is easy to do. If any user gets into your server room, it may be easy for them to do damage to your network. In a Server Core environment, just as we stated, there are no GUI snap-ins. If they don't know the command-line utilities, they can't make changes.

Server Core is an installation option that allows you to set up only limited server roles: DNS, DHCP, File Server, Active Directory, Media Services, and Hyper-V. For many organizations, this is going to be the way you set up Hyper-V, discussed in the "Understanding Virtualization" section of this chapter. This gives you extra security for your Hyper-V environment. By installing Server Core, you automatically create the following limitations:

◆ There is no Windows shell and limited GUI functionality (the Server Core interface is a command prompt).

◆ There is no managed code support in Server Core (all code must be native Windows API code).

◆ Microsoft Installer Package (MSI) support is limited to unattend mode only.

There are multiple editions of Windows Server 2008. Each edition has its specific uses. Table 12.1, taken from Microsoft's website at `www.microsoft.com/windowsserver2008/en/us/r2-compare-roles.aspx`, it shows the new and upgraded features included with Windows Server 2008 R2 (R2 is the latest release of Windows Server 2008) and which edition of Microsoft Windows Server 2008 R2 is required to use the new or upgraded features.

TABLE 12.1:   Server Editions Comparison

SERVER ROLE	ENTERPRISE	DATACENTER	STANDARD	ITANIUM	WEB
Active Directory Certificate Services	X	X	X[1]		
Active Directory Domain Services	X	X	X		
Active Directory Federation Services	X	X			
Active Directory Lightweight Directory Services	X	X	X		
Active Directory Rights Management Services	X	X	X		
Application Server	X	X	X	X	
DHCP Server	X	X	X		
DNS Server	X	X	X		X
Fax Server	X	X	X		
File Services	X	X	X[2]		
Hyper-V	X	X	X		
Network Policy and Access Services	X	X	X[3]		
Print and Document Services	X	X	X		
Remote Desktop Services	X	X	X[4]		
Web Services (IIS)	X	X	X	X	X
Windows Deployment Services	X	X	X		
Windows Server Update Services (WSUS)	X	X	X		

[1] *Limited to creating Certificate Authorities — no other ADCS features (NDES, Online Responder Service). See ADCS role documentation on TechNet for more information.*
[2] *Limited to one standalone DFS root.*
[3] *Limited to 250 RRAS connections, 50 IAS connections, and 2 IAS Server Groups.*
[4] *Limited to 250 Remote Desktop Services connections.*

In the next section, we look at the requirements that are needed to install Windows Server 2008.

Requirements for Windows Server 2008 Installation

Now that you have seen the benefits of Windows Server 2008, let's look at the requirements you need to install Windows Server 2008. If you are wondering why we are covering Windows Server 2008 requirements in a Windows 7 book, it's because Windows 7 will be installed on Windows Server 2008 domains.

This chapter walks you through the installation of Active Directory and then shows you how to add a Windows 7 machine to the domain. Because many readers have not switched to Windows Server 2008, it will help with the Active Directory installation.

Table 12.2, taken directly from Microsoft's website, it shows both the minimum and recommended requirements. I have been an IT manager and consultant for many years and from personal experience, I would only use the recommended requirements or higher.

TABLE 12.2:   Microsoft Windows Server 2008 Installation Requirements

COMPONENT	REQUIREMENT
Processor	◆ Minimum: 1 GHz (x86 processor) or 1.4 GHz (x64 processor) ◆ Recommended: 2 GHz or faster Note: An Intel Itanium 2 processor is required for Windows Server 2008 for Itanium-based systems.
Memory	◆ Minimum: 512 MB of RAM ◆ Recommended: 2 GB of RAM or greater ◆ Maximum (32-bit systems): 4 GB (Standard) or 64 GB (Enterprise and Datacenter) ◆ Maximum (64-bit systems): 32 GB (Standard) or 2 TB (Enterprise, Datacenter, and Itanium-based systems)
Available disk space	◆ Minimum: 32 GB ◆ Recommended: 40 GB or greater Note: Computers with more than 16 GB of RAM will require more disk space for paging, hibernation, and dump files.
Drive	DVD-ROM drive
Display and peripherals	◆ Super VGA (800×600) or higher-resolution monitor ◆ Keyboard ◆ Microsoft mouse or compatible pointing device

The minimum requirements will allow the Windows Server 2008 operation system to install, but it will not be practical for any real-world situation. To make sure the requirements have not changed, visit Microsoft's website at www.microsoft.com/windowsserver2008/en/us/system-requirements.aspx.

One nice feature that Microsoft gives you is that if anyone is interested in evaluating Windows Server 2008, you can do so for no cost. When evaluating Windows Server 2008, the installation does not require a product activation or product key. Any Microsoft Windows Server product can be installed without activating the software for 60 days.

But let's say at the end of the 60 days you still need more time to finish your evaluation. You may reset your evaluation three more times (60 days each). This will allow you to evaluate the product for up to 240 days. At the end of the 240 days, the Windows Server 2008 product will need to be uninstalled or a valid product key and activation will be required.

Installing Windows Server 2008

Now that we have seen the benefits, editions, and requirements of Windows Server 2008, let's go ahead and install the product.

INSTALLING WINDOWS SERVER 2008

If you have already installed Windows Server 2008, you can skip the following steps. Just make sure that Windows Server 2008 64-bit version was the version installed. Hyper-V (discussed in the "Understanding Microsoft's Hyper-V Technology" section later in this chapter) must be run on a 64-bit version of Server 2008. If you have a 32-bit version of Windows Server 2008, complete the steps with a 64-bit Windows Server 2008 R2 version.

Perform the following steps to walk through installing Windows Server 2008 Enterprise Edition. If you do not have Windows Server 2008 Enterprise, download a trial version at Microsoft's website: www.microsoft.com/downloads.

1. Insert the Windows Server 2008 64-bit edition CD into the CD-ROM drive and reboot the machine. Make sure the computer can boot off the CD-ROM drive.

2. A window shows that files are loading onto the machine. After this screen finishes, another screen appears that asks you to specify your Language, Time, and Keyboard settings. Choose the settings that fit your system (normally just left at the defaults for US residents). Click Next.

3. At the Install Windows screen, click the Install Now arrow.

4. The next screen asks which version of Windows Server 2008 you would like to install. The choices you see might not be the same as the graphic (depending on the CD you have). Choose Windows Server 2008 Enterprise (Full Installation) and click Next. If you do not have Enterprise Edition, choose Standard (Full Installation).

5. At the License Terms screen, after reading the license select the I Accept The License Terms check box and click Next.

6. At the Which Type Of Installation Do You Want? screen, choose Custom (Advanced).

7. When the Where Do You Want To Install Windows? screen appears, choose the hard drive where you would like to install the operating system. Click Next.

8. The Installing Windows screen appears that shows the status of your install. Reboot after the install completes.

9. After you reboot, the system asks you to change the Administrator password at first login. Click OK and then enter and reenter the password **P@ssw0rd**. Click the arrow to the right of the password boxes.

10. When the Password Has Been Changed screen appears, click OK.

Now that you have installed the 64-bit version of Windows Server 2008 Enterprise Edition, perform the following steps to install Active Directory. Do not follow these steps if you are on a live network.

Perform the following steps in a test environment:

1. To install Active Directory, start the Active Directory Installation Wizard by clicking Start and typing **dcpromo in the Start Search box**. Press the Enter key.

2. When the Welcome screen appears, select Use Advanced Mode Installation and then click Next.

3. At the Operating System Compatibility screen, click Next.

4. The Choose A Deployment Configuration screen appears. Choose the second option, Create A New Domain In A New Forest. Then click Next.

5. The Name The Forest Root screen appears and asks you to enter the Full DNS name of your domain. For example, you can type **mycompany.com**. Enter your domain DNS name and click Next (use **mycompany.com** if you do not have a domain name).

6. After the DNS name is verified, a NetBIOS name box will appear with your default NetBIOS name (example: mycompany). A NetBIOS name can be up to 15 characters. To make it easier to remember and type the name, you should limit yourself to the English alphabet characters and numbers. Leave the default and click Next.

7. The Set Forest Function Level screen appears. Use the pull-down menu and choose Windows Server 2003 or Windows Server 2008 and click Next.

8. The Additional options screen appears next. Make sure DNS is checked (DNS is a requirement for Active Directory). Click Next.

9. A TCP/IP Static IP screen may appear. If it doesn't, go on to the next step. If the box does appear, choose the first option, Yes, and then make sure you configure a static IP address for your computer.

10. At the Database And Log Folders screen, you specify the file system locations for the Active Directory database and log file.

11. Accept the defaults and click Next.

12. At the Directory Services Restore Mode Administrator Password screen, provide a Directory Services Restore Mode Administrator password. This password is used to restore Active Directory in the event of its loss or corruption. This password does not have to correspond with passwords set for any other account. For now, make the password **P@ssw0rd**.

13. After you confirm the password, click Next.

14. The Active Directory Installation Wizard presents a summary of the installation options you've selected. Click Next to begin the Active Directory installation process. As Active

Directory is installing, you'll see a small window containing a graphic of a book that is being written to.

15. After you install Active Directory, you are prompted to reboot the system. After the reboot, you can access the administrative tools that are related to the configuration and management of Active Directory.

After the Active Directory database is installed, you need to verify the installation by clicking Start ➢ Administrative Tools ➢ Active Directory Users And Computers. If Active directory opens properly, then you completed the Active Directory installation correctly.

Perform the following steps to create a new user account in Active Directory:

1. From the Windows Server 2008 machine, click Start ➢ Administrative Tools ➢ Active Directory Users And Computers.

2. Expand the domain and right-click the Users OU. Choose New ➢ User.

3. Create a new user using your information. You will log on as this user in the next section.

In the next section, we show you how to add a Windows 7 machine to the Active Directory domain.

Adding Windows 7 to the Domain Environment

In a corporate environment, the client machines (Windows XP, Windows Vista, and Windows 7) will be connected to the domain environment. There are two ways to connect the Windows 7 machine to the domain. You can connect the Windows 7 machine to the domain from the Windows 7 operating system or from Active Directory.

It does not matter which way you choose to connect the machine to the domain. We usually connect the Windows 7 machine through the Windows operating system, but either way does the same task.

Having the Windows 7 machine on the domain offers many benefits to administration, such as the following:

◆ You can deploy Group Policy Objects (GPOs) from one location instead of Local Group Policy Objects (LGPOs) on each machine (see Chapter 9, "Managing Security").

◆ Users can back up their data to a server. This way, the nightly backups cover user information. Most Windows 7 machines will *not* be backed up separately.

◆ You can manage users and groups from one central location (Active Directory) instead of on each Windows 7 machine.

◆ You can manage security to resources on servers instead of resources on each Windows 7 machine.

Perform the following steps to connect a Windows 7 machine to a Windows Server 2008 domain:

1. On the Windows 7 machine, click Start and then right-click Computer. Choose Properties from the context menu.

2. In the Computer Name, Domain, And Workgroup section, click the Change Settings link.

3. Click the Change button next to the To Rename This Computer Or Change Its Domain Or Workgroup section.

4. In the Member Of section, click the Domain radio button and type the name of the Windows Server 2008 domain previously created, as shown in Figure 12.4.

FIGURE 12.4
Changing a workgroup
machine to a domain

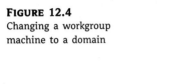

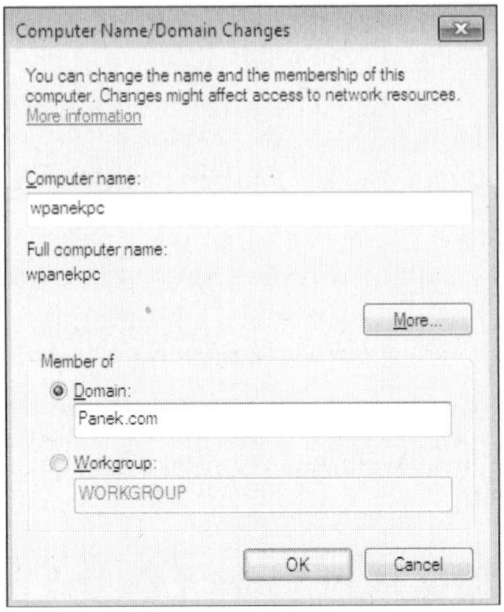

5. A Credentials dialog box appears that asks for the administrator's username and password. Enter the Administrators username and password and then click OK.

6. A dialog box stating that you are part of the domain appears. Click OK and reboot the machine.

7. From the Windows 7 machine, log onto the domain with your username and password.

You also have the ability to create the computer account in the Active Directory Users and Computers MMC snap-in.

Perform the following steps to add the Windows 7 machine to the domain from the Active Directory snap-in:

1. From the Windows Server 2008 machine, click Start ➢ Administrative Tools ➢ Active Directory Users And Computers.

2. Expand the domain and right-click the Computers OU. Choose New ➢ Computer.

3. In the Computer Name field, type the name of the Windows 7 computer. Click OK.

4. Double-click the new Windows 7 computer in the right-hand window to open its properties.

5. Take a look at the different tabs and then click the Cancel button.

In the next section, we look at one of the most exciting technologies to hit the market in a long time: virtualization.

Understanding Virtualization

Server virtualization gives an organization the ability to run multiple operating systems, called virtual machines, on a single machine. The ability to run multiple operating systems on a single machine will help an organization reduce their hardware costs and allow an organization to reduce their IT department overhead.

Many organizations have started to move their servers over to virtualized servers. But you do not need to just use virtualization for your servers. You can also use virtualization for client operating systems like Windows 7. In this section, we look at the two of the most common ways to use Microsoft products to virtually set up Windows 7. We also examine Microsoft's Virtual PC and Hyper-V. Microsoft has just released a new version of virtualization, called Hyper-V, with the Windows Server 2008 operating system and that's where we'll start.

Understanding Microsoft's Hyper-V Technology

Hyper-V is not Microsoft's first attempt at virtualization. Microsoft has been doing virtualization for years. There were two versions of virtualization that IT teams have used in the past. The two Microsoft virtualization products that you might have used before are Microsoft Virtual PC and Microsoft Virtual Server 2005.

Microsoft *Hyper-V* is the next-generation hypervisor-based virtualization technology. The Windows hypervisor is a thin layer of software that sits between the hardware and the Windows Server 2008 operating system. This thin layer allows one physical machine to run multiple operating systems in different Hyper-V virtual machines all at the same time. The hypervisor is the mechanism that is responsible for maintaining isolation between the different Hyper-V partitions.

With the release of Microsoft Windows Server 2008, Microsoft has now incorporated server virtualization into the operating system with the release of Hyper-V. This gives an organization the ability to take full advantage of the next generation of 64-bit server hardware.

Let's imagine an IT department for any size organization. You come in one morning before everyone else (common in our field) and see that one of your servers has crashed. The first thing that's going to happen is your heart drops into your stomach. After that, you start trying to fix the error and you might need to even rebuild the machine. Now your heart is racing and your blood pressure is going through the roof because you need to get this server up and running before anyone else comes into work. We have all been there before.

Now let's imagine the same situation but all of our servers are running Hyper-V. When you come in and see your crash, you know you can relax. All you need to do is move the Hyper-V virtual machine to another machine and you are back up and running. This is what Hyper-V can do for you. Hyper-v is a role-based feature that allows an organization to have multiple virtual machines (multiple operating systems, including Windows 7) on a single Windows Server 2008 machine.

A *virtual machine (VM)* is an implementation of an operating system that runs in its own virtualization window. The advantage to using virtual machines is that you can have multiple VMs on the same Windows Server 2008 machine. Each VM can have its own unique resources running on its operating system. An administrator can now run multiple operating systems (including non-Windows-based systems) or run multiple server roles in their own virtual machines, thus allowing an organization more flexibility without the need for more servers.

One of the greatest advantages of Hyper-V technology is that you have the ability to run both 32-bit and 64-bit applications within the virtual environment. Let's take a look at some more benefits of running Hyper-V.

BENEFITS OF HYPER-V

Microsoft's Hyper-V is a virtualization platform that gives you the ability to manage all your physical and virtual resources from a single set of integrated management utilities. Microsoft's Hyper-V can help an organization with all of the following:

Server Consolidation This is one of the major benefits that Hyper-V offers. Server consolidation allows an organization to run many versions of server (even non-Microsoft versions) on a single box. Each one of these versions is isolated from the other versions running on the same machine. This allows an organization to have a lower total cost of ownership (TCO) while maintaining all the services and servers that are required to make the network operate properly.

Downtime and Recoverability Two major concerns that all organizations face are downtime and recoverability. Downtime includes not only unscheduled events (such as machine errors or hardware failure) but also scheduled events like backups and maintenance. Microsoft's Hyper-V has many features like live backup that help reduce the server downtime for an organization.

Recoverability is also something that all IT staff members should be concerned about. Most organizations could not afford to lose their data and still stay in business. Disaster recoverability is supported by Hyper-V through clustering and backups, thus reducing downtime and saving an organization money.

Testing and Development One of the nice benefits of using Microsoft's Hyper-V is the ability to test or develop software in a safe virtual machine operating system. Any operating system, including Windows 7, can be used in a Hyper-V environment.

If you have been in this industry long enough, you have run into the situation of loading a service pack or utility and watching your system crash because of that install. By testing it in Hyper-V, an administrator can reduce the chances of network downtime on a live server.

Dynamic Datacenter Hyper-V virtualization allows you to design and create a dynamic network environment that not only addresses network problems but anticipates higher demands of network resources.

FEATURES OF HYPER-V

Now that you have seen some of the benefits of Microsoft Hyper-V, let's look at some of the new features included with Microsoft Hyper-V:

Symmetric Multiprocessors (SMP) Support Hyper-V allows a virtual machine environment to use up to four processors, allowing for SMP support.

New Architecture Design Hyper-V was designed to run on a 64-bit processor that allows an administrator to use many different types of devices. This 64-bit architecture also allows for better system performance.

Operating System Support   Hyper-V allows an organization to run both Microsoft and non-Microsoft operating systems (Windows, Linux, UNIX, etc.), giving an organization more flexibility. The operating systems can be both 32-bit and 64-bit versions.

Virtual Machine Migration   A nice feature of Hyper-V is the ability to migrate virtual machines from one server to another without long periods of downtime. Let's say that you have a server that is having hardware problems; you can switch the virtual machine to another server running Hyper-V without rebuilding the bad machine immediately.

Network Load Balancing   Hyper-V gives an organization the ability to use Network Load Balancing (NLB). The NLB can be placed across multiple virtual machines even if they are on different physical machines.

Hardware Architecture   With the new Hyper-V hardware architecture, all hardware resources in a virtual machine (disk, network card, RAM, and so forth) have access to those resources on the physical machine.

Scalability   Microsoft's Hyper-V gives an organization the ability to place large number of virtual machines on the same physical machine. This gives an organization the ability to grow a network without purchasing additional hardware.

Now that you understand the benefits and features of Hyper-V, in the next section we install Hyper-V.

INSTALLING HYPER-V ON WINDOWS SERVER 2008

When you install Hyper-V onto a server, you have two options for the way you install Hyper-V on a server:

♦ You can install Hyper-V onto a Windows Server 2008 machine that had a full operating system installation.

♦ You can install Hyper-V onto a Windows Server 2008 server core installation.

When you install Hyper-V on a full installation of Microsoft Windows Server 2008, you can enjoy the advantages of having the traditional full GUI. This makes it easier for you to manage, configure, and maintain Hyper-V and the Windows environment. This is also a much more comfortable environment for newer administrators who might not be familiar with a command line–driven operating system.

Because the Windows Server 2008 full installation has a GUI environment, installing Hyper-V becomes a much easier task. Windows Server 2008 includes a new feature called *Server Manager*. Server Manager is a Microsoft Management Console (MMC) snap-in that lets you view information about server configuration and the status of roles that are installed, and includes links for adding and removing features and roles.

The following is a list of some of the roles that you can install and manage by using Server Manager:

♦ Active Directory Certificate Services

♦ Active Directory Domain Services

♦ Active Directory Federation Services

- Active Directory Lightweight Directory Services
- Active Directory Rights Management Services
- Application Server
- Availability and Scalability
- DHCP Server
- DNS Server
- Fax Server
- File Services
- Hyper-V
- Network Policy and Access Services
- Print Services
- Streaming Media Services
- Terminal Services
- Troubleshooting
- UDDI Services
- Web Server
- Windows Deployment Services

Before Server Manager, Windows Server 2003 administrators had to use many utilities like Manage Your Server, Configure Your Server, and Add or Remove Windows Components to install sever roles and features. Server Manager allows you to manage your server's features and roles from one central utility.

Perform the following steps to install Hyper-V on a Windows Server 2008 machine:

1. Start the Server Manager application by clicking Start ➤ Administrative tools ➤ Server Manager.

2. In the left-side pane, click Roles.

3. In the right-hand pane, click the Add Roles link.

4. When the Before You Begin window appears, click Next.

5. At the Select Server Roles screen, click the Hyper-V check box and click Next.

6. At the Introduction To Hyper-V screen, click Next.

7. The Create Virtual Networks screen appears; click the check box for your network card and then click Next.

8. At the Confirm Installation Selections screen, click the Install button.

9. The Progress screen appears next and shows you the progress of the installation. After you reboot, you need to log in with the same user who started the process. After the Results screen appears, click Finish.

Now that we have just installed Microsoft Hyper-V, we want to verify that it is up and running. To do this, start the Hyper-V Manager.

Perform the following steps to verify that the Microsoft Hyper-V role was installed onto your machine:

1. Open the Hyper-V Manager by clicking Start ➢ Administrative Tools ➢ Hyper-V Manager.

2. In the left-hand window, click your server name under Microsoft Hyper-V Servers.

3. If there are no errors or messages, close Hyper-V Manager.

4. Verify that the Microsoft Hyper-V services are up and running properly by clicking Start ➢ Administrative Tools ➢ Services.

5. Scroll down and verify that there are two services running under Microsoft Hyper-V (Image Management Service and Network Management Service).

6. Close the Services snap-in.

In the next section, we install the Windows 7 operating system in Hyper-V as a virtual machine.

CREATING A HYPER-V WINDOWS 7 VIRTUAL MACHINE

A virtual machine is an operating system that is running within the Hyper-V virtual environment. You can run multiple virtual machines on the same physical machine. By placing multiple virtual machines on the same physical machine, Hyper-V allows you to maximize performance by utilizing hardware resources.

The hypervisor is a 64-bit mechanism that allows Hyper-V to run multiple virtual machines on the same physical machine. The hypervisor's job is to create and manage the partitions between virtual machines. The hypervisor is a thin software layer that sits between the virtual machines and the hardware.

Virtual machines are full operating systems that run in a virtualized environment. The end users who connect to the virtual machines cannot tell the difference between a normal machine and a virtualized machine. Because of this, you can set up your virtual machine environment the same way you would set up a normal machine.

Perform the following steps to install Windows 7 as a virtual machine on Hyper-V:

1. Start the Hyper-V Manager by clicking Start ➢ Administrative Tools ➢ Hyper-V Manager.

2. When the Hyper-V Manager starts, click the New ➢ Virtual Machine link in the Actions section.

3. Click Next at the Before You Begin screen.

4. At the Specify Name And Location screen, type **Win7VM** in the Name field. Leave the default location. Click Next.

5. At the Assign Memory screen, type **1024***MB* and click Next.

6. At the Configure Networking screen, choose your network adapter from the Connection Type drop-down list. Click Next.

7. At the Connect Virtual Hard Disk screen, click Create A New Virtual Hard Disk.

8. Type **Win7.vhd** and make the hard drive size 20 GB. Click Next.

9. At the Summary screen, check the "Start the virtual machine after it is created" check box and click Finish.

10. When the Win7VM starts, you receive a boot failure. Click the Media menu option. Click DVD Drive and then capture your DVD drive. Place the Windows 7 DVD into the media device. Then press Enter.

11. The Windows 7 installation should start. Install the Windows 7 Enterprise Edition as normal.

WINDOWS HYPER-V

To learn more about Microsoft Hyper-V, see *MCTS: Windows Server Virtualization Configuration Study Guide: Exam 70-652,* by William Panek (Wiley, 2008).

Now it might not be feasible to set up a Windows Server 2008 machine with Hyper-V to run Windows 7. So there is a better way for client operating systems: Microsoft Virtual PC.

Understanding Microsoft Virtual PC

Microsoft also has a virtualization environment that can operate on its client software called Virtual PC. Virtual PC allows you to create and manage virtual machines without the need of a server operating system. The advantage here is that you can run server operating systems in a client environment like Windows XP, Windows Vista, or Windows 7.

Virtual PC gives you the ability to set up virtualization on a client operating system. This is beneficial for anyone in the industry who has to do testing or configuration. Virtual PC is not really meant to run a network like Hyper-V, but it does give you the ability to test software and patches before installing them live on a network. Also, it is beneficial to research problems in a controlled environment and not on a live server where you can end up doing more damage than good.

Finally, Virtual PC gives you a training advantage. Think about having the ability to train users on a real product like Windows Server 2008 or Windows 7 without having to purchase additional equipment. Virtual PC allows you to train users on products and software while using only one machine.

🌐 Real World Scenario

USING VIRTUAL PC

As an instructor and as a consultant, I can't begin to explain how valuable Microsoft Virtual PC can be as a tool. I have used it on many occasions to either test a piece of software before installation or find an answer to a problem in a controlled environment.

At the time this book was written, I use Microsoft Windows Vista on my laptop. On that same laptop I have a version of Virtual PC with both Windows Server 2008 and Windows 7 operating system virtual machines.

While I am on a client site or while I am in the classroom, having a way to test and research problems using multiple operating systems on one client computer system is an invaluable resource.

To run Virtual PC, you need a minimum of a 400 MHz Pentium-compatible processor (1.0 GHz or faster recommended), that requires at least 35 MB of free disk space. You can load Virtual PC on Windows 7, Windows Vista with SP1 (Enterprise, Business, Ultimate), or Windows XP with SP3.

Perform the following steps to download and configure Virtual PC:

1. Download Microsoft Virtual PC (currently version 2007) at www.microsoft.com/windows/virtual-pc/download.aspx.

2. After the download completes, install the application on your system.

3. After the product installs, open the Virtual PC application by clicking Start ➢ All Programs ➢ Virtual PC.

4. When you start Virtual PC, the New Virtual Machine Wizard automatically appears. Click Next.

5. At the Options screen, click the Create A Virtual Machine radio button.

6. At the Virtual Machine Name And Location screen, type **VirtualWin7** and then click Next.

7. At the Operating System screen, choose Other from the drop-down list (we are going to install Windows 7 32-bit). Click Next.

8. At the Memory screen, choose the Adjust The RAM radio button and set it to 1024 (512 minimum if needed). Click Next.

9. At the Virtual Hard Disk screen, click the New Virtual Hard Disk radio button and click Next.

10. At the Virtual Hard Disk Name And Location screen, accept the default location and click Next. You can change the name or location if needed.

11. At the Completing The New Virtual Machine screen, verify the settings and click Finish.

12. The Virtual PC Console now shows the VirtualWin7 virtual machine. Click the virtual machine and choose Settings from the Actions menu.

13. The Settings for VirtualWin7 appear. You can change or verify your settings here for this virtual machine. Click CD/DVD Drive and verify that you are using the local DVD drive. Click OK.

14. Put the Windows 7 32-bit DVD in the physical drive. At the Virtual PC Console screen, click VirtualWin7 and click Start.

15. Install Windows 7 on the virtual machine. If for any reason the DVD does not get recognized, click the CD menu and choose the Use Physical CD option. Press Enter and finish the install.

16. After Windows 7 is installed, close the VirtualWin7 virtual machine and save the changes.

Now that we have created a Windows 7 virtual machine for Virtual PC, let's go ahead and start the Windows 7 operating system on the virtual PC.

Perform the following steps to run the Windows 7 virtual PC virtual machine:

1. Open Microsoft Virtual PC.

2. Click the Windows 7 machine (VirtualWin7) and click Start.

3. When Windows 7 starts, log in as normal.

VIRTUAL PC COMMANDS

To do a Ctrl+Alt+Del in Virtual PC, you can use Right Alt+Del. You can go into a full-screen mode by clicking Right Alt+Enter. Enter the same command to get out of full-screen mode. When you use the mouse within Virtual PC, to release the mouse and go back to the host machine, press the Right Alt key.

Implementing Windows 7 in a Virtual PC environment allows you to start testing and learning about the new operating system before implementing it in your organization. The one downside to Virtual PC is that at the time this book was written, Virtual PC does not support 64-bit operating systems. Make sure that all operating systems that you use in Virtual PC are 32-bit and check Microsoft's website for any changes.

Virtualization is a fast-growing technology that many IT departments have embraced. If you have not started using virtualization yet, start doing your homework now. Virtualization can save your organization money and downtime and make you look great as the IT person who implemented it.

The Bottom Line

Connect Windows 7 to the domain.   In almost all corporate environments, the client machines (Windows 7) will be connected to the domain environment. Having the Windows 7 machine on the domain offers many benefits, including:

◆ You can deploy GPOs from one location instead of LGPOs on each machine (see Chapter 9, "Managing Security").

◆ Users can back up their data to a server. This way, the nightly backups cover user information. Most Windows 7 machines will *not* be backed up separately.

◆ You can manage users and groups from one central location (Active Directory) instead of on each Windows 7 machine.

◆ You can manage security to resources on servers instead of resources on each Windows 7 machine.

Master It   You are the administrator of a large organization that has decided to implement the Windows 7 operating system on all machines. As you load Windows 7 onto the machines, you need to join them to the domain. How do you accomplish this goal?

Configure Hyper-V.   Microsoft *Hyper-V* is the next-generation hypervisor based virtualization technology. With the release of Microsoft Windows Server 2008, Microsoft has now incorporated server virtualization into the operating system with the release of Hyper-V. This gives an organization the ability to take full advantage of the next generation of 64-bit server hardware.

Master It   You are the administrator for a large computer company. You need to set up a machine that can run multiple versions of Windows 2008 and Windows 7 for testing and evaluation. What Microsoft server product would you install to solve this issue?

Use Microsoft Virtual PC.   Microsoft also has a virtualization environment that can operate on its client software called Virtual PC. Virtual PC allows you to create and manage virtual machines without the need of a server operating system. The advantage here is that you can run server operating systems in a client environment like Windows XP, Windows Vista, or Windows 7.

> **Master It**   You are asked by your organization to set up a training room. This training room will be required to run multiple operating systems, including Windows Server 2008, Windows Vista, and Windows 7. This solution is for training only. How can you implement the computers?

Chapter 13

Configuring Internet Explorer 8

Windows Internet Explorer (IE) has been the web browser for the Microsoft operating systems since its introduction as Internet Explorer version 1 in 1995. As the Internet and the World Wide Web have increased exponentially in both content and features, Microsoft has continually enhanced and added new functionality to their world-class browser up to the current version, Internet Explorer 8 (IE8).

With the increase in functionality and ease of use for the browsers, there has been an increase in the use of websites for providing content for end users in both the public space (Internet browsing) and private corporate browsing of resources. With the introduction of IE8, Microsoft has taken the usability end users desire to new levels, as well as providing a good deal of security enhancements to end users, giving the best and easiest browsing environment to the user sitting in front of their computer as well as providing a balance of security information about the sites and pages being viewed. IE8 tries to inform the user of potential issues through security enhancements while allowing administrators to enforce security with the least amount of inconvenience to the end users.

In this chapter, you'll learn how to:

◆ Use IE8 accelerators and Web Slices

◆ Configure Pop-up Blocker in IE8

◆ Use the InPrivate security feature of IE8

◆ Configure security for IE8

Overview of IE8

Windows IE8 is the latest web browser developed and released by Microsoft in the popular Internet Explorer series. IE8 was released in March 2009 and available to download for Windows XP and Server 2003 with at least SP2 in both the 32-bit and 64-bit operating systems. IE8 is available for Windows Vista and Server 2008 in both the 32-bit and 64-bit versions. It is also being shipped with Windows 7 (both 32 bit and 64 bit). IE8 is the successor to IE7, released in 2006. With the explosion of Internet use and even inexperienced end users browsing the Internet for personal reasons as well as browsing the Web for work-related tasks, enhancing the user interface (UI) while providing better levels of security (which include privacy) has been the focus in the development of IE8.

IE8 is loaded with new user features to provide end users with a better and simpler way to get the information they desire from their browsing experience.

Using New IE8 Features

The new features added to IE8 are designed to give the end user an easy way to browse the Internet for the information they're looking for while providing a secure environment for the network by recognizing potentially bad sites (those attempting to sneak viruses or Trojans into the network), phishing sites (those that attempt to steal private information about the user), or invasive sites that users may go to either on purpose or inadvertently. We will explore the security and safety features of IE8 later in this chapter.

Let's look at the user experience additions to IE8 first. Microsoft has added accelerators to give users a faster way to access online services; Web Slices, which let users see if parts of a website have changed that they might be watching, such as a stock quote; and Compatibility View, which ensures older web pages display appropriately in IE8.

Defining IE8 Accelerators

IE8 includes a new feature that allows you to gain access to Internet services with a click. By highlighting a word on a web page and clicking the accelerator icon, you have access to a various range of services by default and can add more accelerators if you desire. In Figure 13.1, you can see the word *cryptographic* highlighted and the accelerator icon selected. Click the accelerator icon to bring up a list of currently available services available.

FIGURE 13.1
Accelerator icon

The default set of accelerator services are shown in Figure 13.2 and are available to launch a web page to provide information about the selected text. In our example, let's search Bing for the term *cryptographic* by choosing Search With Bing.

Figure 13.2 shows the default set of accelerator services installed by default in IE8, but there are several more currently available and more to be available as time goes on. You add more accelerators from the same menu by selecting All Accelerators and then clicking Find More Accelerators, as shown in Figure 13.3.

Adding accelerators to your IE8 will certainly provide a more feature-rich and efficient browsing experience. Most of the time when browsing, a second browser or new tab is opened to do further research about the page you are currently viewing. Sometimes this is just for a quick look at a new piece of information or to look up something. If you're used to going to a certain page to find the "extra" information, this would be a great candidate to add to your accelerators.

FIGURE 13.2
Choosing the Search
With Bing accelerator

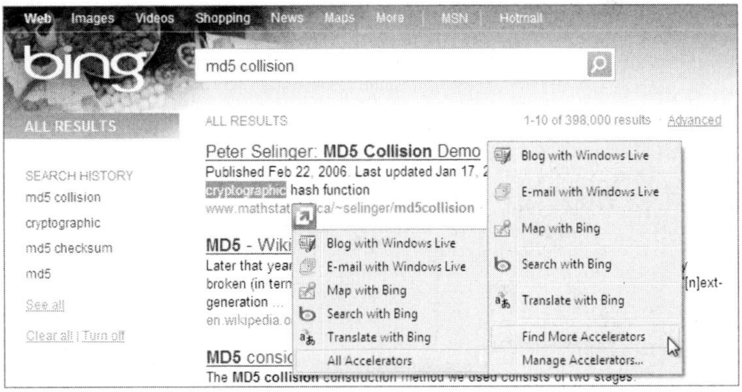

FIGURE 13.3
Clicking Find More
Accelerators

ADDING THE DEFINE WITH BING ACCELERATOR TO IE8

Perform the following steps to add an accelerator to IE8 from a currently open web page:

1. Open IE8 and open a web page.

2. Select a word or phrase and click the accelerator icon.

3. Choose All Accelerators, and then click Find More Accelerators.

4. Review the available accelerators and select the Define With Bing accelerator, as shown in Figure 13.4. (This might not be available on the first page of accelerators.)

5. A confirmation box appears that asks if you're sure you want to add this accelerator and if you want to make it the default for this accelerator category. Select the check box to make it the default and click Add.

6. You can verify the installation of the Define With Bing accelerator by returning to the web page (or going to any web page), highlighting a word or phrase, and clicking the accelerator icon. The Define With Bing option is now available.

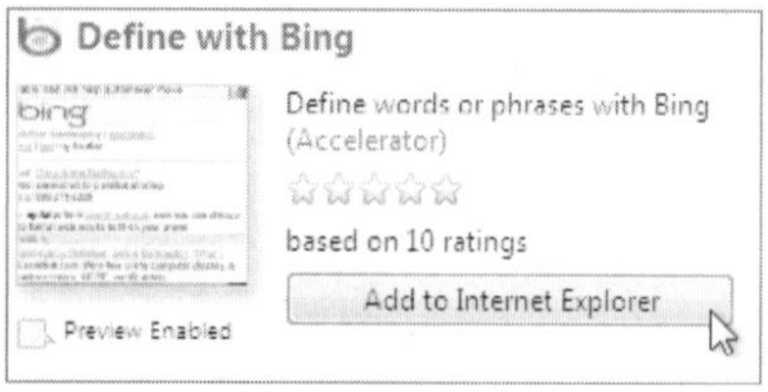

FIGURE 13.4
The Define With Bing
accelerator

You can also add the Define With Bing accelerator directly from the IE8 menus, which is also where you can manage any of the accelerators you have installed (which includes deleting them).

MANAGING IE8 ACCELERATORS

Perform the following steps to manage the installed accelerators or add new accelerators directly from the IE8 program interface:

1. Open IE8.

2. Click Tools ➢ Manage Add-ons.

3. In the Manage Add-ons window, select Accelerators in the Add-on Types section.

4. Select the accelerator in the right pane you would like to manage or click Find More Accelerators in the bottom left of the Manage Add-ons window to add more accelerators to IE8.

HANDLING ACCELERATORS IN IE8

Let's take a look at some of the various capabilities of the accelerators in IE8. In the previous section, we installed the Define With Bing accelerator. We discussed the addition of the Define With Bing accelerator as a quick launch of Bing with a define search functionality implemented in a new tab of IE8. This is true, but the accelerator provides an even more useful function by giving you a "preview" of the search without opening a new tab. If you select a word in a web page you are viewing and would like a definition of the word, you can open the Accelerators menu by clicking the icon and simply pausing over the Define With Bing option. IE8 will use Bing and display a quick definition in the current window, as shown in Figure 13.5.

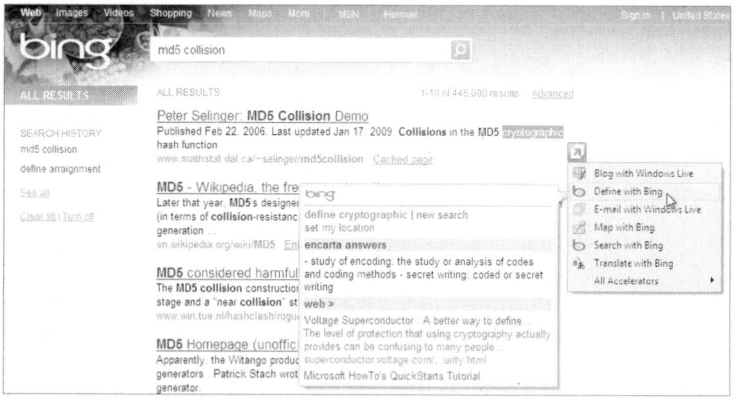

FIGURE 13.5
Viewing a quick
definition using an
accelerator

If you think this is cool, hold on — it gets even better. The default Map With Bing accelerator works like Define With Bing and will open a new tab in IE8 with a highlighted location address entered and searched with Bing. The Map With Bing accelerator also has the preview capability and will show you an insert in your current page with the map of the address if you hover over the address, as shown in Figure 13.6 (where we searched for the latitude and longitude of a lighthouse in Maine).

FIGURE 13.6

Quick map from an accelerator

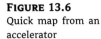

WHICH ACCELERATORS SHOULD YOU USE?

The list of accelerators providing Internet services is extensive at this time, with accelerators available for most of your favorite providers. We've used examples from Bing here, but if you prefer other search engines and mapping providers, they already have accelerators available. eBay, Facebook, Hotmail, Google, LinkedIn, Trip Advisor, Currency Converter, Walmart, Tech-Net, MSDN, UPS Tracking, and USPS Tracking are just a short list of accelerators available. As you get used to using the accelerators, the functionality they provide will make the browsing experience so much faster you'll wonder what you did without them.

As with accelerators, there are more new services available in IE8, such as Web Slices, as you'll see in the next section.

Defining IE8 Web Slices

Web Slices in IE8 allows the browser to check for updates to web page content that you may frequently want to have. How many times in the course of the day do you check your local weather or stock quotes or even watch an auction item on eBay? Most of the time you either keep a tab open and refresh it periodically or even return to the website with the content you would like to review. With Web Slices, you can add the piece of the web page with the content you're looking for to the new Favorites toolbar and IE8 will check it for you and give you a visual clue when the content changes. You can control how often IE8 checks for changes as well as have IE8 play a sound when Web Slice content is found on a page — and even when an update to content is discovered.

Web Slice content is being added to provider pages continually and its functionality will grow over time. Even at the time Windows 7 and IE8 are being released, the available content makes this new feature a welcome addition. If Web Slice content is available on a web page, the green Web Slice icon becomes active on the Favorites toolbar; it also becomes visible as you hover over the available Web Slice content in the page itself. Figure 13.7 shows the Web Slice icon in the IE8 new Favorites toolbar.

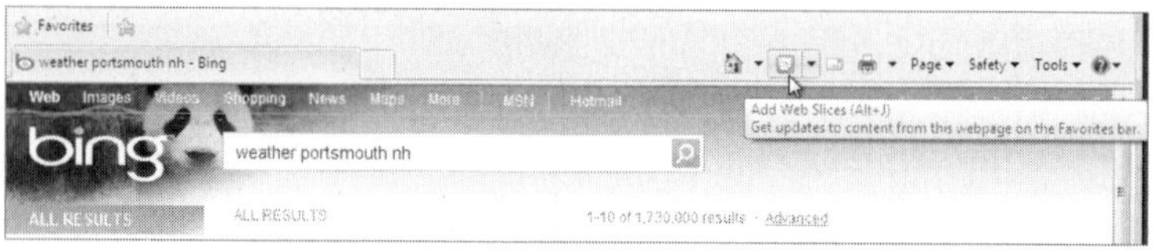

FIGURE 13.7
Web Slice icon in the
Favorites toolbar

Figure 13.8 shows a Bing query for a weather forecast for Portsmouth, New Hampshire, and the option icon available to add the forecast content as a Web Slice to the IE8 Favorites toolbar. Click the down arrow associated with the Favorites toolbar's Web Slice icon to display all the Web Slices available on the current web page. In the case of eBay, for example, all the items that match your search will be individual Web Slices you can pick from, allowing you to watch just one (or more if you add more than one Web Slice) item.

FIGURE 13.8
Web Slice icon within a
web page

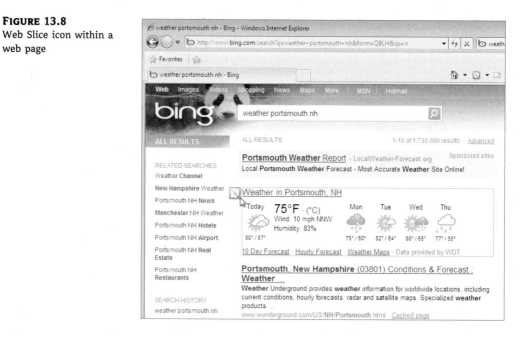

Clicking the Web Slice icon on the web page content presents the user with a confirmation box for adding the Web Slice to the Favorites toolbar. Once accepted, the Web Slice is available to be viewed at any time, even if you browse away from the originating page. Figure 13.9 shows the Web Slice content for the weather forecast added.

FIGURE 13.9
Web Slice content from
the Favorites toolbar

After you add the Web Slice to IE8, the browser periodically checks the source of the content for changes. If there are changes to the content, the Web Slice favorite text changes to bold and the background color flashes a color that indicates an update has been detected. Adding a Web Slice to your browser is a simple task you will find extremely convenient.

ADDING A STOCK QUOTE WEB SLICE TO IE8

You might like to monitor a company's stock prices throughout the course of the day.
Perform the following steps to add Microsoft's stock quote to your IE8 interface:

1. Open IE8 and browse to `www.bing.com`.

2. Enter `msft` into the search box in Bing and click the search button.

3. Choose the drop-down arrow from the Web Slice icon in the IE8 new Favorites toolbar and select Microsoft Corp Web Slice.

4. Select the Add To Favorites Bar button in the Internet Explorer confirmation window.

5. Verify that the Web Slice is available in the IE8 Favorites toolbar.

6. Click the down arrow of the Bing Microsoft Corp Web Slice and you are presented with the current information from the Web Slice of the original page, with updated information if it's available.

You could have also added the Web Slice by clicking the Web Slice icon associated with the content on the page. After you add the Web Slice, you can change certain parameters associated with it, such as how often the content is checked for updates, or to add a sound association with Web Slices.

After you add Web Slices to IE8, you might want to tweak the properties to allow a more frequent update check. The default update interval for a Web Slice is dependent on the web site content developer. The eBay interval shows up as 3,600+ seconds for an item expiring a long time from when the Web Slice was added. The weather Web Slice from Bing defaults to 360 seconds. You can change the properties for the Web Slice timing by adjusting the values from the properties pages of the Web Slice. Right-click (alternate mouse click) the Web Slice from the Favorites toolbar and select Properties to open the properties dialog box, as shown in Figure 13.10.

FIGURE 13.10
Web Slice Properties
dialog box

MANAGING IE8 WEB SLICES

Perform the following steps to change the update time interval for a Web Slice:

1. Perform the tasks in the earlier section "Adding a Stock Quote Web Slice to IE8" if you have not done so.

2. Right-click (alternate mouse click) the Bing Microsoft Corp Web Slice in the Favorites toolbar and select Properties.

3. Click the Use Custom Schedule radio button.

4. Click the down arrow to open the Frequency drop-down list and choose a new interval.

5. Click OK to close the Properties box and save your changes.

You can also set other properties for a Web Slice from the Properties dialog box as well by clicking the Settings button in the Update Schedule section, as shown in Figure 13.11. You can set sound options and display options for the Web Slices from the Feed And Web Slice Settings page.

If you have to enter credentials for a Web Slice, you can add or modify the information on the Web Slice's Properties dialog box by clicking the Settings button next to the User Name And Password field. You can change the display text as well as the URL for the Web Slice in the Properties dialog box.

After you finish with a Web Slice, remove it from the Favorites toolbar by right-clicking it and selecting Delete from the context menu; you are asked to confirm the deletion. The alternate click context menu also provides shortcuts to Web Slice properties, such as choosing to bold a new entry and modifying the text or icons shown on the Favorites toolbar. You will find Web Slices a fast and convenient way to keep up-to-date with content you review periodically throughout the day or would like to keep track of web content that may need to be addressed as it changes.

As IE continues to advance, content providers can make use of the new features, but there might be older pages that don't display correctly. IE8 adds Compatibility View, thus allowing IE8 to present older content correctly.

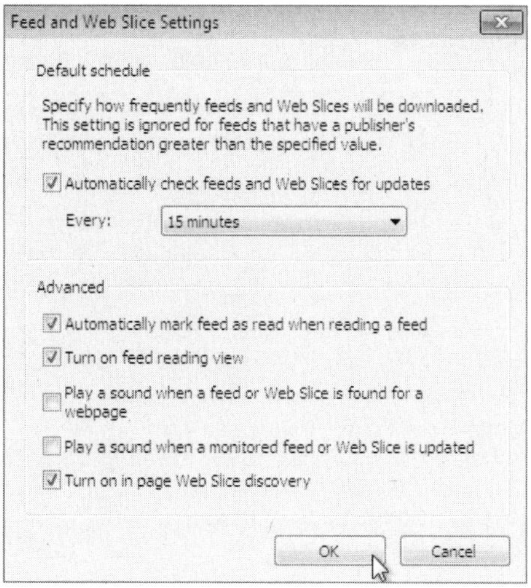

FIGURE 13.11
Feed And Web Slice
Settings

Browsing with IE8's Compatibility View

IE8 is a new release of Microsoft's web browser included in Windows 7 and some websites may not be updated to use the new features of IE8 or display their content correctly. Problems may exist with displaying misaligned images or text. By using Compatibility View, IE8 will display a web page the way it would have been displayed in IE7 (which should correct any display issues). To display a page in Compatibility View, click the Compatibility View button in the IE8 address bar, as shown in Figure 13.12.

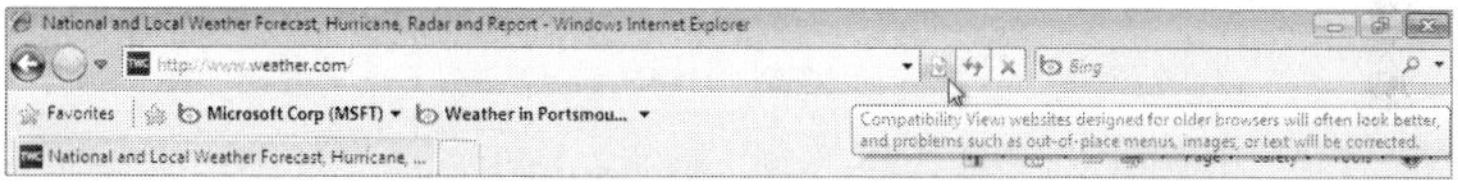

FIGURE 13.12
Compatibility View

Once you choose Compatibility View for a website, you will not need to make the choice again; IE8 displays the site in Compatibility View the next time you browse to the same website. If the website is updated in the future or you decide you would prefer to see it in the native IE8 standard mode, you can simply click the Compatibility View button again to return to the standard view. You can also enable this option by choosing Tools ➤ Compatibility View. In addition, a Compatibility View Settings option in the Tools menu lets you manage the sites currently set to Compatibility View. You can add or delete sites using the Add and Remove buttons, as shown in Figure 13.13. Many companies today have an extensive website for their users who may take time to update to IE8 features. The Compatibility View Settings page has the default setting for all intranet sites to be displayed in Compatibility View. You also have the choice to display all websites in Compatibility View.

Compatibility View helps in the transition to the new IE8 that allows users to view pages in a consistent manner. The new features — accelerators, Web Slices, and Compatibility View — are all a definite plus in the overall browsing experience. IE8 also includes a wide range of enhancements and updated features.

FIGURE 13.13
Compatibility View
Settings

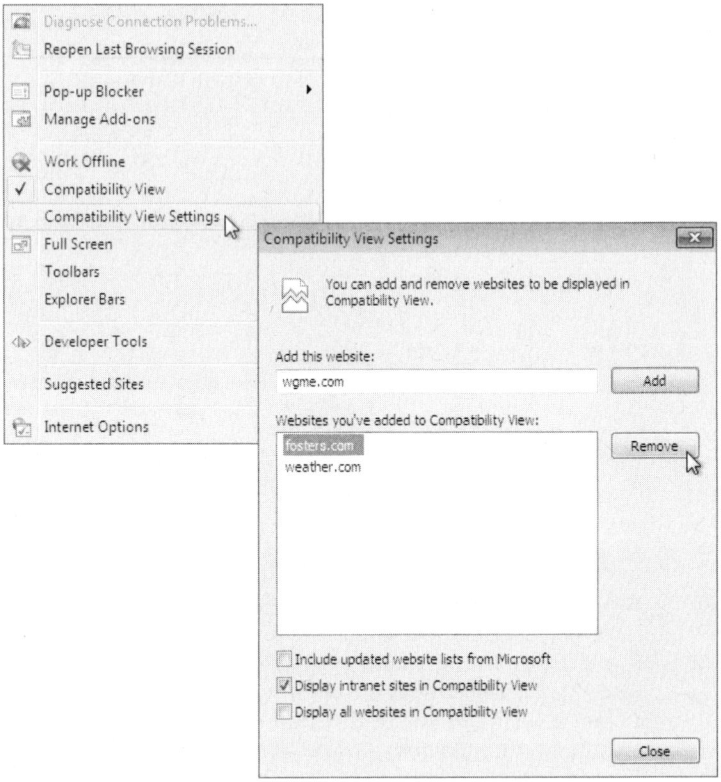

Using Updated Features of IE8

Windows Internet Explorer has included features through all releases that provide users with a simple way to get information from the Internet as well as browse more efficiently. IE8 takes many of the existing functionality and adds to it. Updated features include the Smart Address Bar, enhanced tab browsing, tab grouping, improved boom, and better Find On Page functionality.

Exploring Address Bar and Tab Updates

The address bar now offers information to the user rather than just waiting for input and processing the data. IE8 adds intelligence to the address bar and refers to it as a Smart Address Bar. Once upon a time, we had to open separate browsers if we wanted to surf to more than one website at a time. Earlier versions of IE added a tab functionality to allow more than one website or multiple pages of the same website to be open at the same time within on browser. This multisite single-browser capability lets users open separate tabs for each session. This is good, but in previous versions of IE, the view was just a tab with a site and didn't offer much information to an end user. Windows IE8 has added enhanced tab browsing and grouping by giving users more information while surfing the Web. Let's start by taking a look at the Smart Address Bar.

BROWSING WITH THE SMART ADDRESS BAR

Windows IE8 shows you options on places to browse as you type the address of the site you are planning to go to. Previous versions of the Internet Explorer address bar have presented the user with history options, but the Smart Address Bar enhances the input by displaying the history with a different color text as you type in a new address. The Smart Address Bar also offers options as you type to open the new page in a new tab as shown in Figure 13.14.

FIGURE 13.14
Smart Address Bar

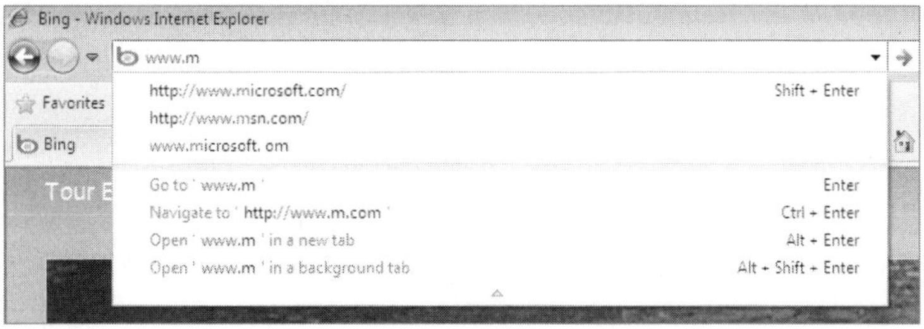

In previous versions of IE, the address bar would also show you each page you browsed to in a specific site; if you browsed to 20 pages in a news website, you'd have 20 history entries in your address bar. The new IE8 Smart Address Bar only displays the main site address. IE8 populates the Smart Address Bar by searching across your history, favorites, and RSS (Really Simple Syndication) feeds you have subscribed to. If you mistyped a website, it will also show up in the Smart Address Bar, but you can select and delete the unwanted entry.

Another feature enhanced in IE8 is the tabs we open instead of multiple browsers. It's easy to get overwhelmed while browsing if you have too many tabs open. IE8 now gives us enhanced tab browsing, which sets up tab groups. If a second tab is opened from a page in another tab, the second tab is placed next to the originating tab in the tab bar and then color coded so each related tab is the same color. This way, you can quickly see the tabs that have related content. If you close a tab but there are still related tabs, IE8 will open the related tabs rather than just drop you into unrelated content.

IE8 offers improved functionality in the way tabs are managed as well. By right-clicking a tab, you open the context menu shown in Figure 13.15, allowing you to close the individual tab, close the whole tab group, or close the other tabs (except the selected tab). Another nice feature, as shown in Figure 13.15, is the Refresh All option, which refreshes all the available tabs.

Also part of enhanced tab browsing are the options IE8 presents when you open a new tab. IE7 displayed a thumbnail view of your browsing history, but IE8 provides a whole new layer of functionality. When you open a new tab in IE8, you can choose to make it an InPrivate session (which we will discuss in the "Using the New Security and Safety Features of IE8" section later in this chapter). IE8 lets you reopen your last browsing session (maybe you closed the whole session by mistake) or reopen specific previously opened websites. The user can choose to launch an accelerator directly into a new tab as well.

OPENING A NEW TAB AND LAUNCHING THE SEARCH WITH BING PAGE

Perform the following steps to open a new tab and start a search in Bing:

1. Open IE8.

2. Click the New Tab area of the tab bar or press Ctrl+T to open a new tab.

3. In the Use An Accelerator section of the new tab, choose Search With Bing.

4. The Bing page opens and you can enter your search criteria.

FIGURE 13.15
Tab group context menu

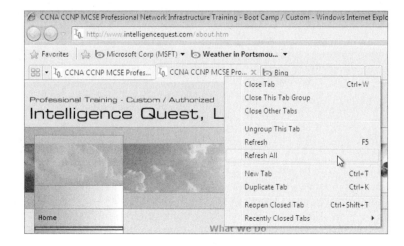

Using Find On Page and Improved Zoom

When you view web pages, there are many times when you would like to be able to search for a word or phrase on a page, assuming you can see the small words. You can use the improved Find On Page functionality in IE8 and then use the improved zoom feature to better read or see the information.

THE FIND ON PAGE ANNOYANCE

It has always been a gripe of users and administrators that when we search on the page for some text, a separate dialog box pops up in which we need to enter the search parameter. Once we start the search, text is blocked by the search dialog box, and you have to move it to see content, and sometimes even other occurrences of the search term, on the page. Finally we have a more convenient way of searching web pages for terms.

SEARCHING WITH THE IMPROVED FIND ON PAGE

IE8 has a redesigned Find On Page that adds a new Find On Page toolbar. You can activate the Find On Page toolbar by pressing Ctrl+F or by selecting Edit ➢ Find On Page. The Edit menu itself might be a problem for you as IE8 does not display the classic Windows menus by default. In order to see the Windows menus, you need to press the Alt key.

Perform the following steps to activate the better Find on Page toolbar:

1. Open IE8 and browse to a page with text available for you to search through.

2. Press the Alt key to activate the Windows classic menus, as shown in Figure 13.16.

3. Click Edit ➢ Find On This Page. Alternatively, press the Ctrl+F.

   The Find On Page toolbar becomes active, as shown in Figure 13.17.

4. Enter text to search for in the Search box of the Find On Page toolbar. You should notice the matching characters become highlighted as you type them into the search box.

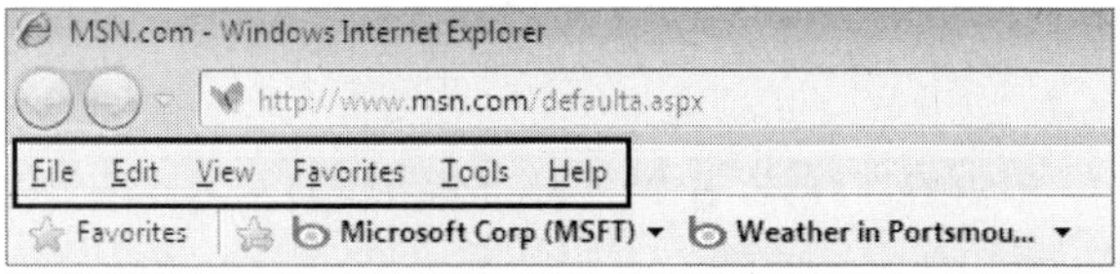

FIGURE 13.16
Legacy menu bar

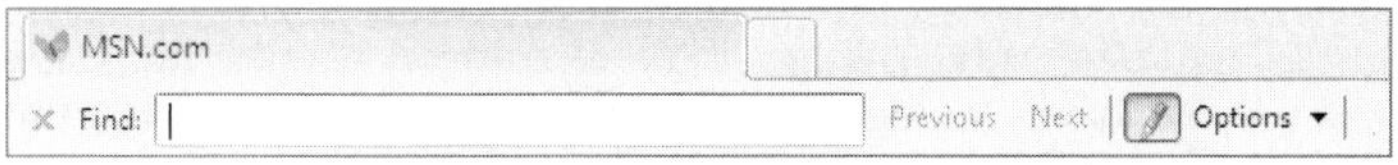

FIGURE 13.17
Find On Page toolbar

As you type characters into the Find On Page toolbar, you should also notice the next and previous buttons are now part of the toolbar, not located in a dialog box in the page (which has always been an annoyance). The toolbar also shows you a hit count on the number of times the search criteria has been met on the current page. Each instance of a match for the criteria is highlighted for easier location on the web page. You can toggle the highlighting feature on and off by clicking to toggle the highlighting button in the Find On Page toolbar. You also have the option to search on the whole word or to match case using the Options drop-down box.

Say you've searched for text on a web page and found the item you're looking for but would like to zoom in to see it better. This is where the improved zoom functionality of IE8 comes into play.

VIEWING WEB CONTENT WITH IMPROVED ZOOM

Choosing the Zoom button or the Zoom drop-down list box in the lower-right corner of IE8, as shown in Figure 13.18, lets you zoom into or out of a web page. You can also press Ctrl++ (plus sign) or Ctrl+– (minus sign) to zoom in or out, respectively.

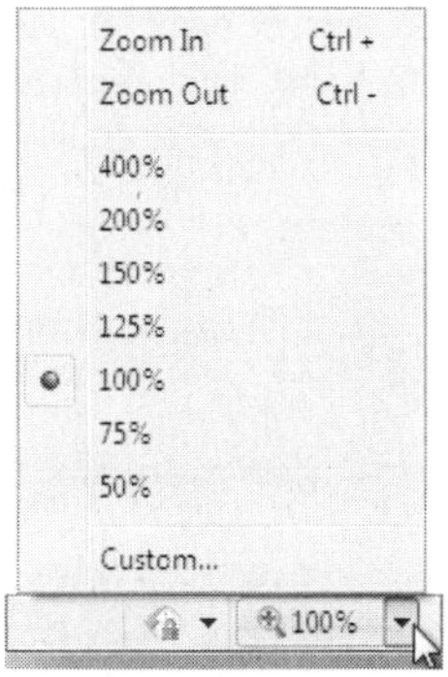

FIGURE 13.18
Zoom options in IE8

The IE8 zoom has been enhanced from previous versions with an adaptive Page Zoom feature. In previous versions, the page just zoomed to the upper-left corner of the current page, requiring the user to use the scroll bars to find the data they had centered on their screen. Unless the data you want is in the upper-left corner (not very likely), scrolling is necessary and not friendly or enjoyable. The improved feature zooms around the content you are viewing in the page, so you may not have to move the content you have zoomed in to but will have to scroll only in order to view more data than you can see initially.

The new and enhanced user features aren't the only great improvements to IE8; there are numerous new and improved security and safety features as well.

Using IE8's New Security and Safety Features

IE8's new security and safety features are designed to help protect users from malicious attacks or attempts to get personal information without their knowledge. Because we all use the Internet and our corporate intranets to provide information every day, online crime has risen dramatically. The new type of criminal we face are known as cybercriminals and are using extremely deceptive and sophisticated methods for getting information from users. Malware is one type of method in which a cybercriminal will try to steal private information through software pretending to be an expected website. This malware could be a program running on your PC that reads everything you type (including login information from a web browser) and reports the information back to a cybercriminal. Phishing is another technique used by cybercriminals to gain personal information from users. Phishing can be perpetrated by the cybercriminal pretending to be a legitimate website, such as the user's banking site or credit card site, and convincing the user to enter information into a fraudulent page.

New features of IE8 help to identify malware and phishing schemes and make it easier for users to quickly identify potential issues. This in turn allows administrators to spend less time "fixing" the network and "fixing" user-compromised data. Domain highlighting, the Cross-Site Scripting (XSS) filter, click-jacking prevention, SmartScreen filters, InPrivate browsing, and InPrivate filtering are new additions to IE8.

Understanding Domain Highlighting

When a user surfs to a website, they normally type in a URL in the form of `www.bing.com`. This URL displays in the address bar of the browser, and the user can see it during the entire browsing session. This may or may not be apparent to the user as it is nondescript text and nothing jumps out at the user. In IE8, the displayed URL is shown to the user with the domain highlighted, such as `www.bing.com`. As the user continues to surf to other pages within Bing, the domain portion, `bing.com`, remains clear (the other text softens to gray). That way, if the user is redirected to another site, there is a visual clue that jumps out at the user.

🌐 Real World Scenario

GETTING USERS TO HELP THEMSELVES WITH SECURITY

One of the biggest issues we face working with users is getting them to think outside the box while they're using a browser. The main problem is that users often expect the world to be a kind place and that no one is going to try to trick them. How many times have we told users — both well versed in technology and not quite so well versed — that they should not click links in an email? How many times have we told users to make sure they get the lock icon if they're surfing to a secure site and to check the protocol being used (https: instead of http:)? Educating the user and getting them to "do what you say" are two completely different things.

We have set up phishing websites and had corporate users go to the site (unknown to them it was a fake) and enter company credentials to gain access. The phishing site was not the correct name for the company, and in some cases where the connection was meant to be secure, we did not use https: and the users being tested still entered their credentials.

We have contemplated numerous times just what we can do to help users to see that there is a problem and provide some feedback. Although not a perfect solution (some users just won't look), the domain highlighting feature of IE8 appears to be a step in the right direction. The fact that the link changes as the user surfs and that the domain name appears in bold at least has a few users looking and asking the question, "Is this the right place?" Other features in IE8 as allows us as administrators to control the users, but with domain highlighting users are at least pondering the domain changes and wondering whether the change is good or bad.

If you look at Figure 13.19, you can see the same search string issued in both IE7 and IE8. Notice how much better bing.com stands out in the IE8 address bar.

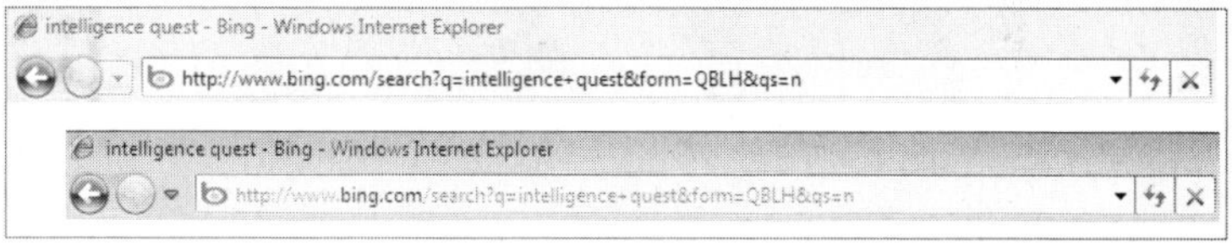

FIGURE 13.19
Domain highlighting in IE8

Domain highlighting and user education are a good starting place for security and safety, but are there features that can be added to proactively help the user? The answer is yes. One of the common phishing/malware activities is XSS, where the user inadvertently runs a script in a website link exploiting a flaw in a website, or click-jacking where a user clicks a link that says one thing on the page but sends them somewhere else. IE8 has proactive software to help identify these types of phishing/malware attacks before they can happen.

Defending Against XSS and Click-Jacking

XSS attacks attempt to exploit vulnerabilities that exist in the websites you use. XSS attacks are set up by inserting a malicious website address in a link a user might click in an email. The data in the link direct the browser to a legitimate website that has been compromised to contain malicious code that can capture keystrokes, therefore letting the cybercriminal capture a user's login credentials. IE8 includes an XSS filter that attempts to detect these types of attacks and disable the harmful scripts. Users surfing to a website that has been compromised can be detected and IE8 can modify the request, avoiding the potential risk. A message appears at the top of the IE8 page that indicates to the user "Internet Explorer has modified this page to help prevent cross-site scripting." Figure 13.20 shows the message displayed when issuing a malformed query to a search engine. The user can click the message to get further information about the compromise.

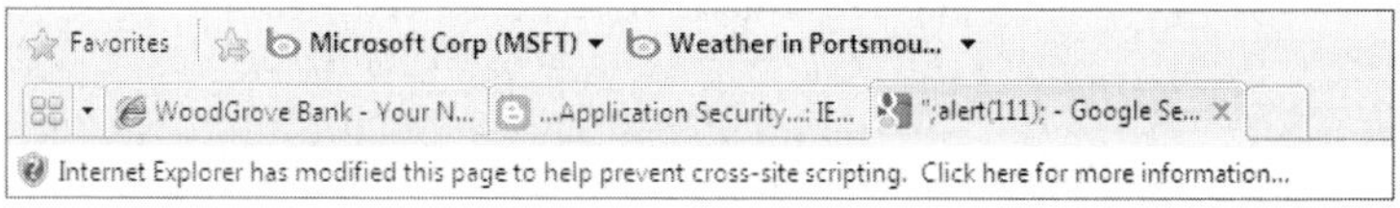

FIGURE 13.20
Cross-site scripting filter message

As with all of our technology and cybercrime, it's a cat and mouse game between the administrators and users with the cybercriminals. Every time the good guys find a way to block or mitigate an attack, the bad guys (good/bad, we guess, depends on your point of view . . .) find a different way to perpetrate an exploit. Click-jacking is a growing threat to our online community; a savvy cybercriminal can create a website where a real page is placed in a frame in the attacker's page. Clicking an item in the attacker's page allows the attacker to manipulate your input and have you view an advertisement at best or change your browser parameters at worst. IE8 includes code that allows developers not to let their websites be inserted into a frame in the IE8 interface, helping to mitigate the click-jacking event. The XSS filter and click-jack prevention code offer protection against malicious code in the website.

There is also a set of tools included in IE8 that help prevent the user from visiting a website that has been reported as unsafe or from downloading content that has been reported as unsafe. This protection is known as SmartScreen filtering.

Working with SmartScreen Filters

Microsoft maintains a database of unsafe websites that is checked while a user is browsing through websites. If the user chooses an unsafe website, IE8 blocks the user's request and presents a page that displays that the page has been identified as unsafe, as shown in Figure 13.21, and changes the background color of the address bar to reflect the same. The user can continue to the web page if they are confident of the safety of the website by choosing More Options and continuing to the website. This functionality is part of the IE8 suite of technologies helping to protect users from the deceptive practices of cybercriminals. The SmartScreen filters also have the ability to block malware or phishing from within initially safe sites by including specific pages as unsafe in the Microsoft unsafe website database.

FIGURE 13.21
SmartScreen filter of an unsafe website

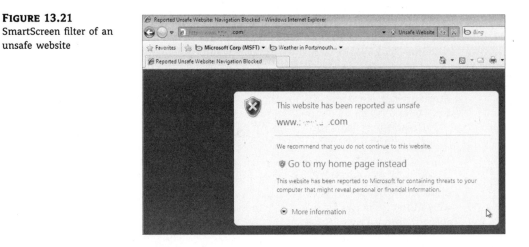

Another new feature related to SmartScreen filters is the ability to protect the user from unsafe downloads. If a user attempts to download a file and the file has been reported as unsafe (and accepted into the Microsoft database as unsafe), an Unsafe Download security warning dialog box is generated and the user is prevented from downloading the file. As with the unsafe website filter, the user can still continue the download if they are confident the file they are requesting is safe, as shown in Figure 13.22.

FIGURE 13.22
SmartScreen filter of an
unsafe download

Administrators do have the option of configuring Group Policy for IE8 to disable the ability of the users to download unsafe files if this is desired. You can manage SmartScreen Filtering functionality from the Safety menu of IE8. Figure 13.23 shows the option Turn Off SmartScreen Filter. Using the SmartScreen filter menu, you can check whether the current site has been reported as unsafe. (for instance, say you turned off SmartScreen filtering but would like to check a specific site).

FIGURE 13.23
SmartScreen Filter
options

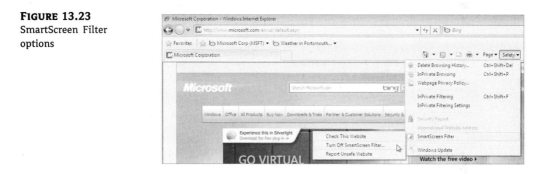

The SmartScreen filter feature also gives you the ability to report a website as unsafe. Once your report is submitted, Microsoft will review the site and add it to their database if they determine it meets the criteria they have put in place for an unsafe website.

Microsoft has also added two new features for the safety of users by protecting their personal information: InPrivate browsing and InPrivate filtering.

Browsing with InPrivate Browsing and InPrivate Filtering

InPrivate browsing provides a level of privacy to users using IE8. The privacy maintained with InPrivate browsing relates to current browsing where an InPrivate session has been enabled. The InPrivate session prevents the browsing history from being recorded, nor will temporary Internet files be retained. Cookies, usernames, passwords, and form data will not remain in IE8 following the closing of the InPrivate session, as well leaving no footprints or data pertaining to the InPrivate browsing session. This is a good method of protecting user data if you are not surfing from your own machine or are surfing from a public location (always a bad place to leave personal information). InPrivate browsing can also be used if you don't want anyone to be able to see data from your Internet browsing session.

There are several ways to launch an InPrivate IE8 browsing session. One way is to open a new tab and select the Open An InPrivate Browsing Window option from the Browse With

InPrivate section. This opens a new tab, and the tab is an InPrivate session. You can also choose to open IE8 and start an InPrivate session directly by clicking Safety ➢ InPrivate Browsing. You can also open a new IE8 browser and press Ctrl+Shift+P. Figure 13.24 shows an InPrivate session launched with Ctrl+Shift+P; you are taken to `login.live.com`. This ensures any of your login and browsing information is not saved to this computer.

FIGURE 13.24
InPrivate browsing session

InPrivate browsing keeps information from being saved to the local machine while you're in the session, but don't get lulled into a false sense of security; malware, phishing, and other compromises that send data out of the local machine are still valid and can provide personal information to a cybercriminal.

InPrivate filtering takes a slightly different approach in providing security and safety to the user who is surfing using IE8. Many websites gather content from different sources as they present a web page to you. Some of these sources are websites outside the main location and provide third-party companies with tracking information about where you surf and what you look at. This information can then be used to provide statistics as well as advertisements back to you. InPrivate filtering provides an added layer of control for the user to decide what information third-party websites have access to while browsing, thus limiting the ability for third-party websites to track your browsing usage.

InPrivate filtering is not enabled by default and must be enabled per browsing session. InPrivate filtering is enabled from the Safety menu in IE8, as shown in Figure 13.25. You can alternatively use Ctrl+Shift+F to enable InPrivate filtering.

After you choose InPrivate Filtering, you are given the option to have IE8 automatically block some third-party content or choose to let the user select which third-party providers receive the user's browsing information, as shown in Figure 13.26. You can always go back and change the options later or turn off InPrivate filtering if you desire.

After you enable InPrivate filtering, you can see which pages have been blocked as third-party queries from the InPrivate Filtering Settings dialog box. The InPrivate Filtering Settings dialog box is an alternate location for enabling (or disabling) InPrivate filtering, as shown in Figure 13.27. You open InPrivate Filtering Settings from IE8's Safety menu.

Along with the new security and safety features of IE8, there are several enhancements to existing features as well, which we'll discuss in the next section.

FIGURE 13.25
Enabling InPrivate filtering

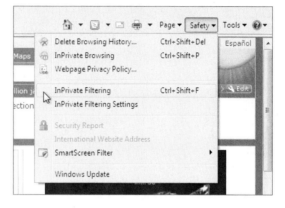

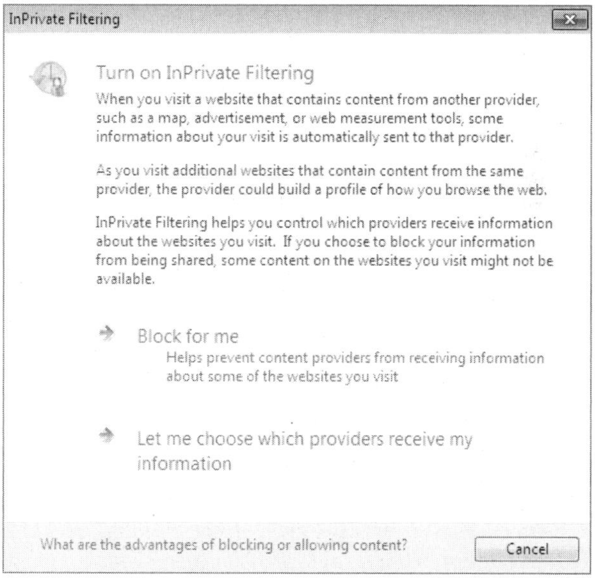

FIGURE 13.26
InPrivate Filtering options

FIGURE 13.27
You can enable
(or disable) InPrivate
filtering here.

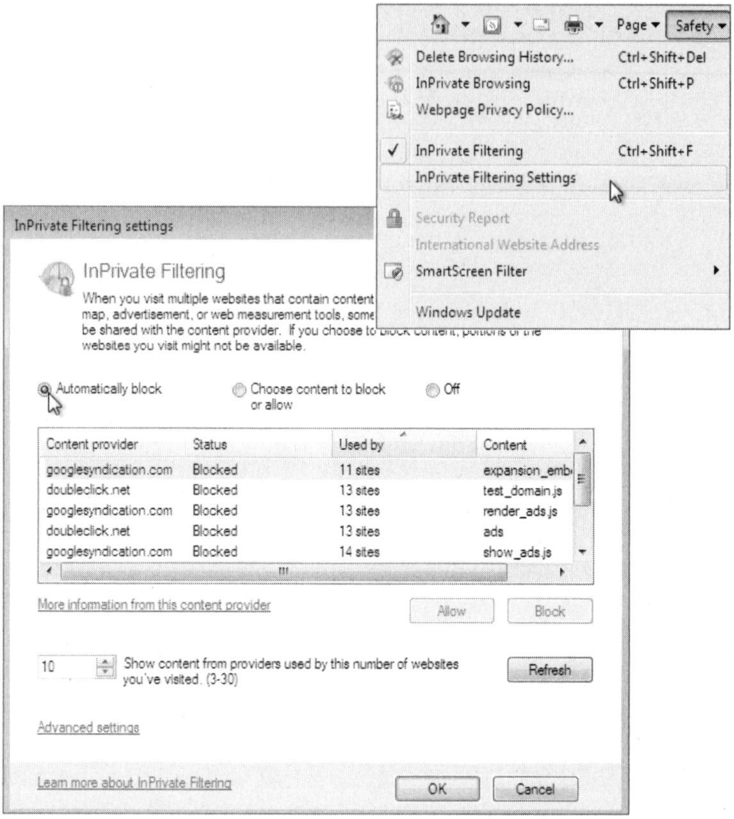

Using IE8's Enhanced Security and Safety Features

Among the enhancements to the security and safety features of IE8 are data execution prevention and an updated Automatic Crash Recovery function, as well as an enhanced Delete Browsing History feature.

Protecting the User with Data Execution Prevention

Data execution prevention (DEP) is enabled by default in IE8 and is a security feature of the browser. DEP helps to prevent malicious code from being run (or executed) in memory when it should not. Viruses, Trojans, and other dangerous software might try to execute code when they should not be able to. DEP prevents certain types of applications that are known to be malicious from writing to executable memory space. The various types of malicious code that are prevented are constantly being updated, and IE8 provides the latest information for the best layer of protection.

Along with DEP, IE8 includes an enhanced Automatic Crash Recovery feature to give a user a more seamless surfing experience even when something goes wrong.

Dealing with Automatic Crash Recovery

When dealing with legacy Internet Explorer versions, users would have multiple browsers open and the same time. With our new implementations, we use the same instance of Internet

Explorer running with individual tabs open for multiple websites. In the legacy implementation, if one IE crashes due to an application fault, the other browsers would remain active. If all the sites you are browsing to are in one application, the potential for an all-out failure is present. Automatic Crash Recovery uses tab isolation so only a single tab is affected in case of an application or browser add-in failure. If a tab experiences a fault, the main IE8 browser application remains stable as well as the other tabs. IE8 also uses a better crash recovery model; if one (or more) of the tabs closes or crashes unexpectedly, the remaining tabs are automatically reloaded and you are returned to the site(s) you were on before the fault. This provides the user with a cleaner experience and less to think about in times of peril.

Another enhancement to the security and safety functionality of IE8 is the update to the Delete Browsing History functionality.

Controlling Your Browsing with Enhanced Delete Browsing History

With previous versions of Internet Explorer, you had the ability to delete your web browsing history and individual components (such as temporary Internet files, cookies, form data, and passwords) on an individual basis or delete them all at once. IE8 provides better control of what you want to delete (and keep, for that matter) with a check box selection. You access this option on IE8's Safety menu or by pressing Ctrl+Shift+Del. You are then presented with the Delete Browsing History dialog box, as shown in Figure 13.28, where you can decide what to delete and what not to delete.

FIGURE 13.28
Enhanced Delete
Browsing History
dialog box

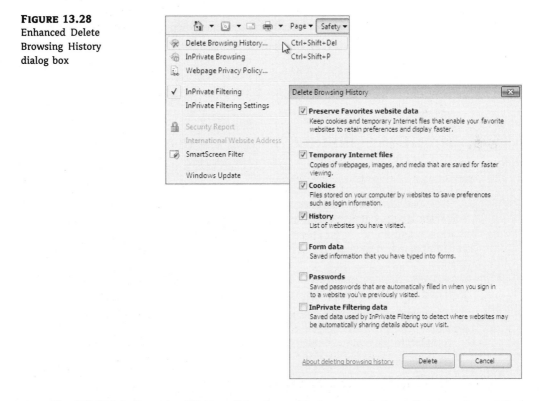

The IE8 Delete Browsing History dialog box adds two new features that complement the new functionality in IE8 by including InPrivate filtering data as a component and allows you to delete (or keep) browsing history specific to your Favorites website data. This is a welcome addition to IE8 that gives users better control and an easier experience to keep their personal data out of the eyes of others. With all of the new and enhanced features of IE8, it is still the same browser we have become used to. IE8 should just be more helpful as we continue to use it and configure it as we have done in previous versions.

Using IE8

IE8 is used to surf the Internet as well as corporate intranets using HTTP, HTTPS, and FTP on a day-to-day basis. We have become used to surfing, but utilizing the browser's enhancements might not be something we're all familiar with. IE8 includes many features included in legacy Microsoft browsers that you might find useful if you have not discovered them. A search box tied to an Internet search engine, automatic Really Simple Syndication (RSS) feed detection and updating, add-on support providing third-party utilities, and a Pop-up Blocker are available to provide a better surfing experience. IE8 also includes Protected Mode functionality to help shield the user from malicious code.

Taking Advantage of the Instant Search Box

The Instant Search box of IE8 provides quick access to Internet search capabilities without the need to install a third-party toolbar or open more tabs to load a search engine page. The Instant Search box is located in the upper-right corner or IE8 and defaults to Bing as its search provider, as shown in Figure 13.29. By clicking the down arrow associated with the search box, you can configure other search providers as well as choose a different default if you so desire.

FIGURE 13.29
Instant Search box
in IE8

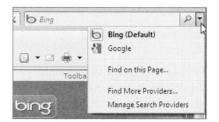

After you have more than one search provider listed, you can simply choose which provider you want to use, enter the search term, and hit Enter. You will also notice that as you add characters and words to the Instant Search box, IE8 will make suggestions and show visuals of potential search responses, allowing you a preview and the ability to select a previewed search result.

ADDING A NEW SEARCH PROVIDER TO THE INSTANT SEARCH BOX

There might be times when you want to have the option to choose between two search providers when you are looking for something on the Internet.

Perform the following steps to add a new search provider to the Instant Search box:

1. Open IE8.

2. Choose the drop-down arrow from the Instant Search box in the upper-right corner of IE8.

3. Click the Find More Providers option.

4. Choose a search provider from the Microsoft Add-ons Gallery: Search Providers page (Wikipedia Visual Search, for example).

5. Click the Add button in the Add Search Provider dialog box.

6. Choose the drop-down arrow from the Instant Search box and note that you can now use the new provider to perform an Internet search.

MANAGING SEARCH PROVIDERS

If you have included more than one search provider, you might want to manage them by changing the search order and having the search providers preview content.

Perform the following steps to change the search order of the search providers:

1. Open IE8 and add a search provider to the Instant Search box if you haven't already done so (see "Adding a New Search Provider to the Instant Search Box" earlier).

2. Click the down arrow associated with the Instant Search box located in the upper-right corner of IE8.

3. Select the Manage Search Providers option.

4. In the Manage Add-ons window, select Search Providers in the Add-on Types section.

5. Select a search provider in the right side of the Manage Add-ons window.

6. Use the Move Up or Move Down text item below the Search Providers box to change the order of the search providers.

You also have the ability in IE8 to use RSS feeds and get a visual when there is updated content for you to read.

Configuring RSS

RSS is a content syndication technology that enables a website to syndicate content via an RSS file formatted in XML (known as a feed). As you visit sites that have an RSS feed available, you can subscribe to the feed and any updates to the content will be automatically downloaded to the host machine. IE8 monitors and downloads the content and makes it available. Microsoft has added RSS support across many of its websites to enable users to automatically get updates and information about Microsoft products whenever new information is published. TechNet and the MSDN Microsoft sites are examples using RSS feed to distribute information to users via RSS.

In IE8, any website that has an RSS feed is indicated by an orange Feeds icon. Clicking the orange icon lets the user pick from any of the feeds available on the page and keeps the content updated by checking periodically to see whether the data has changed. This is similar to the way Web Slices work (described earlier in this chapter). The timing and other options for the RSS feed and Web Slice updates are found in the same configuration pages. Figure 13.30 shows two RSS feeds that are available on the TechNet home page (note that no Web Slices are available in the page).

SUBSCRIBING TO AN RSS FEED

Perform the following steps to subscribe to a Microsoft TechNet RSS feed:

1. Open IE8.

2. Enter **technet.microsoft.com** in the address bar and press Enter.

3. Click the down arrow associated with the RSS feed icon in the tab bar.

4. Click the Featured TechNet Downloads RSS Feed option.

5. In the TechNet Featured Download page, you are given the option to subscribe to the feed. Click the subscribe link.

6. Click the Favorites star to open the Favorites window.

7. Select the Feeds tab to see that you have subscribed to the TechNet feed; by selecting the TechNet option, you can view the feed data.

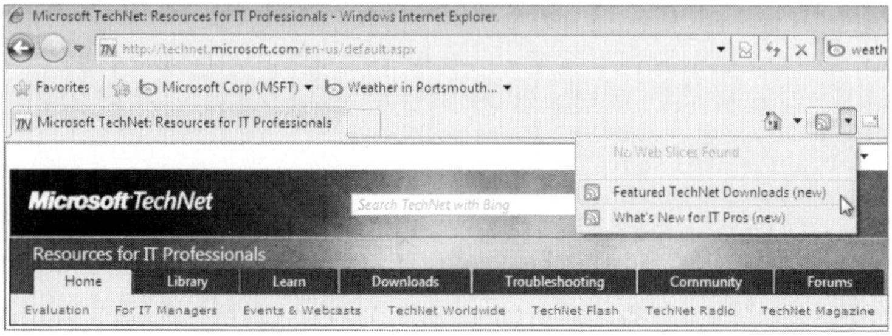

FIGURE 13.30
RSS feed availability in a website

MANAGING AN RSS FEED

After you subscribe to an RSS feed, you can configure several options for the feed, such as how often the feed is checked for updates, whether attachments associated with the feed are downloaded, or how many updates should be saved.

Perform the following steps to modify the properties of an RSS feed:

1. Open IE8 and click the Favorites star to open the Favorites window.

2. Click the Feeds tab and right-click an RSS feed that you have subscribed to (if you need to subscribe to a feed, see the previous section, "Subscribing to an RSS Feed").

3. View the properties of the RSS feed and modify as desired.

As with the Instant Search box and RSS feeds, there are other features that might enhance your browsing experience but that are not specifically provided by Microsoft. These features might come in the form of an add-on.

Installing Add-ons to IE8

IE8 provides the ability to install add-ons to extend the functionality of the browser. Add-ons can improve the user experience by providing a simpler approach to resources, enhancing security, or simply providing enjoyment (a joke-of-the-day add-on, for example). Add-ons can be created by Microsoft, but many times you will find third party add-ons to be equally as useful.

To enable, disable, or install add-ons, select Tools ➢ Manage Add-ons. This opens the Manage Add-ons dialog box. In the Add-on Types pane, select Toolbars And Extensions, and you can change the properties for installed add-ons in the right pane. By selecting an item, you can toggle it from enable to disabled, or vice versa, by clicking the button in the lower right. In Figure 13.31, you can see that the Shockwave Flash Object add-on is selected and enabled; the button in the lower left would be used to disable this add-on.

FIGURE 13.31
Manage Add-ons
dialog box

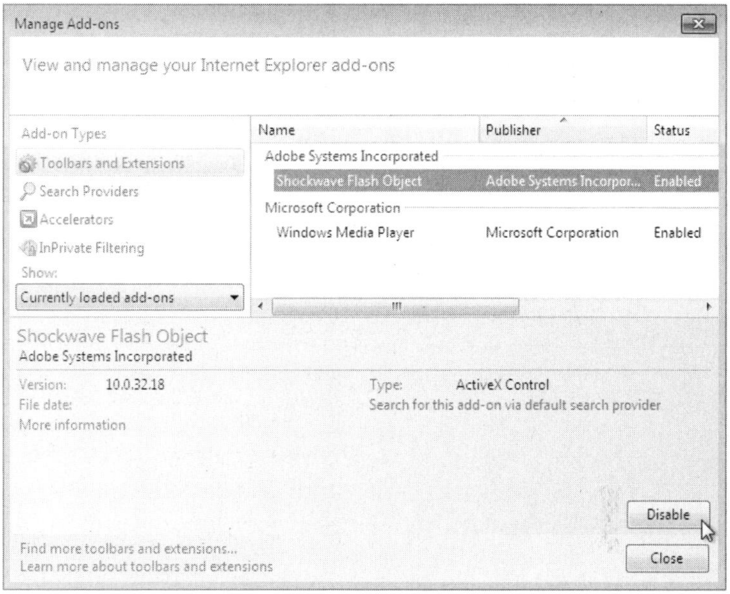

If you were looking for more add-ons for your IE8, you could click Find More Toolbars And Extensions in the lower left of the Manage Add-ons windows. You can install and manage toolbars as well as search providers and Extensions from the Manage Add-ons window.

Another feature of many websites is the pop-up windows the website developers include. IE8 includes functionality to block pop-ups dynamically.

Controlling Pop-ups with IE8's Pop-up Blocker

IE8 includes the Pop-up Blocker feature, which prevents pop-up pages from being displayed. Most of the time advertisers and marketers use these pop-up pages to get users to view content in an attempt to convince them to click and buy. Not all pop-ups are malicious or advertisement-related and may actually provide useful information. IE8's Pop-up Blocker is enabled by default, but does inform the user anytime a pop-up page is blocked. When a pop-up is blocked, the user has the option immediately to allow the pop-up to display. Figure 13.32 shows the message in IE8; as you can see, the user could allow the pop-up to be displayed.

FIGURE 13.32
Pop-up Blocker message

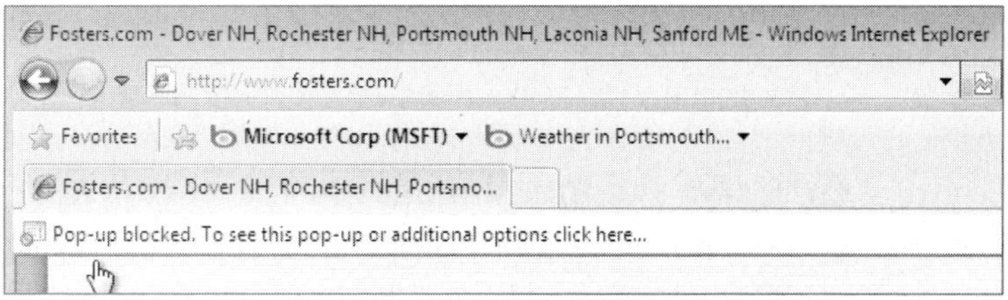

You can also allow a pop-up to be displayed from a website where it was blocked by IE8 by selecting Tools ➢ Pop-up Blocker ➢ Temporarily Allow Pop-ups or from the Pop-up Blocker selection of the Tools menu. The option Always Allow Pop-ups From This Site is also available, as well as the ability to open the Pop-up Blocker Settings page, as shown in Figure 13.33. The Pop-up Blocker Settings dialog box allows you to manage which sites will not have pop-ups blocked.

FIGURE 13.33
Pop-up Blocker Settings
dialog box

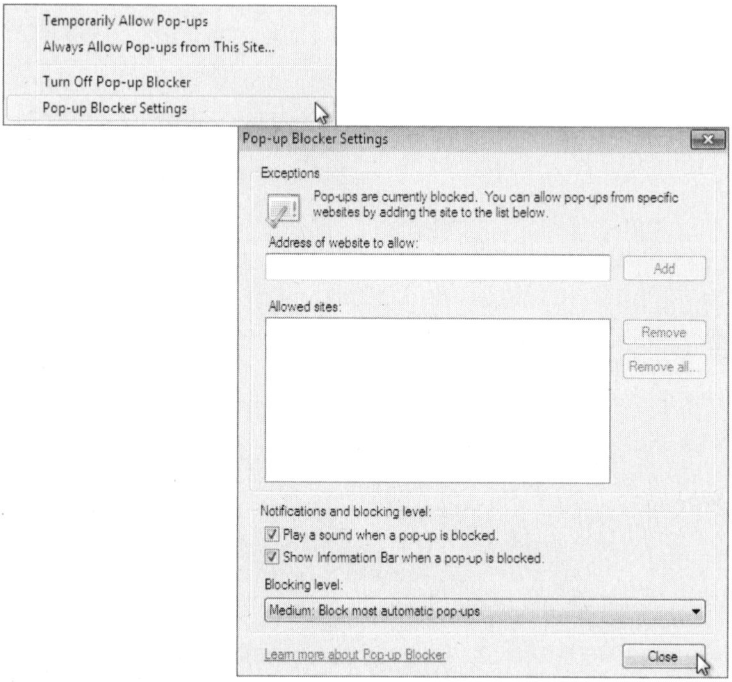

In addition to providing the ability to create and maintain a list of approved sites for pop-ups, the Pop-up Blocker Settings dialog box lets you configure notification options. You can enable or disable the playing of a sound when a pop-up is blocked or control whether or not the information bar is displayed. The Blocking Level drop-down list gives you better control of which pop-ups are blocked and provides three levels of control:

◆ High: Block All Pop-ups (press Ctrl+Alt to override)

◆ Medium: Block Most Automatic Pop-ups

◆ Low: Allow Pop-ups from Secure Sites

By default, IE8 has the Blocking Level set to Medium.

CHANGING THE BLOCKING LEVEL FOR POP-UP BLOCKER

Perform the following steps to change the Blocking Level to Low for Pop-up Blocker:

1. Open IE8..

2. Select Tools ➢ Pop-up Blocker Settings.

3. Click the down arrow next to the Blocking Level drop-down list box.

4. Click the Low: Allow Pop-ups From Secure Sites option.

5. Click the Close button to exit the Pop-up Blocker Settings dialog box.

ADDING A WEBSITE TO THE ALLOWED SITES FOR POP-UP BLOCKER

Perform the following steps to manually add a site for IE8 to allow pop-ups:

1. Open IE8.

2. Select Tools ➤ Pop-up Blocker Settings.

3. Enter a website for which you want to allow pop-ups to be displayed in the Address Of Website To Allow text box.

4. Click the Add button to include the desired website in the Allowed Sites text box.

5. Click the Close button to exit the Pop-up Blocker Settings dialog box.

Using Protected Mode for IE8

Protected Mode is a feature of Windows 7 for IE8 that forces IE8 to run in a protected, isolated memory space, thus preventing malicious code from writing data outside the Temporary Internet Files directly unless the program trying to write the information is specifically granted access by the user. Protected Mode is enabled by default and displayed in the lower-right corner of the IE8 window. You can install software through IE8, but you will need to explicitly allow the modification of the file structure of Windows 7 if the software is going to install outside the protected directory. You can switch out of Protected Mode using the Security tab of IE8's Internet Options dialog box. To access this dialog box, select Tools ➤ Internet Options; or type **internet options** in the Start menu's search box in Windows 7. You also have the option of double-clicking Protected Mode: On at the bottom right of the IE8 interface to open just the Security tab of Internet Options, as shown in Figure 13.34.

To change the Protected Mode settings, click to select or deselect the Enable Protected Mode (Requires Restarting Internet Explorer) check box. Microsoft recommends that Protected Mode remain active as it provides a greater level of security and safety for the user and does not prohibit an action (installing a program from IE8); it just requires interaction from the user to allow the modification.

Configuring IE8 Options

In addition to security and usability options that you can configure in IE8, you can configure other options for managing the browser. Many of the configurations we have discussed in this chapter have used the Safety or Tools options to quickly change individual parameters. The ability to change the individual parameters is also available from within the Internet Properties tabbed dialog box. This dialog box offers general parameters, security parameters, privacy configurations, content control, connection settings, program options, and advanced settings available for Internet options.

GENERAL PARAMETERS IN INTERNET PROPERTIES

You can open the Internet Properties dialog box by selecting Tools ➤ Internet Properties or by typing **internet options** in the Start menu's search box Windows 7. The General tab, as shown in Figure 13.35, allows you to change the default home page that displays when IE8 is launched. An interesting feature here is that you can have more than one default home page. By entering more than one page in the Home Page text box, every time IE8 is launched each of these pages will open in its own tab.

FIGURE 13.34
Security tab of IE8's
Internet Options

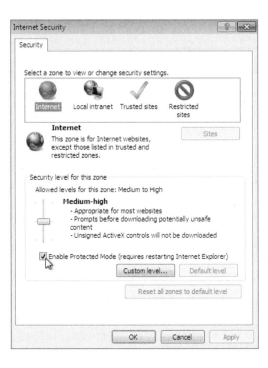

FIGURE 13.35
General tab of IE8's
Internet Properties

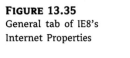

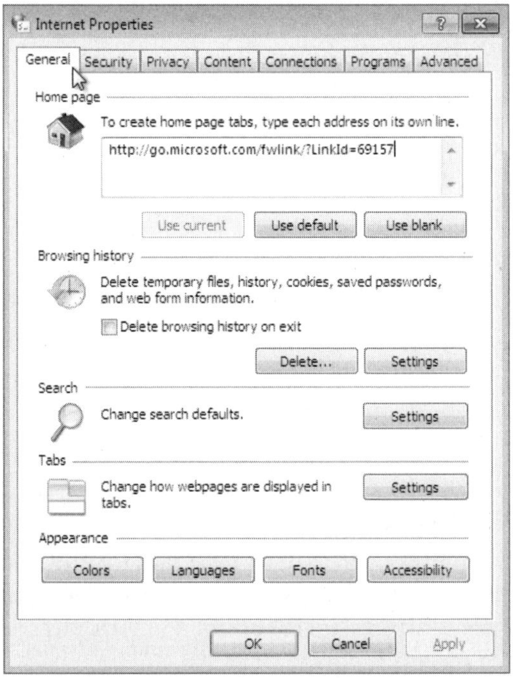

The General tab also allows you to control your browsing history settings, search settings, tabs, and the appearance (including accessibility options) of the IE8 interface.

SECURITY PARAMETERS IN INTERNET PROPERTIES

The Security tab of IE8's Internet Properties dialog box not only gives you access to control Protected Mode (as seen earlier in this section), but also gives you the ability to set security settings on the specific zones you may browse to. The zones are the Internet, Local Intranet, Trusted Sites, and Restricted Sites. You can set the behavior of IE8 individually for each zone and even individual sites within each zone.

PRIVACY CONFIGURATIONS IN INTERNET PROPERTIES

The Privacy tab, as shown in Figure 13.36, allows you to manage privacy settings for the Internet zone; this is the cookie management for specific sites.

FIGURE 13.36
Privacy tab of Internet Properties

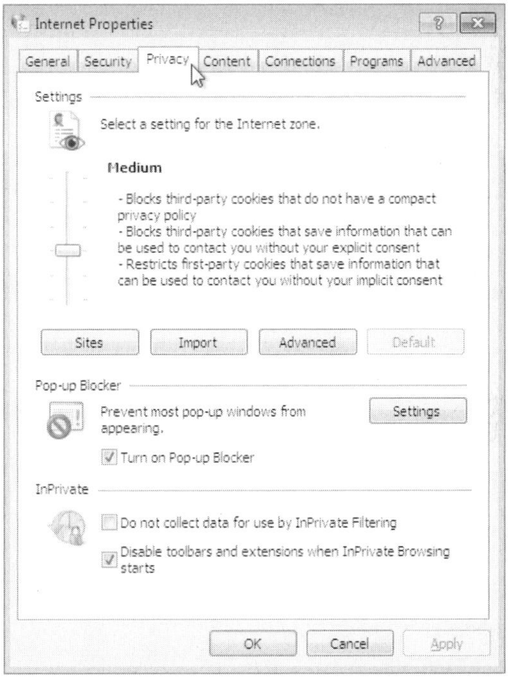

You can also control the settings for Pop-up Blocker and your InPrivate filtering and InPrivate browsing here.

CONTENT CONTROL IN INTERNET PROPERTIES

Figure 13.37 shows the Content tab of IE8's Internet Properties. Parental controls let you manage which sites are available through web filtering and monitoring of website access using the Activity Monitor. There has to be a privileged account with a password set to enforce parental controls. InPrivate browsing is also not allowed when parental controls are in place.

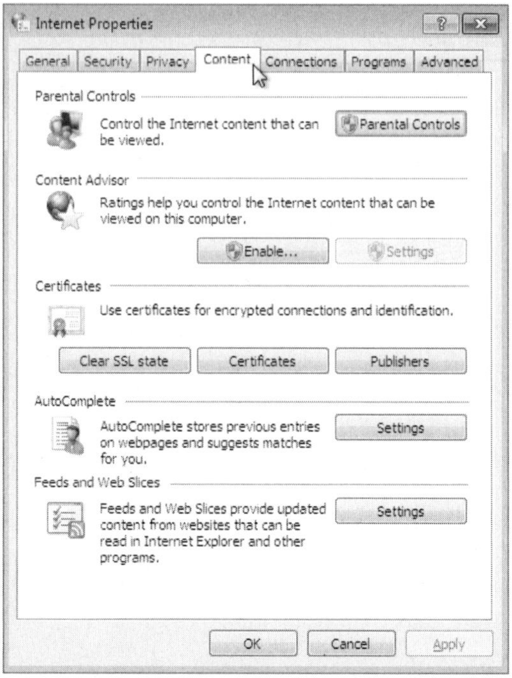

FIGURE 13.37
Content tab of Internet
Properties

You can enable Content Advisor settings on the Content tab. Content Advisor displays rated sites as users browse to different locations. Certificate management for secure browsing is managed through the Content tab as well. You have the ability to manage AutoComplete functionality and manage RSS feeds and Web Slice data here too.

CONNECTION SETTINGS IN INTERNET PROPERTIES

The Connections tab of IE8's Internet Properties dialog box allows you to manage the way IE8 gains access to the network. You can initiate the Connect To The Internet Wizard on this tab as well as set up a virtual private network. If you are using dial-up networking, you can also configure this connection from the Connections tab. Local area network (LAN) general settings are configured on this tab. You can specify a proxy server if you need to use one (this is typical across many corporate sites as well as to provide a better level of anonymity for Internet surfing).

PROGRAM OPTIONS IN INTERNET PROPERTIES

The Programs tab of the IE8 Internet Properties dialog box allows you to control which browser you are using as your default web browser. You can manage add-ons specific to IE8 on the Programs tab as well. You can set up an application to allow for HTML editing and set up default programs to be used for Internet services such as email.

ADVANCED SETTINGS IN INTERNET PROPERTIES

The Advanced tab, as shown in Figure 13.38, of the IE8 Internet Properties dialog box allows you to configure advanced configuration settings for IE8. Some of the advanced configuration items include accessibility settings, browsing settings, international browsing settings, encoding settings, multimedia parameters, printing parameters, and general security settings. You can control whether links are underlined, whether pictures should be displayed, which versions of the secure communication protocols or SSL are used, background colors, and many other parameters.

FIGURE 13.38
Advanced tab of Internet Properties

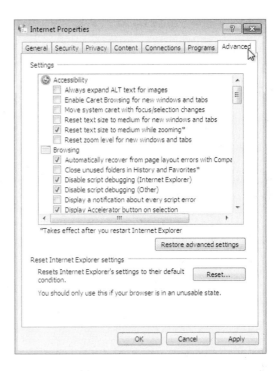

In addition to being able to change the advanced settings, you also have the option to restore advanced settings to their original configurations or to even reset the Internet Explorer settings (clicking this option resets all IE8 settings, not just the advanced settings, to the default configuration).

IE8, with all of its new and exciting features for user browsing, safety, and security, provides a solid foundation for users to enjoy Internet surfing and gives administrators comfort with the knowledge that their users will be on the network safely. Many of the enhancements provide administrators with more peace of mind about the integrity of the network as well as being able to suppress the intentions of cybercriminals without dramatically affecting the surfers. Kudos to Microsoft and Windows IE8!

The Bottom Line

Use IE8 accelerators and web slices. IE8 has added accelerators and Web Slices to its arsenal of features available to users to make browsing more efficient. Accelerators add a quick launch feature to services such as searching, while Web Slices add the ability to receive updates to content that changes dynamically.

Master It You would like to add the ability to see Microsoft's stock price reflected in your browser throughout the course of the day. It seems as though adding a Web Slice would be the most efficient way of getting this information. You have been told that Microsoft belongs to NASDAQ and would like to see a quick definition of the term. You know that there's an accelerator that provides a definition. How can you accomplish these tasks using IE8?

Configure Pop-up Blocker in IE8. Pop-ups are used within websites to launch a separate window with additional content from the site. Most of the time this is an advertisement or some other unwanted content, and it is blocked by default in IE8. However, there are some sites that use pop-ups to present information that you would like to see, but IE8 still blocks it.

Master It You routinely browse to your local newspaper's website to see what's happening in the local area as well as the world. It is extremely annoying that they use a pop-up for breaking news. You know the pop-up gives you good information and would like to see the content any time you surf to the site. How will you disable pop-ups from occurring anywhere within the local newspaper website?

Use the InPrivate security feature of IE8. InPrivate browsing is a new addition that allows a separate browsing session to be initiated where none of the browsing history, cookies, or other data pertaining to the session are retained on the local machine.

Master It You have entered an Internet cafe and are going to use one of the local machines to surf around the Internet for a bit. You would like to make sure that nothing you do is recorded on the Internet cafe computer. You notice that the Internet cafe is using Windows 7 and realize you can feel confident that your browsing history, cookies, and other data will not be kept on the local machine. How will you surf privately?

Configure security for IE8. IE8 allows you to change the security settings for different zones or areas where you will be browsing. The default settings are Medium for both the Internet and Intranet zones.

Master It You have decided that you would like to increase the security settings for sites you browse to in both the Internet and Intranet zones. You would like to set the security to the highest available level. How will you accomplish this task?

Chapter 14

Installing and Configuring Applications

Windows 7 introduces a new way to use many built-in programs of Vista by incorporating them into an online feature to make access and collaboration even easier than in previous versions. Live Essentials is a downloadable program suite that provides email and calendaring in an online format. Vista and previous versions of Windows introduced Mail, Calendar, and Contacts, a Getting Started welcome center, Fax and Scan, Media Player, and Media Center. These applications gave users quick access to features they would use on a day-to-day basis, but only on the local machine. Windows 7 utilizes Live Essentials for Mail and Calendar to make online access to those applications available, but it also allows offline access to users' data, which enhances and simplifies application use. It is still fairly straightforward to install, repair, change, and uninstall other commercial applications as well.

Having everyday applications available in Windows 7 results in efficient productivity for users as well as administrators because users will spend less time installing and updating applications. With the new online collaboration of Live Essentials, functionality previously available only in Windows Vista is now available from any Internet-accessible location, thus improving the quality of the user experience.

Windows 7's built-in applications also allow you to use your PC as a hub for multimedia by providing functionality to access audio and video that is stored on your PC from the Internet. You can also send the same audio and video to other media-capable devices within your local network.

In this chapter, you'll learn how to:

◆ Use Windows 7's Getting Started feature

◆ Manage Live Essentials' Mail features

◆ Play a saved digital video in Windows Media Center

◆ Use Repair to fix a corrupted application

Getting Started in Windows 7

Windows Vista provides you with a welcome center that launches automatically by default after you log in. This window displays the edition of Windows Vista that's installed, the CPU, the amount of RAM, the video card, and the computer name. Windows 7 also feature a welcome center, where you are presented with a Getting Started window, as shown in Figure 14.1.

FIGURE 14.1
Getting Started in
Windows 7

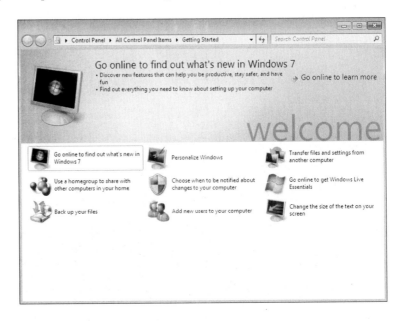

The Getting Started window does not show you the hardware configuration of your PC or which version of Windows 7 you have, but it does offer several links to the following features of Windows 7 that are commonly set up when you first get started:

◆ Go Online To Find Out What's New In Windows 7

◆ Use A Homegroup To Share With Other Computers In Your Home

◆ Back Up Your Files

◆ Personalize Windows

◆ Choose When To Be Notified About Changes To Your Computer

◆ Add New Users To Your Computer

◆ Transfer Files And Settings From Another Computer

◆ Go Online To Get Windows Live Essentials

◆ Change The Size Of The Text On Your Screen

All of the items in the Getting Started window are available from various locations in the Windows 7 interface, and you can even launch them individually from the Start menu's search box. Rather than search around, use Getting Started to gain access by typing **Getting Started** into the search box.

You can also open the Getting Started window with these steps:

1. Click Start ➢ Control Panel.

2. Choose System And Security.

3. On the left side of the System And Security screen, click Control Panel Home, as shown in Figure 14.2.

4. In the All Control Panel Items window, choose Getting Started, as shown in Figure 14.3.

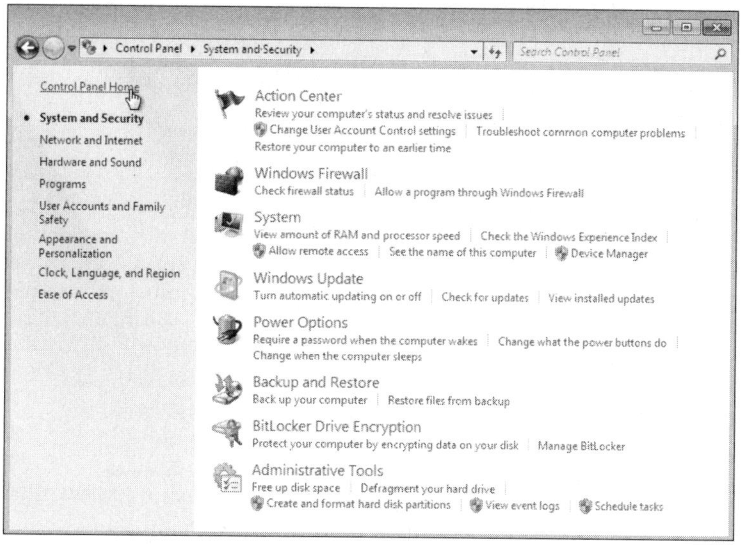

FIGURE 14.2
Select Control
Panel Home.

FIGURE 14.3
Choose Getting Started
in the All Control Panel
Items window.

If you need to access the hardware configuration of your PC or version of Windows 7, you can still do so from the System window in Control Panel. The easiest way is to type **system** in the Start menu's search box and select System from the Control Panel section, as shown in Figure 14.4.

FIGURE 14.4
Choosing System from
Windows 7 search
results

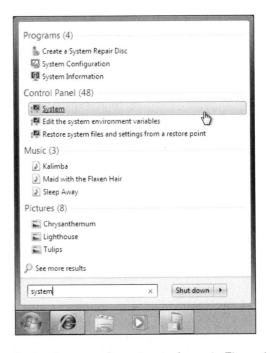

The System window that shows the hardware configuration is shown in Figure 14.5.

You can also choose Start ➤ Control Panel ➤ System And Security ➤ System or choose Start, right-click Computer in the Start menu, and select Properties to access the System window.

FIGURE 14.5
Windows 7 System
window

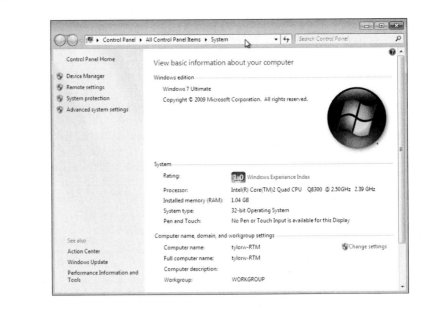

Although Getting Started allows you access to many of the common initial configuration tasks, you should note that there is no task to configure email. In fact, in Windows 7 no email client is available from the distribution — you must download it, which we discuss in the next section.

Accessing Email in Windows 7

Windows Mail was introduced in Vista as the replacement for Outlook Express. Windows Mail added new functionality, such as junk email filters. In Windows 7, the Windows Mail program is not available (nor is Outlook Express). Microsoft has opted to include the email program in its Live Essentials download. Why did Microsoft do this? The company seems to have decided that having the users install the more collaborative applications after the fact will give the users better control over which applications they install. The basic installation of Windows 7 has become so streamlined that we barely have to stop and make any decisions. After the installation, users can simply install or uninstall programs as desired. If they have to go online to get their applications, users will be more inclined to use Windows Live, a set of collaborative servers. Again, what does this mean? Live Messenger includes a set of contacts, so why not use the same contacts list for email? Many of the web-based email providers (Yahoo! and Google, for example) also provide contacts, messaging, and email. Your Windows Live account, Live Mail, Live Messenger, and other collaborative programs that might become available in the future can share your collected information across the applications.

MICROSOFT LIVE ESSENTIALS

You can get the Essentials bundle from `http://download.live.com`. After the web page loads, you may want to take a few minutes to review the available items. Once you decide, click the Download button and either save the file to run later or run the downloaded file directly. After you run the downloaded file, you will be shown the installation options.

Installing Live Mail

To use Live Mail in Windows 7, you must download and run the installation of the Live Essentials programs. You can choose which applications associated with Live Essentials you want to install. Selecting the Mail option will install Live Mail. Setting up an email account is the first task you'll undertake after you install Live Mail.

Setting Up Email Accounts with Live Mail

After you install Live Mail, you will set up an email account for access. Assuming you have an SMTP server account, you set up the configuration just as you would with Windows Mail or Outlook Express. With your login credentials, SMTP server, and POP3 server parameters, you are able to compose and read email. In the Windows Live Mail window shown in Figure 14.6, you click Add E-mail Account to launch a wizard that prompts you for configuration parameters.

Perform the following steps to set up a new email account:

1. Open Live Mail by choosing Start ➤ Windows Live Mail.

2. If this is the first time Live Mail has been opened, the Add E-mail Account wizard starts. If this is not the first time Live Mail has been opened, you must select Add E-mail Account in the main window, as shown in Figure 14.6.

3. Type the email address of the account you are adding, the email account password, and the display name for the account.

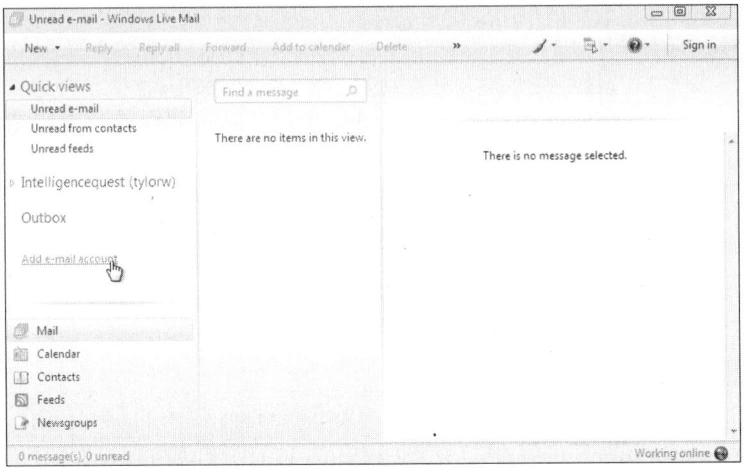

FIGURE 14.6
Click Add E-mail
Account in Live Mail.

4. Select the check box in the bottom left of the wizard to manually configure server settings for the email account, and then click Next.

5. Enter the parameters for your email account incoming and outgoing mail server type, along with their authorization parameters, and click Next.

6. Choose Finish, and your new email account is added to Live Mail.

There are several other parameters that you can use to configure the way Live Mail behaves. Next, we'll show you how to use the Options dialog box to customize Live Mail's actions.

Configuring Options in Live Mail

Live Mail will work as soon as you configure an email account, but you might want to tweak it for personalized experience. To access the Options dialog box, press the Alt key to activate the standard menu bar. Click Tools ➤ Options to open the Options dialog box, as shown in Figure 14.7.

The General tab of the Options dialog box (see Figure 14.8) lets you configure general options, specify how messages are to be sent and received, and select default messaging programs. New options are available in Live Mail that allow you to automatically log on to Windows Live Messenger and to participate in the Windows Live improvement program by allowing Microsoft to collect information about your system and how you use the program (this option is not selected by default).

The Read and the Receipts tabs, as shown in Figure 14.9, allow you to configure the behavior of Windows Mail when messages are read and received. You can also use the Read tab to specify newsgroup behavior and to select the default font and encoding method to be used for reading messages. Use the Receipts tab to configure whether read receipts are requested or sent. You can also configure Secure receipts.

FIGURE 14.7
Live Mail Options
dialog box

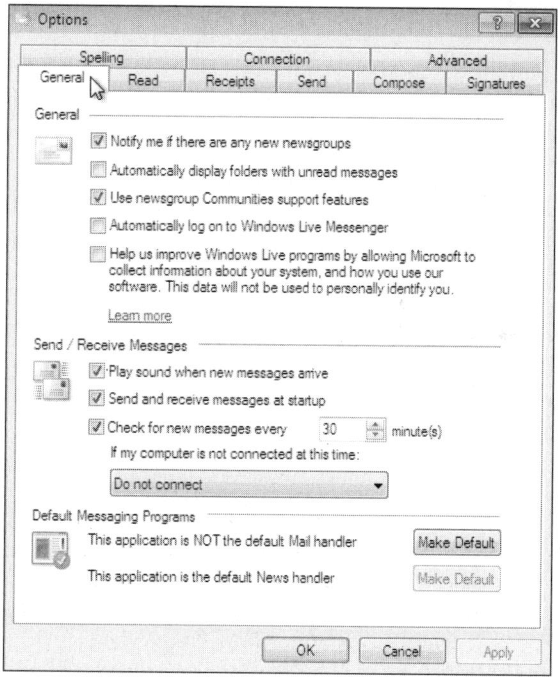

FIGURE 14.8
The General tab of
Live Mail's Options
dialog box

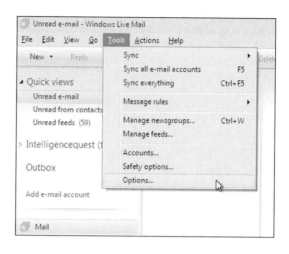

Use the Send tab to configure the behavior of Live Mail when messages are sent. You can also use this tab to configure whether mail and newsgroup messages are sent in HTML or plain text. The Compose tab lets you configure the default font, stationery, and business card that are used for sending mail and newsgroup messages. The Send and Compose tabs are shown in Figure 14.10.

FIGURE 14.9
The Read and Receipts tabs of Live Mail's Options dialog box

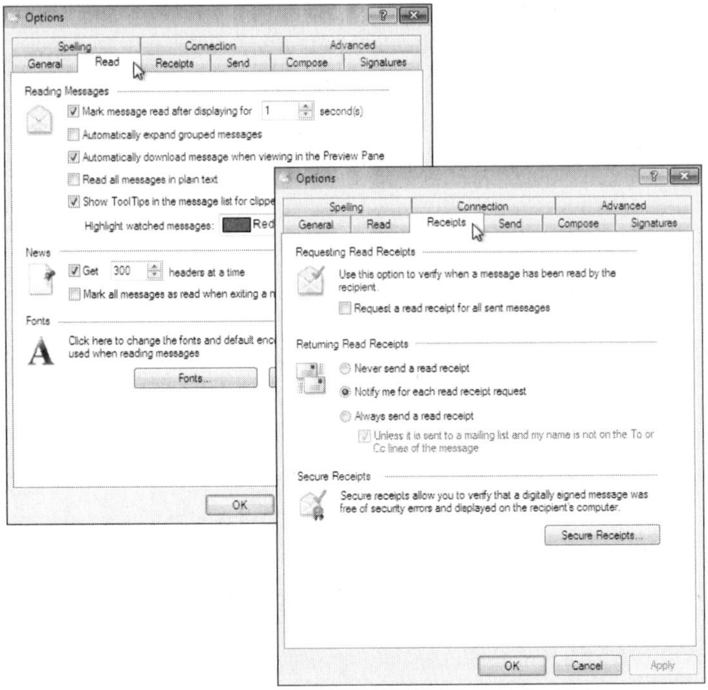

FIGURE 14.10
The Send and Compose tabs of Live Mail's Options dialog box

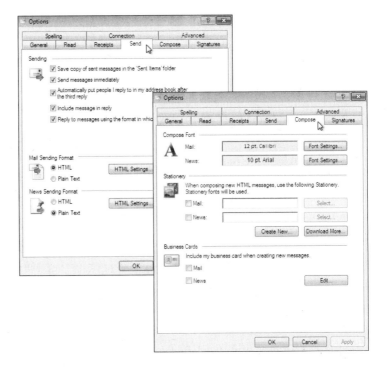

The Signatures tab, shown in Figure 14.11, lets you add, remove, and configure signatures. Signatures are the text automatically added to the bottom of outgoing messages. They are configured as straight text or added as a file.

FIGURE 14.11

The Signatures tab of Live Mail's Options dialog box

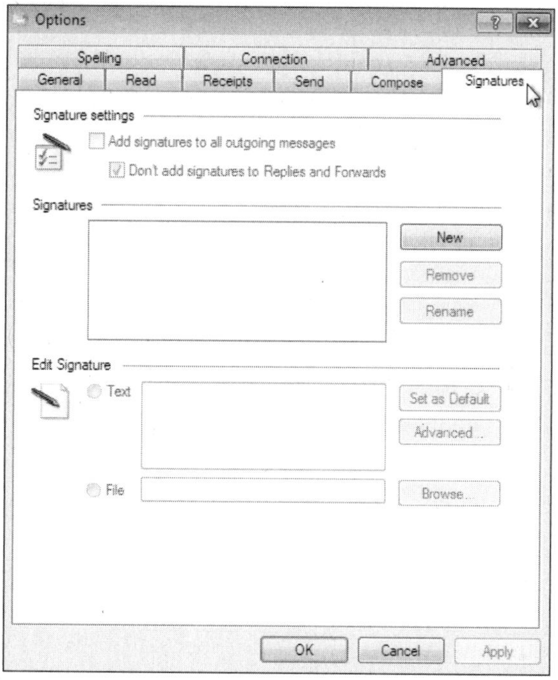

On the Spelling tab (see Figure 14.12), you configure whether Windows Mail will check for spelling errors either before sending or while you are typing the message (the latter is a new feature of Live Mail). The Spelling tab features options for automatically correcting common capitalization and spelling mistakes as well as checking spelling in the current input language. The Spelling tab also lets you choose to ignore spelling when words are in uppercase or contain numbers, and whether the original text is checked for spelling.

The Connection tab (see Figure 14.13) lets you configure dial-up and Internet connection behavior. Live Mail uses the same Internet Connection settings that Internet Explorer uses. The Connection tab also lets you sign in to your Windows Live account or tell Live Mail to stop signing you in.

The last tab in the Options dialog box is the Advanced tab, as shown in Figure 14.14. You use the Advanced tab to configure IMAP settings, message threads, replies, and forwards. You can also click the Maintenance button to open the dialog box shown in Figure 14.15, which lets you configure maintenance tasks — such as whether deleted items are emptied on exit and how the database is compacted. The Maintenance dialog box also lets you clean up your newsgroup messages and change the location of your message storage, known as the Store Folder. You can configure the troubleshooting logs from the Maintenance window as well.

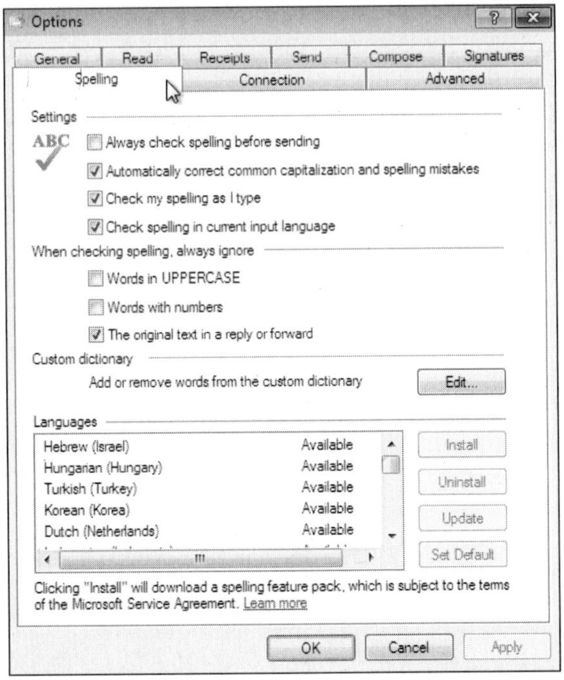

FIGURE 14.12
The Spelling tab of
Live Mail's Options
dialog box

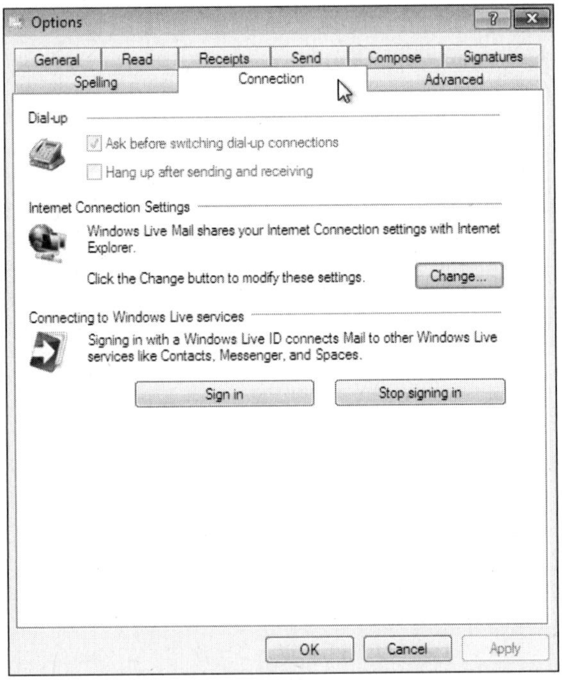

FIGURE 14.13
The Connection tab
of Live Mail's Options
dialog box

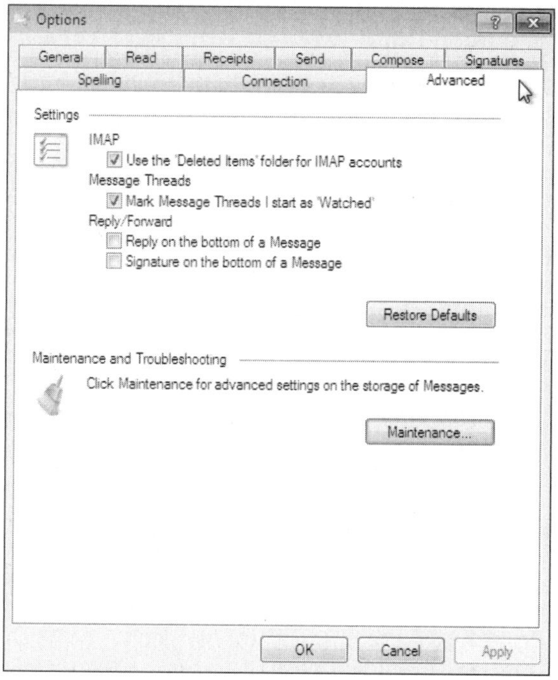

FIGURE 14.14
The Advanced tab of
Live Mail's Options
dialog box

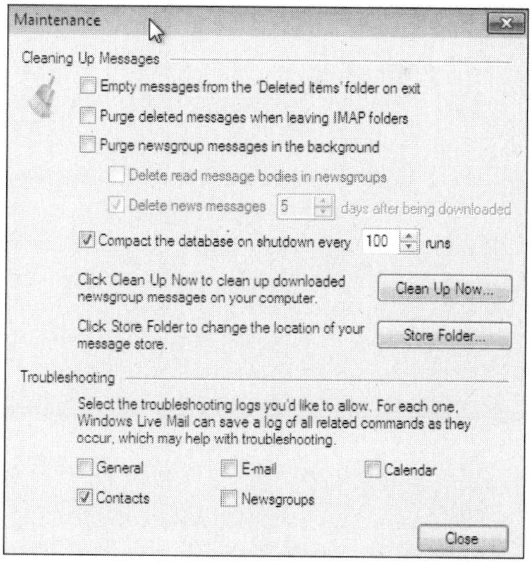

FIGURE 14.15
Click the Maintenance
button to open this
dialog box.

The security configuration for virus protection features, such as whether an application
attempts to send an email on your behalf, was formerly found on the Security tab in Windows Mail's Options window. In Live Mail, these configurations are found in the Safety
window.

Setting Up Safety Parameters in Live Mail

Live Mail includes enhanced safety features to help protect users and give them a better email experience by

- Identifying and handling junk email

- Setting up blocked sender and safe sender lists

- Configuring disallowed top-level domains (international countries and entities)

- Filtering phishing email

- Adding security features

You configure these features in the Safety Options dialog box of Live Mail. To access this window, activate the standard menu bar by pressing Alt and then select Tools ➤ Safety Options. This dialog box includes individual tabs for configuring the safety parameters.

The Options tab of the Safety Options dialog box, as shown in Figure 14.16, allows you to configure the junk mail settings for Live Mail.

FIGURE 14.16
The Options tab of Live Mail's Safety Options dialog box

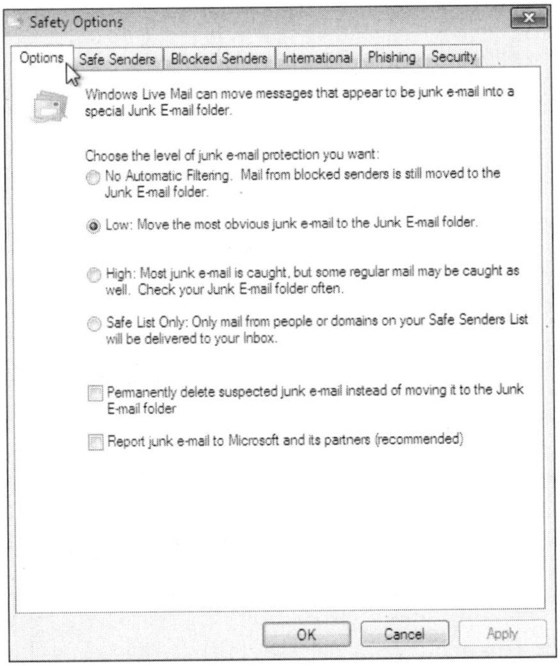

The Options tab lets you choose the level of junk mail:

- No Automatic Filtering

- Low

- High

- Safe List Only

Two options at the bottom of this tab are "Permanently delete suspected junk e-mail instead of moving it to the Junk E-mail folder" and "Report junk e-mail to Microsoft and its partners (recommended)."

The Safe Senders and Blocked Senders tabs are shown in Figure 14.17. These tabs allow you to configure a list of addresses you want to always allow or block.

FIGURE 14.17
The Safe Senders and Blocked Senders tabs of Live Mail's Safety Options dialog box

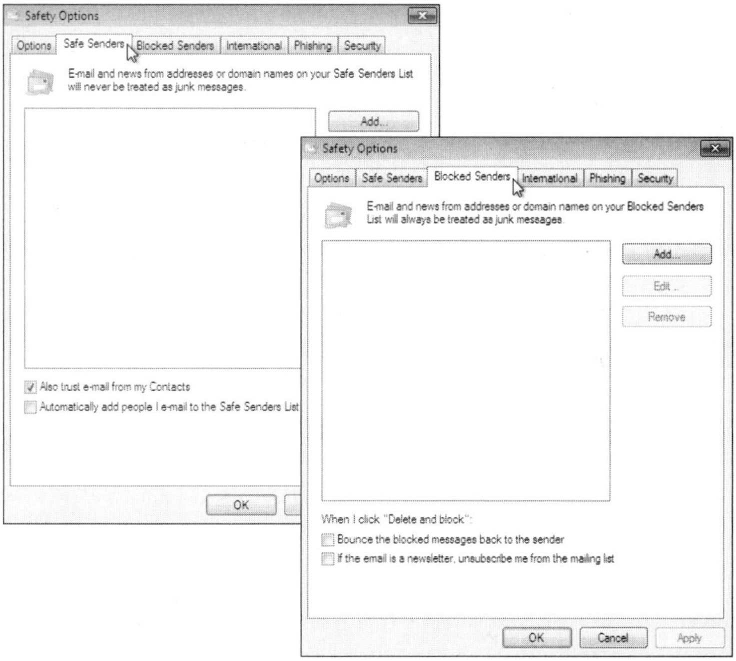

The International tab allows you to choose which top-level domains you would like to block and which character sets may be present in an email you choose to block. Figure 14.18 shows the International tab of as well as the Blocked Top-Level Domain List and Blocked Encodings List tabs.

ACCESSING EMAIL ON THE WEB USING LIVE MAIL ONLINE

One great feature of Live Mail is the ability to integrate your local email with a web-based email that gives you access to your email from any location with Internet access. The email you access on the Web will initially be your Live email account, but you can even add your other accounts to the web-based version. Using web-based email has proven to be convenient for many users. Live Mail will boost your productivity and user experience to new levels of usefulness by integrating your web-based email with your local email program.

Live Mail conveniently integrates your email contacts and messaging. Also, having a calendar available for keeping track of appointments as well as setting up free time will make Live Mail one stop closer to a complete collaborative solution.

FIGURE 14.18

The International, Blocked Top-Level Domain List, and Blocked Encodings List tabs of Live Mail's Safety Options dialog box

Using the Live Mail Calendar

Windows Vista includes a program called Windows Calendar that allows you to create events and appointments in a local calendar and then publish the local calendar and perhaps even share it. In Windows 7, the calendar functionality is appropriately part of Live Mail. This calendar is stored in your Live account, making it available anytime you log in. You may want to use it only locally like the Vista version, but having it online makes the calendar even more functional.

Calendar is available from within the Live Mail program; you launch the Calendar program from the lower-left pane. You are presented with the Calendar window shown in Figure 14.19. A toolbar is available that lets you change your view from month to week or to the day.

The toolbar also gives you the ability to add new events or create new calendars, as shown in Figure 14.20. By creating new calendars, you can have multiple calendars all tied to Live Mail. You can also create a new email message, photo email, news message, or contact by using the New menu.

So far we've looked at a local implementation of Calendar, but if you have a Live account, you can sign up for a Live.com mail account and your calendar will then be available any time you log into Live. You can share any of the calendars you have created with friends or colleagues, and you can have one collaborative location. Be assured that you do not have to share all or any of your calendars if you choose not to.

In addition to integrating your email and calendar functionality with a web presence as well as local access, Live Mail provides you with the ability to add friends and colleagues to a common database accessible from your local machine or online.

FIGURE 14.19
Live Mail Calendar

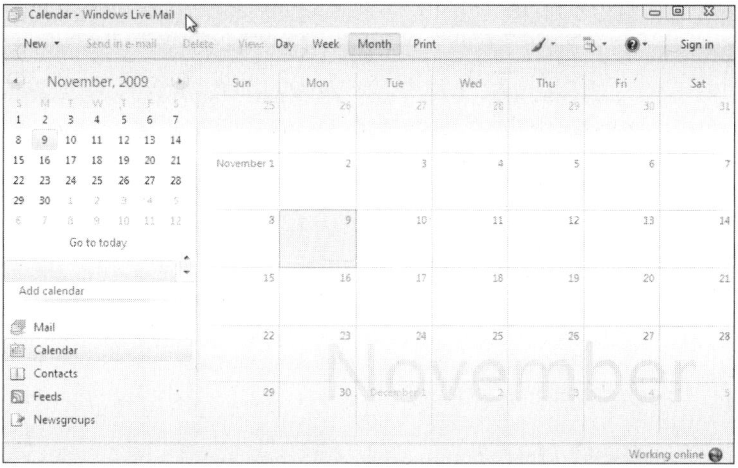

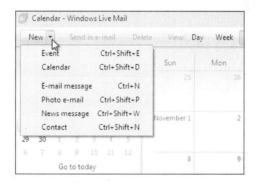

FIGURE 14.20
Live Mail Calendar's
New menu

Real World Scenario

USING EMAIL AND A CALENDAR IN WINDOWS 7

The authors have been using web-based email for a long time, and most of the administrators and users we know do the same. Yes, we have our corporate emails; we can access them using Outlook Web Access and even have them sent to our mobile devices. But we all use web-based email as well. We have even become quite fond of Google's calendar as it allows us to keep track of teaching schedules, our consulting team's schedule, and our personal schedule — all of which we can make available to colleagues and family selectively. The corporate Outlook has a great calendaring function, but alas, this is stuck to our corporate account.

Live Essentials' Mail program allows us to have the same Google email and calendar functionality we have become attached to. You can set up all your email accounts (yep, even Gmail), your contacts, and your calendars in Live Mail and have your consolidated messaging at every

Internet connection. Our consulting team has recommended the Live Essential solution to many clients, who have been pleased with the ease of integration into these collaborative features. We don't think we'll migrate our users away from Exchange and Outlook, but for some, this will be the most convenient and most inclusive solution for our messaging pleasure.

Using Live Mail Contacts

Live Mail Contacts is a component in the Live suite that is used to store contact information for individuals. You can access Contacts by selecting Contacts in the lower-left pane in Live Mail. The Contacts window, shown in Figure 14.21, lets you create, modify, and delete contacts and contact groups. You can also use your default email program to compose an email message to the selected contact.

FIGURE 14.21
Live Mail Contacts window

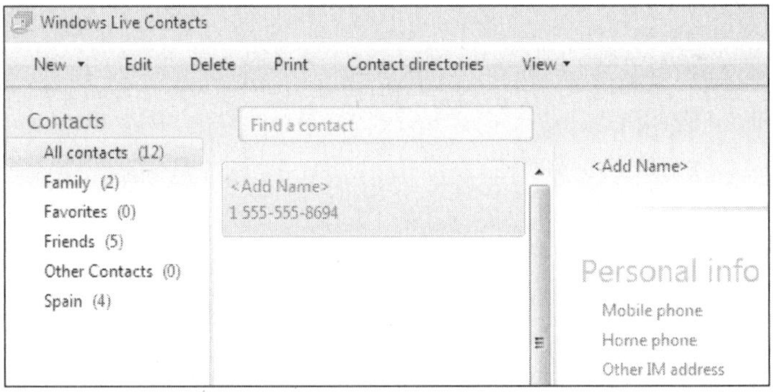

Adding a new contact is as simple as clicking New ➤ Contact, as shown in Figure 14.22.

FIGURE 14.22
Choose New ➤ Contact to add a new contact.

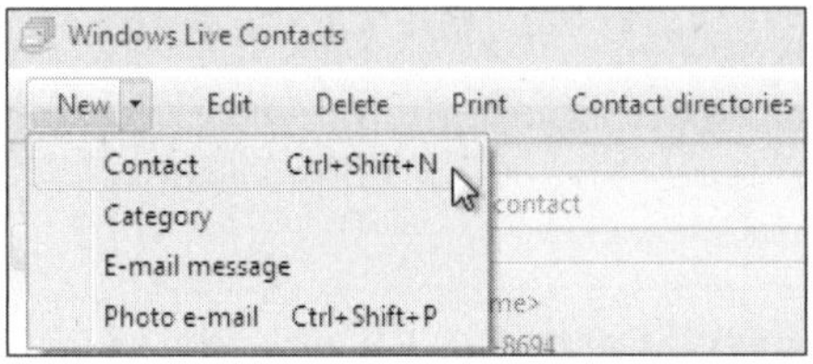

Within each contact, you can record a great deal of information by clicking the Quick Add button (as shown in Figure 14.23). This information includes the following:

◆ First name

◆ Last name

◆ Personal email

◆ Home phone

◆ Company

You can go even further with your contact information by adding many personal items to the contact information, such as the following:

- Additional contact information

- Personal information

- Work information

- Internet Messaging (IM) information

- Notes

- Digital IDs

As with Live Mail and Calendar, the contact information can also be made available to your Live account so your contacts are never more than an Internet connection away. Live Mail provides a set of applications available to you as a Windows 7 user and administrator. Some applications come installed in Windows 7 by default that provide more features and functionality to the users, such as Windows Fax and Scan.

Integrating Windows Fax and Scan

Windows Fax and Scan enables you to send and receive faxes without a fax machine. You can also use Windows Fax and Scan to scan documents so that you can fax or email them. To configure fax support and set fax properties, select Start ➤ All Programs ➤ Windows Fax And Scan. The Windows Fax and Scan application starts, as shown in Figure 14.24.

FIGURE 14.24
Windows Fax and Scan

Configuring Fax Support

Windows 7 allows you to add and configure fax support. You can add fax support to your computer even if a fax machine is not available. You configure fax support through the Windows Fax and Scan application.

ADDING A FAX ACCOUNT

Before you can send or receive faxes, you must first create an account. To create an account, click Tools ➤ Fax Accounts and then click Add to create an account. You are prompted to connect to a fax modem on your computer or to a fax server.

SETTING FAX PROPERTIES

To configure fax settings, click Tools ➤ Fax Settings. The Fax Settings dialog box displays and has four tabs with options and information for your fax support, as follows:

General   Displays the device name and provides the ability to configure the device parameters to send and receive faxes.

Tracking   Enables you to set up notification options for fax events and configure the Fax Monitor to display progress when faxes are sent or received. You can also configure sound options in the Tracking tab.

Advanced   Enables you to configure which folder is used for receiving faxes. Sent faxes will also be stored in the specified folder. It also allows you to include a banner with the fax. The

Advanced tab lets you configure the number of redials to perform, and the start and end times for sending faxes.

Security   Enables you to configure which users or groups can send and receive faxes and who can manage fax configuration.

STARTING THE FAX SERVICE

After you configure fax support, you need to start the Fax Service in Windows 7.
Perform the following steps to start the service:

1. Right-click Computer on the Start menu and select Manage from the context menu.

2. Expand Services and Applications and then Services.

3. Double-click Fax Service and click the Start button.

4. Select Automatic as the Startup Type and click OK.

5. Close the Computer Management window.

Managing Imaging Devices

A scanner is a device that can read text or graphics that are on paper and translate the information to digital data that the computer can understand. After you install a scanner on a Windows 7 computer, you can manage the device through the Windows Fax and Scan application.

If the scanner is a USB scanner, simply connecting the device to the computer should install the appropriate driver, and the scanner will be available in the Windows Fax and Scan application. To configure a scanner that is attached to your computer, click Scan in the lower-left corner of the Windows and Fax application, and then click Tools ➢ Scan Settings, which opens the Scan Profiles dialog box.

If you have a scanner installed on your computer, perform the following steps to view and configure its properties:

1. Select Start ➢ All Programs ➢ Windows Fax And Scan.

2. In the Windows Fax and Scan application, click Scan in the lower-left corner.

3. Select the scanner to modify and then click the Edit button.

4. Modify the settings as desired and then click Save Profile.

5. Click Close to close the Scan Profiles dialog box.

6. Close the Windows Fax and Scan application.

Windows 7 has even more applications installed and available for your convenience, such as Media Player for listening to audio and viewing video.

Using Windows Media Player 12

Windows Media Player 12, shown in Figure 14.25, enables you to play digital media, organize your media files, burn CDs and DVDs, synchronize files to a portable music player, and shop for digital media online. To open Windows Media Player 12, choose Start ≫ All Programs ≫ Windows Media Player.

Understanding the Windows Media Player 12 Interface

The new version of Windows Media Player in Windows 7 has a different look and feel than previous versions. Microsoft is following their goals of making the user experience easier by rearranging menu items to a more logical placement. Windows Media Player 12 has two views you can toggle between:

◆ The Library view (the default view when opening Windows Media Player 12 from the Start menu)

◆ The Now Playing view

Toggle between the Library and Now Playing views by clicking the icon in the lower right of the Library view or the upper-right of the Now Playing view, as shown in Figure 14.26.

Windows Media Player 12 organizes your media into several categories available in the Library view. The categories include:

Playlists   Choosing Save List from your list of songs saves the list as a playlist, which makes it available for future access.

Music   Any digital music Windows Media Player 12 has discovered on your PC is located in this category. Media files discovered include MP3, WMA, WAV, and so forth.

Videos   Any videos you have saved from cameras or have downloaded are saved in this category. Media files discovered for this category include AVI, MPEG, WMV, DivX, and so forth.

Pictures   Media Player saves digital pictures on your PC in this category and can display them to you. File types discovered for this category include JPEG, GIF, and so forth.

Recorded TV   If your PC has the hardware installed to capture TV, any recorded programs are saved into the Recorded TV category.

Other Libraries   The Other Libraries category holds media that is stored on other Windows 7 machines in the same HomeGroup as your PC. This category might also hold items you've added that Windows Media Player 12 doesn't recognize.

The following tabbed menu items are available in the Library view of Windows Media Player 12:

Play   Used to play a CD or DVD, create and clear playlists, and see what's currently being played.

Burn   Used to burn music to a CD or data to a CD or DVD. You can burn at various speeds, apply volume leveling to audio CDs, and convert music to a different bit rate.

Sync   Used to perform two-way synchronization of data between your computer and a portable media device, a flash memory device, or a Portable Media Center.

You can use Windows Media Player 12 as a launching spot to shop online for digital media. Select the drop-down list box in the lower-left corner, as shown in Figure 14.27, to access the Browse All Online Stores option.

FIGURE 14.27
Media options in
Windows Media
Player 12

When you play, burn, or sync a protected file, Windows Media Player checks to see whether you have valid media usage rights. If you have valid rights, you are allowed to play, burn, or sync the file. Normally, media usage rights are automatically downloaded for you. So why can't you play your file if you've got a connection to the Internet? Check to see if Download Usage Rights Automatically When I Play Or Sync A File is selected on the Privacy tab of the Options dialog box. If it is enabled, you might have to restore your media usage rights from the online store where you purchased your digital media. Playing a music CD in Windows Media Player 12 can be as simple as inserting the CD into your PC.

Playing Music CDs in Windows Media Player 12

Playing an audio CD in Windows 7 should be straightforward, because Windows Media Player 12 recognizes the insertion of a music CD into your PC and launches the Player view automatically. Some CDs that contain digital music might prompt Windows 7 to display a dialog box that asks you what you want to do. This happens sometimes when you create your own music CDs and Windows 7 simply sees the music as files. The dialog box offers you the option to play the audio CD, which launches Windows Media Player 7.

If by some chance another program plays your audio CD, then Windows Media Player 7 might not be the default program for playing audio CDs. Perhaps the file format on the CD is captured by another program. You can close the other program and launch Windows Media Player 12 from the Start menu and choose to play an audio CD.

Playing music CDs in Windows 7 using Windows Media Player 12 is fairly simple, but what about movies? Windows Media Player 12 also recognizes DVDs.

Playing DVDs in Windows Media Player 12

Windows Media Player 12 will react similarly to DVDs as it does for CDs: it will launch automatically into the Now Playing view when you insert a video DVD in your PC's DVD drive. Being able to play multiple media formats without user intervention is another way Microsoft is trying to make the music and movie experience simple.

To play your DVD movie in full-screen view, press and hold the Alt key and then press Enter. Return to the windowed view by pressing the same keystrokes. While in full-screen view, moving your mouse cursor will bring up the play controls, but they will disappear after a few moments of not moving the cursor.

You can play other video files in the same interface as the DVD movie screen as well. You can double-click movies that you have captured on a digital camera or from an Internet source in the Videos library and control them just as you would a DVD movie. What if you have a TV tuner built in or added to your PC? Windows 7's Media Center lets you control this added input.

Controlling Digital Media with Windows Media Center

Windows Media Center is included in the Home Premium, Professional, and Ultimate editions of Windows 7. Windows Media Center adds the ability to watch, pause, and record live TV (as long as you have the appropriate TV tuner hardware installed). You can also view online entertainment within Windows Media Center from around the world. Windows Media Center plays CDs, DVDs, music, and video much the same way Windows Media Player does, but with more controls available to the user. One thing Windows Media Center does that Windows Media Player does not do is make your PC into a digital video recorder (DVR).

DISPLAYING TV PROGRAMS IN WINDOWS MEDIA CENTER

To play TV programs and use the DVR capabilities of Windows Media Center, you need to make sure a few items are present. You need a TV tuner to received broadcast signals and select TV channels. Some TV tuners you can purchase for your PC come with a remote that will integrate into Windows Media Player. If your TV tuner doesn't have a remote, you can still use your keyboard and mouse for control. You also need a TV signal. You might be able to capture over-the-air signals, but remember, this is only a digital signal now and your tuner will have to decode these signals or you'll still need an external converter. You also have to make sure you have a version of Windows 7 that has support for Windows Media Center. Probably the best enhancement you can select is a TV tuner that has a TV output as well. TV programs on your computer's monitor will look good, but being able to display any of your digital media on the big screen of a television, even HD programming, will best contribute to your viewing pleasure.

When you launch Windows Media Center for the first time, you are prompted to go through a setup wizard. Windows Media Center is a little more intense than most. There is an express mode, but it will still take you a few minutes for the install application to go through your PC looking for music, videos, and so forth; to ask you questions about your home network and Internet connections; to ask which area of the world you live in (for a TV programming guide); and even ask you for the provider for your TV programming (if you have the TV tuner installed). If you don't know all the answers, you can guess and go back later to change any incorrect parameters if you need to. Changing the parameters after the fact is your first exercise in using the Windows Media Center menu structure.

Using Windows Media Centers Menus

Windows Media Center offers a lot of options for users, and creating access to the options in a convenient manner was an obvious challenge. The Microsoft team seems to have found a great solution by using both vertical and horizontal scrolling for the menu structure. Keep in mind that Windows Media Center is designed to be at home equally on a TV screen as well as a PC monitor. Figure 14.28 shows Windows Media Center as it may appear upon launching if the last thing you were doing was browsing music.

FIGURE 14.28
Windows Media Center's
main screen

To browse through the various categories offered by Windows Media Center, you use the vertical scrolling options. You access the up and down arrows to scroll through the categories by moving your mouse cursor to a position above or below the categories, and the scroll arrows appear as shown in Figure 14.29.

FIGURE 14.29
Windows Media Center
category selection scroll
arrows

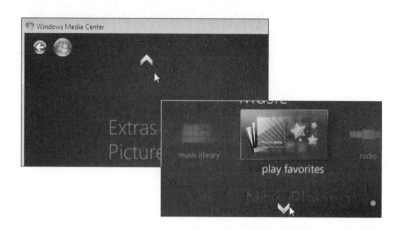

After you find the category you are looking for, you can scroll through the items within that category by scrolling horizontally. Access the horizontal scroll arrows by moving your mouse cursor to the left or right of the category item, and Windows Media Center will display the appropriate arrow. Figure 14.30 shows the left scroll arrow displayed for the Extras category.

FIGURE 14.30
The left scroll arrow
displayed for the Extras
category

You can scroll through the following categories in the Windows Media Center:

Extras   The Extras category displays miscellaneous items such as an Extras library where you can find Windows 7 games, Explore option, Internet TV, News, a Learn How item for inter-active help, and new hardware Extenders for Windows Media Center allowing access to your audio and video content on your local network.

Pictures + Videos   Pictures + Videos gives you access to your picture library, video library, and favorites lists.

Music   The Music category gives you access to your music library, favorites music lists, the ability to search for music, and a radio option that has the ability to capture radio signals being carried by your TV provider (if you have the tuner installed).

Now Playing   If you want to go back to what you were listening to or watching before you accessed the menu structure, you can return by selecting the Now Playing category.

Movies   The Movies category allows you to access your movie library, which is where you will find any recorded video you have, movie guides, and movie trailers. You can even play a DVD.

TV   The TV category follows the Movies category in structure, allowing you access to recorded video, TV guides and schedules, live TV setup, and search functionality (by title, actor, director, and so forth).

Sports   If you're looking for sports scores, team player information, or sports league information, the Sports category is where you would look.

Tasks   The Tasks category is where you visit (or revisit) to change your setup options. Figure 14.31 shows the Tasks category with the Settings option selected. Click the Settings box to access the setup parameters and make changes if necessary.

FIGURE 14.31
The Tasks category with the Settings option

Along with the standard categories of files you can access on your local machine with Windows Media Center, you can also access other devices on your network and enjoy media stored available elsewhere.

Accessing Other Devices on Your Network with Windows Media Center

You can have one of your machines set up to use a TV and sound system for viewing and listening to your digital media, utilizing the functionality of Window Media Center. If you have some of your media resources stored on other devices in your network, Media Center provides a central location for accessing the resources and playing them for you. Media Center has the ability to connect to your networked Xbox 360, displaying its library of music, photos, and movies. You can use the Windows 7 HomeGroup functionality to allow other Windows 7 machines on your network to supply music, photos, and video as well.

Windows Media Center, Windows Media Player, and Windows Fax and Scan are programs installed in Windows 7 by default. Live Essentials is a package downloaded and installed via the Web. What if you have purchased a software program and need to install it? Relax, we've come a long way and Windows 7 will protect itself while allowing applications to be installed and then cleanly uninstall themselves when required.

Installing and Uninstalling Applications in Windows 7

Using the built-in applications in Windows 7 is all well and good, but there will certainly be other applications that will need to be installed. Microsoft might be the author of the applications, or it might be other software vendors. You may install from a CD or DVD or download the installation files from a website and then install the application. No matter which way you get the application, you will more than likely have to go through an installation process.

Installing an Application from a Disk

One of the operating system protection features of Windows 7 is that in order to install an application, you must have administrator privileges on the machine. You must be able to enter the username and password of an administrator of the local machine in order for the application to install and make the necessary configuration changes. This requirement applies to any installation location, not just from a CD or DVD disk.

LAUNCHING THE INSTALLATION PROGRAM

Most commercial programs you purchase will be delivered via DVD or CD media and should come with a set of installation instructions. Just like everything else in our computing world, program installation is designed to be simple and seamless, and most written instructions state that you should insert the DVD or CD into the drive and follow the on-screen instructions.

To start an application installation, follow these steps:

1. Close any programs you might be running on your machine. This step is not required, but it's always a good idea.

2. Insert the application installation media into the appropriate disk drive.

3. Wait for the automated installation program to launch (this might take a moment or two).

4. Follow the on-screen instructions.

Normally the on-screen instructions are in the form of a wizard and will walk you through a series of questions (the fewer the better) as you click the Next button to continue. It's nice that most vendors include a default set of answers where possible so that many times you can just "next through the installation" and make changes to the configuration later if necessary. When all is done, you're normally presented with a confirmation screen saying all is well and you can click the Finish button to exit the installation.

There might be times when the automated start does not occur when you insert the installation disc. Why? Well, some users disable the Autorun feature so they don't get prompted each time a disc is inserted.

If your installation does not start automatically, perform the following steps to start the installation:

1. Choose Start ➤ Computer to open the computer window where you can access the drives in your PC.

2. Double-click the drive where you inserted the installation disc to start the automated setup program.

You might be one more step away from launching the application installation if the automated installation does not launch from the previous steps. You might need to locate the setup application and launch it manually.

Perform the following steps to manually launch an application installation:

1. Choose Start ➤ Computer to open the computer window where you can access the drives in your PC.

2. Right-click the drive where you inserted the installation disc and select Explore from the context menu.

3. Locate the application installation program, normally named `setup.exe`, and double-click the file; this should launch the setup program, thus allowing the installation to commence.

After the installation starts, you normally are presented with an installation wizard that provides a series of installation prompts as you progress through the installation.

DEALING WITH THE STANDARD INSTALLATION PROMPTS

There are several standard prompts you may encounter as you install your application. You will be prompted for the following in most wizard-based installations:

A Serial Number, Registration Number, or Product Key   Most current commercial installation programs require some sort of validation that you have purchased a license to run the application. This is in the form of a serial number, registration number, or license key that is unique to your installation. The installation wizard prompts you for this parameter and will not continue without it. In some cases you can continue and use the application on a trial basis without entering a value, but you will most certainly need to purchase the license to fully use the product or continue beyond a trial period.

An End-User License Agreement (EULA)   Almost all commercial and most shareware/freeware applications want you to read and agree to a legal document outlining your rights to the program as well as retained rights from the vendor to the use of their program. The EULA is this agreement, and you won't be able to continue with the installation unless you agree to abide by its terms. Most of the time, you will not read this document as it is long and boring, but you *really* should. It may also outline multiple machine usage, copying of the disk for backup, and even whether you can sell the program to someone else when you're done with it.

Type of Application Installation   The goal of most vendors is to make the installation as simple as possible, but there might be times when you want to add your input to the installation by configuring advanced options. Most programs offer two types of installation: Express, where most (if not all) of the installation questions are answered by default for you by the software vendor, and Advanced, where you are given the opportunity to answer most of the configuration questions as the application installation wizard progresses.

Where to Install the Program Icon   After the installation, you want to run the application (that's why you are installing it). Most setup programs give you the option of adding the program icon to the desktop and/or adding it to the Start menu. It will be added to your program menu even if you don't choose either of the two options.

Installation Summary   Most current installation programs present the user with an installation summary at the completion of the installation, with any parameters you configured displayed.

After you install the program, you can run it by clicking the desktop icon (if you added it), choosing Start and selecting the application (if you added it to the Start menu), or choosing Start ➤ All Programs and finding the application in its All Programs folder. Even though you provided answers to configuration questions (or were provided with defaults), many programs will still ask you application-specific questions when you initially launch the program.

Occasionally files associated with an application might become corrupted or an application file might get inadvertently deleted; in this case, you may need to repair the installation.

Repairing or Changing an Application

In some cases, you might need to revisit an application's installation options. If you chose one type of installation — Express, for example — and then realize there are more components that you need, you might want to change the installed application items. Because these components were part of the install, you need to go through the installation process again to change them. You can use the Change option for your installation from Control Panel.

Perform the following steps to access the Change option for an application:

1. Choose Start, type **control** in the search box, and press Enter (you can also select Control Panel from the Start menu).

2. In Control Panel, select Programs.

3. In the Programs window, select Programs And Features.

4. In the Programs And Features window, select the application you want to change and then choose Change from the menu.

After you perform the previous steps, a new instance of the application installation program starts and you can change the original options to meet your needs. Figure 14.32 shows the choices for step 2, 3, and 4 selections that were used in the previous task.

FIGURE 14.32
Accessing the Change menu from Control Panel

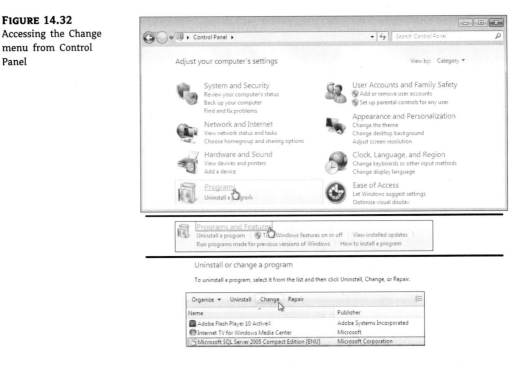

This process works well to add options, but maybe you just need the installation to rerun because one of the application files has been deleted or because one of the application files has been corrupted. In this case you would want to repair the installation. You can follow the pre-vious step to access the Repair option, but choose Repair instead of Change.

Bear in mind that with the Repair and Change options, the progression will change from application to application. In fact, some application installations won't offer the Change or Repair option. In most cases, repairing or changing an application will require you to have the original installation media (so you'll have the original files). If you simply don't need the application any longer, you may choose to uninstall the application.

Uninstalling an Application

If you no longer need an application, you can stop using it and even delete the icon from your desktop, but the application will still be installed using disk space and maybe using memory and CPU resources (if the application launches any components as Windows 7 starts). If you know you are not going to use the program anymore, uninstalling the application is the best course of action.

Perform the following steps to uninstall an application:

1. Choose Start, type **control** in the search box, and press Enter (you can also select Control Panel from the Start menu).

2. In Control Panel, select Programs.

3. In the Programs window, select Programs And Features.

4. In the Programs And Features window, select the application you want to change and then choose Uninstall from the menu.

Finding an application in Control Panel's Programs And Features window assumes the application vendor followed Windows 7 guidelines and included it there. If the program does not appear in the Programs And Features window, you might still be able to uninstall it conventionally by finding the application's uninstall program in its program directory (choose Start ➢ All Programs). Find the application you want to uninstall in All Programs, right-click, and choose Uninstall, or you can locate the uninstall program in the application's All Programs folder.

Some applications or services you use within Windows 7 are not actually installed after the fact — they are Windows features. You have the ability to change these features as well.

Modifying Windows 7 Features (Built-in Programs)

Windows 7 comes with many programs and services that enhance the functionality of Win-dows 7 and are known as Windows features. You can turn on features, turn off features, and change some of the features options from the Windows Features dialog box.

Perform the following steps to access the Windows Features dialog box:

1. Choose Start, type **control** in the search box, and press Enter (you can also select Control Panel from the Start menu).

2. In Control Panel, select Programs.

3. In the Programs window, select Programs And Features.

4. In the Programs And Features window, select the Turn Windows Features On Or Off from the menu in the left column to launch the Windows Features dialog box.

5. In the Windows Features dialog box, select the Windows Feature check box you would like to activate, or deselect to turn off a feature. You can also click the plus sign to expose more subfeatures to turn on or off, as shown in Figure 14.33.

We've gone through quite a few examples in this chapter about programs and features available in Windows 7. We discussed the new and exciting features of many existing programs as well as the introduction of Live Essentials as a web-based collaboration of programs and utilities. The best way to fully understand Windows 7 is to experience it. Get into the operating system, look around, and enjoy.

FIGURE 14.33
Windows Feature selection window

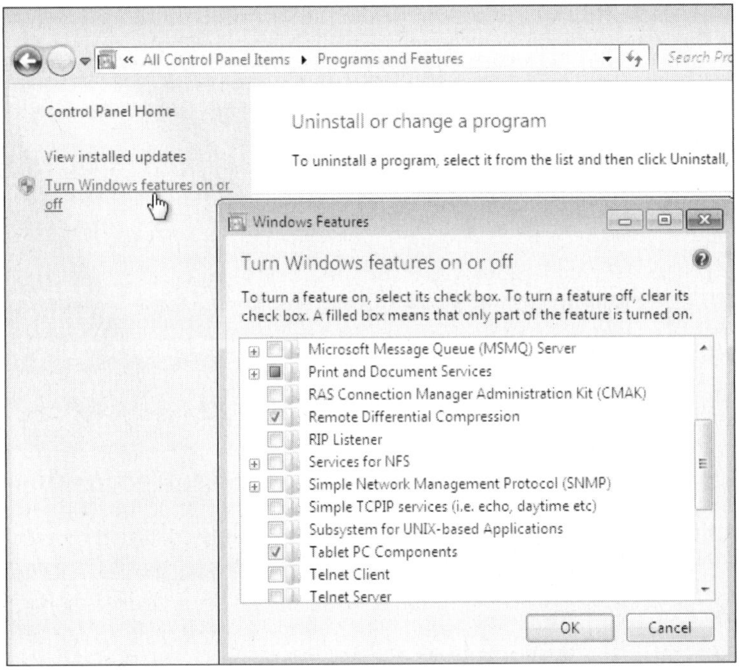

Real World Scenario

USING OTHER PROGRAMS INSTALLED IN WINDOWS 7

There are several other programs, like games, installed in Windows 7 by default. Although not overly functional as far as productivity, they look cool and provide an idea of just what Windows 7 graphical components have to offer. The Accessories folder has another series of applications to offer that provide simple, yet valuable tools, as shown here:

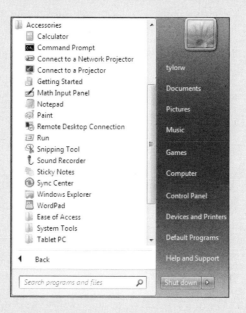

The authors use many of these programs on a regular basis. If we have a quick text file to look at, we'll use WordPad or Notepad; if we need to look at our network configuration, we open the command prompt. For any graphic we want to modify, we use Paint (that's the program we used for every screen shot in this book). Take a look at Calculator. The same functionality is there as in previous versions of Calculator, but now in Windows 7, there's even more. Check out the following image to see the four views now available (in addition to Programmer and Statistics from earlier versions).

Along with the new views are some basic unit conversions, date calculations, and worksheet templates for calculations such as mortgages, vehicle leases, and fuel economy. We know this program, Calculator, seems like such a simple thing, but it is probably one of the best modifications for the simplest task we've seen in a long time.

The Bottom Line

Use Windows 7's Getting Started feature.   The Getting Started screen in Windows 7 offers the user several quick links for configuring some of Windows 7's features and online resources.

Master It   You recently installed Windows 7 and when logging in you saw the Getting Started window, but immediately closed it and starting exploring your new operating system. You remember seeing something about accessing online resources and would like to go back to Getting Started to see if you can find out more about Windows 7. How will you get back to Getting Started and find the online resources you saw previously?

Manage Live Essentials' Mail features.   Live Essentials is a program suite for collaborative or online programs that includes Live Mail (taking the place of Windows Mail). There are several configurable Live Mail convenience features.

Master It   You have downloaded Live Essentials from download.live.com and installed the program. You selected several of the Live Essential programs, including Live Mail. You have set up Live Mail and it's working just fine. You saw a colleague using Live Mail and it was making spelling suggestions as your colleague wrote the email (just as Word does), and you want to make this option available in your Live Mail. How do you enable the spelling suggestions?

Play a saved digital video in Windows Media Center.   Windows Media Center has the ability to play music, TV, and video; launch applications; and even gather Internet statistics for sports teams. Media Center is an entertainment portal that provides superior functionality from a simple interface.

Master It   You have downloaded a digital video from your camera and placed it into the Video library in Windows 7. You know you can play it in Media Player, but would like to play it in Windows Media Player on your large-screen TV and listen to the audio on your entertainment center. You have installed the required hardware to use your TV and audio system. How do you find the video and play the movie?

Use Repair to fix a corrupted application.   You can use Control Panel's Programs And Features application to repair or change installation items in Windows 7.

Master It   You installed an application some time ago from a CD and it's been running fine. While cleaning up, you deleted some files you thought were not being used and now your application won't run. You would like to repair the installation. How do you repair an application in Windows 7?

Chapter 15

Maintaining and Optimizing Windows 7

If you want an optimized Windows 7 installation, you must monitor its reliability and performance. Windows 7 comes with many tools to track memory, processor activity, the disk subsystem, and the network subsystem, as well as other computer subsystems. Tools are available to provide baseline statistics for each of the subsystems so that you can track changes over time and better evaluate issues that pertain to the Windows 7 machine and make changes to proactively affect declining performance.

In this chapter, you'll learn how to monitor, maintain, troubleshoot, and optimize Windows 7 using the following utilities: Performance Monitor, Reliability Monitor, System Information, Task Manager, several system tools, System Configuration, Task Scheduler, and Event Viewer. Each of these tools provides information about the operating system and hardware status.

Windows 7 has a full backup and restore application to allow you to maintain a backup copy of any of the Windows 7 component files and data files that are considered critical to the operation of your day-to-day business. You can use the backup of the files to restore them if they become unusable (corrupted, deleted, or even modified and you want to go back to the original).

You'll also learn about system recovery and troubleshooting. In this chapter, we'll show you how to safeguard your computer and how to recover from a disaster. The benefit of having a disaster recovery plan is that when you expect the worst to happen and are prepared for it, you can easily recover from most system failures.

In this chapter, you'll learn how to:

◆ Use Performance Monitor to view CPU usage

◆ Maintain Windows 7 with system tools

◆ Schedule a task to launch daily

◆ Back up critical data files

Understanding Windows 7 Performance Optimization

Before you can optimize the performance of Windows 7, you must monitor the operating systems' critical subsystems to determine how each is currently performing and what (if anything) is causing system bottlenecks that negatively affect performance. Windows 7 ships with many tools that you can use to monitor system performance. The monitoring tools enable you to assess your server's current health and determine what requirements to improve its present condition are available.

Performance Monitor is a tool that you can used to perform the following tasks:

♦ Create baselines.

♦ Identify system bottlenecks.

♦ Determine trends.

♦ Test configuration changes or tuning efforts.

♦ Create alert thresholds.

Creating Baselines

A baseline is a snapshot of how your system is currently performing. Suppose that your computer's hardware has not changed over the last six months, but the computer seems to be performing more slowly now than it did six months ago. If you have been using the Performance Monitor utility and taking baseline logs, as well as noting the changes in your workload, you can more easily determine what resources are causing the system to slow down. If you simply note Windows 7 seems to be running more slowly, without any supporting statistics, you will not have any idea what is causing your issues.

You should create baselines at the following times:

♦ When the system is first configured, without any load

♦ At regular intervals of typical usage

♦ Whenever any changes are made to the system's hardware or software configuration

Baselines are particularly useful for determining the effect of changes that you make to your computer. For example, if you are adding more memory to your computer, you should take baselines before and after you install the memory to determine the effect of the change. Along with hardware changes, system configuration modifications can affect your computer's performance, so you should create baselines before and after you make any changes to your Windows 7 configuration.

MAKING CHANGES TO WINDOWS 7

For the most part, Windows 7 is a self-tuning operating system. If you decide to tweak the operating system, take baselines before and after each change. If you don't notice a performance gain after the tweak, consider returning the computer to its original configuration; some tweaks might cause more problems than they solve.

IDENTIFYING SYSTEM BOTTLENECKS

A bottleneck is a system resource that is inefficient compared with the rest of the computer system as a whole. The bottleneck can cause the rest of the system to run slowly.

You need to pinpoint the cause of a bottleneck to correct it. Consider a system that has a Pentium 4 3.0 GHz processor with 1024 MB of RAM. You might consider changing to a more advanced processor. However, if your applications are memory-intensive and lack of memory is your bottleneck, upgrading your processor will not eliminate the bottleneck.

By using Performance Monitor, you can measure the performance of the various parts of your system, which allows you to identify system bottlenecks in a scientific manner. You will learn how to set counters to monitor your network and spot bottlenecks in the "Managing System Performance" section later in this chapter.

DETERMINING TRENDS

Many of us tend to manage situations reactively instead of proactively. With reactive management, you focus on a problem when it occurs; with proactive management, you take steps to avoid the problem before it happens. In a perfect world, all management would be proactive. Performance Monitor is a great tool for proactive network management. If you are creating baselines on a regular basis, you can identify system trends. For example, if you notice average CPU utilization increasing 5 percent every month, you can assume that within the next six months, you're going to have a problem. Before performance becomes so slow that your system is not responding, you can upgrade the hardware.

Testing Configuration Changes or Tuning Efforts

When you make configuration changes or tune your computer, you might want to measure the effects of those changes. Performance Monitor allows you evaluate your machines' subsystems before changes are made and while you are in the process of making changes. When you make configuration changes, the following recommendations apply:

Make only one change at a time.   If you are making configuration changes for tuning, and you make multiple changes at one time, it is difficult to quantify the effect of each individual change. In addition, some changes might have a negative impact that, if you have made multiple changes, may be difficult to identify.

Repeat monitoring with each individual change you make.   This will help you determine whether additional tuning is required.

As you make changes, check the Event Viewer event log files.   Some performance changes will generate events within Event Viewer that should be reviewed. Event Viewer is covered in more detail in the "Using Event Viewer" section later in this chapter.

Using Alerts for Problem Notification

Performance Monitor provides another tool for proactive management in the form of alerts. Through data collector sets, you can specify alert thresholds (when a counter reaches a specified value) and have the utility notify you when these thresholds are reached. For example, you could specify that if one of your hard drives logical disks has less than 10 percent of free space, you want to be notified. Once alerted, you can add more disk space or delete unneeded files before you run out of disk space. Setting up Performance Monitor and using its capabilities is a boon to you as an administrator to keep Windows 7 optimized.

Optimizing Windows 7 with Performance Monitor

The Performance Monitor utility is used to measure the performance of a local or a remote computer on the network. Performance Monitor enables you to do the following:

◆ Collect data from your local computer or remote computers on the network. You can collect data from a single computer or multiple computers concurrently.

◆ View data as it is being collected in real time, or historically from collected data.

◆ Have full control over the selection of what data will be collected by selecting which specific objects and counters will be collected.

◆ Choose the sampling parameters that will be used, meaning the time interval that you want to use for collecting data points and the time period that will be used for data collection.

◆ Determine the format in which data will be viewed: inline, histogram bar, or report views.

◆ Create HTML pages for viewing data.

◆ Create specific configurations for monitoring data that can then be exported to other computers for performance monitoring.

VIEWING PERFORMANCE MONITOR ON REMOTE MACHINES

To view data on remote computers, you need to have administrative rights to the remote computer, the Remote Registry Service must be enabled and running on the remote computer, and Windows Firewall must be set to allow the connection.

Through Performance Monitor, you can view current data or data from a log file. When you view current data, you are monitoring real-time activity. When you view data from a log file, you are importing a log file from a previous session.

To access Performance Monitor, choose Start ≻ Control Panel ≻ System And Security ≻ Administrative Tools, and then double-click Performance Monitor; or you can type **perfmon** in the Start menu's search box. Figure 15.1 shows the main Performance Monitor window when it is initially opened without configuration.

When you first start Performance Monitor, the Overview Of Performance Monitor page is displayed. This page gives a quick snapshot of what resources are being used in your computer in the System Summary pane. Notice the four initial resources tracked are Memory, Network Interface, Physical Disk, and Processor Information. You can view detailed information about each resource by clicking the Open Resource Monitor link.

Using Resource Monitor

The Resource Monitor window was integrated into the Reliability and Performance utility of Windows Vista, but has been given its own dialog box in Windows 7. Figure 15.2 shows the Resource Monitor dialog box (which you can open from Performance Monitor or by typing **Resource Monitor** (or **resmon**) into the Start menu's search box.

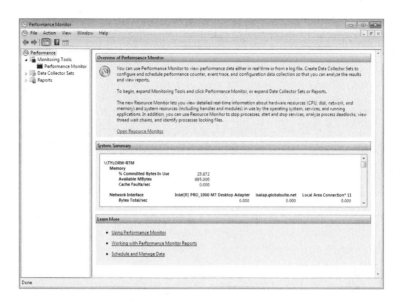

The Overview tab of the Resource Monitor dialog box is open by default and gives you a fair amount of detail. The main window provides an overview of the four major subsystems monitored by default (CPU, Disk, Network, and Memory). You expand or compress each of the four items by clicking the arrow in the left of the item title bar, as shown in Figure 15.3. For example, if you want to view details about the memory being used by the processes of Windows 7, click the arrow to expand Memory and you can view each process, process ID, and memory allocation by physical, shared, and private allotment.

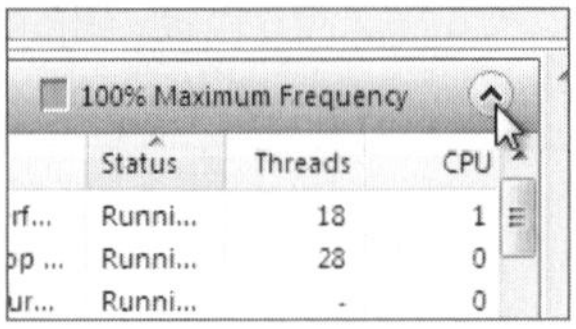

FIGURE 15.3
Expand or collapse
Resource Monitor items.

The other tabs of the Resource Monitor dialog box offer detailed information about each of the major subsystems of Windows 7. The CPU tab displays the individual processes currently running on the machine, the process IDs (PIDs), a brief description, the running status of the process, how many threads the process is running, current CPU utilization, and average CPU utilization. You can also expand the Services, Associated Handles, and Associated Module items for more detail on each of these items. The CPU tab, shown in Figure 15.4, also offers a graphical representation of real-time statistics for CPU total usage by percentage and Service CPU usage as a percentage on the right of the screen.

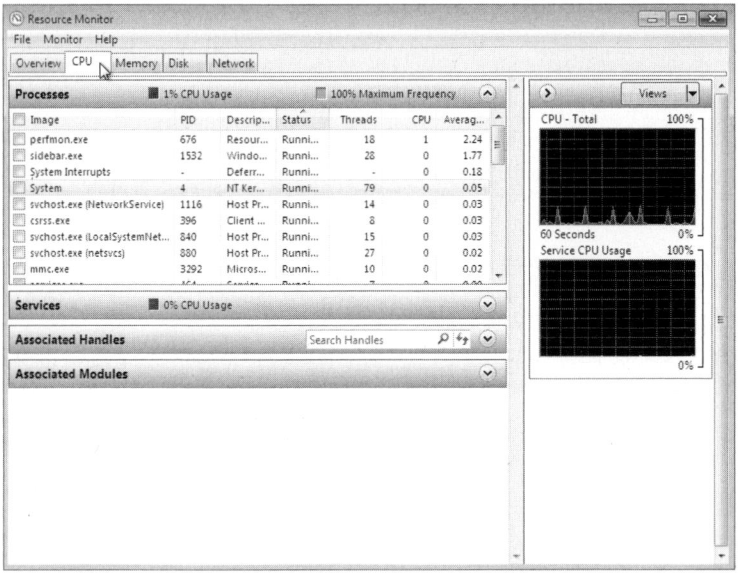

FIGURE 15.4
The CPU tab of Resource
Monitor

The Memory tab of Resource Monitor shows the process information as displayed on the CPU tab with an overview of memory allocation in the form of a graphical representation. The right side of the display also shows you real-time information of the physical memory and the currently allocated memory, called the Committed Charge and Hard Faults/Sec (the number of memory accesses that are not actually in RAM, but in a page file waiting to be used). The Memory tab is shown in Figure 15.5.

The Disk tab of Resource Monitor (Figure 15.6) is used to display the disk activity of your machine. The items available to view are Processes With Disk Activity, Disk Activity, and Storage. The Disk tab includes a real-time graphical representation of disk transfer in KB/Sec and disk queue length (the amount of transfer currently waiting for transfer to RAM for processing).

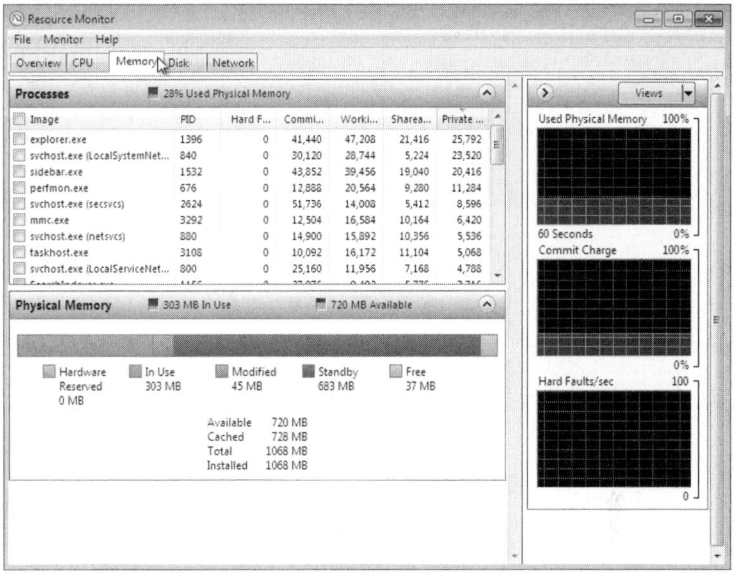

FIGURE 15.5
The Memory tab of
Resource Monitor

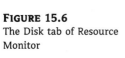

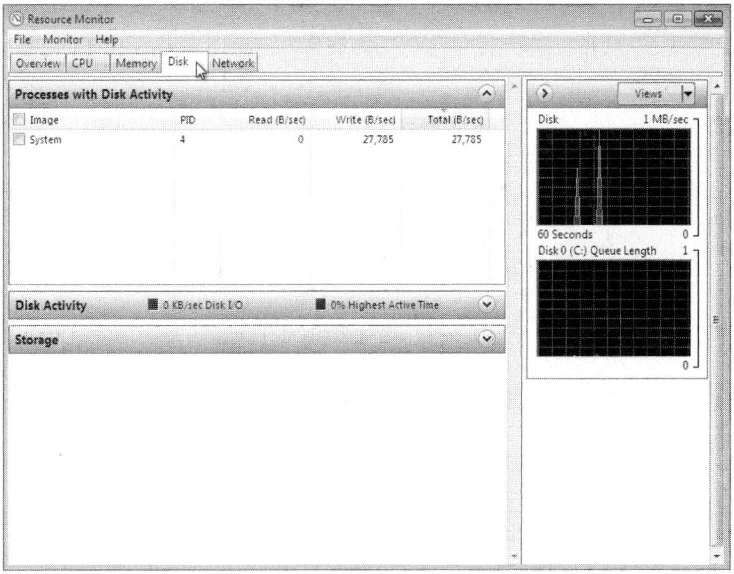

FIGURE 15.6
The Disk tab of Resource
Monitor

The Network tab of Resource Monitor (Figure 15.7) shows network utilization as well as network protocol information. The items available for detailed information include Processes With Network Activity, Network Activity, TCP Connections, and Listening Ports. We've had this information available to us in previous versions of Windows, but this is one convenient location for a slew of useful network information. The Network tab offers a huge amount of useful network information (we have opened the Listening Ports item in the figure) as well as the real-time graphical information for network data transfer, open TCP connections, and local area connection usage as a percentage. You can view any of these counters in Resource Monitor as well as Performance Monitor. The key counter value guidelines (what's good/what's not good) are included in the "Key Counters" sections later in this chapter.

FIGURE 15.7
The Network tab of
Resource Monitor

THE GREAT NETWORK TAB IN RESOURCE MONITOR

One of the authors is a packet sniffer and network utilization geek and has been for some time. He constantly talks with other administrators about resources being used in their servers and client machines that are associated with many network attributes. It's always important for him to see just which applications are using the network in terms of the ports they have open on his machine. He uses TCPView on a regular basis (downloadable from http://technet.microsoft.com) and has even been known to fire up Netstat (the ever popular command-line utility that shows network status) to see what's happening. Making the association to the ports open, the processes using resources, the applications associated with the ports and processes and just how much bandwidth is being used has always had him looking between applications and utility outputs. The author has a regimen that he uses and recommends to administrators to monitor this information, but Resource Monitor's Network tab has now consolidated this information into one convenient spot with a regular data display as well as real-time graphical views. This author returns to Resource Monitor time and time again to see what his Windows 7 machine is doing and has come across many of his colleagues doing the same thing. If you've ever considered looking at the connections being made into or out of your computer, you will love the Network tab of Resource Monitor (and the other tabs are pretty good too).

For monitoring system activity other than what is provided by the Resource Overview and Resource Monitor, you must use more of the Performance Monitor features.

Utilizing Customized Counters in Performance Monitor

You can add numerous counters from any of the subsystems within Windows 7. To access the configurable Performance Monitor window, select the Performance Monitor item in the left pane, as shown in Figure 15.8.

FIGURE 15.8
Customizable
Performance Monitor
window

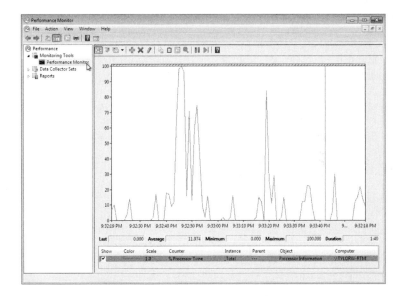

Customizable counters are listed at the bottom of the Performance Monitor window. By default, only the % Processor Time counter is tracked for the local computer. The fields just above the counter list will contain data based on the counter that is highlighted in the list, as follows:

Last Displays the most current data

Average Shows the average of the counter

Minimum Shows the lowest value that has been recorded for the counter

Maximum Shows the highest value that has been recorded for the counter

Duration Shows how long the counter has been tracking data

Before we add counters to Performance Monitor, let's discuss the three Performance Monitor views.

SELECTING THE APPROPRIATE VIEW

Click the Change Graph Type button on the Performance Monitor toolbar to see your data in one of three views, as shown in Figure 15.9.

Line View The line view is Performance Monitor's default view. It's useful for viewing a small number of counters in a graphical format. The main advantage of line view is that you can see how the data has been tracked during the defined time period.

FIGURE 15.9
Change Graph Type
button

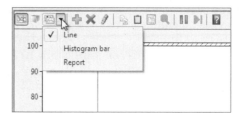

Histogram View   The histogram view, shown in Figure 15.10, shows the Performance Monitor data in a bar graph. This view is useful for examining large amounts of data. However, it shows performance only for the current period. You do not see a record of performance over time, as you do with the line view.

FIGURE 15.10
Performance Monitor
histogram view

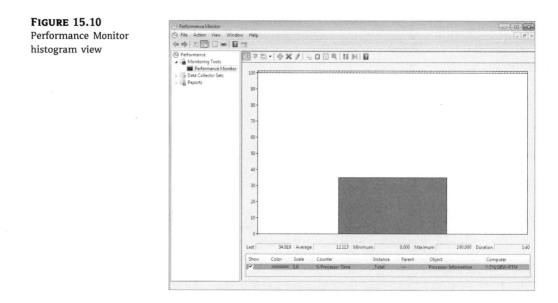

Report View   The report view, shown in Figure 15.11, offers a logical text-based report of all the counters that are being tracked through Performance Monitor. Only the current session's data is displayed. The advantage of report view is that it allows you to easily track large numbers of counters in real time. It is important to note that when you view data in real-time format, the data can appear skewed as applications and processes are started. It is typically more useful to view data as an average over a specified interval.

ADDING COUNTERS

As mentioned previously, you can add customized counters to Performance Monitor to track data.

Follow these steps to add counters:

1. In Performance Monitor, click the Add button on the toolbar, which looks like a green plus sign (+). This brings up the Add Counters dialog box.

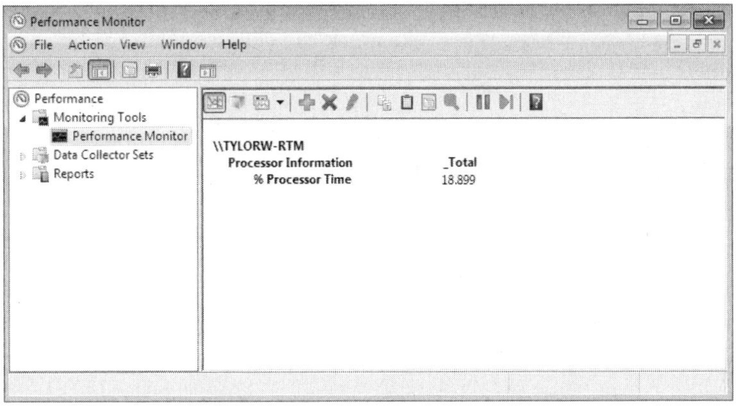

FIGURE 15.11
Performance
Monitor report view

SEEING DETAILS ABOUT COUNTER OBJECTS

To see information about a specific counter, in the Add Counters dialog box select the counter from the list and select the Show Description check box beneath the list on the left. Performance Monitor displays detail text regarding the highlighted counter.

---

2. In the Add Counters dialog box, ensure that the Select Counters From The Computer drop-down list displays <Local Computer> so that you can monitor the local computer. Alternatively, to select counters from a specific computer, pick a computer from the drop-down list.

MONITORING REMOTELY

You can monitor remote computers if you have administrative permissions. This option is useful when you do not want the overhead of the Performance Monitor graphics running on the computer you are trying to monitor. Although Microsoft has minimized the effect of running Performance Monitor, even without the graphical display, there will be minimal impact of running the data collection of Performance Monitor within the counter statistics. You can connect to another machine by selecting Connect To Another Computer in the context window of Performance within the Performance Monitor window as shown here:

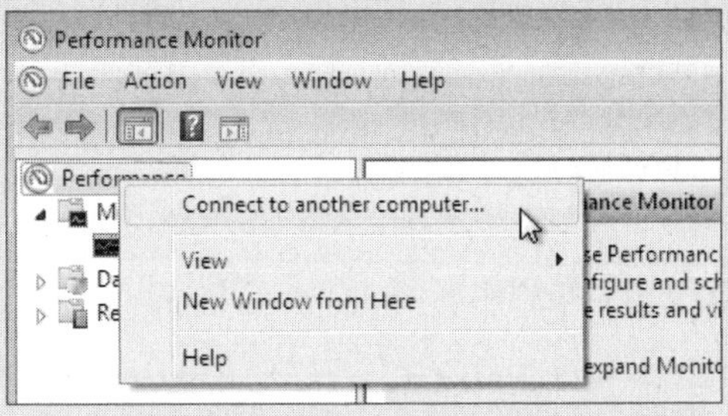

3. Select a performance object from the drop-down list. All Windows 7 system resources are tracked as performance objects, such as Cache, Memory, Paging File, Process, and Processor.

VIEWING COUNTER OBJECTS IN PERFORMANCE MONITOR

All the objects together represent your total system. Some performance objects exist on all Windows 7 computers; other objects appear only if specific processes or services are running. For example, if you want to track the physical disk's level of activity, choose the PhysicalDisk performance object.

---

4. Select the counter or counters within the performance object that you want to track. Each performance object has an associated set of counters. Counters are used to track specific information regarding a performance object. For example, the PhysicalDisk performance object has a % Disk Time counter, which will tell you how busy a disk has been in servicing read and write requests. PhysicalDisk also has % Disk Read Time and % Disk Write Time counters, which show you what percentage of disk requests are read requests and what percentage are write requests, respectively.

5. Select <All Instances> to track all the associated instances or pick specific instances from the list box.

USING INSTANCES WITHIN PERFORMANCE MONITOR

An instance is a mechanism that allows you to track the performance of a specific object when you have more than one item associated with a specific performance object. For example, suppose your computer has two physical drives. When you track the PhysicalDisk performance object, you can track one or both of your drives. If a counter has more than one instance, you can monitor the sum of all of the instances by selecting the _Total option.

---

6. Click the Add button to add the counters for the performance object.

7. Repeat steps 2 through 6 to specify any additional counters you want to track. When you finish, click OK.

After you've added counters, you can select a specific counter by highlighting it in Performance Monitor. To highlight a counter, click it and then click the Highlight button (which looks like a highlighter) on the Performance Monitor toolbar, or select the counter and press Ctrl+H.

To stop showing data for a counter, deselect the check box under Show for that counter. To remove a counter, highlight it in Performance Monitor and click the Delete button on the toolbar. The Delete button looks like a red X.

MANAGING PERFORMANCE MONITOR PROPERTIES

To configure the Performance Monitor properties, click the Properties button on the Performance Monitor toolbar and the Performance Monitor Properties dialog box opens, as shown in Figure 15.12.

FIGURE 15.12
Performance
Monitor Counter
Properties
dialog box

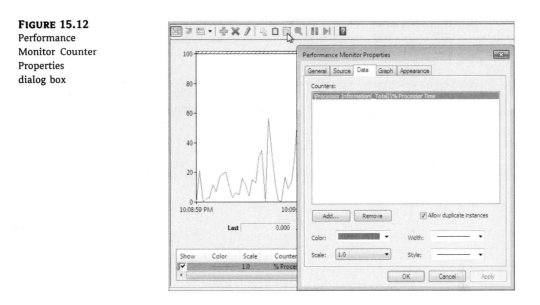

The Performance Monitor Properties dialog box has the following five tabs:

General Tab The General tab of the Performance Monitor Properties dialog box, as shown in Figure 15.13, contains the following options:

◆ The display elements that will be used — legend, value bar, and/or toolbar

◆ The data that will be displayed — default (for reports or histograms, this is current data; for logs, this is average data), current, minimum, maximum, or average

◆ How often the data is updated, in seconds

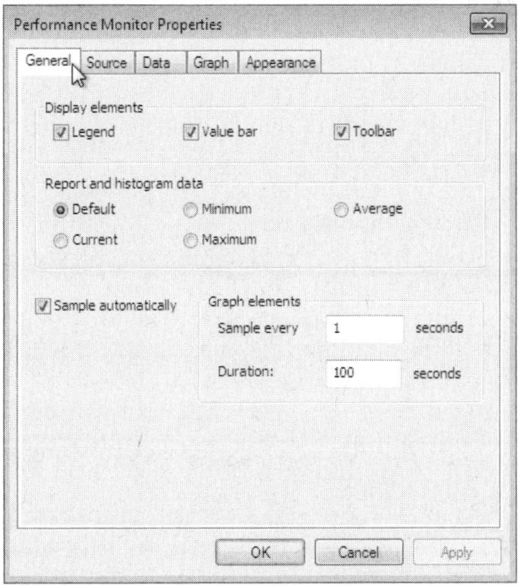

FIGURE 15.13
The General tab of the
Performance Counter
Properties dialog box

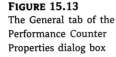

Source Tab The Source tab, shown in Figure 15.14, allows you to specify the data source. This can be current activity, or it can be data that has been collected in a log file or database. If you import data, you can specify the time range that you want to view.

Data Tab The Data tab (the default tab that is active when the properties window opens, as shown in Figure 15.12 earlier) lets you specify the counters that you want to track. You can add and remove counters by clicking the Add and Remove buttons. You can also select a specific counter and define the color, scale, width, and style that are used to represent the counter in the graph.

Graph Tab The Graph tab, shown in Figure 15.15, contains the following options, which you can apply to the line or histogram bar view:

◆ Whether the data will scroll or wrap (line view only)

◆ A title

◆ A vertical axis label

◆ Whether you will show a vertical grid, a horizontal grid, vertical scale numbers, and/or time axis labels

◆ The minimum and maximum numbers for the vertical scale

Appearance Tab The Appearance tab of the Performance Monitor Properties dialog box, shown in Figure 15.16, has options for customizing the colors and fonts used in the Performance Monitor display.

After you have set counters and viewed them in real time, you might be interested in collecting the data over time and saving it to a file for maintaining a baseline of data for comparison. You do this in Performance Monitor by using data collector sets.

Managing Performance Monitor Data with Collector Sets

The Data Collector Sets portion of Performance Monitor is shown in Figure 15.17. Data collector sets are used to collect data into a log so that the data can be reviewed and saved for comparison at a later date (a process called base lining). You can view the log files with Performance Monitor, as described in the previous section "Managing Performance Monitor Properties."

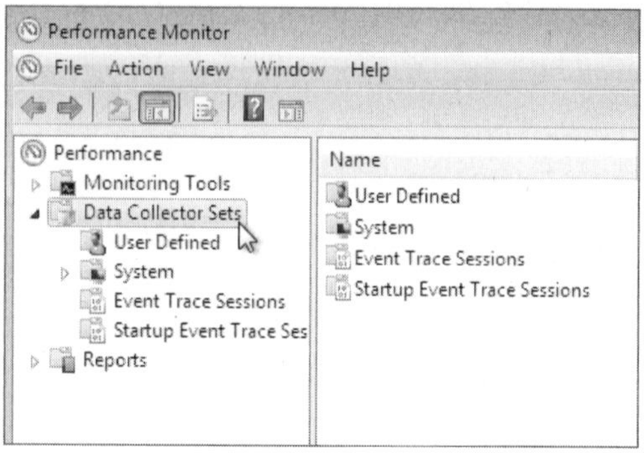

FIGURE 15.17
Configuring
Performance
Monitor data
collector sets

When you create a data collector set, right-click User Defined and choose New Data Collector Set from the context menu to launch the Create New Data Collector Set Wizard. You can let Windows 7 use a standard data collector set or you can define data logs from the following options:

♦ Performance counters

♦ Event trace data

♦ System configuration information

There are two built-in data collector sets that track multiple counters for system diagnostics and system performance. You can also create your own user-defined data collector sets and save them for later use. You can view the reports from these data collector sets within the Reports folder in Performance Monitor.

CREATING A USER-DEFINED DATA COLLECTOR SET

Performance counter logs record data about hardware usage and the activity of system services. You can configure logging to occur manually or on a predefined schedule.

Perform the following steps to create a data log:

1. Expand Data Collector Sets, right-click User Defined, select New, and select Data Collector Set from the pop-up menu.

2. In the Create New Data Collector Set dialog box that appears, type a name for the collector set and choose whether to create the set from a template or to create it manually; then click the Next button.

3. If you chose to create the set from a template, follow the prompts to create the set. After the set is created, you can modify it.

   If you chose to create the set manually, you are asked whether you want to create data logs or a performance counter alert. Data logs can consist of the following types of data:

   ♦ Performance counters

   ♦ Event trace data

   ♦ System configuration information

   After you select the data you want to collect, click Next.

4. Add the performance counters you want to collect and click Next after each data type.

5. You are asked where to save the data. Browse to the location, click OK, and then click Next.

6. You are asked under which user account the data collector set should run, and whether the data collector set should be edited, started, or saved. After you make your selections, click Finish.

CREATING AN ALERT

Alerts can be generated when a specific counter rises above or falls below a specified value. You can configure alerts to log an entry in the application event log and/or start a data collector set. Creating an alert is similar to creating a performance counter data log except you are required to specify the alert conditions. You create an alert by creating a user-defined collector set and manually specifying counters. In the Create New Data Collector Wizard, you select the Performance Counter Alert radio button. For example, you might configure a performance counter alert that will log an entry whenever the % Free Space counter for C: falls below 5 percent. After you create the alert, you can modify the alert parameters by right-clicking the data collector and selecting Properties.

After you create the data collector sets and set the alerts, you will want to run the sets and save the logs periodically. Reviewing the logs gives you a proactive approach to managing your Windows 7 performance.

Simply creating the logs and saving them is not enough; you need to evaluate the data using previous logs to determine trends that allow you to manage your system's performance.

Managing System Performance

By analyzing data, you can determine whether any resources are placing an excessive load on your computer that is resulting in a system slowdown. The following list gives some of the causes of poor system performance:

◆ A resource is insufficient to handle the load that is being placed upon it, and the component might need to be upgraded, or additional components might be required.

◆ If a resource has multiple instances, the resources might not be evenly balancing the workload, and the workload might need to be balanced over the multiple instances more effectively.

◆ A resource might be malfunctioning. In this case, the resource should be repaired or replaced.

◆ A specific program might be allocated resources improperly or inefficiently, in which case the program needs to be rewritten or replaced by another application.

◆ A resource might be configured improperly and causing excessive resource usage and has to be reconfigured.

You should monitor four main subsystems. Configure counters in your data collector set for each of the following:

◆ The memory subsystem

◆ The processor subsystem

◆ The disk subsystem

◆ The network subsystem

Each subsystem should be examined over time to evaluate Windows 7 performance.

MONITORING AND OPTIMIZING MEMORY

When the operating system needs a program or process, the first place it looks is in physical memory. If the required program or process is not in physical memory, the system looks in logical memory (the page file). If the program or process is not in logical memory, the system then must retrieve the program or process from the hard disk. It can take thousands of times longer to access information from the hard disk than to get it from physical RAM. If your computer is using excessive paging, that is an indication that your computer does not have enough physical memory.

Insufficient memory is the most likely cause of system bottlenecks. If you have no idea what is causing a system bottleneck, memory is usually a good place to start checking. To determine how memory is being used, examine the following two areas:

Physical Memory The physical RAM you have installed on your computer. You can't have too much memory if you are below your operating system's maximum. It's a good idea to have more memory than you think you will need just to be on the safe side. As you've probably noticed, each time you add or upgrade applications, you require more system memory.

Page File Logical memory exists on your hard drive. If you are using excessive paging (swapping between the page file and physical RAM) or hard page faults, it's a clear sign that you need to add more memory.

The first step in memory management is determining how much memory your computer has installed and what the appropriate memory requirements are based on the operating system requirements and the applications and services you are running on your computer.

KEY COUNTERS TO TRACK FOR MEMORY MANAGEMENT

The following are the three most important counters for monitoring memory:

Memory > Available MBytes Memory > Available MBytes measures the amount of physical memory that is available to run processes on the computer. If this number is less than 20 percent of your installed memory, it indicates that you might have an overall shortage of physical memory for your computer, or you possibly have an application that is not releasing memory properly. You should consider adding more memory or evaluating application memory usage.

Memory > Pages/Sec Memory > Pages/Sec shows the number of times the requested information was not in memory and had to be retrieved from disk. This counter's value should be below 20; for optimal performance, it should be 4 or 5. If the number is above 20, you should add memory or research paging file use more thoroughly. Sometimes a high Pages/Sec counter is indicative of a program that is using a memory-mapped file.

Paging File > % Usage Paging File > % Usage indicates the percentage of the allocated page file that is currently in use. If this number is consistently over 70 percent, you might need to add more memory or increase the size of the page file. You should track this counter in conjunction with Available MBytes and Pages/Sec.

These counters work together to show what is happening on your system. Use the Paging File > % Usage counter value in conjunction with the Memory > Available MBytes and Memory > Pages/Sec counters to determine how much paging is occurring on your computer.

Along with memory counters, processor (or CPU) counters are valuable in evaluating Windows 7 performance.

Managing Processor Performance

Processor bottlenecks can develop when the threads of a process require more processing cycles than are currently available. In this case, the process will wait in a processor queue and system responsiveness will be slower than if process requests could be immediately served. The most common causes of processor bottlenecks are processor-intensive applications and other subsystem components that generate excessive processor interrupts (for example, disk or network subsystems).

In a workstation environment, processors are usually not the source of bottlenecks; however, you should still monitor this subsystem to make sure that processor utilization is at an efficient level. There are several standard counters you should monitor to track processor utilization.

KEY COUNTERS TO TRACK FOR PROCESSOR

You can track processor utilization through the Processor and System objects to determine whether a processor bottleneck exists. The following are the most important counters for monitoring the system processor:

Processor > % Processor Time   Processor > % Processor Time measures the time that the processor spends responding to system requests. If this value is consistently above an average of 85 percent, you might have a processor bottleneck. The Processor > % User Time and Processor > % Privileged Time counters combine to show the total % Processor Time counter. You can monitor these counters individually for more detail.

Processor > Interrupts/Sec   Processor > Interrupts/Sec show the average number of hardware interrupts received by the processor each second. If this value is higher than 3,000, you might have a problem with a program or hardware that is generating spurious interrupts (this value will vary in optimization based on the processor type; you'll need to do a little research for your specific processor to see the appropriate value).

System > Processor Queue Length   System > Processor Queue Length is used to determine whether a processor bottleneck is due to high levels of demand for processor time. If a queue of two or more items exists for an extended period of time, a processor bottleneck might be indicated. If you suspect that a processor bottleneck is due to excessive hardware I/O requests, you should also monitor the System > File Control Bytes/Sec counter.

TUNING AND UPGRADING THE PROCESSOR

If you suspect that you have a processor bottleneck, you can try the following solutions:

♦   Use applications that are less processor-intensive.

♦   Upgrade your processor.

♦   If your computer supports multiple processors, add one.

The memory and processor subsystem objects are important counters to evaluate in determining your Windows 7 performance. You should look at the hard drive or disk subsystem to look for issues as well.

Managing the Disk Subsystem

Disk access is the amount of time your disk subsystem takes to retrieve data that is requested by the operating system. The two factors that determine how quickly your disk subsystem will respond to system requests are the average disk access time on your hard drive and the speed of your disk controller.

KEY COUNTERS TO TRACK FOR THE DISK SUBSYSTEM

You can monitor the PhysicalDisk object, which is the sum of all logical drives on a single physical drive, or you can monitor the LogicalDisk object, which represents a specific logical disk. Here are the more important counters for monitoring the disk subsystem:

PhysicalDisk > % Disk Time and LogicalDisk > % Disk Time PhysicalDisk > % Disk Time and LogicalDisk > % Disk Time shows the amount of time the disk is busy because it is servicing read or write requests. If your disk is busy more than 90 percent of the time, you will improve performance by adding another disk channel and splitting the disk I/O requests between the channels.

PhysicalDisk > Current Disk Queue Length and LogicalDisk > Current Disk Queue Length PhysicalDisk > Current Disk Queue Length and LogicalDisk > Current Disk Queue Length indicates the number of outstanding disk requests that are waiting to be processed. On average, this value should be less than 2.

LogicalDisk > % Free Space LogicalDisk > % Free Space specifies how much free disk space is available. This counter should be at least 15 percent.

TUNING AND UPGRADING THE DISK SUBSYSTEM

When you suspect that you have a disk subsystem bottleneck, the first thing you should check is your memory subsystem. Insufficient physical memory can cause excessive paging, which in turn affects the disk subsystem.

If you do not have a memory problem, try the following solutions to improve disk performance:

◆ Use faster disks and controllers.

◆ Confirm that you have the latest drivers for your disk adapters.

◆ Use disk striping to take advantage of multiple I/O channels.

◆ Balance heavily used files on multiple I/O channels.

◆ Add another disk controller for load balancing.

◆ Use Disk Defragmenter to consolidate files so that disk space and data access are optimized.

After you evaluate the first three subsystems — memory, processor, and disk — you also need to look at the network subsystem to optimize your Windows 7 performance.

Optimizing the Network Subsystem

Windows 7 does not have a built-in mechanism for monitoring the entire network. However, you can monitor and optimize the traffic that is generated on your Windows 7 machine. You can monitor the network interface (your network card) and the network protocols that have been installed on your computer.

Network bottlenecks are indicated when network traffic exceeds the capacity that can be supported by the local area network (LAN). Typically, you would monitor this activity on a network-wide basis — for example, with the Network Monitor 3.3 (available for download at www.microsoft.com).

KEY COUNTERS TO TRACK FOR THE NETWORK SUBSYSTEM

If you are using the Performance Monitor utility to monitor local network traffic, the following two counters are useful for monitoring the network subsystem:

Network Interface > Bytes Total/Sec   Network Interface > Bytes Total/Sec measures the total number of bytes sent or received from the network interface and includes all network protocols.

TCPv4 > Segments/Sec   TCPv4 > Segments/Sec measures the number of bytes sent or received from the network interface and includes only the TCPv4 protocol.

TUNING AND UPGRADING THE NETWORK SUBSYSTEM

You can use the following guidelines to help optimize and minimize network traffic:

◆   Install only the network protocols you need.

◆   Use network cards that take advantage of your bus speed.

◆   Use faster network cards — for example, 100Mbps Ethernet or 1Gbps Ethernet instead of 10Mbps Ethernet.

Microsoft added a feature to Windows Vista's Performance Monitor called Reliability Monitor (hence the Windows Vista tool named Reliability and Performance Monitor). In Windows 7, Microsoft has removed the tool from Performance Monitor and Reliability Monitor is a separate tool.

Using Reliability Monitor

Reliability Monitor (see Figure 15.18) is a stand-alone feature in Windows 7 that provides an overview of the stability of your Windows 7 computer. You can access Reliability Monitor by typing **reliability monitor** in the Start menu's search box and selecting View Reliability Report from the resulting list.

If a problem is causing system instability, Reliability Monitor can provide details about it. The data is collected and stored in the following five categories in the lower half of the display window:

Application Failures   Programs that hang or crash

Windows Failures   Includes operating system and boot failures

Miscellaneous Failures   Includes unexpected shutdowns

Warnings   Items that are detrimental, but not failures

Information   Information messages that Windows 7 issues

The upper half of the graphical display indicates the relative reliability of your Windows 7 machine on a scale of 1 to 10 (with 10 representing completely reliable). To display the tracked reliability items in the time view (which you can change to display by days or weeks), click View By: Days | Weeks in the upper left of the Reliability Monitor window. You can view the details about failures, warnings, and informational messages by clicking the icon in the graphical window for the time period displayed.

FIGURE 15.18
Windows 7's Reliability
Monitor

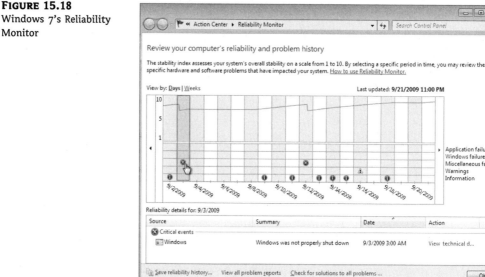

If you notice a recurring problem, choose Check For Solutions To All Problems at the bottom of the window and let Windows 7 check the issues and report potential solutions. You can view all the problems Reliability Monitor has detected by choosing View All Problem Reports, also located at the bottom of the window. By selecting Save Reliability History, you can save the current report in XML format.

Using Performance Monitor, Reliability Monitor, and Resource Monitor to manage your Windows 7 computer will make your administrative tasks simpler. Several other tools are also available for you to learn about your system information.

Using Windows 7 Tools to Discover System Information

Windows 7 contains many other tools to discover system information about your computer. In this section, we'll explore three of them:

- System Information

- Task Manager

- Performance Information and Tools

Getting System Information

You can use the System Information utility, shown in Figure 15.19, to learn details about your hardware, software, and resources. Type **msinfo32** in the Start menu's search box to launch this utility.

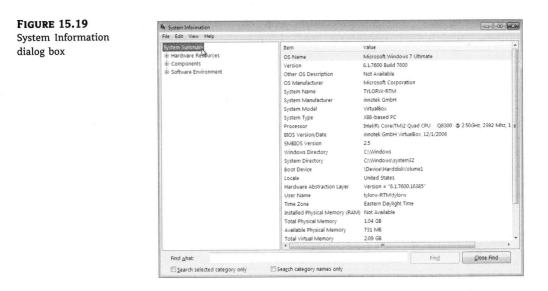

A great deal of your systems information is available within this application. Click the fields in the left pane and details are displayed in the right pane. You can also search for a term by typing it in the Find What field at the bottom of the page. This utility has been available in many releases of the Windows product.

Using Task Manager

The Task Manager utility shows the applications and processes that are currently running on your computer, as well as CPU and memory usage information. To access Task Manager, press Ctrl+Alt+Delete and click Start Task Manager. Alternatively, right-click an empty area in the Taskbar and select Task Manager from the context menu, or type **task manager** in the Start menu's search box. The Task Manager dialog box has the following six main tabs:

- Applications
- Processes
- Services
- Performance
- Networking
- Users

Managing Application Tasks in Task Manager

The Applications tab of the Task Manager dialog box, shown in Figure 15.20, lists all the applications that are currently running on the computer. For each task, you will see the name of the task and the current status (Running, Not Responding, or Stopped).

To close an application, select it in Task Manager and click the End Task button at the bottom of the dialog box. To make the application window active, select it and click the Switch To button. If you want to start an application that isn't running, click the New Task button and specify the location and name of the program you wish to start.

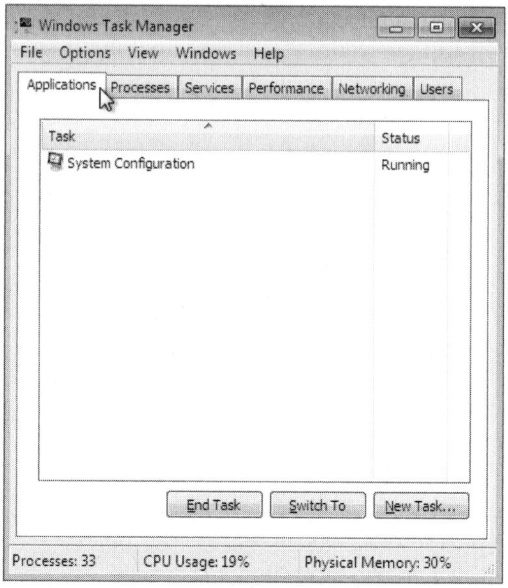

FIGURE 15.20
Applications tab in Task Manager

MANAGING PROCESS TASKS IN TASK MANAGER

The Processes tab of the Task Manager dialog box, shown in Figure 15.21, lists all the processes that are currently running on the computer. This is a convenient way to get a quick look at how your system is performing. For each process, you will see the Image Name (the name of the process), the User Name (the user account that is running the process), CPU (the amount of CPU utilization for the process), Memory (Private Working Set) (the amount of memory that is being used by the process), and Description (a description of the process).

From the Processes tab, you can organize the listing and control processes as follows:

◆ To organize the processes, click the column headings. For example, if you click the CPU column, the listing will start with the processes that use the most CPU resources. If you click the CPU column a second time, the listing will be reversed so that the processes that use the least CPU resources are listed first.

◆ To manage a process, right-click it and choose an option from the context menu. You can choose to end the process, end the process tree, debug the process, specify virtualization, create a dump file, or set the priority of the process (to Realtime, High, Above Normal, Normal, Below Normal, or Low). If your computer has multiple processors installed, you can also set processor affinity (the process of associating a specific process with a specific processor) for a process.

◆ To customize the counters that are listed, select View ➢ Select Columns. This brings up the Select Columns dialog box where you can select various information you want to see listed on the Processes tab.

FIGURE 15.21
Processes tab in Task Manager

SHOWING PROCESSES OF OTHER USERS IN TASK MANAGER

By default, only your processes are shown. To display processes from all users, including System, Local Service, and Network Service, click Show Processes From All Users.

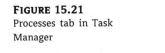

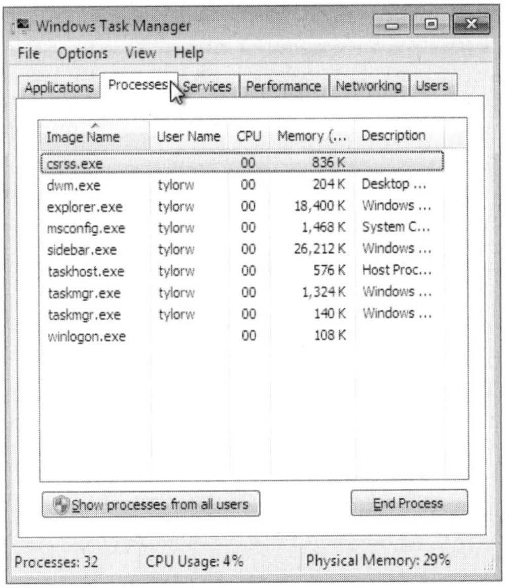

On the Processes tab in Task Manager, you can also stop a process and manage process priority:

Stopping Processes You might need to stop a process that isn't executing properly. To stop a specific process, select the process you want to stop in the Task Manager's Processes tab and click the End Process button. Task Manager displays a Warning dialog box. Click the End Process button to terminate the process. If you right-click a process, you can end the specific process or you can use the option End Process Tree. The End Process Tree option ends all processes that have been created either directly or indirectly by the process.

Managing Process Priority To change the priority of a process that is already running, use the Processes tab of Task Manager. Right-click the process you want to manage and select Set Priority from the context menu. You can select from Realtime, High, Above Normal, Normal, Below Normal, and Low. As you might expect, applications launch at Normal priority by default.

Perform the following steps to set a process priority and end a process from within Task Manager:

1. Right-click an empty space on your Taskbar and select Task Manager from the context menu.
2. On the Applications tab, click the New Task button.

3. In the Create A New Task dialog box, type **calc** and click OK.

4. Click the Processes tab. Right-click calc.exe and select Set Priority, then select Low. In the Warning dialog box, click the Change Priority button to continue.

5. Right-click calc.exe and select End Process. In the Warning dialog box, click the End Process button.

⊕ Real World Scenario

RESTARTING YOUR WINDOWS 7 DESKTOP

Windows 7 is much better at closing all graphical displays when programs close or crash than other Windows legacy operating systems. But, I have still had issues when something seems to stay on my desktop when it shouldn't. A piece of a window, some graphic component, or just some distracting piece of garbage that is not supposed to be there is just hanging around. Most of the time you'll see users reboot their machine to clean up the desktop, I know I used to. Using the Process tab of Task Manager can provide a solution to this problem. If you select the explorer.exe process and end it, you will see your desktop programs, icons, and random stuck graphics go away (and not come back). You can then just restart the explorer.exe process (the desktop) by choosing File ➤ New Task and typing explorer.exe to bring back your desktop (Task Manager stays with the ending of the explorer process). This is a much faster and more efficient way of restoring your desktop without rebooting.

MANAGING SERVICES IN TASK MANAGER

The Services tab of the Task Manager dialog box, shown in Figure 15.22, lists all the services that can run on the computer. For each service, you will see the Name (the name of the service), the PID (the associated process identifier), Description (a description of the service, Status (whether a process is Running or Stopped), and Group (the service group).

To start a stopped service, click the service and select Start Service. To stop a running service, click the service and select Stop Service. You can also open the Services tool by clicking the Services button. The Services tool allows you to specify whether a process starts automatically, automatically with a delayed start, manually, or is disabled.

MANAGING PERFORMANCE TASKS IN TASK MANAGER

The Performance tab of Task Manager, shown in Figure 15.23, provides an overview of your computer's CPU and memory usage. This information is similar to the information tracked by Performance Monitor.

The Performance tab shows the following information:

◆ CPU usage, in real time and in a history graph

◆ Memory usage, in real time and in a history graph

◆ Physical memory statistics

◆ Kernel memory statistics

◆ System totals for handles, threads, processes, uptime, and the pagefile

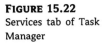

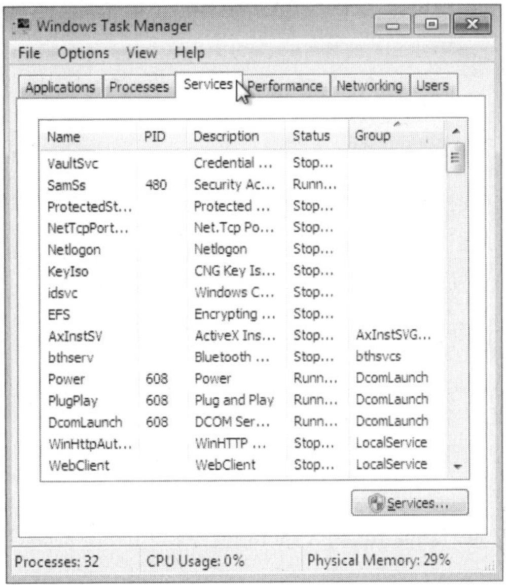

FIGURE 15.22
Services tab of Task
Manager

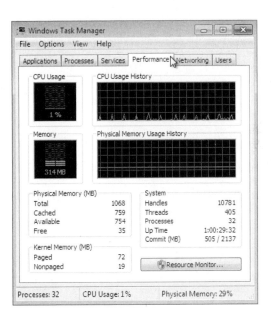

FIGURE 15.23
Performance tab of Task
Manager

Click the Resource Monitor button to launch the Resource Monitor that you can also find in Performance Monitor.

MANAGING NETWORKING TASKS IN TASK MANAGER

The Networking tab of Task Manager, shown in Figure 15.24, provides an overview of your networking usage. Statistics for each adapter are displayed at the bottom of the tab.

FIGURE 15.24
Networking tab of Task
Manager

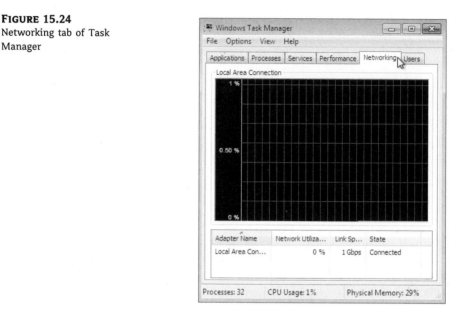

MANAGING USERS IN TASK MANAGER

The Users tab of Task Manager, shown in Figure 15.25, shows the active and disconnected users on your computer. For each user, you will see the User (the name of the user), the ID (the current user ID), Status (whether Active or Disconnected), Client Name, and Session (whether the user is connected via the console session or by another method, such as Remote Desktop).

FIGURE 15.25
Users tab of Task
Manager

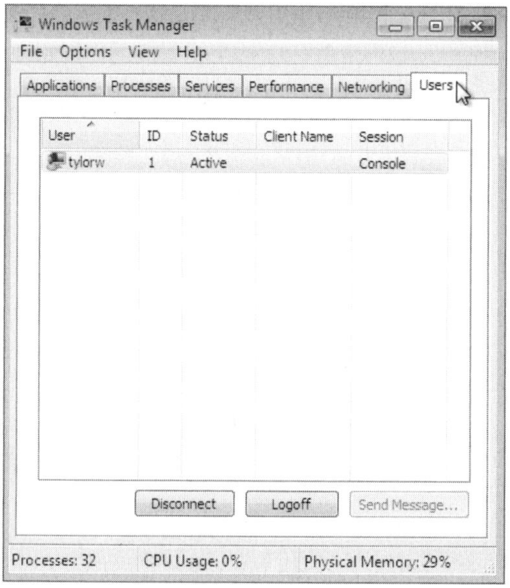

To send a message to a user, select the user and click the Send Message button. To connect to a user session, right-click the user and select Connect. To disconnect a user session, select the user and click the Disconnect button. To log off a user, select the user and click the Logoff button.

Next let's look at another tool available in Windows 7 that reveals how well your machine is working: Performance Information and Tools.

Scoring Windows 7 with Performance Information and Tools

If you enjoy seeing how well your computer performs by running benchmarking applications that provide a score rating, then you will love Performance Information and Tools, shown in Figure 15.26. This utility provides you with a numerical score that lets you know how well your system performs. To launch Performance Information and Tools, click Start ➤ Control Panel ➤ System and Maintenance ➤ Performance Information and Tools, or type **performance information** in the Start menu's search box.

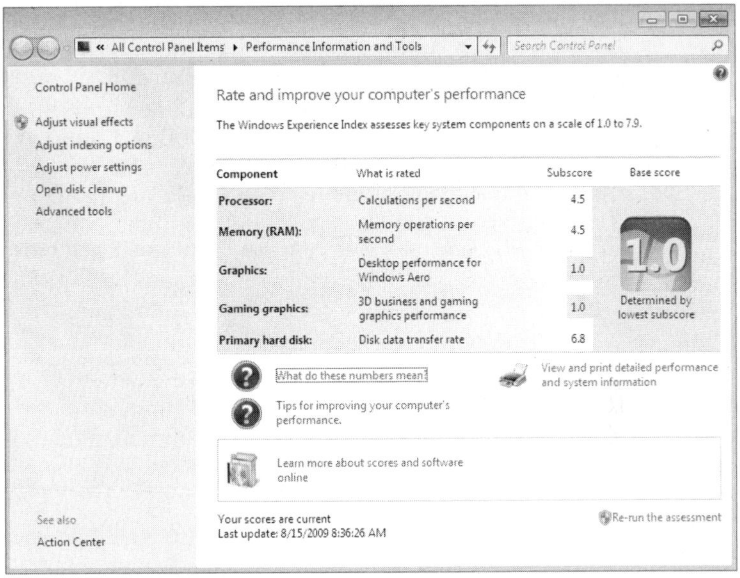

FIGURE 15.26
Performance Information and Tools window

The main pane reveals a calculated score, called the Windows Experience Index. The Windows Experience Index base score is calculated by taking the lowest subscore among five rated components:

- Processor, based on calculations per second

- Memory (RAM), based on memory operations per second

- Graphics, based on Windows Aero performance

- Gaming Graphics, based on 3D graphics performance

- Primary Hard Disk, based on disk transfer rate

A computer with a base score of 1 or 2 will be able to perform only the most basic tasks. A base score of 3 indicates that a computer can run Windows Aero and all but the most advanced Windows 7 features. A computer with a base score of 4 or 5 should be able to run all Windows 7 features, as well as play graphics-intensive 3D games.

Each component subscore determines how well each individual component performs. Because the base score is equal to the lowest component subscore, the Windows Experience Index base score should give you an overview of how well your computer will run applications. This enables application developers to give their applications a numerical rating so that consumers can easily determine whether the application will run well on their computer. If an application requires a higher base score than your computer has, it might be time to upgrade your hardware. After you install new hardware, you can select Update My Score to have Windows 7 recalculate your Windows Experience Index base score.

The left pane of Performance Information and Tools contains useful links to help you improve the performance of your computer. Click Adjust Visual Effects to open the Visual Effects tab of the Performance Options dialog box, which you can use for configuring how Windows will graphically display windows, menu items, and icons. Click Adjust Indexing Options to launch Indexing Options, which can improve the speed of searching files on your computer. Click Adjust Indexing Options to launch the Indexing Options dialog box, where you can choose which resources on your Windows 7 machine are included in indexing. Click Adjust Power Settings to launch Power Options, which you can use to adjust your power plan. Click Open Disk Cleanup to launch Disk Cleanup Options so that you can clean up unnecessary files on your hard disk. Finally, click Advanced Tools to launch a list of tools that you can use to further improve your computer's performance:

- Clear all Windows Experience Index scores and re-rate the system

- View Performance Details in Event Log

- Open Performance Monitor

- Open Resource Monitor

- Open Task Manager

- View Advanced System Details in System Information

- Adjust the Appearance and Performance of Windows

- Open Disk Defragmenter

- Generate a System Health Report

The Performance Information and Tools menu is a great display of your system and a launching point for many tools in Windows 7. Another useful tool that has been around in many versions of Windows and is still available in version 7 is the System Configuration utility, or MSConfig.

Using System Configuration

You can use the System Configuration utility to help you view and troubleshoot how Windows 7 starts and what programs and services launch at startup. You might recognize this utility as `msconfig.exe`. To launch it, run `msconfig.exe` from the Start menu's search box. Use the

General tab, shown in Figure 15.27, to specify startup options. You can choose from the following three startup options:

◆ Normal Startup, which loads all device drivers and services

◆ Diagnostic Startup, which loads basic services and drivers

◆ Selective Startup, from which you can choose whether or not to load system services, load startup items, and use the original boot configuration

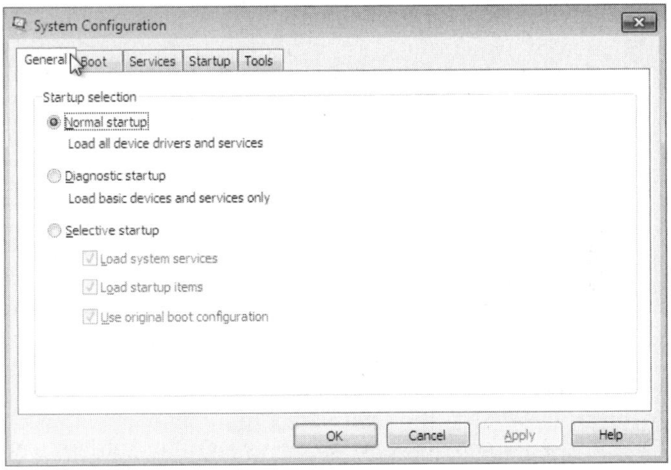

FIGURE 15.27
General tab in System Configuration

Use the Boot tab, shown in Figure 15.28, to configure whether Windows boots in Safe Mode, runs an Active Directory repair, boots to a graphical user interface (GUI), logs boot information, boots in VGA mode, and displays driver names while booting. Select any of the options on this screen to change the settings on the General tab; conversely, select Normal Startup on the General tab to clear the settings on the Boot tab.

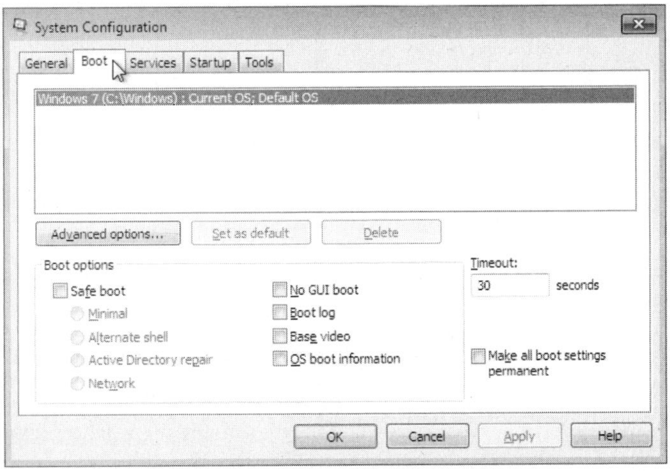

FIGURE 15.28
Boot tab in System Configuration

Use the Services tab to list Windows 7 services and indicate which services are running. You can deselect services on this tab so that they do not launch at startup. Select any of the services on this screen to change the settings on the General tab; conversely, select Normal Startup on the General tab to clear the settings on the Services tab. The Services tab of the System Configuration tool is shown in Figure 15.29.

FIGURE 15.29
Services tab in System
Configuration

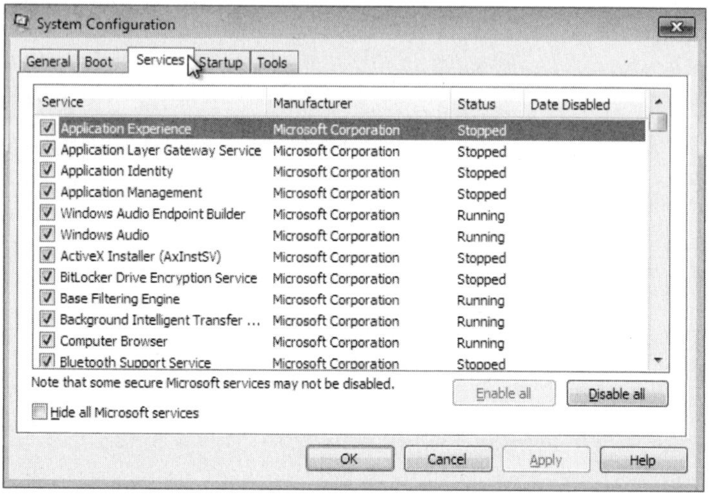

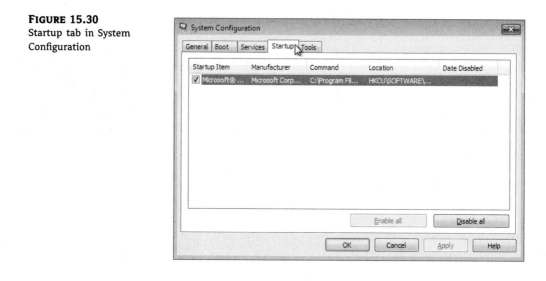

Use the Startup tab, shown in Figure 15.30, to show applications that start when Windows 7 starts. You can deselect applications on this tab so that they do not launch at startup. If you've read through the previous two paragraphs, you can probably guess that selecting any of the services on this screen changes the settings on the General tab, and selecting Normal Startup on the General tab clears the settings on the Startup tab.

FIGURE 15.30
Startup tab in System
Configuration

Use the Tools tab, shown in Figure 15.31, to view the tools you can launch from System Configuration. Simply click the tool name and click Launch to launch the tool. You can launch the following tools from this tab:

- About Windows
- Change UAC Settings
- Action Center
- Windows Troubleshooting
- Computer Management
- System Information
- Event Viewer
- Programs
- System Properties
- Internet Options
- Internet Protocol Configuration
- Performance Monitor
- Resource Monitor
- Task Manager
- Command Prompt
- Registry Editor
- Remote Assistance
- System Restore

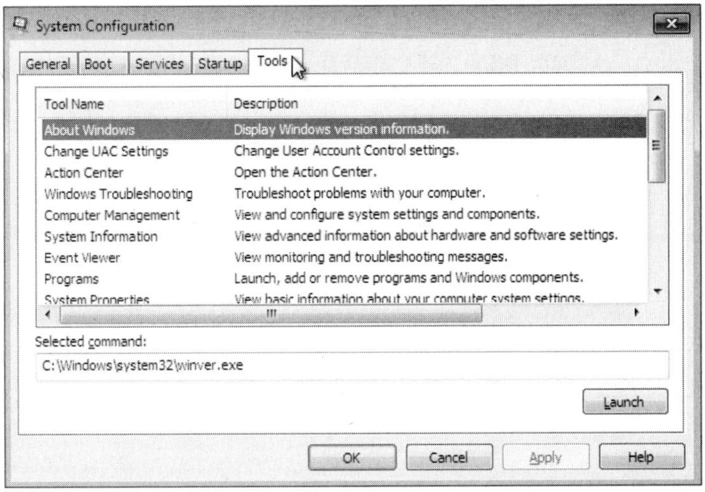

FIGURE 15.31
Tools tab in System Configuration

From the Tools tab you can launch many of the utilities offered by Windows 7 manually. You might have some tools or programs you want to launch automatically and run at a predetermined time; this ability is available using Task Scheduler.

Setting Up Task Scheduler

Use the Task Scheduler utility in Windows 7 to schedule actions to occur at specified intervals. Windows 7 Task Scheduler (shown in Figure 15.32) can be accessed by typing **task scheduler** in the Start menu's search box.

FIGURE 15.32
Windows 7 Task
Scheduler

After the Task Scheduler starts, you can create a scheduled task.

Creating a Scheduled Task

You can create a basic task by selecting the Create Basic Task item in the Actions pane in the right side of Task Scheduler, as shown in Figure 15.33.

FIGURE 15.33
Creating a basic task in
Task Scheduler

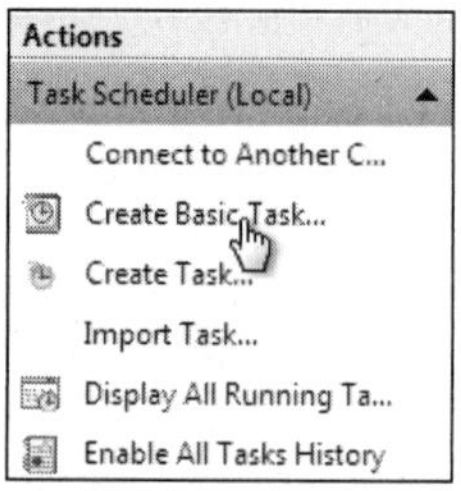

By creating a basic task, a Task Manager wizard lets you set any of your Windows programs to run automatically at a specific time and at a set interval, such as daily, weekly, or monthly. For example, you might schedule an application to run daily at 2:00 a.m. Actions can be performed at the following events (called triggers) available in the Task Manager wizard:

◆ Daily, or once every number of days (such as once every three days)

◆ Weekly, or on certain days of the week, or every number of weeks (such as every four weeks on Monday)

◆ Monthly, or on selected days of the month, or only on selected months

◆ One time only

◆ When the computer starts

◆ When you log on

◆ When a specific event is logged

If you've chosen a time trigger, you configure the time/date when the action will occur. When a trigger is activated, Task Scheduler can perform the following actions:

◆ Start a program.

◆ Send an email.

◆ Display a message.

Perform the following steps to set up a scheduled task to launch Windows 7 Calculator at a predetermined weekly time:

1. Select Start and type **task scheduler** in the Start menu's search box or choose Start ➢ Control Panel ➢ System And Security ➢ Administrative Tools ➢ and double-click Task Scheduler.

2. In the Actions pane of the Task Scheduler window, select Create Basic Task.

3. The Create Basic Task wizard appears; type **Monday's calculator** as a name for your task, enter a description, and then click Next.

4. Select how often you want the action to occur; we will select Weekly and click Next to continue.

5. Specify that the action should occur every Monday at 9 a.m. and click Next.

6. Select the Start A Program radio button and click Next.

7. Browse for the Calculator application at C:\%windir%\system32\calc.exe; click Next.

8. The final screen shows your selections for the scheduled task; click Finish.

Select the Windows folder in the left pane and then select the arrow to expand the folder's contents to reveal a complete set of preconfigured tasks. Figure 15.34 shows the Windows folder expanded and the Defrag task selected. You can view the Defrag task settings, edit the task, and even run the Defrag task manually if you desire.

FIGURE 15.34
Task Scheduler
preconfigured
Defrag task

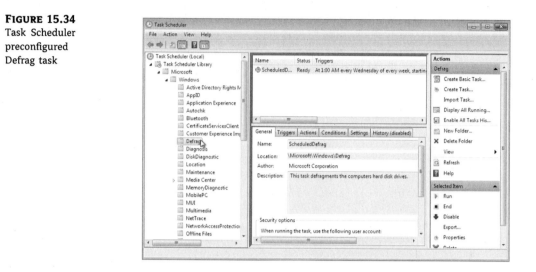

Task Scheduler also allows you to run tasks manually by selecting the task and clicking Run in the right pane. Select a task and click Disable to disable a task.

Managing Scheduled Task Properties

You can manage a scheduled task through its properties dialog box. To access this dialog box, right-click the task you want to manage and choose Properties from the context menu, as shown in Figure 15.35.

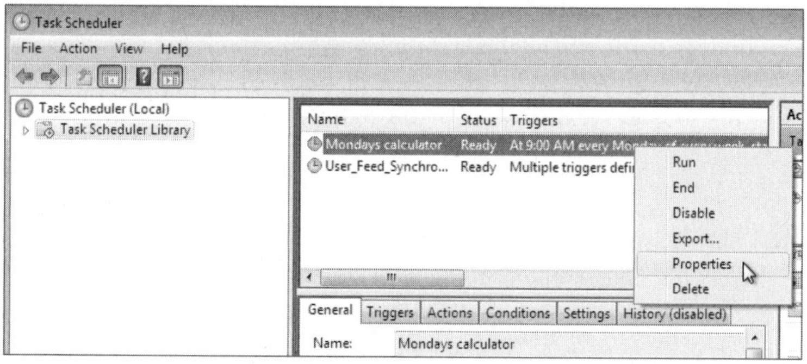

FIGURE 15.35
Right-click the task you
want to manage and
choose Properties.

The scheduled task's properties dialog box has six tabs for configuration, as follows:

◆ General

◆ Triggers

◆ Actions

◆ Conditions

- Settings
- History

Each options tab is described here:

General Tab   On the General tab, you can configure the following options:

- The description of the task
- The username or group to be used to run the specified task
- Whether the task is run when the user is logged off
- Whether the task is hidden

Triggers Tab   The Triggers tab shows the schedule configured for the task. You can click Edit to edit the trigger, which brings up the Edit Trigger dialog box. You can also click New to create a new trigger or click Delete to delete an existing trigger.

Actions Tab   The Actions tab shows the action that is configured for the task. You can click Edit to edit the action, which brings up the Edit Action dialog box. You can also click New to create a new action or click Delete to delete an existing action.

Conditions Tab   The Conditions tab shows the conditions associated with the task. The options in the Idle section are useful if the computer must be idle when the task is run. You can specify how long the computer must be idle before the task begins and whether the task should be stopped if the computer ceases to be idle. The options in the Power section are applicable when the computer on which the task runs is battery powered. You can specify that the task should not start if the computer is running from batteries and choose to stop the task if battery mode begins. You can also select whether to wake the computer in order to run the task. The option in the Network section defines whether the task starts when a particular network connection is available.

Settings Tab   The Settings tab shows the settings that affect the task's behavior with the following settings:

- Whether the task can be run on demand
- Whether the task should be restarted if it is missed
- How often the task should be restarted if it fails
- When to stop the task if it runs a long time
- Whether you can force the task to stop
- When the task should be deleted
- What actions should occur if the task is already running

History Tab   The History tab shows historical information regarding the task, including the task's start time, stop time, and whether the task completed successfully. Once set up, the scheduled task should commence at the appropriate time; if not, you might need to troubleshoot it.

Troubleshooting Scheduled Tasks

If you are trying to use Task Scheduler and the tasks are not properly being executed, one of the following troubleshooting options might resolve the problem:

◆ If a scheduled task does not run as expected, right-click the task and select Properties. In the Task Scheduler Library, ensure that the task status is Ready. In the task's properties page, verify the schedule has been defined on the Triggers tab.

◆ If the scheduled task is a command-line utility, make sure that you have properly defined the command-line utility, including any options that are required for the utility to run properly.

◆ Verify that the user who is configured to run the scheduled task has the necessary permissions for the task to be run.

◆ Within the Task Status section, check the task status to see when the task last ran successfully, if ever.

◆ Verify that the Task Scheduler service has been enabled on the computer if no tasks can be run on the computer.

Task Scheduler is a great utility that you can use to run scheduled maintenance applications and proactively maintain a Windows 7 system. If there are issues that occur within Windows 7, you use a different utility, called Event Viewer, to view these events.

Using Event Viewer

Event Viewer, shown in Figure 15.36, enables you to view event logs that are created by the operating system. This utility is useful when troubleshooting problems that occur on your computer.

FIGURE 15.36
Windows 7 Event
Viewer

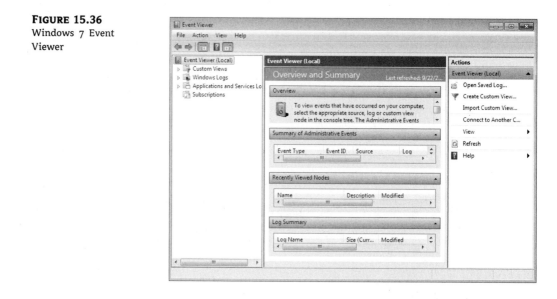

Whenever an error occurs, an event is usually placed in one or more event logs. To open Event Viewer, click Start ➢ Control Panel ➢ System And Security ➢ Administrative Tools ➢ View Event Logs, or you can type **event viewer** in the Start menu's search box.

Whereas old versions of Event Viewer contained only the Application, Security, and System logs, the Windows 7 version of Event Viewer contains the following logs:

◆ Application

◆ Security

◆ Setup

◆ System

◆ Forwarded Events

The Application log is used to log events relating to applications, such as whether an application, driver, or service fails. The Security log is used to log security events, such as successful or failed logon events. The Setup log is used only by domain controllers, so it doesn't have much practical use in Windows 7. The System log is used to log events concerning the operating system and related services. The Forwarded Events log is used to collect events that have been forwarded from other computers.

To configure log settings, right-click the log that you want to configure and select Properties. The Log Properties dialog box appears. The application log properties are shown in Figure 15.37.

The Log Properties dialog box shows the following information:

◆ The full name of the log

◆ Where the log is stored

◆ The size of the log

◆ When the log was created, modified, and accessed

◆ Whether logging is enabled for the log

◆ The maximum log size in KB

◆ The action that occurs when the log reaches the max size

The left pane of Event Viewer is where you find the Windows logs noted previously, but it also contains other logs and views that can be helpful when troubleshooting a specific application. The Custom Views section can be used to create a view that contains only the information you want to see, such as only events in a particular log or only Critical events. One custom view, Administrative Events, is created for you by default, as shown in Figure 15.38.

The Administrative Events view contains Critical, Error, and Warning events from all logs, enabling you to easily view only the most important events. Another section in the left pane contains logs that relate to Applications and Services, as shown in Figure 15.39.

The Microsoft folder within the Application and Services Log contains many other logs related to specific Microsoft components and applications.

The Subscription folder enables you to receive event logs from other computers. Having other machines send its event to one machine is useful to us as it gives us one central to view events from multiple locations. To use subscriptions, you must start the Windows Event Collector Service.

FIGURE 15.37
Event Viewer Application log properties

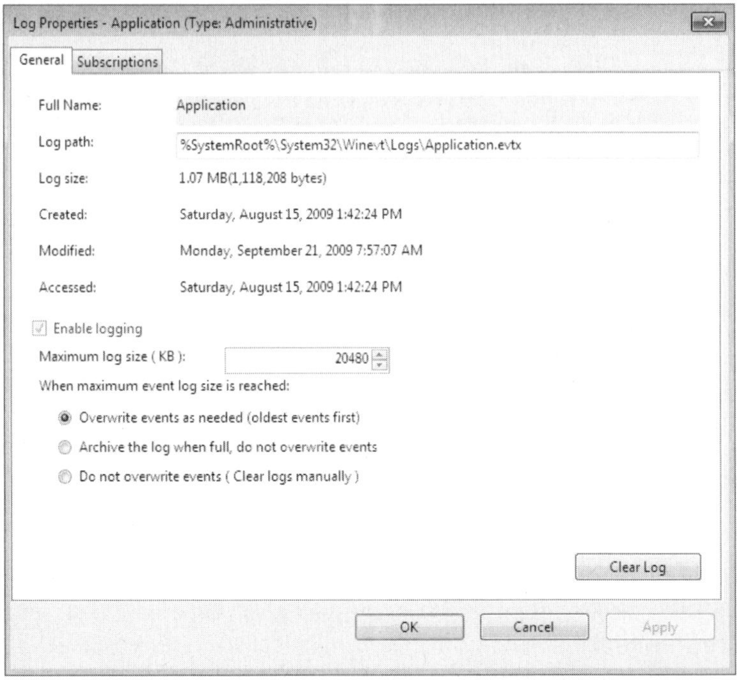

FIGURE 15.38
Event Viewer Custom Views section: Administrative Events

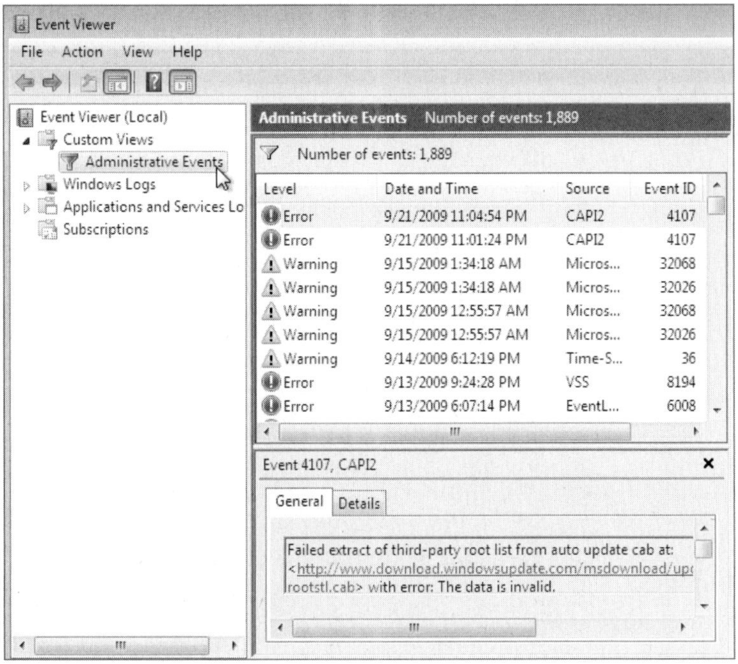

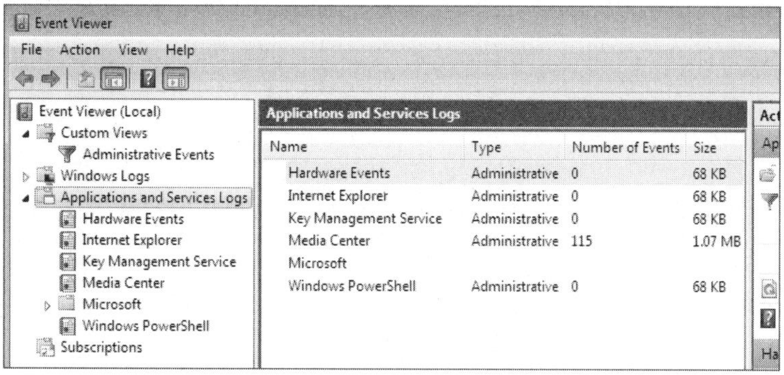

FIGURE 15.39
Event Viewer
Application and
Services Logs

The center pane of Event Viewer displays the events and information that relates to those events. You can also view a summary of your administrative events, which contains a count of Critical, Error, Warning, Information, Audit Success, and Audit Failure events. A count of these events is displayed for the last hour, day, and week, and the total number of events is also provided. Each event is assigned an event level of Critical, Error, Warning, Information, or Verbose.

The right pane of Event Viewer enables you to perform actions related to items you have selected in the left and center panes. You can save logs, open saved logs, create or import views, clear logs, filter logs, and find logs with certain keywords. You can also attach a task to an event. Clicking Attach Task To This Event opens the Create Basic Task wizard in Task Scheduler so that you can easily create a task related to the selected event.

Perform the following tasks to view events in Event Viewer and set log properties:

1. Select Start ➢ Control Panel ➢ System And Security ➢ Administrative Tools ➢ View Event Logs, or type **event viewer** in the Start menu's search box.

2. Open Windows Logs and click System in the left pane of the Event Viewer window to display the System log events.

3. Double-click the first event in the center pane of the Event Viewer window to see its Event Properties dialog box.

4. After you view the event properties, click the Close button to close the dialog box.

5. Right-click System in the left pane of the Event Viewer window and select Properties.

6. Configure the System log to archive the log file when it is full by clicking Archive The Log File When Full; Do Not Overwrite Events; click OK to close the dialog box.

7. Right-click System in the left pane of the Event Viewer window and select Filter Current Log.

8. Select the Critical and Error check boxes; then click OK (you will see only Critical and Error events listed in the System log).

9. Right-click System and select Clear Log.

10. A dialog box appears that asks if you want to save the System log before you clear it; click the Save And Clear button.

11. Specify the path and filename for the log file, and then click the Save button (the events will be saved in an `.evtx` file, and the events will be cleared from the System log).

Event Viewer is one of the first places to look when you suspect Windows 7 is not behaving correctly. But what if you know Windows 7 is having a problem and you need to restore the configuration or restore files? You need to use Windows 7 Backup and Restore.

Maintaining Windows 7 with Backup and Restore

The Windows 7 Backup and Restore utility allows you to create and restore backups. Backups protect your data in the event of system failure by storing the data on another medium, such a hard disk, CD, DVD, or network location. If your original data is lost due to corruption, deletion, or media failure, you can restore the data using your saved backup.

To access Backup and Restore (Shown in Figure 15.40), type **backup and restore** in the Start menu's search box or select Start ➤ Control Panel ➤ System And Security ➤ Backup And Restore.

Creating a Backup

You can see in Figure 15.40 that no backups of this Windows 7 machine have been taken. To set up a backup, choose the Set Up Backup link to launch a wizard that takes you through the process of creating a backup. The Backup wizard first asks you for a location to save your backup. This location can be a hard disk (removable or fixed), a CD, a DVD, or even a network location (if you have Windows 7 Premium or Ultimate).

FIGURE 15.40
Windows 7 Backup and Restore

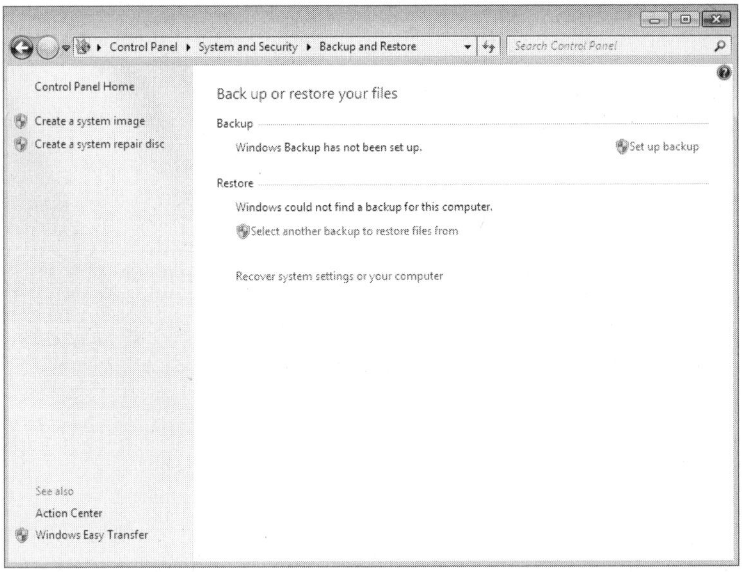

Next you are asked to either let Windows 7 choose the files and folders to back up or let you manually select the resources you want to back up. In your manual selection you can choose just the data libraries of Windows 7 for you as a user, or other users. You can also choose to create a backup of the Windows 7 systems files. If you want to choose other files and folders, you have the option of selecting any resources individually on your hard disk(s).

The final page of the wizard allows you to view the items you have selected as well as set up a schedule for your backups to occur. If you're happy with the setup, click the Save Settings And Run Backup button. The backup commences and you are able to restore the resources if necessary in the future. Figure 15.41 shows this author's Windows 7 machine right after he chose to save settings and run the backup. You can see the backup in progress and the history of his backups.

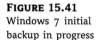

FIGURE 15.41
Windows 7 initial backup in progress

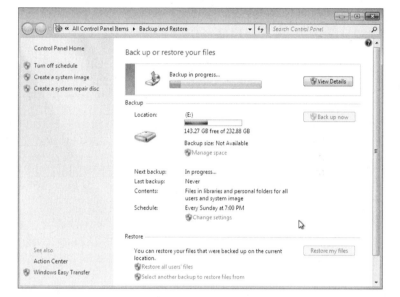

After you have created your backup, you can restore systems files and user data files with the restore utility.

Restoring Files from a Backup

If you have lost or destroyed files that you still want on your Windows 7 system, you can restore them from your backup. To restore files to your computer, launch the Backup and Restore program by typing **backup and restore** in the Start menu's search box. Assuming the media where your backup was saved is available, you can click the Restore My Files button, as shown in Figure 15.42.

FIGURE 15.42
Click the Restore My Files button to launch a restore wizard.

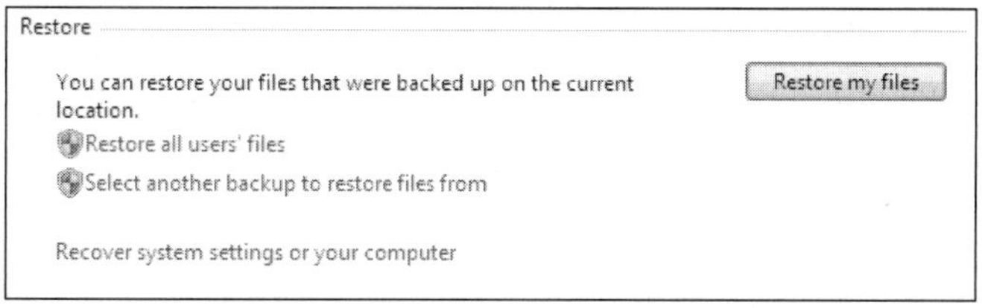

> ### Restore
>
> You can restore your files that were backed up on the current location.   **Restore my files**
> 🛡Restore all users' files
> 🛡Select another backup to restore files from
>
> Recover system settings or your computer

Clicking the Restore My Files button launches a restore wizard that prompts you to search for the files you want to restore. You can select multiple files and folders to restore. When you have selected all the files and folders you want to restore, click Next and you will have one final option: to restore to the original location or to pick an alternate location for restoration. After you make the restore location decision, click Restore and the restore operation commences and your original files and folders are available for you from the backup media.

You also have options in the Backup and Restore window to restore all users' files and to select another backup to restore files from. You would use this second option if you have saved your backup to multiple locations, and the last one (the one listed in the backup section) is not the set of backup files you want to use in your current session. Other than just files and folders, you have the choice to use other advanced backup options.

Using Advanced Backup Options

In the main backup and restore window, you have options in the left pane (as shown in Figure 15.43): Turn Off Schedule, Create A System Image, and Create A System Repair Disc.

FIGURE 15.43
Other backup options

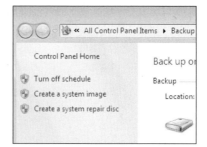

Choosing Turn Off Schedule lets you take your backup out of the current backup scheduling as seen in Task Scheduler. Create A System Image lets you back up critical operating system files for restoration later if your operating system has become corrupted. Create A System Repair Disc allows you to create a bootable disc that will store a limited setup, repair utilities, and the ability to restore your backup files if necessary.

There's one more option for restoring your Windows 7 configuration: System Protection.

Using System Protection

System Protection is a feature of Windows 7 that creates a backup and saves the configuration information of your computer's system files and settings on a regular basis. System Protection saves previous versions of saved configurations rather than just overwriting them. This makes it possible to return to multiple configurations, known as restore points, in your Windows 7 history. These restore points are created before most significant events, such as installing a new driver. Restore points are also created automatically every seven days. System Protection is turned on by default in Windows7 for any drive formatted with NTFS.

You manage System Protection and the restore points from the System Protection tab of the System Properties dialog box. You access this tab directly by typing **restore point** in the Start menu's search box, as shown in Figure 15.44.

Clicking the System Restore button launches the System Restore wizard, which walks you through the process of returning Windows 7 to a previous point in time. Also on the System Protection tab of the System Properties dialog box you'll find the Protection Settings section, where you can configure any of your available drives. Select the drive on which you would like to modify the configuration and click the Configure button. The System Protection configuration dialog box for the drive appears, as shown in Figure 15.45.

FIGURE 15.44
The System Protection tab of the System Properties dialog box

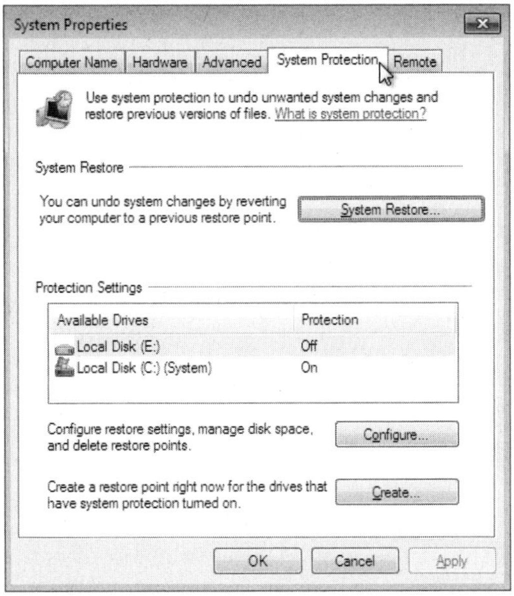

FIGURE 15.45
Drive Protection properties in System Protection

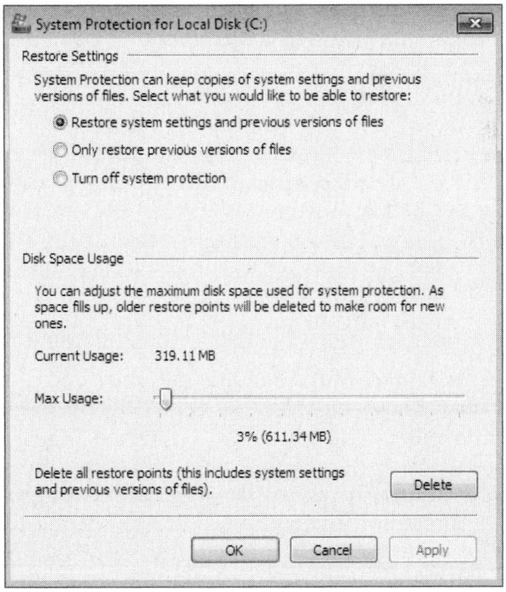

The System Protection for the selected disk properties box allows you to enable or disable system protection for the drive. When you enable protection, you can opt for previous versions for files or previous versions of files and system settings. You also have the ability to set the maximum usage your restore points will use for storage. One final function of the System Protection dialog box for the selected disk is to delete all restore points (including system setting and previous versions of files) by clicking the Delete button.

The Bottom Line

Use Performance Monitor to view CPU usage.   Performance Monitor gives you a way to view real-time statistics of several of the Windows 7 subsystems.

Master It   You recently installed a new Windows 7 application. It seems as though your machine is operating more slowly than normal. Someone told you to look at how busy your CPU is while the application is running. How will you view the CPU utilization while the application is running?

Maintain Windows 7 with system tools.   There are several system tools within Windows 7 to help you monitor and maintain your operating system. These tools include Task Manager, Performance Information and Tools, and System Configuration (MSConfig).

Master It   After you install a new application on your Windows 7 machine, you find that it is causing you problems in performance. The longer the application runs, the more your machine seems to lag. After a period of time, the application no longer responds. It even displays "Not Responding" in its title bar and the whole application interface has become translucent. You would like to shut the application down but can't even click the close "X" in the upper-right corner. How can you force the application to close?

Schedule a task to launch daily.   There are times when you would like an application to run periodically to perform some function on your Windows 7 machine. You can use Task Scheduler to perform this operation.

Master It   You are concerned about security on your local machine and have purchased a software product to collect security information such as open ports, applications that are running, and services that are enabled. The application has the ability to take a snapshot of several of the security parameters you're concerned with and save them to a log file; you just have to run the application. You would like to run the program daily and save the logs so you can review them periodically at your convenience. How can you run the program daily without having to launch it manually?

Back up critical data files.   You can use the Backup and Restore application in Windows 7 to make backup copies of operating system and critical data files that might be needed even if they're deleted by mistake or become corrupted.

Master It   Your main application that stores critical financial data files for your company is stored locally on your Windows 7 machine. You're nervous that these files can severely impact your day-to-day operation if they somehow become corrupted or are deleted. You would like to save a copy of the whole financial data folders so you can recover any or all of the data files with minimal impact. How can you back up the critical files in Windows 7?

Appendix A

The Bottom Line

Each of The Bottom Line sections in the chapters suggest exercises to deepen skills and understanding. Sometimes there is only one possible solution, but often you are encouraged to use your skills and creativity to create something that builds on what you know and lets you explore one of many possible solutions.

Chapter 1: Overview of Windows 7

Choose a client operating system.   Choosing the right client operating system is a task that all IT professionals will have to face. The proper operating system is dependent on the client's hardware and job function.

Master It   You are a consultant who needs to set up a new Windows Server 2008 network for one of your clients. The end-user machines must be able to work on the new network, but new equipment is not possible due to financial constraints. How should you determine which operating systems will go on each machine?

Solution   The first step would be check all the end users' hardware and then choose the operating system based on hardware requirements. Because you are working with Windows Server 2008, Windows XP with SP2 or higher, Windows Vista, or Windows 7 will all work properly.

Understand the newest features of Windows 7.   There are many new features in Windows 7, among them a new Windows Taskbar and Jump Lists, Preview pane, Windows Touch, XP Mode, simpler home networking, and Device Stage.

Master It   You are a consultant who needs to quickly set up a home network for one of your clients. Which operating system would you use?

Solution   Using Windows 7, you create a new HomeGroup by choosing Control Panel ➤ Networking. When you create the HomeGroup, a password will be created. Use this password to connect all of the other Windows 7 machines to this network.

Explain the Windows 32-bit and 64-bit architecture.   The terms 32-bit and 64-bit refer to the CPU, or processor. The number represents how the data is processed. It is processed as 2^{32} or 2^{64}. The larger the number, the larger the amount of data can be processed at any one time.

Master It   How do you decide which operating system, 32-bit or 64-bit, you want to assign to your users?

Solution Determine which applications and job functions your users will be completing. Depending on job functions, decide whether users will need more than 4 GB of RAM. If they do, install Windows 7 64-bit. If they don't, install Windows 7 32-bit.

Chapter 2: Installing Windows 7

Determine the hardware requirements for Windows 7. One of the most important tasks in installing Windows 7 is to verify that the machines that you want to install Windows 7 can handle the installation. The following hardware requirements are for Windows 7:

CPU (processor)	1 GHz 32-bit or 64-bit processor
Memory (RAM)	1 GB of system memory
Hard disk	16 GB of available disk space
Video adapter	Support for DirectX 9 graphics with 128 MB of memory (to enable the Aero theme)
Optional drive	DVD-R/W drive
Network device	Compatible network interface card

Master It You are a consultant who is hired by an organization to migrate the users from Windows Vista and Windows XP to Windows 7. How would you accomplish this?

Solution You have to verify that all the machines can work with Windows 7. To do this, you first need to verify that the machines meet the minimum hardware requirements. Second, check the HCL to verify that the hardware can handle the Windows 7 operating system. Finally, make a plan for the migration of users' data from the previous Windows operating systems to Windows 7.

Determine which version of Windows 7 to install. Microsoft has released six versions of the Windows 7 operating system. It is very important to install the correct version of Windows 7 to match the end user's needs. The six versions are

◆ Windows 7 Starter

◆ Windows 7 Home Basic

◆ Windows 7 Home Premium

◆ Windows 7 Professional

◆ Windows 7 Enterprise

◆ Windows 7 Ultimate

Master It You are an IT manager and you must install a Windows 7 operating system that supports Windows BitLocker. Which edition of Windows 7 could you use?

Solution You have the choice of installing Windows 7 Enterprise or Windows 7 Ultimate. Both of these Windows 7 versions support BitLocker. All of the other Windows 7 versions do not currently support BitLocker.

Install the Windows 7 operating system.   Installing Windows 7 is an easy process but it is important to plan the installation before actually installing the operating system.

You can install Windows 7 either from the bootable DVD or through a network installation using files that have been copied to a network share point. You can also launch the `setup.exe` file from within the Windows Vista operating system to upgrade your operating system.

The Windows 7 DVD is bootable. To start the installation, you simply restart your computer and boot to the DVD. The installation process will begin automatically.

> **Master It**   Your company has purchased a new computer that meets all the minimum requirements for installing Windows 7. They need Windows 7 installed on the machine. How can you install Windows 7?

> **Solution**   Using the Windows 7 DVD, boot the computer off the installation disk. The Windows 7 installation will begin. Follow the installation process to complete the installation.

Migrate users from Windows XP to Windows 7.   Since the upgrade option from Windows XP to Windows 7 is not available, you can use Windows Easy Transfer to integrate settings from Windows XP to Windows 7 on the same computer.

The first step in this migration process is to copy your files to a removable media such as an external hard drive or thumb drive or to a network share. After the installation of the Windows 7 operating system, you can then migrate these files onto the Windows 7 system.

> **Master It**   Your organization needs to convert all Windows XP machines to Windows 7. What steps should you take to complete the upgrade?

> **Solution**   First, you must make sure that the Windows XP machines meet the minimum hardware requirements for Windows 7. Then, using the Windows Easy Transfer utility, copy all of your Windows XP data to a removable media. Install Windows 7 to the machine and then migrate the data from the removable media back into Windows 7.

Chapter 3: Automating the Windows 7 Installation

Use the Microsoft Deployment Toolkit (MDT) 2010.   Microsoft Deployment Toolkit (MDT) 2010 is a way of automating desktop and server deployment. The MDT gives you tools for deployment of desktops and servers through the use of a common console. It allows for quicker deployments and standardized desktop and server images and security. MDT 2010 also allows for Zero Touch deployments of Windows 7, Windows Server 2008, Windows Vista, Windows Server 2003, and Windows XP.

> **Master It**   Your organization has asked you to set up one application that all administrators can use to configure and deploy Windows desktop operating systems. Which utility should you use?

> **Solution**   By installing and using the MDT 2010, you can use the Deployment Workbench to have one central application that all administrators can use to deploy Windows. MDT 2010 also allows you to set up Zero Touch deployments of Windows.

Take advantage of the Windows Deployment Services (WDS).   WDS is an updated version of Remote Installation Services (RIS). WDS is a suite of components that allows you to remotely install Windows 7 on client computers.

A WDS server installs Windows 7 on the client computers. The WDS server must be configured with the Preboot Execution Environment (PXE) boot files, the images to be deployed to the client computers, and the answer file. WDS client computers must be PXE capable.

> **Master It**   You are hired as a consultant by a large organization with multiple locations. The organization wants to have the ability to deploy Windows 7 remotely. How can you set this up?

> **Solution**   You can use (WDS) to remotely install the Windows 7 operating system. The client machines must be PXE compatible, and you must also have a DNS server, Active Directory server, and a DHCP server that can respond to PXE requests.

Utilize the Windows Automated Installation Kit (Windows AIK).   The Windows AIK is a set of utilities and documentation that allows you to configure and deploy Windows operating systems. You can use the Windows AIK to capture Windows Images with ImageX, configure and edit your images by using the Deployment Image Servicing and Management (DISM) utility, create Windows PE images, migrate user data and profiles using the User State Migration Tool (USMT), and centrally manage volume activations by using the Volume Activation Management Tool (VAMT).

> **Master It**   You need to configure and deploy Windows operating systems by using images. How can you accomplish this task?

> **Solution**   By installing and using the Windows AIK, you can deploy Windows operating systems by using images. The Windows AIK will also allow you to manage these images all in one application.

Make the most of the Microsoft Assessment and Planning (MAP) Toolkit.   MAP is a utility that will locate computers on a network and then perform a thorough inventory of these computers. To obtain this inventory, MAP uses multiple utilities like the Windows Management Instrumentation (WMI), the Remote Registry Service, or the Simple Network Management Protocol (SNMP).

Having this information will allow you to determine if the machines on your network will be able to load Windows 7, Windows Vista, Server 2008, Microsoft Office 2007, and Microsoft Application Virtualization. One advantage of using MAP when determining the needs for Windows 7 is that MAP will also advise you of any hardware upgrades needed for a machine or device driver availability.

> **Master It**   You are a consultant who is hired by an organization to migrate the computers from Windows XP to Windows 7. How would you accomplish this?

> **Solution**   You can use MAP to run an inventory report on all the Windows XP machines. You can use this report to verify which machines can be upgraded to Windows 7 and which machines need to be updated to allow an installation of Windows 7.

Chapter 4: Configuring Disks

Understand the different file systems.   When you select a file system, you can select FAT32 or NTFS. You typically select file systems based on the features you want to use and whether you will need to access the file system using other operating systems. If you have a FAT32 partition and want to update it to NTFS, you can use the Convert or Disk Management utility.

Master It   You are the system administrator for your organization and you have to install a new Windows 7 laptop for a salesperson who goes on the road. Data protection and hard drive space are important features that must be included on the Windows 7 laptop. How would you configure the file system?

Solution   By installing the Windows 7 laptop with NTFS as the file system, you will meet the requirements needed for the salesperson. NTFS has many benefits over using FAT32, including Encryption and Compression. These two features will allow you to set up the laptop the way the company needs it.

Identify disk storage types.   Windows 7 supports three types of disk storage: basic, dynamic, and GUID partition table (GPT). Basic storage is backward compatible with other operating systems and can be configured to support up to four partitions. Dynamic storage is supported by Windows 2000, Windows XP, Windows Server 2003, Windows Server 2008, Windows Vista, and Windows 7, and allows storage to be configured as volumes. GPT storage allows you to configure volume sizes larger than 2 TB and up to 128 primary partitions.

Master It   Your organization has asked you to configure a Windows 7 Desktop. The Desktop was already installed but the company would like you to reconfigure the disks so that some of the storage areas can be extended. How would you set up the disk storage?

Solution   By configuring the disk storage as dynamic disks, you'd be able to expand your volumes. Dynamic disks can be extended as long as they are formatted as NTFS volumes. GPT storage would not work here because GPT storage has to be set up on a machine with unformatted free space, and because this machine was already installed, the storage would not be unformatted free space.

Understand the benefits of NTFS.   NTFS offers comprehensive folder and file-level security. This allows you to set an additional level of security for users who access the files and folders locally or through the network. NTFS also offers disk management features such as compression, encryption, quotas, and data recovery features.

Master It   You have a Windows 7 machine in your organization that multiple users operate. The users keep complaining that other users are using too much hard disk space. Your organization has asked you to set up disk space limits for the Windows 7 machine. How would you configure this?

Solution   First you need to make sure your file system is using NTFS. If it's using FAT32, convert the file system to NTFS. After the file system is using NTFS, you can enable volume or partition quotas. Placing quotas on this Windows 7 machine ensures that no one user uses too much hard disk space.

Use disk-management utilities. Microsoft Windows 7 includes a few utilities that you can run to help keep your system running efficiently. Two utilities that continue to allow the machine to run at its peak performance are Disk Defragment and Disk Cleanup.

Master It You have users on your network who are complaining that their Windows 7 machines are starting to show slower response times when opening or managing files and applications. What are some of the ways you can help speed up the machines?

Solution Machines can start slowing down over time due to the hard drives getting fragmented or too many temporary files. By running the Disk Defragment and Disk Cleanup utilities, your machine can gain back response times from opening files and applications. Having faster machine responses allows users to work more efficiently.

Chapter 5: Managing the Windows 7 Desktop

Understand the Start menu shortcuts. The Start menu has many default shortcuts that are preloaded when the Windows 7 operating system is created. Some of the default shortcuts are Getting Started, Windows Media Center, Calculator, Sticky Notes, Snipping Tool, Remote Desktop Connection, Startup, and Internet.

Master It You are the system administrator for your organization, and you have salespeople who need an application to start every time they log into the Windows 7 system. How would you configure the application so that it starts when the salespeople log into their machine?

Solution One of the shortcuts on the Start menu is Startup. The Startup shortcut allows an administrator or user to place a shortcut within the Startup and that application will automatically start when the user logs onto the Windows 7 system.

Customize the Start menu and Taskbar. Users can customize the Taskbar and Start menu using the Taskbar And Start Menu Properties dialog box. This dialog box has three tabs: Taskbar, Start Menu, and Toolbars. The easiest way to access the dialog box is to right-click a blank area in the Taskbar and choose Properties from the context menu.

Master It You are the system administrator for your organization, and you have a user who has received a computer that was previously used by another user. The machine was not formatted, but the new user's data was migrated over. The user complains because the Taskbar disappears on its own. The user gets the Taskbar back when the mouse is moved over the bottom of the screen. How can you stop the Taskbar from disappearing?

Solution The Auto-Hide option is enabled for the Taskbar. This option hides the Taskbar but reveals it when the mouse is moved over the bottom of the screen. Auto-Hide is disabled by default, but this machine was being used by a previous user. To disable the Auto-Hide option, click the Auto-Hide check box in the Taskbar And Start Menu Properties dialog box.

Work with regional settings. Multilanguage and regional support is available with Windows 7 that allows the user interface to be presented in different languages and that allows applications to be viewed and edited in different languages. Depending on the level of language support required by your environment, you may use either a localized version of Window Windows 7 or install language files to support multiple languages.

> **Master It** You are the system administrator for an organization that has multiple sites all over the world. You are responsible for rolling out Windows 7 client machines to users in all offices. You have to set up a Windows 7 machine for a user overseas. How do you configure the Windows 7 machine?

> **Solution** Depending on the location of the user, you need to load the Windows 7 operating system that is created for that locale. For example, if the user is in Japan, you need to load a Japanese version of Windows 7.

Use accessibility features. Windows 7 allows you to configure the Desktop so those users with special accessibility needs can use the Windows 7 Desktop more easily. Through its accessibility options and accessibility utilities, Windows 7 supports users with limited sight, hearing, or mobility.

> **Master It** You are the administrator for a mid-sized computer training company. You have a user who has difficulty seeing the Desktop clearly. You have already made the icons larger, but the user is still having issues. What other steps can you show the user so that the Desktop and applications are easier to see?

> **Solution** Windows 7 provides several accessibility utilities for people with limited sight, including the Magnifier, the Narrator, and the On-Screen Keyboard. The Magnifier utility creates a separate window to magnify a portion of your screen. The Narrator utility can read aloud on-screen text, dialog boxes, menus, and buttons, and the On-Screen Keyboard displays a large keyboard on the screen.

Chapter 6: Managing the Interface

Understand Control Panel. Windows 7 uses the Registry when the operating system starts. The Registry is the database used by the operating system to store configuration information. Control Panel is a set of GUI utilities that allow you to configure Registry settings without using a Registry editor.

> **Master It** You are the administrator for a large computer company. One of your salespeople calls and asks you if they can remove an old application from their machine. How would you instruct them to remove the old application properly from the Windows 7 machine?

> **Solution** One of the icons in the Control Panel is Programs and Features. The Programs and Features icon allows you to uninstall, change, or repair programs and features. The Programs and Features icon also allows you to choose which Windows 7 features that you want to install or remove on the Windows 7 machine.

Use the System utility. The System icon is one of the most important icons in Control Panel. The System icon allows you to view which operating system your machine is using; check system resources (processor, RAM); change the computer name, domain, or workgroup; and activate your Windows 7. From the System icon you can also configure the Device Manager, Remote Settings, System Protection, and Advanced settings.

Master It   You are the system administrator for your organization and you have a sales-person who has been trying to activate his legal company version of Windows 7. He gets an error message stating that the product key is invalid. What can you do to help activate the Windows 7 machine?

Solution   You can issue the user a new legal company product key and have the user change the product key. To change the product key, open the System utility and click the Change Product Key link at the bottom of the screen. Have the user enter the new product key and try to reactivate the Windows 7 machine online.

Configure mobile computers.   Windows 7 includes several features that are useful for laptop computers. One of the best features for laptops is configuring the power options. Power options allow you to select a power plan and enable power-management features with Windows 7. By selecting the proper power plan, users can increase the life of their battery.

Master It   You are the administrator for a small company that uses only laptops for their end users. You need to configure the laptops to extend the life of the battery. How would you configure the power options on their laptops?

Solution   You configure power options through the Power Options Properties dialog box. To access this dialog box, open Control Panel and click Power Options. The Power Options dialog box provides the ability to manage power plans and to control power options, such as when the display is turned off, when the computer sleeps, and what the power button does.

Configure services.   A service is a program, routine, or process that performs a specific func-tion within the Windows 7 operating system. Most applications and features use services to help make that application run properly.

Master It   You are the system administrator for your organization and you have a salesper-son who needs a service to start every time she turns on the Windows 7 system. How would you configure the service so that it starts when the salesperson starts her machine?

Solution   You have the ability to configure a service to start automatically in the Ser-vices snap-in. To configure the service to start automatically, double-click the service and change the Startup Type to Automatic. On the General tab you can also configure the service display name, a description of the service, the path to the service executable, the current service status, and the start parameters that can be applied when the service is started.

Chapter 7: Using Remote Assistance and Remote Desktop

Assist novice users with Windows 7.   Remote Assistance is a great collaboration tool used between an expert and a novice user that allows the expert to help the novice by watching the novice user's actions on another machine. If desired, the expert can even request control (which has to be granted by the novice user) to perform an action. Remote Assistance can be used as a teaching tool or simply to fix a problem for a novice user.

Master It   You are an administrator on your local network, and one of your users is trying to find their IP address. You know it's easiest to open the command prompt and type `ipconfig`, but you're not sure if the user can follow your instructions and you would like to watch them so they don't get lost while you give the instructions. You know you've said too many times, "Tell me what you see." You have decided to use Remote Assistance to help the user. Both you and the user needing assistance are using Windows 7. How can you assist your novice user to get the IP address of their machine?

Solution   Where you are both using Windows 7, the easiest solution is to use Easy Connect to provide Remote Assistance. Have the novice user start a Remote Assistance session by typing `msra` in the Start menu's search box. Have the novice user choose Invite Someone You Know To Help You, then choose Use Easy Connect. An invitation will be created and a password given to the novice user that will be conveyed to you (the expert user).

You will now launch Remote Assistance on your machine (by typing `msra` in the Start menu's search box). Choose Help Someone Who Has Invited You. Then select Use Easy Connect and enter the password supplied by the novice user.

The novice user will be asked if they want to accept assistance from you. When the user accepts, you'll be able to see the novice user's Desktop and can instruct them (either via the built-in chat window or by phone) how to view the IP address of the machine. Tell the user to follow these steps: enter `cmd` in the Start menu's Run box; in the command prompt window, enter the command `ipconfig`; and note the IP address in the window. The session can now be terminated and the novice user is very happy — and so are you.

Provide help from Windows 7 to older operating systems.   Remote Assistance is available on legacy operating systems as well as Windows 7. It works the same way on most current operating systems, except that the Easy Connect option (available in Windows 7) is not available on previous operating system versions. To integrate a Windows 7 Remote Assistance session with a previous version, an invitation file or email invitation is a solution. The Remote Assistance established by a file or email invitation will allow an expert user to assist a novice user interactively (both can see what's happening).

Master It   You are the network administrator for your company and you have taken a phone call from a novice user asking for help changing the default printer they are on from one device to another. You know this is a fairly simple operation but would like to be looking over the user's shoulder as the changes are made to avoid any problems that may be created by the change. The novice user is running Windows Vista and you are running Windows 7. How can you have the user request a Remote Assistance session with you so you won't have to physically go to the novice user's location?

Solution   One appropriate solution here is to have the novice user send you a Remote Assistance invitation by email. You should have the novice user start a Remote Assistance session. Instruct the user to type `msra` in the Start menu's search box and then to choose Invite Someone You Trust To Help You. Because they're on Vista, the user can also select Start ➤ Help and Support, choose Windows Remote Assistance in the Ask Someone section, and then click Invite Someone You Trust To Help You. After choosing the Invite option, the novice user must select Use E-mail To Send An Invitation. The user will be asked to enter and confirm a password to give to you, the expert user, to allow you to establish the connection. An invitation file will be created and added as an email attachment within the user's default email program (the novice user must have a default email program configured, or this solution will not work). The novice user will send the email to you. You will receive the email and open the invitation attachment, launching the expert side of the Remote Assistance session. You will enter the password given to you by the novice user. The novice user will still have to accept the Remote Assistance session, and then you can help the novice user change default printers. Ask the user to open Control Panel, select Printers, right-click the printer the user wants to be the default, and choose Set As Default Printer. The novice user is happy and you've avoided another road trip to a user's desk.

Access a machine from a remote location. Remote Desktop is another form of remote access that allows a user to connect to a machine and have access to that machine's resources. The host machine is the machine being connected to; the client machine is where the user accessing the remote resources is located. The host machine can be the end user's in the case of telecommuting or even that of the end user if the user is in a different office for the day.

Master It You are currently working in a remote office and realize you have left an important document on your home office machine. You thought you'd put it on your stick, but alas, it's not there and you don't think asking someone to log into your machine and retrieve it is a good idea (good thinking, by the way). You need to access your machine remotely to get the file. How will you do it?

Solution You use Remote Desktop to gain access to your machine and copy the file to the machine you're sitting at in the remote office. Your account will have been added to the Remote Desktop Users group and the Allow Remote Desktop Connections option will have to be selected on your machine (at the home office). With these criteria met, you can launch Remote Desktop from the machine you're sitting at in the remote office, specify the IP address of your machine in the remote office, and enter your authorizing credentials for your machine. You will then essentially have a remote keyboard, monitor, and mouse to your local machine. Locate the file you need in the remote office, then copy and paste it to the machine you're using. You can log off and continue working as you have the necessary file to complete your task.

Script a session for automated connection. As the network administrator, you need to log in to a server machine on a regular basis to check on its performance and make minor changes. You have been going down to the server room and physically logging in every time you have to make changes or log data. You now know you can use Remote Desktop to access the server and would like to start using the application.

Master It You know you can launch Remote Desktop from the menu structure of Windows 7, but you would like to be able to have an icon on your Desktop to launch a Remote Desktop session with one of the servers you are responsible for. You know that down the road you will have to manage more machines this way, and if you create an icon for one now it will be pretty easy to create more icons later so you can simply double-click any one of the individual icons to initiate the Remote Desktop session to any of several individual servers. You want to create a Notepad file with the appropriate command line to launch a Remote Desktop session to a server at 192.168.1.62 and make it so double-clicking it will initiate the Remote Desktop session.

Solution Open Notepad by typing notepad in the Start menu's search box or choosing Start ➤ All Programs ➤ Accessories ➤ Notepad. Type the command line to launch Remote Desktop with the desired IP parameter: **mstsc.exe /v:192.168.1.62**. Save the file with an intuitive name to your desktop with a .bat extension. You can now double-click the generic icon and a Remote Desktop session to **192.168.1.62** will start; you will still have to enter credentials.

Chapter 8: Configuring Users and Groups

Understand user account types. Windows 7 uses two basic account types: Administrator and Standard User. The Administrator account type provides unrestricted access to performing administrative tasks. Administrator accounts should be used only for performing administrative tasks and should not be used for normal computing tasks.

The Standard User type is the account type that should be applied for every user of the computer. Standard User accounts can perform most day-to-day tasks on the Windows 7 machine.

Master It You are the administrator for a large computer company. You need to set up 20 Windows 7 machines and 20 local user accounts on those machines. When setting up the user accounts, what type of user account should these users have?

Solution These users should be set up with the Standard User account type. Standard User accounts can do the end-user tasks like working with email, Microsoft Office, and so forth. Administrator access not only would allow these users to perform the day-to-day tasks but would also let the users manipulate and change the Windows 7 operating system.

Create accounts. To create user accounts for your Windows 7 users, you have multiple options. To create local user accounts you can use the Local Users and Groups MMC snap-in, or you can use the User Accounts option in Control Panel. To create domain users accounts, you use Active Directory Users and Computers (see Chapter 12 for more information).

Master It You are the administrator for a large computer company. You need to create 20 local users accounts for the 20 new Windows 7 machines that your company has just purchased. How would you accomplish this task?

Solution To create the local accounts, use the Local Users and Groups MMC snap-in. In the Local Users and Groups snap-in, right-click the Users folder and choose New User. Enter the data for the users of that Windows 7 machine. Repeat the process for all local users for all Windows 7 machines.

Configure accounts. When you're configuring users' accounts, you deal with three main categories of properties: General, Member Of, and Profile.

The General tab contains the information you supplied when you set up the new user account, including any Full Name and Description information, the password options you selected, and whether the account is disabled.

The Member Of tab allows you to place this account into local groups on this Windows 7 machine. The Profile tab enables you to configure a user's Profile data, including user profile path, logon scripts, and home folder locations.

Master It   You are the administrator for a small pottery company. Your users are complaining that when they work on any machine that is not their own, the desktop settings are different. This is causing an issue for your users. What can you do to make sure that all users have their own desktop settings no matter which machine they are working on?

Solution   To solve this problem you can set up roaming profiles. A roaming profile is stored on a network server and allows users to access their user profile, regardless of the client computer to which they're logged on. Roaming profiles provide a consistent Desktop for users who move around, no matter which computer they access.

Understand local groups.   Groups are a way to make sure that similar users get access to similar resources without having to add individual user accounts to each resource. Groups are an important part of network management.

Windows 7 includes built-in local groups, such as Administrators and Backup Operators. These groups already have all the permissions needed to accomplish specific tasks. Windows 7 also uses default special groups, which the system manages. Users become members of special groups based on their requirements for computer and network access.

You can create and manage local groups through the Local Users and Groups utility. The Local users and Groups snap-in allows you to add groups, change group membership, rename groups, and delete groups.

Master It   You are the administrator for a large organization. You have decided to set up local groups on all the Windows 7 machines so that all salespeople have access to the same resources. How do you accomplish this goal?

Solution   You can create, manage, disable, and delete groups in the Local Users and Groups. You would need to create a Sales group and add all salespeople into this group. Then give this group access to all the sales resources.

Chapter 9: Managing Security

Understand Local Group Policy Objects.   Local Group Policy Objects (LGPOs) are a set of security configuration settings that are applied to users and computers. LGPOs are created and stored on the Windows 7 computer.

If your Windows 7 computer is a part of a domain, which uses the services of Active Directory, then you typically manage and configure security through Group Policy Objects (GPOs). LGPOs are rules that can be placed on either users or computers.

Master It   You are the administrator for a large computer company. You need to make sure that all of the Windows 7 machines reset their passwords every 45 days. How can you accomplish this?

Solution   You can set up an LGPO on these Windows machines or set up a GPO for the domain that sets the Maximum Password Age. The Maximum Password Age forces users to change their password after the maximum password age is exceeded. Setting this value to 0 will specify that the password will never expire.

Understand User Account Control (UAC). User Account Control (UAC) enables nonadministrator users to perform standard tasks, such as install a printer, configure a VPN or wireless connection, and install updates, while preventing them from performing tasks that require administrative privileges, such as installing applications.

Master It You are the administrator for a small plumbing company. You need to set 20 Windows 7 machines so that the users can always run applications with elevated privileges. How do you accomplish this goal?

Solution You can enable an executable file to run with elevated privileges. To do so, on a one-time basis, you can right-click a shortcut or executable and select Run As Administrator.

But what if you need to configure an application to always run with elevated privileges? Log in as an administrator, right-click a shortcut or executable and select Properties. On the Compatibility tab, check the Run This Program As An Administrator check box.

Configure NTFS security. NTFS permissions control access to NTFS files and folders. The person who owns the object has complete control over the object. You configure access by allowing or denying NTFS permissions to users and groups.

NTFS permissions are cumulative, based on group memberships if the user has been allowed access. This means that the user gets the highest level of security from all the different groups they belong to. However, if the user had been denied access through user or group membership, those permissions override the allowed permissions.

Master It You are the administrator for a small organization that has decided to use NTFS on each Windows 7 machine. The company needs to make sure that all files and folders are secure. How do you make sure that all files and folders are secure on the Windows 7 NTFS drives?

Solution You can secure all of the Windows 7 drives by using NTFS file and folder level security. Giving access to just the users who are supposed to access these drives verifies that unauthorized users will not get data from these drives.

Manage shared permissions. Sharing is the process of allowing network users access to a resource located on a computer. A network share provides a single location to manage shared data used by many users. Sharing also allows an administrator to install an application once, as opposed to installing it locally at each computer, and to manage the application from a single location.

Master It You are the administrator for a large computer company. You need everyone in the company to have access to the reports folder on Server A. How should you give everyone enough access to change and create reports?

Solution On Server A, share the reports folder and give the Everyone group the Change permission to the folder. By giving Everyone the Change permission, all users will be able to create and modify reports.

Chapter 10: Configuring Hardware and Printers

Use Device Manager. Device Manager is the primary management tool for installing, configuring, troubleshooting, and updating hardware devices and their associated driver components.

Master It You recently updated a piece of hardware on one of your servers; you have added a video capture card that will be tied in to the security system in the server room. You did all the necessary due diligence before installing the hardware and verifying prerequisites successfully. The card seems to have installed correctly from the manufacturer's setup program. Now that you're trying to use the connected camera to capture video, you cannot get it to work correctly. You need to verify that Windows 7 sees the device and believes the status is good. How will you do it?

Solution You should look for the device in Device Manager. This will verify that the operating system recognized the device. You need to also look at the properties of the device by right-clicking the device and selecting Properties from the context menu. The General tab provides a Device Status window that reports how Windows 7 is viewing the device/device driver communication.

Manage and update device drivers. Device Manager shows you the driver status as seen by Windows 7 for the hardware installed in your machine. If there is a problem, you should be able to see that a problem exists.

Master It After installing a video capture card into one of your servers, you find that it is misbehaving. You see in Device Manager that the device driver is not communicating with the device. Researching the manufacturer's website, you find they have identified a bug in the driver code and offer an updated device driver. How will you install the new device driver on your server?

Solution Download the updated driver from the hardware vendor and save it. You will use Device Manager to update the device driver. Find the hardware in question in Device Manager, right-click the device, and select Properties. On the Driver tab, click the Update Driver button to launch the Update Driver Software Wizard. Choose Browse My Computer For Driver Software and locate the updated driver. Select the driver and click OK. The new driver will be installed and the hardware will now work.

Install, uninstall, and disable hardware. Device Manager in Windows 7 gives you the ability to install, uninstall, and disable hardware installed in your machines. Troubleshooting hardware issues many times requires actions to be performed from Device Manager.

Master It You have recently changed a piece of hardware you had installed to a device with more functionality from a different vendor. You physically disconnected the old device and installed the new device. You are using a server health program that monitors your servers, including the one with the new hardware. Your health program is now showing the old hardware as failed (although it does not even exist in the machine now). You must uninstall the old device's software components so Windows will not try to report its status.

Solution Use Device Manager to remove the software components for the missing hardware. Locate the old hardware in Device Manager and right-click it. From the context menu, choose Uninstall. Confirm the un-installation and you will no longer have the issue with the software of the server.

Manage I/O and removable storage devices.   Device Manager is the central application for controlling hardware installed in your machines, which includes I/O devices such as your keyboard and mouse. Ease Of Access features allow you to control keyboard and mouse behavior.

Master It   Managing I/O devices for users is not normally a concern, but you are now opening an office and have inexperienced users who are having problems following the mouse they are learning to use. You need to turn on the option to have mouse trailers available and would also like the users to be able to find the mouse on the screen easily. How will you do it?

Solution   Access the Ease Of Access Center found in Control Panel to turn on mouse pointer trails and the location of mouse pointer functionality. Open Control Panel and select Ease Of Use. Select the Make The Mouse Easier To Use option and then choose Mouse Properties. On the Pointer Options tab, click Display Pointer Trails and click Show Location Of Pointer When I Press The CTRL Key option.

Install and configure printers.   Printers and print devices can be one of the most problematic areas for IT staff to handle. Every user will need to have at least one printer installed on their machine. Although many times this is an automated process, it is possible to manually install the software printer on the end user's machine.

Master It   You are completing the installation of several new machines in a remote office. The last Windows 7 machine you are setting up has a specific requirement to connect to a network printer in the main office, which is not part of your automated installation. How do you install the network printer in the local machine?

Solution   In Windows 7, you choose the Devices And Printers applet from the Start menu. From this window you choose the Add A Printer menu item to launch the Add Printer Wizard. You select the Add A Network, Wireless Or Bluetooth Printer option and supply the required parameters to connect to the print device in the main office.

Chapter 11: Configuring Network Connectivity

Set up hardware to provide network connectivity.   After installing a new piece of hardware into Windows 7, the operating system goes through a process of discovery and installation. This goes smoothly most of the time, although occasionally, you must step in as the administrator and correct an issue.

Master It   You have just installed a new network adapter into one of your Windows 7 machines. The operating system discovered the new device and installed the driver, but the adapter doesn't work. You checked Device Manager and the network adapter appears to have been installed with a generic network adapter driver. You have a disk with the correct driver for Windows 7. How do you install a network adapter driver from a disk supplied by the hardware vendor to allow Windows 7 to use the NIC to connect to the network?

Solution   First, open Device Manager by clicking Start and typing **Device Manager** into the Start menu's search box. Then, double-click Network Adapters in Device Manager to list the network adapters if this is where the misidentified adapter has been added. (Or double-click Other Devices if this is the Device Manager option that has the misidentified NIC.) Right-click the misidentified network adapter and select Properties. Click the Driver tab for the network adapter properties dialog box and click the Update Driver button. Choose Browse My Computer For Driver Software. Click the Browse button in the Update Driver Software screen and locate the driver file on the hardware vendor's disk. The new drivers will install and the network card will work. You can close the windows still open from the install and return the machine to service.

Connect to network devices.   Windows 7 offers many enhancements for administrators to connect to network devices. One option that can make implementation easier is to connect to a network capable projector.

Master It   One of your training rooms has a new overhead projector that has the capability of being connected to the network and displaying information from the connection. Tim, the instructor, just received a new machine in the classroom running Windows 7 and has asked you to configure the machine to use the network projector to present his PowerPoint presentations. The projector has an IP address of 172.25.2.100. How will you set up a network projector option in Windows 7 to allow PowerPoint to display using the current network infrastructure rather than a video cable in your classroom?

Solution   Select Start and then type **Network Projector** into the Start menu's search box (you can also choose Start ➢ All Programs ➢ Accessories ➢ Connect To A Network Projector) to initiate the connection process. Click Search For A Projector to locate a projector connected to your wired or wireless network. If no projectors are found, you can go back and enter the name or IP address of a projector. If you know the name or IP address, you can simply choose Enter The Projector Address during the initial wizard progression. You might also need the password of the projector if there is a password configured.

Set up peer-to-peer networking.   Having the ability to share resources has been one of Windows' main features since network capability was added to the operating system. Each release of Windows has added new or enhanced functionality to peer-to-peer networking and Windows 7 is no exception with the addition of HomeGroups.

Master It   How can you use the HomeGroup functionality in Windows 7 to allow users in the remote office to share file and printer resources with each other?

Solution   Click Start and then type **Network and Sharing Center** in the Start menu's search box. In the Network And Sharing Center, select Choose Homegroup And Sharing Options. If a HomeGroup has been created on one of the machines in the Windows 7 network, the machine will be displayed in the screen here; if not, click the Create A Homegroup button. In the Network And Sharing Center choose Change The Password; change the password to a secure password (you can leave it to the default and just note it for the other Windows 7 machines if you choose). On the other Windows 7 machines that need to be members of the HomeGroup, in the Network And Sharing Center choose Homegroup And Sharing Options, click the Join button, and enter the password. If the default libraries to be shared are not correct, you can modify here as well.

Configure network protocols. In order to allow machines to communicate through a network, network protocols must be installed and configured on each device. As administrators, we can use dynamic methods to configure our users' machines, but sometimes we may need to manually configure the network protocol.

Master It As a network administrator, you are responsible for ensuring users have a proper network configuration to access the network. Your network is set up for DHCP for the client machines. One of your users currently set up as a DHCP client needs to have a static IP address due to the use of a specific application. How do you configure a Windows 7 client machine that is set up as a DHCP client to have a Static IPv4 address of 172.16.1.50 with a subnet mask of 255.255.255.0 and a default gateway of 172.16.1.1?

Solution From the Network And Sharing Center, choose Local Area Connection in the View Your Active Networks section. Click the Properties button in the Local Area Connection Status properties dialog box. Select Internet Protocol Version 4 (TCP/IPv4) and click the Properties button. Click Use The Following IP Address radio button. Enter the IP address, subnet mask, and default gateway parameters. You should enter a static DNS server for the configuration as well.

Chapter 12: Networking with Windows Server 2008

Connect Windows 7 to the domain. In almost all corporate environments, the client machines (Windows 7) will be connected to the domain environment. Having the Windows 7 machine on the domain offers many benefits, including:

◆ You can deploy GPOs from one location instead of LGPOs on each machine (see Chapter 9, "Managing Security").

◆ Users can back up their data to a server. This way, the nightly backups cover user information. Most Windows 7 machines will *not* be backed up separately.

◆ You can manage users and groups from one central location (Active Directory) instead of on each Windows 7 machine.

◆ You can manage security to resources on servers instead of resources on each Windows 7 machine.

Master It You are the administrator of a large organization that has decided to implement the Windows 7 operating system on all machines. As you load Windows 7 onto the machines, you need to join them to the domain. How do you accomplish this goal?

Solution There are two ways to connect the Windows 7 machine to the domain. You can connect the Windows 7 machine to the domain from the Windows 7 operating system or from Active Directory.

Configure Hyper-V. Microsoft Hyper-V is the next-generation hypervisor based virtualization technology. With the release of Microsoft Windows Server 2008, Microsoft has now incorporated server virtualization into the operating system with the release of Hyper-V. This gives an organization the ability to take full advantage of the next generation of 64-bit server hardware.

Master It   You are the administrator for a large computer company. You need to set up a machine that can run multiple versions of Windows 2008 and Windows 7 for testing and evaluation. What Microsoft server product would you install to solve this issue?

Solution   Microsoft Hyper-V allows an organization to run both Microsoft and non-Microsoft operating systems (Windows, Linux, Unix, and so forth), giving an organization more flexibility. The operating systems can be both 32-bit and 64-bit versions.

Use Microsoft Virtual PC.   Microsoft also has a virtualization environment that can operate on its client software called Virtual PC. Virtual PC allows you to create and manage virtual machines without the need of a server operating system. The advantage here is that you can run server operating systems in a client environment like Windows XP, Windows Vista, or Windows 7.

Master It   You are asked by your organization to set up a training room. This training room will be required to run multiple operating systems, including Windows Server 2008, Windows Vista, and Windows 7. This solution is for training only. How can you implement the computers?

Solution   Virtual PC gives you the ability to set up virtualization on a client operating system. This is beneficial for anyone in the industry who has to do testing or configuration. Virtual PC is not meant to run a network like Hyper-V, but it does give you the ability to test software, install patches, and do training in a controlled environment and not on a live server where you can end up doing more damage than good.

Chapter 13: Configuring Internet Explorer 8

Use IE8 accelerators and web slices.   IE8 has added accelerators and Web Slices to its arsenal of features available to users to make browsing more efficient. Accelerators add a quick launch feature to services such as searching, while Web Slices add the ability to receive updates to content that changes dynamically.

Master It   You would like to add the ability to see Microsoft's stock price reflected in your browser throughout the course of the day. It seems as though adding a Web Slice would be the most efficient way of getting this information. You have been told that Microsoft belongs to NASDAQ and would like to see a quick definition of the term. You know that there's an accelerator that provides a definition. How can you accomplish these tasks using IE8?

Solution   First, use Bing to look up Microsoft's stock quote. Open IE8 and go to Bing (if it's not already your home page) by typing `www.bing.com` in the address bar.

Enter **Microsoft Stock** in the search box and click the search icon.

There will be an entry for Microsoft showing current information regarding its stock quote. Fortunately the word NASDAQ is also available in the entry. Highlight the word NASDAQ and the accelerator icon appears. Click the accelerator icon and hover over the Define With Bing option; a box will appear with the Encarta definition of NASDAQ.

Hovering over the Microsoft Stock search item in Bing displays a framed box that contains the Web Slice icon. Click the Web Slice icon, and a confirmation box displays. Choose to add the Web Slice to your Favorites toolbar. You can now click the Microsoft Corp favorite and the Web Slice will be displayed to you. Any time IE8 detects a change to the content of the Web Slice, the favorite will flash and the Microsoft Corp text will become bold (indicating updated content is available).

Configure Pop-up Blocker in IE8.   Pop-ups are used within websites to launch a separate window with additional content from the site. Most of the time this is an advertisement or some other unwanted content, and it is blocked by default in IE8. However, there are some sites that use pop-ups to present information that you would like to see, but IE8 still blocks it.

Master It   You routinely browse to your local newspaper's website to see what's happening in the local area as well as the world. It is extremely annoying that they use a pop-up for breaking news. You know the pop-up gives you good information and would like to see the content any time you surf to the site. How will you disable pop-ups from occurring anywhere within the local newspaper website?

Solution   Browse to your local news website and note the message from IE8 that indicates the pop-up has been blocked. You have a couple of choices to allow the pop-ups to be displayed, the easiest of which is to click the message and choose Allow Pop-ups for this site. You can also choose Tools ➢ Pop-up Blocker and add the news site to the Allowed Sites list in the Pop-up Blocker Settings dialog box.

Use the InPrivate security feature of IE8.   InPrivate browsing is a new addition that allows a separate browsing session to be initiated where none of the browsing history, cookies, or other data pertaining to the session are retained on the local machine.

Master It   You have entered an Internet cafe and are going to use one of the local machines to surf around the Internet for a bit. You would like to make sure that nothing you do is recorded on the Internet cafe computer. You notice that the Internet cafe is using Windows 7 and realize you can feel confident that your browsing history, cookies, and other data will not be kept on the local machine. How will you surf privately?

Solution   Knowing the Internet cafe is using Windows 7 means that you can use IE8 as your browser and you will be able to use InPrivate browsing.

Launch IE8 and choose Safety ➢ InPrivate Browsing (or simply press Ctrl+Shift+P for InPrivate browsing). You should verify that the address bar now indicates InPrivate, and you can feel confident that no information about your surfing will be recorded on the local machine. You must remember to close the browser before you leave the machine as the data from your session will still be available as long as that browsing session is active.

Configure security for IE8.   IE8 allows you to change the security settings for different zones or areas where you will be browsing. The default settings are Medium for both the Internet and Intranet zones.

Master It   You have decided that you would like to increase the security settings for sites you browse to in both the Internet and Intranet zones. You would like to set the security to the highest available level. How will you accomplish this task?

Solution Open IE8 and choose Tools ➢ Internet Options. On the Security tab, you can select the zones that you want to change the level. Click Internet, and move the slider in Security Level For This Zone to High. There is a brief description of High, and you can compare this to the default Medium. Click Local Intranet in Select A Zone To View Or Change Security Settings. Move the slider to High for the Local Intranet zone as well. If either of these is too restrictive and you cannot access the sites and data you need, you can always go back and try a lower level, thus providing the highest but not restrictive security levels for your browsing pleasure and safety.

Chapter 14: Installing and Configuring Applications

Use Windows 7's Getting Started feature. The Getting Started screen in Windows 7 offers the user several quick links for configuring some of Windows 7's features and online resources.

Master It You recently installed Windows 7 and when logging in you saw the Getting Started window, but immediately closed it and starting exploring your new operating system. You remember seeing something about accessing online resources and would like to go back to Getting Started to see if you can find out more about Windows 7. How will you get back to Getting Started and find the online resources you saw previously?

Solution Choose Start, type **getting started** in the search box, and press Enter. The Getting Started window will appear. You will see a Getting Started option called "Go online to find out what's new in Windows 7." Select this option and a link will appear in the upper right that reads Go Online To Learn More. Click this link to launch Windows Internet Explorer 8 and the Windows 7 web page.

Manage Live Essentials' Mail features. Live Essentials is a program suite for collaborative or online programs that includes Live Mail (taking the place of Windows Mail). There are several configurable Live Mail convenience features.

Master It You have downloaded Live Essentials from download.live.com and installed the program. You selected several of the Live Essential programs, including Live Mail. You have set up Live Mail and it's working just fine. You saw a colleague using Live Mail and it was making spelling suggestions as your colleague wrote the email (just as Word does), and you want to make this option available in your Live Mail. How do you enable the spelling suggestions?

Solution Launch Live Mail and log in if you have created your Live account (you don't have to log in to make the option change). Press the Alt key to display the menu bar and select Tools Options. In the Options window, select the Spelling tab. On the Spelling tab, click the Check My Spelling As I Type option. Click OK to save your change and return to the Live Mail program.

Play a saved digital video in Windows Media Center. Windows Media Center has the ability to play music, TV, and video; launch applications; and even gather Internet statistics for sports teams. Media Center is an entertainment portal that provides superior functionality from a simple interface.

Master It You have downloaded a digital video from your camera and placed it into the Video library in Windows 7. You know you can play it in Media Player, but would like to play it in Windows Media Player on your large-screen TV and listen to the audio on your entertainment center. You have installed the required hardware to use your TV and audio system. How do you find the video and play the movie?

Solution   Launch Windows Media Center. From the Windows Media Center program interface, scroll down to Pictures+Videos (using the up or down scroll arrow at the top or bottom of the Categories column). After you have selected Pictures+Videos, scroll horizontally left or right (using the left and right arrows at the left edge or right edge of the screen in the row containing Pictures+Videos) to the Video Library item. Click Video Library and you will be able to select the digital video you placed in your Video library. You can then double-click the movie or click the play button in the bottom right of the Windows Media Center screen to play the movie.

Use Repair to fix a corrupted application.   You can use Control Panel's Programs And Features application to repair or change installation items in Windows 7.

Master It   You installed an application some time ago from a CD and it's been running fine. While cleaning up, you deleted some files you thought were not being used and now your application won't run. You would like to repair the installation. How do you repair an application in Windows 7?

Solution   To repair an installation in Windows 7, open Control Panel and select Programs. From In the Programs window, select Programs And Features. In the Programs and And Features window, click the application you want to repair and then click the Repair menu item. An installation wizard will launch (just like the original) launch and will let you choose to repair your application (it will replace the deleted file without changing configuration parameters). Don't forget to have the original media available — you will probably need it.

Chapter 15: Maintaining and Optimizing Windows 7

Use Performance Monitor to view CPU usage.   Performance Monitor gives you a way to view real-time statistics of several of the Windows 7 subsystems.

Master It   You recently installed a new Windows 7 application. It seems as though your machine is operating more slowly than normal. Someone told you to look at how busy your CPU is while the application is running. How will you view the CPU utilization while the application is running?

Solution   Choose Start, type **performance monitor** into the search box, and press Enter. Performance Monitor launches and CPU utilization is the default counter displayed. You can note the base utilization before you launch the new application and then launch the new program. Watching Performance Monitor gives you an idea of whether the new application is overutilizing your CPU. You can also click the plus button to add other CPU counters to better view what's happening inside the machine in real time.

Maintain Windows 7 with system tools.   There are several system tools within Windows 7 to help you monitor and maintain your operating system. These tools include Task Manager, Performance Information and Tools, and System Configuration (MSConfig).

Master It   After you install a new application on your Windows 7 machine, you find that it is causing you problems in performance. The longer the application runs, the more your machine seems to lag. After a period of time, the application no longer responds. It even displays "Not Responding" in its title bar and the whole application interface has become translucent. You would like to shut the application down but can't even click the close "X" in the upper-right corner. How can you force the application to close?

Solution   You can use Task Manager to end the application. Launch Task Manager by typing **task manager** in the Start menu's search box. On the Applications tab, locate the misbehaving application in the Task column. Select the hung application and click the End Task button. This will close the application. You can then troubleshoot any issues and restart the application to see if it's causing you problems.

Schedule a task to launch daily.   There are times when you would like an application to run periodically to perform some function on your Windows 7 machine. You can use Task Scheduler to perform this operation.

Master It   You are concerned about security on your local machine and have purchased a software product to collect security information such as open ports, applications that are running, and services that are enabled. The application has the ability to take a snapshot of several of the security parameters you're concerned with and save them to a log file; you just have to run the application. You would like to run the program daily and save the logs so you can review them periodically at your convenience. How can you run the program daily without having to launch it manually?

Solution   The best solution to automatically run your security logging application is by using Task Scheduler. Launch Task Scheduler by typing **task manager** in the Start menu's search box. Select Create A Basic Task from the Actions pane and follow the wizard to specify the time schedule you would like have the program run. You will also specify the program within the wizard and have the option to pass parameters into the program (which might be needed to pass optional switches depending on the application). Once you finish the wizard, your task will be scheduled and will run at the scheduled time. You can then review the output logs at your convenience while being confident the logs will always be generated.

Back up critical data files.   You can use the Backup and Restore application in Windows 7 to make backup copies of operating system and critical data files that might be needed even if they're deleted by mistake or become corrupted.

Master It   Your main application that stores critical financial data files for your company is stored locally on your Windows 7 machine. You're nervous that these files can severely impact your day-to-day operation if they somehow become corrupted or are deleted. You would like to save a copy of the whole financial data folders so you can recover any or all of the data files with minimal impact. How can you back up the critical files in Windows 7?

Solution   You can use the Windows 7 Backup and Restore application to save your data files. Launch the Backup and Restore application by typing **backup and restore** into the Start menu's search box. Click the Set Up Backup option to launch the Backup wizard.

You can choose just the financial data files and/or directories (as well as other critical files) while you're here. You should also consider backing up the operating system files, but you don't have to. After you are finished with the wizard, your initial backup commences and you have a copy of today's data. You can now recover the data as of the time and day the backup was taken. You might also want to consider scheduling the backup to occur periodically using Windows 7's Task Scheduler to make sure you always have as close to a current set of critical data files as possible.

Index

Note to the Reader: Throughout this index **boldfaced** page numbers indicate primary discussions of a topic. *Italicized* page numbers indicate illustrations.